Due Diligence in the International Legal Order

Due Diligence in the International Legal Order

Edited by

HEIKE KRIEGER

ANNE PETERS

LEONHARD KREUZER

OXFORD
UNIVERSITY PRESS

OXFORD
UNIVERSITY PRESS

Great Clarendon Street, Oxford, OX2 6DP,
United Kingdom

Oxford University Press is a department of the University of Oxford.
It furthers the University's objective of excellence in research, scholarship,
and education by publishing worldwide. Oxford is a registered trade mark of
Oxford University Press in the UK and in certain other countries

First Edition published in 2020

Published in the United States of America by Oxford University Press
198 Madison Avenue, New York, NY 10016, United States of America

British Library Cataloguing in Publication Data

Data available

Library of Congress Control Number: 2020940074

ISBN 978–0–19–886990–0

DOI: 10.1093/oso/9780198869900.001.0001

Acknowledgements

The finalisation of this book manuscript in early 2020 has been dominated by the Corona pandemic—not only because editors and authors are in confinement due to health measures taken by their governments but because the responses to the spread of the Covid-19 virus lay bare both the importance and weakness of due diligence. Probably some states, beginning with China where the virus was first documented, have been violating their due diligence obligations enshrined in the International Health Regulations.[1] To all appearances, China has informed the World Health Organization too late about the virus, and some governments have reacted slowly and hesitantly or even counter-productively.[2] But it is highly unlikely that inter-state responsibility will be activated. The reasons are not only strategic considerations of governments which themselves would risk being accused of negligence, and the difficulty of finding an international forum,[3] but also the complexity of assessing the damage caused, and the softness and vagueness of the due diligence standard which barely lends itself to create 'hard' state responsibility.[4] The pandemic and the global struggle against it may or may not foster changes in the international landscape—changes which are anyhow already under way.[5] Will the 'retreat into nativism'[6] continue? Or will states and other global actors such

[1] Gian Luca Burci, 'The Outbreak of COVID-19 Coronavirus: Are the International Health Regulations Fit for Purpose?' *EJIL: Talk!*, 27 February 2020, available at: https://www.ejiltalk.org/the-outbreak-of-covid-19-coronavirus-are-the-international-health-regulations-fit-for-purpose/ (accessed 20 April 2020); Antonio Coco/Talita de Souza Dias, 'Due Diligence and COVID-19: States' Duties to Prevent and Halt the Coronavirus Outbreak', Parts I-III, *EJIL: Talk!*, 24 and 25 March 2020, available at: https://www.ejiltalk.org/part-i-due-diligence-and-covid-19-states-duties-to-prevent-and-halt-the-coronavirus-outbreak/ (accessed 20 April 2020) .

[2] Russell Miller/William Starshak, 'China's Responsibility for the Global Pandemic', *JustSecurity*, 31 March 2020, available at: https://www.justsecurity.org/69398/chinas-responsibility-for-the-global-pandemic/ (accessed 20 April 2020).

[3] Peter Tzeng, 'Taking China to the International Court of Justice over COVID-19', *EJIL: Talk!*, 2 April 2020, available at: https://www.ejiltalk.org/taking-china-to-the-international-court-of-justice-over-covid-19/ (accessed 20 April 2020); Guo Shuai, 'Don't Bother Suing China for COVID-19 Before the ICJ', *China Global Television Network (CGTN)*, 8 April 2020, available at: https://news.cgtn.com/news/2020-04-08/Don-t-bother-suing-China-for-COVID-19-before-the-ICJ-PutmYs7u24/index.html (accessed 20 April 2020).

[4] David Fidler, 'COVID-19 and International Law: Must China Compensate Countries for the Damage?', *JustSecurity*, 27 March 2020, available at: https://www.justsecurity.org/69394/covid-19-and-international-law-must-china-compensate-countries-for-the-damage-international-health-regulations/ (accessed 20 April 2020).

[5] See Armin von Bogdandy/Pedro Villarreal, 'International Law on Pandemic Response: A First Stocktaking in Light of the Coronavirus Crisis', *Max Planck Research Paper Series No. 2020-7*, available at: https://papers.ssrn.com/sol3/papers.cfm?abstract_id=3561650 (accessed 20 April 2020).

[6] James Crawford, 'The Current Political Discourse Concerning International Law', *The Modern Law Review* 81 (2018), 1–22, at 22.

as the World Health Organization, the United Nations, and the private health industry reinforce multilateralism and take collective action? In any case, this global emergency has exposed that our understandings of what the rule of law and respect for personal liberties demands needs to be constantly defended.

We would like to express our gratitude to the Max Planck Society for the Advancement of Sciences for enabling the research project 'Towards a Proceduralization of International Law?' which has led to this book. We are grateful for the generous funding of a Max Planck fellowship for Heike Krieger and a research assistance position of Leonhard Kreuzer. We would also like to thank Freie Universität Berlin for its hospitality in hosting and supporting the research group. The Max Planck Society's Harnack House was the most pleasant venue for the authors' workshop in the summer of 2018 which allowed authors to refine their arguments and receive input from colleagues.

Numerous persons have supported us in the preparation of this book. We are indebted to Matthew Milbourne who helped polishing the language of this volume, to the two anonymous reviewers of Oxford University Press whose feedback reassured us that this book is timely and needed, and to Jack McNichol of Oxford University Press for his advice and support. Special thanks are due to our student assistants Nathanael van der Beek, Julian Erben, and Leah Gölz for their skilful and continuous support in the process of editing this book. We thank all participants of the research seminars at the Berlin Potsdam Research Group 'The International Rule of Law—Rise or Decline?' and at the Max Planck Institute for Comparative Public Law and International Law for constructive criticism on earlier drafts of the conclusion.

We hope that this book makes a modest contribution to understanding better the mechanisms and options that the international law of due diligence offers and the dangers it bears.

Heike Krieger, Anne Peters, and Leonhard Kreuzer
Berlin and Heidelberg in April 2020

Table of Contents

List of Abbreviations xi
Editor Information xv
List of Contributors xvii

1. Due Diligence in the International Legal Order: Dissecting the Leitmotif of Current Accountability Debates 1
   Anne Peters, Heike Krieger, and Leonhard Kreuzer

PART I: DUE DILIGENCE AND GENERAL INTERNATIONAL LAW

2. The Historical Roots of the Due Diligence Standard 23
   Giulio Bartolini
3. Due Diligence in the History of the Codification of the Law of State Responsibility 42
   Helmut Philipp Aust and Prisca Feihle
4. Member States' Due Diligence Obligations to Supervise International Organisations 59
   Kristina Daugirdas
5. The Function of the Triad 'Territory', 'Jurisdiction', and 'Control' in Due Diligence Obligations 75
   Federica Violi
6. Due Diligence and the Duty to Protect Human Rights 92
   Björnstjern Baade

PART II: DUE DILIGENCE IN INTERNATIONAL ENVIRONMENTAL LAW

7. Due Diligence in International Environmental Law: A Fine-grained Cartography 111
   Jorge E. Viñuales
8. Due Diligence in the Use of International Watercourses 129
   Malgosia Fitzmaurice

9. Due Diligence in the Law of the Sea 147
Irini Papanicolopulu

10. Due Diligence in International Climate Change Law 163
Lavanya Rajamani

PART III: DUE DILIGENCE IN PEACE AND SECURITY LAW

11. Due Diligence in International Humanitarian Law 183
Marco Longobardo

12. Due Diligence and the Obligation to Prevent Genocide and Crimes Against Humanity 200
Larissa van den Herik and Emma Irving

13. Due Diligence, the UN, and Peacekeeping 217
Nigel D. White

14. Due Diligence in International Anti-terrorism Law: Developments in the Resolutions of the UN Security Council 234
Inger Österdahl

15. Due Diligence in Cyber Activities 252
Eric Talbot Jensen

PART IV: DUE DILIGENCE IN INTERNATIONAL ECONOMIC LAW

16. Due Diligence in International Investment Law: From the Law of Aliens to Responsible Investment 273
Aniruddha Rajput

17. Due Diligence Debates in International Anti-corruption and Money Laundering Law: From Content to the Construction of Risk 288
Radha Ivory

18. Due Diligence in International Tax Law 302
Reuven S. Avi-Yonah and Gianluca Mazzoni

19. Due Diligence in International Trade Law 312
Markus Krajewski

20. Due Diligence in World Bank Project Financing 329
Diane A. Desierto

CONCLUSION

21. Due Diligence and Structural Change in the International Legal Order 351
Heike Krieger and Anne Peters

Index 391

List of Abbreviations

ACHR	American Convention of Human Rights
AEoI	Automatic Exchange of Information
API	First Additional Protocol
API	Advance Passenger Information
ARIO	Draft Articles on the Responsibility of International Organizations
ARSIWA	Draft Articles on the Responsibility of States for Internationally Wrongful Acts
ASM	Agreement on Safeguard Measures
ATC	Agreement on Textiles and Clothing
CBDRRC	Common but Differentiated Responsibilities and Respective Capabilities
CBI	Citizenship by Investment
Convention of Belém do Pará	Inter-American Convention on the Prevention, Punishment and Eradication of Violence Against Women
CRS	Common Reporting Standards
DSU	Dispute Settlement Understanding
ECHR	European Convention on Human Rights
ECtHR	European Court of Human Rights
EECC	Eritrea-Ethiopia Claims Commission
EHSG	Environmental, Health, and Safety Guidelines
EIA	Environmental Impact Assessment
ESA	European Space Agency
ESCP	Environmental and Social Commitment Plan
ESF	Environmental and Social Framework
ESRS	Environmental and Social Review Summary
FATCA	Foreign Accounts Tax Compliance Act of 2010
FATF	Financial Action Task Force
FCCC	Framework Convention on Climate Change
FFI	Foreign Financial Institutions
FTAs	Free Trade Agreements
GATS	General Agreement on Trade in Services
GATT	General Agreement on Tariffs and Trade
GCs/GCI/II/III/IV	Geneva Conventions/Geneva Convention I/II/III/IV
GHG	Greenhouse Gas
HgRs	Hague Regulations
HIPPO	High Level Independent Panel on Peace Operations
IACtHR	Inter-American Court of Human Rights
ICAO	International Civil Aviation Organization

ICCPR	International Covenant on Civil and Political Rights
ICESCR	International Covenant on Economic, Social and Cultural Rights
ICJ	International Court of Justice
ICRC	International Committee of the Red Cross
ICSID	International Centre for Settlement of Investment Disputes
ICT	Information and communications technology
ICTY	International Criminal Tribunal for the former Yugoslavia
IFC	International Finance Corporation
IGAs	Intergovernmental Agreements
IGOs	Intergovernmental Organisations
ILA	International Law Association
ILC	International Law Commission
ILM	International Legal Materials
IPCC	Intergovernmental Panel on Climate Change
IRS	Internal Revenue Service
Istanbul Convention	Council of Europe Convention on preventing and combating violence against woman and domestic violence
ITC	International Tin Council
ITLOS	International Tribunal on the Law of the Sea
MDB	Multilateral Development Banks
MINUSCA	United Nations Multidimensional Integrated Stabilization Mission in the Central African Republic
MINUSTAH	United Nations Stabilization Mission in Haiti
MLC	Maritime Labour Convention
MoUs	Memoranda of Understanding
NDC	Nationally Determined Contributions
NGO	Non-Governmental Organisation
OECD	Organisation for Economic Co-operation and Development
OECD Convention	Convention on the Bribery of Foreign Public Officials in International Business Transactions
OECD Working Group	OECD's Working Group on Bribery in International Transactions
OGPRP	Office on Genocide Prevention and the Responsibility to Protect
PNR	Passenger Name Record
QI	Qualified Intermediary
R2P	Responsibility to Protect
RBI	Residence by Investment
RoE	United Nations Rules of Engagement
Ruggie Principles	United Nations Guiding Principles on Business and Human Rights
SADC	Southern African Development Community

SCM	Agreement on Subsidies and Countervailing Measures
SCSL	Special Court for Sierra Leone
SOFA	Status of Forces Agreement
SOLAS	International Convention for the Safety of Life on Sea
SPS	Agreement on Sanitary and Phytosanitary Measures
SSP	Satellite Sentinel Project
TCNs	Troop Contributing Nations
TiSA	Trade in Services Agreement
UNAMID	United Nations-African Union Mission in Darfur/United Nations African Union Hybrid Operation in Darfur
UNCAC	United Nations Convention against Corruption
UNCITRAL	United Nations Commission on International Trade Law
UNCLOS	United Nations Convention on the Law of the Sea
UNCTC	United Nations Security Council Counter-Terrorism Committee
UNCTED	United Nations Security Council Counter-Terrorism Committee Executive Directorate
UNECE Water Convention	Convention on the Protection and Use of Transboundary Watercourses and International Lakes
UN GGE	United Nations Group of Governmental Experts on Developments in the Field of Information and Telecommunications in the Context of International Security
UNOCT	United Nations Office of Counter-Terrorism
UNODC	United Nations Office of Drugs and Crime
UNOHCHR	United Nations Office of the High Commissioner for Human Rights
UNSC	United Nations Security Council
UNTOC	United Nations Convention against Transnational Organised Crime
Watercourse Convention	United Nations Convention on Non-Navigational Uses of International Watercourses
WFP	United Nations World Food Programme
WHO	World Health Organization
WTO	World Trade Organisation

Editor Information

Heike Krieger holds the Chair for Public Law and International Law at the Freie Universität Berlin. She is Max Planck Fellow at the Max Planck Institute for Comparative Public Law and International Law, Heidelberg, and chair of the Berlin Potsdam Research Group (Kolleg-Forschungsgruppe) 'The International Rule of Law—Rise or Decline?' (funded by the German Research Foundation). Between 2007 and 2014 she acted as a judge of the Constitutional Court of the State of Berlin. She has represented the German parliament before the German Constitutional Court and acted as counsel for the German government before the European Court of Human Rights. She is a member of the Holberg Committee. Her research focuses on general international law, international human rights law, and international humanitarian law.

Anne Peters is Director at the Max Planck Institute for Comparative Public Law and International Law Heidelberg, Professor at Heidelberg, Basel, and Freie Universität Berlin, and a L. Bates Lea Global Law Professor at the University of Michigan. She has been a member of the European Commission for Democracy through Law (Venice Commission) in respect of Germany (2011–2015) and served as the President of the European Society of International Law (2010–2012). She is currently Chairwoman of the German Society of International Law (DGIR). Her research interests relate to public international law including its history, global animal law, global governance, and global constitutionalism, and the status of humans in international law.

Leonhard Kreuzer is Research Fellow at the Max Planck Institute for Comparative Public Law and International Law Heidelberg and a PhD candidate at the Freie Universität Berlin. He is a member of the editorial board of the Völkerrechtsblog.

List of Contributors

Helmut Philipp Aust, Professor of Public and International Law, Freie Universität Berlin.

Reuven S. Avi-Yonah, Irwin I. Cohn Professor of Law, Director of the International Tax LLM Program, University of Michigan.

Björnstjern Baade, Senior Research Fellow, Freie Universität Berlin.

Giulio Bartolini, Associate Professor of International Law, Roma Tre University.

Kristina Daugirdas, Professor of Law, University of Michigan Law School.

Diane A. Desierto, Tenured Associate Professor of Human Rights Law & Global Affairs, Keough School of Global Affairs, University of Notre Dame (USA); Professor of International Law and Human Rights, Philippines Judicial Academy of the Supreme Court of the Philippines.

Prisca Feihle, Research Fellow, Freie Universität Berlin.

Malgosia Fitzmaurice, Professor of International Law, Queen Mary University of London; Member (Associé) of the Institut de Droit International.

Emma Irving, Assistant Professor of Public International Law, Grotius Centre for International Legal Studies, Leiden University.

Radha Ivory, Senior Lecturer, T.C. Beirne School of Law, The University of Queensland, Australia.

Eric Talbot Jensen, Professor of Law, Brigham Young University, Provo, Utah.

Markus Krajewski, Professor of Public Law and Public International Law, University of Erlangen-Nürnberg.

Leonhard Kreuzer, Research Fellow, Max Planck Institute for Comparative Public Law and International Law.

Heike Krieger, Professor of Public Law and International Law, Freie Universität Berlin.

Marco Longobardo, Lecturer in International Law, University of Westminster.

Gianluca Mazzoni, S.J.D. candidate, University of Michigan Law School.

Inger Österdahl, Professor of Public International Law, Uppsala University.

Irini Papanicolopulu, Associate Professor of International Law, University of Milano-Bicocca.

Anne Peters, Managing Director, Max Planck Institute for Comparative Public Law and Public International Law; Professor of Law at the Universities of Heidelberg, Basel and Freie Universität Berlin; L. Bates Lea Global Law Professor, University of Michigan.

Lavanya Rajamani, Professor of International Environmental Law, University of Oxford; Yamani Fellow in Public International Law, St Peter's College, Oxford.

Aniruddha Rajput, Member UN International Law Commission, Consultant, Public International Law and International Arbitration, Withers LLP (London).

Larissa van den Herik, Professor of Public International Law, Grotius Centre for International Legal Studies, Leiden University.

Jorge E. Viñuales, Harold Samuel Professor of Law and Environmental Policy, University of Cambridge; Founder and former Director of the Cambridge Centre for Environment, Energy and Natural Resource Governance (C-EENRG); Member (Associé) of the Institut de Droit International.

Federica Violi, Assistant Professor of International law, Erasmus University Rotterdam.

Nigel D. White, Professor of Public International Law, University of Nottingham; Co-Director, Nottingham International Law and Security Centre.

1

Due Diligence in the International Legal Order

Dissecting the Leitmotif of Current Accountability Debates

Anne Peters, Heike Krieger, and Leonhard Kreuzer

1. Due Diligence: A Familiar Stranger

Due diligence is a prominent concept of international law. It has frequently been referred to in arbitral awards[1] and in international court decisions, notably by the International Court of Justice (ICJ)[2] and the International Tribunal on the Law of the Sea (ITLOS).[3] But the ongoing scholarly debate—mostly on state responsibility[4]—hides the fact that the specific normative content and the systemic relation of due diligence to other international legal or para-legal principles (such as sovereignty, good neighbourliness, good governance, the no harm principle, or corporate social responsibility) is still under-explored.

[1] Permanent Court of Arbitration, *South China Sea Arbitration, Philippines v. China*, Award of 12 July 2016, PCA Case No 2013-19, ICGJ 495, para. 744. See for the old awards notably Giulio Bartolini, 'The Historical Roots of the Due Diligence Standard', chapter 2 of this book, section 2.

[2] ICJ, *Corfu Channel Case (United Kingdom of Great Britain and Northern Ireland v. Albania)*, Judgment of 9 April 1949, ICJ Reports 1949, 4, p. 22; ICJ, *Application of the Convention on the Prevention and Punishment of the Crime of Genocide (Bosnia and Herzegovina v. Serbia and Montenegro)*, Judgment of 26 February 2007, ICJ Reports 2007, 43, para. 430; ICJ, *Pulp Mills on the River Uruguay (Argentina v. Uruguay)*, Judgment of 20 April 2010, ICJ Reports 2010, 14, paras 101, 197, 204, 223; ICJ, *Certain Activities Carried out by Nicaragua in the Border Area (Costa Rica v. Nicaragua) and Construction of a Road in Costa Rica along the San Juan River (Nicaragua v. Costa Rica)*, Judgment of 16 December 2015, ICJ Reports 2015, 665, paras 104, 153, 168, 228.

[3] ITLOS Seabed Disputes Chamber, *Responsibilities and Obligations of States Sponsoring Persons and Entities with Respect to Activities in the Area*, Advisory Opinion of 1 February 2011, ITLOS Reports 2011, paras 110–112, 117–120, 131–132; ITLOS, *Request for an Advisory Opinion Submitted by the Sub-Regional Fisheries Commission (SRFC)*, Advisory Opinion of 2 April 2015, ITLOS Reports 2015, paras 125–132, 146–150.

[4] Contemporary scholarship on due diligence began with the seminal works by Pavlos Alexandrou Zannas, *La responsabilité internationale des États pour les actes de négligence* (Montreux: Ganguin 1952) and Riccardo Pisillo Mazzeschi, *Due Diligence e responsabilità internazionale degli Stati* (Milan: Giuffrè editore 1989). See for recent book-length treatments: Joanna Kulesza, *Due Diligence in International Law* (Leiden: Brill 2016); Société Française pour le Droit International (SFDI)/Sarah Cassella (eds), *Le standard de due diligence et la responsabilité internationale* (Paris: Pedone 2018). The title of the latter volume suggests an inherent link to state responsibility.

Anne Peters, Heike Krieger, and Leonhard Kreuzer, *Due Diligence in the International Legal Order* In: *Due Diligence in the International Legal Order*. Edited by: Heike Krieger, Anne Peters, and Leonhard Kreuzer, Oxford University Press (2020).
 DOI: 10.1093/oso/9780198869900.003.0001.

Due diligence comes from the Latin word *diligentia* which can be translated as care or circumspection. The opposite of (due) diligence is negligence. The Encyclopædia Britannica defines due diligence as 'a standard of vigilance, attentiveness, and care often exercised in various professional and societal settings. The effort is measured by the circumstances under which it is applied, with the expectation that it will be conducted with a level of reasonableness and prudence appropriate for the particular circumstances.'[5]

Diligence is a *qualifier of behaviour* as shown in its adverbial use: an actor can behave diligently—or negligently. Due diligence thus is no free-standing obligation but a *modality* attached to a duty of care for someone or something else (including the duty to prevent and mitigate harm). One might call it an ancillary obligation if one wants to use the language of obligation at all.

Due diligence is needed when a risk has to be controlled or contained, in order to prevent harm and damage done to another actor or to a public interest. The rise of the concept is therefore tied to the rise of the 'risk society'[6] and the idea of risk management. In the standard situation, a state is expected to tackle risks emanating from non-state actors in its territory. But risks can also arise from forces of nature, or be triggered by other types of actors, including third states.

The idea of due diligence has an inbuilt normative (evaluative) component, because the assessment what is 'due' needs a value judgment. This value judgment, the appraisal of what is appropriate or owed (and concomitantly whether due diligence has been observed or not), depends on the (legitimate) expectations directed at the relevant actor's behaviour. These expectations in turn depend on factors attached to the actor itself (notably its capacities), and arise from the social, political, and legal context. Another question is whose expectations count. In a state-centred international legal order, these were the expectations of other states, notably treaty partners. But where other actors' interests are safeguarded by international law, for example the human rights of natural persons, their expectations would seem to matter as well. And when it comes to protecting public goods such as the environmental quality, the question is who may authoritatively formulate the relevant expectations.

Due to its normative colouring, due diligence is inevitably a concept which transgresses the confines of the positive, black letter law and opens a window for

[5] Robert Sprague/Sean Valentine, 'Due Diligence', *Encyclopædia Britannica*, 4 October 2018, available at: https://www.britannica.com/topic/due-diligence (accessed 15 April 2020). Along a similar line, *Black's Law Dictionary* defines due diligence as 'the diligence reasonably expected from, and ordinarily exercised by, a person who seeks to satisfy a legal requirement or to discharge an obligation' and links it to 'reasonable diligence' which is the 'degree of diligence expected from someone of ordinary prudence under circumstances like those at issue', Bryan A. Garner, in Henry Campbell Black (founder), *Black's Law Dictionary* (St. Paul (MN): West Publishing 10th ed. 2014), 553.

[6] Ulrich Beck, *Risk Society: Towards a New Modernity* (London: Sage 1992). See in detail Heike Krieger/Anne Peters, 'Due Diligence and Structural Change in the International Legal Order', chapter 21 of this book, section 1, section 2.1, section 7.

considerations of ethics and politics. Just like 'good faith', 'legitimate expectations', and 'ordre public', due diligence is a concept sitting on the (blurry) boundaries between law and morality and between law and politics. This feature brings to the fore the limits of the law: if the culture of international relations lacks normative ambitions, then an international law of due diligence will not help much.

With this caveat, due diligence might still be an important normative tool to address and grapple with the growing transboundary effects and repercussions of governmental and private activities in an increasingly interconnected, contested, and complex international order. So far primary and secondary rules of international law do not sufficiently address these cross-border effects and the spillovers of decisions taken and activities conducted inside states. This state of affairs has created accountability gaps.[7]

In order to close these accountability gaps, due diligence might offer a way forward: on the level of primary rules, the flexibility of the concept might be welcome. In international law-making processes, it can be employed in a spirit of a constructive ambiguity[8] in order to overcome a deadlock in negotiations. In underdeveloped legal areas, due diligence might fulfil a transitory function towards the creation and emergence of denser and more specific rules.[9] In legal regimes where broad but unspecific obligations of prevention or positive obligations exist, due diligence might consolidate the parameters of what is due[10] and thereby help to operationalise and stabilise these obligations.[11] Generally speaking, the rise of due diligence which is after all mainly a prescription of processes seems to be one manifestation of a much-noted shift towards a proceduralisation in international law.[12]

On the level of secondary norms, due diligence might complement and strengthen the established rules on state responsibility. Article 8 of the ILC Articles

[7] By accountability we understand the relationship between an actor and a forum in which the actor has to explain and justify its conduct against acknowledged benchmarks, and where the actor faces (reputational, political, or even legal) sanctions if the explanation does not satisfy the recipients of accountability, see Mark Bovens, 'Analysing and Assessing Accountability: A Conceptual Framework', *European Law Journal* 13 (2007), 447–468, at 450; Ruth Grant/Robert Keohane, 'Accountability and Abuses of Power in World Politics', *American Political Science Review* 99 (2005), 29–43, at 29. In international law, legal accountability is realised through the principles of international responsibility.

[8] Lavanya Rajamani, 'Due Diligence in International Climate Change Law', chapter 10 of this book, section 1.

[9] See Helmut Philipp Aust/Prisca Feihle, 'Due Diligence in the History of the Codification of the Law of State Responsibility', chapter 3 of this book, section 2.4. See also Timo Koivurova, 'Due Diligence', in Rüdiger Wolfrum (ed.), *Max Planck Encyclopedia of Public International Law* (Oxford: OUP 2010), para. 44. See on the catalysing function of due diligence Yann Kerbrat, 'Le standard de due diligence, catalysateur des obligations conventionnelles et coutumières pour les Etats', in SFDI/Cassella (n. 4), 27–38, at 34.

[10] Highlighting this aspect with regard to positive obligations, Pisillo Mazzeschi, 'Le chemin étrange de la due diligence: d'un concept mystérieux à un concept surévalué', in SFDI/Cassella (n. 4), 323–337, at 336.

[11] On the stabilising function of interactional law-building processes after the conclusion of a treaty Jutta Brunnée/Stephen J. Toope, 'International Law and the Practice of Legality: Stability and Change', *Victoria University of Wellington Law Review* 49 (2018), 429–446, at 441.

[12] See in detail Krieger/Peters, 'Structural Change', chapter 21 of this book, section 6.4.

on the Responsibility of States for Internationally Wrongful Acts (ARSIWA) allows to hold states responsible for behaviour of non-state actors only under limited conditions, notably when a state directs or controls the latter. And Article 16 ARSIWA only regulates complicity and does not cover blameworthy state negligence below that level. Due diligence might bridge the accountability gap left by these provisions. Due diligence might further provide the normative framework for greater accountability of international organisations.[13]

Yet before simply asserting this positive potential of due diligence caution seems warranted. International legal scholars need to examine the following key questions: in which areas does due diligence indeed fulfil the said promises?[14] In which areas can it promote stability and strengthen the international rule of law, in which areas does it rather risk to dilute substantial standards? Does a potential endless malleability render the concept void of any substantial content or overstretch its key elements?

In order to display the full kaleidoscope of current due diligence debates in international law, this volume employs a primarily inductive (bottom-up) approach, looking at very concrete and diverse due diligence norms in a host of specialised fields of international law. The sector-specific chapters do not only cover areas of international law in which the concept of due diligence has already gained prominence, but also areas in which it is currently about to emerge or in which it may gain relevance in the future. This will allow us to draw connections between different areas of international law and provide a comprehensive picture, identifying commonalities in the scope, contents, and operation of due diligence in the various subfields, and differences and frictions among them.

2. Established Aspects of Due Diligence in International Law

Due diligence has emerged in international law as a state-to-state obligation through arbitral decisions, mixed claims commissions, and diplomatic practice in the late nineteenth and early twentieth century.[15] Some essential characteristics of the concept were established already in that period: States' sovereignty

[13] See Nigel D. White, 'Due Diligence, the UN and Peacekeeping', chapter 13; Kristina Daugirdas, 'Member States' Due Diligence Obligations to Supervise International Organisations', chapter 4; Diane A. Desierto, 'Due Diligence in World Bank Project Financing', chapter 20; all in this book. See also Ellen Campbell/Elizabeth Dominic/Snezhana Stadnik/Yuanzhou Wu, 'Due Diligence Obligations of International Organizations under International Law', *New York University Journal of International Law and Politics* 50 (2018), 541–604; Evelyne Lagrange, 'La responsabilité des organisations internationales pour violation d'une obligation de diligence' in SFDI/Cassella (n. 4), 189–229.

[14] For example, the extent to which states have complied with their due diligence obligations under the 2005 International Health Regulations will most likely arise in any retrospect evaluation of the Covid-19 pandemic.

[15] See for the historical evolution of due diligence in international law, Bartolini, 'Historical Roots', chapter 2 of this book, section 1.4.

over their territory has come to be understood as not absolute. Rather, states must take other states' interests diligently into account. The ICJ in the *Corfu Channel* judgment of 1949 counted among the 'general and well-recognized principles': 'every State's obligation not to allow knowingly its territory to be used for acts contrary to the rights of other states'.[16] Due diligence became a 'corollary (. . .) duty' of sovereignty.[17] Obligations of diligence have evolved as integral part of legal norms, most prominently in the law of neutrality, the law of aliens, and in environmental law. Due diligence has not required that harm to the interests of other states is totally prevented, but that states use best efforts or do the utmost to prevent or minimise such harm.[18] Due diligence hence has been established as a best efforts obligation in contrast to result-oriented obligations and in contrast to 'strict liability' (in the sense of responsibility even for certain types of lawful behaviour if a risk materialised and independently of negligence). This feature has later led later to the classification of due diligence as an 'obligation of conduct' and not of 'result'.[19] It was established that the required standard of care has to be determined flexibly and context-dependent and therefore entails 'such diligence as can reasonably be expected if all circumstances and conditions of the case are taken into consideration'.[20] As it is difficult to anticipate all circumstances beforehand, the specific obligations have usually been ascertained ex post.[21] A state's overall governance capacity and its capacity to take measures in the relevant field have influenced the standard's content so as to avoid an undue burden on less capable states. Regardless of capacity, however, a certain minimum standard was said to exist.[22] Furthermore, the predictability and severity of the imminent risk and the level of control have been taken into account. Due diligence ought to be

[16] ICJ, *Corfu Channel Case* (n. 2), 22.

[17] Arbitrator Max Huber, *Case of the Island of Palmas (Netherlands v. USA)*, Award of 4 April 1928, vol. II, UNRIIA, 829–871, 839.

[18] United Nations, International Law Commission, Draft Articles on Prevention of Transboundary Harm from Hazardous Activities, UN GAOR A/56/10, 23 April–1 June, 2 July–10 August 2001, commentary to art. 3, 154, para. 7: 'The duty of due diligence involved, however, is not intended to guarantee that significant harm be totally prevented, if it is not possible to do so. In that eventuality, the State (. . .) [must] exert its best possible efforts to minimize the risk. In this sense, it does not guarantee that the harm would not occur.'

[19] ITLOS Seabed Disputes Chamber, *Responsibilities and Obligations of States* (n. 3), para. 110; ICJ, *Pulp Mills* (n. 2), para. 187; see for a more nuanced classification Krieger/Peters, 'Structural Change', chapter 21 of this book, section 2.3.

[20] Lassa Oppenheim, *International Law. A Treatise, Vol. II, War and Neutrality* (New York/Bombay: Longmans, Green and Co. 1906), 393.

[21] Critical on the indeterminacy of the standard, Edwin M. Borchard (Reporter), Harvard Law School Drafting Committee, 'The Law and Responsibility of States for Damage Done in Their Territory to the Person or Property of Foreigners', *American Journal of International Law* 23 (1929), Supplement: Codification of International Law, 131–239, at 188.

[22] General Claims Commission, *L. F. H. Neer and Pauline Neer (U.S.A.) v. United Mexican States*, Decision of 15 October 1926, vol. IV, UNRIAA, 60, 61; *A. L. Harkrader (U.S.A.) v. United Mexican States*, Decision of 3 October 1928, vol. IV, UNRIAA, 371–373.

exercised in 'exact proportion to the risks':[23] the more control a state possesses over certain parts of its territory or over certain actors, the more stringent the standard will be.[24] The standard has been established as an international one—states are not allowed to rely on (possibly lower) domestic standards or to apply (only) a *diligentia quam in suis*.[25] Furthermore, due diligence has come to be understood as a binding legal obligation, at least in some contexts. In other areas of international law (notably anti-corruption law and international finance law), due diligence refers to voluntary processes of risk-evaluation ('doing due diligence') in order to avoid bad outcomes which might include, but are not limited to, breaches of the law.[26]

Overall, a range of elements of due diligence have already been firmly settled in international law. However, these elements are very abstract and therefore provide only limited guidance for contemporary sector-specific due diligence problems. Furthermore, the parameters remain inconclusive and do not clear up various points of confusion surrounding the idea of due diligence.

3. Due Diligence in-between Primary and Secondary Norms of International Law

Due diligence escapes the categories of primary and secondary rules of international law. Historically, when due diligence emerged in nineteenth-century international practice, international legal doctrine did not yet distinguish between primary and secondary rules. The discussion of due diligence changed significantly when ILC Special Rapporteur Roberto Ago in 1970 introduced the conceptual distinction between primary rules of behaviour and secondary rules of responsibility.[27] Since then, due diligence has mostly been analysed in the context of the secondary rules of state responsibility.[28] In particular, it became a placeholder for the element of 'fault'

[23] Tribunal of arbitration established by Article I of the Treaty of Washington of 8 May 1871, Alabama claims of the United States of America against Great Britain, Award of 14 September 1872, UNRIAA, XXIX, 125–134, 129.

[24] Mixed Claims Commission, *Sambiaggio Case (Italy v. Venezuela)*, Decision of 1903, vol. X, UNRIAA, 499–525, 512.

[25] Max Huber, *British Claims in the Spanish Zone of Morocco*, Award of 13 May 1925, vol. II, UNRIAA, 615, 644.

[26] Neil McDonald, 'The Role of Due Diligence in International Law', *International and Comparative Law Quarterly* 68 (2019), 1041–1054, at 1042; Krieger/Peters, 'Structural Change', chapter 21 of this book, section 4.3.

[27] Roberto Ago, Second Report on State Responsibility, A/CN.4/233, 20 April 1970, YBILC 1970, vol. II, 177–197, para. 11. See on due diligence throughout the ILC codification efforts Aust/Feihle, 'Codification of State Responsibility', chapter 3 of this book, section 2.2.

[28] Riccardo Pisillo Mazzeschi, 'The Due Diligence Rule and the Nature of the International Responsibility of States', *German Yearbook of International Law* 35 (1992), 9–51; Robert P. Barnidge, 'The Due Diligence Principle under International Law', *International Community Law Review* 8 (2006), 81–121; Kulesza, *Due Diligence in International Law* 2016 (n. 4), 7.

which was contentious at the time. Lack of due diligence was—along this line—interchangeably also called 'objective fault'[29] or seen as functionally similar to the culpability or negligence of a state.[30]

Despite the intense discussion of due diligence in the context of secondary norms, the ARSIWA ultimately refrained from establishing due diligence as one of the constituent elements of state responsibility. Instead, the ILC relegated the question which diligence is actually due to the level of primary norms.[31] In line with the ILC Articles, it is nowadays basically agreed both in practice and scholarship that no element of 'fault' is required for establishing the international legal responsibility of a state.[32] Concomitantly, the relevance and doctrinal place of due diligence has been shifted back from the secondary level to the level of primary rules. Due diligence has not only stayed in place in older international legal norms but is also arguably implicit in new treaty provisions which contain primary norms,[33] and is explicit in the Istanbul Convention on Domestic Violence of 2011[34] and in the current draft of a legally binding Instrument to Regulate, in International Human Rights Law, the Activities of Transnational Corporations and other Business Enterprises.[35] Also, the 2001 ILC Draft Articles on Prevention of Transboundary

[29] Karl Zemanek, 'Schuld und Erfolgshaftung im Entwurf der Völkerrechtskommission über Staatenverantwortlichkeit', in Emanuel Diez (ed.), *Festschrift für Rudolf Bindschedler* (Bern: Stämpfli 1980), 315–334, at 323; for further references, see Pisillo Mazzeschi, 'The Due Diligence Rule' 1992 (n. 28), 17.

[30] United Nations, International Law Commission, Report of the International Law Commission on the work of its forty-eighth session, 6 May–26 July 1996, Official Records of the General Assembly, 51st session, Supplement No. 10, A/51/10, art. 22, commentary, 132, para. 9.

[31] United Nations, International Law Commission, Draft Articles on Responsibility of States for Internationally Wrongful Acts, UN GAOR A/56/10, 23 April–1 June, 2 July–10 August 2001, 70, art. 2 (3): 'Whether responsibility is "objective" or "subjective" in this sense depends on the circumstances, including the content of the primary obligation in question. The articles lay down no general rule in that regard. The same is true of other standards, whether they involve some degree of fault, culpability, negligence or want of due diligence (. . .)'.

[32] See, however, Aust/Feihle, 'Codification of State Responsibility', chapter 3 of this book, section 4.

[33] Examples are the Marine Waste Dumping Convention (1972); the Vienna Convention on the Ozone Layer (1985); the Environmental Impact Assessment Convention (1991); the Transboundary Watercourses Convention (1992); the Convention on Non-Navigational Uses of International Watercourses (1997), and more. See for the language of these treaties notes 51–56.

[34] Council of Europe Convention on Preventing and Combating Violence against Women and Domestic Violence, 11 May 2011, CETS 2010, art. 5(1), (2): '(1) Parties shall refrain from engaging in any act of violence against women and ensure that State authorities, officials, agents, institutions and other actors acting on behalf of the State act in conformity with this obligation. (2) Parties shall take the necessary legislative and other measures to exercise due diligence to prevent, investigate, punish and provide reparation for acts of violence covered by the scope.'

[35] Open-ended intergovernmental working group (OEIGWG) on business and human rights, Revised Draft of a Legally Binding Instrument to Regulate, in International Human Rights Law, the Activities of Transnational Corporations and other Business Enterprises, 16 July 2019, art. 5(2): 'For the purpose (. . .) of this Article, State Parties shall adopt measures necessary to ensure that all persons conducting business activities, including those of transnational character, to undertake human rights due diligence as follows: a) Identify and assess any actual or potential human rights violations or abuses that may arise from their own business activities, or from their contractual relationships; b) Take appropriate actions to prevent human rights violations or abuses in the context of its business activities, including those under their contractual relationships; c) Monitor the human rights impact of their business activities, including those under their contractual relationships; d) Communicate to stakeholders and account for the policies and measures adopted to identify, assess, prevent and monitor any actual

Harm from Hazardous Activities which—unlike the ARSIWA—formulate primary obligations spell out a 'duty of prevention' which requires the state of origin to 'take all appropriate measures to prevent significant transboundary harm or at any event to minimize the risk thereof' (Article 3 of the Draft Articles on Prevention).[36] This primary obligation is a due diligence obligation, as the commentary makes clear.[37]

Yet, due diligence is persistently discussed also on the level of secondary rules of responsibility. For instance, in this book, Helmut Aust and Prisca Feihle propose construing the subjective element (namely knowledge) which is—exceptionally—a prerequisite for 'complicity' in the law of state responsibility (Article 16 ARSIWA)[38] in the language of due diligence, but only for specific situations, namely in the event of serious breaches of peremptory norms and within continuous relationships of cooperation.[39]

Generally, how can due diligence be simultaneously relevant on the levels of both primary and secondary norms? One stumbles against the apparent doctrinal inconsistency. Does this dual relevance show that the concept is in itself conceptually flawed and confused? Or does the dual relevance, quite to the contrary, indicate that the concept has a potential to enhance accountability irrespective of doctrinal categories?

4. Normative Quality

The lack of clarity about the status of due diligence as a primary or secondary norm, or both, is matched by a confusing variety of terms used to describe the normative quality of due diligence:[40] It has been referred to as a 'general principle of international law',[41] as an 'obligation or duty',[42] as a

or potential human rights violations or abuses that may arise from their activities, or from those under their contractual relationships.'

36 ILC Draft Articles on Prevention (n. 18).

37 Ibid., 394, art. 3, commentary, 154, paras 7–11.

38 Art. 16 ARSIWA requires that the complicit state 'does so with knowledge of the circumstances of the internationally wrongful act'. Art. 16 is not a 'pure' secondary norm because the conduct by the aiding or assisting state is not as such wrongful. It sits in between primary and secondary norms, just like due diligence.

39 Aust/Feihle, 'Codification of State Responsibility', chapter 3 of this book, section 3.2.

40 Highlighting this variety Alain Pellet, 'Préface', in SFDI/Cassella (n. 4), 5, 6; Sarah Cassella, 'Les travaux de la Commission du Droit International sur la Responsabilité Internationale et le standard de due diligence', in SFDI/ Cassella (n. 4), 1–26, at 13.

41 Olivier Corten, 'La "complicité" dans le droit de la responsabilité internationale: un concept inutile?', *Annuaire Français de Droit International* 57 (2011), 57–84, at 67; Anja Seibert-Fohr, 'From Complicity to Due Diligence: When Do States Incur Responsibility for Their Involvement in Serious International Wrongdoing?', *German Yearbook of International Law* 60 (2017), 667–707, at 681 and 706. See the explicit rejection of this normative quality by Pisillo Mazzeschi, 'Le chemin étrange' 2018 (n. 10), 336.

42 See Jorge E. Viñuales, 'Due Diligence in International Environmental Law: A Fine-grained Cartography', chapter 7 of this book, section 1; ITLOS, *Responsibilities and Obligations of States* (n. 3), para. 111.

'standard',[43] or as a 'concept'.[44] This broad range of categories shows that the international legal discourse has so far not fully conceptualised due diligence. These varying terms are not only a matter of etiquette but implicitly assert a particular normative quality or imply a specific interrelation with international legal norms. As a 'general principle of international law', due diligence could form a basis for more specific customary norms.[45] As a general principle, due diligence would also have to be read and construed in the light of other international legal principles, such as sovereignty or good neighbourliness.[46] Understood as an 'obligation' or 'duty', the function and content of due diligence would likely remain more constrained by the specific norm to which it attaches. A 'standard' of due diligence would rather neutrally suggest a normative expectation. It may well be that 'due diligence' is a placeholder for different types of normative structures with differing functions in the various distinct contexts.[47]

5. Identification of Due Diligence Sources

A further challenge for the analysis of due diligence in international law is the difficulty of comprehensively identifying all due diligence norms. While due diligence is pervasive across different areas of international law, the actual use of the term in treaty provisions is rare.[48] Even where specific treaty clauses seem to point at due diligence obligations, they usually do not mention due diligence explicitly.[49] Implicit references are often, but not always, characterised by employing due diligence 'slang':[50] The treaty language contains obligations to take 'all appropriate

[43] Maja Seršić, 'Due Diligence—Fault-based Responsibility or Autonomous Standard?', in Rüdiger Wolfrum/Maja Seršić/Trpimir M. Šošić (eds), *Contemporary Developments in International Law: Essays in Honour of Budislav Vukas* (Leiden: Brill 2016), 151–170, at 159–160; ILA Study Group on Due Diligence in International Law, Second Report, July 2016, 2–3.

[44] Awalou Ouedraogo, 'La neutralité et l'émergence du concept de due diligence en droit international. L'affaire de l'*Alabama* revisitée', *Journal of the History of International Law* 13 (2011), 307–346, at 330; Pisillo Mazzeschi, 'Le chemin étrange' 2018 (n. 10), 336–337.

[45] See for a qualification of due diligence as a general principle of international law spelled out in specific rules, Corten, 'La "complicité"' (n. 41), 67. ICJ, *Pulp Mills* (n. 2), para. 101 stated that 'the principle of prevention, as a customary rule, has its origins in the due diligence that is required of a state in its territory'. This does not amount to an explicit qualification of due diligence as a general principle but points in this direction. In its draft conclusions on the identification of customary international law the ILC however notably refrained from any assertion of the potential influence of general principles on the identification of customary international law, United Nations, International Law Commission, Draft conclusions on identification of customary international law, UN GAOR A/73/10, 30 April–1 June, 2 July–10 August 2018, 124, para. 6.

[46] On the question whether due diligence should be regarded as a general principle of international law see Krieger/Peters, 'Structural Change', chapter 21 of this book, section 5.

[47] This introduction therefore uses the terms concept, standard, and principle interchangeably.

[48] ILA Study Group on Due Diligence in International Law, First Report, 7 March 2014, 6.

[49] See for one of these rare instances the fairly recent Istanbul Convention on Domestic Violence (n. 34) and the draft Instrument to Regulate, in International Human Rights Law, the Activities of Transnational Corporations and other Business Enterprises, 2019 (n. 35).

[50] Bartolini, 'Historical Roots', chapter 2 of this book, sections 2.3 and 2.4.

measures',[51] 'all appropriate and effective measures',[52] 'all measures necessary',[53] or the parties must 'exert appropriate efforts'[54] to achieve a certain aim, or states must 'have due regard' to other states' rights.[55]

Other treaty provisions do not even employ such 'slang', but have nevertheless been qualified as due diligence norms.[56] Such a qualification might be justified wherever norms are supported by a wider due diligence obligation in a specific area. For example, in environmental law the obligation to undertake an environmental impact assessment is underpinned by the general due diligence obligation to prevent transboundary environmental harm. Or norms that lay down positive

[51] Vienna Convention for the Protection of the Ozone Layer, 22 March 1985, 1513 UNTS 293, art. 2: 'The Parties shall take *appropriate measures* (...) to protect human health and the environment against adverse effects (...)' (emphasis added); Convention on the Protection and Use of Transboundary Watercourses and International Lakes, 17 March 1992, 1936 UNTS 269, art. 2 (1): 'The Parties shall take all *appropriate measures* to prevent, control and reduce any transboundary impact' (emphasis added). See similarly art. 4(2) of the Basel Convention on the Control of Transboundary Movements of Hazardous Wastes and their Disposal of 22 March 1989, 1637 UNTS 57; art. 2(2) of the Convention on the Protection of the Alps of 7 November 1991, OJ EC 1996 L 61, 32–36; arts. 3(1) and 6(1) of the Convention on the Transboundary Effects of Industrial Accidents of 17 March 1992, 2105 UNTS 457; art. 7(1) and (2) of the Convention on the Law of the Non-navigational Uses of International Watercourses of 21 May 1997, 2999 UNTS; Art. 3 No. 10 lit. a) of the Revised Protocol on Shared Watercourses in the Southern African Development Community, 8 August 2000, IUCN (ID: TRE-001267).

[52] Convention on the Prevention of Marine Pollution by Dumping of Wastes and Other Matter, 19 November 1972, 1046 UNTS 120, art. 1: 'Contracting Parties shall individually and collectively promote the effective control of all sources of pollution of the marine environment, and (...) take all practicable steps to prevent the pollution of the sea (...)'; art. 2: 'Contracting Parties shall (...) take *effective measures* individually, according to their scientific, technical and economic capabilities, and collectively, to prevent marine pollution (...) and shall harmonize their policies in this regard'; art. 7 (2): 'Each Party shall take in its territory *appropriate measures* to prevent and punish conduct in contravention of the provisions of this Convention' (emphases added). Convention on Environmental Impact Assessment in a Transboundary Context, 25 February 1991, 1989 UNTS 309, art. 2 (1), (2): '(1) The Parties shall, either individually or jointly, take all *appropriate and effective measures* to prevent, reduce and control significant adverse transboundary environmental impact from proposed activities. (2) Each Party shall take the *necessary legal, administrative or other measures* to implement the provisions of this Convention (...)' (emphases added).

[53] United Nations Convention on the Law of the Sea, 10 December 1982, 1833 UNTS 3, art. 194 (2): 'States shall take all measures necessary to ensure that activities under their jurisdiction or control are so conducted as not to cause damage by pollution to other States and their environment (...)'.

[54] Convention on the Regulation of Antarctic Mineral Resource Activities, 2 June 1988 (so far not in effect), SATCM IV-12-10, art. 7 (5): 'Each Party shall *exert appropriate efforts*, consistent with the Charter of the United Nations, to the end that no one engages in any Antarctic mineral resource activities contrary to the objectives and principles of this Convention' (emphasis added).

[55] UNCLOS, 1982 (n. 53), art. 58(3): '(...) States shall have *due regard* to the rights and duties of the coastal State and shall comply with the laws and regulations adopted by the coastal State in accordance with the provisions of this Convention and other rules of international law in so far as they are not incompatible with this Part' (emphasis added).

[56] See for example Convention on the Prevention and Punishment of the Crime of Genocide, 9 December 1948, 78 UNTS 277, art. 1: 'The Contracting Parties confirm that genocide, whether committed in time of peace or in time of war, is a crime under international law which they *undertake to* prevent and to punish' (emphasis added). The due diligence character of this obligation was highlighted by the ICJ in the Bosnia Genocide Case, ICJ, *Bosnia Genocide* (n. 2), para. 430: 'In this area the notion of "due diligence", which calls for an assessment *in concreto*, is of critical importance.' See also Larissa van den Herik/Emma Irving, 'Due Diligence and the Obligation to Prevent Genocide and Crimes Against Humanity', chapter 12 of this book, section 1.

obligations and require the parties to realise the stipulated normative objective to the widest extent possible, for example in human rights law, might for that reason be qualified as embodying due diligence.[57]

The identification of customary due diligence norms is similarly difficult. State representatives only rarely refer to due diligence explicitly, making the ascertainment of an *opinio iuris* hard. In consequence, it has so far been incumbent mostly on courts and tribunals, such as the ICJ and ITLOS, to find customary due diligence obligations in international law.[58]

Beyond the formal sources of Article 38 ICJ Statute, soft law documents increasingly shape due diligence standards.[59] But the indiscriminate reliance on binding and non-binding due diligence norms might be another source of confusion. Such a critique has been raised against the use of the term in the UN Guiding Principles on Business and Human Rights.[60]

The diversity of due diligence sources raises follow-up questions: do we have to categorically distinguish between 'soft' and 'hard' due diligence norms or do they converge in substance and effect? Could their alignment point towards an elevation of transnational private actors to the status of international legal persons in the due diligence-context?

[57] See for an appraisal of the due diligence dimension of the fundamental right to life under art. 2 ECHR, Björnstjern Baade, 'Due Diligence and the Duty to Protect Human Rights', chapter 6 of this book, section 6.

[58] See above (n. 2) and (n. 3). See on the law-making aspect of judgments on due diligence Serena Forlati, 'L'objet des différentes obligations primaires de diligence: prévention, cessation, répression . . . ?', in SFDI/Cassella (n. 4), 39–66, at 59: 'Sans doute la juridiction internationale exerce une fonction "créatrice" quand elle apprécie le contenu des obligations primaires de diligence.'

[59] This is shown by various chapters in this book: Radha Ivory pointed to the relevance of the standards of the Financial Action Task Force (FATF) for the determination of the due diligence required of state and non-state actors in international anti-corruption law, Radha Ivory, 'Due Diligence Debates in International Anti-Corruption and Money Laundering Law: From Content to the Construction of Risk', chapter 17 of this book; Markus Krajewski highlighted the relevance of the guidelines of the EU Commission for assessing trade-related policy initiatives. Cf. European Commission, Guidelines on the analysis of human rights impacts in impact assessments for trade-related policy initiatives of 19 July 2015, available at: http://trade.ec.europa.eu/doclib/docs/2015/july/tradoc_153591.pdf (accessed 15 April 2020); Markus Krajewski, 'Due Diligence in International Trade Law', chapter 19 of this book. Reuven Avi-Yonah and Gianluca Mazzoni analysed the relevance of OECD Common Reporting Standards for international Tax Law, Reuven Avi-Yonah/Gianluca Mazzoni, 'Due Diligence in International Tax Law', chapter 18 of this book.

[60] See Baade, 'Human Rights', chapter 6 of this book, section 2.1, discussing the 'Ruggie Principles', UN, Human Rights Council, Human rights and transnational corporations and other business enterprises, Resolution 17/4, A/HRC/RES/17/4, 6 July 2011, para. 1. See for the controversy Jonathan Bonnitcha/Robert McCorquodale, 'The Concept of 'Due Diligence' in the UN Guiding Principles on Business and Human Rights', *European Journal of International Law* 28 (2017), 899–919; John Gerard Ruggie/John F. Sherman III, 'The Concept of "Due Diligence" in the UN Guiding Principles on Business and Human Rights: A Reply to Jonathan Bonnitcha and Robert McCorquodale', *European Journal of International Law* 28 (2017), 921–928.

6. Due Diligence Requirements

It is difficult to define *ex ante* what due diligence demands.[61] The requirements of due diligence are context-dependent, often highly discretionary. In practice, the 'optimal' diligence probably never plays a role. When a dispute arises, the question is rather the bottom line. Court or other monitoring bodies will have to decide when due diligence was breached, not what would have been best. Early cases often had a strong repressive tilt, concentrating on due diligence violations for failure to diligently prosecute and punish offenders. Yet with the increasing relevance of due diligence in treaty and customary norms and accompanying case law[62] a more diverse range of due diligence requirements has evolved. Tentatively, two broad categories can be identified:[63]

- Obligations with regard to a state's institutional capacity[64] such as legislative or administrative safeguard measures (e.g., sanctioning of violations by enacting criminal law provisions or by establishing quasi-judicial procedures for concerned persons[65] in administrative processes), or suitable monitoring mechanisms (e.g., periodic inspection measures with regard to hazardous activities).[66]
- Procedural obligations to notify, to inform, to consult, to cooperate, to conduct risk assessments,[67] to monitor, to warn,[68] to publicly explain, or to take feasible precautions.

[61] See for an overview of the relevant parameters Pierre d'Argent/Alexia de Vaucleroy, 'Le contenu de l'omission illicite: la non utilisation de moyens raisonnables', in SFDI/Cassella (n. 4), 255-280.

[62] See on the specification of due diligence requirements through case law Baade, 'Human Rights', chapter 6 of this book, section 4.

[63] Koivurova, 'Due Diligence' 2010 (n. 9), para. 21; one may alternatively categorise due diligence requirements into preventative measures before the occurrence of harm (e.g., the obligation to conduct a risk assessment) and repressive measures after the occurrence of harm (e.g., the obligation to prosecute and punish). However, such categories would frequently overlap: For example, an effective criminal prosecution *after* the occurrence of harm would require the enactment of a criminal law provision *before* its occurrence.

[64] This category refers to measures akin to those listed in the ILC Draft Articles on Prevention (n. 18), 370, art. 5: 'States concerned shall take the necessary legislative, administrative or other action including the establishment of suitable monitoring mechanisms to implement the provisions of the present articles'.

[65] Ibid., 399, art. 5, commentary, para. 2.

[66] Ibid.

[67] Ibid., 373, art. 7: 'Any decision in respect of the authorization of an activity within the scope of the present articles shall, in particular, be based on an assessment of the possible transboundary harm caused by that activity, including any environmental impact assessment.'

[68] For an example of a notification obligation see ibid., art. 8 (1): 'If the assessment (. . .) indicates a risk of causing significant transboundary harm, the State of origin shall provide the State likely to be affected with timely notification of the risk and the assessment and shall transmit to it the available technical and all other relevant information on which the assessment is based.' See for an example of a consultation obligation, ibid., art. 9 (1): 'The States concerned shall enter into consultations, at the request of any of them, with a view to achieving acceptable solutions regarding measures to be adopted in order to prevent significant transboundary harm or at any event to minimize the risk thereof (. . .)'.

Does the increasing specification make it easier to predict what due diligence requires *ex ante*? Is a trend towards more timely, more permanent, and more stringent risk containment discernible? Does the concretisation in various issue areas mean that due diligence is becoming more effective as a legal concept? Or rather to the contrary: does the growing detail strip off the concept's proprium—its inherent flexibility and its link to obligations of conduct? Is due diligence simply 'overrated'?[69]

7. Outline of the Book

The lack of conceptual, terminological, and source-related clarity motivates the basic question this book seeks to address: Can we identify a common content, scope, and function of due diligence in international law? The cross-cutting and bottom-up approach pursued in this book means to take a step back, and to map how the concept of due diligence has played out throughout various areas of international law in order to arrive at some generalisable conclusions.

For this purpose, the book is divided into four parts: due diligence and general international law (Part I), due diligence in international environmental law (Part II), due diligence in international peace and security law (Part III), and due diligence in international economic law (Part IV). The areas chosen represent the most important constellations in which due diligence plays an established role.[70] The breadth of these categories highlights that due diligence is no longer relevant only for isolated or specific areas of international law but has become a central leitmotif of international accountability debates.

7.1 Due Diligence and General International Law (Part I)

Part I surveys overarching and central aspects of the concept starting with the historical roots of due diligence in international law. Giulio Bartolini's analysis reveals that the key features of due diligence already emerged in the nineteenth century, such as the utilisation of due diligence 'slang' in the formulation of treaty obligations or the relevance of the available means at the disposal of a state. Also

[69] Pisillo Mazzeschi, 'Le chemin étrange' 2018 (n. 10), 323 (translation by the authors).

[70] The book does not contain chapters on international disaster law and global health, fields in which due diligence has only recently received attention; see Gian Luca Burci, 'The Outbreak of COVID-19 Coronavirus: Are the International Health Regulations Fit for Purpose?', *EJIL: Talk!*, 27 February 2020, available at: https://www.ejiltalk.org/the-outbreak-of-covid-19-coronavirus-are-the-international-health-regulations-fit-for-purpose/ (accessed 13 April 2020); Antonio Coco/Talita de Souza Dias, 'Due Diligence and COVID-19: States' Duties to Prevent and Halt the Coronavirus Outbreak', Parts I-III, *EJIL: Talk!*, 24 and 25 March 2020, available at: https://www.ejiltalk.org/part-i-due-diligence-and-covid-19-states-duties-to-prevent-and-halt-the-coronavirus-outbreak/ (accessed 13 April 2020).

the degree of control of a state, the predictability of harm, and its likely severity have been traditional parameters for assessing which amount of diligence is due (chapter 2).

Zooming in on the traditional core field, Helmut Philipp Aust and Prisca Feihle examine due diligence in the history of the codification of the law of state responsibility. Their chapter scrutinises the often-overlooked work of the ILC First Special Rapporteur Francisco V. García-Amador, as well as the further evolution of the codification process under the ILC Special Rapporteurs Roberto Ago and James Crawford. The role due diligence played in the early drafting history serves as the basis for arguing that it can be helpful to conceptualise due diligence as sitting in-between the level of primary and secondary rules of international law. The chapter thus questions the popular narrative of a migration of due diligence from the level of secondary rules to the primary rules. For the later-on adopted secondary rules, the authors explore how due diligence could re-enter current debates on state responsibility in some unexpected contexts, especially within remaining subjective elements in the ARSIWA (chapter 3).

Due diligence obligations also play a prominent part in the ILC Draft Articles on the Responsibility of International Organizations. Kristina Daugirdas highlights that the Draft Articles are insufficient to address the complex response needed for an effective accountability mechanism for international organisations. The chapter postulates due diligence obligations of states to supervise international organisations and examines international organisations' own due diligence obligations to mitigate the accountability gap (chapter 4).

Due diligence is traditionally contingent upon the triad 'territory', 'jurisdiction', and 'control'. Federica Violi's chapter on territorial sovereignty and jurisdiction shows how difficult it is to neatly delineate these terms. She also enquires whether international legal discourse and practice is moving beyond the above-mentioned triad and has notably severed due diligence from its traditional territorial basis. Instead of being linked to territory, due diligence obligations could flow from an actor's capacity to influence, or from its power or authority (chapter 5).

The shift from territory to function is also visible in international human rights law. Björnstjern Baade analyses due diligence in this core area of international law and identifies the dual function of due diligence: First, due diligence implies a general duty to mitigate risks for human rights no matter their source. Second, due diligence standards have become an efficient tool for operationalising human rights treaty obligations (chapter 6).

7.2 Due Diligence in International Environmental Law (Part II)

International environmental law is arguably the area in which due diligence most prominently evolved. Jorge Viñuales traces the concept's relevance throughout environmental treaties, soft law instruments, and judicial and quasi-judicial decisions. His chapter provides a 'fine-grained cartography' of the operative parameters in international environmental law. It also examines how the growing recognition of the need to protect the environment per se influences the due diligence standard (chapter 7).

Malgosia Fitzmaurice's chapter on the law of international watercourses examines the interrelation of due diligence in general environmental law with international watercourses law. Her analysis of due diligence in multilateral and regional watercourses treaties illustrates the concept's primary function in this area as a normative tool to balance the interests of upstream and downstream states (chapter 8).

The next issue area in which due diligence fares prominently is the law of the sea. Irini Papanicolopulu examines due diligence obligations in the United Nations Convention on the Law of the Sea (UNCLOS).[71] Her chapter also studies the topical link between due diligence and the precautionary principle addressed by advisory opinions of the International Tribunal for the Law of the Sea[72] (chapter 9).

Due diligence may also be utilised for realising interests of the international community. Lavanya Rajamani's chapter on international climate change law illustrates the augmented role of due diligence in this area after the turn to flexible obligations of conduct in the Paris Agreement of 2015.[73] The chapter also points at the close link between due diligence and other legal or para-legal principles in this area, such as the precautionary principle, the expectation of good faith, and common but differentiated responsibilities (chapter 10).

7.3 International Peace and Security Law (Part III)

The prevention of threats for international peace and security is a *raison d'être* of the entire international legal order. Prevention can be informed and guided by due diligence obligations. Part III of the book analyses the relevant issues, in the law *contra bellum*, the law *in bello*, and anti-terrorism.

Marco Longobardo's chapter focusses on five issues of international humanitarian law: The duty to ensure respect for international humanitarian law, the conduct of hostilities, the protection of civilians and of persons *hors de combat*, the administration of occupied territories, and the law of non-international armed conflicts. His analysis shows that due diligence plays a significant role in

[71] UNCLOS, 1982 (n. 53).

[72] ITLOS, *Responsibilities and Obligations of States* (n. 3), para. 132.

[73] United Nations Framework Convention on Climate Change, Conference of the Parties, Decision 1/CP.21 ('Paris Agreement'), 13 December 2015, FCCC/CP/2015/10/Add, 1.

international humanitarian law, in line with the traditional equation of due diligence obligations with obligations of conduct (chapter 11).

In their chapter on the prevention of genocide and crimes against humanity, Larissa van den Herik and Emma Irving examine the dynamic character of due diligence as a potential catalyst of new obligations. Using the ICJ judgment in the *Bosnia Genocide* case as a starting point, they identify emerging due diligence requirements in this area, such as the need to publicly justify actions and omissions in the context of imminent risks of genocide and crimes against humanity, and a potential duty to employ available technology to mitigate risks as early and effectively as possible (chapter 12).

Nigel D. White analyses due diligence obligations in UN peacekeeping operations. He examines customary human rights law, the internal law of the UN, general principles of international law, and the model Status of Forces Agreement as potential due diligence sources. His analysis underscores the difficulty of heightening the accountability of international organisations (chapter 13).

Inger Österdahl's chapter on anti-terrorism law exemplifies the need for international risk containment and the difficulty to achieve this aim in each and every case. Her analysis of Security Council resolutions on counter-terrorism focusses on the question to what extent such resolutions have consolidated specific counter-terrorism duties of states and, if so, what these duties are (chapter 14).

The lack of consensus on a regulation of cyber activities by international law has stimulated a discourse on due diligence in cyber space. Eric Talbot Jensen analyses the thin understanding of cyber due diligence in the Tallinn Manual 2.0 of 2017 and criticises the reluctance of various states to commit to a more robust understanding of due diligence. Jensen favours a vigorous understanding of due diligence because this might deploy a stabilising potential in the cyber area (chapter 15).

7.4 International Economic Law (Part IV)

Several areas of international economic law exemplify how states and other actors are interconnected, how transnational interactions are growing, and how concomitant problems of allocating accountability for extraterritorial or transboundary harm arise. Pertinent issue areas are investment law, international anti-corruption and money-laundering law, international tax law, and international trade law.

Aniruddha Rajput analyses due diligence in international investment law. His chapter traces how due diligence requirements for the protection of foreign investment already emerged in the historical law of aliens, preceding investment treaties. The chapter also shows that due diligence obligations are becoming reciprocal: not only are host states obliged to act diligently but also investors must exercise due diligence when developing the potential of their investment (chapter 16).

In international anti-corruption and money-laundering law, risk governance which impacts on due diligence plays an important role. Radha Ivory examines the two-fold direction of international due diligence norms in this field, both horizontal (state-to-state) and transversal (state-to-business). She also identifies a de facto binding effect of Financial Action Task Force recommendations via enforcement mechanisms, and finally sees a structural shift towards risk management (chapter 17).

Reuven S. Avi-Yonah and Gianlucca Mazzoni analyse due diligence in international tax law. They examine the impact of the OECD Common Reporting Standards of 2014 for the states' due diligence and ask how a complementary accountability of public and private actors in this area could be strengthened (chapter 18).

Markus Krajewski maps due diligence obligations in international trade agreements. He attributes a crucial role to due diligence in this area which is often overlooked. In addition, his chapter examines due diligence in the negotiation and implementation of trade agreements, especially in the context of sustainable development and human rights impact assessments (chapter 19).

Diane A. Desierto analyses due diligence of the World Bank with regard to project financing, an area in which the diversity of actors and frequent operational complexity necessitate accountability enquiries. Her contribution delineates diligence parameters of the World Bank in the planning, execution, and supervision of project funding (chapter 20).

In the concluding chapter, Heike Krieger and Anne Peters pull together the threads and discuss whether and how due diligence both manifests and drives structural change in international law (chapter 21).

8. Due Diligence as an Indicator of Structural Change in the International Legal Order?

The range and the content of topics dealt with in this volume suggest that the increasing relevance of due diligence might indicate structural change in the international legal order. Due diligence is closely linked to several other trends which seem to respond to ongoing and arguably deepening challenges to international law. These include the putative erosion of the international rule of law,[74] the

[74] Heike Krieger/Georg Nolte, 'The International Rule of Law—Rise or Decline? Approaching Current Foundational Challenges', in Heike Krieger/Georg Nolte/Andreas Zimmermann (eds), *The International Rule of Law—Rise or Decline?* (Oxford: OUP 2019), 3–30.

pluralisation of international legal subjects,[75] the de-formalisation,[76] and finally the proceduralisation[77] of international law.

The identification and assessment of such structural change to which the rise of due diligence might both contribute and respond depends on how the observers perceive and frame the overall state of the international legal order. A popular narrative describes international law as a legal order composed of different layers which have grown over time.[78] The oldest layer of an 'international law of co-ordination' aimed at preserving the status quo against changes and disruption, basically refrained from determining in substance how societies within states should develop, and rather foresaw only some rules for joint action.[79] In such a legal order, accountability primarily operates retrospectively and seeks to restitute the status quo ante while creating incentives to behave in accordance with the law. This first layer of international law centres around single states focusses on the protection of bilateral relations, national interests, and goods, and sees co-operation as the exception not the rule.

While these considerations are still relevant, international law has broadened its objectives and instruments for ordering constantly evolving and increasingly complex global affairs. The moves of international law after 1945 and again after 1990 have been described as a turn to a law of cooperation.[80] According to Wolfgang Friedman, the 'universal international law of co-operation' is 'the body of legal rules regulating universal human concerns, the range of which is constantly expanding' and it 'extends from matters of international security to questions of international communication, health and wealth.' It builds on a 'community of interests and values', a community which encompasses a large number of new states and new actors ranging from state agencies to private groups.[81]

More recently, notably in the 1990s, a third layer of international law has been added. It consists of a host of multilateral treaty regimes, equipped with international institutions including international courts and tribunals. These institutions have engaged in intense law production which has given rise to

[75] Math Noortmann/August Reinisch/Cedric Ryngaert (eds), *Non-State Actors in International Law* (Oxford/Portland, Oregon: Hart Publishing 2015).

[76] Joost Pauwelyn/Ramses Wessel/Jan Wouters (eds), *Informal International Lawmaking* (Oxford: OUP 2012).

[77] Jochen Rauber, 'Zukunftsorientierung und Prozeduralisierung im öffentlichen Recht—Parallelen in der Entwicklung von innerstaatlicher und völkerrechtlicher Ordnung', *Archiv des öffentlichen Rechts* 143 (2018), 67–121, at 102–119.

[78] Joseph Weiler, 'The Geology of International Law', *Heidelberg Journal of International Law* 64 (2004), 547–562.

[79] The dichotomy 'law of coordination' versus 'law of cooperation' is from Wolfgang Friedman, *The Changing Structure of International Law* (New York: Columbia UP 1964). See for a succinct portrayal of both layers (which Wolfrum calls 'different techniques of legal regulation') Rüdiger Wolfrum, 'International Law', in Rüdiger Wolfrum (ed.), *Max Planck Encyclopedia of Public International Law* (Oxford: OUP 2015), paras 39–65.

[80] Friedman, 'Changing Structure' 1964 (n. 79).

[81] Ibid., 365, 366.

sophisticated—often conflictual—interaction with the national law of states. This third layer of law and actors has been analysed and conceptualised by theories of constitutionalisation and global constitutionalism,[82] of global administrative law,[83] in concepts of global governance,[84] or international public authority.[85] These approaches are mostly complementary. All seem to agree that the law has responded to ongoing economic, technical, cultural, and social connectivity, and that the 'level' of regulation (international or national) and the 'form' (hard or soft law) seems to become less important. From the perspective of global constitutionalism, the rise of due diligence might signal a kind of de-constitutionalisation of international law, because this term is taken from the reservoir of tort law, contract law, and criminal law, but is not a typical constitutional principle. A Global Administrative Law approach would conceptualise due diligence as a kind of administrative procedure and inquire into its effectiveness and legitimacy. Through the lens of global governance, due diligence appears as a governance strategy for regulating the globalised 'risk society' which has emerged in the second half of the twentieth century.[86]

The following chapters' meticulous analyses of the very specific operations of due diligence in the particular issue areas of international law steer far from these grand narratives. But they provide the material for a bottom-up analysis of the interplay between the rise of due diligence and other strands of the current evolution of the international legal order. In our concluding chapter[87] we will pull the threads together in order to examine notably how due diligence tackles pressing accountability challenges in the international order, and thereby both manifests and contributes to a transformation of international law.

[82] Anne Peters, 'Constitutionalization', in Sahib Singh/Jean d'Aspremont (eds), *Concepts for International Law: Contributions to Disciplinary Thought* (Cheltenham: Edward Elgar 2019), 141–153.

[83] Benedict Kingsbury/Nico Krisch/Richard Stewart, 'The Emergence of Global Administrative Law', *Law and Contemporary Problems* 68 (2005), 15–61; Sabino Cassese, 'Administrative Law without the State? The Challenge of Global Regulation', *New York University Journal of International Law and Politics* 37 (2005), 663–694.

[84] James N. Rosenau/Ernst-Otto Czempiel (eds), *Governance without Government: Order and Change in World Politics* (Cambridge: Cambridge Studies in International Relations 1992); Commission on Global Governance, *Our Global Neighborhood* (Oxford: OUP 1995).

[85] Armin von Bogdandy/Matthias Goldmann/Ingo Venzke, 'From Public International to International Public Law: Translating World Public Opinion into International Public Authority', *European Journal of International Law* 28 (2017), 115–145.

[86] Weiler, 'Geology' 2004 (n. 78), 550.

[87] Krieger/Peters, 'Structural Change', chapter 21 of this book.

PART I
DUE DILIGENCE AND GENERAL INTERNATIONAL LAW

2

The Historical Roots of the Due Diligence Standard

Giulio Bartolini

1. Due Diligence in a Historical Perspective: A Move from Secondary to Primary Rules

For a long period, due diligence did not attract autonomous attention and scholars embedded elements pertaining to this standard within broader theoretical discussions on issues related to the role of fault or the attribution of wrongful acts for activities of private individuals.[1] Indeed, 'it was not until the nineteenth century that due diligence began to take shape and was applied as both a duty and a constraint upon state behaviour'.[2] During this formative moment, due diligence was progressively used in its contemporary manifestation: as a legal benchmark for assessing which measures a state is required to take in order to comply with obligations of conduct characterised by a component of *alea* in the fulfilment of the required goal.[3] The shift was probably linked to several different elements.

First, due diligence acted 'as the counterbalance to state sovereignty':[4] while sovereignty implied a state's exclusive jurisdiction over its territory, due diligence obligations emphasised certain measures states were expected to undertake in order to protect the interests of other states. This standard was thus instrumental in giving guidance on corollary duties of protection provided by the rule on territorial sovereignty. Second, the inherently flexible character of due diligence, namely its being

[1] Jan Hessbruegge, 'The Historical Developments of the Doctrine of Attribution and Due Diligence in International Law', *New York University Journal of International Law and Policy* 36 (2004), 265–306; Giuseppe Palmisano, 'Fault', in Rüdiger Wolfrum (ed.), *Max Planck Encyclopedia of Public International Law* (Oxford: OUP 2007).

[2] International Law Association (ILA), Study Group on Due Diligence in International Law, First Report, 7 March 2014, 2; Riccardo Pisillo Mazzeschi, 'Le chemin étrange de la due diligence: d'un concept mystérieux à un concept surévalué', in Société Française pour le Droit International (SFDI)/Sarah Cassella (eds), *Le standard de due diligence et la responsabilité internationale* (Paris: Pedone 2018), 323–337: 'due diligence (. . .) saw its light, at the international level, in the famous 1872 Alabama award' (author's translation) 5.

[3] Riccardo Pisillo Mazzeschi, 'The Due Diligence Rule and the Nature of the International Responsibility of States', *German Yearbook of International Law* 35 (1992), 9–51, at 30.

[4] Joanna Kulesza, *Due Diligence in International Law* (Leiden/Boston: Brill 2016), 58.

Giulio Bartolini, *The Historical Roots of the Due Diligence Standard* In: *Due Diligence in the International Legal Order.*
Edited by: Heike Krieger, Anne Peters, and Leonhard Kreuzer, Oxford University Press (2020).
DOI: 10.1093/oso/9780198869900.003.0002.

able to accommodate different concerns,[5] favoured its emergence and thereby permitted the avoidance of cumbersome standards of protection disproportionately limiting state sovereignty. As recognised by Clyde Eagleton, while 'the exclusive control which the state has over its own territories' would apparently imply state responsibility 'for all injurious acts occurring therein, the community of nations (…) has alleviated the force of the principle in practice by the rule of due diligence'.[6] Third, and most significantly, 'once the "turn to arbitration" had been established',[7] case law largely assumed a 'creative' function,[8] providing the possibility to 'empirically establish the rules of law'[9] related to due diligence through a bottom-up approach not dissimilar to contemporary reappraisals. Indeed, academic contributions in the nineteenth and early decades of the twentieth centuries largely replicated formulas inferred from practice.[10] Consequently, putting due diligence obligations to the test of dispute settlement mechanisms permitted the identifying of normative benchmarks capable of filling this flexible concept with more specific content and clarifying the supposed standard of conduct required in concrete contexts. Fourth, once early codifications favoured the emergence of treaty provisions requiring positive measures and a series of combined efforts to be put in place by a state's apparatus, the drafting of such rules and provisions to entail due diligence obligations thus granted states the necessary flexibility to avoid overly strict standards. And finally, the progressive qualification of acts of private individuals as mere 'catalyst' events,[11] and thereby potentially implying state responsibility mainly for omissions attributable to its organs, favoured the rise of due diligence in order to identify measures required by these obligations.

2. Mapping Early Examples of Due Diligence Obligations

This section aims to provide a survey of international obligations recognised at an early stage in practice and by scholars to have a potential due diligence component. Even if it could be maintained that only a quantitatively limited number of

[5] Riccardo Pisillo Mazzeschi, *Due Diligence e responsabilità internazionale degli Stati* (Milano: Giuffrè 1989), 44.

[6] Clyde Eagleton, *The Responsibility of States in International Law* (New York: New York University Press 1928), 94.

[7] Kathryn Greenman, 'Aliens in Latin America: Intervention, Arbitration and State Responsibility for Rebels', *Leiden Journal of International Law* 31 (2018), 617–639, at 624.

[8] For contemporary case law, see Serena Forlati, 'L'objet des différentes obligations primaires de diligence: prévention, cessation, répression … ?', in SFDI/Sarah Cassella (eds), *Le standard de due diligence et la responsabilité internationale* (Paris: Pedone 2018), 59–63.

[9] Edwin Borchard, 'La responsabilité internationale des États à la Conférence de la codification de La Haye', *Revue de droit international et de législation comparée* 58 (1931), 37–60, at 60 (author's translation).

[10] Pisillo Mazzeschi, 'Le chemin' 2018 (n. 2), 325.

[11] Roberto Ago, Fourth Report on State Responsibility, YBILC 1972, vol. II, paras 61–136, para. 140.

due diligence obligations were recognised in the nineteenth and early twentieth century, it should be emphasised how they were able to cover a significant portion of issues relevant for an international legal order depicted along the lines of co-existence,[12] thus confirming the continuing relevance of this topic.

2.1 Protection of Foreigners

An obligation on states to provide protection to foreigners and their properties is one of the earliest rules of customary law.[13] Several activities characterised as having a due diligence component were progressively associated with the obligation of states to prevent and repress the detrimental activities of private individuals. Due diligence as the proper standard to assess conducts required in concrete contexts was so widely established that it was officially recognised both in the 1929 codification project of the Harvard Law School[14] and as the basis of discussions submitted by the preparatory committee for the 1930 League of Nations Conference on Codification. In particular the basis of discussions claimed that a state could be held responsible for a wrongful act when it 'has failed to show in the protection of such foreigner's person or property such diligence as, having regard to the circumstances and to any special status possessed by him, could be expected from a civilized State', and required, in similar terms, the exercise of 'diligence in detecting and punishing the author of the damage'.[15]

Nineteenth- and early-twentieth-century case law, and complemented by scholars,[16] had indeed confirmed as a leitmotif references to due diligence in the context of evaluating the required efforts of states in using their apparatus to prevent injuries to aliens. For instance, the *Youmans* case referred to possible failures 'to exercise due diligence to protect'[17] aliens. Similarly, the adoption of 'reasonabl[e]'[18] measures were requested in other cases. Likewise, due diligence characterised actions requiring states to investigate and apprehend those private

[12] Wolfang Friedmann, *The Changing Structure of International Law* (London: Stevens & Sons 1964).

[13] Emer de Vattel, *The Law of Nations or the Principles of Natural Law Applied to the Conduct and to the Affairs of Nations and of Sovereigns*, 1758, Book II, Chapter VIII, para. 104, translation of the edition of 1758 by Charles Fenwick (Washington: Carnegie Institution of Washington 1916), vol. III, 145.

[14] Harvard Law School, 'The Law and Responsibility of States for Damage Done in Their Territory to the Person or Property of Foreigners', *American Journal of International Law* 23 (1929), Supplement, 131–239, at 134, arts 10–11.

[15] The basis of discussion, (No. 10, 17, and 18) are reproduced in Francisco García Amador, International Responsibility: Second Report, A/CN.4/106, 15 February 1957, 124, para. 14.

[16] Charles Calvo, *Le droit international théorique et pratique, Tome I* (Paris: Guillaumin 3rd ed. 1880), 425–427; Amos Hershey, *The Essentials of International Public Law* (New York: The Macmillan Company 1912), 162.

[17] General Claims Commission (Mexico-USA), *Youmans*, 23 November 1926, UNRIAA, vol. IV, 114.

[18] Claims Commission (Venezuela-USA), *De Brissot and others Case*, in John Moore, *History and Digest of the International Arbitrations to which the United States Has Been a Party*, vol. III (Washington: Government Printing Office 1898), 2968.

individuals responsible for injuries to aliens.[19] For instance, in the *Sewell* case, Mexico was held responsible because of a 'lack of diligence in the pursuit and apprehension of the culprits'.[20] Similarly, the *Janes* case mentioned a 'duty of diligently prosecuting and properly punishing the offender'.[21] Also in the case of the *Spanish Zone of Morocco*, the lack of effective sanctioning via criminal and civil law led to international responsibility.[22] In other cases, the failure of states 'to exercise properly their functions'[23] of repression was the key legal parameter, while once 'reasonable diligence'[24] had been recognised by concerned states, international responsibility was denied.

2.2 Protection of Other States

The protection to be provided to other states involved different scenarios. First, regarding representatives of foreign states, a customary rule characterised by a due diligence obligation imposed more demanding measures in comparison to 'common' cases dealing with aliens, due to the relevance of protected interest. Indeed, as recognised by Emer de Vattel:

> it is true that the sovereign should protect every man who happens to be in his States (. . .) but this care is due in a higher degree to a foreign minister.[25]

This position was not challenged by subsequent authors. Johan Caspar Bluntschli, for example, claimed:

> this general duty increases and it could be said that it is brought to a higher level with regard to representatives of foreign states.[26]

Also international practice confirmed that a higher diligence was required with regard to representatives of foreign states. The American-Mexican General Claims Commission held that regarding 'the safety of a consular officer (. . .) due account

[19] Eagleton, *Responsibility* 1928 (n. 6), 92.
[20] General Claims Commission (Mexico-USA), *Sewell*, 24 October 1930, UNRIAA, vol. IV, 632.
[21] General Claims Commission (Mexico-USA), *Janes*, 16 November 1925, UNRIAA, vol. IV, 87.
[22] Max Huber, *Affaire des biens britanniques au Maroc espagnol (Spain v. UK)*, 1 May 1925, UNRIAA, vol. II, 644.
[23] Mixed Claims Commission (Italy-Venezuela), *Poggioli*, 1903, UNRIAA, vol. X, 689.
[24] Claims Commission (Venezuela-USA), *Wippermann*, 2 July 1868, in Moore, *History* 1898 (n. 18), 3041; General Claims Commission (Mexico-USA), *Neer*, 15 October 1926, UNRIAA, vol. IV, 62; General Claims Commission (Mexico-USA), *Miller*, 26 September 1928, UNRIAA, vol. IV, 336–337.
[25] de Vattel, *The Law* 1758 (n. 13), 371, Book III, Chapter VII, para. 82.
[26] Johan Caspar Bluntschli, *Le droit international codifié* (Paris: Libraire de Guillaumin et Cie 2nd ed. 1874), 140. Similarly, see Lassa Oppenheim, *International Law: A Treatise: Peace*, vol. I (London: Longmans 1905), 438.

[shall] be taken of his special position',[27] as was echoed regarding assaults against another Mexican consul in 1907.[28] This approach was similarly endorsed by the Committee of Jurists appointed by the Council of the League of Nations for the *Tellini* case: while in such scenarios a state needs to 'take all reasonable measures' for the prevention and repression of such injures, '[t]he recognised public character of a foreigner and the circumstances in which he is present in the territory entail upon the State a corresponding duty of special vigilance on his behalf'.[29] This position was firm enough to be endorsed by the preparatory committee for the 1930 League of Nations Conference on Codification, according to which 'the fact that a foreigner is invested with a recognized public status imposes upon the State a special duty of vigilance'.[30] The notion of due diligence also emerged in relation to duties to prevent the use of a state's territory for activities carried out by private individuals potentially detrimental to other states.

A first scenario pertained to the law of neutrality, especially when the subject of due diligence was significantly debated during the *Alabama* case,[31] bringing leading scholars to affirm that it permitted the judicial 'consecration' of due diligence with regard to the law of neutrality.[32] However, references to the obligations of neutral states to adopt appropriate efforts to prevent such activities were already recognised by scholars prior to the *Alabama* arbitration. Laurent-Basil Hautefeuille emphasised how:

> The neutral sovereign must control with the utmost care that warships of belligerents will not leave their ports or other areas under their domain stronger and better equipped than they were before getting in.[33]

Authors such as Bluntschli pinpointed the due diligence component of these obligations as the need to exercise strict surveillance[34] in such scenarios, or to do everything possible to avoid the departure of troops from its territory, as maintained through an extensive literature review by Charles Calvo.[35]

27 General Claims Commission (Mexico-USA), *Chapman*, 24 October 1930, UNRIAA, vol. IV, 634.

28 General Claims Commission (Mexico-USA), *Mallén*, 27 April 1927, UNRIAA, vol. IV, 173.

29 League of Nations, *Official Journal* 4 (1924), 524.

30 Basis of discussion No. 10 (n. 15).

31 On the *Alabama* case, see below section 3 and Jorge E. Viñuales, 'Due Diligence in International Environmental Law', chapter 7 of this book, section 2.1.

32 Awalou Ouedraogo, 'La neutralité et l'émergence du concept de due diligence en droit international. L'affaire de l'Alabama revisité', *Journal of the History of International Law* 13 (2011), 307–346, at 335.

33 Laurent-Basil Hautefeuille, *Des droits et des devoirs des nations neutres en temps de guerre maritime*, vol. I (Paris: Libraire de Guillaumin 3rd ed. 1868), 233 (author's translation).

34 Bluntschli, *Le droit international* 1874 (n. 26), 422.

35 Charles Calvo, 'Les trois règles de droit maritime proposée par le Traité de Washington', *Revue de droit international et de législation comparée* 6 (1874), 453–552, at 514–521.

Nevertheless, the *Alabama* award was a pioneer in that it tested the general references to due diligence included in the so-called three rules of Washington expressed in Article VI of the bilateral treaty of 1871, which aimed to provide guidance to the arbitrators against concrete events. In particular, the award was significant both for highlighting factors influencing this standard, as explored in paragraph 3, and to promote subsequent codification framed in due diligence terms. The rules on the duties of neutral states, as provided by the Institut de Droit International at The Hague session of 1875, confirmed a duty to survey these activities,[36] while the Hague Convention concerning the Rights and Duties of Neutral Powers in Naval War[37] clearly endorsed due diligence parameters. In particular, the Convention's Article 8 stated that a 'neutral State is bound to employ the means at its disposal to prevent the fitting out or arming of any vessel within its jurisdiction'; it also has to 'display the same vigilance to prevent the departure from its jurisdiction' of military vessels belonging to belligerent states, as echoed by Article 25 on the prevention of any violations of the Convention.

Early codifications pertaining to neutral states confirmed how due diligence added elements of flexibility to the required measures. Article 57 of the Regulations annexed to the Second Hague Convention on the Laws and Customs of War of 1899[38] imposed that when neutral states intern troops belonging to belligerent armies they should do so 'as far as possible, at a distance from the theatre of war', while Article 59 required them 'to adopt such measures of safety and control as may be necessary' for the transit back to the belligerent parties of their wounded or sick. Once attention moved towards obligations of third states in civil wars, references to due diligence were maintained, such as in the 1900 resolution of the Institut de Droit International.[39] Finally, in Article 1 of the 1928 Havana Convention on Rights and Duties of States in Case of Civil Wars, the parties agreed to 'use all means at their disposal to prevent the inhabitants of their territory' from participating in or amassing the means for engaging in civil strife.[40]

Furthermore, in light of the duties connected to territorial sovereignty, some scholars affirmed more general obligations on states to prevent private individuals from carrying out detrimental activities against other states, especially with regard to hostile propaganda, conspiracies, or raids, where references to due diligence

[36] Institut de Droit International, *Annuaire de l'Institut de droit international* 1 (1877), 139–140.

[37] Convention concerning the Rights and Duties of Neutral Powers in Naval War (XIII), 18 October 1907, translated in James Scott (ed.), *The Proceedings of the Hague Peace Conference: The Conference of 1907*, vol. I (New York: OUP 1920), 672–677.

[38] Regulations Respecting the Laws and Customs of War on Land, 29 July 1899, translated in ibid.

[39] Institut de Droit International, *Annuaire de l'Institut de droit international* 18 (1900), 227.

[40] Convention on Duties and Rights of States in the Event of Civil Strife, 20 February 1928, 134 LNTS 47.

were sometimes present.[41] The echo of such references was also present in domestic and international case law.

For instance, in 1887 the US Supreme Court in the *Arjona* case cited de Vattel on the wrongful act committed by states that protect false coiners[42] to justify domestic legislation aimed at repressing such activities and stated that the 'law of nations requires every national government to use "due diligence" to prevent a wrong being done within its own dominion to another nation with which it is at peace, or to the people thereof'.[43] Similarly, in 1875 the American-Mexican Claims Commission analysed, with negative conclusions, whether 'there was a want of due diligence on the part of the Mexican authorities in preventing' the robbery of cattle at the Texas border.[44] Subsequently, the dissenting opinion of Judge John Moore in the *Lotus* case referred to the above-mentioned *Arjona* case and maintained that 'it is well settled that a State is bound to use due diligence to prevent the commission within its dominions of criminal acts against another nation or its people'.[45] A similar line of reasoning was upheld in affirming the responsibility of Canada in the *Trail Smelter* case. Due diligence was relevant here in reaching this conclusion, which was arrived at by way of reference to 'international decisions, in various matters, from the Alabama case onward', and to the writings of Eagleton, according to whom '[a] State owes at all times a duty to protect other States against injurious acts by individuals from within its jurisdiction'.[46] The *Trail Smelter* award found in this an expression of a 'general principle'.[47]

2.3 International Humanitarian Law

Even if the majority of early treaty provisions referred to negative obligations or obligations of result, some positive obligations drafted to incorporate a due diligence standard were present. Even if early treaties only went as far as mentioning terms and phrases associated with 'due diligence slang', such as 'necessary steps' or 'as far as possible', their content clearly indicated how this legal parameter was the point of reference for their interpretation, as maintained in contemporary provisions.[48]

[41] Calvo, *Le droit* 1880 (n. 16), 425–426; Alphonse Rivier, *Principes du droit des gens*, vol. I (Paris: Arthur Rosseau 1896), 266; Robert Phillimore, *Commentaries upon International Law*, vol. I (London: Butterworths 1871), 255–261.

[42] de Vattel, *The Law* 1758 (n. 13), 46, Book I, Chapter X, para. 108.

[43] US Supreme Court, *United States v. Arjona*, 7 March 1887, 120 U.S. Reports 1887, 484.

[44] Umpire Thornton, *Dickens Case (USA v. Mexico)*, 3 December 1875, in Moore, *History* 1898 (n. 18), 3037.

[45] Permanent Court of International Justice, *The Case of the S.S. Lotus (France v. Turkey)*, Dissenting Opinion by Moore, 7 September 1927, Series A, No. 10, 88.

[46] Eagleton, *The Responsibility* 1928 (n. 6), 80.

[47] *Trail Smelter Case (USA v. Canada)*, Decision of 16 April 1938, UNRIAA, vol. III, 1963.

[48] Gabriella Venturini, 'Les obligations de diligence dans le droit international humanitaire', in SFDI/ Sarah Cassella (eds), *Le standard de due diligence et la responsabilité internationale* (Paris: Pedone 2018),

Such provisions mainly aimed at introducing margins of appreciation helpful in front of complexities present in conflicts. For instance, in dealing with the conduct of hostilities, Articles 26 and 27 of the Regulations annexed to the 1899 Hague Convention on War on Land—as reiterated in the Regulations to the Fourth Hague Convention of 1907[49]—clarified that the commander 'before commencing a bombardment (…) should do all he can to warn the authorities', and that 'in sieges and bombardments all necessary steps should be taken to spare as far as possible' some specifically protected edifices. The law of occupation similarly introduced provisions parameterised through due diligence, like Article 43 of the 1899 and 1907 Hague Regulations claiming that the occupying power 'shall take all steps in his power to re-establish and ensure, as far as possible, public order and safety', while other provisions balanced the need to apply the standards mentioned in treaty provisions with the caveat 'as far as possible'.[50]

Interestingly, references to due diligence obligations emerged once codification efforts progressed, apparently with the aim of smoothing over solutions held in previous treaties. A test case is offered by the obligation to search for wounded combatants, originally expressed in peremptory terms by Article 6 of the 1864 Geneva Convention, whereby 'wounded or sick combatants (…) shall be collected and cared for'.[51] This same duty was confirmed by Articles 3 and 4 of the 1929 Geneva Convention on the Wounded and Sick,[52] which required more generally that 'after each engagement the occupant of the field of battle shall take measures to search for the wounded and dead', a terminology finally modified by Article 15 of the First Geneva Convention of 1949 which refers to 'all possible measures'[53] and clearly pinpoints due diligence elements. Similarly, whether Article 3 of the 1906 Geneva Convention required belligerents to conduct 'a careful examination (…) of the bodies of the dead prior to their interment or incineration', Article 4 of the 1929 Geneva Convention requested, more smoothly, that belligerents should conduct 'if possible, [a] medical examination'.

Similarly, once more structured and positive obligations complemented the original negative ones, due diligence acquired an additional role, as can be seen in the

135–144; see Marco Longobardo, 'Due Diligence in International Humanitarian Law', chapter 11 of this book, section 2.1.

49 For 1899, see Scott, *Conference of 1899* 1920 (n. 38); for 1907, see Regulations concerning the Laws and Customs of War on Land, 18 October 1907, translated in Scott, *Conference of 1907* 1920 (n. 37), 623–631.

50 Articles 48 and 51 of the 1899 Hague Regulations applied this standard for the collection of taxes and tools 'in accordance with the rules of assessment and incidence in force'. According to art. 52 (3) of the 1907 Hague Regulation, '[c]ontributions in kind shall, as far as possible, be paid for in cash'.

51 Convention for the Amelioration of the Condition of the Wounded in Armies in the Field, 22 August 1864, in Dietrich Schindler/Jiri Toman, *The Laws of Armed Conflicts: A Collection of Conventions, Resolutions and Other Documents* (Leiden: Martinus Nijhoff 1988), 280–281.

52 Convention for the Amelioration of the Condition of the Wounded and Sick in Armies in the Field, 27 July 1929, in ibid., 326–334.

53 Geneva Convention for the Amelioration of the Condition of the Wounded and Sick in Armed Forces in the Field, 2 August 1949, 75 UNTS 31.

1929 Geneva Convention on Prisoners of War, which substantially supplemented previous basic provisions. First, Article 2 required the protection of prisoners of war, particularly 'from insults and from public curiosity', prefiguring current obligations that imply a due diligence component.[54] Other provisions provided flexibility in relation to complex conflict situations, imposing 'as soon as possible' to evacuate prisoners to areas far from the hostilities (Article 7); pass on data to the Information Bureau and enable for correspondence (Article 8); and move prisoners to internment camps located in climatically favourable locations (Article 9). Similarly, the request not to mix 'prisoners of different races and nationalities' was to be realised only 'as far as possible' (Article 9); while detaining powers were required 'to take all necessary hygienic measures' regarding the camps (Article 13).

Finally, a number of obligations addressed a state's institutional capacity to facilitate the respect of protected interests: Article 26 of the 1906 Geneva Convention requested that states 'take the necessary steps to acquaint their troops (…) with the provisions of this convention', while Article 27, dealing with criminal prosecution, requires measures 'to prevent the use, by private persons or by societies' of protected emblems. However, their qualification as due diligence obligations is debatable, as explored for similar human rights provisions.

2.4 Human Rights Law

In pre-World War II treaties some obligations characterised by a due diligence component were present, which aimed to address the potential detrimental role played by private individuals in fulfilling the expected treaty goals, for example those dealing with slavery, human trafficking, or working conditions. These treaties included general duties of protection parameterised by provisions pointing to 'due diligence slang'. Furthermore, draft techniques subsequently associated with due diligence obligations could be recorded, namely the inclusion of ancillary guidance to states on measures potentially helpful to realising the protected goal.

Mention should be made to Article 2 of the 1926 Slavery Convention, providing states with a general positive obligation '[t]o prevent and suppress the slave trade', whose implementation was conditioned by due diligence parameters, as expressed by Article 3 imposing on states 'to adopt all appropriate measures with a view to preventing and suppressing the embarkation, disembarkation and transport of slaves in their territorial waters'. This treaty also provided an early example of an obligation of progressive realisation,[55] that is, requesting states '[t]o bring about,

[54] Silvia Sanna, 'Treatment of Prisoners of War', in Andrew Clapham/Paola Gaeta/Marco Sassoli (eds), *The 1949 Geneva Conventions: A Commentary* (Oxford: OUP 2015), 981–982.

[55] On such obligations, see Riccardo Pisillo Mazzeschi, 'Responsabilité de l'état pour violations des obligations positives relatives aux droits de l'homme', *Recueil des Cours de l'Académie de Droit International de la Haye* 338 (2008), 290–297.

progressively and as soon as possible, the complete abolition of slavery in all its forms' (Article 2(b)).

The 1910 Convention for the Suppression of the White Slave Traffic,[56] the 1921 International Convention for the Suppression of the Traffic in Women and Children,[57] or the 1933 International Convention for the Suppression of the Traffic in Women of Full Age[58] mainly requested states to provide criminal repression for activities prohibited under these treaties, a measure characterised by a due diligence component. According to Articles 2 and 3 of the 1921 Convention for the Suppression of the Traffic in Women and Children, '[p]arties agree to take all measures to discover and prosecute persons who are engaged in the traffic in children of both sexes' and 'to take the necessary steps to secure punishment of attempts to commit (...) the offences specified' in the Convention, as complemented by the requirement in the 1933 Convention for the Suppression of the Traffic in Women of Full Age 'to take the necessary steps to ensure that these offences shall be punished in accordance with their gravity'.[59] Other provisions provided flexibility through due diligence obligations, as Article 3 of the 1910 Convention for the Suppression of the White Slave Traffic illustrates, according to which states 'undertake, within legal limits, and as far as possible, to send back to their country of origin those women and girls who desire it', or 'as far as can be done, to entrust temporarily (...) the victims' to charitable institutions, while Article 7 of the 1921 Convention for the Suppression of the Traffic in Women and Children imposed 'such administrative and legislative measures as are required to check the traffic'.

Furthermore, to give more content to general due diligence obligations, provisions suggesting detailed activities addressing institutional capacity building were included. For instance, the request 'that all necessary measures are taken to safeguard the health of the workers and to guarantee the necessary medical care' for individuals obliged to compulsory labour, as provided by Article 17 of the Forced Labour Convention,[60] was further exemplified by making reference to measures implying periodic medical examinations and the maintaining of adequate medical services, as well as the supply of benefits such as water or food. Such provisions were thus prefiguring contemporary treaties where institutional or procedural measures aiming at minimising abstract risks are required in order to perform an auxiliary role for the fulfilment of more general due diligence obligations.

Finally, states were required to adopt legislative measures to repress those individual acts contrary to protected interests, as provided by Article 6 of the

[56] International Convention for the Suppression of the White Slave Traffic, 4 May 1910, 98 LNTS 101.

[57] International Convention for the Suppression of the Traffic in Women and Children, 30 September 1921, 9 LNTS 415.

[58] International Convention for the Suppression of the Traffic in Women of Full Age, 11 October 1933, 150 LNTS 431.

[59] See arts 2 and 3 of the 1933 Convention, and arts 1–3 of the 1910 Convention.

[60] Convention concerning Forced or Compulsory Labour, C29, 28 June 1930.

1926 Slavery Convention,[61] which required states 'to adopt the necessary measures in order that severe penalties may be imposed' in case domestic laws were inadequate, as maintained by Articles 3 of the 1910 and 1933 Conventions on trafficking. However, as such measures are not characterised by a particular latitude of *alea* and leaving no significant room for states with regard to the content of measures to be adopted, it is doubtful that they involve a due diligence component.[62]

3. Factors Influencing the Application of the Due Diligence Standard

Early practice also highlighted factors influencing the application of this standard, providing concrete content to a 'flexible concept'[63] whose theoretical challenges were already identified in 1874 by Federico Sclopis in the *Alabama* case, according to whom:

> Due diligence by itself does not mean anything. What is due diligence for a men or a government is no longer as such with another men and another more powerful state.[64]

This argument was reiterated in the early twentieth century, when scholars emphasised the difficulties in providing due diligence with a concrete content,[65] as reaffirmed by the report of the Harvard Law School, which stated that 'what is "due diligence" in a given case is often difficult to determine',[66] and maintained by Charles de Visscher at the 1930 League of Nations Conference on Codification.[67] However, as pinpointed by Eagleton, even if 'it is impossible to state this rule with precision', an examination of case law permits one 'to study other cases, and to judge according to the circumstances in any particular situation'.[68] Indeed, judicial practice permitted to define the rules of law dealing with due diligence,[69] favouring

[61] Slavery Convention, 25 September 1926, 60 LNTS 253.

[62] Pisillo Mazzeschi, 'Responsabilité' 2008 (n. 55), 311–334; Helene Raspail, 'Due diligence et droits de l'homme', SFDI/Sarah Cassella (eds), *Le standard de due diligence et la responsabilité internationale* (Paris: Pedone 2018), 130–131.

[63] ILA, Study Group on Due Diligence, First Report 2014 (n. 2), 2.

[64] Albert de Lapradelle/Nicolas Politis, *Recueil des arbitrages internationaux, Tome II: 1856-1872* (Paris: Pedone 1923), 857 (author's translation).

[65] Edwin Borchard, *The Diplomatic Protection of Citizens Abroad* (New York: Banks Law 1915), 217–218; Frederick Sherwood Dunn, *The Protection of Nationals* (Baltimore: John Hopkins Press 1932), 145–146.

[66] Harvard Law School, 'The Law' 1929 (n. 14), 188.

[67] 'Nous avons vainement cherché le moyen de préciser la teneur de l'obligation. Il a été reconnu qu'il était impossible de le faire', Société des Nations, Actes de la conférence pour la codification du droit international, vol. IV, Procès-verbaux de la troisième commission, 1930, 144.

[68] Eagleton, *Responsibility* 1928 (n. 6), 88.

[69] Borchard, *Diplomatic Protection* 1915 (n. 65), 60.

the emergence of theoretical references for subsequent debates on the 'variable criteria'[70] for its application, an aspect which remains an object of contemporary debates.

3.1 The Required Degree of Diligence

One of the most debated issues regarding the required standard of due diligence was already identified at the time, namely the contraposition between the *diligentia quam in suis* parameter, i.e., the domestic level normally applied by a state for its own affairs, and the request to meet an international standard, capable of eventually imposing stricter conditions according to potential objective parameters.[71]

The *Alabama* case already exemplified this theoretical division, with the UK favouring the *diligentia quam in suis* standard[72] and claiming that it was unreasonable and impractical to demand that a civilised government employ a higher standard internationally than it employs domestically;[73] while for the US due diligence should be proportionate to the relevance of the issue, regardless of the standard of care employed domestically.[74] The *Alabama* award has been constantly recognised as endorsing this latter position,[75] especially once it claimed that due diligence ought to be exercised 'in exact proportion to the risks to which either of the belligerents may be exposed', claiming that the UK 'cannot justify itself for a failure in due diligence on the plea of insufficiency of the legal means of action which it possessed'.[76] This solution was nonetheless subject to criticism, mainly regarding the difficulties in parameterising risks.[77] Some scholars preferred to maintain that required state measures were to be in line with national standards, as was expressed by Gustave Rolin-Jaequemyns, who argued that the dominant principle should be good faith and good willingness, assessed with regard to the standard of care employed domestically.[78] Nonetheless, a significant caveat was already

[70] Pierre d'Argent/Alexia de Vaucleroy, 'Le contenu de l'omission illicite: la non utilisation de moyens raisonnables', SFDI/Sarah Cassella (eds), *Le standard de due diligence et la responsabilité internationale* (Paris: Pedone 2018), 255–280, at 273.

[71] Pisillo Mazzeschi, *Due Diligence* 1989 (n. 5), 254–260.

[72] Ouedraogo, 'La neutralité' 2011 (n. 32), 341.

[73] For the UK position, see de Lapradelle/Politis, *Recueil* 1923 (n. 64), 796; for the memorial, see 792–800, 852-853.

[74] For the US position, see ibid., 789; for the memorial, see ibid., 784–792, 853–855.

[75] Paulos Zannas, *La responsabilité internationale des États pour les actes de négligence* (Montreux: Ganguin et Laubscher 1952), 98–100.

[76] *Alabama Claims of the United States of America against Great Britain*, Award of 14 September 1872, UNRIAA, vol. XXIX, 129.

[77] See James Lorimer, 'Observations sur les trois règles de droit des gens maritime, proposées par le Traité de Washington', *Revue de droit international et de législation comparée* 6 (1874), 542–548, at 544; William Lawrence, 'Observations sur les trois règles de Washington', *Revue de droit international et de législation comparée* 6 (1874), 570–574, at 574.

[78] Gustave Rolin-Jaequemyns, 'Les trois règles de Washington', *Revue de droit international et de législation comparée* 6 (1874), 561–569, at 568.

expressed: whether or not the level of domestic vigilance could be supported, it was necessary to ascertain if 'those institutions are such that the state can be described as well-ordered to an average extent',[79] thus introducing an international parameter.

Similar issues emerged concerning the protection of foreigners. In some cases, formal preference was expressed for domestic standards, as was maintained in the *Spanish Zone of Morocco*. Max Huber held that:

> The State is only required to exercise the degree of surveillance corresponding to the means at its disposal (…). This vigilance (…) can be characterized, using by analogy a term from Roman law, as a diligentia quam in suis.[80]

This solution was circumscribed, however, as it was required to ascertain that 'the general security in the countries of their residence does not fall below a certain level, and, at least, their protection by justice does not become purely illusionary',[81] pointing to the minimal characteristics of the domestic apparatus.

A preference was usually expressed for the need to meet international parameters through such formulas as: the 'insufficiency of governmental action so far short of international standards that every reasonable and impartial man would readily recognize its insufficiency';[82] the need to ascertain 'whether the investigation that took place was below the minimum standard required by international law';[83] or cases where the treatment of aliens and nationals was considered to be below 'ordinary standards of civilization'.[84] A preference for international standards was reiterated by scholars,[85] and finally proposed at the 1930 League of Nations Conference on Codification, where reference was made to the need 'to show such diligence in the protection of foreigners as (…) could be expected from a civilized State'.[86]

Still, even if an international standard emerged as a parameter, its identification remained an unsolved question, as was emphasised by references made to general concepts—such as 'reasonableness'—to provide it with content. This latter term was largely influenced by the reasonableness standard of *bonus pater familias* in Roman law, a concept mentioned both in international practice[87] and by international law scholars.[88] However, this term hardly enabled the expected measures

79 William Hall, *A Treatise of International Law* (Oxford: Clarendon Press 3rd ed. 1890), 216–217.
80 *Spanish Zone* (n. 22), 644 (author's translation)
81 Ibid., 641–642.
82 General Claims Commission (Mexico-USA), *Neer* (n. 24), 61–62.
83 General Claims Commission (Mexico-USA), *Harkrader*, 3 October 1928, UNRIAA, vol. IV, 373.
84 General Claims Commission (Mexico-USA), *Roberts*, 2 November 1926, UNRIAA, vol. IV, 80.
85 Eagleton, *Responsibility* 1928 (n. 6), 83–84.
86 Basis of discussion No. 10, 17, and 18 (n. 15).
87 Claims Commission (Venezuela-USA), *Wippermann* (n. 24), 3041; General Claims Commission (Mexico-USA), *Neer* (n. 24), 61; *Spanish Zone* (n. 22), 644.
88 Lassa Oppenheim, *International Law: A Treatise: War and Neutrality*, vol. II (London: Longmans 1906), 393.

to be clearly identified,[89] and basically only an examination of the elements relevant for the cases under discussion permitted the relevant measures to be eventually pinpointed.

3.2 Means at the Disposal for the Concerned State

An element currently debated is the possibility of balancing the performance of due diligence obligations in light of available means for the concerned state; this issue was already discussed in early practice. Some primary rules included this parameter, like the above-mentioned Articles 8 and 25 of the thirteenth Hague Convention of 1907 (where a neutral state was required to use the means at its disposal),[90] which was later reiterated by the 1928 Havana Convention on Maritime Neutrality (whose Article 26 required the state to 'exercise the surveillance made possible by means at its disposal').[91] These formulas, inferred from eighteenth-century friendship and commerce treaties, where parties pledged to use all means in their power to protect and defend any vessels belonging to the other state and its citizens,[92] were apparently included to balance solutions expressed in the *Alabama* case.[93] Similarly, in the *Salvador Prats* case, related to losses suffered in 1868 during the US Civil War, the umpire, aiming to identify a theoretical definition of due diligence, affirmed that 'the extent of the duties is to be commensurate with the extent of means for performing the same, and that he who has employed all the means within his reach has perfectly fulfilled his duty'.[94]

However, the risk of paying too much deference to the existing means at a state's disposal could lead to unjustified reductions in the extent of relevant obligations. Emphasis was put on the need to dispose of some basic capacities, as exemplified by the *Montijo* case, where Panamanian authorities were unable to retake control of a ship captured by rebels, and the umpire held that:

> It is true that it did not have the means to do so, as it did not have at its disposal sufficient forces (…) for such a task; but the lack of forces leaves the obligation

[89] D'Argent/de Vaucleroy, 'Le contenu' 2018 (n. 70), 261–273.

[90] On this aspect see above (n. 37).

[91] Convention on Maritime Neutrality, 20 February 1928, 135 LNTS 187.

[92] See *Traité d'amitié et de commerce entre le Roi de France et les Provinces-unies de l'Amérique*, 1778, in Georg Friedrich de Martens, *Recueil des principaux traités, Tome I: 1761-1778* (Göttingen: Dieterich 1791), 688.

[93] According to de la Pradelle/Politis, *Recueil* 1923 (n. 64), 971–972: 'Depuis la fin du XVIII siècle, il s'était dégagé (…) l'idée que le devoir d'un pays neutre est d'empêcher sur son territoire tout acte préjudiciable à l'un des belligérants, non d'une manière absolue, mais simplement par l'usage de tous les moyens en son pouvoir.'

[94] *Prats Case*, Opinion of Mr. Palacio (without date), in Moore, *History* 1898 (n. 18), 2894.

> intact (. . .) If it promises protection (. . .) it must provide for the means to make it effective.[95]

Similarly, in the *Mead* case, the Mexican claim to lack military forces in the area, having been diverted to other territories, was criticised by the commission:

> [T]here are of course limits to the extent to which they can justify a failure effectively to deal with lawlessness. And conditions (. . .) in this region may also reveal both the necessity for urgent measures as well as a censurable failure of efforts.[96]

Likewise, in the *Spanish Zones of Morocco*, Huber emphasised that protection should not go below a certain level.[97]

These approaches implied that a state is required to have at its disposal a minimal—though sufficient from an international standard perspective—level of state apparatus to perform their required obligations, with the need to build its machinery to the level sufficient to meet due diligence obligations, regardless of actual capacity. Failing in this regard, as already evoked by Calvo,[98] and irrespective of making use of existing means, a state would have been per se unable to exercise the required due diligence—as maintained by scholars—for the protection of aliens[99] and the law of neutrality.[100] For instance, Maurice Bourquin, referring to theories expressed by Dioniso Anzilotti (according to whom a state could not benefit from the deficiencies of its apparatus),[101] maintained that a state cannot escape its responsibility for activities required by due diligence obligations by invoking a general deficiency in its political organisation.[102] According to these perspectives, activities required by due diligence obligations could not just be parameterised by means effectively at a state's disposal but should be extended to the means a state ought to have at its disposal to comply with the internationally required diligence,[103] bringing contemporary scholars to argue that a state's duty to have at its disposal a sufficient apparatus to protect aliens implies an obligation of result.[104]

[95] Colombia-USA, *Montijo*, 25 July 1875, in Albert de Lapradelle/Nicolas Politis, *Recueil des arbitrages internationaux, Tome III* (Paris: Pedone 1954), 678 (author's translation).

[96] General Claims Commission (Mexico-USA), *Mead*, 29 October 1930, UNRIAA, vol. IV, 654–655.

[97] *Spanish Zone* (n. 22), 641–642.

[98] Calvo, *Le droit* 1880 (n. 16), 427.

[99] See Eagleton, *Responsibility* 1928 (n. 6), 89–90; Dunn, *Protection* 1932 (n. 65), 145–146.

[100] Giuseppe Ottolenghi, *Il rapporto di neutralità* (Torino: UTET 1907), 117–118.

[101] Dioniso Anzilotti, 'La responsabilité internationale des États à raison des dommages soufferts par des étrangers', *Revue générale de droit international public* 13 (1906), 5–29, at 27.

[102] Maurice Bourquin, 'Crimes et délits contre la sureté des États étrangers', *Recueil des Cours de l'Académie de Droit International de la Haye* 16 (1927), 117–246, at 240.

[103] Zannas, *La responsabilité* 1952 (n. 75), 84.

[104] Pisillo Mazzeschi, *Due Diligence* 1989 (n. 5), 230–234.

3.3 The Predictability of the Wrongful Act and the Level of Risk

The potential harm and elements of risk that the concerned state ought to have knowledge of, especially in light of any information brought to its attention prior to the events in question taking place, were already identified as elements influencing the performance of due diligence obligations.[105] It was emphasised in several cases that warnings provided to local authorities by aliens or representatives of foreign states with regard to concrete threats could assume relevance,[106] as the relevance of the risk was considered a sliding-scale element in assessing expected measures. Additional measures to those normally in place could thus be required.[107] Even in the *Alabama* case this element, underlined in the US memorial,[108] played a role once the tribunal assessed how the UK government had 'omitted, notwithstanding the warnings and official representations made by the diplomatic agents of the United States (…) to take into due time any effective measure of prevention',[109] and subsequently specified how the required measures should be 'in exact proportion to the risks'.[110]

Such evaluations did not imply that states would be automatically relieved of their responsibilities if sufficient warnings were lacking. Case law emphasised a preference for an objective responsibility such that the determining factor is not whether the state has knowledge of the potential risks but rather that the state ought to have known about the potential risks. As emphasised in the *Mead* case:

> [R]equests of aliens to authorities for protection may obviously be very important evidence of warning as to the need of such measures. But (…) obviously the fact that requests for protection are not made in a given case does not relieve authorities from their solemn responsibilities.[111]

Furthermore, both the public character of events able to cause prejudices on aliens and their gravity, which implies an expectation that the relevant authorities would have knowledge of their occurrence[112] (that is, on the basis that 'the facts were known to the competent authorities, either because they were of public notoriety or because they were brought to their knowledge in due time'[113]), were considered to be relevant elements in assessing a potential lack of required due diligence.

[105] André Decencière-Ferrandière, *La responsabilité internationale des États à raison des dommages subis par des étrangers* (Paris: Librairie Arthur Rosseau 1925), 121.

[106] Mixed Claims Commission (Italy-Venezuela), *Revesno et al.*, 1903, UNRIAA, vol. X, 583.

[107] General Claims Commission (Mexico-USA), *Kennedy*, 6 May 1927, UNRIAA, vol. IV, 198–199.

[108] See de Lapradelle/Politis, *Recueil* 1923 (n. 64), 788.

[109] *Alabama Claims* (n. 76), 130.

[110] Ibid., 129.

[111] General Claims Commission (Mexico-USA), *Mead* (n. 96), 655.

[112] General Claims Commission (Mexico-USA), *Austin*, 24 October 1930, UNRIAA, vol. IV, 625.

[113] Claims Commission (UK-Mexico), *Mexico City Bombardment Claims*, 15 February 1930, UNRIAA, vol. V, 80.

Conversely, the unexpected nature of such events was maintained as a mitigating or excluding factor in assessing responsibility.[114] Scholars, therefore, confirmed how the flexible character of due diligence obligations could also be influenced by the potential foreseeability of events, which could impose a different degree of necessary measures,[115] with additional protective measures required in case of deteriorating security conditions, regardless of any forewarning.[116]

3.4 The Level of Control Exercised by the State

Another element capable of influencing due diligence obligations was already identified in the level of control exercised by states with regard to areas where detrimental activities took place.

In some cases, elements that are capable of delaying those activities required by due diligence obligations, like geographical remoteness or communications difficulties, were apparently relevant to the potential exoneration of states from responsibility. For example, in the *Buckingham* case, in relation to the murder of a British citizen, the British-Mexican Claims Commission emphasised that 'the oil camp where the murder was committed is in a very remote situation, and its connections with the rest of the country are scarce and arduous'.[117] Indeed, in light of the technological capacity and the means of communication at the state's disposal at the time, scholars admitted that these factors could be taken into account in evaluating the performance of due diligence obligations,[118] an element nowadays having a minor relevance in light of developments affecting societies.

Difficulties in exercising proper control were particularly evaluated in cases of riots or events that occurred in areas controlled by opposition forces. For instance, in the *Egerton and Bernet* case decided in 1895, the British-Chilean Mixed Commission, while claiming that military authorities must do everything in their power to ensure respect for the property of the peaceful inhabitants, denied responsibility in cases of rebellion, civil war, or local troubles.[119] This stance was later maintained in other cases.[120]

[114] Claims Commission (USA-Mexico), *Mills*, 6 July 1870, in Moore, *History* 1898 (n. 18), 3034; Claims Commission (Venezuela-USA), *Wippermann* (n. 24), 3040–3041.

[115] Pasquale Fiore, *Nouveau Droit International Public*, vol. I (Paris: Durand et Pedone 1885), 580; Eagleton, *Responsibility* 1928 (n. 6), 91.

[116] Bourquin, 'Crimes' 1927 (n. 102), 236.

[117] Claims Commission (Mexico-UK), *Buckingham*, 3 August 1931, UNRIAA, vol. V, 288.

[118] Lawrence, 'Observations' 1874 (n. 77), 634; Alfred Verdross, 'Règles générales du droit international de la paix', *Recueil des Cours de l'Académie de Droit International de la Haye* 30 (1929), 271–517, at 446.

[119] Reproduced in Henri La Fontaine, *Pasicrisie internationale: 1794-1900* (Bern: Stämpfli 1902), 456.

[120] General Claims Commission (Mexico-USA), *Coleman*, 3 October 1928, UNRIAA, vol. IV, 366–367.

However, in such circumstances practice has rarely automatically exonerated states: their activities were still parameterised against those due diligence measures expected of them. Through this standard it was thus possible to rebut positions held by those scholars, especially those from Latin America (Calvo or Arias would be apt examples in this regard), more willing to exonerate states from responsibility,[121] and therefore kept open the possibility of recognising potential wrongful acts in exceptional circumstances. For instance, in 1903 the US-Spanish Claims Commission maintained, as a driving principle, the non-responsibility of Spain for rebel acts, unless it could be 'proved in any particular case before this Commission that the Spanish authorities by the exercise of due diligence might have prevented the damages done'.[122] In a few cases Spain was condemned in light of specific events: had Spain performed 'reasonable diligence'[123] then they would have been able to prevent the detrimental effects for occurrences where military contingents providing protection did not make any effort or prevented claimants from removing their goods. This approach was confirmed in 1903 by the Italian-Venezuelan Mixed Claims Commission: even if the principle was maintained that Venezuela would have been responsible if it 'failed to exercise due diligence to prevent damages from being inflicted by revolutionists (…) no such want of diligence [was] alleged and proved',[124] which was later reaffirmed by case law[125] and doctrine.[126]

4. Conclusions

Historically, due diligence was therefore progressively recognised as a component of international obligations and its increasing relevance could be linked to several factors: a protective counterbalance to state sovereignty; a tool providing flexibility to the challenges faced by states in guaranteeing the protection of interests expressed in primary rules; and a law-making approach for emerging positive treaty obligations. Early case law nonetheless permitted states to avoid making this concept a hollow and abstract one through the progressive identification of legal benchmarks capable of influencing its application.

[121] For a critical assessment, see Greenman, 'Aliens' 2018 (n. 7), 619–624.

[122] Samuel Crandall, 'Principles of International Law Applied by the Spanish Treaty Claims Commission', *American Journal of International Law* 4 (1910), 806–822, at 808.

[123] For case law, see ibid., 818–820.

[124] Mixed Claims Commission (Italy-Venezuela), *Sambiaggio*, 1903, UNRIAA, vol. X, 524.

[125] See *Spanish Zone* (n. 22), 642; British-Venezuelan Commission, *Aroa Mines*, 1903, UNRIAA, vol. IX, 445.

[126] Borchard, *Diplomatic Protection* 1915 (n. 65), 228–235; Eagleton, *Responsibility* 1928 (n. 6), 125–131.

The survey outlined in this chapter has illustrated that early solutions have managed to influence subsequent debates, especially once due diligence obligations assumed a pivotal role in the law-making processes that characterised the 'coexistence' era of the international legal order, being them the 'privileged tool of the international law of cooperation', due to their flexibility and adaptability.[127]

[127] D'Argent/de Vaucleroy, 'Le contenu' 2018 (n. 70), 255.

3

Due Diligence in the History of the Codification of the Law of State Responsibility

Helmut Philipp Aust and Prisca Feihle

1. Introduction

State responsibility has intrigued international lawyers for the last fifty years, if not more. At the same time, it is a relatively new field insofar as it has only materialised as a distinct sub-branch of international law after World War II. Before, rules existed which were retrospectively counted as belonging to the field of state responsibility. But these rules were largely concerned with questions of injuries to aliens. In this subject area, the number of inter-state claims and first attempts at working with forms of international arbitration generated the material for thinking about questions of responsibility in a structured manner.[1] Yet, before the post-World War II order, it was unusual to think of state responsibility as a general field which applied also to other rules of international law.[2]

When the International Law Commission (ILC) put state responsibility on its agenda, it was still a subject area very much characterised by this tradition. Yet, the first ILC Special Rapporteur, Francisco V. García-Amador considered it not possible to just continue codifying this field along the lines of the previous attempts from the interwar era. His idea was to connect state responsibility with the newly emerging norms of human rights law. As it is well known, García-Amador was not successful. The ILC hardly discussed his reports. The Commission only breathed new life into the topic of state responsibility after Roberto Ago became the second Special Rapporteur. His stroke of genius was to relaunch the entire project of state responsibility and restrict its scope to what he identified as 'secondary rules'. With this concept, he meant rules independent of the material content of international

[1] Hersch Lauterpacht, 'Survey of International Law in Relation to the Work of Codification of the International Law Commission', in Elihu Lauterpacht (ed.), *Hersch Lauterpacht, International Law: Collected Papers, Vol. 1 The General Works* (Cambridge: CUP 1970), 445–530, at 513.

[2] For the historical development of the field of state responsibility, see James Crawford, *State Responsibility: The General Part* (Cambridge: CUP 2013), 3–44.

Helmut Philipp Aust and Prisca Feihle, *Due Diligence in the History of the Codification of the Law of State Responsibility*
In: *Due Diligence in the International Legal Order*. Edited by: Heike Krieger, Anne Peters, and Leonhard Kreuzer, Oxford University Press (2020). © The Several Contributors. DOI: 10.1093/oso/9780198869900.003.0003.

law which would only come to apply once there was a breach of the respective primary, i.e., substantive, rule.

Which role did due diligence play in all this? A powerful narrative in the literature on due diligence is that it first developed in the realm of state responsibility—and hence as a secondary rule—before then later migrating and diversifying into primary rules. This chapter wishes to question this orthodoxy and shine a different light on the place of due diligence in the field of state responsibility. To this end, it draws in particular on the much-neglected[3] work of García-Amador. As it emerges from the corpus of his reports, due diligence was alive and well as a notion of international law before Ago introduced the category of secondary rules. García-Amador's work is intriguing in the sense that it was undertaken at a critical juncture in the history of the field of state responsibility, at a time that one can still count as a pre-history of the modern law of state responsibility.

Methodologically, this chapter does not conduct an analysis of due diligence within a specific field of international law in order to draw generalisable conclusions. Instead, the chapter focuses on the role of due diligence within the development of the law of state responsibility. The development of this field is both distinct from the 'primary' rules of international law and related to it—as it aims to provide general rules for the attribution of responsibility and its consequences. The historical pedigree of the law of state responsibility as concerned with the question of reparation for injuries to aliens also provided manifold examples for the emergence of the notion of due diligence in international law. Against this background we argue that a reassessment of García-Amador's work provides the ground for the argument that due diligence is a notion which sits in-between the level of primary and secondary rules of international law. In order to unfold this argument, the next section will look at the evolution of due diligence in the work of the ILC. Herein, we will proceed in three steps, following along the evolution of the ILC project from García-Amador over Ago to its conclusion under Special Rapporteur James Crawford.[4] In particular, we will retrace the deletion of 'primary rules' together with 'subjectivity' from the law of state responsibility. The standard narrative is

[3] See, for example, the depiction of the development of due diligence in Riccardo Pisillo Mazzeschi, 'Le chemin étrange de la Due Diligence: D'un concept mystérieux à un concept surévalué', in Société Française pour le Droit International (SFDI)/Sarah Cassella (eds), *Le standard de due diligence et la responsabilité internationale* (Paris: Pedone 2018), 323–337, at 323–327, leaving the role of García-Amador completely aside, even naming Ago as the first Special Rapporteur (at 326).

[4] The analysis excludes the work of the third and fourth Special Rapporteurs Riphagen and Arangio-Ruiz. With their focus on the consequences of a breach of an international obligation, considerations of due diligence were not essential within their reports. Only in his last report, Riphagen assigns the 'obligation of due diligence' to the level of primary rules where an element of fault is necessary for a breach of an international obligation, Willem Riphagen, Seventh Report on State Responsibility, A/CN.4/397 and Add. l, 4 March and 23 April 1986, YBILC 1986, vol. II (part I), 1–19, at 8; see also Joanna Kulesza, Due Diligence in International Law (Leiden: Brill 2016), 148–149. Arangio-Ruiz mentions 'a lack of "due diligence" (...) on the part of the injured State' as a concomitant cause leading to a reduction of the compensation, Gaetano Arangio-Ruiz, Second Report on State Responsibility, A/CN.4/425 and Add. I, 9 and 22 June 1989, YBILC 1989, vol. II (part I), 1–58, para. 47.

that all traces of fault were purged from the law of state responsibility, which thus coalesced around an objective understanding of responsibility. This is also one of the key arguments for the view that due diligence migrated from the realm of secondary rules to the level of primary rules. As we will demonstrate in the third section, however, this is only partly true. There are some remnants both of substantive questions relating to the content of specific obligations and of subjectivity in the 2001 Draft Articles on the Responsibility of States for Internationally Wrongful Acts[5] (ARSIWA) (section 3.1). What is more, due diligence also re-enters the debates about the ARSIWA in some unexpected contexts. In particular, this chapter will focus on the role that due diligence might have to play for the understanding of the rules on complicity in the field of international responsibility (Article 16 ARSIWA) (section 3.2).

2. The Evolution of Due Diligence in the Drafting History of the Articles on State Responsibility

The ILC Commentary to the ARSIWA excludes 'due diligence' from their content, together with other elements of subjectivity.[6] This stands in contrast to the attention the notion of due diligence received in the codification history of state responsibility under the ILC right from the beginning.

2.1 Pre-Histories: Due Diligence in the Early Work of the International Law Commission

As the first Special Rapporteur on the topic of state responsibility, García-Amador produced six reports between 1956 and 1961. Whereas the first report covered the topic of state responsibility in a general manner,[7] from the second report onwards García-Amador focused on injuries to aliens.[8] Today this limitation might seem surprising. But the topic of injuries to aliens—then arguably resting on a customary law basis recognised in case law of the nineteenth to early twentieth century—was also in previous codification efforts a focal point for the consideration of

[5] United Nations, ILC, Responsibility of States for Internationally Wrongful Acts, annexed to UN GAOR A/RES/56/83, 12 December 2001.

[6] ILC, Commentary to the Draft Articles on State Responsibility, YBILC 2001, vol. II (part II), 30–143, art. 2, para. 3.

[7] Francisco García-Amador, First Report on State Responsibility, A/CN.4/96, 20 January 1956, YBILC 1956, vol. II, 173–231.

[8] For an analysis of García-Amador's approach and its rejection see Daniel Müller, 'The Work of García Amador on State Responsibility for Injury Caused to Aliens', in James Crawford/Alain Pellet/Simon Olleson (eds), *The Law of International Responsibility* (Oxford: OUP 2010), 69–74. For a critical analysis of the trajectory of García-Amador's work see also Philip Allott, 'State Responsibility and the Unmaking of International Law', *Harvard International Law Journal* 29 (1988), 1–26, at 4–5.

state responsibility.[9] In what was quite an innovation at the time, he included in his draft articles an enumeration of fundamental human rights each state would have to guarantee.[10] When criticised by his fellow Commission colleagues, García-Amador did not give in to the suggestion to exclude issues raising 'substantive questions'.[11] In his view, his suggested provisions included the general conditions giving rise to state responsibility. He did not understand his project to restate or define exact obligations for the treatment of aliens—apart from the provisions on fundamental human rights,[12] which he deemed a necessary element in order to connect the traditional law of reparations for injuries to aliens with new developments in the field of human rights protection.[13] His reluctance to exclude substantive issues per se is, in the established narrative, the main reason for the failure of his efforts in advancing the codification of state responsibility. However, this feature is also essential for understanding the position of due diligence in his work.

García-Amador envisaged states to be responsible 'for injuries caused to an alien by acts of ordinary private individuals, if the organs or officials of the State were manifestly negligent in taking the measures which are normally taken to prevent or punish such acts'.[14] Under similar conditions, state responsibility would arise for injuries resulting from internal disturbances.[15] Thus García-Amador outlined his understanding of due diligence within the context of state responsibility for injuries to aliens caused by acts of private individuals but also extended the scope of his considerations to acts of third parties in general including acts of other states.[16] In his reports García-Amador also shed light on his broader understanding of due

[9] Giulio Bartolini, 'The Historical Roots of the Due Diligence Standard', chapter 2 of this book, section 2.1. On due diligence in the work of private expert bodies and within the League of Nations' codification process of the inter-war period see also Timo Koivurova, 'Due Diligence', in Rüdiger Wolfrum (ed.), *Max Planck Encyclopedia of Public International Law* (Oxford: OUP 2010), para. 4.

[10] Francisco García-Amador, Second Report on State Responsibility, A/CN.4/106, 15 February 1957, YBILC 1957, vol. II, 104–130, at 112–113 (draft arts 5 and 6).

[11] Francisco García-Amador, Third Report on State Responsibility, A/CN.4/111, 2 January 1958, YBILC 1958, vol. II, 47–73, at 48, para. 4.

[12] Ibid., 48–49, para. 7.

[13] For García-Amador the formulation of certain fundamental human rights provided for a synthesis of the conflicting principles of an 'international standard of justice' and the 'principle of the equality of nationals and aliens', see García-Amador, Second Report, 1957 (n. 10), 113–114, paras 2–4; for an analysis of García-Amador's general aim to ensure that 'international law should meet the legitimate concerns of both developed and developing nations', see Francisco Orrego Vicuña, 'In Memoriam Francisco V. García-Amador', *University of Miami Inter-American Law Review* 25 (1993), 5–14, at 7.

[14] García-Amador, Second Report, 1957 (n. 10), 121, draft art. 10.

[15] Ibid., 121, draft art. 11. For a similar location of due diligence in the previous work of the League of Nations and private expert bodies, see e.g., the Bases of Discussion drawn up in 1929 by the Preparatory Committee of the Conference for the Codification of International Law (The Hague 1930), Bases of Discussion 10, 17, 18, 19, 22a, 22d (reprinted in García-Amador, First Report, 1956 (n. 7), Annex 2); as well as the Draft Convention on 'Responsibility of States for Damage Done in their Territory to the Person or Property of Foreigners' prepared by Harvard Law School (1929), draft arts 10–12 (reprinted in García-Amador, First Report, 1956 (n. 7), Annex 9).

[16] García-Amador, First Report, 1956 (n. 7), paras 41–45.

diligence. The terminology varies between a 'duty', 'concept or rule', or 'standard'.[17] The general aim of the obligations to 'prevent and punish' is to justify state responsibility on separate grounds for constellations in which an injury stems from an act not attributable to the state itself. García-Amador identifies a 'principle' of a 'presumption against responsibility': states are generally not responsible for injuries caused by private individuals unless there is a lack of diligence in the prevention or punishment.[18] Responsibility thus rests on a specific conduct contrary to international law.

According to García-Amador, the term of due diligence should be understood as emphasising the efficiency and care to be used.[19] The standard thus establishes a subjective condition for state responsibility. What is more, for García-Amador the 'rule of "due diligence" is the expression *par excellence* of the so-called theory of fault (*culpa*)' in the law of state responsibility.[20] In this regard we can connect his statements concerning due diligence (or the related terms of 'vigilance' and 'negligence'[21]) with his general idea of state responsibility. To him responsibility is in principle of an objective nature. Subjective elements are only necessary when specifically required. The rule of due diligence—as outlined in his draft articles—would establish such a requirement with regard to constellations concerning acts of private individuals and internal disturbances.[22] This subjective element would be 'so closely linked to the conduct of the organ or official (...) [that] it is the negligence or volition [itself] which constitutes the conduct contrary to international law'.[23]

Accordingly, the main approach of the first ILC Special Rapporteur is to identify the general conditions giving rise to responsibility on the one hand. On the other hand, he did not refuse to go beyond this scope by stating specific requirements, such as the (primarily) subjective requirement of due diligence for particular constellations. At the same time those additional requirements do not simply reframe specific substantive rules. Instead they are also based on an abstraction. García-Amador depicts that the content of diligence depends on the circumstances of each case and the respectively applicable rules.[24] Using the distinction only introduced

[17] García-Amador, Second Report, 1957 (n. 10), 121–122, paras 2–3, see also Francisco García-Amador, 'State Responsibility—Some New Problems', *Recueil des Cours de l'Académie de Droit International de la Haye* 94 (1958-II), 369–487, at 401–405.

[18] García-Amador, Second Report, 1957 (n. 10), 122–123, para. 9.

[19] Ibid., 122, para. 4; see also Riccardo Pisillo Mazzeschi, 'The Due Diligence Rule and the Nature of the International Responsibility of States', *German Yearbook of International Law* 35 (1992), 9–51, at 42–44; Kulesza, *Due Diligence* 2016 (n. 4), 1–2, 13–17, 262–270.

[20] García-Amador, Second Report, 1957 (n. 10), 122, para. 7; critical Kulesza, *Due Diligence* 2016 (n. 4), 143.

[21] As the term for a failure to comply with the due diligence standard, Koivurova, 'Due Diligence' 2010 (n. 9), para. 1.

[22] Francisco García-Amador, Fifth Report on State Responsibility, A/CN.4/125, 9 February 1960, YBILC 1960, vol. II, 41–68, para. 88; see also Pisillo Mazzeschi, 'Due Diligence Rule' 1992 (n. 19), 18–19: García-Amador's approach would be an 'eclectic theory'.

[23] García-Amador, Fifth Report, 1960 (n. 22), para. 88.

[24] García-Amador, Second Report, 1957 (n. 10), 122–123, paras 7–9.

later on by Ago,[25] we could retrospectively reconceptualise due diligence as envisaged by García-Amador to sit in-between the layers of 'primary' and 'secondary rules'. His statements concerning responsibility for acts of private individuals link those distinct levels. On the 'primary' side he adapts the specific requirements to individual cases according to the applicable rules and circumstances. More on the 'secondary' side, he establishes a—rather vague[26]—rule to the effect that in the case of acts of individuals, states are internationally responsible for not preventing or punishing such acts if they failed to exercise due diligence.

2.2 All Substance Removed? The Ago Revolution and its Impact on Due Diligence

After García-Amador left the ILC without his efforts leading to the adoption of his suggested draft articles, Roberto Ago took over as Special Rapporteur. The basis for his success was a renunciation of García-Amador's focus on injuries to aliens under which—according to Ago—constant disagreement over substantive questions had paralysed the codification process. The 'Ago Revolution' brought about the distinction between 'primary rules' concerning substantive rules in different fields of international law and 'secondary rules' on general questions of state responsibility. The demand for a strict limitation of the codification work on 'secondary rules' had to affect the way in which due diligence was discussed—given its position between substantive rules and general questions of state responsibility in García-Amador's approach.[27] Yet far from allocating questions of due diligence to the level of primary rules and, thus, pushing them outside of the scope of the codification process, Ago positioned due diligence in the realm of secondary rules. Whereas some of Ago's findings indicate a certain continuity to García-Amador's approach, there is also substantial difference in other parts. Ago differentiated between 'subjective' and 'objective' elements of state responsibility, the 'subjective' elements referring to the attribution of an act to the state, whereas the 'objective' elements consist in the breach of an international obligation.[28] Ago discusses the notion of due diligence in the context of both elements.[29]

[25] Roberto Ago, Second Report on State Responsibility, A/CN.4/233, 20 April 1970, YBILC 1970, vol. II, 177–197, para. 11.

[26] On the virtues of flexibility see García-Amador, Second Report, 1957 (n. 10), 122, para. 7.

[27] García-Amador—further defending his approach of including human rights into the law of state responsibility for injuries to aliens—criticised the strict distinction of secondary and primary rules in his later work on state responsibility, Francisco García-Amador, *The Changing Law of International Claims* vol. I (New York/London/Rome: Oceana Publications 1984), 47–48, 73–74.

[28] Roberto Ago, First Report on State Responsibility, A/CN.4/217 and Add. 1, 7 May 1969 and 20 January 1970, YBILC 1969, vol. II, 125–156, para. 91.

[29] See also Andrea Gattini, 'Smoking/No Smoking: Some Remarks on the Current Place of Fault in the ILC Draft Articles on State Responsibility', *European Journal of International Law* 10 (1999), 397–404, at 398.

A first more extensive discussion relating to due diligence appears in the context of 'subjective elements' of responsibility on attribution, more specifically, in the part on 'conduct of private individuals' and thus somewhat parallel to García-Amador's approach. Ago argued that acts of private individuals are generally not attributed to the state. However, he did not end with a rule on non-attribution, but considered an alternative basis for state responsibility in such constellations. It is in this context that Ago discussed state responsibility for a failure to either prevent or punish certain acts which he depicts as 'two aspects of the same obligation to provide protection'.[30] These remarks are not entirely consistent with his general approach towards state responsibility. At first, they seemingly take a stand on the content of relevant (primary) obligations. Probably because he was well aware of this ambiguity, he stressed again the importance of excluding substantive aspects. Accordingly, despite the frequent reference to guarantees to protect aliens in this part, 'the aim must still be to seek to define the principles governing the international responsibility' and not to 'yield to the facile temptation to seek to define (. . .) other rules which are only relevant to our purpose from the aspect of a failure to fulfil the obligations they prescribe'.[31] In what comes close to an attempt to square the proverbial circle in this regard, Ago submitted a draft Article 11[32] which stipulated, on the one hand, that the conduct of private individuals would, as a rule, not be considered an act of the state. Yet, in a second paragraph, he underlined that this rule would be without prejudice to the attribution to the state of any omission when its organs ought to have prevented or punished the conduct of an individual.

Whereas García-Amador had attempted to establish a case-specific standard for state responsibility in relation to acts of private individuals, Ago merely hinted at the possibility that responsibility can flow from a separate omission of the state itself. Yet this raises the question of whether draft Article 11(2) had any meaningful content at all.[33] If it does not define the standard of due diligence for such cases and refers to the level of primary rules, why include it at all? This question foreshadows later concerns by Special Rapporteur Crawford who—carefully applying Ockham's razor to the existing draft articles adopted on first reading—opted to delete draft Article 11 for precisely that reason.

Ago also included due diligence into his considerations of the 'objective element' of state responsibility, i.e., the breach of an international obligation. Here, Ago introduced a draft Article 23 which—in a somewhat circular manner—stipulated that

[30] Roberto Ago, Fourth Report on State Responsibility, A/CN.4/264 and Add. 1, 30 June 1972 and 9 April 1973, YBILC 1972, vol. II, 71–160, para. 67.

[31] Ibid., para. 71.

[32] Ibid., para. 146.

[33] See also Gattini, 'Smoking/No Smoking' 1999 (n. 29), 399 (draft art. 11(2) a compromise solution with no real content).

> (t)here is no breach by a State of an international obligation requiring it to prevent a given event unless, following a lack of prevention on the part of the State, the event in question occurs.[34]

Ago's understanding of such an 'obligation of prevention' appears to be concerned with an obligation of result as opposed to one of conduct according to his particular usage of this distinction.[35] To Ago, obligations of result would touch upon state sovereignty to a lesser degree, leaving it to the state to decide on the necessary measures.[36] Those obligations of prevention à la Ago rather pertained to the category of obligations of result because such obligations required the occurrence of an 'external event', which could consist in the commission of an injury by private individuals, for instance. Seen from this perspective, the notion of due diligence then served as a transmission device between the external conduct as such not attributed to the state and the ensuing responsibility of the state for the breach of an obligation of prevention.

The notion of due diligence was thus not excluded altogether with the introduction of the distinction between 'secondary' and 'primary rules'. Ago's discussion of due diligence both in the context of attribution and the obligations of prevention is ambiguous with respect to the question of whether the statements referred to the level of 'primary' or 'secondary rules'. Whereas Ago presented his considerations of due diligence to be relevant for the question of general principles of state responsibility, his analysis of their content in some parts seems very close to what he considers as being outside the scope of codification as belonging to the primary rule level in other parts.

[34] Roberto Ago, Seventh Report on State Responsibility, A/CN.4/307 and Add.1 & 2 and Corr.1 & 2, 29 March, 17 April, and 4 July 1978, YBILC 1978, vol. II, part I, 31–60, para. 19; see further Andrea Gattini, *Zufall und force majeure im System der Staatenverantwortlichkeit anhand der ILC-Kodifikationsarbeit* (Berlin: Duncker & Humblot 1991), 201–204.

[35] For critical views, see Pierre-Marie Dupuy, 'Reviewing the Difficulties of Codification: On Ago's Classification of Obligations of Means and Obligations of Result in Relation to State Responsibility', *European Journal of International Law* 10 (1999), 371–385, at 378–380; Crawford, *State Responsibility: The General Part* 2013 (n. 2), 227–228; Constantin Economides, 'Content of the Obligation: Obligations of Means and Obligations of Result', in James Crawford/Alain Pellet/Simon Olleson (eds), *The Law of International Responsibility* (Oxford: OUP 2010), 371–381, at 376; Andrea Gattini, 'Breach of International Obligations', in André Nollkaemper/Ilias Plakokefalos (eds), *Principles of Shared Responsibility in International Law: An Appraisal of the State of the Art* (Cambridge: CUP 2014), 25–59, at 37–38.

[36] Roberto Ago, Sixth Report on State Responsibility, A/CN.4/302 and Add.1, 2, & 3, 15 April, 7 June, 5 and 14 July 1977, YBILC 1977, vol. II, part I, 3–44, paras 14–15; Dupuy, 'Ago's Classification' 1999 (n. 35); Gattini, 'Breach' 2014 (n. 35), 35–37.

2.3 Furthering the Exclusion of Substance and Subjectivity: Crawford's Continuation

In contrast to Ago's sometimes ambiguous inclusion of due diligence in the realm of secondary rules, Crawford clearly assigns due diligence to the level of primary rules and excludes it thereby explicitly from the codification process. It can thus be said in more than one way that Crawford accomplished the mission first set out by Ago. By defending the differentiation of 'primary' and 'secondary rules' as preventing the necessity to 'resolve a myriad of issues about the content or application of particular rules',[37] he seemed to push the distinction even further than Ago did.[38]

A central consideration for Crawford was that the articles did not establish any general requirement of fault.[39] Crawford accordingly identified that Ago's draft article concerning acts of private individuals was difficult to square with that axiomatic position. In particular, the 'negative attribution rule' of former draft Article 11 would lack 'any independent content' as it would not touch upon the decisive question: the extent of the obligation of a state to prevent such acts from occurring. Therefore, he suggested its deletion.[40] To Crawford, the draft article addressed a non-problem while not dealing with a real problem he saw as related to these questions, i.e., the subsequent adoption of conduct of non-state actors by a state.[41] In general, the substantive question of a separate basis for responsibility with regard to non-attributable acts of individuals was consequently left to the level of primary rules. The chapter on attribution suggested by Crawford refrained from hinting to the possibility of responsibility based on separate grounds. Instead, it limited itself to clarifications within the Commentary in this regard.

Likewise, in his assessment of Ago's differentiation between obligations of conduct, of result and of prevention, the main criticism was that this distinction transgressed the boundary between primary and secondary rules.[42] In line with sceptical governmental comments,[43] Crawford held that Ago's articles in this context were 'either (…) circular (for primary rules of a certain content, this is their

[37] James Crawford, First Report on State Responsibility, A/CN.4/490 and Add. 1–7, 24 April, 1, 5, 11, and 26 May, 22 and 24 July, 12 August 1998, YBILC 1998, vol. II, part I, 1–80, para. 16.

[38] Similarly, Koivurova, 'Due Diligence' 2010 (n. 9), paras 5 and 27.

[39] Crawford, First Report, 1998 (n. 37), para. 105; also Crawford equates due diligence with other subjective elements of state responsibility, Crawford, *State Responsibility: The General Part* 2013 (n. 2), 37–38.

[40] Crawford, First Report, 1998 (n. 37), paras 244–245. This also affected the article with respect to acts of other subjects of international law (ibid., paras 246–252).

[41] Ibid., para. 246. This led him to suggest a separate draft article later adopted as article 11 ARSIWA.

[42] James Crawford, Second Report on State Responsibility, A/CN.4/498 and Add.1–4, 17 March, 1 and 30 April, 19 July 1999, YBILC 1999, vol. II, part I, 3–100, para. 3.

[43] France stated that these considerations related to 'rules of substantive law' thus lying outside the scope of the draft, the United Kingdom found this article to be 'uncontroversial but also unnecessary', Crawford, Second Report, 1999 (n. 42), para. 56.

content)' or they would create a presumption of the interpretation of certain primary rules.[44]

2.4 Analysis: Due Diligence from García-Amador to Crawford

Analysing the ways in which the treatment of due diligence in the codification history evolved shows that the exclusion of due diligence from the scope of the ARSIWA came along with the gradual removal of 'subjective requirements' as well as 'substantive questions' from the scope of the ILC project.[45] It is in this evolution that considerations of due diligence as linking the rules on state responsibility to specific primary obligations were lost.[46] The distinction of 'secondary' and 'primary rules' first led to an inclusion of due diligence into the realm of the secondary rules under Ago. It was only under Crawford that due diligence was assigned to the level of primary rules in furtherance of the main conceptual distinction introduced by Ago. This shifting treatment also contributes to our finding that due diligence is best understood as a normative standard located in-between the layers of secondary and primary rules.[47]

At the same time, the exclusion of due diligence was also triggered by the elimination of subjective elements within the ILC project. García-Amador, Ago, and Crawford seem to agree on the fact that due diligence—at least primarily—pertains to the realm of subjective elements of responsibility. Such a location of due diligence conflicts with views putting forward an objectified notion of due diligence.[48]

It was under García-Amador's approach that due diligence could be analysed in a productive manner as sitting in-between substantive questions and general principles of state responsibility. In advancing his envisaged protection of human rights through rules of state responsibility, due diligence could be interpreted in parallel to the principle of 'abuse of rights' as a form of a transitory rule that (temporarily)

[44] Ibid., para. 90.

[45] This could be read in line with Allott's harsh criticism of the ILC's work on state responsibility: the attempt for establishing universally coherent rules on state responsibility was at the same time 'particularizing in substance', Allott, 'Unmaking of IL' 1988 (n. 8), 25.

[46] For a parallel—more general—finding that the ILC's efforts 'to introduce conceptual innovations (on occasion) has resulted in a step backwards', Orrego Vicuña, 'In Memoriam' 1993 (n. 13), 7.

[47] See also Sarah Cassella, 'Les travaux de la Commission du Droit International sur la Responsabilité Internationale et le standard de due diligence', in SFDI/Sarah Cassella (eds), *Le standard de due diligence et la responsabilité internationale* (Paris: Pedone 2018), 1–26, at 14–18; Kulesza, *Due Diligence* 2016 (n. 4), 130–131, 262–270.

[48] For an objectified understanding of due diligence, see Pisillo Mazzeschi, 'Due Diligence Rule' 1992 (n. 19) and Kulesza, *Due Diligence* 2016 (n. 4). Martti Koskenniemi, 'Doctrines of State Responsibility', in James Crawford/Alain Pellet/Simon Olleson (eds), *The Law of International Responsibility* (Oxford: OUP 2010), 45–51, at 50 notes that—concerning the role of fault—a 'great burden fell upon the intermediate doctrine of "due diligence", which has tended to make the distinction between fault and objective responsibility vanish'.

allows for capturing constellations that—in specific fields or in future times—find a more specific regulation.[49]

Requiring a clear classification of due diligence within the distinction of secondary and primary rules finally led to its progressive exclusion from the codification.

3. Remaining Traces of Due Diligence in the Contemporary Law of State Responsibility

The ARSIWA maintained Crawford's explicit exclusion of due diligence. In a strong reaffirmation of the elimination of 'primary rules' from the scope of the articles, the Commentary states that:

> [w]hether responsibility is 'objective' or 'subjective' in this sense depends on the circumstances, including the content of the primary obligation in question. (...) The same is true of other standards, whether they involve some degree of fault, culpability, negligence or want of due diligence. Such standards vary from one context to another for reasons which essentially relate to the object and purpose of the treaty provision or other rule giving rise to the primary obligation. Nor do the articles lay down any presumption in this regard as between the different possible standards.[50]

The ARSIWA, thus, consider due diligence as closely linked to questions of substantive elements and subjective requirements for responsibility. Yet it can be wondered whether this exclusion was successful in its entirety. According to our view, certain aspects of due diligence remained within the ARSIWA and its accompanying commentary. In the following, we attempt to detect traces of due diligence in the remaining aspects relating to the content of obligations, namely the 'obligations of prevention' (section 3.1). What we can also see is that the concept of due diligence reappears in different contexts of the contemporary law of state responsibility, especially with respect to notions of subjectivity in what is otherwise perceived to be an objective regime of responsibility (section 3.2). Even if, following the diversification of international law, due diligence obligations are now embedded within different specialised fields of international law,[51] this part of our

[49] Similarly, Koivurova, 'Due Diligence' 2010 (n. 9), para. 44.

[50] ILC, Commentary, 2001 (n. 6), art. 2, para. 3.

[51] For the changing context of due diligence being elaborated in more detailed primary rules, see ILA, Study Group on Due Diligence in International Law, Second Report, 12 July 2016, 5–6; assessing a corresponding parallel between historical and contemporary analysis of due diligence through specific case law, see Bartolini, 'The Historical Roots of the Due Diligence Standard', chapter 2 of this book, section 3; considering the continuous role of due diligence where complex primary obligations are already in place, Serena Forlati, 'L'objet des différentes obligations primaires de diligence: prévention,

chapter attempts to assess in how far the notion of due diligence still has—and could further have—a role to play on the level of the law of state responsibility.[52]

3.1 Remaining Traces of 'Obligations of Prevention'

Due diligence as we encountered it in the drafting history reappears in connection to some articles of the ARSIWA and particularly within clarifications in the Commentary.[53] Most of these references pertain to what can be summarised as 'obligations of prevention'.[54]

Within the chapter on attribution, the Articles themselves do not contain a rule on non-attribution similar to Ago's suggestion anymore. However, it is the ILC Commentary which clarifies that there is the possibility of responsibility of a state in relation to acts of private individuals,[55] or insurrectional or other movements,[56] for a failure to take necessary measures of prevention. In addition, the Commentary implies an underlying interaction between rules of attribution on the one hand and responsibility on a separate basis as under due diligence obligations on the other. For the situation of an excess of authority, it states that the distinction 'between unauthorized but still "official" (...) and "private" conduct (...) may be avoided if the conduct complained of is systematic or recurrent, such that the State knew or ought to have known of it and should have taken steps to prevent it'.[57] Also, the Commentary foresees the possibility of responsibility because of a 'failure to take sufficient action' before a state acknowledges and adopts a certain conduct (leading to its attribution under Article 11 ARSIWA) in order to 'avoid gaps in the extent of responsibility' for a 'continuing act'.[58]

Similarly, traces of due diligence can be detected in the chapter on the breach of an international obligation. In particular, Article 14 ARSIWA on breaches extending in time and Article 15 ARSIWA on breaches consisting of a composite act, recall considerations of due diligence. Generally leaving aside the categorisation of

cessation, répression ... ?', in SFDI/Sarah Cassella (eds), *Le standard de due diligence et la responsabilité internationale* (Paris: Pedone 2018), 39–66, at 62–63.

[52] For the similar claim that the strict distinction between primary and secondary rules hinders the analysis of the notions of negligence and due diligence in a more general way, see Cassella, 'Les travaux de la Commission du Droit International sur la Responsabilité Internationale et le standard de due diligence' 2018 (n. 47), 17–18, 21.

[53] Kulesza, *Due Diligence* 2016 (n. 4), 136–149 and 163 underlines the continuous relevance of due diligence in the realm of state responsibility especially for omissions.

[54] For the link between obligations of prevention and due diligence, see also Cassella, 'Les travaux de la Commission du Droit International sur la Responsabilité Internationale et le standard de due diligence' 2018 (n. 47), 15–16.

[55] ILC, Commentary, 2001 (n. 6), chapter II (attribution), para. 4.

[56] Ibid., art. 10, para. 15.

[57] Ibid., art. 7, para. 8.

[58] Ibid., art. 11, para. 4.

'obligations of conduct' and 'of result',[59] a distinction is retained with regard to the extension in time of the breach of an obligation according to Article 14. Somewhat similar to Ago's approach, the category of 'obligations of prevention' appears in Article 14(3) and is further discussed in the Commentary as 'best efforts obligations, requiring States to take all reasonable or necessary measures to prevent a given event from occurring, but without warranting that the event will not occur',[60] thus retaining Ago's requirement of the occurrence of an external event in this regard.

Thereby, obligations of prevention still—implicitly—have their place within the ARSIWA, specifically for the constellations for which García-Amador had drafted substantial obligations. They provide a separate basis for responsibility with regard to acts of private individuals (and other subjects of international law) which cannot be attributed to the state. More precisely, the considerations of obligations of prevention in the articles and the Commentary rather clarify that the non-attribution of the conduct in question does not exclude responsibility on a separate basis. For the involvement of states in the internationally wrongful acts of non-state actors, the ARSIWA do not foresee indirect responsibility for complicity as they do in the state-to-state constellation in Article 16 ARSIWA.[61] In this conception, the basis of responsibility is not to be found in the ARSIWA, but within specific primary rules.

3.2 Lingering Subjectivity and Due Diligence: The Case of Complicity

In line with an understanding of due diligence as a subjective condition of state responsibility, it is another provision of the ARSIWA where due diligence could potentially make a somewhat unexpected re-entry into the law of state responsibility. Article 16—concerning aid or assistance to another state for the commission of an internationally wrongful act—is one of the few provisions in the ARSIWA where a subjective element is expressly required in order to trigger responsibility. Of course, Article 16 ARSIWA is not to be equated with a due diligence obligation. Rather, we argue that for *specific* constellations, a reference to due diligence considerations can be helpful to determine the subjective element required for a state to become responsible for its aid or assistance.[62]

[59] Ibid., art. 12, para. 11; see also Koivurova, 'Due Diligence' 2010 (n. 9), at 6, who claims that 'in 2001, all primary norm classifications had been eliminated'.

[60] ILC, Commentary, 2001 (n. 6), art. 14, para. 14.

[61] Considering the progressive development of a non-state complicity rule given the increased influence of non-state actors in order to fill 'the proverbial secondary rule vacuum' (at 406)—as an alternative to direct state responsibility based on a violation of a primary obligation of prevention—is Richard Mackenzie-Gray Scott, 'State Responsibility for Complicity in the Internationally Wrongful Acts of Non-State Armed Groups', *Journal of Conflict and Security Law* 24 (2019), 373–407.

[62] In this way, our suggestion differs from approaches which—in order to harmonise the concepts of complicity and due diligence—rely on an openness of Article 16 ARSIWA to be interpreted as generally

Linking the concept of complicity with the notion of due diligence stands *prima facie* in contrast to approaches emphasising their distinction. In this sense, the Commentary to the ARSIWA states that Article 16 forms one exception to the general principle of independent responsibility[63]—to which the responsibility for a breach of a separate due diligence obligation with regard to another state's action pertains. Furthermore, there are suggestions claiming that the concept of complicity is unnecessary precisely because of the possible reliance on a general principle of due diligence.[64] Others support a recourse to the notion of due diligence stemming from primary rules for indirect forms of participation in serious violations of international law below the level of complicity.[65] Nevertheless, drawing this connection between Article 16 ARSIWA and due diligence can be justified for two reasons. Firstly, there is a structural parallel between complicity and due diligence. Both concepts sit in-between the layers of secondary and primary rules.[66] Secondly, both notions concern constellations in which state responsibility does not rest on attribution of the acts of other states, but on separate grounds related to such acts.

Generally, it is a matter of dispute what the subjective element in Article 16 lit. a) ARSIWA requires.[67] This lack of clarity is fuelled by language in the ILC Commentary which can be read to the extent that knowledge is not enough to make a supporting state responsible but that rather some form of wrongful intent would be required.[68] With the growing recognition the provision has received—both by the confirmation of its customary law status by the ICJ[69] and in governmental practice—the discussion around the subjective element has not gone away.[70] In

not requiring a subjective element based on an objective reading of the conception of fault therein which would, thus, come close to the concept of negligence, see Massimo Starita, 'Négligence illicite et responsabilités multiples: Partage ou cumul de responsabilités?', in SFDI/Sarah Cassella (eds), *Le standard de due diligence et la responsabilité internationale* (Paris: Pedone 2018), 297–320, at 311–315. For the general claim that the concept of due diligence has replaced the concept of fault in contemporary international law, see Pisillo Mazzeschi, 'Le chemin étrange de la Due Diligence' 2018 (n. 3), 337.

63 ILC, Commentary, 2001 (n. 6), chapter IV, paras 1–5.

64 Olivier Corten, 'La 'complicité' dans le droit de la responsabilité internationale: Un concept inutile?', *Annuaire Français de Droit International* 57 (2011), 57–84, at 67–70.

65 Anja Seibert-Fohr, 'From Complicity to Due Diligence: When Do States Incur Responsibility for their Involvement in Serious International Wrongdoing?', *German Yearbook of International Law* 60 (2017), 667–707.

66 Article 16 ARSIWA is not clearly primary as it does not stipulate an independent legal content, but defining it as secondary is also difficult as the conduct engaged in by the aiding or assisting state as such is not wrongful. It only becomes wrongful due to the connection with the wrongful conduct of another state.

67 See further Helmut Philipp Aust, *Complicity and the Law of State Responsibility* (Cambridge: CUP 2011), 235–237.

68 ILC, Commentary, 2001 (n. 6), art. 16, para. 3.

69 ICJ, *Case Concerning the Application of the Convention on the Prevention and Punishment of the Crime of Genocide (Bosnia and Herzegovina v. Serbia and Montenegro)*, Judgment of 26 February 2007, ICJ Reports 2007, 43, para. 420.

70 Most recently discussed in Harriet Moynihan, 'Aiding and Assisting: The Mental Element under Article 16 of the International Law Commission's Articles on State Responsibility' *International and Comparative Law Quarterly* 67 (2018), 455–471.

the meantime, a number of intermediate positions have been formulated, most recently coalescing around the formulation that states must not hide behind 'wilful blindness' against the consequences of their cooperation with other states.[71]

It is at this point where the notion of due diligence re-enters the picture.[72] Already during the drafting history there was some support to construe the subjective element of Article 16 ARSIWA in the language of due diligence.[73] However, there are still good reasons against due diligence as a blanket standard for the interpretation of Article 16 ARSIWA. Already the requirement of knowledge indicates that it is normally not required of states to make pro-active inquiries whether aid or assistance rendered in good faith may contribute to the commission of internationally wrongful acts.[74] Rather, such a duty might stem from an 'obligation of prevention' laid down in specific (now) primary rules. However, it is inherently plausible to hold that no state should be capable of hiding behind a fake veil of ignorance in order to continue supplying, for instance, a notorious regime with arms and other forms of military support in order to help that regime suppress political opposition.[75] In our view, a shift in the subjective element under Article 16 ARSIWA by relying on the notion of due diligence could be adequate in certain constellations, namely with regard to serious breaches of peremptory norms and within continuous relationships of cooperation.

Firstly, the rules on serious breaches of peremptory norms (Articles 40, 41 ARSIWA) set forth a separate obligation of non-assistance. Neither Article 41(2) nor its accompanying commentary require a mental element of the kind of Article 16 lit. a) ARSIWA.[76] Besides the importance of the values protected by peremptory norms, this difference is justified by the time element. Article 41 ARSIWA is set against massive breaches of peremptory norms which have produced some kind of status. This follows from the formulation in Article 41(2)

[71] Vaughan Lowe, 'Responsibility for the Conduct of other States' *Kokusaiho Gaiko Zassi* 101 (2002), 1–15, at 10; Miles Jackson, *Complicity in International Law* (Oxford: OUP 2015), 162.

[72] Also identifying that Article 16 ARSIWA tends to reintroduce the notion of due diligence is Corten, 'Complicité: Concept Inutile?' 2011 (n. 64), 84. However, Corten questions the utility of the concept of complicity given the possibility to rely on a general principle of due diligence. In contrast, we suggest to refer to due diligence in order to clarify the subjective element required by Article 16 ARSIWA within specific constellations. See also Stefan Talmon, 'A Plurality of Responsible Actors: International Responsibility for Acts of the Coalition Provisional Authority' in Phil Shiner/Andrew Williams (eds), *The Iraq War and International Law* (Oxford: Hart 2008), 185–230, at 219.

[73] See to this the statement of the Netherlands, in: ILC, State responsibility: Comments and observations received from Governments, A/CN.4/515, 19 March 2001, 28.

[74] See also Lowe, 'Responsibility for other States' 2002 (n. 71), 10.

[75] Ibid. On the interconnectedness between applying a test of 'wilful blindness' within the subjective element for complicity and considerations of negligence and due diligence, see also Mackenzie-Gray Scott, 'Complicity to Non-State Armed Groups' 2019 (n. 61), at 393–394, also pointing to the potential ensuing conceptual difficulty of 'blurring the line between primary and secondary rules'.

[76] The Commentary explains this lack of a subjective element in the following way: 'There is no need to mention such a requirement in article 41, paragraph 2, as it is hardly conceivable that a State would not have notice of the commission of a serious breach by another State.' (ILC, Commentary, 2001 (n. 6), art. 41, para. 11).

ARSIWA that it is about not aiding or assisting in the maintenance of the situation brought about by the breach (together with the separate yet related obligation of non-recognition).[77] Here it is arguable that if such serious breaches occur, the conditions under which aid or assistance trigger responsibility change radically. It is the time between the beginning of the serious breach and the moment when the consolidation of the outcome of this breach is at stake that the notion of due diligence might have a fruitful role to play.

Secondly, this rationale could apply also for Article 16 ARSIWA for situations where aid or assistance to a wrongful act is having a continuing character in the sense of Article 14(2) ARSIWA. An additional argument flows from the rationale set out in Article 14(3) ARSIWA according to which a 'breach may be progressively aggravated by the failure to suppress it'.[78] Here, it is arguable that an ongoing relationship of cooperation helps to shift the subjective standard. If states find out that there are reasonable grounds to believe that aid or assistance becomes entangled in wrongful conduct of another state, they have good reasons to re-assess their previous assumption that they can deliver such aid or assistance in good faith.[79] The notion of due diligence might be helpful in order to determine what is expected of state officials in such situations. This is especially the case when a partner state has a bad track record with respect to compliance with international law.[80]

Interpreted along these lines, Article 16 ARSIWA would not suffocate international cooperation by an undue requirement to conduct a pre-support assessment of whether assistance might contribute to wrongful conduct. Yet it would also not turn Article 16 ARSIWA into a fig leaf behind which states can hide by pointing towards a lack of knowledge and/or intent with respect to the outcomes of their cooperative relationship. Reintegrating due diligence into the realm of state responsibility—and thus transgressing specific regimes of primary rules—would provide criteria for specific situations in which no special rule exists.[81] If one follows this argument, due diligence would fittingly re-enter the law of state responsibility at a juncture where the boundary between primary and secondary norms is blurry anyway.

[77] Also emphasising that it is not only the unlawful act, but also the 'factual situation created by the breach' which is 'tainted' and falls under art. 41, para. 2 ARSIWA, Dire Tladi, Third Report on Peremptory Norms of General International Law (jus cogens), A/CN.4/714, 12 February 2018, para. 99.

[78] ILC, Commentary, 2001 (n. 6), art. 14, para. 14.

[79] Similar considerations can be found in policy documents like the UN Human Rights Due Diligence Policy seeking to ensure that UN units do not become implicated in serious violations of international law, Helmut Philipp Aust, 'The UN Human Rights Due Diligence Policy: An Effective Mechanism against Complicity of Peacekeeping Forces?', *Journal of Conflict & Security Law* 20 (2015), 61–73.

[80] This suggestion can be read in parallel to Lowe who noted that the concept of complicity will become most efficient if it becomes entrenched in the mindset of bureaucracies, Lowe, 'Responsibility for other States' 2002 (n. 71), 14.

[81] Despite the conceptual differences, our approach, thus, would partly ascribe a similar function to the notion of due diligence as Corten's suggestion of a reliance on a general principle of due diligence, Corten, 'Complicité: Concept Inutile?' 2011 (n. 64), 68.

4. Conclusion: Due Diligence in-between Primary and Secondary Rules

Accordingly, we have seen that the codification history of the law of state responsibility paints a more variegated picture with respect to due diligence than it is usually assumed. In particular, it should not be assumed too lightly that due diligence first materialised as a secondary rule to migrate later into the domain of primary rules. The much-neglected work of the first ILC Special Rapporteur on the matter, Francisco V. García-Amador, shows that due diligence as a notion was already part of the arsenal of international law before a meaningful distinction between primary and secondary rules developed. What is more, García-Amador's work also invites us to reconsider this distinction more generally. With respect to due diligence, we have formulated the argument that this notion can be best understood as sitting in-between the categories of primary and secondary rules. It connects general rules on responsibility with specific requirements of conduct, especially with respect to obligations of prevention which are difficult to conceptualise on a purely secondary level. This difficulty points towards certain limitations that come along with a rigid distinction between secondary and primary rules.[82] This chapter has also shown that over the further course of the ILC work the 'ghost' of García-Amador was not fully exorcised from the project. In fact, the second ILC Special Rapporteur Roberto Ago was quite close in his approach to the one of García-Amador—despite the clearly announced intention to break radically with the work of his predecessor. The turn to an exclusive focus on secondary rules was then further radicalised by Special Rapporteur James Crawford. He purged the Articles themselves from most traces of subjectivity as well as norms which could be seen to relate to the substantive side, i.e., the primary rules.

Nonetheless, even then it was not possible to rid the ARSIWA completely from connections with due diligence. What is more, we have also shown how the notion re-enters the law of state responsibility in some rather unexpected places, such as within the provision on complicity (Article 16 ARSIWA). Conspicuously, this provision itself defies a clear positioning with respect to its character as primary or secondary. Taken together, we view the notion of due diligence as a fruitful and flexible instrument to attune the law of state responsibility to different situations in which care and oversight is required of states in order not to trigger wrongful conduct which might then give rise to state responsibility.

[82] See also Cassella, 'Les travaux de la Commission du Droit International sur la Responsabilité Internationale et le standard de due diligence' 2018 (n. 47), 14–18.

4
Member States' Due Diligence Obligations to Supervise International Organisations

Kristina Daugirdas[*]

1. Introduction

There are two reasons to consider obligations to supervise international organisations as a distinct category of due diligence obligations. First, due diligence obligations typically require states to regulate third parties in some way. But it is harder for states to regulate international organisations unilaterally than to regulate private actors within their own territories. International law protects individual states' authority to regulate people and activities within their territories through a variety of mechanisms, including through the prohibition on intervention. To be sure, international law also imposes some constraints; human rights law is an especially important example here. But states retain significant discretion about whether and how to regulate third parties within their territory.

By contrast, international law protects the autonomy of international organisations, in part by limiting the authority of individual member states to unilaterally influence international organisations. The charters of international organisations typically prohibit states from issuing instructions to international civil servants.[1] International organisations also usually have comprehensive immunities from national legal process, in part to shield them from the influence of individual states.[2] When an organisation's member states act collectively through the governance mechanisms established in that organisation's charter, however, they exercise broad authorities over such organisations and their officials.

Second, due diligence obligations with respect to international organisations also merit attention because they may compensate for the dearth of mechanisms to hold international organisations accountable when they cause harm. These

* For their excellent comments and suggestions, I am grateful to Monica Hakimi, Leonhard Kreuzer, Heike Krieger, Anne Peters, and the other participants in the workshop on Due Diligence in International Law hosted by the Max Planck Institute in Berlin.

[1] See, e.g., Charter of the United Nations, 26 June 1945, art. 100.

[2] See, e.g., Convention on the Privileges and Immunities of the United Nations, 13 February 1946, 1 UNTS 15; Convention on the Privileges and Immunities of the Specialized Agencies, 21 November 1947, 33 UNTS 261.

Kristina Daugirdas, *Member States' Due Diligence Obligations to Supervise International Organisations* In: *Due Diligence in the International Legal Order.* Edited by: Heike Krieger, Anne Peters, and Leonhard Kreuzer, Oxford University Press (2020).
 DOI: 10.1093/oso/9780198869900.003.0004.

accountability concerns are especially acute when it comes to private individuals who are harmed by such organisations' activities.[3] Immunity from legal process in national courts bolsters international organisations' autonomy—but it also closes down national courts as a venue for victims to seek recourse. Individuals and entities with pre-existing contractual relationships may have access to alternative venues—but tort victims generally do not.[4]

The chapter turns next to elaborating on this latter point: Section 2 explains why the possibility that international organisations might incur responsibility for violations of international law does not solve the problem of international organisations' accountability to tort victims. Section 3 describes some specific examples of due diligence obligations that states have under current law. Section 4 shows how the International Law Commission's Draft Articles on the Responsibility of International Organizations (the ARIO), adopted in 2011, establish some more general, cross-cutting obligations on states to act (or refrain from acting) in particular ways vis-à-vis international organisations. None of these provisions is explicitly labelled a due diligence obligation—but they have some features that characterise due diligence obligations. Section 5 critiques the ARIO for framing these obligations too narrowly. Section 6 argues in favour of establishing a due diligence obligation on member states to prevent international organisations from abusing their immunities.

2. The Problem: Limitations of the Responsibility of International Organisations

The possibility that international organisations might incur responsibility for violations of international law offers, at best, only a partial and incomplete solution to the problem of international organisations' lack of accountability to tort victims. These limitations result partly from the scope of the ARIO and partly from practicalities related to implementation.

To start, for states and international organisations alike, the law of international responsibility kicks in only where there is a violation of international law. But key aspects of the sources and content of international organisations' international obligations remain unsettled and controversial. Some obligations are clear: international organisations are bound by their own charters and by treaties to which they are parties. But the extent to which customary international law binds

[3] See, e.g., Anne Peters, 'International Organizations and International Law', in Jacob Katz Cogan/ Ian Hurd/Ian Johnstone (eds), *The Oxford Handbook on International Organizations* (Oxford: OUP 2017), 33–59.

[4] Individuals employed by international organisations will usually have access to an administrative tribunal.

international organisations remains contested. Scholars have taken different positions on the question.[5] International organisations themselves have said relatively little.

Another limitation of responsibility is that international organisations can harm individuals without violating any international obligations. An international organisation official driving a car might get into an accident that causes injuries or deaths. Or an international organisation that is a party to contracts under national law might fail to pay its creditors. In fact, the incident that galvanised concerns about the accountability of international organisations involved exactly this problem. The International Tin Council (ITC) had been created to keep the price of tin within an agreed range. To achieve this goal, the ITC's buffer stock manager bought tin when the price dipped below the agreed range and sold tin when the price exceeded it.[6] On 24 October 1985, the ITC's buffer stock manager announced that the ITC lacked sufficient funds to honour its contracts. The ITC had accumulated a stockpile of more than 100,000 tons of tin—and £900 million of debt.[7] The ITC's inability to pay its creditors caused them significant financial harm, though it does not appear that the ITC or its officials violated any international obligations. The buffer stock manager had broad authority to buy and sell tin under the international agreement that established the ITC, and the contracts between the ITC and its creditors were ordinary commercial contracts under English law.[8] Without a violation of international law, there is no international responsibility.

Where international organisations do have international obligations, the victims of breaches may encounter problems seeking recourse when those obligations are violated. If the victim is a state or international organisation, then that state or organisation can directly pursue the claim against the breaching organisation through diplomatic channels. If the victim is an individual, however, this route is unavailable. In theory, a state could pursue such a claim against an international organisation on behalf of its nationals. In practice, governments may be reluctant to do so—especially if they rely on the international organisation for various types of assistance. For example, in 2010 United Nations peacekeepers inadvertently brought cholera to Haiti. The resulting epidemic has sickened hundreds of thousands of Haitians and killed more than nine thousand.[9] There are strong arguments

[5] Kristina Daugirdas, 'How and Why International Law Binds International Organizations', *Harvard International Law Journal* 57 (2016), 325–381; August Reinisch, 'Sources of International Organizations' Law: Why Custom and General Principles Are Crucial', in Jean d'Aspremont/Samantha Besson (eds), *Oxford Handbook of the Sources of International Law* (Oxford: OUP 2018), 1007–1024; Jan Klabbers, 'Sources of International Organizations' Law: Reflections on Accountability', in ibid., 987–1006.

[6] Eric J. McFaddon, 'The Collapse of Tin: Restructuring a Failed Commodity Agreement', *American Journal of International Law* 80 (1986), 811–830.

[7] Ibid., 812–813.

[8] Romana Sadurska/Christine Chinkin, 'The Collapse of the International Tin Council: A Case of State Responsibility?', *Virginia Journal of International Law* 30 (1990), 845–890, at 858–859, 865.

[9] United Nations, Report by the Secretary-General, A New Approach to Cholera in Haiti, A/71/620, 25 November 2016.

that the United Nations has a treaty obligation to develop a mechanism for providing redress to these victims.[10] Yet the United Nations has denied any such obligation. The Haitian government has not seriously challenged this position,[11] and the United Nations successfully invoked its immunity when the victims sued it in a US court.[12] There are some isolated cases where international organisations have established special institutions to hear individuals' claims.[13] On the whole, however, the ARIO remain 'underinstitutionalised,' and injured individuals are only rarely able to enlist courts or other dispute settlement bodies to hear their claims.[14]

Even if it were clear that an international organisation was responsible for a particular violation of international law, that international organisation may lack the capacity to take the steps that the ARIO would require. These include ceasing the wrongful conduct and making full reparation for the injury caused, which may involve paying compensation.[15] Although international organisations are independent from their member states as a formal legal matter, as a practical matter they remain quite dependent on their member states for financial and other resources. Even when international organisations are willing to make full reparation, they may lack the ability to do so without the support of their member states.

Finally, the status of the ARIO as customary international law remains doubtful, at least for now. When the International Law Commission (ILC) adopted the ARIO in 2011, it acknowledged that a number of the articles 'are based on limited practice' and thus the Commission's work reflected more progressive development and less codification than the corresponding Draft Articles on State Responsibility (ARSIWA).[16] Since then, evidence that more of the ARIO's provisions have ripened into customary international law remains rather scant.[17]

[10] Convention on UN Privileges and Immunities, 1946 (n. 2), art. VIII sec. 29; Frédéric Mégret, 'La responsabilité des Nations Unies aux temps du Choléra', *Revue belge de droit international* 46 (2013), 161–189; Kristen E. Boon, 'The United Nations as Good Samaritan: Immunity and Responsibility', *Chicago Journal of International Law* 16 (2016), 341–385, at 354–362.

[11] Kristina Daugirdas, 'Reputation and the Responsibility of International Organizations', *European Journal of International Law* (2014), 991–1018, at 1004; Kristina Daugirdas, 'Reputation and Accountability: Another Look at the United Nations' Response to the Cholera Epidemic in Haiti', *International Organizations Law Review* 16 (2019), 11–41, at 32.

[12] Kristina Daugirdas/Julian Davis Mortenson, 'U.S. Federal Court of Appeals Upholds United Nations' Immunity in Case Related to Cholera in Haiti', *American Journal of International Law* 111 (2017), 155–196, at 168–169.

[13] One example is the Kosovo Human Rights Advisory Panel.

[14] Niels Blokker, 'Member State Responsibility for Wrongdoings of International Organizations: Beacon of Hope or Delusion?', *International Organizations Law Review* 12 (2015), 319–332.

[15] United Nations, International Law Commission (ILC), Draft Articles on the Responsibility of International Organizations, with Commentaries, in Report on the Work of Its Sixty-Third Session, A/66/10, 2011 [hereinafter ARIO], art. 31.

[16] Ibid., cmt. 5.

[17] United Nations, Report of the Secretary-General, Responsibility of International Organizations: Comments and Information Received from Governments and International Organizations, A/72/80, 26 April 2017; United Nations, Report of the Secretary-General, Responsibility of International Organizations: Compilation of Decisions of International Courts and Tribunals, A/72/81, 26 April 2017.

Thus, the further development of the law of international organisations responsibility in recent years is not, by itself, enough to close the accountability gap created by international organisations immunity. Under these circumstances, the appeal of due diligence obligations with respect to international organisations becomes clearer. If member states policed international organisations more carefully, those organisations may be less likely to cause harm, or be more likely to provide recourse when they do.

It is necessary to specify, however, what any possible due diligence obligations might require states to do. To what end should states be obliged to act? Firstly, states could have due diligence obligations to prevent international organisations from engaging in activities that would violate their own international obligations. Secondly, states could have due diligence obligations to prevent international organisations from violating the organisations' own international obligations—and to ensure that the ARIO's requirements are satisfied in the event that such violations occur. Finally, states could have due diligence obligations to prevent international organisations from causing harm to third parties regardless of whether that harm results from a violation of international law.

3. Existing Due Diligence Obligations

There are some examples of states having international obligations that extend to their interactions with international organisations of which they are members. All of these examples fall within the second category outlined above—they involve obligations on member states to take steps to assure that international organisations do not engage in activities that would violate the member states' obligations. In other words, these obligations are designed to ensure that states do not exploit international organisations to evade their own international obligations.[18]

One example is expressly codified in the UN Convention on the Law of the Sea (UNCLOS). UNCLOS requires states parties to ensure that activities within the Area—i.e., the 'seabed and ocean floor and subsoil thereof, beyond the limits of national jurisdiction'—are undertaken consistently with requirements set out in the UNCLOS.[19] This obligation applies to activities carried out by states themselves, as well as to activities carried out by their nationals or others within their effective control.[20] But that is not all—UNCLOS also requires states parties 'that are members of international organizations [to] take appropriate measures to ensure the implementation of this article with respect to such organizations'.[21]

[18] This apprehension corresponds to a particular view of international organisations as vehicles through which states operate; see Daugirdas, 'How and Why' (2016) (n. 5), at 328.

[19] United Nations Convention on the Law of the Sea, 10 December 1982, 183 UNTS 397, art. 139(1).

[20] Ibid.

[21] Ibid., art. 139(3).

Another example comes from the International Covenant for Economic, Social and Cultural Rights (ICESCR). Article 2(1) of the ICESCR requires each state party 'to take steps, individually and through international assistance and co-operation, especially economic and technical, to the maximum of its available resources, with a view to achieving progressively the full realization of the rights recognised in the present Covenant by all appropriate means, including particularly the adoption of legislative measures'.[22] The Committee on Economic, Social, and Cultural Rights has encouraged certain states 'to do all [they] can to ensure that the policies and decisions' of the International Monetary Fund and the World Bank 'are in conformity with the obligations of States parties to the Covenant, in particular the obligations contained in Article 2.1 concerning international assistance and cooperation'.[23]

A third example comes from the case law of the European Court of Human Rights (ECtHR). On several occasions, the court has concluded that states did violate—or would violate—their obligations under the European Convention on Human Rights unless they assured that international organisations in which those states participated protected rights enumerated in the European Convention on Human Rights. For example, the court rejected an argument that Germany had violated its obligation to guarantee a right of access to courts by according comprehensive immunities from legal process to the European Space Agency (ESA).[24] The court emphasised that 'a material factor' in its decision was the availability of a 'reasonable alternative means to protect effectively [the challengers'] rights under the Convention'.[25] Specifically, the ESA had established an independent body to adjudicate employment disputes with the organisation.[26] The court did not frame its analysis in due diligence terms—indeed, the ECtHR focused on the result (the existence of an alternative mechanism for resolving disputes) rather than on Germany's efforts to establish such a mechanism. If Germany had tried but failed to establish such a mechanism, it seems likely that the ECtHR would have found a violation. Still, the court's opinion surely created an incentive for Germany to ensure that the ESA and other international organisations heeded the rights protected by the European Convention.[27]

22 International Covenant on Economic, Social and Cultural Rights, 16 December 1966, 999 UNTS 3, art. 2.

23 United Nations, Committee on Economic, Social and Cultural Rights, Concluding Observations (Belgium), E/C.12/1/Add.54, 1 December 2000, para. 31; see also United Nations, Committee on Economic, Social, and Cultural Rights, Concluding Observations (Morocco), E/C.12/Add.55, 1 December 2000, para. 38: 'The Committee strongly recommends that Morocco's obligations under the Covenant be taken into account in all aspects of its negotiations with international financial institutions (...) to ensure that economic, social and cultural rights, particularly of the most vulnerable groups of society, are not undermined.'; Ana Sofia Barros, 'Member States and the International Legal (Dis)order', *International Organizations Law Review* 12 (2015), 333–357, at 351 (collecting additional examples of such comments).

24 ECtHR, *Waite and Kennedy v. Germany*, Judgment of 18 February 1999, Application No. 26083/94.

25 Ibid., para. 68.

26 Ibid., para. 69.

27 Pierre Klein, 'The Attribution of Acts of International Organizations', in James Crawford/Alain Pellet/Simon Olleson (eds), *The Law of International Responsibility* (Oxford: OUP 2010), 297–315, at

4. Due Diligence Obligations in the Draft Articles on the Responsibility of International Organizations

Some scholars have suggested the desirability of going further and establishing cross-cutting due diligence obligations on states to supervise international organisations.[28] This section maps the steps that the ARIO take in this direction. Although the Commission has described the ARIO as a set of secondary rules, the ARIO include a number of primary obligations.[29] These provisions supplement the discrete due diligence obligations described in section 3, though, as noted earlier, they do not (yet) reflect customary international law.

4.1 Preventing Circumvention: Member State Responsibility for Contributing to Acts of International Organisations Internationally Wrongful if Committed by the Member State Itself

The ARIO delineate several ways that a state might incur international responsibility for contributing to conduct by an international organisation that would be internationally wrongful if the state had engaged that conduct itself. Two provisions closely track provisions of the ILC's ARSIWA that give effect to the principle that 'a State should not be able to do through another what it could not do itself'.[30] A state will incur international responsibility if it aids or assists an international organisation in engaging in conduct that violates an international obligation that binds both the state and the international organisation.[31] Likewise, the ARIO provide that a state will incur international responsibility if it directs and controls such an act by an international organisation.[32] Direction and control requires more forceful conduct than providing aid and assistance, where the assisting state plays 'a mere supporting role'.[33] But even aid and assistance requires some affirmative,

311 (describing other cases of the ECtHR suggesting that states parties to the European Convention on Human Rights have due diligence obligations with respect to international organisations to which they have transferred the exercise of certain competences).

28 Sadurska/Chinkin, 'Collapse' 1990 (n. 8), 887 ('[A]lthough we argue for the existence in international law of a duty on member States of an organization to supervise its functioning in order to prevent damage to third parties, it must be admitted that such a duty is not firmly established.'); Ian Brownlie, 'The Responsibility of States for the Acts of International Organizations', in Maurizio Ragazzi (ed.), *International Responsibility Today* (Leiden: Martinus Nijhoff 2005), 355–362.

29 André Nollkaemper/Dov Jacobs, 'Shared Responsibility in International Law: A Conceptual Framework', *Michigan Journal of International Law* 34 (2013), 359–438, at 409–412.

30 United Nations, ILC, Draft Articles on Responsibility of States for Internationally Wrongful Acts, with Commentaries, Report on the Work of Its Fifty-Third Session, A/56/10, 2001, [hereinafter ARSIWA], art. 17 cmt. 8.

31 ARIO, 2011 (n. 15), art. 58.

32 Ibid., art. 59.

33 ARSIWA, 2001 (n. 30), ch. IV cmt. 6.

concrete action. An omission is not enough to trigger responsibility under these provisions[34] (nor even is incitement of wrongful conduct, provided that it's not accompanied by concrete support).[35] Thus, the obligations in these provisions do not establish an affirmative obligation on member states to supervise international organisations.

The ARIO also address circumvention: Article 61 provides that '[a] State member of an international organization incurs international responsibility if, by taking advantage of the fact that the organization has competence in relation to the subject-matter of one of the State's international obligations, it circumvents that obligation by causing the organization to commit an act that, if committed by the State, would have constituted a breach of the obligation'.[36] The act need not be internationally wrongful for the international organisation concerned.[37] To incur responsibility under this provision, the state must intend to avoid compliance, and the organisation must have competence in relation to the subject matter of the state's international obligations.[38] The Commission does not elaborate much on what kind of conduct on the part of a state would qualify as causing an organisation to act in a particular way, saying only that there must be a 'significant link between the conduct of the circumventing member state and that of the organization'.[39]

4.2 Contributing and Responding to Violations of International Organisations' Obligations

The ARIO also address member states' obligations in connection with conduct by international organisations that violates the international obligations of the latter but not the former. Strikingly, under the ARIO, member states have no cross-cutting obligations to refrain from aiding and assisting or directing and controlling acts by an international organisation that violate an international obligation of the organisation without simultaneously violating an international obligation of the state providing aid or assistance.[40]

The result differs in the more extreme case of a member state coercing action by an international organisation that violates the organisation's international

[34] ICJ, *Case Concerning Application of the Convention on the Prevention and Punishment of the Crime of Genocide (Bosnia and Herzegovina v. Serbia and Montenegro)*, Judgment of 26 February 2007, ICJ Reports 2007, 43, paras 420 and 432.

[35] ARSIWA, 2001 (n. 30), ch. IV cmt. 9.

[36] ARIO, 2011 (n. 15), art. 61.

[37] Ibid., art. 61(2).

[38] Ibid., art. 61 cmt. 6.

[39] Ibid., art. 61 cmt. 7.

[40] This situation is not covered by ARIO, 2011 (n. 15), arts 58 or 59 because states engaging in aid or assistance or direction and control incur responsibility only where 'the act would be internationally wrongful if committed by that State'. Ibid., art. 58(1)(b), art. 59(1)(b).

obligations.[41] Where a state coerces such conduct, it is the state rather than the international organisation that incurs responsibility. The idea is that the state is the real actor, while the coerced organisation is a 'mere instrument'.[42] The threshold for establishing coercion is high: as the Commission explained, the act must have 'the same essential character as *force majeure*'.[43]

Separately, the ARIO impose affirmative obligations on member states to respond to breaches of international law by international organisations in two situations. First, just like the ARSIWA, the ARIO provide that, where an international organisation has committed a serious breach of a peremptory norm, states and international organisations alike 'shall cooperate to bring to an end through lawful means' any such breach.[44] Notably, this obligation is not limited to member states—it applies to states (and international organisations) across the board.

The second provision concerns the consequences of an 'ordinary' breach of international law (i.e., a breach of a norm other than a peremptory norm of international law). Under the ARIO, an international organisation that has violated an international obligation must cease the wrongful act, if it is continuing;[45] it must 'offer appropriate assurances and guarantees of non-repetition, if circumstances so require';[46] and it must 'make full reparation for the injury caused by the internationally wrongful act'.[47] The ARIO addresses member states' obligations only with respect to the last of these requirements, providing that 'members of a responsible international organization shall take all the appropriate measures that may be required by the rules of the organization in order to enable the organization to fulfil its obligations [to make full reparation]'.[48]

Stepping back, then, this is where things stand with respect to the three possible categories of due diligence obligations outlined above. As described in section 3, under existing law, there are some circumstances where states may incur international responsibility for failure to take steps to assure that international organisations act consistently with the state's own international obligations. That is, there are examples where states may incur responsibility for their omissions with respect to supervising international organisations. Whether and when states' obligations extend to their interactions with international organisations will require evaluation on a norm-by-norm basis; the isolated examples described in section 3 do not add up to a general positive obligation of member states to assure that the conduct of international organisations conforms to each state's own international obligations. As described in section 4.1, ARIO adds some general obligations on states

41 Ibid., art. 16.
42 Cf. ARSIWA, 2001 (n. 30), art. 18 cmt. 4.
43 Cf. ibid., art. 18 note (2).
44 ARIO, 2011 (n. 15), art. 42(1).
45 Ibid., art. 30(1).
46 Ibid., art. 30(2).
47 Ibid., art. 31.
48 Ibid., art. 40.

not to aid or assist, direct, and control, or cause conduct by international organisations that would violate states' own international obligations.

When it comes to states' obligations to supervise international organisations' compliance with the organisations' international obligations, as section 4.2 describes, the ARIO impose some discrete across-the-board obligations to respond to serious breaches of peremptory norms and to enable international organisations to fulfil their obligations to make full reparations. To a large degree, however, the ARIO allow member states to be quite standoffish when an international organisation of which they're a member state breaches an international obligation. The ARIO do not require states to take any affirmative steps to assure that international organisations comply with their own obligations in the first instance. Even more notably, under the ARIO, member states do not incur responsibility for aiding and assisting or directing and controlling an act by an international organisation that constitutes a violation of the organisation's own international obligations.

Finally, neither the ARSIWA nor the ARIO impose any obligations on states with respect to actions by international organisations that cause harm without violating international law.

5. A Missed Opportunity

In developing articles on international responsibility, the ILC had to wrestle with fundamental questions about the ways that states and international organisations do, and should, interact with one another.[49] In my view, the Commission took inadequate account of the differences between state-state relationships and member state-international organisation relationships. As a result, when it comes to the provisions enumerated above, the ARIO track the ARSIWA too closely.

The ARSIWA largely leave states free to ignore other states' international obligations. State A has no obligation to help ensure that state B will comply with state B's obligations. Likewise, if state B has an obligation that state A does not share, then state A has no obligations to refrain from conduct that would undermine state B's ability to comply that obligation.[50] Indeed, the Commission notes, in many cases a state can take affirmative action to incite other states to violate their international obligations without incurring international responsibility.[51] There are exceptions, though, wherever states have taken on international obligations that prohibit such indifference or incitement. The Genocide Convention

[49] David J. Bederman, 'Counterintuiting Countermeasures', *American Journal of International Law* 96 (2002), 817–832 (observing that the state responsibility regime goes 'to the intellectual core of public international law by delimiting the character of states and the nature of their obligations when they interact with one another').

[50] ARSIWA, 2001 (n. 30), art. 16(b) and art. 17(b).

[51] Ibid., ch. IV cmt. 9.

is an important one; it requires states parties to take affirmative steps to prevent genocide extraterritorially.[52] When it comes to responding to violations of international law, the ARSIWA require action only where the violation constitutes a serious breach of a peremptory norm.[53] Taken in in their entirety, the ARSIWA permit states to be indifferent to whether or not other states comply with their international obligations the vast majority of the time.

The Commission offers some explanations for these rules in its commentary. One is the pacta tertiis rule, which provides that the obligations that state B has to state C have no impact on the rights or obligations of state A.[54] Pacta tertiis is a classic rule of international law, one that reinforces the role of consent in creating international obligations. Separately, the Commission explained that it sought to reduce the burden on states in relation to their interactions with one another: 'States engage in a wide variety of activities through a multiplicity of organs and agencies'; 'a State providing financial or other aid to another State should not be required to assume the risk that the latter will divert the aid for purposes which may be internationally unlawful'.[55] The international law prohibition on intervention also aligns with the Commission's approach by reinforcing the basic idea that it's appropriate for states to have a laissez-faire attitude with respect to other states' choices on key choices about whether and how to govern their territories. As the International Court of Justice (ICJ) explained, states may not engage in coercive acts that bear on 'matters in which each State is permitted, by the principle of sovereignty, to decide freely'. These matters include the 'formulation of foreign policy'.[56]

Whatever the merits and drawbacks of the Commission's approach when it comes to relations between states, it's a mismatch when it comes to relations between member states and international organisations. To start, duties of co-operation and good faith apply to states' interactions with the international organisations of which they are members. As the ICJ explained in its 1980 advisory opinion regarding efforts to move a regional office of the World Health Organization (WHO) away from Alexandria, Egypt, this general obligation of co-operation and good faith generated some concrete requirements in that setting, including an obligation to consult in good faith and to provide a reasonable period of notice in the event that either the WHO or Egypt wished to relocate the office.[57] The court went on to explain that the 'paramount consideration' for both parties

[52] See Larissa van den Herik/Emma Irving, 'Due Diligence and the Obligation to Prevent Genocide and Crimes Against Humanity', chapter 12 of this book, section 1.

[53] ARSIWA, 2001 (n. 30), art. 40 (defining such a breach as 'serious' 'if it involves a gross or systematic failure by the responsible State to fulfil the obligation').

[54] Vienna Convention on the Law of Treaties, 23 May 1969, 1155 UNTS 331, art. 34 ('A treaty does not create either obligations or rights for a third State without its consent.').

[55] ARSIWA, 2001 (n. 30), ch. IV cmt. 8.

[56] ICJ, *Military Activities in and against Nicaragua (Nicaragua v. United States of America)*, Judgment of 27 June 1986, ICJ Reports 1986, 14, para. 205.

[57] ICJ, *Interpretation of the Agreement of 25 March 1951 Between the WHO and Egypt*, Advisory Opinion of 20 December 1980, ICJ Reports 1980, 73.

'in every case must be their clear obligation to co-operate in good faith to promote the objectives and purposes of the Organization as expressed in its Constitution'.[58]

In addition, international organisations' international obligations have consequences for member states when they act collectively through intergovernmental organs like the UN General Assembly or the World Health Assembly. The reason is that any international obligation that binds an organisation binds its organs as well. The ICJ affirmed as much in a 1954 advisory opinion that addressed whether the General Assembly has a legal right to refuse to give effect to awards made by the United Nations Administrative Tribunal in favour of staff members.[59] The court asserted that the General Assembly had no such right, at least so long as the tribunal was not acting ultra vires. The court's analysis was straightforward. It observed that the General Assembly empowered the tribunal to make final judgments that were binding on the United Nations.[60] The court continued:

> As this final judgment has binding force on the United Nations Organization as the juridical person responsible for the proper observance of the contract of service, that Organization becomes legally bound to carry out the judgment and to pay the compensation awarded to the staff member. It follows that the General Assembly, as an organ of the United Nations, must likewise be bound by the judgment.[61]

Under these circumstances, it is inappropriate for the organisation's member states to be indifferent as to whether General Assembly's actions accord with this obligation. Member states ought to exercise their governance authorities in a way that allows the organisation to comply with its international obligations.

In developing the ARIO, the ILC did not take adequate account of these features of international organisation-member state relationships. In particular, certain provisions described in section 4.2 are deficient. The Commission should have made clear that member states would incur responsibility by aiding and assisting or directing and controlling acts by international organisations that violate the latter's international obligations. This omission does not matter when an international organisation's obligations coincide with those of its member states. But in some important cases, their obligations diverge. One important example was referenced earlier: the United Nations' treaty obligation to provide for alternative mechanisms of resolving certain categories of disputes that cannot be heard by national courts on account of the immunity of the United Nations or its officials.[62]

58 Ibid., para. 49.

59 ICJ, *Effect of Awards of Compensation Made by the United Nations Administrative Tribunal*, Advisory Opinion of 13 July 1954, ICJ Reports 1954, 47.

60 Ibid., at 53.

61 Ibid.

62 See Convention on UN Privileges and Immunities, 1946 (n. 2), art. VIII sec. 29.

Separately, the Commission's enumeration of member states' obligations is too narrow when it comes to the consequences of violations by international organisations. As noted in section 4.2, the ARIO instructs member states to take affirmative steps to ensure that organisations will be able to implement their obligation to make full reparation.[63] Surely the capacity of international organisations to pay compensation is an especially salient concern. In its commentary, the Commission explains that 'an obligation for members to finance the organization as part of the general duty to cooperate with the organization may be implied under the relevant rules'.[64] But member states' duty of cooperation is broader than that—and the Commission should have reminded states that this duty extends to assuring international organisations can implement all of the obligations triggered by a violation of international law.[65]

6. Wanted: Due Diligence Obligations to Prevent Abuse of International Organisations' Immunities

Keeping in mind the accountability gap described in section 2, there is one place where establishing a due diligence obligation on the part of member states would be especially attractive: a due diligence obligation to ensure that international organisations do not abuse their immunities.

Treaties that accord privileges and immunities to international organisations and international organisation officials often include provisions that are designed to ensure that such immunities are not abused.[66] To take just one example, the Convention on the Privileges and Immunities of the Specialized Agencies sets out a dispute resolution procedure if any state party to the convention 'considers that there has been an abuse of a privilege or immunity conferred by this Convention'.[67]

In addition, there are examples of both international organisations and states taking steps to prevent abuses of immunity by assuring that individuals injured by international organisations are not left without any kind of recourse or remedy. Thus, in 1946, the UN General Assembly adopted a resolution that noted the United Nations' intention to 'prevent the occurrence of any abuse' in connection with its privileges and immunities and instructed the Secretary-General to ensure that 'the drivers of all official motor-cars of the United Nations' are properly insured'.[68] Indeed, the aftermath of the International Tin Council's collapse can be

[63] See ARIO, 2011 (n. 15), art. 30(1).
[64] Ibid., art. 40 cmt. 5.
[65] See *supra* (nn. 43–45).
[66] Peter H. F. Bekker, *The Legal Position of Intergovernmental Organizations* (Dordrecht: Martinus Nijhoff 1994), 185–190 (collecting examples); C. Wilfred Jenks, *International Immunities* (London: Stevens and Sons Limited 1961), 41–45 (same).
[67] Convention on Specialized Agencies' Privileges and Immunities, 1947 (n. 2), art. VII sec. 24.
[68] UN, General Assembly, Resolution A/RES/22(I)A-F, part E, 13 February 1946.

seen in these terms. Even after the ITC's creditors lost every one of the multiple lawsuits they brought in UK courts, the ITC reached an out-of-court settlement with them, agreeing to pay just under £200 million, or about 35% of the total amount creditors claimed they were owed.[69] Each of the ITC's member states contributed funds to allow the ITC to make that settlement payment.[70] As these examples illustrate, a due diligence obligation to prevent an abuse of international organisations' immunities would extend to cases where international organisation caused harm without violating international law.

This proposal might be attacked from two sides: that it will do too little and fail to meaningfully address the accountability gap and, from the other side, that it will do too much, and prompt states to micromanage international organisations and destroy their autonomy. This latter objection echoes the objection that Rosalyn Higgins articulated in a 1995 report for the Institute of International Law. In the wake of the ITC's collapse, there were calls to make member states secondarily liable for international organisations' debts, thereby allowing creditors to proceed directly against member states to collect them, at least when procedures directly against the organisation were unavailable. Higgins saw a strong policy argument against such secondary liability:

> [I]f members know that they are potentially liable for contractual damages or tortious harm caused by the acts of an international organization, they will necessarily intervene in virtually all decision-making by international organizations. It is hard to see how the degree of monitoring and intervention required would be compatible with the continuing status of the organization as truly independent, not only from the host state, but from its membership.[71]

Heeding this concern, the ARIO set out a rule that, as a baseline matter, rejects such secondary liability.[72]

To be sure, the goal of a due diligence obligation to prevent international organisations from abusing their privileges and immunities would be to prompt states to be more active. The autonomy concern is unfounded or, at a minimum, overstated. First, the due diligence obligation would *not* make states secondarily

[69] Kenneth Gooding, 'Tin Creditors' £182.5m Accord', *Financial Times* (23–24 December 1989), 22; Reuters, 'Tin Council Pays Creditors', *International Herald Tribune* (2 April 1990), 11.

[70] Ibid.

[71] Rosalyn Higgins, 'The Legal Consequences for Member States of the Non-Fulfilment by International Organizations of Their Obligations Toward Third Parties', *Yearbook of the Institute of International Law* 66 (1995), 252.

[72] ARIO, 2011 (n. 15), art. 62 (setting out the baseline rule that 'membership does not as such entail for member States international responsibility when the organization commits an internationally wrongful act' as well as exceptions where a member state has accepted responsibility for the organisation's act towards an injured party or of a state has led an injured party to rely on its responsibility, for example by 'lead[ing] a third party reasonably to assume that [it and/or other member states] would stand in if the responsible organization did not have the necessary funds for making reparation').

liable for international organisations' debts, nor would it permit any persons or entities to proceed directly against member states to collect them. Any actions against member states would concern only their individual efforts (or lack thereof) to ensure that international organisations do not abuse their immunity. Indeed, provided they used their best efforts to avoid such abuse, states could avoid responsibility even if the organisation did abuse its immunities. Second, such an obligation would not license states to ignore their international obligations to respect international organisations' independence and autonomy. There's a parallel here to states' obligation to prevent genocide extraterritorially: in implementing that obligation, states must respect international law prohibitions on use of force and intervention.[73]

Separately, it's important to consider the way that such a due diligence obligation would strengthen the position of international organisations vis-à-vis their member states. Consider again the United Nations' response to cholera in Haiti. Although the United Nations has denied any legal obligation to compensate Haitian victims, in 2016 Secretary-General Ban Ki-moon acknowledged the organization had a moral responsibility to act, and proposed a $400 million 'new approach' that would involve two tracks: (i) renewed efforts to eliminate cholera in Haiti, and (ii) a package of material assistance and support to those individuals and communities most severely impacted by cholera.[74] States roundly endorsed the new approach with their words, less so with their actions: collectively UN member states have supplied only $9 million to date—some 2% of the amount Ban sought—notwithstanding the many entreaties Ban and his successor Antonío Guterres have made.[75]

Now suppose that the argument was available that member states had a legal obligation to fund the new approach—that failure to do so would constitute a breach of states' due diligence obligation to prevent abuses of immunity. The Secretary-General could deploy the legal argument to support his appeals for funding—and also to bolster efforts to fund the new approach through the regular budget (and assessed contributions) rather than only through voluntary contributions.[76] After all, legal positions taken by the UN secretariat are often quite influential. Scholars of the UN Secretary-General have cited the issuance of legal opinions as one especially important tool for influencing debate and action by member states and others.[77]

[73] ICJ, *Bosnia Genocide* (n. 34), para. 430.

[74] Daugirdas/Mortenson, 'Court Upholds United Nations' Immunity' 2017 (n. 12), 168–169.

[75] UN Haiti Cholera Response Multi-Partner Trust Fund, http://mptf.undp.org/factsheet/fund/CLH00 (accessed 31 January 2019).

[76] Guterres raised this possibility in 2017. Rick Gladstone, 'After Bringing Cholera to Haiti, U.N. Can't Raise Money to Fight It', *New York Times* (19 March 2017).

[77] Thomas Franck, *Nation Against Nation* (Oxford: OUP 1985), 126–127; Ian Johnstone, 'The Secretary-General as Norm Entrepreneur', in Simon Chesterman (ed.), *Secretary or General?* (Cambridge: CUP 2007), 123–138.

In addition, to the extent that views within individual national governments are mixed, a legal argument could strengthen the position of national government officials who favour funding the new approach over those who oppose it.[78] It is impossible to say precisely how much difference the legal argument would make—but plausible to believe that it would make some.

In the end, due diligence obligations on the part of states to supervise international organisations are not a panacea for deficiencies in international organisations' accountability to individuals who are harmed by the organisations' activities. There are good reasons, however, to believe that further developing such obligations would have positive consequences.

[78] Antonia Chayes/Abram Chayes, *The New Sovereignty* (Cambridge Mass.: Harvard University Press 1995), 4 (describing how compliance with international obligations is the 'normal organisational presumption' within government bureaucracies).

5

The Function of the Triad 'Territory', 'Jurisdiction', and 'Control' in Due Diligence Obligations

*Federica Violi**

1. Introduction

The most notable formulation of the notion of due diligence refers back to a dictum of the International Court of Justice (ICJ) in the *Corfu Channel* case:

> It is every State's obligation not to allow knowingly its territory to be used for acts contrary to the rights of other States.[1]

While the quote above refers to the (mis)use of 'territory', the scope of application of due diligence obligations also extends towards acts or activities under the 'jurisdiction' or 'control' of states. More radically, Olivier Corten suggests that due diligence could be seen as having a tendency to be emancipated from its territorial dimension (be it de iure or de facto) altogether.[2] Taking this argument as an appropriate cue, this chapter seeks to explore the territorial, jurisdictional, and control components of due diligence; tries to identify how the scope of application of due diligence rules has been interpreted in various fields of international law; and determine whether it is possible to discern a consistent meaning attributed to each of the three components.

Such an endeavour requires an analysis that looks transversally at different areas of international law where due diligence is articulated in specific rules. This chapter looks at human rights, international environmental law, the law of the sea, and the law of occupation. The analysis starts with a short overview of the triad of

* The author wishes to thank Anastasia Karatzia, Alessandra Arcuri, Marjolein Schaap, Pedro Alejandro Villarreal, Federica Favuzza, and the editors for their valuable comments on earlier versions of this chapter. The usual disclaimers apply.

[1] ICJ, *Corfu Channel Case (United Kingdom v. Albania)*, Judgment of 9 April 1949, ICJ Reports 1949, 4, p. 22.

[2] Olivier Corten, 'La complicité dans le droit de la responsabilité internationale: un concept inutile?', *Annuaire Français de Droit International* 57 (2011), 57–84, at 70.

Federica Violi, *The Function of the Triad 'Territory', 'Jurisdiction', and 'Control' in Due Diligence Obligations* In: *Due Diligence in the International Legal Order*. Edited by: Heike Krieger, Anne Peters, and Leonhard Kreuzer, Oxford University Press (2020). © The Several Contributors. DOI: 10.1093/oso/9780198869900.003.0005.

territory, jurisdiction, and control, and its function within the context of due diligence (section 2). It proceeds by disentangling the meaning of territory (section 3), jurisdiction, and control in the different areas where they appear, while at the same time scrutinising whether these might also entail a non-spatial character (section 4). Finally, some normative thoughts are provided regarding whether current international law can move away from the territoriality principle and encompass other forms of organising power, where due diligence obligations are allocated on the basis of different connecting factors and not borne (exclusively) by states (section 5).

2. The Link between 'State' and 'Risk' in the Context of Due Diligence

Due diligence is strictly connected with the notion of risk.[3] Either the risk is yet to occur and the efforts of a state are aimed at preventing it, or the harm has already materialised and the efforts of a state are aimed at rectifying it. The presence of risk justifies the construction of due diligence obligations as obligations of conduct,[4] when obtaining a certain result would be excessively burdensome for states.

Territory, jurisdiction, and control perform a specific function in the context of due diligence, in that this triad epitomises the link between state and risk, 'le lien de rattachement'.[5] In other words, the connection this triad exposes is not between a state and a certain wrongful conduct, as if we were to establish attribution; rather, the triad embodies risk proximity and defines the scope of application of due diligence obligations, based on the assumption that risk proximity enables a state to act upon a certain risk. This link is further qualified by a significant, albeit not a standalone, factor: the predictability or knowledge of risk.[6] The risk needs to be

[3] Generally on due diligence, see Anne Peters/Heike Krieger/Leonhard Kreuzer, 'Due Diligence in International Law: Dissecting the Leitmotif of Current Accountability Debates', chapter 1 of this book; Joanna Kulesza, *Due Diligence in International Law* (Leiden/Boston: Brill Nijhoff 2016); Riccardo Pisillo Mazzeschi, 'The Due Diligence Rule and the Nature of the International Responsibility of States', *German Yearbook of International Law* 35 (1992), 9–51; Riccardo Pisillo Mazzeschi, *Due Diligence e responsabilità internazionale degli Stati* (Milano: Giuffrè 1989).

[4] Extensively Pisillo Mazzeschi, *Due Diligence* 1989 (n. 3), 387.

[5] Pasquale De Sena, 'La "due diligence" et le lien entre le sujet et le risque qu'il faut prévenir: quelques observations', in Société Française pour le Droit International (SFDI)/Sarah Cassella (eds), *Le standard de due diligence et la responsabilité internationale* (Paris: Pedone 2018), 243–254.

[6] ICJ, *Corfu Channel* (n. 1), para. 22; *Trail Smelter Case (United States v. Canada)*, Decisions of 16 April 1938 and 11 March 1941, vol. III, UNRIAA, 1905–1982, at 1965; ICJ, *Legality of the Threat or Use of Nuclear Weapons*, Advisory Opinion of 8 July 1996, ICJ Reports 1996, 226, para. 29; ICJ, *Case concerning the Gabčíkovo-Nagymaros Project (Hungary v. Slovakia)*, Judgment of 25 September 1997, ICJ Reports 1997, 7, para. 54; ICJ, *Pulp Mills on the River Uruguay (Argentina v. Uruguay)*, Judgment of 20 April 2010, ICJ Reports 2010, 14, para. 119; ECtHR, *Osman v. the United Kingdom*, Grand Chamber Judgment of 28 October 1998, Application No. 23452/94, para. 101; ECtHR, *Mastromatteo v. Italy*, Grand Chamber Judgment of 24 October 2002, Application No. 37703/97, para. 74; ITLOS Seabed Disputes Chamber, *Responsibility and Obligations of States Sponsoring Persons and Entities with Respect to Activities in the Area*, Advisory Opinion of 1 February 2011, ITLOS Reports 2011, para. 162.

predictable or known for such obligations to arise.[7] In this sense, predictability and knowledge contribute to defining the scope of application: in order to be able to avert or repress a certain occurrence, a state should or ought to have known about the risk and have the effective power and tools to intervene.[8]

As will be seen in the next two sections, once risk proximity is established, the actual degree of diligence that can be expected from a state can be influenced by a number of factors, including the state's level of knowledge or control over its territory. In this sense, due diligence constitutes an elastic and variable standard.[9]

3. Territory in the Definition of the Standard of Due Diligence

Territory seems the main and natural locus of due diligence obligations. Territorial sovereignty entails the effective exercise of state authority, and hence, one might say, a state's ability to prevent or repress harmful activities from being conducted in its territory. In other words, territory seems to embody the most obvious risk proximity. While this might appear quite straightforward, it requires further elaboration.

Two considerations are in order. Firstly, as mentioned above, territorial control is a factor that may influence the standard of conduct that can be expected from the territorial sovereign.[10] The purpose of assessing territorial control is to verify in concreto what a state could have effectively done to comply with its obligation to prevent or repress.[11] Thus the degree of effective control becomes a factor when measuring the standard of diligence requested in a specific circumstance.[12] The capacity of states might be reduced,[13] for example, when a state is unable to control its entire territory[14] or as a consequence of the presence of insurrectional

[7] In this sense, see ICJ, *Case Concerning Application of The Convention on the Prevention and Punishment of the Crime of Genocide (Bosnia and Herzegovina v. Serbia and Montenegro)*, Judgment of 26 February 2007, ICJ Reports 2007, 43, para. 431.

[8] This chapter endorses an objective understanding of knowledge. At the level of international responsibility, see Helmut Aust/Prisca Feihle, 'Due Diligence in the History of the Codification of the Law of State Responsibility', chapter 3 of this book.

[9] See Pisillo Mazzeschi, *Due Diligence* 1989 (n. 3), 261; International Law Association, Study Group on Due Diligence in International Law, Second Report, 12 July 2016, 10.

[10] See, already at an early stage, *Home Frontier and Foreign Missionary Society of the United Brethren in Christ (United States v. Great Britain)*, Decision of 18 December 1920, vol. VI, UNRIAA, 44; *Leonor Buckingham (Great Britain v. United Mexican States)*, Decision of 3 August 1931, vol. V, UNRIAA, 286.

[11] Pisillo Mazzeschi, *Due Diligence* 1989 (n. 3), 263.

[12] On the connection with international responsibility, see Robert Barnidge, 'The Due Diligence Principle under International Law', *International Community Law Review* 8 (2006), 81–121, at 105.

[13] On the notion of capacity as foundation of power, see André Nollkaemper, 'Power and Responsibility', in Adriana Di Stefano (ed.), *A Lackland Law? Territory, Effectiveness and Jurisdiction in International and EU Law* (Turin: Giappichelli 2015), 19–44.

[14] See also ICJ, *Military and Paramilitary Activities in and against Nicaragua (Nicaragua v. United States of America)*, Judgment of 27 June 1986, ICJ Reports 1986, 14, para. 157.

movements.[15] However, since the international legal order remains for the most part territorially-based, territorial sovereignty still generates the presumption that states exercise control over their territory. While this does not equate to a presumption of knowledge,[16] the absence of effective control does not automatically preclude wrongfulness. In fact, this absence might also point towards a 'censurable failure of efforts to deal with lawlessness'.[17] Secondly, territorial control seems to be less relevant in recent practice, especially because of the emerging specification and technicalities of due diligence obligations, which reduce the elasticity of the standard. In this regard, the detailed monitoring and assessment actions that states are required to undertake to prevent or mitigate climate change-related risks under Articles 7 and 8 of the Paris Agreement offer a good example.[18] The above notwithstanding, new situations might revive the need to verify the level of territorial control a state possesses when assessing due diligence obligations. This is true, in particular, when a territorial state retains its title but voluntarily relinquishes its control, where no other country is involved.

This scenario of reduced effective control is reflected in a variety of situations that are characterised by an unclear legal status and denote a voluntary lack of control by the territorial states in question. Examples range from excised territories from migration in Australia, Guantanamo Bay, or land rented out to private actors for investment purposes. Although the terminology found in the literature varies,[19] the common element is that the territorial state has divested itself from exercising control over its territory, for example, by way of agreements or other legal tools such as investment contracts. This chapter argues that in these situations the territorial sovereign nevertheless fully retains its due diligence obligations both to prevent and repress. While it is true that the territorial state might be unable to exert effective control over those contested areas, the 'lawlessness' situations came about precisely through these prior arrangements.[20] If we are to assume that a country

[15] See, e.g., Max Huber, *Affaire des biens britanniques au Maroc espagnol (Spain v. UK)*, 1 May 1925, UNRIAA, vol. II, 642.

[16] See ICJ, *Corfu Channel* (n. 1), 18; Olivier De Schutter, 'Globalization and Jurisdiction: Lessons from the European Convention on Human Rights', *Baltic Yearbook of International Law* 6 (2006), 185–247, at 226; see also Ian Brownlie, *System of The Law of Nations: State Responsibility Part I* (Oxford: OUP 1983), 45.

[17] *Mrs. Elmer Elsworth Mead (Helen O. Mead) (USA v. United Mexican States)*, Decision of 29 October 1930, vol. IV, UNRIAA, 653.

[18] United Nations, Paris Agreement to the United Nations Framework Convention on Climate Change, 12 December 2015, US TIAS No. 16-1104.

[19] Péter Szigeti, 'The Illusion of Territorial Jurisdiction', *Texas International Law Journal* 52 (2017), 369–399: refers to those areas as 'anomalous zones'; Saskia Sassen, 'Land Grabs Today: Feeding the Disassembling of National Territory', *Globalizations* 10 (2013), 25: refers to 'holes in the tissue of territorial sovereignty'; the present author has referred to 'de facto enclaves', Alessandra Arcuri/Federica Violi, 'Reconfiguring Territoriality in International Economic Law', *Netherlands Yearbook of International Law* 47 (2017), 175–215.

[20] In the case of lease of territory, however, the allocation of due diligence obligations depends on the terms of the lease agreements. See also Szigeti, 'The Illusion' 2017 (n. 19), 389; James Crawford, *Brownlie's Principles of International Law* (Oxford: OUP 2012), 215.

shall not knowingly allow the misuse of its territory, the voluntary divestment of its powers of control[21] to other actors cannot constitute the basis to claim a reduced ability to prevent or repress. In other words, a state cannot escape its obligations by contracting out its powers to another (mostly unaccountable) entity. Reasoning otherwise would provide countries unwilling to comply with their obligations an excuse not to control their territory.[22]

4. Jurisdiction and/or Control: What's in a Name?

Due diligence obligations extend to activities under the jurisdiction and control of states. Both concepts define the scope of application and embody the connection with risk. Hence these require a thorough interpretation in order to identify the exact extent of states' due diligence duties. This section looks at how the risk proximity enshrined in jurisdiction and control has been interpreted in the context of due diligence obligations in various fields of international law and whether it is possible to identify a uniform interpretative trend.

4.1 The Human Rights Regime

Jurisdiction is a controversial notion. Under international law, it traditionally indicates the limits of a state's entitlement to perform prescriptive, adjudicative, and enforcement acts. In the human rights regime, however,[23] extensive studies[24] have shown that jurisdiction enshrines the vertical relationship between states and individuals. This relationship does not need to be sanctioned de iure; it depends on a de facto exercise of legal and political authority, which entails effective territorial control or control over affected individuals. If established, it triggers the application

[21] See Federica Violi, 'The Regulatory Vicious Circle of Investment Operations in Agriculture', Margherita Alabrese (ed.), *Current Issues in Agricultural Law in a Global Perspective* (Berlin: Springer 2017), 311–340.

[22] *Spanish Zone in Morocco* (n. 15), 615.

[23] The (European) Convention on the Protection of Human Rights and Fundamental Freedoms, 4 November 1950, 213 UNTS 221 (art. 1), the American Convention on Human Rights, 22 November 1969, 1144 UNTS 123 (art. 1), and the International Covenant on Civil and Political Rights, 16 September 1966, 999 UNTS 171 (art. 2) explicitly refer to 'jurisdiction'.

[24] Aravind Ganesh, 'The European Union's Human Rights Obligations Towards Distant Strangers', *Michigan Journal of International Law* 37 (2016), 475–538; Samantha Besson, 'The Extraterritoriality of the European Convention on Human Rights: Why Human Rights Depend on Jurisdiction and What Jurisdiction Amounts To', *Leiden Journal of International Law* 25 (2012), 857–884; albeit taking a different stance, see Marko Milanovic, *Extraterritorial Application of Human Rights Treaties: Law, Principles, and Policy* (Oxford: OUP 2011), 119, 137; Pasquale De Sena, *La nozione di giurisdizione statale nei trattati sui diritti dell'uomo* (Turin: Giappichelli 2002), 217.

of negative and positive human rights obligations.[25] Therefore, risk proximity in the realm of human rights is realised through de facto authority, understood here as the power to 'speak the law'[26] and require compliance. This and the following subsection mainly look at two issues. Firstly, whether the traditional delimitating notion of jurisdiction has any role to play in the human rights positive duties context (4.1); and secondly, whether jurisdiction for the purposes of applying human rights treaties has ever been severed from the spatial scope of application of due diligence obligations (4.2).

The question of the role of jurisdiction in human rights positive duties refers to a situation in which the territorial state retains its title, yet another state exercises control over an area of the former's territory. This can be well illustrated through the ECtHR's *Ilaşcu v. Moldova* case,[27] which relates to the arrest and detainment of Ilia Ilaşcu and three others by the Transdniestrian government. It is generally recognised that Moldova's authority over the Transdniestrian region is constrained, and that Russia exerts significant[28] de facto authority over the very same area.[29]

Instead of considering Russia as the sole state maintaining jurisdiction for the purposes of Article 1 ECHR—and thus implicitly bearing all obligations[30]—the Strasbourg judges held that:

> [E]ven in the absence of effective control over the Transdniestrian region, Moldova still has a positive obligation under Article 1 of the Convention to take the diplomatic, economic, judicial or other measures that [are] in its power to take and are in accordance with international law to secure to the applicants the rights guaranteed by the Convention.[31]

Moldova was thus expected to exert all possible efforts to ensure that rights were respected in an area where it had lost full control.[32] The foundation for such an obligation still resides with the country's jurisdiction under Article 1 of the Convention, which, according to the court, was not removed by a de facto situation of constraint.[33] In other words, here the ECtHR applied the presumption

[25] Extensively: Ganesh, 'The European Union's HR Obligations' 2016 (n. 24), and Besson, 'The Extraterritoriality of the ECHR' 2012 (n. 24); see Björnstjern Baade, 'Due Diligence and the Duty to Protect Human Rights', chapter 6 of this book.

[26] As referred to in Ganesh, 'The European Union's HR Obligations' 2016 (n. 24), 503.

[27] ECtHR, *Ilaşcu and Others v. Moldova and Russia*, Grand Chamber Judgment of 8 July 2004, Application No. 48787/99.

[28] Yet not equal to military occupation.

[29] ECtHR, *Ilaşcu* (n. 27), para. 392. The methodological flaws of the reasoning of the Court have been highlighted in Milanovic, *Extraterritorial Application* 2011 (n. 24), 185; De Schutter, 'Globalization and Jurisdiction' 2006 (n. 16), 221.

[30] Kjetil Mujezinovic Larsen, '"Territorial Non-Application" of the European Convention on Human Rights', *Nordic Journal of International Law* 78 (2009), 78–93, at 85.

[31] ECtHR, *Ilaşcu* (n. 27), para. 331.

[32] Importantly here the presumption is that the authorities acting in Transdniestria are not de iure or de facto organs of Moldova; they are considered private actors.

[33] ECtHR, *Ilaşcu* (n. 27), para. 333.

by which facts occurring within a certain territory are under the jurisdiction of the territorial sovereign.[34] That is, even when constrained, jurisdiction in its traditional international law meaning still gives rise to positive duties.[35] However, positive obligations might be tailored to what the territorial state can effectively do.[36] The mechanism introduced by the ECtHR in *Ilaşcu* illustrates what was discussed above in terms of territorial control and flexibility: objective factors might alter the primary standard of conduct that is expected of a state.[37] Yet a state cannot hide 'behind its inability to control portions of its national territory in order to escape its obligations to do everything which it legally and practically can do in order to secure the rights of the Convention on all its territory'.[38] At the same time the state exercising de facto authority bears other due diligence obligations derived from its shared portion of jurisdiction. In the *Ilaşcu* case, for example, Russia did not prevent the detention, abuse, and ill-treatment of the applicants mainly due to a lack of control and supervision over the perpetrators.

4.2. An Anomaly? Due Diligence Obligations for Domestic Activities with Extraterritorial Effects

A recent advisory opinion of the Inter-American Court of Human Rights (IACtHR)[39] has opened new scenarios with regard to 'domestic activities with extraterritorial effect'.[40] The case related to the risk of potential environmental harm generated by a series of infrastructural works in the wider Caribbean region. The court reformulated the original question of Colombia to include issues involving general environmental (due diligence) obligations[41] deriving from the duty to respect and ensure human rights, and in particular the right to life and personal integrity.

In this advisory opinion, the 'lien de rattachement' with the risk has played out somewhat differently. According to the IACtHR, if an emission originating in a certain state has a causal nexus with the harm suffered by individuals in another

[34] De Schutter, 'Globalization and Jurisdiction' 2006 (n. 16), 226.

[35] ECtHR, *Ilaşcu* (n. 27), para. 313.

[36] Besson, 'The Extraterritoriality of the ECHR' 2012 (n. 24), 879.

[37] Larsen, '"Territorial Non-Application" of the ECHR' 2009 (n. 30), 84.

[38] ECtHR, *Ilaşcu* (n. 27) seems to leave open the possibility that there might be situations that amount to 'shared' jurisdiction; see De Schutter, 'Globalization and Jurisdiction' 2006 (n. 16), 221.

[39] IACtHR, Advisory Opinion OC-23/17 of 15 November 2017, Requested by the Republic of Columbia, paras 62–63, 101–103.

[40] See, among others, Antal Berkes, 'A New Extraterritorial Jurisdictional Link Recognised by the IACtHR', *EJIL: Talk!*, 28 March 2018, available at: https://www.ejiltalk.org/a-new-extraterritorial-jurisdictional-link-recognised-by-the-iacthr/ (accessed 29 August 2019); Pedro Villarreal, 'Stretching Abstract Reasoning to its Limits: The IACtHR and the Right to a Healthy Environment', *Völkerrechtsblog*, 6 April 2018, available at: https://voelkerrechtsblog.org/stretching-abstract-reasoning-to-its-limits/ (accessed 29 August 2019).

[41] Namely, extending the duty to prevent transboundary harm also to individuals.

state, this would be sufficient to establish the human rights jurisdiction of the emitting state over the victims if the territorial state knew about the risk and could have prevented it. As highlighted by Antal Berkes, following the reasoning of the IACtHR, 'the knowledge on the risk of wrongful acts and the capacity to protect due to its effective control over activities within its territory'[42] would be enough to establish control over individuals for the purposes of extraterritorial jurisdiction. Basically, a territorial link with the risk is paired with the extraterritorial reach of human rights jurisdiction. Clearly, this potentially encompasses a wide variety of situations and could exacerbate the burden of states. While knowledge and capacity might trigger certain due diligence obligations,[43] this hybrid construction creates a situation in which (territorial) jurisdiction over the activities is extended extraterritorially through causality. Relying on the causal nexus, the court equated jurisdiction with causality and ultimately with imputability, thus altering the vertical understanding of human rights jurisdiction, and eventually risk proximity.[44]

4.3. International Environmental Law

The relevant due diligence provisions in international environmental law require states to ensure that activities within their jurisdiction or control do not cause significant damage to the environment of other states (or of areas beyond the limits of national jurisdiction). The ICJ has recognised this norm as customary international law on several occasions.[45]

The phrase 'jurisdiction or control' suggests that the two notions do not form a pair but are alternatives. The Commentaries to the 2001 Articles on Prevention of Transboundary Harm from Hazardous Activities,[46] the 2006 Draft Principles on the Allocation of Loss in the case of Transboundary Harm arising out of Hazardous activities,[47] and the 1987 Report on the International Liability for Injurious Consequences Arising out of Acts Not Prohibited under International Law offer an indication of what the two notions entail in international environmental law.[48]

[42] Berkes, 'A New Extraterritorial Jurisdictional Link' 2018 (n. 40).

[43] See below section 5; cf. Larissa van den Herik/Emma Irving, 'Due Diligence and the Obligation to Prevent Genocide and Crimes Against Humanity', chapter 12 of this book.

[44] Besides the methodological flaws of the Court's reasoning, we might expect similar issues in the future, see n. 41; see also Ellen Hey/Federica Violi, 'The Hard Work of Regime Interaction: Climate Change and Human Rights', in Mededelingen van de Koninklijke Nederlandse Vereniging voor Internationaal Recht nr. 145, *Climate Change: Options and Duties under International Law* (The Hague: Asser Press 2018), 5–24.

[45] See n. 6.

[46] United Nations, International Law Commission (ILC), Report of the International Law Commission on the Work of its Fifty-Third Session, A/56/10, 23 April–1 June and 2 July–10 August 2001, 151, para. 9.

[47] ILC, Report of the International Law Commission on the Work of its Fifty-Eighth Session, A/61/10, 1 May–9 June and 3 July–11 August 2006, 134, para. 25.

[48] ILC, Report of the International Law Commission on the Work of its Thirty-Ninth Session, A/42/10, 4 May–17 July 1987. See also Comments and Observations received from Governments,

All three instruments consider jurisdiction as having the de iure meaning it carries under general international law, territorially or otherwise connoted,[49] thus losing the vertical de facto significance it carries in the context of human rights. The de facto component is instead taken over by the notion of control. Interestingly, the phrase refers to activities within a state's jurisdiction or control, and not to activities *within a territory* under a state's jurisdiction or control. It seems reasonable to explore whether the formula refers to state control over the activities[50] or control over territory. The first hypothesis would extend the scope of application of due diligence obligations to situations where the state itself has control over potentially harmful activities, regardless of where these are located. This would open Pandora's box in relation to what is meant by 'control', and therefore under what conditions risk proximity would materialise and how this would affect the degree of diligence. The 1987, 2001, and 2006 commentaries lean towards effective control over the territory[51] where such harmful activities are conducted. In support of this interpretation, the International Law Commission (ILC) refers to the Namibia advisory opinion[52] where the ICJ maintained that physical control over a territory would trigger responsibility for affecting other states. Similarly, the wording of Article IV of the 1977 Environmental Modification Convention[53] refers to the obligation of states to prevent any activity that violates the Convention *anywhere* under their jurisdiction and control, loading the latter with a spatial meaning. Somewhat differently, an earlier report on the Draft Articles on Prevention of Transboundary Damage from Hazardous Activities refers to instances of 'short-time effective control by a State over activities which are under the jurisdiction of another State'.[54] However, the reactions of states to this report[55] seem to show a preference for maintaining a territorial dimension under the notion of 'control'.

A/CN.4/481 and Add.1, 14 April and 6 May 1997, 45, para. 162. Note that these Principles were never adopted; they are used here only in support of the analysis.

[49] E.g., the flag state of a vessel, ILC, Report 2001 (n. 46), 151, para. 10.

[50] This might range from financial or technical support to ownership and shareholding of companies. Control over territory in this context does not seem to be linked to a specific account of authority as understood in the HRs regime.

[51] ILC, Report 2001 (n. 46), 151, para. 12; ILC, Report 1987 (n. 48), 45, para. 160.

[52] See ICJ, *Legal Consequences for States of the Continued Presence of South Africa in Namibia notwithstanding Security Council Resolution 276 (1970)*, Advisory Opinion of 21 June 1971, ICJ Reports 1971, 16, para. 118.

[53] Environmental Modification Convention, 10 December 1976, 1108 UNTS 152.

[54] ILC, Report of the International Law Commission on the Work of its Fiftieth Session, A/53/10, 20 April–12 June and 27 July–14 August 1998, 25, para. 11.

[55] ILC, Third report on international liability for injurious consequences arising out of acts not prohibited by international law (prevention of transboundary damage from hazardous activities), by Mr. Pemmaraju Sreenivasa Rao, Special Rapporteur, A/CN.4/510, 9 June 2000, 116, para. 6. The division of either spatial (control over territory) or causal (control over activities) connection between the harm and the state of origin was considered confusing by states. See UK's suggestion (A/CN.4/509). See also Venezuela (Official Records of the General Assembly, Fifty-Third Session, Sixth Committee, 15th Meeting (A/C.6/53/SR.15, 28 October 1998, para. 27).

Throughout the literature, scholars have mainly taken the same stance,[56] with some seemingly leaving the door open to the hypothesis of de facto control over activities by states in areas beyond national jurisdiction. Under Annex VI on Liability Arising from Environmental Emergencies of the 1991 Protocol on Environmental Protection to the Antarctic Treaty,[57] an Operator is considered to be 'of the State Party', even in absence of 'formal authorisation', as long as the activities are subject to a 'comparable regulatory process'.[58] Such an open-ended definition seems to allow for a situation where de facto control over the activities is paired with a more relaxed de iure jurisdiction, and would be sufficient to establish the necessary link for the purposes of the due diligence obligations included in Article 10 of the same Annex VI.

4.4. Law of the Sea

Article 194 of the United Nations Convention on the Law of the Sea (UNCLOS)[59] equally employs the formula of 'activities under states' jurisdiction or control' in the context of due diligence obligations to prevent environmental harms.[60] As is well known, there is no 'territorial' state in the law of the sea. Waters are divided according to a 'zonal approach',[61] where rights and duties for port, coastal, flag, and sponsoring states are articulated (albeit not always comprehensively) within the Convention. While 'jurisdiction' refers to the rights UNCLOS grants to states, the meaning of 'control' remains unclear. Generally speaking, besides the territorial sea, where the coastal state exercises territorial sovereignty, all other zones are subject to sovereign 'rights', that is, functional competences attributed to states for the pursuit of specific objectives. There is no appurtenance relationship with the zones, nor the possibility of appropriation. In areas beyond national jurisdiction, the flag state has an almost exclusive jurisdiction over its vessels. The question is therefore

[56] René Lefeber, *Transboundary Environmental Interference and the Origin of State Liability* (The Hague: Kluwer Law International 1996), 10–11; referring also to ICJ, *Certain Phosphate Lands in Nauru (Nauru v. Australia)*, Order of 13 September 1993, ICJ Reports 1993, 322, where Australia was the former mandatory.

[57] The Antarctic Treaty, 1 December 1959, 402 UNTS 71.

[58] The previous Convention on the Regulation of Antarctic Mineral Resource Activities of 1988 ('Wellington Convention') (did not enter into force) was clearer and explicitly open to such an option; art. 1 requested a 'genuine link', available at: www.ats.aq/documents/recatt/Att311_e.pdf (accessed 21 February 2019).

[59] United Nations Convention on the Law of the Sea, 10 December 1982, 1833 UNTS 3.

[60] See, among others, *In the matter of South China Sea Arbitration (Philippines v. China)*, Award of 12 July 2016, PCA Case No 2013-19, ICGJ 495; *In the matter of the Chagos Marine Protected Areas (Mauritius v. United Kingdom)*, Final Award of 18 March 2015, PCA Case No 2011-03, ICGJ 486; ITLOS, *Responsibility and Obligations in the Area Opinion* (n. 6).

[61] The author will only refer to UNCLOS for the purposes of this chapter, as the backbone and most comprehensive law of the sea framework. For a comprehensive analysis, see Irini Papanicolopulu, 'Due Diligence in the Law of the Sea', chapter 9 of this book.

whether any (residual) meaning can be attributed to de facto 'control', divorced from a competence formally stipulated under the Convention. In the recent award in the *South China Sea* case, the conclusions of the arbitral tribunal on the violations of, among others, Article 194 were based on the jurisdiction of China as the flag state of the infringing vessels.[62] It is notable that, at a certain point, the tribunal does refer to the 'de facto' control of China over the waters surrounding the marine features under dispute. However, the tribunal did not derive any potential obligations for China from the fact of control.[63] Also, the preparatory works of UNCLOS show certain difficulties that states had in dealing with the 'jurisdiction or control' formula. The only reference the present author was able to find in relation to the issue is a footnote to a preparatory document, which reads as follows:

> some delegations felt that 'or control' should be retained, while others felt it should be deleted. Some delegations thought that the meaning of 'control' in this context should be clarified. It was stressed that the above sentence relates to a State's control over activities and not areas of control.[64]

Scholars have interpreted the two notions by differentiating 'jurisdiction', as a competence *ratione loci*, from 'control', as competence *ratione materiae*.[65] This would correspond, for example, to a vessel flying a foreign flag (control)[66] within the territorial sea (jurisdiction) of another state. Thus, the formula would seem to include all diverse sovereign rights that are attributed de iure under UNCLOS. The spatial dimension of control over areas is excluded. More generally, the intricate web of rights and duties comprised in UNCLOS does not easily accommodate effective control disarticulated from any formal competence.

A similar situation exists for those provisions related to activities conducted in the zone known as the Area. UNCLOS encompasses one relevant due diligence provision seemingly severing effective control from jurisdiction. Article 139 specifies that those states effectively controlling natural or juridical persons (operating in 'the Area') shall ensure that these subjects will conduct their activities in conformity to the Convention.[67] However, a closer look shows that a de iure link is nonetheless required. Under Article 153, in cases where a company is effectively controlled by a state other than its state of nationality, both the controlling and the national states will share the obligation to ensure that the company's activities comply with the relevant provisions. Yet again, it seems that the attempt is to

[62] *South China Sea Arbitration* (n. 60), paras 822–944.
[63] Ibid., para. 745.
[64] UN Doc. A/AC.138/SC.III/L.39 (WG2/Paper No. 8/Add.2), 1973, as cited in Myron H. Nordquist (ed.), *United Nations Convention on the Law of the Sea, 1982: A Commentary* (Dordrecht/Boston/London: Martinus Nijhoff 2002), 56.
[65] Ibid., at 76.
[66] See UNCLOS, 1982 (n. 59), art. 94.
[67] ITLOS, *Responsibility and Obligations in the Area Opinion* (n. 6), para. 107.

not leave any possible gap for effective control deprived of an accompanying de iure link.

4.5 Law of Occupation

Due diligence obligations feature prominently in the law of occupation. Article 43 of the Hague Regulations includes a general due diligence duty for the occupying power, which is further articulated into other more specific due diligence obligations.[68] Article 43 explicitly indicates that these obligations arise when the 'authority of the legitimate power' has 'in fact passed into the hands of the occupant'. Thus, the connection with the risk is enshrined here in the notion of authority. The normative content of the term is not free of ambiguity and has fuelled both scholarly and judicial debate.[69] Authority is largely understood to be 'substantiated'[70] by effective control, which is considered to lie at the core of the notion of occupation. The terms 'actually' and 'established' in Article 42 Hague Regulations suggest that, in order to initiate the occupation, the forces of the foreign power must gain actual control over the occupied territory[71] with the territorial sovereign losing its ability to exercise any authority. That is, the occupying power needs to be effectively able to assume and exercise its authority over the occupied territory. This is also due to the nature of the authority referred to in Article 42, which entails instructing legal and 'political direction' over the population,[72] and assuming governmental functions more generally, in place of the local government. It would otherwise be difficult to imagine how the foreign forces could discharge their duties. Notwithstanding the last dictum of the ICJ in *Democratic Republic of Congo v. Uganda*, which has seemingly restricted the notion of occupation to the actual exercise of authority,[73] legal scholarship and international case law have consistently upheld the position that actual control over territory coupled with the ability to exercise authority over the population is sufficient for occupation to materialise, in order to avoid both abuse and escaping duties imposed on the occupant. On the other side of the spectrum,

[68] Gabriella Venturini, 'Les obligations de diligence dans le droit international humanitaire', in SFDI/ Sarah Cassella (eds), *Le standard de due diligence et la responsabilité internationale* (Paris: Pedone 2018), 135–144; see also Marco Longobardo, 'Due Diligence in International Humanitarian Law', chapter 11 of this book.

[69] For general accounts on the issue, see Yoram Dinstein, *The International Law of Belligerent Occupation* (Cambridge: CUP 2009), 31; Eyal Benvenisti, *The International Law of Occupation* (Oxford: OUP 2012), 43; see also the extensive literature cited in Tristan Ferraro, 'Determining the Beginning and End of an Occupation Under International Humanitarian Law', *International Review of the Red Cross* 94 (2012), 133–163; Marco Longobardo, *The Use of Armed Force in Occupied Territory* (Cambridge: CUP 2018), 36.

[70] Ferraro, 'Determining the Beginning and End of an Occupation' 2012 (n. 69), 140.

[71] Benvenisti, *Law of Occupation* 2012 (n. 69), 50.

[72] Ferraro, 'Determining the Beginning and End of an Occupation' 2012 (n. 69), 148.

[73] ICJ, *Case Concerning Armed Activities on the Territory of the Congo (DRC v. Uganda)*, Judgment of 19 December 2005, ICJ Reports 2005, 168, para. 173.

some jurisprudence has displayed a tendency to lower the threshold in certain situations. According to the International Criminal Tribunal for the former Yugoslavia in *Naletilic*:

> the application of the law of occupation as it [a]ffects 'individuals' as civilians protected under Geneva Convention IV does not require that the occupying power have actual authority.[74]

Such a stance seems to assimilate the scope of application of due diligence obligations included in Geneva Convention IV Section III with 'capacity', thus extending the link with the risk to situations where effective control has not yet fully materialised, as is already the case for other duties of international humanitarian law.[75] The debate on the matter is far from settled.[76] However, rather than a modification of the notion of occupation, the decision of the Tribunal appears to extend the scope of application of the provisions above so as to include, for example, situations of invasion.[77]

5. A Functional Shift from the Triad?

As mentioned in section 1 of this chapter, some authors have contemplated whether the principle of due diligence should be severed from its territorial dimension. Some international humanitarian law obligations, and genocide related provisions, as articulated in the findings of the ICJ in *Bosnia v. Serbia*,[78] arguably already rely on the 'capacity to influence' as a standalone factor to establish a connection with the risk. As such, this capacity is disentangled from either physical control over territory or jurisdiction, albeit within the limits of what is allowed under international law.

Some margin of detachment from the territorial or jurisdictional paradigm might also be found in those due diligence obligations to promote, like Article 2

[74] ICTY, *Prosecutor v. M. Naletilic and V. Martinovic*, Judgment of 31 March 2003, IT-98-34-T, para. 221.

[75] Longobardo, *The Use of Armed Force* 2018 (n. 69); see also Serena Forlati, 'L'objet des différentes obligations primaires de diligence: prévention, cessation, répression ... ?', in SFDI/Sarah Cassella (eds), *Le standard de due diligence et la responsabilité internationale* (Paris: Pedone 2018), 39–65.

[76] Longobardo, *The Use of Armed Force* 2018 (n. 69), 39. See also a reference to a potential duty to protect in Benvenisti, *Law of Occupation* 2012 (n. 69), 51.

[77] Ferraro, 'Determining the Beginning and End of an Occupation' 2012 (n. 69), 138; Dapo Akande, 'Classification of Armed Conflicts: Relevant Legal Concepts', in Elizabeth Wilmshurt (ed.), *International Law and the Classification of Conflicts* (Oxford: OUP 2012), 32, 45.

[78] ICJ, *Bosnia Genocide* (n. 7), para. 430. See Larissa van den Herik/Emma Irving, 'Due Diligence and the Obligation to Prevent Genocide and Crimes Against Humanity', chapter 12 of this book.

of the International Covenant on Civil and Political Rights (ICESCR),[79] which are seemingly[80] not limited by a jurisdiction clause. This general obligation to progressively achieve full realisation of the rights included in ICESCR is enforced through the adoption of more specific domestic and international measures. While some of these measures might be territorially connoted—such as the proper functioning of the domestic judiciary—the general obligation they contribute to enforce is not territorially connoted per se, thus there might be instances of non- or extraterritorial-specific due diligence obligations.[81]

Finally, two normative points are in order. Territoriality has been subject to significant criticism in the last decade because of its alleged inability to function as an ordering principle for the allocation of power and authority in the current international realm (section 5.1). Our globalised, interconnected world has put this paradigm in question and several authors have suggested potential alternatives to territorial jurisdiction along the lines of functionalism, where the state—while being one of the actors in the global arena—would not be the only one contributing to the functioning of a certain system or subsystem of international law (section 5.2).

5.1. Alternatives to the Existing Paradigm?

Regardless of the legality, legitimacy, and feasibility of a functional approach severed from territory,[82] the question is whether it is possible to conceive alternative links that could redefine territoriality and jurisdiction. Cedric Ryngaert has recently suggested that both notions might be redesigned in light of other concepts, such as community, temporality, or justice.[83] While admitting, and rightly so, that these do not currently constitute concrete alternatives to political geography and the exercise of authority connected to it (namely territoriality), he suggests that

[79] International Covenant on Economic, Social and Cultural Rights, 16 December 1966, 993 UNTS 3; see Riccardo Pisillo Mazzeschi, 'Responsabilité de l'État pour violation des obligations positives relatives aux droits de l'homme', *Recueil des Cours de l'Academie de Haye* 333 (2008), 175–506, at 175.

[80] A discussion on the territorial delimitation of ICESCR is beyond the scope of this chapter. The presumption, for the sake of the argument, is that Art. 2 ICESCR is not limited by a jurisdictional requirement.

[81] An example might be the voting attitude of states within international organisations, in the case of the adoption of acts or decisions that might undermine human rights or generate a regression thereof. In the context of international financial institutions, see Pasquale De Sena, 'International Monetary Fund, World Bank and Respect for Human Rights: A Critical Point of View', *Italian Yearbook of International Law* 10 (2010), 247–274.

[82] Cedric Ryngaert, 'Territory in the Law of Jurisdiction: Imagining Alternatives', *Netherlands Yearbook of International Law* 47 (2017), 49–82; Arcuri/Violi, 'Reconfiguring Territoriality' 2017 (n. 19); Luca Pasquet, 'Jurisdiction ed elemento territorial: Riflessioni su un mondo multilivello, interconnesso e specializzato', in Adriana Di Stefano (ed.), *A Lackland Law? Territory, Effectiveness and Jurisdiction in International and EU Law* (Turin: Giappichelli 2015), 143–164.

[83] Ryngaert, 'Territory' 2017 (n. 82), 59.

these might still de iure condendo have an impact on how we understand jurisdiction, and hence, for our purposes, on how we conceptualise the link between risk and the exercise of power. In the case of due diligence, the idea of temporality might be interesting for obligations to prevent future harms—for example, to avert the risk of adverse climate change impacts. Deploying the notion of ‘territorial-extension’ developed by Joanne Scott,[84] Ryngaert shows how the extension of the EU Aviation Directive on carbon dioxide emission allowances to non-EU companies might have been justified ‘on the basis of a temporal version of jurisdiction’.[85] While still at an embryonic stage, such a perspective might be interesting in the information technology sphere, where simultaneity is often the rule and implies that different actors are able to act upon a certain risk or harm at the same time. The main question here is how to avoid pluralism and conflict, but the idea that criteria other than territorial or personal jurisdiction might better encapsulate the link between the risk and a state in due diligence obligations might deserve further rethinking.

5.2. Reconstructing the Link with the Risk for Non-State Actors

As a final normative reflection, it might be worth exploring whether ‘control over territory’ on the part of multinational enterprises could be conceptualised as triggering due diligence obligations.[86] Without delving into the theoretical and legal foundations of these duties, one can enquire at an abstract level whether the control that investors exercise over investment areas through their property and contractual rights[87] might be framed as the same *lien de rattachement* that serves as a basis for the due diligence obligations of states. The objective here is not to delve into the substantive content of these obligations, but rather to: (a) detect patterns that have been identified in assessing and justifying the connection between a duty bearer and the risk; and (b) assess whether these can, at least to a certain extent, be reproduced for private investors. While extending dynamics and mechanisms that are properly state-centric might be perceived as invalid or arbitrary, the point is to offer an exploratory basis to engage in the discussion regarding the participation of

[84] Joanne Scott, ‘Territorial Sovereignty and Territorial Extension in an Inter-Connected World’, in Richard Rawlings/Peter Leyland/Alison Young (eds), *Sovereignty and the Law: Domestic, European and International Perspectives* (Oxford: OUP 2013), 269–285; however, a territorial trigger was still present, namely in EU airports or aviation areas.

[85] Ryngaert, ‘Territory’ 2017 (n. 82): Directive 03/87/EC, as amended by Regulation (EU) No 421/2014, [2014] OJ L 129/1.

[86] Jonathan Bonnitcha/Robert McCorquodale, ‘The Concept of “Due Diligence” in the UN Guiding Principles on Business and Human Rights’, *European Journal of International Law* 28 (2017), 1–25: the authors show how the notion of due diligence for multinational enterprises is used inconsistently within the UNGPs, mixing company due diligence to manage internal risk with human rights due diligence to prevent or remedy external risk.

[87] See above section 3.

non-state actors in international law. In the absence of a coherent legal framework articulating due diligence obligations for multinational enterprises, it appears safe to take a stringent view and adopt a notion of 'authority' as a parameter, understood as the power to frame the law and demand compliance through enforcement, combined with effective control over the investment areas.[88] It is submitted here that these interdependent elements would be fulfilled in the context of certain investment operations, since they create a situation by which investors can 'lawfully' claim authority and demand compliance, thus exerting features of both structural and institutional power.[89] In this sense, scholars have already pointed out how multinational enterprises are steadily taking on 'law-making' capacities,[90] and constructing legal enclaves where the territorial state exerts a minimal role.[91] Investment operations are typically implemented via state contracts, and concluded between host countries and investors. These contracts are generally included within the framework of bilateral investment treaties. A lot has been said about the nature of these instruments and the hybridism thereof. What is relevant here is that often state contracts enjoy a formidable hierarchical position, both for the status they enjoy under domestic law[92] and through the protection offered by bilateral investment treaties, which at a general level[93] might imply the international responsibility of the state for the violation of contractual clauses, and can be challenged through international arbitration.[94] Besides the formal-relational qualities of state contracts, the compelling force thereof is also derived by the actual content of these transactions. Contractual clauses tend very often to significantly restrict the state's right to regulate. These clauses (i) constrain the host state's power to govern in public matters (ranging from public health to the environment) and (ii) affect the host country's population by significantly circumscribing and redirecting the scope of public decision-making. On the opposite side, investors are generally granted a generous and discretionary array of rights, which sometimes even includes powers connected to 'maintaining' security. The combination of these elements show that a formally private or, at best, hybrid contract exhibits public functions and that 'the state and the private party share authority over the contract's disposition'.[95] Thus, through these contracts, investors enjoy the power

[88] See above section 4.1.

[89] On these definitions, see André Nollkaemper, 'Power and Responsibility' 2015 (n. 13), 32.

[90] Julian Arato, 'Corporations as Lawmakers', *Harvard Journal of International Law* 56 (2015), 229–295.

[91] This author has already explored this aspect in Arcuri/Violi, 'Reconfiguring Territoriality' 2017 (n. 19); and 'The Practice of Land Grabbing and its Compatibility with the Exercise of Territorial Sovereignty', in Francesca Romanin Jacur/Angelica Bonfanti/Francesco Seatzu (eds), *Natural Resources Grabbing: An International Law Perspective, Legal Studies on Access and Benefit-Sharing* (Boston: Martinus Nijhoff 2015), 17–37.

[92] These are often placed above ordinary law; see Violi, 'The Regulatory Vicious Circle' 2017 (n. 21), 322.

[93] Ibid.

[94] See Aniruddha Rajput 'Due Diligence in International Investment Law', chapter 16 of this book.

[95] Arato, 'Corporations as Lawmakers' 2015 (n. 90), 241.

of dictating legal norms that overrule domestic law and rewrite public choice, and can demand compliance thereof through a strong system of enforcement. This is coupled with a starkly autonomous power of control over the areas and activities of investment, which results in a free decision-making space that also includes the possibility of directly enforcing contractual rights upon third parties. The combination of these factors, sanctioned by international law, seems sufficient to establish a reasonable link between the investor and a risk connected to the investment areas. This 'authority' appears to embody the ability of an investor to act upon a potential risk, since it provides the necessary 'powers and tools'. The next step, which is outside the scope of this chapter, would be to understand what risks or substantive duties could be commensurate to the investors' 'authority', and how to coordinate those with the due diligence obligations of states. On the other hand, the danger might be that such a construct would contribute to justifying such 'enclavisations', rather than altering them, and minimise the role of the state.

6. Conclusions

This chapter has shown that risk proximity as the link between duty-bearer and risk is not always homogenous in the different fields of international law under scrutiny. However, most international instruments still require jurisdiction (in either sense, and mostly spatially connoted), or at least control over territory for risk proximity to materialise. The reason is mostly that an inordinate enlargement of states' due diligence obligations might overburden states, dilute the link with the risk, and create legal uncertainty.

This chapter has also shown that in certain areas of international law there are some tendencies to either divert from or expand the interpretation of the triad in constructing risk proximity. These tendencies display a certain unease in grappling with the meaning of these notions, thus making it difficult to establish what conditions must be fulfilled for due diligence obligations to arise. In fact, current developments are such that the most common understandings of risk proximity do not always reflect an effective link between duty-bearer and risk. This might be the case because these common understandings no longer describe a proper allocation of power and the ability to act upon risks. While some of these tendencies appear methodologically flawed, others offer viable alternatives. The challenge will be to explore them and understand how to legitimately allocate power to discharge duties in a way that properly reflects risk proximity.

6
Due Diligence and the Duty to Protect Human Rights

Björnstjern Baade

1. Introduction

By now, most, if not all, substantive human rights give rise to a duty to protect that is derived from the effective interpretation of a substantive right in conjunction with the respective human rights treaty's general protection clause (e.g., Article 1 European Convention on Human Rights (ECHR)).[1] This duty to protect requires the state to act in protection of a right, including against private actors, without having to guarantee success.[2] Because of this feature, it is generally understood to be an obligation of due diligence.[3]

In human rights law, the term 'due diligence' is used to describe the standard of conduct necessary to comply with a duty to protect.[4] While it is often highlighted as a tool that allows to oblige states to protect human rights against conduct not directly attributable to them,[5] this chapter will explore an additional and more

[1] For the ECHR, see Heike Krieger, 'Funktionen von Grund- und Menschenrechten', in Oliver Dörr/ Rainer Grote/Thilo Marauhn (eds), *EMRK/GG: Konkordanzkommentar* (Tübingen: Mohr Siebeck 2nd ed. 2013), 287–365, paras 28–30; cf. Eva Brems, 'Procedural Protection', in Eva Brems/Janneke Gerards (eds), *Shaping Rights in the ECHR* (Cambridge: CUP 2013), 137–161, at 138.

[2] See, with further references, William Schabas, *The European Convention on Human Rights: A Commentary* (Oxford: OUP 2015), 125.

[3] Anja Seibert-Fohr, 'Die völkerrechtliche Verantwortung des Staats für das Handeln von Privaten: Bedarf nach Neuorientierung?', *Heidelberg Journal of International Law* 73 (2013), 37–60, at 50.

[4] International Law Association (ILA), Study Group on Due Diligence in International Law, First Report, 7 March 2014, 14; Timo Koivurova, 'Due Diligence', in Rüdiger Wolfrum (ed.), *The Max Planck Encyclopedia of Public International Law* (Oxford: OUP 2010), para. 5; UN, Commission on Human Rights, The Due Diligence Standard as a Tool for the Elimination of Violence against Women, Report of the Special Rapporteur on violence against women, its causes and consequences (Yakin Ertürk), E/CN.4/2006/61, 20 January 2006, para. 14: 'yardstick'.

[5] African Commission on Human and Peoples' Rights, *Noah Kazingachire et al. v. Zimbabwe*, Decision of 2 May 2012, Application No. 295/04, paras 133–134; Robert Barnidge, Jr., 'The Due Diligence Principle Under International Law', *International Community Law Review* 8 (2006), 81–121, at 121; UN, Human Rights Committee, General Comment No. 36 on article 6 of the International Covenant on Civil and Political Rights, on the right to life, 30 October 2018, CCPR/C/GC/36, paras 7, 21; UN, CEDAW Committee, General Recommendation No. 19 on Violence Against Women, 1 February 1992, A/47/38, para. 9; UN, General Assembly, Declaration on the Elimination of Violence against Women, Resolution 48/104, 20 December 1993, art. 4 c; UN, Human Rights Committee,

Björnstjern Baade, *Due Diligence and the Duty to Protect Human Rights* In: *Due Diligence in the International Legal Order.* Edited by: Heike Krieger, Anne Peters, and Leonhard Kreuzer, Oxford University Press (2020).
DOI: 10.1093/oso/9780198869900.003.0006.

general conceptualisation of due diligence as a duty to mitigate risk (section 2).[6] It will explore which balancing factors play a role in the assessment (section 3) and how they are operationalised in individual cases (section 4). Finally, the systemic dimension (section 5), as well as the promise and limits of due diligence in general (section 6), will be considered.

2. A Duty to Mitigate Risk No Matter its Source

The duty to protect human rights requires states to safeguard human rights, prima facie, from any infringement no matter its source.[7] Initially developed to ensure the enjoyment of rights against infringement by non-state actors (section 2.1.1),[8] or by official misconduct (section 2.1.2),[9] it was also extended to infringements caused by natural hazards (section 2.1.3). This duty may require preventive and reactive action by states: they must safeguard the human right in question by preventing harm in the first place, and take remedial action if harm nonetheless occurs. The former is regularly referred to as the 'substantive aspect' of the duty to protect by the European Court of Human Rights (ECtHR), the latter as part of the 'procedural aspect'.[10] The duty to protect may also include the duty to commit non-state actors to a due diligence standard.

2.1 Against Non-State Actors

The function most commonly associated with states' due diligence obligations in human rights law is the protection of individuals from the infringement of their rights by other individuals.[11] Most prominently and pervasively, due diligence obligations have been established with regard to gender-based violence,[12] but also

General Comment No. 31 on the Nature of the General Legal Obligation Imposed on States Parties to the Covenant, CCPR/C/21/Rev.1/Add. 1326, 29 March 2004, para. 8.

6 Very clearly stated in ECtHR, *Karaahmed v. Bulgaria*, Judgment of 24 February 2015, Application No. 30587/13, para. 100; cf. Anja Seibert-Fohr, 'From Complicity to Due Diligence: When Do States Incur Responsibility for Their Involvement in Serious International Wrongdoing?', *German Yearbook of International Law* 60 (2017), 667–707.

7 With regard to the right to life: ECtHR, *Case of Öneryildiz v. Turkey*, Grand Chamber Judgment of 30 November 2004, Application No. 48939/99, para. 71.

8 Barnidge, 'Due Diligence' 2006 (n. 5), 91–97.

9 Cf. Heike Krieger, 'Positive Verpflichtungen unter der EMRK: Unentbehrliches Element einer gemeineuropäischen Grundrechtsdogmatik, leeres Versprechen oder Grenze der Justiziabilität?', *Heidelberg Journal of International Law* 74 (2014), 187–213, at 191.

10 See, e.g., ECtHR, *Budayeva and Others v. Russia*, Judgment of 20 March 2008, Application Nos 15339/02 et al., para. 131.

11 For examples see Schabas, *ECHR* 2015 (n. 2), 125–139.

12 For example, arts 8 and 7 of the Convention of Belém do Pará (*infra*); see on these, Laurence Burgorgue-Larsen/Amaya Úbeda de Torres, 'Women's Rights', in Laurence Burgorgue-Larsen/Amaya

human trafficking and domestic servitude,[13] arbitrary deprivation of liberty,[14] harassment, threats, and violence on account of one's 'race',[15] religion,[16] or journalistic work.[17] For preventing and sanctioning serious violations, an effective (criminal) justice system must be in operation, in particular regarding the right to life.[18]

As (re)stated in the UN's Guiding Principles on Business and Human Rights,[19] states' duty to protect also extends to business activities under their jurisdiction.[20] In particular, the ECtHR, the Inter-American Court of Human Rights (IACtHR), and recently also the UN Committee on Economic, Social and Cultural Rights[21] have developed due diligence obligations for states to provide adequate protection against industrial activities that are potentially hazardous to humans.[22] These activities must be appropriately regulated so as to minimise risks, which may include environmental impact studies, licensing, and supervision.[23]

International due diligence responsibilities addressed directly at business entities, as in Guiding Principles no. 11 and 13, are, *de lege lata*, social and not legal norms.[24] Various NGOs have criticised this state of affairs and called for stronger

Úbeda de Torres (eds), *The Inter-American Court of Human Rights* (Oxford: OUP 2011), 411–452, paras 17.26–17.32, who explicitly refer to a duty of due diligence.

[13] ECtHR, *Rantsev v. Cyprus and Russia*, Judgment of 7 January 2010, Application No. 25965/04, paras 286–288; ECtHR, *Case of C. N. v. the United Kingdom*, Judgment of 13 November 2012, Application No. 4239/08, paras 65–69.

[14] ECtHR, *El-Masri v. 'The Former Yugoslav Republic of Macedonia'*, Grand Chamber Judgment of 13 December 2012, Application No. 39630/09, paras 233, 242.

[15] ECtHR, *Case of R. B. v. Hungary*, Judgment of 12 April 2016, Application No. 64602/12, paras 81–84.

[16] ECtHR, *Members of the Gldani Congregation of Jehovah's Witnesses and Others v. Georgia*, Judgment of 3 May 2007, Application No. 71156/01, paras 95–97, 129–135.

[17] ECtHR, *Özgür Gündem v. Turkey*, Judgment of 16 March 2000, Application No. 23144/93, paras 38–46.

[18] ECtHR, *Nikolova and Velichkova v. Bulgaria*, Judgment of 20 December 2007, Application No. 7888/03, para. 57; see for more ECtHR case law: Krešimir Kamber, *Prosecuting Human Rights Offences* (Leiden/Boston: Brill 2017), 217–356.

[19] Endorsed by UN, Human Rights Council, Human rights and transnational corporations and other business enterprises, Resolution 17/4, A/HRC/RES/17/4, 6 July 2011, para. 1.

[20] A draft treaty on business and human rights, created on behalf of the UN Human Rights Council (see Resolution 26/9 of 14 July 2014), reaffirms and elaborates on this principle: Open-ended intergovernmental working group (OEIGWG) on business and human rights, The Revised draft on a Legally Binding Instrument to Regulate, in International Human Rights Law, the Activities of Transnational Corporations and other Business Enterprises, 16 July 2019 (Revised Draft Treaty on Business and Human Rights).

[21] UN, Committee on Economic, Social and Cultural Rights, General Comment No. 24 (2017) on state obligations under the International Covenant on Economic, Social and Cultural Rights in the context of business activities, E/C.12/GC/24, 10 August 2017, paras 14–22.

[22] ECtHR, *Öneryildiz v. Turkey* (n. 7), para. 71.

[23] Ibid., para. 90; IACtHR, *Opinión Consultativa Solicitada por la República de Colombia: Medio Ambiente y Derechos*, Advisory Opinion of 15 November 2017, OC-23/17, paras 149–152.

[24] John Ruggie/John Sherman III., 'The Concept of 'Due Diligence' in the UN Guiding Principles on Business and Human Rights: A Reply to Jonathan Bonnitcha and Robert McCorquodale', *European Journal of International Law* 28 (2017), 921–928, at 923–924. In the Guiding Principles, the term 'responsibilities' is used exactly to denote this legal quality. The Revised Draft Treaty on Business and Human Rights (n. 20) does not change this on the international level: while underlining businesses' 'responsibility' in the preamble, the operative paragraphs directly only oblige state parties. But, in particular in art. 5, it requires states to bind businesses to human rights under their national law.

(legal) safeguards and remedies.[25] While improvements to the protection of human rights from adverse impact by business activities are clearly warranted, this should not detract from the fact that the existing social obligations of businesses can, to a certain extent, effect change also on a domestic legal level.[26] The Guiding Principles may serve as a commonly accepted starting point for discussions among victims of human rights violations, civil society actors, businesses, and governments. It is noteworthy that, even though social in character, businesses' due diligence obligations include a standard of conduct similar to the one described in this chapter, e.g., it takes into account a business's capacity under Guiding Principle no. 14.

Whether the term 'due diligence' is used coherently in the Guiding Principles has recently become controversial. It has been argued that the term is used not only as a standard of conduct, but, in particular in Guiding Principles nos. 15–21, in the sense of the term established in business usage, that is as a process conducted by a company to mitigate financial, reputational, legal or other risks *to itself*.[27] While this may seem at odds with the character of human rights (and the persons enjoying them) as ends in themselves, this framing may actually improve the Guiding Principles' effectiveness. This framing could be used to address businesses with a concept that they already employ in other areas. It recruits businesses for the protection of human rights by emphasising the importance of human rights compliance for businesses' primary operational principle: economic self-interest.[28]

For states, even other man-made risks, such as traffic accidents[29] and medical negligence,[30] may trigger due diligence obligations. Furthermore, when the media negatively report on a person, a balance must be struck, ultimately by states' courts, between that person's right to a private life and the freedom of expression of journalists. The ECtHR regards the most important factor to be whether journalists

[25] See for an overview of this critique: Robert Blitt, 'Beyond Ruggie's Guiding Principles on Business and Human Rights: Charting an Embracive Approach to Corporate Human Rights Compliance', *Texas International Law Journal* 48 (2012), 33–62, at 52–56.

[26] Beata Faracik, *Implementation of the UN Guiding Principles on Business and Human Rights* (European Parliament: Belgium 2017), 24–56; Humberto Cantú Rivera, 'The United Nations Guiding Principles on Business and Human Rights in the European Union: From Regional Action to National Implementation' in Jena Martin/Karen Bravo (eds), *The Business and Human Rights Landscape* (CUP: Cambridge 2016), 498–529, at 527.

[27] Jonathan Bonnitcha/Robert McCorquodale, 'The Concept of "Due Diligence" in the UN Guiding Principles on Business and Human Rights', *European Journal of International Law* 28 (2017), 899–919, at 901–906; *contra* this assertion Ruggie/Sherman, 'Due Diligence' 2017 (n. 24), at 923–925; see also Jonathan Bonnitcha/Robert McCorquodale, 'The Concept of "Due Diligence" in the UN Guiding Principles on Business and Human Rights: A Rejoinder to John Gerard Ruggie/John Sherman, III', *European Journal of International Law* 28 (2017), 929–933; cf. Björnstjern Baade, 'Protect Respect and Remedy: A Framework for Business and Human Rights', *Bulletin of International Legal Developments* 13 (2008) 152–154, at 153.

[28] Cf. Surya Deva, 'Guiding Principles on Business and Human Rights: Implications for Companies', *European Company Law* 9 (2012), 101–109, at 106, 109.

[29] ECtHR, *Case of Zubkova v. Ukraine*, Judgment of 17 October 2013, Application No. 36660/08, para. 35.

[30] ECtHR, *Asiye Genç v. Turkey*, Judgment of 27 January 2015, Application No. 24109/07, paras 73–87.

diligently researched the veracity of the allegations levelled: their research on the issue must be adequate, that is in accordance with the standards of the profession, and establish a 'sufficient factual basis'.[31]

2.2 Against Official Misconduct

Due diligence obligations also protect against misconduct by officials. In the context of enforced disappearances, the IACtHR was the first to develop them in this manner.[32] This is necessary despite the fact that states are strictly responsible for the actions of their organs. Due diligence obligations fulfil two functions in this context. Firstly, due diligence obligations serve to compensate for a lack of evidence if official misconduct cannot be ascertained with the necessary degree of certainty.[33] They oblige the state to conduct an effective investigation if credible allegations are levied against its own organs.[34] This makes up for the de facto lack of effective investigatory powers of international bodies. But even when it is clear that state agents were the actors who caused infringements, a *proprio motu* investigation may be warranted, for example with regard to the right to life and freedom from torture.[35] This is necessary for the effective protection of rights because, even when state authorship is clearly established by the facts, not all facts relevant to a measure's lawfulness might be known. Secondly, due diligence obligations also, and more directly, aim at preventing future violations. More recently, the ECtHR had occasion to emphasise that the duty to protect extends to protecting persons within one's jurisdiction from other states.[36] Even more, the ECtHR found the territorial state to be directly responsible for the conduct of foreign state agents acting on its territory with its 'acquiescence or connivance'.[37] But this finding is hard to square with the general law of state responsibility and should be avoided since it is unnecessary: the duty to protect, which also demands protection against other states, is sufficient to address such issues.[38]

[31] ECtHR, *Case of Prager and Oberschlick v. Austria*, Judgment of 26 April 1995, Application No. 15974/90, para. 37; ECtHR, *Medžlis Islamske Zajednice Brčko and Others v. Bosnia and Herzegovina*, Grand Chamber Judgment of 27 June 2017, Application No. 17224/11, paras 87, 117.

[32] IACtHR, *Case of Velásquez-Rodríguez v. Honduras*, Judgment of 29 July 1988, Series C No. 4, para. 172: 'not directly imputable to a State (...) because the person responsible has not been identified'.

[33] Cf. Krieger, 'Positive Verpflichtungen' 2014 (n. 9), 191; see, e.g., ECtHR, *Mikayil Mammadov v. Azerbaijan*, Judgment of 17 December 2009, Application No. 4762/05, paras 117–133.

[34] ECtHR, *Hentschel and Stark v. Germany*, Judgment of 9 November 2017, Application No. 47274/15, paras 70–71, 80–82: 'arguable claim'.

[35] ECtHR, *Kelly and Others v. the United Kingdom*, Judgment of 4 May 2001, Application No. 30054/96, para. 94.

[36] ECtHR, *El-Masri v. FYRM* (n. 14), paras 233, 239.

[37] Ibid., para. 206; ECtHR, *Case of Abu Zubaydah v. Lithuania*, Judgment of 31 May 2018, Application No. 46454/11, paras 641–644, 581: 'settled case-law'.

[38] Seibert-Fohr, 'Complicity' 2017 (n. 6), 680.

2.3 Against Natural Hazards

Finally, a due diligence obligation to protect human rights can also be triggered by natural hazards. Examples from international jurisprudence include mudslides, falling trees, and sickness.[39]

3. Due Diligence as a Standard of Conduct

Due diligence is the standard used to determine whether positive human rights obligations, which safeguard a legal interest and are characterised by their generality and initial indeterminacy, have been complied with.[40] Recently, the IACtHR confirmed this reading by clarifying that due diligence obligations are obligations of conduct that require 'appropriate measures'.[41]

In human rights law, this standard of conduct is developed from the even more general standard of reasonableness, which requires striking a fair balance between the individual and community interests involved. The case-by-case balancing that reasonableness requires is applied to the general and indeterminate positive obligations and takes the specific form of due diligence. Three general factors need to be assessed in every case: a foreseeable risk (section 3.1) to a legally protected interest (section 3.2) and countervailing interests, in particular the capacity to act in protection of the right and other human rights (section 3.3).[42] Though commonly assumed to be,[43] these factors are not separate requirements *before* a reasonableness or proportionality test is conducted; they are part of the same assessment. Moreover, no fault[44] in the sense of a negligent state of mind is required.[45] This standard emerges clearly from the jurisprudence of the various human rights courts and treaty bodies.

[39] IACtHR, *Medio Ambiente* (n. 23), para. 125; ECtHR, *Budayeva and Others v. Russia* (n. 10), paras 147–160; ECtHR, *Case of Ciechońska v. Poland*, Judgment of 14 June 2011, Application No. 19776/04, paras 68–79; ECtHR, *Gagiu v. Romania*, Judgment of 24 February 2009, Application No. 63258/00, para. 57. For further cases, see Schabas, *ECHR* 2015 (n. 2), 133. See also Krieger, 'Funktionen' 2013 (n. 1), para. 57.

[40] Cf., contrasting specific obligations to protect the environment and general due diligence obligations, IACtHR, *Medio Ambiente* (n. 23), para. 126; but see, arguing that art. 8 of the Convention of Belém do Pará (*infra*) is too widely worded to be a due diligence obligation, Jeremy Sarkin, 'A Methodology to Ensure that States Adequately Apply Due Diligence Standards and Processes to Significantly Impact Levels of Violence Against Women Around the World', *Human Rights Quarterly* 40 (2018), 1–36, at 20.

[41] IACtHR, *Medio Ambiente* (n. 23), paras 123, 140, 174.

[42] Koivurova, 'Due Diligence' 2010 (n. 4), paras 17, 19.

[43] Seibert-Fohr, 'Complicity' 2017 (n. 6), 693; Cordula Dröge, *Positive Verpflichtungen der Staaten in der Europäischen Menschenrechtskonvention* (Heidelberg: Springer 2003), 288.

[44] Giuseppe Palmisano, 'Fault', in Rüdiger Wolfrum (ed.), *The Max Planck Encyclopedia of Public International Law* (Oxford: OUP 2007), para. 28.

[45] Cf. ibid., paras 16–17, 42–44; Riccardo Pisillo Mazzeschi, 'The Due Diligence Rule and the Nature of the International Responsibility of States', *German Yearbook of International Law* 35 (1992), 9–51, at 15.

Even though a duty to protect and thus a due diligence standard are derived from various rights, the factors developed for one right are, generally, applied *mutatis mutandis* to other rights.[46] The similarities often outweigh the differences, and some harmful conduct can engage due diligence obligations with regard to multiple rights: for example, rape engages Articles 3 and 8 of the ECHR.[47] For these reasons, statements of a general nature on the due diligence standard employed in human rights law can adequately be made.

3.1 A Foreseeable Risk

A factor of crucial importance is always whether and to what extent the harm caused was foreseeable.[48] In human rights law, this refers to 'constructive' or 'objective', not actual, knowledge of the risk,[49] namely it suffices that the obligation's addressee ought to have known about the risk.[50]

Objective foreseeability is a necessary requirement for a due diligence obligation to exist,[51] but it is not a binary requirement. Foreseeability can have different degrees. How close or remote the risk ought to have seemed is a sliding-scale factor in the assessment of what reaction would have been reasonable.[52] Reflecting this, the IACtHR makes a difference between general and 'strict' due diligence, the latter referring to a more imminent, rather than an abstract, danger.[53] If it is uncertain whether there is a risk at all, precautions may nonetheless be required when there are 'plausible indications' for severe and irreversible harm.[54]

3.2 An Interest Protected by Human Rights

The abstract weight of the right at stake is just as important as the specific risk to it in the individual case.[55] The more important the protected interest, the more necessary it is to take action.[56] This is reflected in ECtHR jurisprudence when the

[46] Kamber, *Human Rights Offences* 2017 (n. 18), 339.

[47] ECtHR, *M. C. v. Bulgaria*, Judgment of 4 December 2003, Application No. 39272/98, para. 148.

[48] Seibert-Fohr, 'Complicity' 2017 (n. 6), 695; Pisillo Mazzeschi, 'Due Diligence Rule' 1992 (n. 45), 44.

[49] Robert Kolb, 'Reflections on Due Diligence Duties and Cyberspace', *German Yearbook of International Law* 58 (2015), 113–128, at 125.

[50] See, e.g., ECtHR, *Opuz v. Turkey*, Judgment of 9 September 2009, Application No. 33401/02, paras 129–130, 133–136.

[51] ECtHR, *Mikayil Mammadov* (n. 33), para. 111.

[52] See, e.g., ECtHR, *Mukhitdinov v. Russia*, Judgment of 21 May 2015, Application No. 20999/14, para. 62; Kolb, 'Due Diligence and Cyberspace' 2015 (n. 49), 123; Dröge, *Positive Verpflichtungen* 2003 (n. 43), 297.

[53] IACtHR, *González et al. (Cotton Field) v. Mexico*, Judgment of 16 November 2009, Series C No. 205, paras 281–283.

[54] IACtHR, *Medio Ambiente* (n. 23), paras 175–180.

[55] Seibert-Fohr, 'Complicity' 2017 (n. 6), 696.

[56] IACtHR, *Medio Ambiente* (n. 23), para. 142; Sarkin, 'Violence Against Women' 2018 (n. 40), 18.

court requires states to do 'everything' within their power to protect life (as an interest of fundamental importance), while they only need to do 'what is reasonable' to protect property.[57]

3.3 Countervailing Interests

As in any human rights balancing exercise, countervailing public and private interests are a legitimate part of the equation. Firstly, a characteristic factor of the due diligence standard is capacity. Secondly, other human rights and legitimate interests affected by possible due diligence measures have to be considered.

Whether and to what extent the state disposes of the means to safeguard the protected interest, namely its capacity, is a consideration that needs to be factored in. But this does not mean that it is necessary to show in each case that the harm could have been averted (almost) for certain. It may be sufficient that the means available could have had real prospects of doing so.[58]

Limited financial resources, or even a lack of effective control over territory, may exclude certain measures.[59] But due diligence may also include the obligation to *build* the necessary capacity.[60] On a basic level there is a 'minimum of proper organisation' a state needs to have in order to meet the due diligence standard regardless of actual capacity.[61] Moreover due diligence may, to some degree, require (re)considering the allocation of resources so as to enable the state to respond to threats. But an 'impossible or disproportionate burden' must not be imposed on the state.[62]

Individual rights may also preclude certain due diligence measures. From its very beginning, human rights jurisprudence has emphasised that the due diligence standard does not require its addressee to violate other rules of international law.[63] According to this systematic interpretation, absolute rights, the infringement of which cannot be justified—like the specific protections against arbitrary deprivation of liberty or against torture, e.g., in Article 5(2)–(4) ECHR and Article 3 ECHR—must not be violated in order to comply with due diligence obligations. In

[57] ECtHR, *Budayeva and Others v. Russia* (n. 10), para. 175.

[58] Ibid., paras 158, 173: imprecisely termed 'causal link'; ECtHR, *Finogenov and Other v. Russia*, Judgment of 20 December 2011, Application Nos 18299/03 et al., paras 255, 264–265; ECtHR, *Opuz v. Turkey* (n. 50), para. 136.

[59] ECtHR, *Case of Ilaşcu and Others v. Moldova and Russia*, Grand Chamber Judgment of 8 July 2004, Application No. 48787/99, para. 331.

[60] ILA, Study Group on Due Diligence in International Law, Second Report, 12 July 2016, 20; ILA, Study Group on Due Diligence in International Law, First Report, 7 March 2014, 18–20.

[61] IACtHR, *Medio Ambiente* (n. 23), para. 144; cf. Kolb, 'Due Diligence and Cyberspace' 2015 (n. 49), 117; Pisillo Mazzeschi, 'Due Diligence Rule' 1992 (n. 45), 29.

[62] ECtHR, *Case of Osman v. the United Kingdom*, Grand Chamber Judgment of 28 October 1998, Application No. 23452/94, para. 116.

[63] Ibid.

contrast, relative rights, such as those enshrined in Article 18 of the International Covenant on Civil and Political Rights (ICCPR), become part of the balancing exercise called for by the due diligence obligation.[64]

For example, in the context of gender-based violence, the rights of potential perpetrators and the right of the possible victim to a private life must be taken into account as countervailing interests when considering, for example, to order a spouse to leave the shared home. At the same time, an appropriately heavy weight must be given to the fundamental interests of life and liberty protected in this context.[65] When it comes to surveillance measures, it is likewise necessary to strike a fair balance between the duty to protect and countervailing privacy interests.[66]

4. How Due Diligence Is Operationalised in Human Rights Law

In order to operationalise due diligence, the above-mentioned factors must be balanced, and some general statements can be made concerning their interaction and the role of international review bodies (section 4.1). But from a theoretical perspective due diligence remains a very abstract standard. Much like the general reasonableness standard it seems at first glance to offer almost endless interpretative possibilities and thus no real standard at all for measuring state conduct by. However, this holds true only when the standard is considered in the abstract. Since it applies to a very wide range of conduct, it is impossible to exhaustively define what it will require in each and every case.[67] Nevertheless, in individual cases and even with a view to systemic requirements, convincing legal answers can be given.

Even though human rights courts and treaty bodies generally only rule on the question of whether the specific measures that were in fact adopted were sufficient in the case at hand, this involves pointing out the measures that could have been adopted to comply with the due diligence standard, because only the possible and reasonable can be required of the state. What is possible and reasonable in a certain situation may be surprisingly specific: reality (section 4.2) as well as path-dependency effects (section 4.3) may narrow down the range of choices, and in practice many standards are developed from clear instances of malpractice and abuse by state organs (section 4.4).

[64] Cf. ECtHR, *Opuz v. Turkey* (n. 50), para. 129.

[65] UN, CEDAW Committee, *Fatma Yildirim (deceased) v. Austria*, View of 1 October 2007, Communication No. 6/2005, paras 12.1.5, 12.3(b); ECtHR, *Opuz v. Turkey* (n. 50), para. 147.

[66] Karine Bannelier-Kristakis, 'Cyber Diligence: A Low-Intensity Due Diligence Principle for Low-Intensity Cyber Operations?', *Baltic Yearbook of International Law* 14 (2014), 23–39, at 38.

[67] See, in detail, Björnstjern Baade, 'The ECtHR as a Guardian of Discourse', *Leiden Journal of International Law* 32 (2018), 335–361, at 344–345.

4.1 The Balancing Process and the Limits of International Control

The foreseeability of the risk, the nature of the right protected, and the capacity to act in protection of it—all these factors interact with one another in the balancing process. Merely speculative risks to human rights will generally not trigger a due diligence obligation to protect them with all available resources.[68] But a small degree of foreseeability may be countered by a severe risk to a very important interest. Generally, the more foreseeable and severe a risk is, the more necessary it is to take action.[69] If the protected interest is of low importance, this will affect the action required by the duty to protect. There may even be no obligation to take measures at all, for example when merely a remote risk to an interest of low importance is at stake. But it is perfectly conceivable that a duty exists to protect an interest of low importance against a clearly foreseeable infringement that could be averted with simple, low-cost measures.

This balancing exercise is reviewed by international bodies to render effective both the duty to protect and the due diligence standard. But there are limits to the control that may be exercised. States necessarily enjoy a margin of appreciation in fulfilling due diligence obligations, that is authorities retain the power to make 'operational choices' regarding priorities and resources.[70] It is not for international bodies to micromanage national institutions.[71] In particular, enquiring into specific resource allocations may easily prove too intrusive.[72] States' sovereign right to manage their own budgets accords them a wide margin of appreciation in this regard.[73] Generally, due diligence may require (costly) action more easily in specific cases for protection against concrete risks than with regard to more general measures aimed at mitigating abstract risks.[74]

4.2 The Constraining Force of Reality

Courts and tribunals operationalise the due diligence standard by gradually lowering its level of abstraction. The fluid standard of due diligence, which generally allows for various diverging measures to comply with it, tends to become more

[68] Kolb, 'Due Diligence and Cyberspace' 2015 (n. 49), 123.

[69] ECtHR, *Budayeva and Others v. Russia* (n. 10), paras 147–160.

[70] ECtHR, *Opuz v. Turkey* (n. 50), paras 129, 165; ECtHR, *Finogenov and Others v. Russia* (n. 58), para. 213; ECtHR, *Di Sarno and Others v. Italy*, Judgment of 10 January 2012, Application No. 30765/08, para. 110.

[71] Explicitly, ECtHR, *Gürtekin and Others v. Cyprus*, Decision of 11 March 2014, Application Nos 60441/13 et al., para. 28.

[72] Sarkin, 'Violence Against Women' 2018 (n. 40), 33.

[73] Cf. Krieger, 'Positive Verpflichtungen' 2014 (n. 9), 193.

[74] See below section 4.3 and section 5.3 for examples.

rigid when applied to the individual case at hand. In reality, the number of measures available to effectively protect a human right is finite. Among these, states may generally choose; however, at times only one available measure may be sufficiently effective.

For example, in a case before the ECtHR, a man in police custody died of a heart attack. Expert evidence before the court found that the man's broken sternum could have been the result of cardiac massage or a blow to the chest that then caused the heart attack. The facts could have been established by determining the age of a bruise on his sternum, which could not have been caused by cardiac massage. Instead of pointing to these two possibilities and conducting a simple tissue test, the doctor performing the autopsy determined by a naked-eye inspection that the bruise was old and therefore reported only that the broken sternum could have been caused by a cardiac massage.[75]

The court found a violation of the right to life in the following manner. Firstly, it interpreted Article 2 of the ECHR to identify the very general duty to protect the right to life, which calls for the application of a due diligence standard.[76] Secondly, it lowered the level of abstraction to the still generalised but more specific duty to effectively investigate deaths (potentially) caused by the use of force. This duty (regularly referred to by the ECtHR as the 'procedural aspect' or 'procedural limb' of the duty to protect) flows from the application of the more general due diligence standard to the case at hand, namely to a death potentially caused by the use of force. It may require, 'where appropriate', a *lege artis* autopsy.[77] Finally, the court found the autopsy to be of 'crucial importance' in the case at hand and 'consider[ed] that the defects in the autopsy examination fundamentally undermined any attempt to determine police responsibility'.[78]

Considering the high importance of the right to life, and that the state was clearly capable of conducting the tissue test, which was the only effective measure to determine what had happened to the victim, the fluid requirements of the due diligence standard crystallised into the duty to take this one specific measure. In theory, the state would have had the right to substitute this test with an equally effective measure, but for all practical purposes there was only that measure because only it was effective in the specific circumstances of the case.

[75] ECtHR, *Salman v. Turkey*, Grand Chamber Judgment of 27 June 2000, Application No. 21986/93, paras 39–45.
[76] Ibid., para. 104.
[77] Ibid., paras 104–105: 'by implication'.
[78] Ibid., paras 106–107.

4.3 Path-Dependency Effects

When multiple measures could be effective in addressing a risk, path-dependency effects may work to narrow down the range of choices: once the state chooses a specific way of meeting its due diligence obligations, additional corollary actions may be required in order to actually render the option chosen effective.

For example, in *Budayeva v. Russia*, a small town located in the Greater Caucasus Mountains was hit by mudslides almost annually for decades, which is why a mud retention collector and a dam had been built and operated successfully. In 1999, however, these facilities were damaged. Authorities were alerted to the need to repair them by a scientific state agency. However, no action was taken until the next year, when the same agency called for the setting up of observation posts, which also was not done. The town was hit, without warning, by a first mudslide, after which the villagers were evacuated. But residents returned prematurely, uninformed of a second and even stronger mudslide yet to come. At least eight villagers died.[79]

Again, the court initially referred to the general duty to protect life and then specified it again to a still general but more specific duty to mitigate risks due to natural hazards.[80] Relying on the dam and the collector as measures to meet its due diligence obligations in this context, the state would have had to repair them to anticipate the clearly foreseeable harm.[81] Having failed to do so, it would have been necessary, in order to mitigate the (now increased) risk, to inform the population of the impending danger. The state was in that context under a duty to enable itself to warn the population appropriately by setting up observation posts.[82] This followed from its choice to rely on the dam and the collector, and its failure to repair them. Again, the state would have been perfectly within its rights to substitute these measures with similarly effective actions.[83] But, for all practical purposes, there were only these measures in the specific facts of the case.

4.4 *Ex-Negativo* Reasoning

Many of the more specific due diligence requirements are developed *ex negativo* in human rights jurisprudence, namely from instances of obvious malpractice. Many defects that appear in practice are so blatant that no margin of appreciation, however great, could tolerate them. In murder investigations for example, authorities must gather and properly record evidence: in particular and as appropriate by

[79] ECtHR, *Budayeva and Others v. Russia* (n. 10), paras 147–149.
[80] Ibid., paras 128, 137, cf. 151.
[81] Ibid., para. 151.
[82] Ibid., paras 152–155.
[83] Ibid., para. 156.

visiting the crime scene, taking photographs, making a map, taking measurements, conducting a forensic examination of the victim and of the evidence.[84] Recently, the ECtHR ruled that video evidence used in a case against a police unit may not be edited (i.e., partially deleted) by a member of said unit before the investigation.[85] As in the two cases cited above, international bodies will often rely on expert evidence and generally accepted standards for concluding which measures could have been taken.

5. Due Diligence and Systemic Issues

The operation of a due diligence standard regularly has implications not only for the individual case but for entire areas of human rights protection.[86] Due to its generality and comprehensive outlook, the due diligence standard is particularly well-suited to tackle structural (i.e., persistent systemic) problems (section 5.1).[87] Systemic requirements derived from due diligence particularly emphasise the duty not only to provide remedies for violations already committed but to prevent future ones.[88] It may, inter alia, be necessary for states to take action on an institutional level (section 5.2) and establish procedures designed to mitigate abstract risks to human rights, such as training programmes for state agents, the collection of information, and informing and educating the public (section 5.3).[89] Again, in theory, states would have the right to substitute these measures with equally effective ones. In reality, however, no similarly effective measures will be available. For all practical purposes, states have to take these measures to comply.

5.1 The Systemic Dimension of Violations in General

Generally, if individual cases reveal a pattern of violations, due diligence requires a systemic response.[90] Failure to take such an approach may result in findings of violation in individual cases. This requirement was developed with a view to the prohibition of discrimination (e.g., in Article 24 of the American Convention

[84] E.g., ECtHR, *Kelly and Others v. the United Kingdom* (n. 35), para. 96; see for more cases involving all these issues Kamber, *Human Rights Offences* 2017 (n. 18), 244–246.

[85] ECtHR, *Hentschel and Stark v. Germany* (n. 34), paras 95–96.

[86] Cf. Koivurova, 'Due Diligence' 2010 (n. 4), para. 21.

[87] Cf. Sarkin, 'Violence Against Women' 2018 (n. 40), 28.

[88] Joanna Bourke-Martignoni, 'The History and Development of the Due Diligence Standard in International Law and Its Role in the Protection of Women against Violence', in Carin Benninger-Budel (ed.), *Due Diligence and Its Application to Protect Women from Violence* (Leiden/Boston: Martinus Nijhoff 2008), 47–61, at 54–55.

[89] See, e.g., UN, CEDAW Committee, *A. T. v. Hungary*, View of 26 January 2005, Application No. 2/2003, paras 9.4–9.6.

[90] IACtHR, *González et al. v. Mexico* (n. 53), paras 293, 455.

on Human Rights). The Inter-American Commission on Human Rights and the ECtHR have held that, according to the available statistical data, domestic violence disproportionately affects women and that an overall unresponsive and dismissive attitude of the judicial system fails to provide women equal protection of the law.[91]

In order to monitor and evaluate due diligence measures with regard to such systemic issues, states may also have to gather empirical data.[92] Article 8 lit. (h) of the Inter-American Convention on the Prevention, Punishment and Eradication of Violence Against Women (Convention of Belém do Pará) and Article 11 of the Council of Europe Convention on preventing and combating violence against women and domestic violence (Istanbul Convention) specifically oblige states to conduct research and gather statistical and other information in order to assess the effectiveness of due diligence measures and adjust them accordingly.[93] Moreover, the information available to the various organs of a state must be shared among themselves, as necessary, to fulfil due diligence duties.[94]

5.2 General Institutional Capacity Building

In order to diligently protect certain rights, states may be obliged to adopt legislative and administrative measures. For example, there must be clear legal criteria and guidelines for police officers' use of firearms.[95] Forced labour, slavery, and rape must be effectively penalised.[96] A criminal code that provides for a suspended sentence if rape victims marry their rapists fails to effectively penalise rape just like a criminal offence of rape that requires the victim's physical resistance as part of the *actus reus* in addition to the victim's lack of consent.[97]

When sufficiently severe dangers are sufficiently foreseeable, states must take reasonable measures to guard against these dangers and enable themselves to respond appropriately when the risk materialises, such as in the aforementioned disaster-relief case.[98]

The same applies to dangers that regularly emanate from non-state actors. In particular, Article 20 of the Istanbul Convention and Article 8 lit. (d) of the

[91] IACommHR, *Maria da Penha v. Brazil*, Report No. 54/01 of 16 April 2000, Case 12.051, paras 4 5–50, 55–58 61.4.; ECtHR, *Opuz v. Turkey* (n. 50), paras 183–202; ECtHR, *Nachova and Others v. Bulgaria*, Grand Chamber Judgment of 6 July 2005, Application Nos 43577/98 et al., para. 160.

[92] UN, Report on Violence against Women, 2006 (n. 4), para. 37.

[93] Sarkin, 'Violence Against Women' 2018 (n. 40), 20–22.

[94] Kolb, 'Due Diligence and Cyberspace' 2015 (n. 49), 124.

[95] ECtHR, *Makaratzis v. Greece*, Grand Chamber Judgment of 20 December 2004, Application No. 50385/99, paras 56–72.

[96] ECtHR, *M. C. v. Bulgaria* (n. 47), paras 148–166; ECtHR, *Case of C. N. V. The United Kingdom* (n. 13), paras 70–82.

[97] ECtHR, *M. C. v. Bulgaria* (n. 47) para. 166; UN, Report on Violence against Women, 2006 (n. 4), para. 54.

[98] ECtHR, *Budayeva and Others v. Russia* (n. 10).

Convention of Belém do Pará require states to take the necessary measures and undertake progressively to provide specialised services to facilitate recovery from violence, such as counselling, financial assistance, housing shelters, and child care.

For cases in which due diligence requires a criminal investigation, the state organs investigating must be independent, in particular from security forces involved in the incident under investigation. The proceedings must be transparent and capable of investigating effectively, inter alia, by compelling witnesses.[99] In a similar vein, the due diligence obligation of businesses to conduct an environmental impact study for hazardous activities is underpinned by an institutional duty to have the study done by an independent and capable institution.[100]

5.3 Specific Procedural Risk Mitigation

Procedurally, it may also be necessary to establish training programmes.[101] Under the ECHR, law-enforcement officers must be trained to use their firearms only when absolutely necessary and on the fundamental value of the right to life.[102] They must also be trained for mass gatherings as far as practically feasible.[103] Training for state officials is also called for with regard to gender-based violence in soft law instruments,[104] and enshrined specifically in Article 15 Istanbul Convention.

Finally, duties to inform and educate the public about risks can derive from due diligence obligations. States may have to provide information about public health hazards (e.g., when residential buildings are exposed).[105] A fortiori, citizens must be informed about life-threatening emergencies (e.g., as in the above-mentioned mudslide).[106]

Moreover, it is advocated that the public should be made aware of and educated about certain issues (e.g., via advertisement campaigns and within formal education structures) in order to influence the societal atmosphere in which human rights violations flourish, in particular with regard to gender-based violence.[107] On a regional level, specialised instruments contain due diligence obligations in this regard: Article 8 of the Convention of Belém do Pará obliges states to undertake progressive measures to promote awareness of women's rights; Article 2(2) of

99 ECtHR, *Kelly and Others v. the United Kingdom* (n. 35), para. 136.

100 IACtHR, *Medio Ambiente* (n. 23), para. 163.

101 UN, General Assembly, Resolution 61/143, A/RES/61/143, 19 December 2006, para. 8 (m).

102 ECtHR, *Giuliani and Gaggio v. Italy*, Grand Chamber Judgment of 24 March 2011, Application No. 23458/02, para. 250.

103 Ibid., para. 255.

104 UN, Report on Violence against Women, 2006 (n. 4), para. 38.

105 ECtHR, *Di Sarno and Others v. Italy* (n. 70), paras 107, 113: 'procedural obligation'.

106 ECtHR, *Budayeva and Others v. Russia* (n. 10), para. 152; ECtHR, *Öneryildiz v. Turkey* (n. 7), paras 89–118.

107 UN, Report on Violence against Women, 2006 (n. 4), para. 42; UNGA, Resolution 61/143, 2006 (n. 101), para. 8 (n).

the Protocol to the African Charter on Human and People's Rights on the Rights of Women in Africa (Maputo Protocol) requires states to commit themselves to modify discriminatory social and cultural patterns; and Articles 13 and 14 of the Istanbul Convention require states parties to promote awareness of gender-based violence and to include teaching material on gender equality at all levels of education.

6. Conclusion: The Promise and Limits of Risk Mitigation

Some understand the due diligence standard to require from its addressee less than a 'full' positive obligation.[108] Some even frame it as being a shield used by actors (in particular businesses) to avoid liability.[109] The vagueness of due diligence is thought to complicate monitoring.[110] Clear obligations of result are consequently sometimes seen as more appropriate to the realisation of human rights.[111]

Such criticism should be rejected. Due diligence reconciles the duty to protect—which is uncontroversially necessary to effectively safeguard human rights—with other interests. Any attempt at optimising the duty to protect so as to eradicate any risk to the protected interests would have seriously negative repercussions. Firstly, it would tend to be totalitarian. Any attempt at eradicating *all* risk from people's lives would have to excessively infringe on their liberty, which human rights are precisely meant to protect. Secondly, a categorical duty to protect would overburden state organs and individuals (indirectly) addressed by due diligence obligations. The need to provide perfect protection, which often cannot be met in reality, would paralyse them in their decision-making. Due diligence is a pragmatic standard that strives to minimise risks to human rights no matter the source of the risks,[112] but without disproportionately limiting individual freedom or state sovereignty[113]—a sovereignty, it should be stressed, that for many states means democratic self-governance.[114]

[108] Menno Kamminga, 'Due Diligence Mania', in Ingrid Westendorp (ed.), *The Women's Convention Turned 30* (Cambridge: Intersentia 2012), 407–413, at 411; Holly Cullen, 'The Irresistible Rise of Human Rights Due Diligence: Conflict Minerals and Beyond', *George Washington International Law Review* 48 (2016), 743–780, at 749: who perceives a conflation of the two standards in human rights law.

[109] Kamminga, 'Due Diligence Mania' 2012 (n. 108), 410–413.

[110] Julie Goldscheid/Debra Liebowitz, 'Due Diligence and Gender Violence: Parsing its Power and its Perils', *Cornell International Law Journal* 48 (2015), 30–1345, at 320; Rikki Holtmaat, 'Preventing Violence Against Women: The Due Diligence Standard with Respect to the Obligation to Banish Gender Stereotypes on the Grounds of Article 5 (a) of the CEDAW Convention', in Carin Benninger-Budel (ed.), *Due Diligence and Its Application to Protect Women from Violence* (Leiden/Boston: Martinus Nijhoff 2008), 61–89, at 88.

[111] Holtmaat, 'Preventing Violence Against Woman' 2008 (n. 110), 88.

[112] Cf. Ruggie/Sherman, 'Concept of Due Diligence' 2017 (n. 24), 924.

[113] Cf. Krieger, 'Positive Verpflichtungen' 2014 (n. 9), 196–199.

[114] Cf. Baade, 'Guardian of Discourse' 2017 (n. 67), at 335.

In light of the emphasis that jurisprudence puts on the effectiveness of protection,[115] the critique that due diligence would allow for a merely 'formal' show of compliance while remaining substantially ineffective,[116] or that it subtracts from substantive rights,[117] seems generally unfounded. Quite the contrary, due diligence has proven to be an important, additional tool in addressing systemic human rights issues. But a crucial condition for its effectiveness is that compliance with the necessarily flexible standard is reviewed by other actors than the obligation's addressee. Human rights courts and treaty bodies may conduct such reviews, but other states, civil society, and scholars may likewise hold actors to account to some degree.

[115] ECtHR, *Opuz v. Turkey* (n. 50), para. 192; IACHR, *Lenahan (Gonzales) v. United States of America*, Judgment of 21 July 2011, Case No. 12.626, para. 212.
[116] Seeing this danger, Sarkin, 'Violence Against Women' 2018 (n. 40), 36.
[117] Cf. Brems, 'Procedural Protection' 2013 (n. 1), 159.

PART II

DUE DILIGENCE IN INTERNATIONAL ENVIRONMENTAL LAW

7

Due Diligence in International Environmental Law

A Fine-grained Cartography

Jorge E. Viñuales

1. Introduction

It is the fate of duties—as of other norms—deliberately formulated in a broad and open-ended manner to cause some malaise among lawyers, who expect them to have sufficient normative density to be defined not only in *concreto* but also in *abstracto*. The duty requiring states to exercise due diligence so as to avoid causing 'significant' harm to the environment, is no exception to the fate of broad duties. Circumscribing its contours in *abstracto* is a difficult exercise, not because one cannot comment on it but because such commentary—to be of some value—must try to accurately reflect the practical operation of the norm, which in turn requires the surveying of a range of contexts where the norm 'operates', both in adjudication and elsewhere. Two main inquiries can be conducted in this regard.

First, one can discuss the conceptual limits arising from the very formulation of the duty, as it appears in treaties, soft-law instruments, and judicial and quasi-judicial decisions, as well as other authorities. This first inquiry focuses on: (i) identifying the norms from which this duty arises; (ii) determining who are the duty-bearers; (iii) who are the correlative right-holders; (iv) what type of action/inaction is covered by the duty, (v) what outcome it seeks to govern; and (vi) what the outer limits of the duty are. Secondly, one can focus on the 'degree' of due diligence, namely what makes the targeted behaviour 'duly' diligent: (i) the choice of means in discharging this duty; (ii) with the level of diligence depending on the time, the type of activity and the capacity of the state in question; and (iii) the scope of the duty, which encompasses both the adoption of relevant measures and their proactive enforcement.

In this chapter I conduct both inquiries in order to clarify the normative requirements arising from this duty with respect to environmental protection. My purpose is to provide a fine-grained analysis of the materials, rather than focusing on the broad implications of due diligence for environmental protection. The chapter

Jorge E. Viñuales, *Due Diligence in International Environmental Law* In: *Due Diligence in the International Legal Order*. Edited by: Heike Krieger, Anne Peters, and Leonhard Kreuzer, Oxford University Press (2020).
DOI: 10.1093/oso/9780198869900.003.0007.

first seeks to distil from a number of old precedents several significant features relating to both inquiries (section 2). I then turn to the post-1945 law of environmental protection to clarify the due diligence duty from the two aforementioned perspectives (section 3). In conclusion, I make some observations about the wider implications of the fine-grained inquiry conducted in this chapter (section 4).

2. A Tale of Two Precedents

2.1 The Characterisation of Due Diligence in the Alabama Arbitration

The 1872 *Alabama Claims* arbitration is known for providing an authoritative statement on several rules of international law and also represents a prominent illustration of the benefits of international arbitration, even in a highly political dispute between two major powers.[1] In the specific context of due diligence, the reasoning of the arbitration court provided four important considerations that are still relevant today, including for action/inaction relating to environmental protection. The first consideration was that:

> the 'due diligence' referred to in the first and third of the said rules [Article VI of the compromis] ought to be exercised by neutral governments in exact proportion to the risks to which either of the belligerents may be exposed, from a failure to fulfil the obligations of neutrality on their part.[2]

In casu, the court noted that the circumstances were such that the UK was held to 'all possible solicitude for the observance of the rights and duties involved in the proclamation of neutrality',[3] or in other words to the highest level of due diligence. This observation is important for at least three reasons. First, it links due diligence to 'risk', which is different from actual damage. Secondly, the degree of diligence is not static; it varies with the level of risk (no sliding scale of diligence is envisaged on the basis of a state's capabilities and resources, although this was argued by counsel for the US). Thirdly, the duty of due diligence, however demanding (in this case

[1] The place of this arbitration in discussions of due diligence in international environmental law has been overshadowed by references to the *Trail Smelter* arbitration. This neglect also concerns other areas of international law. As noted in the chapter by Helmut Aust/Prisca Feihle on 'Due Diligence in the History of the Codification of the Law of State Responsibility', chapter 3 of this book, section 2.1, it is often thought that due diligence emerged from the codification work of the law on state responsibility. On the history of the concept, see Giulio Bartolini, 'The Historical Roots of the Due Diligence Standard', chapter 2 of this book, section 2.

[2] *Alabama Claims of the United States of America against Great Britain*, Decision of 14 September 1872, vol. XXIX, UNRIAA, 125-134, 129.

[3] Ibid., 130.

the court set the bar to the highest 'possible solicitude'), does not amount to strict liability. In fact, the court found that for some specific vessels manufactured in the UK, the latter had met the requirements of due diligence, despite the occurrence of undesirable results. None of these points are obvious, even today, and they are all significant for international environmental law as it presently operates.

A second consideration arising from this case is the significance of representations by the aggrieved state (the US representative had informed the UK government that vessels were being built for possible use in the Civil War), which should have triggered 'in due time' at least some 'effective' measures of prevention. Thus, action by a possibly aggrieved state (a state at risk), although not a requirement, may catalyse the duty of due diligence or, more specifically, may at the very least be instrumental in setting the time for action.

A third consideration is the fact that subsequent measures could have cured the initial negligence, although the UK failed to take such action or did so in a manner 'so imperfect as to lead to no result, and therefore cannot be considered sufficient to release Great Britain from the responsibility already incurred'.[4] The latter point suggests that the duty of due diligence is a continuous rather than a discreet one: due diligence must be constantly exercised. This is important from a litigation perspective.

As a fourth and final consideration, the formulation of the due diligence rule in Article VI of the compromis makes it clear that a state's failure to effectively control the actions of 'all persons within its jurisdiction' may be a breach of the duty of due diligence. This simple point is significant because it clearly covers the actions of private persons and makes due diligence relevant for extraterritorial situations, much like in today's discussions of human rights extraterritoriality and their link to environmental principles. The duty of due diligence therefore finds a solid basis in the *Alabama Claims* arbitration. Its contribution to the clarification of the duty of due diligence thus warrants comparison with the *Trail Smelter* case, at the very least to highlight areas of convergence and divergence.

2.2 From *Alabama* to *Trail Smelter*

It must be mentioned that the *Alabama* precedent was invoked before the *Trail Smelter* tribunal and duly noted by it.[5] Significantly, the latter tribunal recognised the *Alabama* decision as the start of a relevant line of precedents—although it eventually relied on the domestic practice of Switzerland and the US, as both were federal systems and had faced disputes among 'quasi-sovereign' entities. This was

[4] Ibid., 130.

[5] *Trail Smelter Arbitration*, Decisions of 16 April 1938 and 11 March 1941, vol. III, UNRIAA, 1905-1982, 1963.

possible because Article VI of the compromis specifically required the tribunal to apply 'the law and practice followed in dealing with cognate questions in the United States of America as well as international law and practice'. In a famous and often-quoted statement, the tribunal held that it:

> finds that the *above decisions, taken as a whole*, constitute an adequate basis for its conclusions, namely, that, under the principles of international law, as well as of the law of the United States, no State has the right to use or permit the use of its territory in such a manner as to cause injury by fumes in or to the territory of another or the properties or persons therein, when the case is of serious consequence and the injury is established by clear and convincing evidence.[6]

If, among 'the above decisions, taken as a whole', one is to include international decisions, the only explicitly identified precedent of unquestionable authority is indeed the *Alabama* decision. On this point, there is a clear convergence between the two decisions.

Further convergence can be found in that states may be responsible for allowing private parties to use their territory in harmful ways, irrespective of any attribution inquiry. The relevant conduct of the state is indeed its own inaction, not the action of the private person. Two other points of convergence are the reference to the notifications by the aggrieved state, although the *Trail Smelter* decision does not attach any significant relevance to this point, and, much more importantly, the continuous character of the duty of due diligence, which is formulated in the *Trail Smelter* decision in terms that are so advanced[7] that they could be considered progressive even for an international tribunal deciding a dispute today. The drawback is that the content of due diligence is not spelt out in general terms and remains embedded in, indeed consubstantial with, the technical specifications—akin to the modern 'standards'—provided by the tribunal and cannot be detached from them.

There is, however, some divergence between the two decisions, in that the *Trail Smelter* award provides, quite unexpectedly, a more limited statement of the duty of due diligence. First, unlike the *Alabama* decision, the *Trail Smelter* award makes no explicit reference to the possibility of curing a breach through subsequent action. The attempts of the smelter to manage the initial complaints from farmers in Washington are mentioned as part of the factual record, but the award does not derive any legal principle from them. Secondly, and more significantly, the rule stated in the *Trail Smelter* case concerns actual 'damage' and not any damage but 'material' damage.[8] Thus, the regime set out in the award, which is the embodiment of the

[6] Ibid., 1965 (emphasis added).

[7] The tribunal indeed set up a provisional regulatory regime and then a permanent one to be implemented by Canada, with the explicit possibility of adjusting the system if the circumstances (or their scientific understanding) changed. See ibid., 1966.

[8] Ibid., 1980 (emphasis added).

diligence due by Canada in this case, is aimed only at preventing 'material' damage, not any damage, let alone risk. By contrast, the *Alabama* rule is not confined to damage but encompasses 'risk' as well. That was a result of the circumstances of the case, which were so serious as to require 'all possible solicitude' from the UK. But a similar argument can be made for ultra-hazardous activities such as the generation of nuclear energy or the production of highly toxic substances, in that due diligence is not only 'required' from the state where the operations take place but also 'actionable'—namely it can be legally and specifically demanded—by potentially affected states irrespective of the occurrence of damage. Such is the rule in Article 3 of the 2001 International Law Commission's Articles on Prevention: '[the] State of origin shall take all appropriate measures to prevent significant transboundary harm or at any event to minimise the risk thereof'.[9] The commentary of this provision expressly relies on the *Alabama* case.

The basic conclusion to be drawn from the foregoing paragraphs is that both the *Alabama* arbitration and the *Trail Smelter* case remain relevant, even today, to a proper understanding of the broad parameters of the duty of due diligence (formulation of the duty) and the finer-grained questions of degree (degree of due diligence). Together, they 'unpack' most of the issues and set a broad perimeter within which the more recent instruments, cases, and commentary unfold. In the next section I focus on the post-1945 international law, paying particular attention to the case law of the last decade, which has made an important contribution to the clarification of due diligence.

3. The Duty of Due Diligence in Contemporary International Environmental Law

3.1 Preliminary Observations

Against the backdrop set by the *Alabama* and *Trail Smelter* precedents, subsequent developments have added further specificity (particularly regarding the operation of due diligence in an 'environmental' context), together with further elaboration of elements that were only flagged in those precedents and, last but not least, also some new elements not foreseen at the time. The two precedents nevertheless remain authoritative.

With these clarifications in mind, I now turn to the two different inquiries identified in the introduction. For each of them, the discussion relies on a combined assessment of the two aforementioned precedents and of more recent developments.

[9] United Nations, International Law Commission (ILC), Draft Articles on the Prevention of Transboundary Harm from Hazardous Activities, A/RES/56/82, 12 December 2001.

3.2 First Inquiry: Formulation of the Duty

3.2.1 Due Diligence and the Prevention Principle

In the context of environmental protection, the formulation of the duty of due diligence largely overlaps with the formulation of the principle of prevention provided in Principle 2 of the Rio Declaration on Environment and Development:

> States have, in accordance with the Charter of the United Nations and the principles of international law, the sovereign right to exploit their own resources pursuant to their own environmental and developmental policies, and the responsibility to ensure that activities within their jurisdiction or control do not cause damage to the environment of other States or of areas beyond the limits of national jurisdiction.[10]

To state that due diligence 'largely' overlaps with the principle of prevention implies that there are differences. I would like to state these differences in a form that is not merely a conceptual elaboration of these two norms but one that is practically relevant.

The first difference stems from the broader scope of the duty of due diligence, which applies to several types of harm and risk other than environmental harm or risk thereof (as emphasised in the *Alabama* arbitration). The second difference is that the duty to prevent environmental harm (the prevention principle) concerns—as we recall from the *Trail Smelter* arbitration—only harm of a certain magnitude ('material' harm[11] or 'significant' harm[12] or risk of thereof.[13] By contrast, the duty of due diligence is not similarly limited and, hence, action/inaction that results in harm or risk to the environment but which is below the threshold of significance required to trigger a breach of the prevention principle remains governed by (and could potentially constitute a breach of) the duty of due diligence. That much can be learnt from the *Alabama* arbitration, where due diligence is not limited by either upper or lower bounds in the magnitude of harm or risk.[14] This is not a purely theoretical point. By way of illustration, a state may be required or entitled, under the duty of due diligence, to take precautionary measures even in

[10] United Nations, General Assembly, Rio Declaration on Environment and Development, A/CONF.151/26, 13 June 1992, Rev.1; On prevention, see Leslie-Anne Duvic-Paoli/Jorge E. Viñuales, 'Principle 2: Prevention', in Jorge E. Viñuales (ed.), *The Rio Declaration on Environment and Development: A Commentary* (Oxford: OUP 2015), 107–138; Leslie-Anne Duvic-Paoli, *The Prevention Principle in International Environmental Law* (Cambridge: CUP 2018).

[11] *Trail Smelter* (n. 5), 1980.

[12] See ILC, Prevention Articles 2001 (n. 9), art. 2(a); ICJ, *Pulp Mills on the River Uruguay (Argentina v. Uruguay)*, Judgment of 20 April 2010, ICJ Reports 2010, 14, para. 101.

[13] ILC, Prevention Articles 2001 (n. 9), art. 3.

[14] *Alabama Claims* (n. 2), 129.

the absence of scientific certainty as to the existence of risk of significant harm.[15] Such a requirement/justification would not flow from the prevention principle, which only operates when there is risk. Nor would it flow, at least in the absence of an applicable treaty, from the precautionary approach/principle, whose customary grounding is still debated.[16] It would derive instead from the duty of due diligence, which is unquestionably grounded in general international law since at least the period of the *Alabama* arbitration and has a scope that is not limited to the risk of 'significant' environmental harm. The latter does not mean that any harm or risk thereof may be subject to the duty of due diligence (this sort of 'absolute integrity' theory was early on discarded by international tribunals[17]) but only that this duty is not necessarily subject to the same definition of 'significance' or of 'risk' as the prevention principle.

Aside from these two differences, however, the operation of due diligence and prevention in an environmental context overlap. They do so to a point that the duty of due diligence must be considered as defining the 'responsibility to ensure', as stated in Principle 2 of the Rio Declaration, in a form of articulation similar to that identified in other contexts.[18] Thus, as far as environmental protection is concerned, the duty of due diligence rests upon the prevention principle, which finds expression in several other norms that I have analysed elsewhere.[19]

3.2.2 Duty-bearers

With respect to the duty-bearers of these two articulated norms, one can identify three situations. First, it is well established that states are subject to both the prevention principle and the duty of due diligence, and all the authorities mentioned in this chapter analyse the situation of states as duty-bearers. Secondly, there is some authority for the proposition that at least some international organisations that have been entrusted with, and have effectively taken up, the discharge of some state activities (for example the regulation of fisheries) are likewise subject to the duty of due diligence.[20] It is unclear whether the 'degree' of due diligence expected

[15] See ITLOS Seabed Disputes Chamber, *Responsibilities and Obligations of States Sponsoring Persons and Entities with Respect to Activities in the Area*, Advisory Opinion of 1 February 2011, ITLOS Reports 2011, paras 125-135, particularly paras 131 and 135.

[16] See Pierre-Marie Dupuy/Jorge E. Viñuales, *International Environmental Law* (Cambridge: CUP 2nd ed. 2018), 70–73.

[17] See *Lake Lanoux Arbitration (Spain v. France)*, Decision of 16 November 1957, vol. XII, UNRIAA, 281-317.

[18] See ICJ, *Legality of the Threat or Use of Nuclear Weapons*, Advisory Opinion of 8 July 1996, ICJ Reports 1996, 226, para. 25.

[19] See, e.g., Jorge E. Viñuales, 'The Rio Declaration on Environment and Development: Preliminary Study', in Jorge E. Viñuales (ed.), *The Rio Declaration on Environment and Development: A Commentary* (Oxford: OUP 2015), 1–64; Duvic-Paoli/Viñuales, 'Principle 2' 2015 (n. 10); Jorge E. Viñuales, 'Protección Ambiental en el Derecho Consuetudinario Internacional', *Revista Española de Derecho Internacional* 69/2 (2017), 71–91.

[20] ITLOS, *Request for an Advisory Opinion Submitted by the Sub-Regional Fisheries Commission (SRFC)*, Advisory Opinion of 2 April 2015, ITLOS Reports 2015, 4, para. 168.

from such organisations could in all points be equated with that of states, given the fact that enforcement of such delegated powers remains, both legally and practically, fully in the hands of states. But this is something that relates to the second inquiry, namely that concerning the degree of due diligence, rather than the broad parameters of the duty of due diligence.[21] Thirdly, a range of other subjects of international law—from peoples, to indigenous, tribal, and other groups, as well as a wide variety of individuals (from multinational companies to physical persons)—could potentially be subject to the duty of due diligence and the prevention principle as they arise from international law. There is much disagreement about this point and the matter is not settled.[22] That said, the logic that should guide any consideration on this point is the same as for states and international organisations, namely that it is not merely the formal but the effective ability of such subjects to discharge the duty that is decisive. This point must not be misunderstood: with regards to the duty of due diligence, one must distinguish between matters of *formulation* and matters of *degree*. Peoples, groups, corporations, and individuals are, by their very definition, capable of discharging certain duties. Hence, it would technically (as a matter of formulation) be entirely possible to subject them to a duty of due diligence, which would be sufficient to settle matters of formulation. Matters of degree, however, present a different set of difficulties, which will be discussed later.[23]

3.2.3 Right-holders

The question of duty-bearers must be clearly distinguished from that of the correlative question of right-holders, which is far more complex. It must be noted that it is conceptually possible for a duty and, specifically, for the duty of due diligence to be owed to both an object (the environment, which is not, as such, a right-holder) and a subject, who may or may not have a correlative right (for example future generations). For the protection of these kinds of objects and subjects, the main avenue would be the active discharge by the duty-bearers of the duty of due diligence. To the extent that failure to satisfactorily discharge such a duty can be claimed, this would only be possible through the exercise of a right—whether substantive or procedural—by a right-holder. Thus, I will focus here on right-holders. Another clarification is that an obligation whose duty-bearers are mainly (albeit not only) states might entail correlative rights for both states and/or other subjects. Such is the case, for example, for the human rights obligations of states which are

[21] See below section 3.3.

[22] See the ongoing discussions on the possibility to adopt a Global Pact for the Environment: United Nations General Assembly Resolution 'Towards a Global Pact for the Environment', A/72/L.51, 10 May 2018, which would broaden the definition of 'duty-bearer'. Indeed, the Draft Project for a Global Pact for the Environment contains, in art. 2, a duty of care arising for 'every State or international institution, every person, natural or legal, public or private'.

[23] See below section 3.3.

specifically correlative to the rights of individuals. As noted earlier, the duty of due diligence has a broader scope than the prevention principle because it concerns not only the duty to prevent significant environmental harm or risk thereof but also other types of harm or risks thereof.[24]

This difference has practical importance. It means that there are two categories of rights and right-holders 'relevant' for the discharge of the duty of due diligence in the context of environmental protection: those rights arising technically from the prevention principle (category 1) and those other rights arising from either the broader due diligence duty or from other obligations that present a similar symbiosis with the prevention principle (category 2). The distinction is also important because the exercise of the rights encompassed by category 2 may expand the measure of protection afforded to other subjects (again, future generations) or to an object (the environment as such) who are not right-holders, as compared to the protection that could be claimed through the exercise of rights arising technically from the prevention principle only (category 1).

It is useful, therefore, to discuss category 2 first. This category includes a wide range of rights, none of which arise technically from the prevention principle, but whose object is 'relevant' for—that is, tends towards a similar goal as—the rights technically arising from the prevention principle. For example, the rights of access to environmental information, participation in environmental decision-making, and access to justice are certainly relevant to press state authorities to behave diligently with respect to the prevention of environmental harm, but individuals cannot rely solely on the principle of prevention to base their request for such access or participation. This point can be generalised. For example, freedom of speech and freedom of association are certainly relevant in order for civil society to press state authorities to behave diligently with respect to environmental protection, but they do not arise technically from the prevention principle itself. Such relevant rights have their own right-holders, which are not defined by the prevention principle. They are, however, relevant for the discharge of the duties arising from the prevention principle, not only because they aim for a similar or convergent goal but also, in a more technical manner (systemic integration), which will be explained by reference to category 1.

Moving now to category 1, it encompasses those rights (and right-holders) that arise specifically from the prevention principle. In order to clarify them, an additional distinction is needed between those rights that are *specifically* exigible and those which are only *generally* exigible.[25] The best way to explain the

[24] See above section 3.2.1.

[25] Unfortunately, there is no English term capable of fully translating this notion. Approximate English terms include: 'due', 'payable', or 'chargeable'. In French, 'exigible' is generally understood to mean that an existing (binding) obligation falls due and its specific discharge can thereafter be required at any time by the right-holder. An obligation may be 'binding' or 'due' without yet being 'ripe'. The terms 'payable' and 'chargeable' are closer to 'exigible' but they suggest that only sums of money (not specific performance) are concerned.

difference is with an example. The prevention principle, like the duty of due diligence, entails rights upon potentially affected states to require the state of origin of an activity to exercise due diligence to ensure that no significant harm to the environment (or risk thereof) is generated. But such rights do not entitle potentially affected states to require this or that specific measure. Thus, if a government conducts a cost-benefit analysis on a bill or a proposed regulation taking into account only the likely impact on the territory of the state of origin and not on other potentially affected states, then such other states will be entitled to demand that the state of origin exercises general due diligence but not, for example, the specific procedural measure of expanding the cost-benefit analysis. The selection of specific measures to exercise due diligence remains the purview of the state of origin.[26] In rare cases, a third party will identify the specific measures that must be adopted by the state of origin (as was the case in the *Trail Smelter* award, which is very progressive on this point). More often such measures will be defined by treaty, but neither the prevention principle nor the duty of due diligence entitles the right-holders to require the adoption of specific measures by the state of origin. These measures are only *generally* exigible, with two exceptions under which certain measures are *specifically* exigible.

There are two obligations that have been jurisprudentially considered to be technical expressions of the prevention principle[27] and that entail correlative rights to specifically demand the adoption of certain measures: namely the conduct of an environmental impact assessment and notification and consultation in certain specific cases. These rights are held by potentially affected and possibly other states and, unlike the broader right to demand the exercise of due diligence, they are *specifically* exigible, that is, they provide a legal basis to demand from the state of origin the adoption of not just a measure of its own choosing but a specific measure defined internationally. They operate in the same way as a treaty norm requiring a specific measure.

Importantly, the specification of the remaining areas (beyond the two specifically exigible measures mentioned earlier) of generally exigible due diligence is not entirely unconstrained. Whether the state of origin has exercised its discretion in the choice of relevant means can be reviewed by a tribunal (e.g., the partial cost-benefit analysis referred to above would be subject to review) and such an assessment would normally rely—pursuant to the principle of systemic integration[28]—on

[26] ILC, Prevention Articles 2001 (n. 9), comment to art. 3, paras 9, 11 and 12: referring to the *Alabama* case where the court rejected the proposition of the UK that 'due diligence' was a national standard; see also ICJ, *Pulp Mills* (n. 12), para. 205: where the ICJ suggests that the content of a component of the duty of care, namely the customary obligation to conduct an environmental impact assessment, would be left to states.

[27] ICJ, *Pulp Mills* (n. 12), paras 101–102, 144–146, 204; ICJ, *Certain Activities Carried Out by Nicaragua in the Border Area (Costa Rica v. Nicaragua), Construction of a Road in Costa Rica along the River San Juan (Nicaragua v. Costa Rica)*, Judgment of 16 December 2015, ICJ Reports 2015, 665, para. 104.

[28] Vienna Convention on the Law of Treaties, 23 May 1969, 1155 UNTS 331, art. 31(3)(c).

other 'relevant' norms applicable between the parties. For example, the degree of diligence could be assessed in the light of the rights of access to environmental information, participation in environmental decision-making, and access to justice, or of the human rights of the individuals in foreign states who are affected by the action/inaction of the state of origin.

At this stage, the question regarding the correlative right-holders of the prevention principle and the duty of due diligence can receive a general, albeit still incomplete, answer: technically, the correlative right-holders of the prevention principle are states; but other 'relevant' right-holders, whose rights do not technically arise from the prevention principle, include states and other subjects of international law, depending on the nature of the relevant right. A fuller examination of this question cannot be provided here as it would essentially require a survey, an inventory, and a characterisation of a range of obligations and correlative rights. I should, however, mention the specific case of the right to an environment of a certain quality.

I have examined in another context the articulation between the right to an environment of a certain quality, which is still under development, and the prevention principle.[29] In the present development of international law, the most appropriate understanding of the role of this right is as a 'relevant' right pursuing a purpose that is similar (and indeed very close) to that of the prevention principle. This right could and should in my view be relied upon to interpret the degree of due diligence *generally* exigible from a state. There are some subtleties relating to the spatial scope of operation of the two norms,[30] but their normative articulation would not be affected by them.

3.2.4 Type of Conduct Covered

The next parameter of the duty relates to the type of action/inaction. Against the background of the previous discussion, this question is less complex. Any action/inaction by the duty-bearer (states, international organisations, and possibly other subjects of international law) that may generate significant environmental harm or risk thereof in another state or an area beyond its national jurisdiction (and possibly also within the territory or the jurisdiction of the negligent state) is governed

[29] See Jorge E. Viñuales, 'A Human Rights Approach to Extraterritorial Environmental Protection? An Assessment', in Nehal Bhuta (ed.), *The Frontiers of Human Rights: Extraterritoriality and its Challenges* (Oxford: OUP 2016), 177–221.

[30] Indeed, the prevention principle concerns harm to the environment of other states and beyond national jurisdiction (with an interrogation mark for harm to the environment of the state of origin), whereas the right to an environment of a certain quality (healthy, safe, clean, and/or generally satisfactory) concerns harm that happens in the territory of the state where the person is located (with some additional developments needed for an extraterritorial application of this right, which would make it spatially convergent with the scope of the prevention principle). See the account of extraterritoriality in an environmental context provided in ibid., 218–219, which has been followed by the Inter-American Court of Human Rights in its Advisory Opinion of 15 November 2017, OC-23/18, IACtHR (Ser. A), No. 23.

by the duty of due diligence. The only two issues that may require further clarification relate to the acts of private parties and the continuous nature of the action/inaction. However, as mentioned earlier, it seems abundantly clear, since at least the *Alabama* arbitration, that it is the inaction or deficient action of the state itself, as an enabler of the private action, that is governed by the duty of due diligence.

As for the continuous nature of the action/inaction, the main distinction is between the requirements of the duty, which are continuous, and the action/inaction at stake, which does not need to be. The continuous character of the duty[31] is entirely compatible with punctual, and hence discontinuous, interventions. For example, if the authorities are informed of an imminent private initiative and, although they may have not yet taken any action, they specifically intervene to stop the initiative or keep it under control, the continuous requirements of the duty would be met even if they then discontinue the regulatory intervention, as long as they remain generally vigilant.

3.2.5 Outcomes Governed by the Duty

The outcomes that the duty seeks to govern have also been elaborated upon in the previous discussion. Four clarifications are needed for the parameters of the duty to be understood. First, the *Alabama* precedent and the 2001 ILC Articles on Prevention have made clear that the outcome to be prevented is not only a materially negative outcome ('damage' or 'harm') but also the 'risk' thereof, even if the negative outcome does not in fact materialise. The mere generation of 'risk' may be sufficient to trigger the correlative rights identified earlier.

Secondly, unlike the bare duty of due diligence, in the context of environmental protection, only damage, harm, or risk of a certain magnitude ('material' or 'significant') is governed by the prevention principle. I will not attempt to define what is deliberately not defined in the norm—and likely even beyond the possibility of being abstractly defined—but my earlier comment regarding the use of 'relevant' norms to clarify the scope of the prevention principle is also applicable here. The fact that the outcome may amount to a breach of another—distinct but related ('relevant')—norm may either render the harm 'significant' or may be an important indication that such is the case.[32] By contrast, damage, harm, or risk which is not 'material' or 'significant' is not governed by the prevention principle. This point must not be misunderstood. Indeed, such a statement may only be correct retrospectively, once the negative outcome has indeed materialised and is deemed 'immaterial' or 'non-significant', or after a diligent 'risk' assessment has led to the conclusion that any potential damage or harm would be below the threshold of

[31] On the continuous character of the duty see above section 2.1.

[32] See e.g., ECtHR, *Budayeva and others v. Russia*, Judgment of 29 September 2008, Applications No. 15339/02, 21166/02, 20058/02, 11673/02, and 15343/02, paras 128–137; PCA, *South China Sea Arbitration (Republic of the Philippines v. People's Republic of China)*, PCA Case No. 2013-19, Award of 12 July 2016, paras 962–966.

significance. In the latter case, such an assessment would remain subject to a more conclusive (retrospective) assessment of damage or harm. If instead of adopting a retrospective perspective, one adopts a prospective one, any potential outcome remains governed by the duty of due diligence and therefore triggers the correlative rights. Hence, the importance of procedural steps in this context. Even if the outcome places the action/inaction outside the scope of the prevention principle, such action/inaction may remain governed by other norms. For example, the polluter-pays principle requires states to adopt domestic measures for polluters to internalise (that is, to 'bear') the costs they have lawfully caused. In other cases, the action/inaction may not be in breach of the prevention principle and, yet, it may be in breach of another 'relevant' norm (for example obligations requiring public participation).

Thirdly, a difficult question concerns the boundary between 'risk' and outcomes that do not amount to risk. Despite the conceptual difficulties in distinguishing the two, the insurance industry has found the distinction sufficiently solid to build a business around it. Risk, in this context, requires a reliable probability ('high' or 'small', but reliable as opposed to volatile) of a negative outcome. In the absence of any of these two elements (reliable probability and negative outcome), the situation is one of 'uncertainty', which is beyond the scope of prevention and falls under that of precaution.[33]

Fourthly, as noted earlier, the most widely accepted formulation of the prevention principle refers to 'damage to the environment of other states or of areas beyond the limits of national jurisdiction'[34] without explicitly referring to an outcome that would affect only the state of origin. This apparently minor point is systemically important, and I will discuss it in the last section of this chapter. For present purposes, I should only observe that currently there is some authority for the proposition that the prevention principle applies to environmental harm in general, irrespective of where it occurs.[35]

3.2.6 Outer Boundary of the Duty

The final parameter for the formulation of the duty of due diligence in an environmental context relates to its outer boundary. Here again, the *Alabama* precedent provides normative guidance. Whether one uses conceptual categories such as

[33] See Jorge E. Viñuales, 'Legal Techniques for Dealing with Scientific Uncertainty in Environmental Law', *Vanderbilt Journal of Transnational Law* 42 (2010), 437–503; Antônio Augusto Cançado Trindade, 'Principle 15: Precaution', in Jorge E. Viñuales (ed.), *The Rio Declaration on Environment and Development: A Commentary* (Oxford: OUP 2015), 403–428.

[34] See United Nations, Declaration of the United Nations Conference on the Human Environment, A/CONF 48/14/Rev.1, 16 June 1972, principle 21; United Nations, General Assembly, Rio Declaration, 13 June 1992 (n. 10), principle 2.

[35] See ITLOS, *Responsibilities and Obligations in the Area Opinion* (n. 15), paras 142–148; ITLOS, *Request for Advisory Opinion* (n. 20), paras 111, 120; ITLOS, *Dispute Concerning Delimitation of the Maritime Boundary between Ghana and Côte d'Ivoire in the Atlantic Ocean (Ghana v. Côte d'Ivoire)*, Order of 25 April 2016, Case no. 23, paras 68–73; PCA, *South China Sea Arbitration* (n. 32), para. 940.

obligations of means versus obligations of result,[36] fault versus strict (or objective) liability, or some other category, the outer limit of the duty is clear: the mere occurrence of damage is not enough for a breach. This conclusion was reached in the *Alabama* decision in connection with some specific vessels[37] as well as in the 2016 *South China Sea Arbitration* with respect to some specific instances of environmental damage.[38] But more than the mere adoption of measures is required: states must proactively seek to enforce such measures.[39] Thus, this parameter could be conceptually clarified by reference to three stages: the adoption of measures; the enforcement of measures; and the occurrence of the negative outcome. The outer boundary of the duty is located between the second and the third stages.

3.3 Second Inquiry

3.3.1 Overview

The broad parameters of the duty of due diligence in the context of environmental protection thus defined, the second inquiry comes closer to the legal topography and focuses on matters of 'degree' of diligence. This inquiry is difficult because any conclusion relating to the 'degree' of due diligence should have sufficient legal grounding in the relevant authorities. Based on the materials surveyed, which are largely representative of the state of international law on this question, three main criteria have been recognised as capable of graduating the degree of diligence.

3.3.2 Gravity of the Outcome

This question arose already in the *Alabama* case. During the proceedings, counsel for the US had argued that both the gravity of the potential outcome and the 'dignity and strength of the power which is to exercise [the duty]' had to be taken into account in setting the standard of diligence. The tribunal only retained the first criterion,[40] although it did not reject the second. The gravity of the outcome resulting from negligence seems to be the main criterion graduating the level of the due diligence required.[41] But the second criterion mentioned by the US has also received some attention, although not in the manner envisioned at the time of *Alabama*.

[36] ICJ, *Pulp Mills* (n. 12), para. 187; ITLOS, *Responsibilities and Obligations in the Area Opinion* (n. 15), para. 110; ITLOS, *Request for Advisory Opinion* (n. 20), para. 129.

[37] *Alabama Claims* (n. 2), 132 (discussion relating to the vessel 'Retribution').

[38] PCA, *South China Sea Arbitration* (n. 32), paras 972–975. See further ICJ, *Pulp Mills* (n. 12), para. 187; ITLOS, *Responsibilities and Obligations in the Area Opinion* (n. 15), para. 110; ILC, Prevention Articles, 2001 (n. 9), commentary to art. 3, para. 7.

[39] ICJ, *Pulp Mills* (n. 12), para. 197; ITLOS, *Responsibilities and Obligations in the Area Opinion* (n. 15), paras 115 and 239; ILC, Prevention Articles, 2001 (n. 9), commentary to art. 3, para. 10.

[40] *Alabama Claims* (n. 2), 129.

[41] The 'degree of care required is proportional to the degree of risk involved in the business', ILC, Prevention Articles, 2001 (n. 9), commentary to art. 3, para. 18; ITLOS, *Responsibilities and Obligations in the Area Opinion* (n. 15), para. 117.

3.3.3 Capabilities

What could be referred to as the 'capabilities' criterion has featured prominently in discussions about differentiation in international environmental law.[42] It has also been expressly addressed in the advisory opinion of the International Tribunal for the Law of the Sea's Seabed Chamber on the *Responsibility of States Sponsoring Activities in the Area*.[43] In this opinion, the Chamber concluded that 'general provisions concerning the responsibilities and liability of the sponsoring state apply equally to all sponsoring states, whether developing or developed',[44] and that the rationale is to prevent 'states of convenience', that is, states where companies could register themselves to benefit from less demanding requirements. However, the opinion then noted that there may be some variations in the implementation of certain regulations that expressly rely on the precautionary approach. The formulation of the precautionary approach in Principle 15 of the Rio Declaration expressly allows for this approach to be applied by states 'according to their capabilities'. In the context of prevention, the commentary to Article 3 of the ILC Prevention Articles specifically states that:

> The economic level of States is one of the factors to be taken into account in determining whether a State has complied with its obligation of due diligence. But a State's economic level cannot be used to dispense the State from obligation under the present articles.[45]

This somewhat elliptical comment may be understood as stating that all states are subject to the duty of due diligence (they are duty-bearers from the perspective of the duty's formulation) but the degree of due diligence that must be displayed varies. Even under this understanding, the ILC Articles on Prevention would be inconsistent with the conclusion of the Seabed Chamber, at least as a general matter, because the Seabed Chamber's conclusion concerns the specific norms at stake in that case.

The question remains unsettled in the case law, but the need to account for the capabilities of the state in question seems to me unavoidable. The real issue, in my view, is not *whether* such differences can be taken into account but *how* exactly to do so. To take an extreme example, a state whose administrative capabilities have been almost entirely neutralised as a result of civil war or a natural catastrophe could not be expected to duly and regularly follow every detail concerning activities within its territory that may result in environmental harm. But

[42] For an overview of the debate over 'common but differentiated responsibilities', see Philippe Cullet, 'Principle 7: Common but Differentiated Responsibilities', in Jorge E. Viñuales (ed.), *The Rio Declaration on Environment and Development: A Commentary* (Oxford: OUP 2015), 229–244.

[43] ITLOS, *Responsibilities and Obligations in the Area Opinion* (n. 15), paras 158–159.

[44] Ibid., para. 158.

[45] ILC, Prevention Articles, 2001 (n. 9), commentary to art. 3, para. 13.

that may or may not mean that the level of due diligence expected from it is lower. The legal construction of the situation could be that although there is a violation of due diligence, such a violation is justified (for example through the operation of a circumstance precluding wrongfulness). Alternatively, it could be that due diligence depends on the specific circumstances in which the duty is to be discharged and not on the level of development of the state. Still another possibility would be to adjust the duty of due diligence on the grounds that the prevention principle, like the precautionary approach, admits different degrees arising from the reference—in Principle 2 of the Rio Declaration (unlike Principle 21 of the Stockholm Declaration)—to a state's 'own environmental and developmental policies'. Because these and other understandings are equally possible, the question remains unsettled.

3.3.4 Historical Circumstances

The third criterion is related to the previous one. It makes the degree of due diligence dependent on the specific moment in history in which it is assessed. As noted by the Seabed Chamber:

> The content of 'due diligence' obligations may not easily be described in precise terms. Among the factors that make such a description difficult is the fact that 'due diligence' is a variable concept. *It may change over time as measures considered sufficiently diligent at a certain moment may become not diligent enough in light, for instance, of new scientific or technological knowledge.*[46]

Thus stated, changes 'over time' are a proxy for a 'range of circumstances' that are normally expected to change over time, including the dominant scientific understanding of the risks associated with a given activity, the saturation of certain environmental media (even if the scientific understanding remains fundamentally similar), the public perception of a problem (for example changes in the degree of tolerance), and variations in the scale of the activity with implications for the environment.

It is not unreasonable to include in such circumstances the varying capabilities of all states and thereby (possibly) of only some states that are more (less) advanced in dealing with a given risk. All in all, this criterion, despite its solid recognition in the case law, must be handled with great care so as to prevent it from becoming a 'Trojan horse' for illegitimate (ideological) choices.

[46] ITLOS, *Responsibilities and Obligations in the Area Opinion* (n. 15), para. 117 (emphasis added).

4. Conclusion: Due Diligence and the Evolution of International Environmental Law

The cartography of due diligence outlined in this chapter is, above all, an effort aimed at conceptual clarification. Yet, focusing on the textured details of due diligence, however modest the exercise may initially seem, provides a solid basis to chart in actual practice the evolution of the broader international law of environmental protection. I would like to conclude this chapter with some observations emerging from practice. The evolution of due diligence in the context of environmental protection shows two fundamental transformations in the very texture of international law.

First, if the duty of due diligence was initially a legal safeguard against the possibility that a negligent exercise of sovereignty may result in harm to the interests of other states (both the *Alabama* and the *Trail Smelter* arbitrations illustrate this conception), it has since undergone a fundamental transformation requiring the protection of the environment per se, irrespective and even against the interests (if narrowly conceived) of states. This transformation can be traced, in great detail, in the incremental steps made from one case to the other, over time, particularly since the mid 1990s. I have analysed the footprints of this transformation in some detail elsewhere.[47] The key consideration is that due diligence must be exercised to prevent significant environmental damage, harm, or risk thereof, irrespective of whether it may occur. The spatial extension to areas beyond national jurisdiction was stated already in Principle 21 of the 1972 Stockholm Declaration, but it remained unrecognised by the case law until the famous paragraph 29 of the International Court of Justice's 1996 advisory opinion on the *Legality of Nuclear Weapons*.[48] That change, which has since been confirmed by the court and other international tribunals,[49] left open the question of environmental protection in the state of origin of the harmful or risky activity. If due diligence and prevention are about environmental protection per se, one would expect the duty to apply even within that state's own territory and jurisdiction.[50] Significantly, that would leave absolutely no doubt that the value protected is the environment and not the interest of a state in its territory. As noted earlier in this chapter, there is now some authority for the proposition that the environment must be protected irrespective of where it is located, even in disputed

[47] See Jorge E. Viñuales, 'The Contribution of the International Court of Justice to the Development of International Environmental Law', *Fordham International Law Journal* 32 (2008), 232–258.

[48] ICJ, *Legality of Nuclear Weapons Opinion* (n. 18), para. 29: 'The Court also recognises that the environment is not an abstraction but represents the living space, the quality of life, and the very health of human beings, including posterity. The existence of the general obligation of states to ensure that activities within their jurisdiction and control respect the environment of other states or of areas beyond national control is now part of the corpus of international law relating to the environment.'

[49] For an overview of the case law, see Duvic-Paoli/Viñuales, 'Principle 2' 2015 (n. 10).

[50] Ibid., 119.

areas. No case raising a direct clash between the prevention principle and the interests of the territorial state has been decided on by an international court or tribunal. Recognising that states have a due diligence duty to protect their own environment would have repercussions for other imbricated questions, including the identification of the correlative right-holders (Is it any other state, or the international community, or the environment as such, whose interests would be represented by a state or the international community, itself represented by a certain body? Or future generations, also appropriately represented? Or simply individuals, as a result of their human rights?). The inclusion of individuals in the list offers a proxy answer to this question. What I called in my discussion of right-holders 'other relevant norms', such as human rights provisions,[51] are already being used in very clear and practical terms to provide some measure of protection to the environment within a state's own territory and beyond.

Secondly, the transformation of the duty of due diligence from a norm protecting state interests to one protecting the environment per se offers a window into a broader transformation of the structure of international law from a horizontal system into an increasingly vertical one,[52] where some values receive greater objective protection, even if such protection does not reach the level of peremptory norms. The evolution of due diligence is certainly not the only instance of this transformation. Others include the questions of crimes of state, peremptory norms, obligations erga omnes and aggravated responsibility.

The overall point arising from the two foregoing observations, with the many conceptual problems they raise, is simple but important. The need for theory arises from a close, patient, and modest examination of actual practice. Such practical grounding, whether it is the practice of international courts and tribunals or some other parcel of reality, is perhaps the only guarantee that theoretical inquiry will be more than a mere self-referential game.

[51] See above section 3.2.3.

[52] From the perspective of domestic law categories, this transition would make international law less reliant on the form of private law (as once argued by Hersch Lauterpacht) and more on public law categories. See Anne Peters, 'Transnational Law Comprises Constitutional, Administrative, Criminal and Quasi-private Law', in Pieter Bekker/Rudolf Dolzer/Michael Waibel (eds), *Making Transnational Law Work in the Global Economy: Essays in Honour of Detlev Vagts* (Cambridge: CUP 2010), 154–173.

8

Due Diligence in the Use of International Watercourses

Malgosia Fitzmaurice[*]

1. Introduction

The question of due diligence in the use of international watercourses is part and parcel of the broader question of non-navigational uses of international watercourses, which in turn arguably belongs at least in part to the general question of environmental protection.

There is little doubt that some of the general questions relating to due diligence in the use of watercourses are essentially of the same legal character as those underlying international environmental protection. The present chapter will analyse relevant—both general and certain regional—water cooperation treaties and jurisprudence. Soft-law instruments are not discussed in depth: although they are important from the perspective of the codification of norms of international water law, aspects of the due diligence principle are better illustrated through actual treaties that regulate cooperation between states.[1] Again, there is little doubt that the principle of due diligence in international water law reflects much of the rationale present in notions of international environmental law, including the principle of prevention. However, significant differences between due diligence in international watercourse law, environmental law, and the law of the sea are also present, as due diligence in international watercourse law reflects the interplay amongst the two most fundamental principles of the latter: (i) the principle of equitable utilisation;

[*] I would like to offer my thanks Professor Heike Krieger and Professor Anne Peters for inviting me to participate in this important project, and for their comments on my chapter. In this respect, my special thanks go to Mr Leonhard Kreuzer whose incisive comments have significantly improved its content.

[1] The soft-law instruments, which are the most significant to international watercourses, are: the International Law Association, Rules on the Uses of the Waters of International Rivers, August 1966, adopted by the International Law Association at the fifty-second conference, Helsinki, 1966; the 1967 International Law Association Report of the Committee on the Uses of the Waters of International Rivers, London; the International Law Association Report on the Rules on Water Resources, adopted at the seventy-first conference, Berlin, 2004 (ILA Berlin Rules), 337 and 385; and the International Law Commission, Draft Articles on Transboundary Aquifers, YBILC, 2008, vol. II (part 2); the Report, with commentaries in: Official Records of the General Assembly, Sixty-third Session, Supplement No. 10 (A/63/10).

Malgosia Fitzmaurice, *Due Diligence in the Use of International Watercourses* In: *Due Diligence in the International Legal Order*. Edited by: Heike Krieger, Anne Peters, and Leonhard Kreuzer, Oxford University Press (2020). © The Several Contributors. DOI: 10.1093/oso/9780198869900.003.0008.

and (ii) the principle of no significant harm. At first glance it may appear that these two elements are no different from other areas of international law, such as the law of the sea. However, they define the core of international watercourse law, that is, the relationship between upper and lower riparian states. The upper riparian states have supported the principle of equitable utilisation, as adhering to this principle and acting diligently would release them from liability for environmental harm. Lower riparian states have been advocating for the principle of no significant harm, as it would allow them to seek remedies in cases of environmental harm, even if upper riparian states acted in observance of the principle of due diligence. Hence, the International Law Commission and the Sixth Legal Committee have decided to include Article 7(2) of the 1997 Watercourse Convention to grant lower riparian states some compensation in such situations. Where significant harm is nevertheless caused to another watercourse state, the states whose use caused such harm shall, in the absence of an agreement prior to such use, take all appropriate measures—having due regard for the provisions of Articles 5 and 6 and in consultation with the affected state—to eliminate or mitigate such harm and, where appropriate, to discuss the question of compensation.

Further similarities between these three areas exist in the division of the obligations of prevention into *substantive*—such as the requirement of prevention of transboundary pollution—and *procedural*—such as the EIA, requirement for the exchange of information, notification, and the like—which may all sensibly be considered due diligence obligations.[2]

2. Due Diligence in International Watercourse Law

This section is confined to the due diligence principle as it is enunciated in international water law treaties and the relevant case law. Additionally, there is some mention of soft law where necessary.

There are 263 international watercourses globally,[3] many of which are covered by transboundary treaties. It is beyond the scope of the present chapter to provide a full analysis of the majority of these treaties. Instead, this section focuses on a selection of treaties that set out certain general standards that are often found in other (subsequent) treaties, be they regional or more universal in membership.

[2] See, for more detail, Jutta Brunnée, 'International Environmental Law and Community Interests: Procedural Aspects', in Georg Nolte/Eyal Benvenisti, *Community Obligations Across International Law* (Oxford: OUP 2018), 151–175; Jutta Brunnée, 'Procedure and Substance in International Environmental Law: Confused at Higher Level?', *European Society of International Law Reflections* vol. 5 issue 6 (June 2016), at 2, available at: http://esil-sedi.eu/?p=1344 (accessed 31 July 2019).

[3] Flavia Loures/Alistair Rieu-Clarke/Marie-Laure Vercambre, 'Everything you need to know about the UN Watercourses Convention', August 2008, available at: http://assets.wwf.org.uk/downloads/un_watercourses.pdf (accessed 31 July 2019).

At the more universal level, there is the 1997 United Nations Convention on Non-Navigational Uses of International Watercourses (hereinafter the Watercourse Convention),[4] and the Convention on the Protection and Use of Transboundary Watercourses and International Lakes (hereinafter the UNECE Water Convention).[5] The latter is primarily conceived as a regional Convention, within the context of the United Nations Economic Commission for Europe. Since 2013, following the coming into force of amendments adopted in February 2003, the UNECE Water Convention has been opened to all UN member states, and therefore has become open to universal membership.[6]

At the more regional level there is the 2000 Revised Protocol on Shared Watercourses[7] and the 1995 Mekong River Agreement for the Sustainable Development of the Mekong River Basin, which established the Mekong River Commission.[8]

[4] United Nations Convention on Non-Navigational Uses of International Watercourses, 21 May 1997, 36 ILM 700 (1997); Stephen McCaffrey, *The Law of International Watercourses* (Oxford: OUP 3rd ed. 2019); Stephen McCaffrey, 'International Water Law for the 21st Century: The Contribution of the UN Convention', *Journal of Contemporary Water Research and Education* 118 (2001), 11–19; Stephen McCaffrey, 'The UN Convention on the Law of the Non-Navigational Uses of International Watercourses: Prospects and Pitfalls', in Salman Salman/Laurence Boisson de Chazournes (eds), *International Watercourse: Enhancing Cooperation and Managing Conflict Proceedings of a World Bank Seminar* (Washington: World Bank 1998), 17–27; Ryan Stoa, 'The United Nations Watercourses Convention on the Dawn of its Entry into Force', *Vanderbilt Journal of Transnational Law* 47 (2014), 1321–1370.

[5] Convention on the Protection and Use of Transboundary Watercourses and International Lakes, 17 March 1992, 1936 UNTS 269; on this, see Attila Tanzi/Owen McIntyre/Alexandros Kolliolpulos/Alistair Rieu-Clarke/Rémy Kinna (eds), *The UNECE Convention on the Protection and Use of Transboundary Watercourses and International Lakes: Its Contribution to International Water Cooperation* (Leiden: Brill/Nijhoff 2015); Attila Tanzi, 'Comparing the 1992 UNECE Helsinki Water Convention with the 1997 UN New York Convention on international water-course: harmonization over conflict', *Questions of International Law* 8 (2014), 19–33.

[6] For further information on the UNECE Water Convention, 1992 (n. 5), available at: www.unece.org/env/water.html (last accessed 31 July 2019).

[7] This Protocol is established within the Southern African Development Community, which is a regional economic community comprising fifteen member states, namely, Angola, Botswana, Democratic Republic of Congo, Lesotho, Madagascar, Malawi, Mauritius, Mozambique, Namibia, Seychelles, South Africa, Swaziland, Tanzania, Zambia, and Zimbabwe. Established in 1992, the Southern African Development Community is committed to regional integration and poverty eradication within Southern Africa through economic development and ensuring peace and security. The text of the Protocol is available at: https://www.sadc.int/files/3413/6698/6218/Revised_Protocol_on_Shared_Watercourses_-_2000_-_English.pdf (last accessed 11 March 2019).

[8] Agreement on the Cooperation for the Sustainable Development of the Mekong River Basin (with protocol), 5 April 1995, 2069 UNTS 3, signed at Chiang Rai, Thailand by the Governments of the Kingdom of Cambodia, the Lao People's Democratic Republic, the Kingdom of Thailand, and of the Socialist Republic of Vietnam. The text of the treaty is available at: www.mrcmekong.org/assets/Publications/policies/agreement-Apr95.pdf (last accessed 11 March 2019).

2.1 The 1997 Watercourse Convention

The Watercourse Convention contains thirty-seven provisions and is of general importance as it provides the opportunity for adjusting to, and harmonising with, the provisions of other existing watercourse agreements applicable to the parties (cf. Article 3 (2-3)). It applies to the uses of international watercourses and their waters for purposes other than navigation, as well as to measures of protection, preservation, and management related to the uses of those watercourses and their waters (cf. Article 1(1)). The term 'watercourse' in this Convention means a system of surface and ground waters constituting, by virtue of their physical relationship, a unitary whole and normally flowing into a common terminus (cf. Article 2(a)).

The Convention contains several substantive and procedural provisions. The most important substantive provisions are to be found in Articles 5, 6, and 7. These provisions merit attention as they are at the heart of the due diligence principle. Article 8 contains the duty to cooperate in the management of shared resources.

It is indisputable that Article 5 (stipulating the principle of equitable and reasonable utilisation as well as the principle of equitable and reasonable participation), and Article 7 (stipulating the principle of no significant harm) constitute the cornerstones of this Convention and general international law concerning watercourses. Article 6 lists factors for the determination of what may constitute equitable use, including the effects of use on other watercourse states. The principle of equitable and reasonable utilisation concerns the allocation of rights in the use and benefit of shared water resources based on distributive concepts of equity, taking into account all relevant factors.[9] It should be noted that the principle of equitable utilisation has been confirmed by the International Court of Justice (ICJ) in the *Gabčíkovo-Nagymaros* and *Pulp Mills* cases as a fundamental principle of international watercourse cooperation.[10] In the *Pulp Mills* case this principle was linked directly to the concept of sustainable development, where the court had stated that 'interconnectedness between equitable and reasonable utilization of a shared resource and the balance between economic development and environmental protection (…) is the essence of sustainable development'.[11]

The Convention introduces the standard necessary to comply with the principle of no significant harm, requiring states to refrain from actions that could cause substantial damage to another state's water resources.[12] Should damage occur, the

[9] Owen McIntyre, 'Substantive Rules of International Law', in Alistair Rieu-Clarke/Andrew Allan/Sarah Hendry (eds), *Routledge Handbook of Water Law and Policy* (London: Routledge 2017), 234–246, at 238.

[10] ICJ, *Gabčíkovo-Nagymaros Project (Hungary v. Slovakia)*, Judgment of 25 September 1997, ICJ Reports 1997, 7, para. 147; ICJ, *Pulp Mills on the River Uruguay, (Argentina v. Uruguay)*, Judgment of 10 April 2010, ICJ Reports 2010, 14, para. 170.

[11] ICJ, *Pulp Mills* (n. 10), para. 177.

[12] Cf. UN Convention on Non-Navigational Uses of International Watercourses, 1997 (n. 4), art. 7(1), (2), where it states:'(1) Watercourse States shall, in utilizing an international watercourse in their territories, take all appropriate measures to prevent the causing of significant harm to other

principle requires a state to compensate other states for the damage. Articles 5 and 7 may generate tension between upstream and downstream states as the use of watercourses, even when reasonable and equitable on the part of upstream states, may still result in significant harm to downstream states. This tension has yet to be resolved satisfactorily: at present no solution has been found.[13]

The due diligence standard is also reflected in the requirement stipulated in Article 7(1) that states take 'all appropriate measures', and this obligation usually connotes the duty of due diligence.[14] The idea behind this standard is that the harming state has done all that could reasonably be expected from it to avoid the harm caused. As Stephen McCaffrey observes, one of the major features of the due diligence standard regarded as its principal advantage—its flexibility—was instead considered by some ILC members as a drawback. According to their interpretation, such a standard was too vague and subjective to serve as a standard of responsibility and liability. In their view the responsibility to avoid pollution-related harm should be strict, so that states would be unable to evade responsibility by claiming they had exercised due diligence. It should be noted that such a concern must be taken seriously. Conversely, it should be recognised that progress has been made in defining the content of the standard of due diligence as it applies to international environmental law in general. However, in the case of international watercourse law, it may be difficult to establish the existence of generally accepted minimum standards with regard to particular problems, due to the subjective features of each watercourse and the regime that may apply to it.[15] The ILC also found less acceptable the fact that due diligence appears to unduly favour the state causing the harm.[16] It was suggested that the burden of proof should be upon the originating state to clearly show that it had exercised due diligence; should they be unable to do so, they would prima facie be responsible for a breach of the due diligence obligation.

It must also be taken into consideration that Article 5 (with regard to equitable and reasonable utilisation, as well as participation) plays a fundamental role in the relationship between harm and due diligence. The formulation of Article 7 raises

watercourse States. (2) Where significant harm nevertheless is caused to another watercourse State, the States whose use causes such harm shall, in the absence of agreement to such use, take all appropriate measures, having due regard for the provisions of articles 5 and 6, in consultation with the affected State, to eliminate or mitigate such harm and, where appropriate, to discuss the question of compensation'. On the complex relationship between Articles 5 and 6, and Article 7, see Lucius Caflisch, '*Equitable and Reasonable Utilisation and Factors Relevant to Determining Such Utilisation (Articles 5 and 6)*', 77–94; Salman Salman, 'The Obligation Not to Cause Significant Harm', in Laurence Boisson de Chazournes/Makane Moïse Mbengue/Mara Tignino/Komlan Sangbana/Jason Rudall (eds), *The UN Convention on the Law of the Non-Navigational Uses of International Watercourse: A Commentary* (Oxford: OUP 2018), 95–122.

13 Stoa, 'The United Nations Watercourses Convention' 2014 (n. 4), 1321, 1339.

14 McCaffrey, *The Law of International Watercourses* 2019 (n. 4), 498.

15 Ibid., 500.

16 Ibid., 501.

questions as to whether a state causing harm shall be liable for compensation to a state suffering harm, even when the former had complied with the rule of equitable and reasonable utilisation. The formulation of Article 7 appears to indicate prima facie that a state complying with the standard of due diligence and following the requirement of reasonable and equitable utilisation would still be obliged to pay compensation, thus introducing a double due diligence standard of sorts: (i) to take all appropriate measures to prevent causing significant harm to other watercourse states; (ii) if significant harm does occur to other watercourse states, despite taking all appropriate measures, the responsible states have to take all appropriate measures—including consultation with the affected states—to eliminate or mitigate such harm and, where appropriate, to discuss the question of compensation, while maintaining due regard for the provisions of Articles 5 and 6.

This reflects the difficulty of reconciling the standard of equitable utilisation with the principle of no significant harm, and in effect the interests of lower and upper riparian states. Even if the due diligence standard and the principle of equitable and reasonable use have both been upheld by the harming state, it may be equitable to grant the affected state some compensation.

McCaffrey suggests a method of reconciling the above difficulty. He argues that in international watercourses, it is not the causing of significant harm per se that is prohibited but the unreasonable causing of such harm, which in practical terms means that the affected state could tolerate the harm if it was reasonably caused. In relation to equitable utilisation, it means that harm should not be present. In such a situation, McCaffrey argues, 'there is therefore no need to "reconcile" the no harm and equitable utilisation principles. They are, in reality, two sides of the same coin.'[17]

Moreover, the Convention contains several procedural obligations that are part and parcel of the due diligence standard. Firstly, Article 8 includes the duty to co-operate as one of the fundamental principles underlying the Convention. The duty to cooperate contains the obligation to exchange information as set out in Article 9. These obligations are in line with the 2001 ILC Draft Articles on the Prevention of Transboundary Harm from Hazardous Activities.[18] Article 4 introduces a general duty of cooperation and Article 12 introduces a duty to exchange information.

These are quite comprehensive obligations, comprising the obligation to regularly exchange readily available data and information on the condition of the watercourse—in particular those of a hydrological, meteorological, hydrogeological, and ecological nature—and the water quality, as well as any related forecasts. In the event of a request by another watercourse state to provide data or

[17] Ibid., 497.

[18] Text adopted by the Commission at its fifty-third session, in 2001, and submitted to the General Assembly as a part of the Commission's report covering the work of that session. Official Records of the General Assembly, Fifty-sixth Session, Supplement No. 10 (A/56/10), available at: http://legal.un.org/ilc/texts/instruments/english/ draft_articles/9_7_2001.pdf (accessed 31 July 2019).

information that is not readily available, the cooperating state is obliged to employ its best efforts to comply with the request, but may condition its compliance upon payment by the requesting state of the reasonable costs of collecting and, where appropriate, processing such data or information. Watercourse states are to employ their best efforts to collect and, where appropriate, process data and information in a manner that facilitates its utilisation by the other watercourse states to which the data and information is communicated. Although the stronger verbal form 'shall' is used in this provision, it is qualified with 'employ their best efforts', which also reflects the flexibility, if not imprecision, of the due diligence standard.

Part III of the Convention is fully devoted to procedural obligations, such as those pertaining to information concerning planned measures (cf. Article 11); notification concerning planned measures with possible adverse effects, including the period for replying to the notification (cf. Articles 12 and 13); obligations of the notifying state during the reply period (cf. Article 14); and the obligation to reply to notification and the provisions concerning the absence of a reply (cf. Articles 15 and 16). Article 17 concerns the consultations and negotiations regarding planned measures. This provision links the substantive obligations with procedural obligations based on the due diligence standard. It may also be observed that a direct obligation for EIA is absent in the Convention, while the obligation for negotiations and consultations is its key component.

The commentary adopted in relation to Article 7 had stated that the 'obligation of due diligence contained in Article 7 (...) is an obligation of conduct, not an obligation of result'. According to McCaffrey, what is meant is that Article 7 does not require a state to guarantee that no significant harm will be caused to other states sharing a watercourse. He also states that at times the obligations of conduct may be more stringent than those of results, as they deprive the states of the choice of means. An interesting observation was made by the same author that due diligence obligations may necessitate the enacting of national laws, and by failing to do so a state may be in breach of its due diligence obligation even without having caused serious harm.[19] The *Pulp Mills* case appears to corroborate that the general obligations concerning the obligation of prevention are related to those of conduct. Under the treaty between Uruguay and Argentina, both states were obligated to adopt measures to avoid changes to the ecological balance of the river. The obligation to adopt regulatory measures may be regarded as an obligation of conduct.[20]

In conclusion it may be said that the Convention contains the due diligence standard, both in relation to its substantive and procedural obligations.

[19] McCaffrey, *The Law International Watercourses* 2019 (n. 4), 504.

[20] ICJ, *Pulp Mills* (n. 10), para. 187; Ling Chen, 'Realizing the Precautionary Principle in Due Diligence', *Dalhousie Journal of Legal Studies* 25 (2016), 1–23, at 13.

2.2 The UNECE Water Convention

The UNECE Water Convention pertains to the joint management and conservation of shared freshwater ecosystems. It is a framework Convention and, in contrast to the Watercourse Convention, a robust treaty accompanied by numerous Protocols and sets of guidelines. Suffice it to say that both Conventions, although sharing the objective of the protection of international watercourses, differ in a number of substantial ways.[21]

The scope of the Watercourse Convention is based on the notion of a watercourse, which encompasses all tributaries, lakes, aquifers, and other hydrological components connected to a major internationally shared river, whereas the UNECE Water Convention is based on an ecosystem approach (cf. Article 1(2). The UNECE Water Convention provides that 'Parties shall take all appropriate measures to prevent, control and reduce any transboundary impact' (cf. Article 2(1)). Article 2(2)(c) refers to the equitable utilisation principle within the context of harm prevention). According to Atilla Tanzi, the main difference between the two Conventions is the issue of cooperation. The UNECE Water Convention supplements the general obligation of cooperation by requiring watercourse states to enter into agreements to that end, in contrast to the Watercourse Convention Article 8(2) which only states that 'watercourse States may consider the establishment of joint mechanisms or commissions' as a means of cooperation. Tanzi states that such a provision to consider establishing a joint mechanisms or commission has no normative force. The Watercourse Convention provides a more extensive set of procedural obligations than the UNECE Water Convention, particularly in relation to notification and consultation.

The UNECE Water Convention is based on several procedural principles, such as those concerning best environmental practices, EIAs, and other means of assessment (cf. Article 3). The due diligence standard underlies the substantive provisions of the UNECE Water Convention. What is more, the formulation of Article 2(6), according to which '[t]he Riparian Parties shall cooperate on the basis of equality and reciprocity', highlights how equitable and reasonable participation is also one of the fundamental principles linked to due diligence. This Convention appears to include the full set of relevant procedural obligations that constitute the elements of the standard of due diligence.

Article 10 includes the duty to ensure that consultations are conducted on the basis of reciprocity, good faith, and good neighbourliness. Article 9 ('General Obligations') includes the obligation to conduct the EIA in relation to transboundary waters, the obligation to draw up and exchange information, and the obligation to promote cooperation and the exchange of information with the

[21] On this see Stoa, 'The United Nations Watercourses Convention' 2014 (n. 4), 1343.

best available technology and in accordance with the provisions of Article 13. Article 13 develops the obligations deriving from Article 9 concerning the exchange of information to include information about the environmental conditions of transboundary waters; the experience gained in the application and operation of the best available technology, and the results of research and development; emission and monitoring data; measures taken and planned to be taken to prevent, control, and reduce transboundary impacts; and permits or regulations for wastewater discharges issued by the competent authority or appropriate body.

In sum, it may be said that the procedural obligations pertaining to the due diligence standard are more extensive in the UNECE Water Convention than in the Watercourse Convention, despite the more mandatory language of the latter.

3. The Dilemma of Due Diligence: Substantive and Procedural Obligations

In the *Pulp Mills* case the ICJ confirmed the principle of prevention, which is based on due diligence and constitutes a core principle of international environmental law. This principle had initially been acknowledged in the *Corfu Channel* case,[22] then included in the *Nuclear Weapons* Advisory Opinion,[23] and relied upon in the ILC Articles on Prevention.[24]

Recent ICJ cases concerning due diligence, and its substantive and procedural aspects—namely the substantive aspect pertaining to the duty to prevent significant harm; and procedural aspects (namely, those pertaining to EIA, notification, and consultation)—have led to some confusion as to how these interrelate, and the implications this interrelationship has for due diligence. In the *Pulp Mills* case, the court made certain statements that related to the content of the duty of due diligence in relation to a shared watercourse. The court stated that 'a State is thus obliged to use all of the means at its disposal in order to avoid activities which take place in its territory, or in any area under its jurisdiction, causing significant damage to the environment of another state',[25] thus reaffirming the general obligation of prevention. The ICJ specifically referred to the obligation of due diligence in the protection of the shared river: 'Both Parties are therefore called upon, under

[22] ICJ, *Corfu Channel Case (United Kingdom v. Albania)*, Judgment of 9 April 1949, ICJ Reports 1949, 4, p. 22.

[23] ICJ, *Legality of the Threat or Use of Nuclear Weapons*, Advisory Opinion of 8 July 1996, ICJ Reports 1996, 226, para. 29.

[24] United Nations, International Law Commission, Draft Articles on Prevention of Transboundary Harm from Hazardous Activities, YBILC 2001, vol. II (part II), available at: http://legal.un.org/ilc/texts/instruments/english/commentaries/9_7_2001.pdf (accessed 31 July 2019); on the principle of prevention in general, see Leslie Duvic-Paoli, *The Prevention Principle in International Environmental Law* (Cambridge: CUP 2018).

[25] ICJ, *Pulp Mills* (n. 10), para. 101; see also Alan Boyle, 'Pulp Mills Case: A Commentary', 2010, available at: www.biicl.org/files/5167_pulp_mills_case.pdf (last accessed 31 July 2019).

Article 36, to exercise due diligence in acting through the Commission for the necessary measures to preserve the ecological balance of the river.' The exercise of due diligence entails the adoption of appropriate rules and measures;[26] a certain level of vigilance in their enforcement; the exercise of administrative control applicable to public and private operators; careful consideration of the technology to be used; the commission of an EIA; and notification informing and consulting potentially affected states.[27]

The ICJ also confirms explicitly that the obligation is one of due diligence—an obligation of conduct rather than one of result.[28] The court found that the agreement between Argentina and Uruguay should be interpreted:

> in accordance with a practice, which in recent years has gained so much acceptance among states that it may now be taken as a requirement under general international law to undertake an environmental impact assessment where there is a risk that the proposed industrial activity may have a significant adverse impact in a transboundary context.[29]

The court expressed the view that an EIA is a necessary element of the due diligence obligation. Furthermore, the court confirmed that in appropriate circumstances an EIA must be carried out prior to the implementation of a project that is likely to cause significant transboundary harm.[30] It also stated that 'due diligence, and the duty of vigilance and prevention which it implies, would not be considered to have been exercised, if a party planning works liable to affect the régime of the river or the quality of its waters did not undertake an environmental impact assessment on the potential effects of such works'.[31]

The court further stated that the scope and content of an EIA are not specified by general international law. Therefore, it is for each party to determine on a case-by-case basis what is required, while 'having regard to the nature and magnitude of the proposed development and its likely adverse impact'.[32] In this case the ICJ distinguished between two types of obligation—namely substantive and procedural—and stated that they 'complement one another perfectly, enabling the parties to achieve the object of the Statute which they set themselves in Article 1'.[33]

Furthermore, the court stated that procedural obligations have a separate existence: their breach is not contingent on the presence of significant transboundary harm.[34] The substantive aspect of the due diligence obligation does not impose an

26 ICJ, *Pulp Mills* (n. 10), para. 197.
27 Ibid., para. 223.
28 Ibid., para. 187.
29 Ibid., para. 204.
30 Ibid., para. 205.
31 Ibid., para. 204.
32 Ibid., para. 205.
33 Ibid., para. 77.
34 Ibid., paras 77–78.

absolute duty for harm prevention. Rather, it is based on the due diligence principle, that is to say, states must meet the requirements of due diligence in their efforts to prevent significant transboundary impacts.[35] The court stated that the failure to meet the procedural obligation does not automatically equate to a violation of the substantive obligations (such as the duty to prevent harm). The court was of the view that 'nowhere does the 1975 Statute indicate that a party may fulfil its substantive obligations by complying solely with its procedural obligations, nor that a breach of procedural obligations automatically entails the breach of substantive ones',[36] and 'the fact that the parties have complied with their substantive obligations does not mean that they are deemed to have complied ipso facto with their procedural obligations, or are excused from doing so'.[37] Jutta Brunnée observes that '[t]he Court's decision is ambiguous to the extent that its comments on this point focused on the interpretation of the treaty between the parties while, elsewhere in the judgment, it clearly connected procedural duties and due diligence'.[38] She has noted that the same ambiguous handling of due diligence—and the procedural and substantive obligations—by the court was apparent in the *Nicaragua and Costa Rica* cases.[39] Brunnée based her analysis on statements made by the ICJ concerning Costa Rica's complaint of Nicaraguan dredging, where the ICJ observed that 'to fulfil its obligation to exercise due diligence in preventing significant transboundary harm, a state must, before embarking on an activity having the potential adversely to affect the environment of another State, ascertain if there is a risk of significant transboundary harm, which would trigger the requirement to carry out an environmental impact assessment'.[40] If the assessment confirms the risk, due diligence may require the state planning the activity to conform to the duty of notification and consultation in good faith with the potentially affected states.[41] However, in the absence of the necessary risk, 'Nicaragua was free from the obligations to carry out an environmental impact assessment and also from notification or consultation with Costa Rica' regarding its plans.[42] In the *Nicaragua v. Costa Rica* case, the ICJ found that the road-building plans triggered the obligation to undertake an EIA, an obligation that Costa Rica had failed to discharge.[43] The court expressed the view that there was no need to examine whether Costa Rica had breached the duty to notify or consult, as it had already failed to perform

[35] Ibid., para. 197.
[36] Ibid., para. 78.
[37] Ibid., para. 78.
[38] Brunnée, 'Procedure and Substance' 2018 (n. 2), at 3, 4.
[39] ICJ, *Certain Activities Carried Out by Nicaragua in the Border Area (Costa Rica v. Nicaragua) and Construction of a Road in Costa Rica along the San Juan River (Nicaragua v. Costa Rica)*, Judgment of 16 December 2015, ICJ Reports 2015, 665; Brunnée, 'International Environmental Law and Community Interests' 2018 (n. 2), 157.
[40] ICJ, *Costa Rica and Nicaragua* (n. 39), para. 104.
[41] Ibid.
[42] Ibid., para. 108.
[43] Ibid., paras 153–162.

an environmental impact assessment.[44] Brunnée observes that the court's approach may present a dilemma, stating that it was not quite clear whether the court considered procedural duties of states 'to be strictly sequential, with notification and consultation being contingent upon a prior finding of risk through an EIA, or whether it considered the failure to conduct an EIA had already established a failure to act diligently'.[45] As in the *Pulp Mills* case, the ICJ concluded that where evidence of significant transboundary harm is absent, 'there was no violation of the "no harm" rule'.[46] Brunneé concludes that:

> All in all, it appears as if the ICJ distinguishes between the duty to take diligent steps to prevent significant transboundary harm, which it then deals with under the rubric of separate procedural obligations, and the duty to take diligent steps not to cause harm, which it considers cannot be violated simply by a failure to act diligently. While the latter conclusion is clearly correct, it stands to reason that violations of procedural obligations do breach the harm prevention duty, even if no transboundary harm results from that breach. At any rate, the Separate Opinions suggest that the substance-procedure framework of international environmental law, as well as the legal status of the EIA obligation, may be less settled than it might appear at first glance.'[47]

4. The Due Diligence Standard and the Precautionary Principle

The formulations of the precautionary principle in water agreements and other instruments are all based to some degree on the classical formulation in the 1992 Rio Declaration on Environment and Development.[48] That formulation is not strongly worded, couched instead in weak terms and linking it to subjective factors like the capabilities of states and cost effectiveness. In 2011, the Advisory Opinion

[44] Ibid., para. 168: 'The Court reiterates its conclusion that, if the environmental impact assessment confirms that there is a risk of significant transboundary harm, a State planning an activity that carries such a risk is required, in order to fulfil its obligation to exercise due diligence in preventing significant transboundary harm, to notify, and consult with, the potentially affected State in good faith, where that is necessary to determine the appropriate measures to prevent or mitigate that risk (. . .). However, the duty to notify and consult does not call for examination by the Court in the present case, since the Court has established that Costa Rica has not complied with its obligation under general international law to perform an environmental impact assessment prior to the construction of the road.'.

[45] Brunnée, 'Procedure and Substance' 2018 (n. 2), at 4.

[46] Ibid., para. 196.

[47] Ibid., 159.

[48] United Nations, General Assembly, Rio Declaration on Environment and Development, 12 August 1992, A/CONF.151/26. (vol.1), principle 15: 'In order to protect the environment, the precautionary approach shall be widely applied by States according to their capabilities. Where there are threats of serious or irreversible damage, lack of full scientific certainty shall not be used as a reason for postponing cost-effective measures to prevent environmental degradation.'

of the Seabed Disputes Chamber of the International Tribunal on the Law of the Sea (ITLOS) regarding *Responsibilities and Obligations of States Sponsoring Persons and Entities with respect to Activities in the Area* unequivocally stated that the precautionary approach is 'an integral part of the general obligation of due diligence'.[49]

The precautionary principle is also mentioned in the UNECE Water Convention. In Article 2(5), it is stated that in relation to the adoption of 'all appropriate measures', parties 'shall be guided' by the precautionary principle, the polluter-pays-principle, and intergenerational equity. The precautionary principle is defined as follows:

> [t]he precautionary principle, by virtue of which action to avoid the potential transboundary impact of the release of hazardous substances shall not be postponed on the ground that scientific research has not fully proved a causal link between those substances, on the one hand, and the potential transboundary impact, on the other hand.'

It has been observed that the formulation of the precautionary principle in the UNECE Water Convention is also related to the EIA and has to be read together.[50] The formulation in the chapeau to this article, namely the inclusion of the term 'taking all appropriate measures', indicates the due diligence character of the principle in this instrument.

The issue of the precautionary approach arose in the *Pulp Mills* case, where the court made the following statement:

> [W]hile a precautionary approach may be relevant in the interpretation and application of the provisions of the Statute, it does not follow that it operates as a reversal of the burden of the provisions of the Statute, it does not follow that it operates as a reversal of the burden of proof.[51]

Thus the ICJ adopted a rather weak version of the principle, rejecting the reversal of the burden of proof as a consequence of its application.

It may be interesting to note that Argentina argued that Uruguay should bear the burden of proof that the mills of the latter did not cause environmental harm. Argentina sought to argue that this reversal of the burden of proof was justified

[49] ITLOS Seabed Disputes Chamber, *Responsibilities and Obligations of States Sponsoring Persons and Entities with Respect to Activities in the Area*, Advisory Opinion 1 February 2011, ITLOS Reports 2011, para. 131.

[50] Nicolas de Sadeleer/Mehdi Abbas Khayli, 'The Role of the Precautionary Principle in the Convention on the Protection and Use of Transboundary Watercourses and International Lakes', in Attila Tanzi/Owen McIntyre/Alexandros Kolliopoulos/Alistair Rieu-Clarke/Rémy Kinna (eds), *The UNECE Convention on the Protection and Use of Transboundary Watercourses and International Lakes* (Leiden: Nijhoff 2015), 160–175, at 161.

[51] ICJ, *Pulp Mills* (n. 10), para. 164.

under the precautionary principle.[52] Without delving into the substance of this principle, it can nonetheless be stated that this characteristic feature of the principle is not uniformly accepted and remains somewhat controversial.[53]

The view held by the ITLOS Chamber that the precautionary principle has the character of due diligence is further supported by opinions expressed in the literature and judicial practice, which generally take the position that there are certain parallels between an EIA and the precautionary principle, and further that the application of an EIA includes a level of precaution.[54] From this standpoint, there is no doubt that the precautionary principle, as well as the practice of conducting an EIA, is based on the due diligence standard. This argument is strengthened by the formulation of the precautionary approach in the International Law Association (ILA) Berlin Rules, whereby Article 23 states:

> 1. In implementing obligations under this Chapter, States shall apply the precautionary approach. 2. States shall take all appropriate measures to prevent, eliminate, reduce, or control harm to the aquatic environment when there is a serious risk of significant adverse effect on or to the sustainable use of waters even without conclusive proof of a causal relation between an act or omission and its expected effects.

This provision is based on the obligation of taking 'all appropriate measures' when there is a serious risk of significant adverse effects, which is indicative of the due diligence obligation. The Commentary to the ILA Berlin Rules also states that:

> Implementation of the precautionary principle requires careful planning and the evaluation of the likely effects of significant actions before the action is implemented. The primary, but not the only, method that this will occur is through the impact assessment process that is now part of the requirements for the protection of the environment under international law.[55]

This Article, therefore, also evidences a strong link between the precautionary principle and the EIA, thus confirming the view that even if the precautionary

[52] Ibid., para. 160; Daniel Kazhdan, 'Precautionary Pulp: Pulp Mills and the Evolving Dispute between International Tribunals over the Reach of the Precautionary Principle', *Ecology Law Quarterly* 38 (2011), 528–552.

[53] See, e.g., ITLOS, the Separate Opinion of Judge Wolfrum in the MOX Plant case, *MOX Plant Case (Ireland v. United Kingdom)*, Request for provisional measures, Order of 3 December 2001, 134: 'There is no general agreement as to the consequences which flow from the implementation of this principle other than the fact that the burden of proof concerning the possible impact of a given activity is reversed. A State interested in undertaking or continuing a particular activity has to prove that such activities will not result in any harm, rather than the other side having to prove that it will result in harm.'

[54] Kazhdan, 'Precautionary Pulp: Pulp Mills' 2011 (n. 52), 547.

[55] ILA Berlin Rules, 2004 (n. 1), 28.

principle is not analogous to the requirement to conduct an EIA, at least parallels exist, which further suggest a due diligence standard.

However, we may ask whether and to what extent the inclusion of a principle—the status of which in international environmental law is controversial—of such vague content[56] can modify the application of the standard of due diligence. The main issue is whether the interplay of the precautionary principle and due diligence enhances and raises the application threshold of the latter. The complexities of the scope and application of the precautionary principle were well illustrated by the *Gabčíkovo-Nagymaros* case, in which Hungary in its pleadings relied on the principle to justify the suspension and termination of a treaty with Czechoslovakia. Hungary also linked the operation of this principle to the 'grave and imminent' peril of an essential interest of the state in its efforts to invoke a state of necessity. In the event, the ICJ rejected the contentions of Hungary due to the uncertain nature of the risks.[57]

5. Regional Treaties

5.1 The 2000 Revised Protocol on Shared Watercourses

The 2000 Revised Protocol on Shared Watercourses in the Southern African Development Community in its preamble expressly mentions the 1997 Watercourse Convention, and establishes as its purpose the equitable utilisation of shared watercourses, sustainable development, and environmentally sound management (cf. Article 1). It is also based on the notion of 'significant harm', defined as being established by objective evidence without necessarily equating this notion to some substantial obligation per se. The Protocol relies on the provisions of the 1997 Watercourse Convention, in that it includes the standards of equitable utilisation and significant harm, and refers also to the 'double due diligence standard' (cf. Article 3 'General Provisions'). Furthermore, the 2000 Protocol also contains procedural obligations including those pertaining to notification and consultation, which form part of the general obligation of prevention, which is itself based on the notion of due diligence (cf. Article 4 'Specific Provisions'). A similar 2000 interstate agreement concluded amongst some of the states parties to the 2000 Southern African Development Community Protocol, and relying on the 1997 Watercourse Convention and the 2000 Protocol, also contains the notion of equitable utilisation as one of its fundamental principles.[58] It does not, however, include the 'double due diligence standard'. That agreement states:

[56] De Sadeleer/Khayli, 'The Role of the Precautionary Principle' 2015 (n. 50), 163.
[57] Ibid., 169.
[58] The 2000 Agreement between Botswana, Lesotho, Namibia, and South Africa on the establishment of the Orange-Senqu River Commission, available at: https://iea.uoregon.edu/treaty-text/

> 7.3 The Parties shall, in utilising the resources of the River System in their territories, take all appropriate measures to prevent the causing of significant harm to another Party. The term 'significant harm' shall be interpreted in line with the Revised Protocol on Shared Watercourses in the Southern African Development Community (SADC) Region.

The expression 'all appropriate measures' signifies the standard of due diligence.

5.2 The Mekong River Treaty

The Mekong River Treaty is also based on the principle of reasonable and equitable utilisation of the river in the respective territories of its parties (cf. Article 5), as well as on the principle of prevention and cessation of harmful effects (cf. Article 7). The Treaty imposes on parties an obligation 'to make every effort to avoid, minimize and mitigate harmful effects that might occur to the environment, especially the water quantity and quality'. The inclusion of the term 'every effort' in the above formulation indicates a due diligence obligation. However, the substantive provisions regarding the notion of significant harm appear to be of little practical importance. Parties to both these regional agreements rely on cooperation to prevent harm rather than on pursuing questions connected with remedying harm. For instance, Vietnam, which is a downstream riparian state and thus susceptible to harm, 'has a high interest in regional river basin management, particularly through data exchange, joint flood protection and the establishment of binding rules on water quantity and quality'.[59] Therefore, procedural obligations appear more prominent in regional cooperation than unclear substantive obligations, such as the prohibition on causing significant harm.

6. Conclusions

There is little doubt that due diligence is the underlying standard for obligations pertaining to international water law, as exemplified by the 1997 Watercourse Convention (cf. Article 7). During the drafting of that instrument, it was argued that the standard adopted was preferable because of its flexibility. However,

2000-orangesenqucommissionentxt (accessed 11 March 2019); see Inga Jacobs, 'A Community in the Orange: The Development of a Multi-level Water Governance Framework in the Orange-Senqu River Basin in Southern Africa', *International Environmental Agreements: Politics, Law and Economics* 12 (2012), 187–210.

[59] Susanne Schmeier, 'Regional Cooperation Efforts in the Mekong River Basin: Mitigating River-related Security Threats and Promoting Regional Development', *Austrian Journal of South-East Asian Studies* 2 (2009), 28–52.

the standard also generated unfavourable reactions, as it was thought to be too vague and subjective for the purposes of defining state responsibility. However, as McCaffrey observes, the development of the due diligence standard—and the greater precision accorded to its content in general environmental law and in the law of shared resources—has made it more acceptable.[60] The standard of due diligence has gained a considerable significance in procedural water law. If a state makes a prima facie showing that it has incurred significant harm attributable to another state's conduct concerning an international watercourse, the burden is in principle shifted to the alleged source state to prove that it has complied with the obligation of due diligence to prevent harm. If the state has not, or cannot carry out this burden, it is in breach of its due diligence obligation. Even if it has fulfilled its due diligence obligation, said state is obliged to establish that its conduct or use is equitable and reasonable.[61]

The general observations regarding the flexibility, but also the vagueness, of the due diligence standard in international environmental law equally apply to the law on international watercourses.[62] Despite numerous unresolved questions concerning the standard of due diligence in the law of international watercourses, there are certain recurring common parameters in watercourse agreements. In the present author's opinion, such parameters of due diligence are particularly identifiable in relation to procedural obligations, which are included in almost all watercourse agreements. The requirement of cooperation, the exchange of information, and early notification all appear to form common procedural obligations in which the due diligence standard appears to exhibit a certain uniformity in application, despite a certain lack of precision in their formulation in general international environmental law. Substantive law pertaining to international watercourses, in particular the uneasy relationship between principles of no significant harm and equitable utilisation, as well as differences in their formulations in various watercourse agreements, hamper the identification of general parameters of due diligence in the area of substantive law.

In general, the lack of a definitive determination on the part of the ICJ, or other relevant adjudicative fora, on the interplay between the EIA (and other procedural obligations), significant harm, and due diligence leaves states at times perplexed. Nonetheless, both conventional law and the relevant jurisprudence offer some insight into the constitutive elements of the standard of due diligence, that is to say, of both its substantive aspects—including the underlying principles of equitable and reasonable utilisations and no significant harm—as well as its procedural aspects—such as the obligations relating

60 McCaffrey, *The Law of International Watercourses* 2019 (n. 4), 500.
61 Ibid., 505–506.
62 Duvic-Paoli, *The Prevention Principle in International Law* 2018 (n. 24), 201.

to exchange of information, notification, consultations, and EIAs. That said, Leslie Anne Duvic-Paoli is of the view that, '[b]y envisaging prevention within its international legal context and building upon its multiple ramifications, the flexibility that characterizes due diligence is not necessarily synonymous with vagueness'.[63]

[63] Ibid.

9

Due Diligence in the Law of the Sea

*Irini Papanicolopulu**

1. Introduction: A Regime Based on Due Diligence?

The United Nations Convention on the Law of the Sea[1] (UNCLOS or Convention) does not expressly mention 'due diligence',[2] yet it has been observed that the UNCLOS 'regime is mostly based on the due diligence test'.[3] While this may not necessarily be exact in quantitative terms, it is certainly true that many among the most important duties for states under the law of the sea[4] are framed in terms of due diligence obligations.

The link between due diligence and law of the sea rules, however, had not become widely known until in 2011 the International Tribunal for the Law of the Sea's (ITLOS or Tribunal) Seabed Disputes Chamber rendered its first advisory opinion on responsibilities of states with respect to mining operations in the international seabed area. This opinion, complemented in 2015 by an opinion rendered by the full Tribunal in a case concerning the duties of states to prevent illegal fishing, has caused law of the sea scholars to engage with the concept of 'due diligence'.[5]

* I am grateful to Dr Alice Ollino for research assistance during the preparation of this chapter, as well as to the editors and all the participants to the Berlin Workshop for their insightful comments.

[1] United Nations Convention on the Law of the Sea, 10 December 1982, 1833 UNTS 3.

[2] The only explicit reference to 'due diligence' is in art. 12(3)(b)(i) Annex IV UNCLOS (Statute of the Enterprise), which refers to the diligence in the carrying out of activities by the Enterprise. As the name hints, the Enterprise is not a state or a state organ, but rather a private-like actor.

[3] Francisco Orrego Vicuna, 'State Responsibility, Liability, and Remedial Measures Under International Law: New Criteria for Environmental Protection', in Edith Brown Weiss (ed.), *Environmental Change and International Law: New Challenges and Dimensions* (Tokyo: UN University Press 1992).

[4] The law of the sea is traditionally understood to consist of 'the rules and principles that bind States in their international relations concerning maritime matters' (Robin Churchill/Alan Lowe, *The Law of the Sea* (Manchester: Manchester University Press 3rd ed. 1999), 1) although the recent expansion of the subjects of international law may well demand that the definition be extended to include all 'international rules that bind States and other subjects of international law in their marine affairs' (Yoshifumi Tanaka, *The International Law of the Sea* (Cambridge: CUP 2nd ed. 2015), 3). As a consequence, an examination of the law of the sea through the prism of due diligence needs to expand beyond rules concerning protection of the marine environment to include many more rules.

[5] Doris König, 'The Elaboration of Due Diligence Obligations as a Mechanism to Ensure Compliance with International Legal Obligations by Private Actors', in International Tribunal for the Law of the Sea (ed.), *The Contribution of the International Tribunal for the Law of the Sea to the Rule of Law: 1996–2016/ La contribution du Tribunal international du droit de la mer à l'état de droit: 1996–2016* (Leiden: Brill 2018), 83–95; Ida Caracciolo, 'Due diligence et le droit du mer', in Société Française pour le Droit

Irini Papanicolopulu, *Due Diligence in the Law of the Sea* In: *Due Diligence in the International Legal Order.* Edited by: Heike Krieger, Anne Peters, and Leonhard Kreuzer, Oxford University Press (2020). © The Several Contributors. DOI: 10.1093/oso/9780198869900.003.0009.

Furthermore, both the Seabed Disputes Chamber and the ITLOS have elaborated upon the concept of due diligence, its nature, and its implications, providing useful insights by identifying the common features of due diligence obligations, discussing their relationship with other obligations, and addressing issues of state responsibility and compensation. These findings may be applied beyond the specific cases and have therefore attracted the attention of other scholars as well.[6]

2. Conceptualising Due Diligence

While the International Court of Justice had already referred to this concept in the previous year,[7] it is the 2011 Seabed Disputes Chamber opinion that truly conceptualises due diligence, by providing a definition and clarifying its legal nature and its relationship with the law of state responsibility. In the absence of a generally accepted taxonomy, the Seabed Disputes Chamber opinion, as confirmed by the 2015 opinion, has provided a solid basis for the development of the debate on due diligence. Three aspects will be further analysed in this chapter: the definition provided by the Tribunal, which also concerns the nature of due diligence, the common characteristics of due diligence obligations, and the relationship between due diligence and international responsibility.

2.1 A Definition

According to the well-known definition of the Seabed Disputes Chamber, a due diligence obligation:

> is not an obligation to achieve, in each and every case, the result [envisaged by the norm]. Rather, it is an obligation to deploy adequate means, to exercise best possible efforts, to do the utmost, to obtain this result.[8]

International (SFDI)/Sarah Cassella (eds), *Le standard de due diligence et la responsabilité internationale* (Paris: Pedone 2018), 163–185.

[6] Thus the two advisory opinions are regularly cited by all those who discuss due diligence; see, among many others Anne Peters/Heike Krieger/Leonhard Kreuzer, 'Due Diligence in the International Legal Order: Dissecting the Leitmotif of Current Accountability Debates', chapter 1 of this book, section 1; Serena Forlati, 'L'objet des différentes obligations primaires de diligence: prevention, cessation, repression ... ?', in SFDI/Sarah Cassella (eds), *Le standard de due diligence et la responsabilité internationale* (Paris: Pedone 2018), 39–63.

[7] ICJ, *Pulp Mills on the River Uruguay (Argentina v. Uruguay)*, Judgment of 20 April 2010, ICJ Reports 2010, 14, para. 187.

[8] ITLOS Seabed Disputes Chamber, *Responsibilities and Obligations of States with Respect to Activities in the Area*, Advisory Opinion of 1 February 2011, ITLOS Report 2011, 10, para. 110.

The opinion adds that due diligence obligations are obligations of conduct,[9] that they arise out of the necessity to control activities carried out by non-state actors,[10] and that they are distinct from 'direct' obligations of states.[11] All these findings are confirmed in the 2015 ITLOS opinion.[12]

This concept of due diligence adopts the 'obligation' approach, according to which due diligence identifies a certain type of—generally positive[13]—obligations. Rather than being the substantial content of a certain principle or norm,[14] due diligence is thus a feature of certain legal obligations, which distinguishes them from other types of legal obligations.[15] This approach is premised upon the distinction between primary and secondary rules, introduced by Special Rapporteur Roberto Ago in the work of the International Law Commission,[16] and later taken up and extensively discussed by Riccardo Pisillo Mazzeschi in his doctrinal work.[17] Due diligence is thus related to the content of primary obligations, rather than to the secondary rules on state responsibility, albeit, quite obviously, identifying the content of a primary rule will help determine whether a certain conduct has actually breached the rule.[18]

It is implicit in the two opinions that this categorisation is not restricted to a specific field of international law, but is capable of being applied to any activity which requires the state to ensure that a certain result is reached by other actors. The 2011 advisory opinion, in fact, relates to all duties provided under the UNCLOS,[19] which refer both to environmental protection and the protection of human life.

[9] Ibid., para. 110.

[10] Ibid., para 112.

[11] Ibid., para 121.

[12] ITLOS, *Request for Advisory Opinion submitted by the Sub-Regional Fisheries Commission*, Advisory Opinion of 2 April 2015, ITLOS Reports 2015, para. 126–129.

[13] Riccardo Pisillo Mazzeschi, 'Le chemin étrange de la due diligence d'un concept mysterieux à un concept surevalué', in SFDI/Sarah Cassella (eds), *Le standard de due diligence et la responsabilité internationale* (Paris: Pedone 2018), 323–337.

[14] Reference to a substantive 'principle' of due diligence as expressed in the ICJ dictum in the *Corfu Channel* case seems to conflate the substantive content of the rule—which is the obligation of every state to prevent harm to others originating in its territory—with the nature of such obligation, which is a due diligence obligation and thus requiring the state to put in place its best efforts in order to achieve this objective, as perceptively argued by Pisillo Mazzeschi, 'Le chemin étrange de la due diligence' 2018 (n. 13), 334.

[15] Forlati, 'L'objet' 2018 (n. 6), 40. For other concepts see Timo Koivurova, 'Due Diligence', in Rüdiger Wolfrum (ed.), *Max Planck Encyclopaedia of International Law* (Oxford: OUP 2010).

[16] United Nations, Eighth Report on State Responsibility by Mr Roberto Ago, Special Rapporteur: the Internationally Wrongful Act of the State, Source of International Responsibility, A/CN.4/318 and Add.1 to 4, 24 January, 5 February, and 15 June 1979, in particular paras 121 and 145, where he refers to 'obligations of prevention'.

[17] Riccardo Pisillo Mazzeschi, *"Due diligence" e responsabilità internazionale degli stati* (Milan: Giuffrè 1989) and, more recently, Pisillo Mazzeschi, 'Le chemin étrange de la due diligence' 2018 (n. 13), 323–337.

[18] For a thorough discussion of the relationship between primary obligations of due diligence and state responsibility, see Alice Ollino, *Due Diligence Under International Law: Reappraising Its Scope, Functions and Limits* (Milan: Università degli Studi di Milano-Bicocca 2018).

[19] ITLOS Seabed Disputes Chamber, *Responsibilities and Obligations in the Area Opinion* (n. 8), para. 104.

Similarly, the 2015 opinion applies the concept to duties of the flag state vis-à-vis its fishing vessels, which include conservation of marine living resources and administrative, technical, and social matters.[20] Consequently, this concept applies in all those cases in which a treaty provision or rule of customary international law requires a state 'to ensure' a certain result or to reach a certain aim, be it the avoidance of a certain harm or the achievement of a certain result.[21] Furthermore, the notion of a 'due diligence' obligation seems an appropriate way to describe the standard of conduct required by states that are requested to 'take effective measures', or 'to give complete effect'.[22]

The fact that due diligence obligations are obligations of means implies that states may avoid responsibility—even in the face of actual damage occurring—if they are able to prove that they have done their utmost. This has led many authors to conclude that due diligence obligations are 'weaker' than obligations of result.[23] While this may be true in more than one case, the ability of a legal rule to achieve the desired objective depends not so much on its nature—obligation of result or due diligence obligation—but rather on its content. Compliance with vague or generic norms, whatever their nature, will always be more difficult to assess. A provision asking the state to criminalise dumping of radioactive waste at sea—reflecting an obligation of result—is not necessarily 'stronger' than a due diligence obligation to take all necessary measures to ensure that radioactive waste is not dumped at sea. In the former case, the state can acquit itself from responsibility by simply proving that it has adopted the relevant criminal legislation. In the latter case, producing this legislation would not be enough, and the state would also have to prove that it has taken all other measures it can to avoid dumping.

The UNCLOS and most law of the sea treaties do not expressly mention 'due diligence'. The identification of such obligations, therefore, requires an interpretation of their provisions. In many cases, this is relatively easy, as the provision itself refers to the need to *ensure* a certain objective, often complemented by a reference to the 'necessary', '(all) appropriate', or 'effective' measures.

This is the case, for example, for the general duty of the flag state to exercise its jurisdiction and control over ships flying its flag;[24] for the duty to prevent and contrast slavery;[25] for the duty to conserve the living resources of the exclusive

[20] ITLOS, *Request for Advisory Opinion* (n. 12), paras 116–117.

[21] Forlati, 'L'objet' 2018 (n. 6), 54.

[22] Some authors, e.g., Caracciolo, 'Due diligence' 2018 (n. 5), 170, seem to consider also that 'due regard' obligations are obligations of due diligence.

[23] See, for example, Timo Koivurova, 'What is the Principle of Due Diligence?', in Jarna Petman/Jan Klabbers (eds), *Nordic Cosmopolitanism: Essays in International Law for Martti Koskenniemi* (Leiden: Martinus Nijhoff Publishers 2003), 341–349, at 346.

[24] UNCLOS, art. 94: '3. Every State *shall take such measures* for ships flying its flag as are *necessary* to *ensure* safety at sea (...) 4. Such *measures* shall include those *necessary to ensure* (...)' (emphasis added). Caracciolo, 'Due diligence' 2018 (n. 5), 168–169, seems to have some doubts on the general nature of this obligation.

[25] UNCLOS, art. 99: 'Every State shall take *effective measures* to prevent and punish the transport of slaves' (emphasis added).

economic zone[26] and of the high seas;[27] for transit states' duties;[28] for the duties of states sponsoring activities in the international seabed area;[29] for duties relating to the protection of human life;[30] and for the duties of international organisations in the field of technology transfer.[31] In addition, most of the provisions of UNCLOS concerning protection of the marine environment are framed as due diligence obligations, from the general obligation to prevent and control pollution,[32] to rules concerning transboundary pollution,[33] rare or fragile ecosystems,[34] land-based pollution,[35] vessel source pollution,[36] and pollution from activities in the international seabed area.[37]

If one turns to other law of the sea treaties, one can also find due diligence obligations concerning, for example, the need to ensure the safety of navigation,[38] or decent working conditions on board ships.[39] These obligations are however supplemented by—often detailed—rules concerning the concrete measures that states must take and the content of these measures.

In other cases, it is harder to establish whether the obligation contained in a specific provision is a due diligence obligation or not. Contextual interpretation will prove necessary to assess the nature of the obligation. For example, Article 192

[26] UNCLOS, art. 61(2): 'The coastal State […] *shall ensure* through proper conservation and management measures that the maintenance of the living resources in the exclusive economic zone is not endangered by over-exploitation' (emphasis added).

[27] UNCLOS, art. 117: 'All States have the duty to take, or to cooperate with other States in taking, *such measures* for their respective nationals *as may be necessary* for the conservation of the living resources of the high seas' (emphasis added).

[28] UNCLOS, art. 130(1): 'Transit States shall take *all appropriate measures* to avoid delays or other difficulties of a technical nature in traffic in transit' (emphasis added).

[29] UNCLOS, art. 139(1): 'States Parties shall have the responsibility *to ensure* that activities in the Area […] shall be carried out in conformity with this Part' (emphasis added). Notably, the due diligence obligations apply to international organisations as well.

[30] UNCLOS, art. 146: 'With respect to activities in the Area, *necessary measures* shall be taken *to ensure* effective protection of human life' (emphasis added).

[31] UNCLOS, art. 278: 'The competent international organizations (…) shall *take all appropriate measures to ensure*, (…) the effective discharge of their functions and responsibilities' (emphasis added).

[32] UNCLOS, art. 194(1).

[33] UNCLOS, art. 194(2).

[34] UNCLOS, art. 194(5).

[35] UNCLOS, art. 207(2).

[36] UNCLOS, art. 211.

[37] UNCLOS, art. 145: 'Necessary measures shall be taken (…) *to ensure effective protection* for the marine environment from harmful effects which may arise from [activities in the Area]' (emphasis added). As the rest of this provision clarifies, the main duty rests with the International Seabed Authority.

[38] International Convention for the Safety of Life at Sea, 1 November 1974, 1184 UNTS 2, art. 1 (b): 'The Contracting Governments undertake to *promulgate* all laws, decrees, orders and regulations and to *take all other steps* which may be necessary to give the present Convention full and complete effect, *so as to ensure that*, from the point of view of safety of life, a ship is fit for the service for which it is intended' (emphasis added).

[39] Maritime Labour Convention, 23 February 2006, 2952 UNTS 2952, art. IV (5): 'Each Member shall *ensure*, within the limits of its jurisdiction, that the seafarers' employment and social rights (…) are fully implemented' (emphasis added).

of UNCLOS provides that 'States have the obligation to protect and preserve the marine environment' and nothing else. The text of the provision does not mention the need to ensure this objective, the means to be taken, or whether the obligation refers also to actions by private actors. However, the following provisions, that spell out in more detail the duties of states in this regard, are generally drafted as due diligence obligations. For example, they require states to 'take (...) all measures (...) necessary to prevent, reduce and control pollution',[40] to 'take all measures necessary to ensure that activities under their jurisdiction or control are so conducted as not to cause damage by pollution to other States',[41] to 'act so as not to transfer, directly or indirectly, damage or hazards from one area to another'.[42] Since these provisions concern some of the aspects of environmental protection, and given that they are 'only' due diligence provisions, it seems consistent to consider also Article 192 a due diligence provision, as also hinted by the ITLOS in its 2015 advisory opinion.[43]

2.2 The Content of Due Diligence Obligations

As the Seabed Disputes Chamber has noted, '[t]he content of "due diligence" obligations may not easily be described in precise terms'.[44] There are however some common elements that characterise this type of obligation and which have been discussed by the ITLOS and its Seabed Disputes Chamber: reasonableness, flexibility, and objectivity.

The Seabed Disputes Chamber affirmed that 'the "due diligence" obligation "to ensure" requires the sponsoring State to take measures within its legal system and that the measures must be "reasonably appropriate"'.[45] The assessment of reasonableness, however, is affected by the flexibility of due diligence obligations. Due diligence obligations are variable and their content may change over time, in light of new scientific or technological knowledge, but also in respect of the risks involved in the specific activity.[46] It is interesting to note that this applies not only to due diligence obligations relating to the protection of the marine environment, but to any type of due diligence obligations, for example those relating to the safety of vessels and structures used at sea.

Furthermore, flexibility is evidenced by the fact that there is not a predefined list of actions that would allow the state to comply with its due diligence obligation,

[40] UNCLOS, art. 194(1).
[41] UNCLOS, art. 194(2).
[42] UNCLOS, art. 195.
[43] ITLOS, *Request for Advisory Opinion* (n. 12), para. 120.
[44] ITLOS Seabed Disputes Chamber, *Responsibilities and Obligations in the Area Opinion* (n. 8), para. 117.
[45] Ibid., para. 120.
[46] Ibid., para. 117.

since the state is generally requested to adopt *all* 'necessary' or 'appropriate' measures. All the same, judges have identified a certain number of actions that are relevant in assessing compliance with a due diligence obligation: the adoption of laws and regulations;[47] the taking of administrative measures;[48] the exercise of a 'certain level of vigilance in their enforcement and the exercise of administrative control';[49] the enactment of enforcement measures, including 'boarding, inspection, arrest and judicial proceedings';[50] the proper marking of vessels;[51] the creation of monitoring mechanisms;[52] the investigation of any alleged violation and the duty to inform the affected state of the results;[53] and the provision for sanctions 'sufficient to deter violations and to deprive offenders of the benefits accruing from their' illegal activities.[54] From a substantial perspective, the Seabed Disputes Chamber underlined the link between due diligence obligations and the precautionary principle/approach,[55] as well as with the duty to conduct an environmental impact assessment.[56] Many of these actions have been identified by international tribunals in many other contexts, including human rights.[57]

Finally, the Seabed Disputes Chamber took a firm position on the objective or subjective character of due diligence obligations, by stating that no difference in treatment is admitted, unless it is provided by a specific norm.[58] The reasoning of the Seabed Disputes Chamber is particularly relevant, as it highlights a major issue in the application of due diligence obligations. As mentioned earlier, the use of due diligence obligations in law of the sea instruments principally aims at ensuring that states control private activities and the respect by private actors of international standards, without however establishing a strict, objective responsibility regime which would make states responsible for every violation committed by a private actor. Allocation of the duty to control private activities is affected through

47 Ibid., para. 119.
48 Ibid., para. 119; ITLOS, *Request for Advisory Opinion* (n. 12), para. 119.
49 ITLOS Seabed Disputes Chamber, *Responsibilities and Obligations in the Area Opinion* (n. 8), para. 115, citing: ICJ, *Pulp Mills* (n. 7), para. 197.
50 ITLOS, *Request for Advisory Opinion* (n. 12), paras 104–105.
51 Ibid., para. 137.
52 Ibid., para. 138.
53 Ibid., para. 139.
54 Ibid., para. 138.
55 Ibid., para. 131; since precaution is addressed extensively in other chapters of this book (see in particular Jorge E. Viñuales, 'Due Diligence in International Environmental Law', chapter 7 of this book, section 3.2.1, and Malgosia Fitzmaurice, 'Due Diligence in the Use of International Watercourses', chapter 8 of this book, section 4) it will not be further discussed here.
56 ITLOS Seabed Disputes Chamber, *Responsibilities and Obligations in the Area Opinion* (n. 8), paras 145 and 150; see also Permanent Court of Arbitration, *South China Sea Arbitration (Philippines v. China)*, Award of 12 July 2016, PCA Case No 2013-19, ICGJ 495, para. 988.
57 See Björnstjern Baade, 'Due Diligence and the Duty to Protect Human Rights', chapter 6 of this book.
58 ITLOS Seabed Disputes Chamber, *Responsibilities and Obligations in the Area Opinion* (n. 8), para. 158; a notable example is found in UNCLOS, art. 194(1), which expressly refers to the different 'capabilities' of states.

recourse to notions of jurisdiction and control.[59] In the past, jurisdiction actually reflected the close link between a state and a certain actor or vessel. In recent decades, however, it is often the case that activities formally under the jurisdiction and control of a state are carried out by private subjects more closely linked to another state. This is evident in the case of the use of flags of convenience: most vessels registered under the flags of developing states are in reality owned by companies based in developed states.[60] The strict application of the public/private divide, according to which the due diligence obligation would relate to the capacity of the state to ensure compliance with a certain standard, rather than with the capacity of the private actor to comply with that standard, has caused a lowering of protection in shipping which has benefitted private actors to the detriment of communitarian interests of an environmental or social nature.

Conscious of this situation, the Seabed Disputes Chamber explains that '[e]quality of treatment between developing and developed sponsoring States is consistent with the need to prevent commercial enterprises based in developed States from setting up companies in developing States, acquiring their nationality and obtaining their sponsorship in the hope of being subjected to less burdensome regulations and controls'.[61] This statement by the Seabed Disputes Chamber indicates that the Chamber, rather than considering the capacity of the state, prefers to consider the capacity of the non-state actor (private company or other entity) to adopt the best available techniques and comply with the more stringent environmental standards. This is also due to the fact that the fundamental principles included in Part XI of UNCLOS are for the benefit, not of any specific state, but of the international community as a whole.[62]

2.3 Breach and Responsibility

The Seabed Disputes Chamber also addressed the elements necessary for the identification of a breach of a 'due diligence' obligation. As a general rule, the responsibility of a state will be triggered once the private actor that should have been controlled by the state has breached its own duty. Additionally, it is also possible to argue that a state may be responsible for a breach of a due diligence obligation

[59] See, for example, UNCLOS, art. 94(1), which refers to the jurisdiction of the flag state over its vessels as the link for the existence of the due diligence obligation to ensure that the vessel complies with a certain number of rules.

[60] According to the data provided by United Nations Conference on Trade and Development, while the top five flag registries (Panama, Liberia, Marshall Islands, China, Hong Kong SAR, and Singapore) have a market share of 57.8%, the top five ship owners are Greece, Japan, China, Germany, and Singapore and have a market share of 49.5%; see http://unctad.org/en/pages/newsdetails.aspx?OriginalVersionID=1516 (accessed 25 March 2019).

[61] ITLOS Seabed Disputes Chamber, *Responsibilities and Obligations in the Area Opinion* (n. 8), para. 159.

[62] König, 'The Elaboration' 2018 (n. 5), 90.

to prevent a private actor carrying out certain conduct, even if the private actor does not actually perform that conduct. In other words, for the state to be responsible, it would be sufficient that it fails to adopt measures to prevent the negative consequences, without the need to prove that this omission has actually produced harmful consequences, damage in particular.[63] In this respect, due diligence obligations are different from obligations pertaining to prevention envisaged by Article 14(3) of the International Law Commission's Draft Articles on Responsibility of States for Internationally Wrongful Acts.[64] As a consequence, the number of actual violations of the underlying standard of conduct does not matter.[65]

3. Due Diligence Obligations and Other Types of Obligations

In discussing due diligence obligations, the Seabed Disputes Chamber distinguished them from 'direct' obligations of states, that is 'obligations with which they have to comply independently of their obligation to ensure a certain behaviour by' another subject.[66] This distinction points towards two separate issues. The first relates to the need to distinguish between due diligence obligations and other types of obligations. The second concerns the relationship between a due diligence obligation and other related obligations.

3.1 Drawing Distinctions

Once due diligence obligations have been described, it is easier to distinguish them from other types of obligations. In the first place, a distinction needs to be drawn between 'due diligence' obligations and more stringent obligations of result. It is generally accepted that due diligence obligations are not obligations of result—i.e., requiring a state to achieve a certain result—but rather obligations of conduct—i.e., requiring a state to enact a certain conduct, even if this conduct proves not to be sufficient to reach the ultimate aim of the legal regulation. The distinction is

[63] ITLOS Seabed Disputes Chamber, *Responsibilities and Obligations in the Area Opinion* (n. 8), para. 210, which does not require damage for responsibility to arise under general international law—as opposed to the requirement for damage envisaged in UNCLOS, art. 139 (described ibid., para. 176); ITLOS, *Request for Advisory Opinion* (n. 12), para. 146, according to which the responsibility of the flag state for the breach of a due diligence obligation does not depend on the actual conduct of the private actor that should have been regulated by the flag state's regulations; see also ICJ, *Certain Activities Carried Out by Nicaragua in the Border Area (Costa Rica v. Nicaragua)* and *Construction of a Road in Costa Rica along the San Juan River (Nicaragua v. Costa Rica)*, Judgment of 16 December 2015, Separate Opinion of Judge Donoghue, ICJ Reports 2015, 665, para. 9.

[64] James Crawford, *State Responsibility: The General Part* (Cambridge: CUP 2013), 227–228.

[65] ITLOS, *Request for Advisory Opinion* (n. 12), para. 150.

[66] ITLOS Seabed Disputes Chamber, *Responsibilities and Obligations in the Area Opinion* (n. 8), para. 121.

relevant for the purpose of establishing when the rule has been breached. Compare, for example, the duty of the coastal state to 'determine its capacity to harvest the living resources of the exclusive economic zone'[67] with its duty to 'ensure through proper conservation and management measures that the maintenance of the living resources in the exclusive economic zone is not endangered by over-exploitation'.[68] The former is an obligation of result: the coastal state that does not determine its harvesting capacity breaches the rule, no matter what other action it has taken. The second is a due diligence obligation: if the coastal state has done whatever it could to try to prevent overexploitation of its fish stocks, it will not incur into international responsibility, even if eventually the stock is overexploited.

The framing of the obligation in due diligence terms, as opposed to the terms of an obligation of result, reflects the public/private divide. Actions that are undertaken directly by the state are usually framed in terms of obligations of result,[69] while those that require the collaboration of non-state actors, e.g., masters or owners of vessels, are framed as due diligence obligations. In some cases, the UNCLOS itself seems to distinguish between the two cases, by way of two separate provisions. For example, Article 207(1) of UNCLOS provides that: 'States shall adopt laws and regulations to prevent, reduce and control pollution of the marine environment from land-based sources'; while Article 207(2) of UNCLOS provides that 'States shall take other measures as may be necessary to prevent, reduce and control such pollution'. The former is an obligation of result, because the adoption of laws and regulations depends entirely upon the state, namely its legislative power; if the state does not adopt laws, it will incur into international responsibility. The latter is a due diligence obligation, because it involves exercising control over the activities carried out (also) by private actors; therefore, a state may eventually not be held responsible for pollution caused by non-state actors, if it has taken all measures it could.

In this light, and in order not to dilute too much the duties provided for states by the UNCLOS, it seems reasonable to conclude that provisions that require the state to take specific enforcement measures, for example to 'provide for immediate investigation',[70] or to provide for adequately severe penalties,[71] are not due diligence obligations but are rather akin to obligations of result. The reason is that in this case the adoption of the enforcement action depends totally on the state (respectively, its enforcement/judiciary branch and its legislative branch). Therefore, the state cannot free itself from the obligation by invoking the impossibility to control actions committed by others. There may of course be circumstances in which the

[67] UNCLOS, art. 62(2).

[68] UNCLOS, art. 61(2).

[69] See, for example, the various obligations of notification (e.g., UNCLOS, arts 27(3), 73(4), 198, and 231) or of publicity (e.g. UNCLOS, arts 16(2), 21(3), 24(2), 42(3), 47(9), 60(3), and 75(2)).

[70] UNCLOS, art. 217(4).

[71] UNCLOS, art. 217(8).

state is de facto prevented from acting, for example because the building hosting the parliament has collapsed. These instances, however, are already covered by the law on state responsibility, namely circumstances precluding wrongfulness. Accordingly, the conduct of the state will not be in breach of its obligations, not because the state has done everything it could, but because a circumstance precluding wrongfulness, for example force majeure or a fortuitous event, operates.

The second case in which it is necessary to identify due diligence obligations as opposed to other obligations relates to those provisions that seem to contain duties that do not reach the threshold for a due diligence obligation. A provision that merely asks states to try and do something would not appear to be a due diligence obligation. For example, Article 255 of UNCLOS, which provides that 'States shall endeavour to adopt reasonable rules, regulations and procedures to promote and facilitate marine scientific research',[72] cannot be considered as providing a due diligence obligation. In fact this provision does not require the state to do everything it can to achieve the stated aim of promoting and facilitating marine scientific research, but only to 'try and do something'. Consequently, even a weak, half-hearted endeavour might be considered to fulfil its requirements.[73]

In conclusion, due diligence obligations could be considered as located half-way in the sliding scales of behaviour requested by a state to comply with a legal obligation. On one end, there are obligations of result: states must achieve a certain result, otherwise they will breach their obligation. On the other end, there are obligations of conduct which do not reach the level of due diligence: States are just required to try and do something, and any effort will suffice to comply with the obligation.[74] Half-way, there are obligations of due diligence: they do not ask a state to achieve, but to do all it can in order to try and achieve a certain result. In other words, it is only when a legal rule asks the state to put in place, not any effort, but the best possible efforts that we can speak of an obligation of due diligence.

3.2 Establishing Relationships

In distinguishing between obligations, the Seabed Disputes Chamber noted that, while direct obligations of states are separate from due diligence obligations and may generate international responsibility by their own,[75] they are at the same time 'a relevant factor in meeting' due diligence obligations.[76] This statement introduces a

[72] Emphasis added.

[73] This raises the issue of the relationship between due diligence obligations and obligations to negotiate (or other similar obligations).

[74] The legal requirement to do something distinguishes these rules from soft law.

[75] ITLOS Seabed Disputes Chamber, *Responsibilities and Obligations in the Area Opinion* (n. 8), para. 121.

[76] Ibid., para. 123.

significant issue which is not always fully addressed by commentators,[77] namely the relationship between due diligence obligations and other—related—obligations.

One could imagine that, in their 'purest' form, due diligence obligations are broad and open-ended, leaving the choice of means to states as to how to try and reach their purpose. However, intense normative activity during the last decades has significantly reduced, if not eliminated, the number of generic, stand-alone, due diligence obligations. In the law of the sea, we often find provisions that guide states in their exercise of due diligence, by identifying concrete measures that states may or must use (so-called proceduralisation). These rules can be included in the same legal instrument or in a different instrument. For example, while Article 139(1) of UNCLOS contains a broad due diligence obligation that would seem to admit of any means for its fulfilment, Article 4(4) Annex III of UNCLOS expressly obliges a state to adopt 'laws and regulations' and to take 'administrative measures' within its 'legal system'.[78] Similarly, while Article 94(1) of UNCLOS generally provides that '[e]very State shall effectively exercise its jurisdiction and control in administrative, technical and social matters over ships flying its flag', the following paragraphs of this article refer to a wide range of specific measures, which concern both substantial aspects (for example, the master and officers must possess adequate qualifications in 'seamanship, navigation, communications and marine engineering') and procedural aspects (for example, the maintenance of a register of ships). Further detailed obligations are usually included in specialised treaties that deal with issues such as the safety of navigation,[79] pollution of the marine environment by ships[80] or through dumping,[81] the training of masters and crews,[82] and the labour conditions on board vessels.[83]

As Article 94 UNCLOS exemplifies, a general duty of due diligence may be further specified through a number of concrete steps that states may or must take. Usually, these steps are framed as autonomous, yet related, legal obligations.[84] The relationship may be formally established, for example through specific or general references, or indirectly by means of a reference to 'generally accepted international rules and standards'.[85] These further provisions serve a dual purpose. On one hand,

[77] See however Forlati, 'L'objet' 2018 (n. 6), 46–47.

[78] On the relationship between UNCLOS, art. 139 and UNCLOS, art. 4(4) Annex III see ITLOS Seabed Disputes Chamber, *Responsibilities and Obligations in the Area Opinion* (n. 8), paras 118–119.

[79] SOLAS, 1974 (n. 38).

[80] International Convention for the Prevention of Pollution from Ships, 2 November 1973, 1340 UNTS 184.

[81] Convention on the Prevention of Marine Pollution by Dumping of Wastes and Other Matter, 29 December 1972, 1046 UNTS 120.

[82] International Convention on Standards of Training, Certification and Watchkeeping for Seafarers, 7 July 1978, 1361 UNTS 2 (STCW).

[83] MLC, 2006 (n. 39).

[84] However, since in the law of the sea there are already numerous hard law instruments, the analysis in this chapter will not engage with soft law ones—although they also do exist in the law of the sea.

[85] Catherine Redgwell, 'Mind the Gap in the GAIRS: the Role of Other Instruments in LOSC Regime Implementation in the Offshore Energy Sector', *International Journal of Marine and Coastal Law* 29 (2014), 600–621.

they constitute useful guidance for states which do not know how to comply with their general obligations. On the other hand, they prevent blatant non-compliance based on an alleged impossibility to take concrete measures. They are therefore useful in ensuring compliance with the general duty by 'unable' or 'unwilling' states. Furthermore, and since they are formally distinct obligations, a state might incur in responsibility simply for having ignored one of the other duties.

In a broader, systemic, perspective, detailed obligations contained in specific (for example law of the sea) treaties may be useful in substantiating the due diligence duties of states also in other fields (for example human rights law).[86] While human rights treaties only provide general positive duties, often identifying the right to be protected but not the exact steps that must be undertaken, maritime safety and security treaties contain specific guidance to states. The provisions of these treaties are in fact often so detailed that they leave little room for further action by states. When the guidance is particularly detailed, both in stating the aim to be achieved and in detailing the steps that must be followed, it is possible to argue that a state that applies the requirements set down in those provisions in practice complies with its due diligence obligations under the law of the sea, but potentially also human rights and labour law.

Let us consider, for example, the need to ensure that crew members have adequate time to rest. The UNCLOS only hints at this right when it refers to the duty of the flag state to take measures concerning, inter alia, 'labour conditions'.[87] An express recognition of the right to rest is found in Article 7 lit. d) of the International Covenant on Economic, Social and Cultural Rights (ICESCR),[88] which identifies the right ('the right to work'), as well as a specific supplementary right, the right to rest. The same right is recognised in the Maritime Labour Convention (MLC), which extensively regulates hours of work and hours of rest in Regulation 2.3. Clearly, the Provisions of the MLC are much more detailed, in identifying exactly the number of hours of work and rest, the maximum periods of uninterrupted work that the seafarer may be requested to carry out, as well as the exceptions, for example, if work is required for the immediate safety of the ship, persons on board or cargo, or for the purpose of providing assistance to other ships or persons in distress at sea.[89] The only margin of discretion left to the state consists in determining the exact number of hours of work, or hours of rest, keeping within the parameters identified in the MLC. As such, the MLC provisions leave very little for the state to determine. It follows that the state that complies with the requirement

[86] For a full discussion see Irini Papanicolopulu, *International Law and the Protection of People at Sea* (Oxford: OUP 2018).

[87] UNCLOS, art. 94 (3)(b).

[88] International Covenant on Economic, Social and Cultural Rights, 16 December 1966, 993 UNTS 3.

[89] The respective lengths of these provisions illustrate the different details: while ICESCR, art. 7(d) consists of three lines, MLC, reg. 2.3 consists of forty-two lines.

of Regulation 2.3 MLC may reasonably be considered in compliance with its due diligence obligations both under UNCLOS and under ICESCR.

Similar considerations may be advanced with respect to the right to a safe working environment. According to Article 7 lit. b) ICESCR, favourable conditions of work must include safe and healthy working conditions. The entire International Convention for the Safety of Life on Sea (SOLAS), together with other maritime safety treaties, such as the Convention on the International Regulations for Preventing Collisions at Sea,[90] and the International Convention on Standards of Training, Certification and Watchkeeping for Seafarers,[91] could be considered as a practical application of this duty. In fact, SOLAS regulates how ships must be built up to the exact dimensions, but also how they must be equipped and conducted, in order to ensure that they are safe. Given that the ship is the working space for seafarers, a ship which is safe according to SOLAS requirements could also be considered to comply with the requirements of Article 7 lit. b) of the ICESCR.

4. Conclusion

In concluding this overview of due diligence in the law of the sea, some general comments are warranted. First, notwithstanding the absence of norms that expressly mention this phrase, there is abundance of due diligence rules in the law of the sea. Actually, most of the fundamental rules of this branch of international law—and certainly the ones that aim at protecting fundamental interests of the international community, such as the safety of navigation, protection of the marine environment, and, more recently, living and working conditions—are due diligence obligations, and have been so for quite a long time.

Second, the abundance of due diligence obligations in the law of the sea, it is argued, derives directly from the aim of this branch of international law: to control maritime activities, most of which are carried out by non-state actors and take place in areas which are not under the sovereignty of any state. States may—and often will—encounter problems in ensuring that every private actor under their jurisdiction complies with all its obligations all the time and everywhere. The reasons are twofold: first, practical considerations, such as the vastness of marine spaces, the scarcity of adequate means, and the remoteness of the vessel from a state's territory; second, the fact that often private actors are not directly bound by international norms. At the same time, not to hold states accountable at all would produce those situations of gross violations of fundamental norms that have

[90] Convention on the International Regulations for Preventing Collisions at Sea, 20 October 1972, 1050 UNTS 16.

[91] STCW (n. 82).

characterised maritime operations in the past (and which have not been entirely eliminated even today).[92]

Consequently, this is an ideal field for the development of legal rules that provide 'obligations in respect of which, while it is not considered reasonable to make a State liable for each and every violation committed by persons under its jurisdiction, it is equally not considered satisfactory to rely on mere application of the principle that the conduct of private persons or entities is not attributable to the State under international law'.[93] States thus act both as transposers of international law at the domestic level,[94] and as controllers of the activities carried out by non-state actors.

Conversely, due diligence obligations have also been seen as allowing states to escape from stringent duties and permitting for more relaxed standards. This may be true also in the law of the sea; however, it is here argued, this is not necessarily a bad thing but depends on the context and the situation existing before the due diligence obligation is elaborated. If strict standards already exist, and if new obligations are couched in due diligence terms, then this is surely a step back in protection. If, on the opposite, due diligence rules fill gaps in legal regulation—as was the case, for example, for control by the flag state over vessels flying its flag—then these obligations are a significant step forward in pursuing a more stringent protection of commonly shared interests.

Third, in the law of the sea, generic due diligence obligations are often accompanied by detailed provisions on measures to be taken, in the same or other instruments. As a consequence, states are not allowed much leeway in choosing the means to comply with them. General obligations thus set out the objective to be reached, while more detailed rules inform states as to the measures to adopt in order to reach them. While compliance with the detailed obligations may not always ensure compliance with the general one, in many cases it will.

Fourth, this set of interlinked provisions is usually the product of a long process of stratification. The liquid nature of the marine space and the international dimension of most maritime activities have accustomed states to try and adopt uniform legislation. The long history of many international instruments, such as the SOLAS, has permitted for general obligations to be refined over a period of many decades through a trial-and-error process. At its best, the law of the sea provides a good example of what due diligence obligations may achieve: a well-developed set of general principles, rules, and standards, which interact in order to provide an

92 Papanicolopulu, *International Law* 2018 (n. 86), chapter 1.

93 ITLOS Seabed Disputes Chamber, *Responsibilities and Obligations in the Area Opinion* (n. 8), para. 112; this understanding of the origin of due diligence obligations in the law of the sea is shared by law-of-the-sea scholars, see König, 'The Elaboration' 2018 (n. 5), 95; Caracciolo, 'Due diligence' 2018 (n. 5), 165.

94 König, 'The Elaboration' 2018 (n. 5), 86.

ever more stringent regulation of maritime activities and the progressive achievement of communitarian aims.

This process is far from being completed and there are certainly fields of the law of the sea where the main obligations are still quite generic, and states still need to adopt the detailed set of rules that will ensure that adequate measures are taken. Nonetheless, it is important to note that the general principles—'due diligence'—detailed regulation process is today deeply entrenched in the law of the sea and is the one to which actors in this field turn to whenever they need to address a new concern.

Drawing lessons from the use of this type of obligations in the law of the sea, it is possible to conclude that due diligence obligations, by ensuring that states exercise control without the excessive burden of objective responsibility, are a good compromise and one that practically advances the aims of the international community. This conclusion, however, is premised on the need to see due diligence, not as the end of legal regulation, but as an intermediate phase which will then be developed through the adoption of more and more detailed rules and procedures,[95] to be tested and amended as is necessary in the light of new challenges, new knowledge or new technologies.

[95] Forlati, 'L'objet' 2018 (n. 6), 56–57.

10

Due Diligence in International Climate Change Law

*Lavanya Rajamani**

1. Introduction

Climate change, characterised as the 'defining issue of our age',[1] is a complex, polycentric, and seemingly intractable policy challenge.[2] The international community has been grappling with this challenge since the late 1980s. During this time parties have negotiated three instruments—the 1992 Framework Convention on Climate Change (FCCC),[3] the 1997 Kyoto Protocol,[4] and the 2015 Paris Agreement[5]—countless decisions of parties, and several political agreements. They have also engaged in considerable innovation and experimentation in response to evolving geo-political imperatives, increasing scientific certainty, and gathering popular and political salience.

The 1992 FCCC lays out a broad framework, and guiding principles to regulate climate change; the 1997 Kyoto Protocol establishes binding substantive obligations of result (Greenhouse Gas (GHG) mitigation targets and timetables for developed countries); and the 2015 Paris Agreement lays down procedural obligations, and obligations of conduct, in relation to GHG mitigation and transparency for all parties. The evolution of the climate change regime from the 1997 Kyoto Protocol to the 2015 Paris Agreement charts a course from narrow coverage (of

* I am grateful to the editors of this book for their helpful feedback, to Jutta Brunnée for her incisive comments that have fundamentally shaped the contours of this chapter, and to Bhuvanyaa Vijay for her excellent research assistance.

[1] United Nations Secretary General Ban Ki-moon, 'Opening Remarks at 2014 Climate Summit', 23 September 2014, available at: https://www.un.org/sg/en/content/sg/speeches/2014-09-23/opening-remarks-2014-climate-summit (accessed 18 June 2019).

[2] See generally Daniel Bodansky/Jutta Brunnée/Lavanya Rajamani, *International Climate Change Law* (Oxford: OUP 2017), 1–34.

[3] United Nations Framework Convention on Climate Change (FCCC), 9 May 1992, 1771 UNTS 107.

[4] Kyoto Protocol to the United Nations Framework Convention on Climate Change, 11 December 1997, 2303 UNTS 162.

[5] United Nations, FCCC, Decision 1/CP.21: Adoption of the Paris Agreement in the Report of the Conference of the Parties on its twenty-first session, held in Paris from 30 November to 13 December 2015, 29 January 2016, FCCC/CP/2015/10/Add.1, Annex.

Lavanya Rajamani, *Due Diligence in International Climate Change Law* In: *Due Diligence in the International Legal Order.* Edited by: Heike Krieger, Anne Peters, and Leonhard Kreuzer, Oxford University Press (2020). © The Several Contributors.
DOI: 10.1093/oso/9780198869900.003.0010.

a limited number of developed countries) and deep (stringent) commitments to broad (universal) coverage and shallow commitments.

As the regime has evolved, parties have embraced, with ever greater conviction, procedural obligations, and obligations of conduct, thus privileging greater flexibility and autonomy for all parties and permitting increased dynamism in the regime. The emphasis on procedural obligations, and obligations of conduct, and the expanding terrain of flexibility and autonomy for states, has created greater scope for 'due diligence' to play a role in international climate change law. Obligations of conduct and 'due diligence' are closely linked,[6] in that due diligence—characterised as an 'obligation to deploy adequate means, to exercise best possible efforts, to do the utmost, to obtain this result'[7] provides the standard of conduct for such obligations. Due diligence potentially has differing normative quality and functions depending on the context.[8] In the context of international climate change law, due diligence depending on the specific treaty provision from which it emerges could be a normative expectation,[9] an obligation,[10] or a standard. In so far as these treaty provisions and the rules developed thereunder provide specific benchmarks to guide the normative expectation or obligation of due diligence from parties, they contribute to creating a standard for due diligence in the climate change regime. Thus, for instance, the 2018 Paris Rulebook[11] elaborates the Paris Agreement's procedural obligations and obligations of conduct, from which the normative expectation of due diligence emerges, and in so doing contributes towards a due diligence standard for states.

The turn towards procedural obligations (and away from substantive obligations) and towards obligations of conduct (and away from obligations of result) in the climate change regime places considerable demands on due diligence to deliver on the ambition and goals of the climate change regime. The extent to which it will do so depends, in part, on the extent to which a rigorous standard for due diligence is progressively developed, internalised, and implemented. The Paris Rulebook took a first step in this direction, but there is considerable discretion and constructive ambiguity, as we will see, in these rules, which leaves room for further concretisation of the due diligence standard in the climate change regime.

6 ITLOS Seabed Disputes Chamber, *Responsibilities and Obligations of States Sponsoring Persons and Entities with Respect to Activities in the Area*, Advisory Opinion of 1 February 2011, ITLOS Reports 2011, 10, para. 111; drawing on ICJ, *Pulp Mills on the River Uruguay Case (Argentina v. Uruguay)*, Judgment of 20 April 2010, ICJ Reports 2010, 14, para. 187.

7 Ibid., ITLOS Seabed Disputes Chamber, para. 110.

8 Anne Peters/Heike Krieger/Leonard Kreuzer, 'Due Diligence in the International Legal Order: Dissecting the Leitmotif of Current Accountability Debates', chapter 1 of this book, section 4.

9 See, e.g., Paris Agreement, 2015 (n. 5), art. 4.2.

10 See, e.g., Kyoto Protocol, 1997 (n. 4), art. 3.2.

11 The full set of decisions agreed to in Katowice is available at: https://unfccc.int/process-and-meetings/the-paris-agreement/paris-agreement-work-programme/katowice-climate-package (accessed 18 June 2019).

There are numerous primary rules in international climate change law. These include both substantive and procedural obligations, and obligations of conduct that engage due diligence ('best efforts') in delivering results, and obligations of result that require delivery of results. This chapter first identifies the central substantive and procedural obligations, and obligations of conduct and result, in international climate change law. These obligations provide the normative framework for the exercise of due diligence by states in addressing climate change. This chapter next addresses the nature and extent—the standard—of due diligence required of states in international climate change law. There are numerous factors influencing the nature and extent of due diligence required of states in international climate change law. These include: the objective, purpose, and goals of the climate change regime; the discretion permitted to parties in the climate change regime; differentiation in the climate change regime; the nature and degree of harm that would be suffered in the absence of due diligence; and, good faith. Each of these will be explored in turn. This chapter concludes with reflections on the promise and perils of relying on due diligence to deliver on the ambition of the climate change regime.

A few caveats. This chapter only explores key obligations of conduct, and due diligence, in relation to GHG mitigation commitments, rather than in relation to adaptation and the provision of support, to which due diligence requirements could also apply. And, finally, this chapter explores specific elements of due diligence captured in international climate change law, while assuming that elements arising in general international law and international environmental law, apply in tandem, but are covered in other chapters.

2. The Normative Framework for Due Diligence in International Climate Change Law

Due diligence acquires specific content in different areas of international regulation, including through multilateral environmental agreements in international environmental law.[12] The relevant agreements in the international climate change regime are the 1992 FCCC, 1997 Kyoto Protocol, and the 2015 Paris Agreement.

2.1 Framework Convention on Climate Change (FCCC) (1992)

The 1992 FCCC puts in place the framework for climate change regulation. It identifies principles central to addressing climate change, including the principle of common but differentiated responsibilities, and establishes both substantive and

[12] International Law Association (ILA), Study Group on Due Diligence in International Law, Second Report, 12 July 2016.

procedural obligations[13] and obligations of conduct and of result,[14] some of which apply to all parties, and others to developed countries alone.

The FCCC Article 4.1 identifies substantive obligations for 'all Parties', as for instance to formulate and 'implement' national and regional programmes to mitigate climate change and facilitate adaptation to climate change. It also identifies several procedural obligations for all states. FCCC Article 4.1 requires 'all Parties' to develop and submit national inventories of their GHGs; communicate information related to implementation of their GHG mitigation and adaptation programmes; and take climate change considerations into account, to the extent feasible, in their relevant social, economic, and environmental policies. Further, FCCC Article 4.1 requires parties to 'cooperate' in relation to adaptation to the impacts of climate change; technology development, application, and transfer; conservation and enhancement of sinks of GHGs; scientific and technological research;[15] and education, training, and public awareness.[16] These substantive and procedural obligations apply to 'all Parties' but parties are allowed to take 'into account their common but differentiated responsibilities and their specific national and regional development priorities, objectives and circumstances' in fulfilling their obligations.[17]

FCCC Article 12, a key procedural obligation, requires 'each Party' to provide information on national inventories 'to the extent its capacities permit', and efforts to implement the Convention and achieve its objective. The phrase 'to the extent its capacities permit' introduces flexibility into the performance of these obligations. Moreover, this obligation is explicitly differentiated in its application in that the frequency of submissions differs for developed, developing, and least developed countries. The Conference of Parties has since adopted decisions containing detailed guidance on national communications from developed and developing countries, including on the extent of flexibilities permitted.[18]

[13] For a full and fascinating exposition on this under-theorised area see Jutta Brunnée, 'Procedure and Substance in International Environmental Law', *Recueil des Cours de l'Académie de Droit International de la Haye* 405 (2020), 77–240.

[14] For a clarificatory discussion on obligations of conduct and result see Pierre-Marie Dupuy, 'Reviewing the Difficulties of Codification: On Ago's Classification of Obligations of Means and Obligations of Result in Relation to State Responsibility', *European Journal of International Law* 10 (1999), 371–385, at 375.

[15] See also FCCC, 1992 (n. 3), art. 5.

[16] Ibid., art. 6.

[17] Ibid., art. 4.1 chapeau.

[18] See, e.g., United Nations, FCCC, Decision 4/CP.5: Guidelines for the preparation of national communications by Parties included in Annex I to the Convention, Part II: UNFCCC reporting guidelines on national communications, FCCC/CP/1999/6/Add.1, 2 February 2000, 8; United Nations, FCCC, The Marrakesh Accords, Decision 22/CP.7: Guidance for the preparation of the information required under Article 7 of the Kyoto Protocol, FCCC/CP/2001/13/Add.3, 21 January 2002, 14.

The 2010 Cancun Agreements enhanced the frequency[19] as well as review of these reports.[20]

These FCCC obligations, whether substantive and procedural, whether applicable uniformly to 'all Parties' or differently to different groups of parties, are obligations of result, in that, the obligation is to submit national inventories and provide information on implementation, not merely to 'exercise best possible efforts' to do so.

In addition to these FCCC obligations applicable to 'all Parties', the FCCC contains a substantive obligation, characterised as a 'quasi-target',[21] requiring each developed country, listed in Annex I, to take policies and measures on GHG mitigation 'with the aim of returning individually or jointly' to their 1990 levels of GHGs.[22] This substantive obligation to take policies and measures on GHG mitigation is matched with an obligation of conduct in relation to these policies and measures in that developed countries are required to 'aim' to return to their 1990 levels of GHG emissions, and thus are obliged to exercise best possible efforts to reach this level rather than obliged to achieve it.[23]

2.2 Kyoto Protocol (1997)

The Kyoto Protocol establishes substantive GHG mitigation obligations, collective and individual, for developed countries set to timetables,[24] backed by procedural obligations in relation to reporting and review,[25] and a compliance system.[26] These GHG mitigation obligations are internationally negotiated rather than nationally determined, and are thus prescriptive, but the Protocol provides flexibility to parties in how they meet their targets, in particular by permitting them to use market

[19] United Nations, FCCC, Decision 1/CP.16: The Cancun Agreements: Outcome of the work of the Ad Hoc Working Group on Long-term Cooperative Action under the Convention, FCCC/CP/2010/7/Add.1, 15 March 2011, paras 40 and 60 requiring biennial reports from developed countries and biennial update reports from developing countries, respectively.

[20] Ibid., para. 63 establishing international consultations and analysis of biennial reports from developing countries, and paras 44 and 46 establishing international assessment and review of GHG emissions and removals related to targets of developed countries.

[21] Daniel Bodansky, 'The United Nations Framework Convention on Climate Change: A Commentary', *Yale Journal of International Law* 18 (1993), 451–558.

[22] FCCC, 1992 (n. 3), art. 4.2(a), (b).

[23] See Christina Voigt, 'State Responsibility for Climate Change Damage', *Nordic Journal of International Law* 77 (2008), 1–22, at 6; see also, Benoit Mayer, 'Obligations of Conduct in the International Law on Climate Change: A Defence', *Review of European, Comparative and International Environmental Law* 27 (2018), 130–140, at 134.

[24] Kyoto Protocol, 1997 (n. 4), art. 3.

[25] Ibid., arts 5, 7, 8; elaborated through a series of decisions taken by the Conference of Parties, see United Nations, FCCC, The Marrakesh Accords, Decisions 2-24/CP.7, FCCC/CP/2001/13/Add.1-3, 21 January 2002.

[26] Kyoto Protocol, 1997 (n. 4), art. 18; United Nations, FCCC, The Marrakesh Accords, Decision 24/CP.7: Procedures and mechanisms relating to compliance under the Kyoto Protocol, FCCC/CP/2001/13/Add.3, 21 January 2002, 64.

mechanisms.[27] These obligations, substantive and procedural, are obligations of result in that parties are obliged to deliver, whether in relation to GHG mitigation or reporting obligations, rather than exercise best possible efforts to do so. In relation to GHG mitigation targets, this is underscored by the requirement placed on developed countries to make 'demonstrable progress' by 2005 in achieving their targets,[28] and in the consequences identified in the Marrakesh Accords for non-compliance with the established targets.[29]

2.3 Paris Agreement (2015)

The climate regime took a decisive turn towards procedural obligations in the 2015 Paris Agreement. This turn can be sourced to several political and design considerations. The Kyoto Protocol's GHG mitigation targets did not cover either developing countries that were excluded from mitigation commitments or the United States that had rejected the Kyoto Protocol in 2001. As such, the Kyoto Protocol's first commitment period targets covered just 24% of 2010 global GHG emissions,[30] and its second commitment period, which attracted even fewer countries, covers less than 12% of 2012 global GHG emissions.[31] Most developing countries, however, were reluctant to undertake substantive obligations of result, and most developed countries, in particular the US, were keen to ensure parity in the legal character of commitments across developed and developing countries. These developments were matched by a gathering momentum towards greater autonomy and flexibility for all countries. The choice before parties was to 'level up' GHG commitments for all countries to Kyoto-style substantive obligations of result or 'level down' commitments for all countries to the procedural obligations (to submit mitigation actions) and obligations of conduct (in achieving these self-selected mitigation actions) developing countries had under the Cancun Agreements. Given the momentum towards greater autonomy and flexibility for states, levelling down commitments to procedural obligations, and obligations of conduct, proved the more politically palatable option.

The central obligation relating to GHG mitigation in the Paris Agreement, contained in Article 4.2, is a procedural obligation applicable to all parties. Each party is to 'prepare, communicate and maintain' successive nationally determined contributions (NDC) that it intends to achieve. Parties are also obliged to 'pursue domestic mitigation measures, with the aim of achieving the objectives of such

[27] Kyoto Protocol, 1997 (n. 4), arts 6, 12, 17.

[28] Ibid., art. 3.2.

[29] FCCC, Marrakesh Accords, Decision 24/CP.7: Procedures/mechanisms relating to compliance under Kyoto Protocol, 2002 (n. 26), Annex, Section XV, para. 5.

[30] Igor Shishlov/Romain Morel/Valentin Bellassen, 'Compliance of the Parties to the Kyoto Protocol in the First Commitment Period', *Climate Policy* 16 (2016), 768–782.

[31] This includes the emissions share of Australia, Belarus, EU-28, Iceland, Kazakhstan, Norway, Switzerland, Ukraine in 2010, excluding LULUCF. See World Resources Institute (WRI), 'CAIT Climate Data Explorer', 2019, available at: https://cait.wri.org/ (accessed 18 June 2019).

contributions'. The obligation to communicate an NDC is a binding procedural obligation of result, in that parties are obliged ('shall') to submit such NDCs in the stipulated timeframe. The obligation to pursue domestic measures with the aim of achieving the objectives of the NDC is a binding substantive obligation in that parties are obliged ('shall') to pursue domestic measures. However parties are required only to 'aim' at achieving the objectives of their NDCs through their domestic measures, and not obliged to meet the objectives, targets, or goals identified in their NDCs. This is an obligation of conduct, an obligation to exercise best efforts,[32] and is subject to due diligence requirements.[33]

Article 4.2 is set against the backdrop of Article 3, a cross-cutting provision, that requires 'all Parties' 'to undertake and communicate ambitious efforts' and places an expectation on parties that their 'efforts' 'will represent a progression over time (…)'. These are both substantive ('undertake') and procedural ('communicate'), and obligations of conduct ('efforts'), leaving discretion to parties in relation to the nature of these 'efforts' and how these will represent a 'progression' over time. This too demands 'due diligence' from states. The expectation of 'progression' is complemented with an expectation that NDCs will reflect a party's 'highest possible ambition', their 'common but differentiated responsibilities in light of different national circumstances',[34] and 'leadership' from developed countries.[35]

These normative expectations albeit framed in predictive ('will') rather than mandatory ('shall') language, exercise considerable normative pull on parties, and perform multiple functions. In relation to the procedural obligation identified in Article 4.2 to 'prepare, communicate and maintain' NDCs, these expectations import substantive and qualitative elements into what on the face of it appears to be a purely procedural obligation. In framing and implementing their NDCs, parties must factor in these substantive expectations. In relation to the obligation of conduct identified in Article 4.2 to pursue domestic measures with the aim of meeting the objectives of the NDCs, these expectations provide regime-specific markers for due diligence.[36] The domestic measures parties undertake in order to meet the objectives of their NDCs are also expected to factor in these expectations, and the extent to which they do so will determine the extent to which they have demonstrated due diligence.

It is worth noting, however, that these terms—'progression', 'highest possible ambition', and 'leadership'—are neither defined nor explained in the Paris Agreement

[32] See Lavanya Rajamani, 'Ambition and Differentiation in the 2015 Paris Agreement: Interpretative Possibilities and Underlying Politics', *International and Comparative Law Quarterly* 65 (2016), 493–514; Daniel Bodansky, 'The Legal Character of the Paris Agreement', *Review of European, Comparative and International Environmental Law* 25 (2016), 142–150; Ralph Bodle/Sebastian Oberthür, 'The Legal Form of the Paris Agreement and Nature of its Obligations', in Daniel Klein/María Pía Carazo/Meinhard Doelle/Jane Bulmer/Andrew Higham (eds), *The Paris Agreement on Climate Change: Analysis and Commentary* (Oxford: OUP 2017), 91–103.

[33] See also Mayer, 'Obligations of Conduct in the International Law of Climate Change' 2018 (n. 23), 130–140.

[34] Paris Agreement, 2015 (n. 5), art. 4.3.

[35] Ibid., art. 4.4.

[36] I am grateful to Jutta Brunnée for pointing this out to me.

or the 2018 Paris Rulebook, and thus lend themselves to a range of possible interpretations. The Paris Rules require parties to provide information when submitting their NDCs on how they have addressed the normative expectations of progression, highest possible ambition, common but differentiated responsibilities and leadership from developed countries.[37] In the process of negotiating the Katowice rules, a direct trade-off surfaced between the level of detail in the rules, and the autonomy that states enjoy. The more detailed the rules the less discretion states have, and vice versa. For instance, to the extent that parties are able to elaborate a benchmark against which 'progression' or 'highest possible ambition' can be measured, states have less autonomy to define these for themselves. Many parties therefore resisted detailed prescriptive rules to operationalise the Paris Agreement, preferring instead to leave the constructive ambiguity in the Paris Agreement's terms untouched, or to use discretionary language, in effect leaving operational choices and details to states. As a result, the Rules privilege self-identified benchmarks for 'progression', 'highest possible ambition', and 'leadership', and self-justified and self-serving narratives around the extent to which parties have complied with these. In general, the more detailed and prescriptive the rules, the more concrete the standard for due diligence. Paradoxically, however, the more concrete the standard for due diligence in the regime, the less pivotal the normative expectation of due diligence is in guiding state behaviour. If the rules are concrete, parties have little option but to comply with them, yet it is where there is discretion or leeway, that the expectation of due diligence can be most influential in disciplining it.

The multiple functions that particular provisions play, as discussed above, hints at another interesting dimension of the Paris Agreement—there is dynamic interplay between procedural obligations and substantive obligations, between obligations of result and obligations of conduct (with corresponding due diligence requirements). Parties are required to provide information with their NDCs to facilitate the clarity, transparency, and understanding of their NDCs,[38] to account for their NDCs,[39] and to provide information necessary to track progress made in implementing and achieving their NDCs.[40] These are obligations of result, not conduct, in that parties are obliged to provide the information required, and to account for their NDCs, not merely to exercise their best efforts to do so. However, these obligations complement the obligation of conduct parties have to adopt domestic measures aimed at meeting the objectives of their NDCs. This obligation of conduct parties have is a central defining element of the Paris Agreement. The

[37] United Nations, FCCC, Report of the Conference of the Parties serving as the meeting of the Parties to the Paris Agreement on the third part of its first session, held in Katowice from 2 to 15 December 2018, Decision 4/CMA.1: Further guidance in relation to the mitigation section of decision 1/CP.21, Advance version, FCCC/PA/CMA/2018/3/Add.1, 19 March 2019, 11, Annex I, para. 6.

[38] Paris Agreement, 2015 (n. 5), art. 4.8.

[39] Ibid., art. 4.13.

[40] Ibid., art. 13.7.

informational requirements placed on parties in relation to their NDCs improves the quality of the knowledge base that, in turn, will help the regime determine if parties are exercising their best efforts to meet the objectives of their NDCs.

The Paris Agreement, and the Paris Rulebook, relies on procedural obligations, obligations of conduct, normative expectations, and good faith to take the place of substantive obligations of result. The normative expectation of due diligence, by giving life to the obligations of conduct, shaping expectations that parties will deliver on their NDCs, and bolstering good faith, finds its place in the interstices of the normative architecture of international climate change law.

3. Factors that Influence the Nature and Extent of Due Diligence Required of States in International Climate Change Law

The nature and extent of due diligence required of states varies across different areas of international law, and in differing contexts.[41] As the International Tribunal for the Law of the Sea (ITLOS) noted in the *Seabed Mining Advisory Opinion*, '"due diligence" is a variable concept. It may change over time as measures considered sufficiently diligent at a certain moment may become not diligent enough in light, for instance, of new scientific or technological knowledge. It may also change in relation to the risks involved in the activity.'[42] In the field of international climate change law, the nature and extent of due diligence required from states is influenced and shaped by several factors, including the factors outlined in the following.

3.1 Objective, Purpose, and Goals of the Climate Change Regime

The objective, purpose, and goals of the climate change regime have been progressively crystallised from FCCC Article 2 to Paris Agreement Article 2. Article 2.1 Paris Agreement, identifies the goal of '[h]olding the increase in the global average temperature to well below 2°C above pre-industrial levels and pursuing efforts to limit the temperature increase to 1.5°C above pre-industrial levels, ...'. This long-term temperature goal builds on the FCCC objective (FCCC Article 2) of 'prevent[ing] dangerous anthropogenic interference with the climate system' by setting out, in terms of avoided temperature rise, the limits of what is 'dangerous'. It further builds on the FCCC objective by indicating, in terms of avoided

41 ILA, Study Group on Due Diligence, Second Report 2016 (n. 12).

42 ITLOS, *Responsibilities and Obligations in the Area Opinion* (n. 6), para. 117. For a discussion of the link between risk and due diligence in the context of the *Alabama Claims* case, see Jorge E. Viñuales, 'Due Diligence in International Environmental Law', chapter 7 of this book, section 2.1.

temperature, the level at which concentrations of GHGs in the atmosphere must be stabilised.[43] In order to achieve the long-term temperature goal, Article 4.1 requires parties to 'aim' to reach global peaking of GHG emissions as soon as possible, and to undertake 'rapid reductions' thereafter so as to achieve a balance between GHG emissions by sources and removals by sinks—popularly characterised as 'net zero'—in the second half of this century.

The purpose of the Paris Agreement, expressed in Article 2, is not limited to the long-term temperature goal. Article 2.1 lit. b) sets 'long term goals' for adaptation and resilience, and Article 2.1 lit. c) calls for financial flows to be reoriented, consistent with mitigation and adaptation objectives.

The FCCC, the Kyoto Protocol, and the Paris Agreement require parties to report on, and to varying degrees be accountable for, taking policies, measures, and actions in line with the objective, purpose, and goals of the regime. FCCC Article 12.1 lit. c), referred to earlier, requires parties to communicate information the party considers relevant to achieving the objective of the Convention. Kyoto Protocol Article 7 requires parties to incorporate in their national communications information demonstrating compliance with their GHG targets. Paris Agreement Article 14 establishes a global stock take to 'assess the collective progress towards achieving the purpose' of the Paris Agreement. These provisions seek to instil transparency and accountability for aligning national actions, policies, and commitments with the goals of the climate change regime. Such provisions, among other context-setting provisions,[44] suggest that the nature and extent of due diligence required of states must be guided by the objective, purpose, and goals of the climate change regime.

3.2 Discretion Permitted to Parties in the Climate Change Regime

The international climate change negotiations, politically divisive and deeply discordant as they are, have often reached agreement by establishing primary rules that permit parties considerable discretion in application. This is a cross-cutting feature of the climate change regime, and extends across substantive and procedural obligations, as well as obligations of conduct and result. For instance, the chapeau of FCCC Article 4.1 permits parties to 'tak[e] into account their common but differentiated responsibilities and their specific national and regional development priorities, objectives and circumstances (…)'. Other FCCC provisions qualify requirements placed on parties with terms such as 'to the extent feasible'[45]

[43] Jacob Werksman/Lavanya Rajamani, 'The Legal Character and Operational Relevance of the Paris Agreement's Temperature Goal', *Philosophical Transactions A* 376 (2018).

[44] See, e.g., Paris Agreement, 2015 (n. 5), preambular recital 3, arts 3, 4.1.

[45] FCCC, 1992 (n. 3), art. 4.1(f).

and 'to the extent its capacities permit'.[46] Paris Agreement provisions also contain such qualifications, in particular the term 'as appropriate'.[47] Discretion is also available to developed countries in the manner of performance of their commitments. For instance, in relation to their FCCC commitments on technology, a substantive obligation of conduct, developed countries are required to take 'all practicable steps', 'as appropriate'.[48] And, in relation to their Kyoto commitments to implement policies and measures, developed countries are permitted to choose these 'in accordance with its national circumstances'.[49]

More broadly, the climate change regime has evolved from a more to less prescriptive regime. The Kyoto targets were internationally negotiated and subject to obligations of result while the Paris Agreement's NDCs are self-selected, and subject to obligations of conduct in relation to their objectives. The Paris Agreement's normative expectations in relation to these self-selected contributions ('progression', 'highest possible ambition', and 'leadership') serve to provide regime-specific markers for the due diligence parties must exercise in relation to their contributions. Any assessment of the due diligence required of states thus must be guided not just by the discretion permitted to states more broadly in the climate change regime, but also the elaborate tapestry of normative expectations placed on states.[50]

3.3 Differentiation in the Climate Change Regime

The International Law Commission recognises that one of the factors in determining the standard of due diligence required of a state is its 'economic level' or capacity, but notes however that 'a State's economic level cannot be used to dispense the State from obligation under the present Articles'.[51] Differentiation in the climate change regime, however, is a many-headed beast, and is based not just on disparities in economic levels but also on differences in relation to responsibilities for causing climate harm. Arguably, the standard of due diligence in relation to specific obligations of conduct placed on a state in the international climate change regime is shaped by the distinctive content that differentiation has acquired in the climate change regime.

[46] Ibid., art. 12.1(a).
[47] See, e.g., Paris Agreement, 2015 (n. 5), arts 5.1, 7.9, 8.3.
[48] FCCC, 1992 (n. 3), art 4.5.
[49] Kyoto Protocol, 1997 (n. 4), art. 2.1(a).
[50] See Christina Voigt, 'The Paris Agreement: What Is the Standard of Conduct for Parties?', *Questions of International Law* 26 (2016), 17–28, in relation to 'highest possible ambition'.
[51] United Nations, Report of the International Law Commission (ILC) on the work of its fifty-third session, 23 April–1 June and 2 July–10 August 2001, Draft articles on Prevention of Transboundary Harm from Hazardous Activities, with commentaries, UN GAOR 56th Sess., Supp. No. 10, A/56/10, 2001, art. 3, para. 13.

The standard of due diligence in the climate change regime is shaped by the resources and capacities that states have. The climate regime has, since its inception, recognised the vast disparities between developed and developing countries, and differentiated between them with respect to implementation. This takes the form of differentiation in relation to stringency or timing of implementation, such as delayed compliance schedules,[52] permission to adopt subsequent base years,[53] delayed reporting schedules,[54] flexibility in implementation,[55] and softer approaches to non-compliance;[56] and, provisions that differentiate among countries in relation to assistance, i.e., commitments to provide, and eligibility to receive, financial[57] and technological assistance.[58] Such flexibilities and support for developing countries form a fundamental part of the normative architecture of the climate change regime, and thus shape the standard of due diligence required of states in relation to obligations of conduct in the climate regime.

The standard of due diligence in the climate change regime is also, arguably, shaped by the different contributions of states to climate harm. The principle of common but differentiated responsibilities and respective capabilities, the principled basis for differentiation in the climate change regime, differentiates between states both in relation to capacities ('respective capabilities') as well as to contributions to climate harm ('responsibilities').[59] If the differentiation authorised by this principle were solely due to differences in capacities, then the use of the term 'respective capabilities' would be superfluous.[60] Thus the climate regime contains differentiation between developed and developing countries in relation to the central obligations of the regime. The FCCC's GHG stabilisation targets,[61] and the Kyoto Protocol's GHG mitigation targets,[62] apply to developed countries alone. And although the Paris Agreement, by deft sleight of hand, introduced self-differentiation in relation to mitigation, and thus side-stepped the issue of prescriptive differentiation in central obligations, it recognised the importance of the Common but Differentiated Responsibilities and Respective Capabilities (CBDRRC) principle, and the 'leadership' role of developed countries.[63] Article 2.2, a cross-cutting provision, states that the Paris Agreement 'will be implemented to reflect equity and the

[52] See, e.g., Kyoto Protocol, 1997 (n. 4), art. 3.5.
[53] See, e.g., FCCC, 1992 (n. 3), art. 4.6.
[54] Ibid., art. 2.5.
[55] See, e.g., Paris Agreement, 2015 (n. 5), art. 13.2.
[56] See, e.g., FCCC, Marrakesh Accords, Decision 24/CP.7: Procedures/mechanisms relating to compliance under Kyoto Protocol, 21 January 2002 (n. 26).
[57] See, e.g., Paris Agreement, 2015 (n. 5), arts 9.1, 9.3; FCCC, 1992 (n. 3), art. 4.3.
[58] See, e.g., Paris Agreement, 2015 (n. 5), art. 10.6.
[59] This is disputed, however, see for a full discussion Lavanya Rajamani, 'Common but Differentiated Responsibilities', in Ludwig Krämer/Emanuela Orlando (eds), *Principles of Environmental Law: Elgar Encyclopedia of Environmental Law series* (Cheltenham: Edward Elgar, vol. VI, 2018), 291–302.
[60] This interpretation is bolstered by FCCC, 1992 (n. 3), recital 3.
[61] Ibid., arts 4.2(a), (b).
[62] Kyoto Protocol, 1997 (n. 4), art. 3.
[63] Paris Agreement, 2015 (n. 5), arts 4.4, 4.1.

principle of common but differentiated responsibilities and respective capabilities, in light of different national circumstances'. The qualification of the CBDRRC principle by a reference to 'national circumstances' introduced in the Paris Agreement, introduces a dynamic element to the interpretation of the principle—as national circumstances evolve, so too will the common but differentiated responsibilities of states.[64] However, this clause does not seek to shift the bases for differentiation in the climate change regime. Thus differentiation based on contributions to environmental harm, is also, arguably, part of the normative architecture of the climate change regime, and influences the standard of due diligence in relation to the obligations of conduct it contains.

It could be argued that while differences in contributions to climate harm may affect the responsibilities states have, it should not shape the standard of conduct that states have in fulfilling those responsibilities. Two responses may be offered to this intuitively attractive argument. First, this assumes that the conduct of a state in assuming an NDC is distinguishable from its conduct in fulfilling it. However, both the NDCs parties' take on, and the effort that parties will make to implement their NDCs will be shaped by their national circumstances, constraints, and priorities. These circumstances, include their contributions to climate harm. The extent to which states prioritise climate concerns over other pressing concerns such as poverty eradication, and the resources they will devote to implementation of NDCs, will be driven, even if not expressly, by their respective contributions to climate harm, and their perceptions of fairness. Second, the resources and capacities states have are directly linked to their GHG emissions.[65] The lines between assuming NDCs and fulfilling them, and between capacities and contributions to climate harm are drawn in the sand. Both capacities and contributions to climate harm thus shape the standard of due diligence required of states in relation to the obligations of conduct in the climate regime.

If the standard of due diligence, thus influenced, were to be applied to the obligation of conduct in Paris Agreement Article 4.2, the efforts of developing countries in meeting the objectives of their NDCs would be judged both in relation to their capacities as well as their relative contributions to climate harm. There are of course considerable operational challenges in doing so. There are many different ways of assessing contributions of parties to climate harm (cumulative, per capita etc.), and many different time frames that are plausibly argued as relevant (1850 onwards, 1990 onwards etc.). Each of these yields a different set of considerations in relation to burden sharing among states. For instance, cumulative emissions between 1850 and 2012 for Annex I countries is about 2.3 times that of non-Annex I countries,[66]

[64] See Rajamani, 'Ambition and Differentiation' 2016 (n. 32), 493–514.

[65] See Gail Cohen/João Tovar Jalles/Prakash Loungani/Ricardo Marto, 'The Long-Run Decoupling of Emissions and Output: Evidence from the Largest Emitters', *IMF Working Papers* 18/56, 13 March 2018.

[66] CO_2 emissions from Annex I countries from 1850 to 2014 are 957,536 $MtCO_2$ and from non-Annex I are 421,357 $MtCO_2$. For data for Cumulative Total CO_2 Emissions Excluding Land-Use Change and Forestry from 1850 to selected years to 2014, see WRI, 'CAIT Climate Data Explorer' 2019 (n. 31).

and per capita CO_2 emissions for most developing countries, for instance, India's at 1.8 tons, remains significantly below the US average of 15.7 tons, and even that of the EU's at 6.9 tons.[67] Yet, developing country emissions are now 60% of the total global CO_2 emissions.[68] China's economy alone has grown more than ten-fold since 1990[69] and its emissions have quadrupled. Arriving at a subjective standard of due diligence for a particular state will first require an assessment of which factors, time frames, and approaches are relevant, and next, how these translate into a tailor-made standard for that state. These operational difficulties, however, do not detract from the interpretative forces that help determine the standard of due diligence in the climate change regime.

The pervasive and cross-cutting differentiation in favour of developing countries in the climate regime is thus a critical factor in determining the nature and extent of due diligence required of parties in relation to obligations of conduct such as in Paris Agreement's crucial Article 4.2.[70] However, it is worth factoring in that there has been a gradual dilution of differentiation in favour of developing countries over time, and thus the demands of due diligence in specific contexts should be progressively interpreted as more demanding. For instance, in relation to transparency, the Katowice rules phase in uniform reporting requirements on developed and developing countries in 2024,[71] and although it allows each developing country to determine if it needs flexibility in the application of a particular provision, developing countries are required to clarify their capacity constraints, and provide time-frames for improvements.[72] These rules ensure that over time the need for differentiation is diluted, the number of countries that avail special treatment declines,[73] and there is a push over time towards higher standards for developing countries.

More broadly, given the cross-cutting and pervasive nature of differentiation in the climate change regime, it could be argued that the regime reflects a highly contextual standard for due diligence. Admittedly the general rule is that 'if the primary rule does not explicitly concede a lesser expectation of due diligence from

[67] Jos Olivier/Jeroen Peters, 'Trends in Global CO_2 and Total Greenhouse Gas Emissions: 2018 Report', The Hague: PBL Netherlands Environmental Assessment Agency, 2018, available at: https://www.pbl.nl/sites/default/files/cms/publicaties/pbl-2018-trends-in-global-co2-and-total-greenhouse-gas-emissons-2018-report_3125.pdf (accessed 18 June 2019).

[68] Total CO_2 emissions from Annex I countries for 2014 are 12,927 $MtCO_2$ and from non-Annex I are 20,288 $MtCO_2$. See WRI, 'CAIT Climate Data Explorer' 2019 (n. 31).

[69] 'GDP by Country, Statistics from the World Bank, 1960–2017: China' available at: https://knoema.com/mhrzolg/gdp-statistics-from-the-world-bank?country=China (accessed 17 June 2019).

[70] ILA, Study Group on Due Diligence, Second Report 2016 (n. 12).

[71] United Nations, FCCC, Report of the Conference of the Parties serving as the meeting of the Parties to the Paris Agreement on the third part of its first session, held in Katowice from 2 to 15 December 2018, Decision 18/CMA.1: Modalities, procedures and guidelines for the transparency framework for action and support referred to in Article 13 of the Paris Agreement, FCCC/PA/CMA/2018/3/Add.2, Advance version, 19 March 2019, 18, para. 3.

[72] Ibid., para. 6.

[73] Ibid., Annex, Section I. C, para. 6.

developing states, an objective international standard is to be preferred'.[74] However, in the case of the climate change regime, even in the absence of explicit differentiation in a particular rule, the presence of cross-cutting provisions that recognise the need for differentiation in the implementation of the entire agreement render even facially neutral provisions, subject to differentiation. There are two such cross-cutting provisions in the Paris Agreement: Article 2.2 on the CBDRRC principle, discussed above; and Article 4.1 that qualifies the net-zero goal for parties with the phrase, 'on the basis of equity and in the context of sustainable development and efforts to eradicate poverty'.

3.4 The Nature and Degree of Harm that Would Be Suffered in the Absence of Due Diligence

In determining the due diligence required of states, the nature and degree of harm that would be suffered in the absence of due diligence by states or the 'risks involved in the activity'[75] are relevant factors. The International Law Commission notes that the standard for due diligence should be 'appropriate and proportional to the degree of risk of the transboundary harm'.[76] This builds on the *Alabama Claims* decision that due diligence ought to be exercised in 'exact proportion to the risks'.[77] The 'risks involved in the activity' also engage the precautionary principle, which falls within the scope of due diligence.[78] The ITLOS *Seabed Mining Advisory Opinion*, indeed, found the precautionary approach to be 'an integral part of the general obligation of due diligence'.[79] Viñuales explains that the duty of due diligence in relation to environmental harm is broader than the prevention principle in that it is not limited to harm of a certain magnitude (material harm or significant harm), rather even harm falling below this threshold of magnitude is governed by the duty of due diligence.[80] In a similar vein, Brunnée argues that, 'due diligence provides a bridge between the duty to prevent environmental harm, and the proposition that, even in the absence of "full scientific certainty", states must take precautionary measures to "prevent environmental degradation"'.[81] These elements

[74] ILA, Study Group on Due Diligence, Second Report 2016 (n. 12), 19; ITLOS, *Responsibilities and Obligations in the Area Opinion* (n. 6), para. 230.
[75] ITLOS, *Responsibilities and Obligations in the Area Opinion* (n. 6), para. 117.
[76] ILC, Draft Articles, 2001 (n. 51), commentary to art. 3, para. 11.
[77] *Alabama Claims of the United States of America against Great Britain*, Award of 14 September 1872, UNRIAA 29, 124–134, 129. See discussion by Viñuales, 'International Environmental Law', chapter 7 of this book, section 2.1.
[78] See discussion on scope of due diligence being broader than the prevention principle, by Viñuales, 'International Environmental Law', chapter 7 of this book, section 3.2.1.
[79] ITLOS, *Responsibilities and Obligations in the Area Opinion* (n. 6), para. 131.
[80] Ibid.
[81] Jutta Brunnée, 'ESIL Reflection Procedure and Substance in International Environmental Law Confused at a Higher Level?', *European Society of International Law Reflections*, vol. 5, issue 6 (June 2016), available at: https://esil-sedi.eu/?p=1344 (accessed 18 June 2019).

of due diligence in general international law apply to the climate change regime's obligations of conduct. The risks of climate change far exceed the threshold of significant harm, and there is ever-increasing scientific certainty as to the existence of risk of significant harm.

The Intergovernmental Panel on Climate Change finds in its Fifth Assessment Report that 'the warming of the climate system is "unequivocal" ';[82] and in its Special Report on 1.5°C that 'human activities are estimated to have caused approximately 1.0°C of global warming above pre-industrial levels.'[83] The Intergovernmental Panel on Climate Change notes that 'many of the observed changes are unprecedented over decades to millennia'.[84] These changes 'have caused impacts on natural and human systems on all continents and across all oceans',[85] and, '[c]ontinued emission of [GHGs] will cause further warming and (...) increase[e] the likelihood of severe, pervasive and irreversible impacts'.[86] The Special Report on 1.5°C stresses that there are 'robust differences' in impacts between global warming of 1.5°C and 2°C.[87] The risks of 'irreversible' impacts is higher at higher levels of temperature increase.[88]

The enormous risk of potentially irreversible climate impacts at temperatures above 1.5°C suggests a correspondingly high standard of due diligence. But what role can a high standard of due diligence play in the context of the current wholly inadequate NDCs from parties?[89] The United Nations Environment Programme 2018 Emissions Gap Report finds that 'pathways reflecting current NDCs imply global warming of about 3°C by 2100, with warming continuing afterwards'.[90] And, that '[i]f the emissions gap is not closed by 2030, it is very plausible that the goal of a well-below 2°C temperature increase is also out of reach'.[91]

Admittedly, the duty of diligence, however demanding, does not amount to 'strict liability', and notwithstanding full exercise of due diligence, undesirable

[82] Intergovernmental Panel on Climate Change (IPCC), Synthesis Report of the IPCC Fifth Assessment Report (AR5), 'Climate Change 2014', 2014, available at: https://www.ipcc.ch/site/assets/uploads/2018/02/SYR_AR5_FINAL_full.pdf, 2, SPM 1.1 (accessed 18 June 2019).

[83] Intergovernmental Panel on Climate Change, 'Global Warming of 1.5°C', Summary for Policy Makers, 2018, available at: https://report.ipcc.ch/sr15/pdf/sr15_spm_final.pdf, 6 (accessed 18 June 2019).

[84] Intergovernmental Panel on Climate Change, Working Group I, 'Climate Change 2013: The Physical Science Basis', 2013, available at: http://www.climatechange2013.org/images/report/WG1AR5_SPM_FINAL.pdf, 4 (accessed 18 June 2019).

[85] IPCC, 2014 (n. 82), 6, para. SPM 1.3.

[86] Ibid., 8, para. SPM 2.

[87] IPCC, 2018 (n. 83), 9, para. B.1.

[88] Ibid., paras B.2.2, B.4.2.

[89] United Nations, FCCC, Synthesis report on the aggregate effect of INDCs, FCCC/CP/2016/2, 2 May 2016; United Nations, United Nations Environment Programme, Emissions Gap Report, 27 November 2018, available at: https://www.unenvironment.org/resources/emissions-gap-report-2018 (accessed 18 June 2019).

[90] UNEP, Emissions Gap Report 2018, 27 November 2018 (n. 89), Executive Summary, available at: https://wedocs.unep.org/bitstream/handle/20.500.11822/26879/EGR2018_ESEN.pdf?sequence=10, 4 (accessed 18 June 2019).

[91] Ibid.

consequences may ensue.[92] However, the risk of calamitous climate impacts implies a high standard of due diligence for parties in arriving at their NDCs and implementing them, further bolstering the normative expectation of progression and highest possible ambition placed on parties in relation to their NDCs. It is only this that will reflect fealty to the letter and the spirit of the Paris Agreement.

3.5 The Expectation of Good Faith

A final factor influencing the standard of due diligence required of states in the international climate change regime is the expectation of good faith. The International Law Association notes that '[a] State cannot be considered to have acted diligently when the State has acted in bad faith or has knowingly refused to take any measures whatsoever'.[93]

Good faith, implicit in all treaties, generates expectations in relation to performance of treaty obligations that permeate through the entire climate change regime.[94] So for instance, although NDCs under the Paris Agreement are not subject to obligations of result, there is a good faith expectation that parties, will, nevertheless, take all appropriate steps—given the objective of the Paris Agreement and the risks involved in runaway climate change—to the extent their resources and capacities permit, to achieve their self-selected contributions. This expectation is bolstered by the Katowice rules identifying the information necessary to track the progress made by parties in implementing and achieving their NDCs.[95]

4. Conclusion

Due diligence assumes particular significance in the context of the emerging climate regime that is built on procedural obligations, obligations of conduct, normative expectations, and good faith. This regime places considerable demands on the norms of due diligence to deliver on the ambition and goals of the climate change regime. While due diligence offers some promise in this regard, obligations of conduct, and the requirements of due diligence that these place on states, cannot be asked to perform a task that only stringent substantive obligations of result can.

The exercise of due diligence in relation to the obligations of conduct in the climate change regime, in conjunction with rigorous implementation of the full gamut

[92] See discussion by Viñuales, 'International Environmental Law', chapter 7 of this book, section 2.1.

[93] ILA, Study Group on Due Diligence, Second Report 2016 (n. 12).

[94] ILA, Committee on Legal Principles Relating to Climate Change, Declaration of Legal Principles relating to Climate Change, Resolution 2/2014, arts 8, 9.

[95] FCCC, Decision 18/CMA.1: Modalities/procedures/guidelines for transparency framework under Article 13 of the Paris Agreement, 19 March 2019 (n. 71), Annex, Section I. C.

of provisions of the climate change regime, does offer promise. The ambitious objective, purpose and goals of the climate regime, and the calamitous harm that will be suffered in the absence of due diligence demands a high standard of due diligence from states. Admittedly, the climate regime builds on self-determination—a central, defining and unifying feature of the Paris Agreement—and to varying degrees permits parties discretion, differentiation, and flexibility in their application. These could create a pull towards a standard of due diligence in relation to the fulfilment of their NDCs that is subjective, self-selected, and self-justified. However, there is progressive dilution of differentiation in the climate regime, and some forms of differentiation have the potential to assist parties in meeting their commitments. Much will depend on state practice that will emerge in the coming years, and the extent to which states engage in good faith interpretation and application of the standard for due diligence in international climate change law. To the extent that parties can be held (and/or hold themselves) to a high standard of due diligence in the discharge of their obligations of conduct under the climate regime, it may trigger an ever-increasing cycle of ambitious action, which could eventually meet the goals of the climate regime.

PART III

DUE DILIGENCE IN PEACE AND SECURITY LAW

11
Due Diligence in International Humanitarian Law

Marco Longobardo

1. Introduction

This chapter provides one of the first general assessments of the topic of due diligence in international humanitarian law,[1] with reference to the rules protecting potential or actual victims of armed conflicts and the rules on the conduct of hostilities. Accordingly, the chapter does not address due diligence in neutrality, in the law of arms control, or in international human rights law.[2] After some preliminary remarks on the identification of due diligence obligations, the chapter lists which rules of international humanitarian law require the application of due diligence, explores whether references to due diligence in international humanitarian law are consistent with the way in which due diligence is employed in other areas of international law, and whether the notion of diligence strengthens the implementation of international humanitarian law.

2. Due Diligence Obligations in International Humanitarian Law

2.1 Preliminary Remarks

The notion of due diligence is commonly employed in international law as a standard of care[3] that should be applied in order to assess the compliance of states

[1] See Gabriella Venturini, 'Les obligations de diligence dans le droit international humanitaire', in Société Française pour le Droit International (SFDI)/Sarah Cassella (eds), *Le standard de due diligence et la responsabilité internationale* (Paris: Pedone 2018), 135–144; Antal Berkes, 'The Standard of "Due Diligence" as a Result of Interchange between the Law of Armed Conflict and General International Law', *Journal of Conflict & Security Law* 23 (2018), 433–460.

[2] See Riccardo Pisillo Mazzeschi, 'Responsabilité de l'état pour violation des obligations positives relatives aux droits de l'homme', *Recueil des Cours de l'Académie de Droit International de la Haye* 333 (2008), 175–506.

[3] Robert Kolb, 'Reflections on Due Diligence and Cyberspace', *German Yearbook of International Law* 58 (2015), 113–128, at 115, 117.

Marco Longobardo, *Due Diligence in International Humanitarian Law* In: *Due Diligence in the International Legal Order*. Edited by: Heike Krieger, Anne Peters, and Leonhard Kreuzer, Oxford University Press (2020). © The Several Contributors. DOI: 10.1093/oso/9780198869900.003.0011.

with obligations of conduct.[4] These obligations require states to 'deploy adequate means, to do the utmost, to obtain [a certain] result'.[5] However, states may not be held responsible if, notwithstanding their diligent conduct, the result is not obtained.[6] Due diligence requires a judgment on what could and should be reasonably done under specific circumstances, and is usually linked to a state's relationship with the source of risk.[7] Accordingly, while 'the obligation of result is an obligation to "succeed", (…) the obligation of diligent conduct is an obligation to "make every effort" '.[8]

International humanitarian law embodies both obligations of conduct and obligations of result. Due diligence plays no role in relation to negative obligations since a state may implement them only when reaching the negative result.[9] Whereas some positive obligations are obligations of result,[10] other positive international humanitarian law obligations may require the application of due diligence, such as in the case of obligations to *protect* individuals.[11] In order to identify due diligence obligations pertaining to international humanitarian law, it is useful to refer to some textual elements that must be taken into account along with the context, object, and purpose of the relevant provisions.[12] For example, very likely due diligence applies when international humanitarian law provisions are phrased as 'duties of care', or when the performance of a certain conduct is required 'as far as possible', or when states undertake to do 'everything [that] is possible'.

2.2 The Duty to Ensure Respect for International Humanitarian Law and Related Obligations

The duty to ensure respect for international humanitarian law under Article 1 common to the 1949 Geneva Conventions (GCs) and Article 1(2) of the 1977 First Additional Protocol (API) requires an assessment in light of due diligence. Under

[4] Generally, see Anne Peters/Heike Krieger/Leonhard Kreuzer, 'Due Diligence in the International Legal Order: Dissecting the Leitmotif of Current Accountability Debates', chapter 1 of this book, section 1.

[5] ITLOS Seabed Disputes Chamber, *Responsibilities and Obligations of States Sponsoring Persons and Entities with Respect to Activities in the Area*, Advisory Opinion of 1 February 2011, ITLOS Reports 2011, 10, para. 110.

[6] See ICJ, *Application of the Convention on the Prevention and Punishment of the Crime of Genocide (Bosnia and Herzegovina v. Serbia and Montenegro)*, Judgment of 26 February 2007, ICJ Reports 2007, 43, para. 430.

[7] See Pasquale De Sena, 'La "due diligence" et le lien entre le sujet et le risque qu'il faut prévenir: quelques observations', in SFDI/Cassella 2018 (n. 1), 243–254.

[8] Riccardo Pisillo Mazzeschi, 'The Due Diligence Rule and the Nature of the International Responsibility of States', *German Yearbook of International Law* 35 (1992), 9–51, at 48.

[9] See ibid., 46.

[10] Ibid.; International Law Association (ILA), Study Group on Due Diligence in International Law, Second Report, 12 July 2016, 20.

[11] Pisillo Mazzeschi, 'Due Diligence Rule' 1992 (n. 8), 25–30, 34–36.

[12] See Vienna Convention on the Law of Treaties, 23 May 1969, 1155 UNTS 331, art. 31.

these provisions, states 'undertake to respect and to ensure respect for' international humanitarian law 'in all circumstances'. While the duty to 'respect' international humanitarian law is just a repetition of the formula *pacta sunt servanda*[13] for conduct attributable to the state,[14] the duty to 'ensure respect' covers conduct that is *not attributable to the state*, originally in relation to actions of individuals who were not members of the armed forces.[15] Although the conduct of an armed group fighting alongside a state but acting beyond its direct control is not attributable to that state,[16] a less intense link between the state and the armed group is relevant under international law since a state's overall control over the armed group is sufficient to satisfy the definition of an international armed conflict.[17] Under similar circumstances, in the absence of attribution, while the duty imposed on the state to respect international humanitarian law is not applicable, the state is under the duty to ensure respect for international humanitarian law with regard to the armed group's conduct.[18] However, the duty to ensure respect for international humanitarian law goes further: encompassing the duty to protect civilians from international humanitarian law violations committed by armed groups *without* an affiliation to the state,[19] and demanding a less stringent assessment of the state's diligence than in the case of armed groups affiliated with the state or under its overall control.[20] Additionally, the duty to ensure respect for international humanitarian law is applicable also to co-belligerents, as well as private businesses,[21] militaries, and security companies.[22]

[13] Ibid., art. 26.

[14] On the rules of attribution in international humanitarian law, see Marco Longobardo, 'Rapporti fra strumenti di codificazione: il Progetto di articoli sulla responsabilità degli Stati e le convenzioni di diritto internazionale umanitario', *Rivista di Diritto Internazionale* 101 (2018), 433–460.

[15] Marco Sassòli, 'State Responsibility for Violations of International Humanitarian Law', *International Review of the Red Cross* 84 (2002), 401–434, at 412.

[16] See ICJ, *Case Concerning Military and Paramilitary Activities in and against Nicaragua (Nicaragua v. USA)*, Judgment of 27 June 1986, ICJ Reports 1986, 14, para. 115; ICJ, *Bosnia Genocide* (n. 6), para. 400; United Nations, International Law Commission (ILC), Draft Articles on Responsibility of States for Internationally Wrongful Acts, with commentaries, YBILC 2001, vol. II (part II), commentary to art. 8, 47–48.

[17] See ICTY, *Prosecutor v. Tadić*, IT-94-1-A, Appeals Chamber, Judgment of 15 July 1999, para. 145.

[18] See ICJ, *Military and Paramilitary Activities* (n. 16), para. 220 (for a narrow application); Oona Hathaway/Emily Chertoff/Lara Domínguez/Zachary Manfredi/Peter Tzeng, 'Ensuring Responsibility: Common Article 1 and State Responsibility for Non-State Actors', *Texas Law Review* 95 (2017), 539–590.

[19] Dieter Fleck, 'International Accountability for Violations of the *Ius in Bello*: The Impact of the ICRC Study on Customary International Humanitarian Law', *Journal of Conflict & Security Law* 11 (2006), 179–199, at 187–188; ILA, Study Group on Due Diligence in International Law, First Report, 7 March 2014, 13–14.

[20] With reference to the protection of aliens, see Mixed Claims Commission (Italy–Venezuela), *Salvatore Sambiaggio (Italy v. Venezuela)*, RIAA 10 (1902), 499. However, in this case, the focus was not on international humanitarian law.

[21] Robert Kolb, 'Commentaires iconoclastes sur l'obligation de faire respecter le droit international humanitaire selon l'article 1 commun des Conventions de Genève de 1949', *Revue Belge de Droit International* 46 (2013), 513–520, at 515.

[22] Nigel D. White, 'Due Diligence Obligations of Conduct: Developing a Responsibility Regime for PMSCs', *Criminal Justice Ethics* 31 (2012), 233–261.

Common Article 1 of the GCs also has an external scope. For example, states have the duty to act diligently in order to ensure that other states respect international humanitarian law.[23] The duty to ensure respect is not a source of legality for wrongful acts adopted in response to international humanitarian law violations by non-directly injured states; rather, non-directly injured states may adopt countermeasures only on the basis of the secondary rules on the violations of *erga omnes* obligations, which include some international humanitarian law provisions.[24] However, common Article 1 of the GCs is a primary obligation,[25] and it only requires the adoption of inherently lawful but unfriendly measures against states that violate international humanitarian law.[26]

The assessment of due diligence in relation to the duty to ensure respect for international humanitarian law varies.[27] With regard to conduct occurring in the territory of the contracting state, this assessment must take into account the degree of control exercised by the state and the availability of preventive legislative measures and monitoring mechanisms, as in the case of positive international human rights law obligations.[28] With regard to conduct occurring outside a state's territorial boundaries, either by other states or armed groups, the state's commitment to take all measures to prevent international humanitarian law violations should be assessed with the notion of due diligence in light of the state's capacity to influence effectively the action of persons likely to commit, or already committing, international humanitarian law violations and therefore following the same rationale that was applied by the International Court of Justice (ICJ) with regard to the obligation to prevent genocide.[29]

Other autonomous due diligence obligations pertaining to international humanitarian law may be seen as specifications of the duty to ensure respect. First, the rules regarding the dissemination and training of international humanitarian law are regulated by due diligence, since they aim at reducing the risk that states will violate international humanitarian law. Indeed, states must issue instructions to their armed forces regarding compliance with international humanitarian law,[30]

[23] Luigi Condorelli/Laurence Boisson De Chazournes, 'Quelques remarques à propos de l'obligation des États de "respecter et faire respecter" le droit international humanitaire "en toutes circonstances"', in Christophe Swinarski (ed), *Études en l'honneur de Jean Pictet* (Geneva: ICRC 1984), 17–35; Jean-Marie Henckaerts, 'Article 1: Respect and Ensure Respect', in ICRC (ed.), *Updated Commentary on the First Geneva Convention* (Cambridge: CUP 2016), paras 35–67.

[24] Condorelli/Boisson De Chazournes, 'Quelques remarques' 1984 (n. 23), 29–30.

[25] Giorgio Gaja, 'The Protection of General Interests in the International Community', *Recueil des Cours de l'Académie de Droit International de la Haye* 364 (2012), 9–185, at 125.

[26] See also Marco Longobardo, 'The Contribution of International Humanitarian Law on the Development of the Law of International Responsibility Regarding Obligations *Erga Omnes* and *Erga Omnes Partes*', *Journal of Conflict & Security Law* 23 (2018), 383–404, at 392–393.

[27] See Sassòli, 'State Responsibility' 2002 (n. 15), 412; Henckaerts, 'Article 1' 2016 (n. 23), paras 33–35.

[28] See Pisillo Mazzeschi, 'Responsabilité' 2008 (n. 2).

[29] ICJ, *Bosnia Genocide* (n. 6), para. 430.

[30] See, e.g., art. 4 of the 1907 Fourth Hague Convention and Additional Protocol I (API), 8 June 1977, 1125 UNTS 3, art. 87(2).

include international humanitarian law in the 'programmes of military instruction',[31] and integrate international humanitarian law into military training.[32] These duties are worded as obligations of diligent conduct by the relevant conventions and, accordingly, they may be the source of international responsibility.[33]

Similarly, some of the duties connected to the punishment of war criminals under international humanitarian law[34] must be assessed through due diligence.[35] In particular, while the duty to criminalise war crimes is an obligation of result,[36] the duty to prosecute war crimes requires states to act in a diligent way to find and to put war criminals on trial. Although the choice of means for conducting the prosecution remains in the hands of the states parties,[37] the duty requiring the investigation to be *effective* is a duty of due diligence,[38] even in relation to the prosecution of war crimes.

2.3 The Conduct of Hostilities

The rules pertaining to the conduct of hostilities are a mix of obligations of result and obligations of diligent conduct. A number of these rules are described as prohibitions, such as the duty not to direct an attack against civilians, the civilian population, and civilian objects—which must not be made the object of any attack (principle of distinction).[39]

International humanitarian law acknowledges that even if civilians and civilian objects, under the principle of distinction, must not be directly targeted during the conduct of hostilities, they may nonetheless suffer harm indirectly as a consequence of an attack against military targets. While the principle of proportionality requires that the unintended harm against civilian objectives must not be excessive

[31] See Geneva Convention I (GCI), 12 August 1949, 75 UNTS 31, art. 47, and Second Protocol to the Hague Convention of 1954 for the Protection of Cultural Property in the Event of Armed Conflict, 26 March 1999, 2253 UNTS 172, art. 30.

[32] See API 1977 (n. 30), art. 6(1), and Protocol on Prohibitions or Restrictions on the Use of Mines, Booby-Traps and Other Devices, 3 March 1996, 2048 UNTS 93, art. 4(3).

[33] See Marco Longobardo, 'Training and Education of Armed Forces in the Age of High-Tech Hostilities', in Elena Carpanelli/Nicole Lazzerini (eds), *Use and Misuse of New Technologies: Contemporary Challenges in International and European Law* (The Hague: Springer 2019), 73–91, at 87–88.

[34] See, e.g., arts 49, 50, 129, 146, and 50, 51, 130, 146 respectively of the GCs, and API, 1977 (n. 30), art. 83.

[35] Sassòli, 'State Responsibility' 2002 (n. 15), 412; ILA, Study Group on Due Diligence, First Report 2014 (n. 19), 12.

[36] See with reference to the identical obligation under the 1984 UN Conventions against Torture, ICJ, *Obligation to Prosecute or Extradite*, Judgment of 20 July 2012, ICJ Reports 2012, 422, para. 77.

[37] Ibid., para. 86.

[38] ILA, Study Group on Due Diligence, Second Report 2016 (n. 10), 20.

[39] See API, 1977 (n. 30), arts 48, 51(2), 52; if a state does *direct* the attack against civilians, then international law is violated since the principle of distinction is an obligation of result; see ICTY, *Prosecutor v. Kordić et al.*, IT-95-14/2-A, Appeals Judgment of 17 December 2004, paras 55–57.

in light of the expected military advantage of an attack against legitimate targets,[40] the principle of precaution requires the belligerents to undertake every possible measure in order to limit the negative effects of an attack upon protected persons and objects.

The principle of precaution is divided into several different obligations of diligent conduct. First, there is a generic duty of care under Article 27 of the Hague Regulations (HgRs), according to which 'all necessary steps must be taken to spare, as far as possible', non-military objectives; while Article 57(1) of the API posits that '[i]n the conduct of military operations, constant care shall be taken to spare the civilian population, civilians and civilian objects'. Additionally, Article 57(2)(a)(i) of the API demands that 'those who plan or decide upon an attack shall do everything feasible to verify that the objectives to be attacked' are legitimate targets and that the attack is not otherwise prohibited by the API; while, under Article 57(2)(a)(ii) of the API, states must 'take all feasible precautions in the choice of means and methods of attack' to avoid or minimise the negative impacts on civilians and civilian objects. In both provisions, 'feasible' should be interpreted as a 'high'[41] threshold excluding 'precautions that are practically impossible',[42] and the judgment on the feasibility of these measures requires the application of the notion of due diligence.[43] Finally, Article 57(2)(iii)(c) of the API posits a duty to provide for effective advance warning prior to the attack, which is also governed by due diligence, as demonstrated by the wording of the provision requiring warnings 'unless circumstances do not permit'.[44]

Similarly, due diligence is relevant to the implementation of precautions against the harmful effects of an attack. A state does not incur international responsibility in cases of failure to undertake the measures under Article 58 of the API as long as it demonstrates that it acted diligently in light of the specific circumstances at hand.[45] Indeed, this provision demands that states 'shall, to the maximum extent feasible (. . .) endeavour' to take defensive precautions.

Similarly, due diligence also regulates the precautions in attack and against the effects of attack in relation to cultural property. Indeed, Articles 6 and 7 of the

[40] See API, 1977 (n. 30), arts 51(5)(b), 57(2)(b).

[41] ICTY, *Final Report to the Prosecutor by the Committee Established to Review the NATO*, 8 June 2000, para. 29.

[42] Eritrea-Ethiopia Claims Commission (EECC), *Partial Award: Central Front—Ethiopia's Claim 2*, 28 April 2004, UNRIAA 26, 155, para. 110; according to some states, feasible precautions are those that may be practically undertaken in light of both humanitarian and military considerations; see 2020 UNTS 75, 76; 1591 UNTS 462, 464; 1607 UNTS 526, 529; 1477 UNTS 300; see also art. 3(4) of the Protocol II to the 1980 CCW Convention as amended on 3 May 1996.

[43] See US Department of Defence, *The Law of War Manual* (2015, revised in Dec 2016), section 5.2.3.2; see also Jean-François Quéguiner, 'Precautions under the Law Governing the Conduct of Hostilities', *International Review of the Red Cross* 88 (2006), 793–821, at 798.

[44] See Robert Kolb, *Advanced Introduction to International Humanitarian Law* (Cheltenham: Edward Elgar 2014), 170–171; this provision largely reproduces art. 26 HgRs.

[45] See US Department of Defence, *The Law of War* 2016 (n. 3), section 5.14; Quéguiner, 'Precautions' 2006 (n. 43), 820.

Second Protocol to the Hague Convention of 1954 for the Protection of Cultural Property in the Event of Armed Conflict 1999 refers to the duty to take 'feasible' precautions.[46]

Finally, due diligence is relevant as the parameter for assessing the rules on the protection of the environment during armed conflict. According to Article 55(1) of the API, '[c]are shall be taken in warfare to protect the natural environment against widespread, long-term and severe damage'. As an obligation of care, the implementation of this provision must be assessed in light of due diligence, taking into account the preventive measures adopted by states so that their attacks do not result in widespread, long-term, and severe damage to the environment.[47] Similarly, the International Committee of the Red Cross has identified a customary international law rule according to which hostilities must be conducted 'with due regard to the protection and preservation of the natural environment' and 'all feasible precautions must be taken to avoid, and in any event to minimise, incidental damage to the environment',[48] which requires an assessment in light of due diligence.[49] Additionally, the protection of the environment during armed conflict is reinforced by the existence of other specific prohibitions that are not to be assessed under due diligence.[50]

2.4 The Protection of Civilians and Persons *Hors de Combat*

Due diligence plays a significant role for the implementation of a number of obligations regarding the protection of civilians and the protection of persons *hors de combat*. This view is confirmed both by the wording of the relevant provisions, as well as some state practice, and judicial decisions.

Article 27 of the GCIV demands that civilians 'shall be protected'; similarly, there is a basic rule that 'the wounded, sick and shipwrecked, to whichever Party they belong, shall be respected and protected' and they 'shall receive, to the fullest extent practicable (…), the medical care and attention required by their condition'.[51] The obligation at hand must be assessed taking into account due diligence

[46] Second Protocol to the Hague Convention of 1954 for the Protection of Cultural Property in the Event of Armed Conflict, 26 March 1999, 2253 UNTS 172; see Venturini, 'Les obligations' 2018 (n. 1) 137–138.

[47] See Karen Hulme, *War Torn Environment: Interpreting the Legal Threshold* (Leiden: Martinus Nijhoff 2004), 80–88.

[48] See rule 44 in Jean-Marie Henckaerts/Louise Doswald-Beck (eds), *Customary International Humanitarian Law*, vol. I (Cambridge: CUP 2005), 147.

[49] See Michael Bothe, 'Military Activities and the Protection of the Environment', *Environmental Policy and Law* 37 (2007), 232–341, at 236. See also the obligation to invigilate over the activity of corporations under ILC, Draft Articles on the Protection of the Environment in relation to Armed Conflicts, A/CN.4/L.937, 6 June 2019, draft art. 10.

[50] See API, 1977 (n. 30), arts 35(3), 55.

[51] API, 1977 (n. 30), art. 10; see also GCI (n. 31) and Geneva Convention II (GCII), 12 August 1949, 75 UNTS 85, art. 12, and Geneva Convention IV (GCIV), 12 August 1949, 75 UNTS 287, art. 16(1).

since it is a duty to protect individuals (such duties require the application of due diligence).[52] Likewise, the duty to provide medical care, like every duty of care, is governed by due diligence.[53]

Moreover, Article 15 of the GCI provides that belligerents must take 'all possible measures' to search for, collect, and take care of the wounded and sick, and to search for the dead and prevent their being despoiled, employing a wording that suggests the application of the notion of due diligence. Similarly, the duty to identify the dead is an obligation of conduct subject to due diligence.[54] Moreover, due diligence is relevant to the assessment of compliance with the rule on setting up medical establishments and units ('as far as possible') in places where they are safe from attacks against military objectives,[55] and with the rule on taking 'the necessary steps' to make the emblem of medical units clearly visible to the enemy.[56] Additionally, the imposition of a duty to protect coastal rescue crafts 'so far as operational requirements permit'[57] requires an assessment based on due diligence.[58] A reference to due diligence must be read also in the provision demanding that 'sick-bays shall be respected and spared as far as possible'.[59] Due diligence also plays a role with regard to the regime governing the treatment of prisoners of war.[60] While Article 13(1) of the GCIII imposes both negative obligations and obligations of result upon the state with regard to its organs, Article 13(2) of the GCIII demands that detaining states must 'protect' prisoners of war. This provision has been interpreted as pertaining to the duty to undertake positive measures requiring assessment under due diligence by the Eritrea-Ethiopia Claims Commission, according to which states may be 'liable for failing to take effective measures to prevent' abuses by private actors against prisoners of war.[61] Furthermore, other rules pertaining to the protection of prisoners of war require the application of the notion of due diligence, such as the duty to ensure the safety of prisoners of war during evacuation,[62] and the duties to provide adequate food, shelter, healthcare, clothing, and the like to prisoners of war.[63]

[52] Robin Geiß/Helen Durham, 'Article 12: Protection and Care of the Wounded and Sick', in ICRC (ed.), *Updated Commentary on the Second Geneva Convention* (Cambridge: CUP 2017), 483–528, para. 1360.

[53] Ibid., para. 1380.

[54] GCI, 1949 (n. 31), art. 17 and GCII, 1949 (n. 51), art. 20; see also the similar provision in GCII, 1949 (n. 51), art. 18.

[55] GCI, 1949 (n. 51), art. 19(3).

[56] Ibid., art. 42 and API, 1977 (n. 30), art. 18.

[57] GCII, 1949 (n. 51), art. 27.

[58] See Wolff Heintschel von Heinegg, 'Article 27: Protection of Coastal Rescue Craft and Fixed Coastal Installations', in ICRC (ed.), *Updated Commentary on the Second Geneva Convention* (Cambridge: CUP 2017), 749–773, para. 2206.

[59] GCII, 1949 (n. 51), art. 28.

[60] See ILA, Study Group on Due Diligence, First Report 2014 (n. 19), 12.

[61] EECC, *Final Award, Eritrea's Damages Claims*, 17 August 2009, RIAA 26, 631, para. 230; see also ICTY, *Prosecutor v. Mrkšić et al.*, IT-95-13/1-A, Appeals Judgment of 5 May 2009, paras 72–74.

[62] Geneva Convention III (GCIII), 12 August 1949, 75 UNTS 135, art. 20(2).

[63] Ibid., arts 25–27, 29, 30, 34, 38, 51.

2.5 The Law of Occupation

The law of occupation embodies a number of obligations requiring an assessment under due diligence. These obligations pertain mainly to the duties and powers bestowed upon the occupying powers in relation to the administration of the occupied territory. Article 43 of the HgRs, which requires the occupying power to administer the occupied territory in the place of the ousted sovereign while, at the same time, preserving the sovereignty of the latter,[64] provides for the occupying power's duty to 'restore and ensure' public order and civil life.[65] The duty to restore and ensure public order encompasses the 'responsibility for preserving order, punishing crime, and protecting lives and property within the occupied territory',[66] and was implicitly acknowledged by the Supreme Court of Israel as a due diligence obligation.[67] On the other hand, the due diligence obligation to restore and ensure public life concerns the entire social, commercial, and economic life of the occupied territory.[68]

Additionally, the duty to restore and ensure public order encompasses a number of other due diligence obligations related to the administration of an occupied territory, such as the responsibility for the safety of UN facilities and property,[69] and the diplomatic missions of foreign states located in the occupied territory,[70] which must be protected by the occupying powers through the deployment of law enforcement and military units. Furthermore, the occupying power has a duty of vigilance over the conduct of private actors that may violate international humanitarian law and international human rights law,[71] as well as replacing the sovereign with regard to the duty to prevent private actors from using the controlled territory to harm other states.[72] Accordingly, the occupying power must not tolerate

[64] Fourth Hague Convention, 1907 (n. 30), CTS (1907), 77.

[65] The French only authoritative text refers to 'vie publique'.

[66] US, Military Tribunal, Nuremberg, *Willelm List et al.*, Judgment of 19 February 1948, LRTWC 9 (1948), 34, 57; see also US, Supreme Court, *Ochoa v. Hernandez y Morales*, US 230 (1913), 139, 159.

[67] See HCJ 69/81 *Abu Aita v. Regional Commander*, 37(2) PD 197, para. 50(c); Marco Sassòli, 'Legislation and Maintenance of Public Order and Civil Life by Occupying Powers', *European Journal of International Law* 16 (2005), 661–694, at 664–665.

[68] See Supreme Court of Israel, HC 393/82, *A Cooperative Society Lawfully Registered in the Judea and Samaria Region v. Commander of the IDF Forces*, (1983) 37(4) PD 785, para. 18.

[69] See the statements of Germany and China in S/PV.4812, 21 August 2003, 8 and 9–10.

[70] See the remarks by China, ibid., 9–10; and Stefan Talmon, 'Diplomacy under Occupation: The Status of Diplomatic Missions in Occupied Iraq', *Anuario Mexicano de Derecho Internacional* 6 (2006), 461–511, at 502–505.

[71] See EECC, *Partial Award: Central Front* (n. 42), para. 67; ICJ, *Case Concerning Armed Activities on the Territory of the Congo (DRC v. Uganda)*, Judgment of 19 December 2005, ICJ Reports 2005, 168, paras 178, 250; see also Marco Longobardo, 'State Responsibility for International Humanitarian Law Violations by Private Actors in Occupied Territories and the Exploitation of Natural Resources', *Netherlands International Law Review* 63 (2016), 251–274.

[72] See ICJ, *Legal Consequences for States of the Continued Presence of South Africa in Namibia notwithstanding Security Council Resolution 276 (1970)*, Advisory Opinion of 21 June 1971, ICJ Reports 1971, 16, para. 118; Joint Statement of Iraq's Neighbouring States, 2 November 2003', in Stefan Talmon (ed.), *The Occupation of Iraq*, vol. II (Oxford: Hart 2013), 1453–1454.

these activities in the occupied territory, but rather must use its law enforcement and military capabilities to prevent violations of international humanitarian law and international human rights law, as well as the organisation of activities that are harmful to other states. Finally, the occupying power's duties to protect sites of cultural heritage in the occupied territory are subject to the clause 'as far as possible', requiring the application of due diligence.[73]

Other provisions of the law of occupation requiring the application of due diligence include those concerning the occupying power's right to collect taxes and contributions as far as possible in conformity with those in force prior to the occupation;[74] the duty to pay contributions, as far as possible, in cash;[75] the duties to 'facilitate' the identification of children and the work of institutions protecting children;[76] the duty to provide food, medical supplies, and healthcare for the occupied population;[77] the duty to ensure adequate human conditions in cases of evacuation or civilian transfers;[78] the duty to provide adequate human detention conditions;[79] and some duties pertaining to the protection of the environment.[80]

2.6 Due Diligence Obligations in Non-International Armed Conflicts

Due diligence obligations play a significant role in non-international armed conflicts, both in relation to the conduct of states and armed groups. Indeed, as long as one assumes that customary and treaty international humanitarian law binds organised non-state actors,[81] it must be concluded that due diligence obligations pertaining to international humanitarian law are relevant for them as well.

Many treaty rules on the law on non-international armed conflict demands the application of the concept of due diligence. For example, common Article 3(3) of

[73] See Convention for the Protection of Cultural Property in the Event of Armed Conflict with Regulations for the Execution of the Convention, 14 May 1954, 1956 UNTS 3511, art. 5.

[74] Fourth Hague Convention, 1907 (n. 30), arts 48, 51(2).

[75] Ibid., art. 52(3).

[76] GCIV, 1949 (n. 51), art. 50.

[77] Ibid., arts 55, 56, API, 1977 (n. 30), arts 14(1), 69; see Yves Sandoz/Christophe Swinarski/Bruno Zimmermann, (eds), *Commentary on the Additional Protocols of 8 June 1977 to the Geneva Conventions of 12 August 1949* (Leiden: Martinus Nijhoff 1987), paras 2781–2785.

[78] GCIV, 1949 (n. 51), art. 49(3).

[79] Ibid., art. 85.

[80] See ILC, Protection of the Environment in relation to Armed Conflicts, 2019 (n. 49) draft art. 20(2) (on the duty to take 'appropriate measures to prevent significant harm to the environment of the occupied territory that is likely to prejudice the health and well-being of the population of the occupied territory') and draft art. 22 of the same document (according to which '[a]n Occupying Power shall exercise due diligence to ensure that activities in the occupied territory do not cause significant harm to the environment of areas beyond the occupied territory'). Both these duties are in line with the obligations already embodied in HgRs, art. 43.

[81] Special Court for Sierra Leone, *Prosecutor v. Norman*, Decision on Jurisdiction, Appeals Chamber, 31 May 2004, para. 22.

the GCs requires due diligence in assessing compliance with the duty to 'endeavour to bring into force, by means of special agreements' the provisions of the GCs in non-international armed conflicts.[82]

Moreover, two other provisions are clearly drafted with a wording revealing that they are obligations of diligent conduct. Article 8 of the APII—according to which '[w]henever circumstances permit, (. . .) all possible measure shall be taken (. . .) to search for and collect the wounded, sick and shipwrecked, to protect them against pillage and ill-treatment, to ensure their adequate care, and to search for the dead, prevent their being despoiled, and decently dispose of them'—and Article 4(3) lit. b) of the APII—according to which 'all appropriate steps shall be taken to facilitate the reunion of families temporarily separated'—are clearly drafted with a wording revealing that they are obligations of diligent conduct. Similarly, the duties to protect[83] and to search for[84] the wounded, sick, and shipwrecked; the duty to protect religious personnel and medical personnel and units;[85] and the duty to protect civilians, both individuals and the general population,[86] should be assessed under due diligence as every obligation to protect. Moreover, the duty to assist displaced civilians[87] and the duties to provide adequate food, shelter, healthcare, clothing, and the like to internees and detainees must be assessed in light of due diligence.[88]

In addition, there are some customary rules that are applicable to non-international armed conflicts and that require the application of due diligence. To mention one notable example, according to the International Committee of the Red Cross, the due diligence obligations to take constant care to spare the civilian population, individual civilians, and civilian objects, as well as to take all feasible precautions to minimise the accidental loss of civilian life, injury to civilians, and damage to civilian objects are applicable to non-international armed conflicts as well.[89] This conclusion is supported by the fact that specific conventions applicable to non-international armed conflict embody such a duty.[90]

[82] Venturini, 'Les obligations' 2018 (n. 1) 135.
[83] Additional Protocol II (APII), 8 June 1977, 1125 UNTS 609, art. 7.
[84] Ibid., art. 8.
[85] Ibid., arts 9, 11.
[86] Ibid., arts 13, 14.
[87] Ibid., art. 17.
[88] See ibid., art. 5(1)(b).
[89] See Henckaerts/Doswald-Beck, *Customary* 2005 (n. 48), 51–53.
[90] See, e.g., Protocol on Prohibitions or Restrictions on the Use of Mines, Booby-Traps and Other Devices, 3 May 1996, art. 3(10); Second Protocol to the Hague Convention for the Protection of Cultural Property, 26 March 1999, art. 7.

3. The Impact of International Humanitarian Law on the Legal Discourse of Due Diligence

This overview of relevant international humanitarian law rules demonstrates that the notion of due diligence should be applied when complying with the *jus in bello* in a number of cases. More significantly, international humanitarian law reinforces some well-established ideas on due diligence that are relevant to the wider understanding of this notion from a general international law perspective.

Obligations of diligent conduct are as frequent in international humanitarian law as they are for international law in general, especially in relation to the exercise of governmental functions over individuals and territories (such as in occupied territory) and individuals alone (for example, in relation to most duties to protect). Other due diligence obligations pertain to the 'proceduralisation' of the law of armed conflict, as in relation to the precautions in attack, where state conduct may be divided into a series of teleologically linked acts that must be assessed in order to demonstrate compliance with international humanitarian law.[91]

Moreover, it is now generally accepted that due diligence is not a component of state responsibility but rather a notion that must be applied on the basis of the structure of certain primary rules. Accordingly, the Draft Articles on the Responsibility of States are silent on due diligence since this notion is the parameter employed to assess whether the state's behaviour is adequate to implement a specific obligation of conduct.[92] This conclusion is supported by the examination of the role played by due diligence in international humanitarian law, wherein the possibility to apply this notion is a consequence of the structure of some primary rules rather than the result of peculiar norms on state responsibility.

Furthermore, international humanitarian law supports the idea that due diligence must be addressed as an objective standard rather than as a standard linked to fault or negligence.[93] For example, the objective nature of due diligence is particularly clear with regard to the duty to take feasible precautions in attack: State practice, as well as national and international case law, demonstrates that the targeting process is taken into account as a series of acts that are relevant to assess the diligent behaviour of a state organ rather than as elements to ascertain the mental element of the organ (intent or fault).[94]

[91] For more on this, see below section 4.

[92] See ILC, Draft Articles on Responsibility of States for Internationally Wrongful Acts, UN GAOR A/56/10, 23 April–1 June, 2 July–10 August 2001, 70, art. 2, commentary, para. 34; see also Pisillo Mazzeschi, 'Due Diligence Rule' 1992 (n. 8), 49; cf. Kolb, 'Reflections' 2015 (n. 3), 116–117.

[93] See Pisillo Mazzeschi, 'Due Diligence Rule' 1992 (n. 8), 42–44; ILA, Study Group on Due Diligence, Second Report 2016 (n. 10), 4.

[94] See Marco Sassòli, 'Autonomous Weapons and International Humanitarian Law: Advantages, Open Technical Questions and Legal Issues to be Clarified', *International Law Studies* 90 (2014), 308–340, at 332–335.

Moreover, international humanitarian law confirms that there is no due diligence standard applicable to *every* obligation of conduct, but rather different primary obligations may require different standards of care.[95] Indeed, the level of required diligence may vary on the basis of the different expression employed in the relevant treaty provisions (e.g., the difference between the duty to take 'every feasible measure' and duty to 'take adequate care').[96] Similarly, factual circumstances do influence the way in which due diligence obligations must be implemented in different scenarios, even for an identical wording of the relevant provisions (for example, in an occupied territory, the duty to protect prisoners of war requires a higher degree of diligence than the duty to protect the local population, since prisoners of war are under the direct control of the occupying power). Accordingly, it is important to identify the standards of diligence on a case-by-case basis, taking into account the rules on treaty interpretation in order to assess the level of diligence requested by a specific international humanitarian law obligation of conduct.

Finally, international humanitarian law does not consider that an autonomous primary rule entirely based on due diligence exists,[97] but rather takes due diligence into account only in relation to existing obligations. For example, no general principle of due diligence exists with regard to the protection of the environment during an armed conflict,[98] while other due diligence obligations with a wide scope are rooted in the duty to ensure respect for international humanitarian law under common Article 1 of the GCs and the duty to restore and ensure public order and civil life in occupied territory under Article 43 of the HgRs, rather than in a general principle of international law.

4. Conclusion: The Impact of Due Diligence on the Implementation of International Humanitarian Law

In conclusion, one may wonder whether the frequent resort to the notion of due diligence in international humanitarian law is an advantage or a disadvantage for international humanitarian law implementation. Indeed, it is no mystery that implementation is the Achilles heel of the law of armed conflict due to the weakness of its monitoring and implementation mechanisms.

It is indisputable that the effect of due diligence is, 'in some contexts, to dilute the stringency of state obligations'[99] as states may avoid responsibility if they

[95] ILA, Study Group on Due Diligence, Second Report 2016 (n. 10), 20; Joanna Kulesza, *Due Diligence in International Law* (Leiden: Brill 2016), 108.

[96] Cf. US Department of Defence, *The Law of War* 2016 (n. 3), section 5.2.3.1.

[97] See Michael Schmitt, 'In Defense of Due Diligence in Cyberspace', *Yale Law Journal Forum* 125 (2015), 68–81.

[98] Dieter Fleck, 'The Protection of the Environment in Armed Conflict: Legal Obligations in the Absence of Specific Rules', *Nordic Journal of International Law* 82 (2013), 7–20, at 13.

[99] ILA, Study Group on Due Diligence, Second Report 2016 (n. 10), 3.

demonstrate that they have undertaken diligent conduct; indeed, it is easier to ascertain whether a certain event occurred rather than exploring the conduct behind an event and comparing it with the abstractly required diligence.[100] Furthermore, since states enjoy discretional powers with respect to the conduct to be undertaken in order to fulfil a certain obligation, it may be difficult to scrutinise the decision to adopt certain measures instead of others before a competent court.[101] Additionally, the conduct of hostilities is characterised by the 'fog of war', that shroud of uncertainness, secrecy, and imponderable factors that makes it very challenging to assess facts in armed conflict;[102] accordingly, it may be problematic to reconstruct state conduct *ex post facto* and to assess whether the judgments of value undertaken by state organs were diligent enough.

However, there is good reason to embody due diligence obligations in international humanitarian law. If we consider that due diligence obligations pertain to 'a substantial foreseeable risk to a significant legal value which the state can influence, by its available means [in light of] a means-end relationship',[103] it is obvious that they are peculiarly fit to regulate armed conflict scenarios which are inherently hazardous. Indeed, the standard of diligence required is not diminished by the armed conflict but rather is raised: since it is well-established that the standard of care in due diligence obligations increases along with the risk,[104] it follows that, in a situation of armed conflict, where the risks inherent to the conduct of hostilities are dramatically high, the standard of diligence must be set accordingly.[105]

Additionally, the reality of armed conflict demands a certain flexibility of the relevant rules in order to make them practically applicable;[106] this is the tribute to military necessity, in the sense of the will of states to gain military advantage, which has shaped, along with considerations of humanity, the development of international humanitarian law. Due diligence obligations are effective tools to maintain this balance since they permit states that have caused events contrary to international humanitarian law goals to provide an explanation based on the exercise of sufficient due diligence, and to avoid international responsibility. The alternative way would be considering military necessity as a reason to trump the law of armed conflict altogether. It is not a coincidence that due diligence obligations,

[100] Pisillo Mazzeschi, 'Due Diligence Rule' 1992 (n. 8), 50.

[101] See, with regard to the obligation to restore and ensure civil life in occupied territory, Marco Longobardo, 'The Palestinian Right to Exploit the Dead Sea Coastline for Tourism', *German Yearbook of International Law* 58 (2015), 317–352, at 323–338.

[102] See Carl von Clausewitz, *On War* (Princeton: Princeton University Press 1984), 101.

[103] Anja Seibert-Fohr, 'From Complicity to Due Diligence: When Do States Incur Responsibility for Their Involvement in Serious International Wrongdoing?', *German Yearbook of International Law* 60 (2017), 667–708, at 672–675; see also Federica Violi, 'The Function of the Triad "Territory", "Jurisdiction", and "Control" in Due Diligence Obligations', chapter 5 of this book, section 2.

[104] See ILA, Study Group on Due Diligence, Second Report 2016 (n. 10), 12.

[105] See Max Huber, *Affaire des biens britanniques au Maroc espagnol (Spain v. UK)*, 1 May 1925, UNRIAA, vol. II, 614, 645.

[106] See William Boothby, *The Law of Targeting* (Oxford: OUP 2012), 176–182.

which are often usually framed as umbrella obligations covering a certain topic (for example the duty to protect prisoners of war, the duty to maintain and ensure public order in occupied territory), are accompanied by specific obligations of result and negative obligations to protect fundamental humanitarian values (for example, the prohibition of inhuman treatments of prisoners of war and of collective punishments in occupied territory). From this perspective, the combination of due diligence obligations and obligations not related to due diligence maintains the balance between the opposite interests at the foundation of the law of armed conflict, granting operational and legal flexibility to states involved in an inherently hazardous activity as armed conflict.

The degree of flexibility granted by due diligence obligations pertaining to international humanitarian law ensures that the belligerents are liable only for those events they could have prevented diligently in light of their capabilities. For example, in relation to the duty to verify the objective of an attack, states with more advanced technological capabilities must explain why it was not feasible to use them to verify a specific objective, while the same standard of precision is not required of states with less developed means.[107] Similarly, in relation to the choice of the means to launch an attack, states with precision-guided munitions would be required to use them, whereas states with more primitive weapons would not be required to produce the exact same level of precision, since the relevant due diligence obligations take into account what is feasible case-by-case; however, a minimum standard of precision is required by the different *negative obligation* not to launch indiscriminate attacks.[108] Accordingly, far from being a violation of the principle of equality of belligerents,[109] due diligence obligations manage to maintain the *legal* equality of belligerents along with taking into account the *factual* asymmetries that may affect the compliance of belligerents with international humanitarian law.

Furthermore, the fact that an obligation should be assessed in light of due diligence does not mean that obligations do not exist or are not justiciable. For example, it is incorrect to assert that the occupying power's duty to restore and ensure public order in an occupied territory cannot be scrutinised before a competent court.[110] Rather, as demonstrated by international practice, international courts

[107] See Report of the United Nations Fact-Finding Mission on the Gaza Conflict, A/HRC/12/48, 25 September 2009, para. 61; Marco Longobardo, 'L'obbligo di verificare l'obiettivo e le conseguenze di un attacco ai sensi del diritto internazionale umanitario e nuove forme di intelligence: profili di responsabilità internazionale', in Andrea Spagnolo/Stefano Saluzzo (eds), *La responsabilità degli Stati e delle organizzazioni internazionali* (Milano: Ledizioni 2017), 37–59, at 54.

[108] Giulio Bartolini, 'Air Operations Against Iraq (1991 and 2003)', in Natalino Ronzitti/Gabriella Venturini (eds), *The International Humanitarian Law of Air Warfare* (Utrecht: Eleven Publishing 2005), 227–272, at 264.

[109] See Nathan Canestaro, 'Legal and Policy Constraints on the Conduct of Aerial Precision Warfare', *Vanderbilt Journal of Transnational Law* 37 (2004), 431–484, at 465.

[110] See Yoram Dinstein, *The International Law of Belligerent Occupation* (Cambridge: CUP 2009), 92.

and tribunals may consider the occupying power responsible for a failure to implement its duty with diligence.[111]

It is also not entirely correct that it is more difficult to ascertain the violation of a due diligence obligation: such an assertion is only sound with regard to non-diligent conduct that does *not* result in any unlawful event,[112] since states usually bring disputes before international courts and tribunals only when an event has occurred, asserting the violation of a due diligence obligation *ex post facto*.[113] However, when the event does occur, the state under a due diligence obligation must prove that it has acted diligently.[114] This shift of the burden of proof had positive consequences on international humanitarian law implementation in several areas, such as the law of targeting: since states are under a duty to disclose information concerning the targeting process in order to avoid responsibility,[115] as happened in a number of cases before German courts where German military authorities had to describe step-by-step their decisional processes.[116] From the perspective of international humanitarian law compliance, contemporary military operations may be seen as 'processes'[117] rather than individual acts, with each phase open to being scrutinised under international humanitarian law in order to assess whether a belligerent has acted with the requested diligence. This is an important contribution to the implementation of international humanitarian law since, thanks to due diligence: (i) states undertake preventive measures at every phase of a military operation in order to forestall a negative event; (ii) these measures are disclosed in order to demonstrate a diligent conduct if the negative event occurs, furthering the transparency of the conduct of hostilities; and (iii) a culture based on the need to justify actions in armed conflict is nurtured. Accordingly, as a result of the application of the notion of due diligence, international humanitarian law is facing a progressive 'proceduralisation' that contributes to a strengthening of its implementation.

With regard to the law on non-international armed conflict, one may argue that the degree of flexibility introduced by due diligence obligations may be helpful in order to allow armed groups to comply with rules that were drafted with states as

[111] See UN Compensation Commission, *Governing Council Decision no. 9*, (6 March 1992), ILR 109, 593, paras 12–15; ICJ, *Armed Activities* (n. 71), paras 178, 250.

[112] See Pisillo Mazzeschi, 'Due Diligence Rule' 1992 (n. 8), 50.

[113] ILA, Study Group on Due Diligence, Second Report 2016 (n. 10), 7.

[114] See Kulesza, *Due Diligence* 2016 (n. 95), 204–205.

[115] When states refuse to do so, international courts have considered them responsible for the breach of relevant due diligence obligations (EECC, *Partial Award: Central Front* (n. 42), para. 112).

[116] See, e.g., Bundesanwaltschaft, Ermittlungsverfahren wegen des Luftangriffs vom 4. September 2009 eingestellt, 19 April 2010; German Federal Court of Justice, Judgment, 6 October 2016, III ZR 140/15, para. 55.

[117] See Geoffrey Corn, 'War, Law, and the Often Overlooked Value of Process as a Precautionary Measure', *Pepperdine Law Review* 42 (2015), 419–466.

addressees.[118] However, the advantages of due diligence obligations pertaining to international humanitarian law are almost relegated to the law on international armed conflict as most international humanitarian law provisions are shaped with states as potential addressees, so that the relevant tests on what is 'feasible' or 'necessary' are usually based on the capabilities of states. However, this problem is not a consequence of the application of the notion of due diligence but rather pertains to the entire development of international humanitarian law.

In conclusion, the notion of due diligence affects the implementation of international humanitarian law both by avoiding strict liability and strengthening compliance with the law. The fact that many international humanitarian law rules require the application of due diligence is a consequence of the interests pursued by this branch of international law, which combines due diligence obligations and obligations of result in order to strike a balance between military necessity and humanity. Accordingly, due diligence is in most cases a reasonable component of some international humanitarian law obligations.

[118] See Marco Sassòli, 'Taking Armed Groups Seriously: Ways to Improve their Compliance with International Humanitarian Law', *Journal of International Humanitarian Legal Studies* 1 (2010), 5–51, at 15–20.

12

Due Diligence and the Obligation to Prevent Genocide and Crimes Against Humanity

Larissa van den Herik and Emma Irving

1. Introduction

Article I of the Genocide Convention[1] reads, '[t]he Contracting Parties confirm that genocide, whether committed in time of peace or in time of war, is a crime under international law which they undertake to prevent and to punish'. This provision has been characterised as preambular given its soft and vague contents;[2] a legal but non-normative provision which fails to provide any specific direction as to the behaviour it proscribes.[3] The obligation to prevent is not elaborated by subsequent provisions of the Genocide Convention, apart from Article VIII's reference to the UN system, nor do the travaux préparatoires provide any further substantive guidance as to its content. In fact, as William Schabas writes:

> while the Convention has much to say about punishment of genocide, there is little to suggest what prevention of genocide really means. Certainly, nothing in the debates about Article I provides the slightest clue as to the scope of the obligation to prevent.[4]

Nonetheless and as is well-known, in the *Bosnia Genocide* case, the International Court of Justice (ICJ) refuted Serbia's argument that Article I was merely hortatory and held that this provision did create independent obligations for states that were

[1] Convention on the Prevention and Punishment of the Crime of Genocide, 9 December 1948, 78 UNTS 277.

[2] William Schabas, *Genocide in International Law: The Crime of Crimes* (Cambridge: CUP 2nd ed. 2009), 80.

[3] Cf. the different notions of soft law including binding but non-normative norms, as analysed by Jean d'Aspremont, 'Softness in International Law: A Self-Serving Quest for New Legal Materials', *European Journal of International Law* 19 (2008), 1075–1093, at 1084.

[4] Schabas, *Genocide in International Law* 2009 (n. 2), 81; as also cited by Peter Tomka in his Separate Opinion to the ICJ, *Case Concerning Application of The Convention on the Prevention and Punishment of the Crime of Genocide (Bosnia and Herzegovina v. Serbia and Montenegro)*, Judgment of 26 February 2007, Separate Opinion of Judge Tomka, ICJ Reports 2007, 310, para. 66.

Larissa van den Herik and Emma Irving, *Due Diligence and the Obligation to Prevent Genocide and Crimes Against Humanity* In: *Due Diligence in the International Legal Order.* Edited by: Heike Krieger, Anne Peters, and Leonhard Kreuzer, Oxford University Press (2020). © The Several Contributors. DOI: 10.1093/oso/9780198869900.003.0012.

distinct from other provisions of the Convention.[5] The court also concluded that the provision was not territorially limited,[6] and that it was an obligation of conduct and not one of result.[7] The court premised the extraterritorial obligation to prevent on a state's capacity to influence.[8] Having identified such an independent and extraterritorial obligation to prevent, the court underscored the relevance of due diligence in understanding its contents. The main function of the 'notion of due diligence', as the court called it, was thus to substantiate a provision that had previously been labelled as normatively empty,[9] while also allowing for differentiated obligations in a global context. The court did not expressly use a due diligence approach in relation to each specific dimension, but its finding that the obligation to prevent arises, 'at the instant that the State learns of, or should normally have learned of, the existence of a serious risk that genocide will be committed' implies a risk-assessment that, at the very least, has close synergies with procedural due diligence obligations.

This chapter discusses the role of due diligence in operationalising the obligation to prevent genocide, and extends the discussion to cover the customary obligation to prevent crimes against humanity. The chapter takes the Genocide Convention and the ICJ's *Bosnia Genocide* case and the literature thereon as starting points, while also analysing the International Law Commission's (ILC) debates in the context of the draft Convention on Crimes against Humanity. The chapter inquires how legal arguments and constructions in these settings expressly or impliedly draw on due diligence vocabulary and approaches. The aim of the chapter is to determine whether and to what extent there is a unique approach to due diligence in a 'prevention of mass atrocity' setting.

Section 1 introduces the obligation to prevent genocide and crimes against humanity and argues that, despite different legal bases, the obligation to prevent genocide and the obligation to prevent crimes against humanity should be regarded as identical in scope, nature, and contents. Sections 2, 3, and 4 follow the proposed classification of two types of due diligence obligations concerning institutional capacity and procedural obligations.[10] Sections 2 and 3 zero in on the duty bearer and contents of the extraterritorial obligation to prevent respectively, while section 4 explores synergies between procedural due diligence obligations and states' duty of vigilance in the context of genocide and crimes against humanity.

[5] ICJ, *Case Concerning Application of The Convention on the Prevention and Punishment of the Crime of Genocide (Bosnia and Herzegovina v. Serbia and Montenegro)*, Judgment of 26 February 2007, ICJ Reports 2007, 43, paras 162–165.

[6] Ibid., para. 183.

[7] Ibid., para. 430.

[8] Ibid., para. 430.

[9] Cf. ibid., Separate Opinion Judge ad hoc Kreća, 457, paras 113–120; referred to by Orna Ben-Naftali, 'The Obligation to Prevent and to Punish Genocide', in Paola Gaeta (ed.), *The UN Genocide Convention; A Commentary* (Oxford: OUP 2009), 27–57, at 33.

[10] See Anne Peters/Heike Krieger/Leonhard Kreuzer, 'Due Diligence in the International Legal Order: Dissecting the Leitmotif of Current Accountability Debates', chapter 1 of this book, section 6.

Drawing on the International Tribunal for the Law of the Sea's (ITLOS) Seabed Disputes Chamber's Advisory Opinion of 1 February 2011,[11] section 4 specifically inquires how technological developments inform risk-assessments in the context of the obligation to prevent genocide and crimes against humanity and whether new technologies intensify or extend due diligence obligations. Finally, section 5 offers some overarching reflections on due diligence as a means to operationalise the obligation to prevent genocide and crimes against humanity.

2. The Obligation to Prevent Genocide and Crimes Against Humanity

A duty to prevent mass atrocity is morally anchored in considerations of humanity.[12] As noted by Mark Toufayan, the core idea of a duty to rescue other human beings in danger may be traced back to the Code of Hammurabi, the Talmud, the Koran, and the Bible.[13] The concept of Responsibility to Protect can be regarded as the political manifestation of such a duty at the international level. This concept has some legal connotations, as it is linked to the legal categories of genocide and crimes against humanity. From a positivist perspective though, a legal basis for a duty to prevent mass atrocity must be found elsewhere. For genocide, as indicated, Article I of the Genocide Convention specifies a general obligation to prevent, which was vitalised and solidified by the ICJ in its *Bosnia Genocide* judgment. As for crimes against humanity, by lack of a global crimes against humanity convention, an obligation to prevent must be based on customary international law for the time being. Specifications can nonetheless be found in the ILC's draft Articles on crimes against humanity, and also in the reports of ILC rapporteur Sean Murphy. Several draft articles concern prevention, thereby pre-empting a critique often voiced against the Genocide Convention that it was too vague and non-committal on the prevention part.[14] Article 3(2) of the ILC draft Articles on Crimes Against Humanity is patterned upon the Genocide Convention and reads,

[11] In this Opinion, the Chamber held: 'The content of "due diligence" obligations may not easily be described in precise terms. Among the factors that make such a description difficult is the fact that "due diligence" is a variable concept. It may change over time as measures considered sufficiently diligent at a certain moment may become not diligent enough in light, for instance, of new scientific or technological knowledge.' ITLOS Seabed Disputes Chamber, *Responsibilities and Obligations of States Sponsoring Persons and Entities with Respect to Activities in the Area*, Advisory Opinion of 1 February 2011, ITLOS Reports 2011, para. 117.

[12] ICJ, *Reservations to the Convention on the Prevention and Punishment of the Crime of Genocide*, Advisory Opinion of 28 May 1951, ICJ Reports 1951, 15, para. 12.

[13] Mark Toufayan, 'A Return to *Communitarianism*? Reacting to "Serious Breaches of Obligations Arising under Peremptory Norms of General International Law" under the Law of State Responsibility and United Nations Law', *Canadian Yearbook of International Law* 42 (2004), 197–251, 197.

[14] See, e.g., Michael Reisman, 'Acting *Before* Victims Become Victims: Preventing and Arresting Mass Murder', *Case Western Reserve Journal of International Law* 50 (2007), 57–85, at 59, 60.

'each State undertakes to prevent and punish crimes against humanity, which are crimes under international law, whether or not committed in time of armed conflict.' Article 4 of the draft Articles presents a more concrete obligation to take specific legislative, administrative, judicial, or other preventive measures. This provision is copied from human rights treaties and transnational criminal law treaties and, in contrast to draft Article 3(2), it is territorially and jurisdictionally limited.[15]

Initially, the commentary to draft Article 3(2), then draft Article 2, stated that, 'the content of this general obligation will be addressed through the various more specific obligations set forth in the draft articles that follow, beginning with draft Article 4'.[16] Such a statement links the two provisions and seems to deny a separate existence for the general obligation. In his first report, the Special Rapporteur had, instead, differentiated more clearly between the different function and scope of the two prevention provisions, and connected the general prevention provision of then draft Article 2 expressly with its counterpart in the Genocide Convention. The general and extraterritorial obligation to prevent in then draft Article 2 is effectively an obligation to rescue with extraterritorial reach, just like Article I of the Genocide Convention. These are emergency obligations when atrocity crimes are on the verge of being committed or to prevent further escalation when they are already ongoing. Draft Article 4, instead, is more truly preventative in nature as it obliges states to take measures in their own territory ensuring that the conditions in which crimes against humanity can be committed do not arise. Given the different territorial scope and function of the two provisions, it is important to underscore the autonomous status of what is now draft Article 3(2), which is not only an opening provision but instead has as much independent legal value as the ICJ attributed to Article I of the Genocide Convention. In the final commentaries, this is indeed explicitly recognized in commentary 8 to draft Article 3(2).

This chapter zeroes in on the general obligation to prevent of Article I of the Genocide Convention and draft Article 3(2) on crimes against humanity, which can also be called obligations to rescue. The chapter makes the claim that these are twin-provisions, not only in terms of having autonomous legal standing but also as regards contents. While generally appreciating the ICJ's observation that 'the content of the duty to prevent varies from one instrument to another according to the wording of the relevant provisions, and depending on the nature of the acts to be prevented',[17] the obligation to prevent genocide and the obligation to prevent crimes against humanity can nonetheless be regarded as being the same in contents, scope, and nature. Such a conclusion is supported, in a literal sense, by

[15] For a discussion of more territorially and/or jurisdictionally limited due diligence obligations, also in the human rights field, see Federica Violi, 'The Function of the Triad "Territory", "Jurisdiction", and "Control" in Due Diligence Obligations', chapter 5 of this book, section 4.1.

[16] United Nations, General Assembly, Report of the Sixty-seventh session, A/70/10, 4 May–5 June and 6 July–7 August 2015, 53.

[17] ICJ, *Bosnia Genocide* (n. 5), para. 429.

the equivalent wording of the respective provisions ('undertake to prevent'), and the express references of the Rapporteur to the ICJ *Bosnia Genocide* case in his reports. More substantively, the sameness of the two provisions flows from the similarity in structure of the two international crimes, the substantive overlap between the definitions of genocide and crimes against humanity,[18] and the fact that they are mentioned equally in preventive and Responsibility to Protect contexts. For these reasons, the nature, scope, and contents of an obligation to prevent cannot but be identical for these two crimes despite their differing legal basis.[19] Pursuant to this position, dicta of the ICJ as regards the scope, nature, and contents of the obligation to prevent genocide apply *mutatis mutandis* to the obligation to prevent crimes against humanity, and discussions in the context of the ILC's work on crimes against humanity also inform the obligation to prevent genocide.

3. The Nature and Scope of the Obligation to Prevent: Capacity of the Duty Bearer as the Linking Pin

Obligations to prevent are generally hard to classify under international law.[20] Toufayan has made the point that the obligation to prevent genocide specifically is of sui generis character given the highly political, social, and cultural interests at stake and the same argument can be made for crimes against humanity.[21] There is also general agreement that the obligation must be one of conduct and not of result, and that a state can only be held responsible for failure to prevent if genocide has actually been committed.[22] Those dissenting voices that rather regard the obligation to prevent genocide as one of result, have broader difficulties with the ICJ's extensive interpretation.[23] They see the obligation to prevent genocide as mostly

[18] Philippe Sands details how the intellectual fathers of respective crimes, Lemkin and Lauterpacht, agreed on the value of human life as central, but had different views on approach. Lemkin underlined the necessity to focus on protection of the group as such, whereas Lauterpacht favoured a more individualised approach, Philippe Sands, *East West Street: On the Origins of Genocide and Crimes against Humanity* (London: Weidenfeld and Nicholson 2016), e.g., 378–381.

[19] As also suggested in the report of the Dutch Advisory Committee on Issues of Public International Law (CAVV), 'Advisory report on the scope for and the significance and desirability of the use of the term "genocide" by politicians', March 2017, available at: https://cms.webbeat.net/ContentSuite/upload/cav/doc/Report_no._28_on_the_use_of_the_term__genocide__by_politicians.pdf (accessed 6 February 2019).

[20] See also the discussion between Crawford and Dupuy: James Crawford, 'Revising the Draft Articles on State Responsibility', *European Journal of International Law* 10 (1999), 435–460, and Pierre-Marie Dupuy, 'Reviewing the Difficulties of Codification: on Ago's Classification of Means and Obligations of Result in Relation to State Responsibility', *European Journal of International Law* 10 (1999), 371–385.

[21] Mark Toufayan, 'The World Court's Distress when Facing Genocide: A Critical Commentary on the Application of the Genocide Convention Case (*Bosnia Herzegovina v. Yugoslavia (Serbia and Montenegro)*', *Texas International Law Journal* 40 (2005), 233–261, at 255.

[22] ICJ, *Bosnia Genocide* (n. 5), paras 432, 427, 431; cf. United Nations, ILC, Draft Articles on Responsibility of States for Internationally Wrongful Acts, Supplement No. 10 (A/56/10), ch. IV.E.1, November 2001, art. 14(3).

[23] See, e.g., ICJ, *Bosnia Genocide* (n. 5), Declaration of Judge Leonid Skotnikov, 366, 378–379.

political in nature and they insist on territorially limited obligations based on notions of control rather than influence.[24]

In the *Bosnia Genocide* case, the court did not pronounce on potential ius cogens status of the obligation to prevent genocide, although its use of a slightly less demanding standard of proof might be indicative of the view that this status does not attach specifically to the obligation to prevent.[25] While some scholars still derive ius cogens status of the obligation to prevent from the peremptory character of the principal prohibition of genocide, arguing that the normative status of the prohibition would otherwise be rendered meaningless,[26] one can also argue that ius cogens status of a principal prohibition does not necessarily radiate to all ancillary rights and obligations surrounding the principal norm. In sum, the ius cogens status of the obligation to prevent remains undecided. It is also unclear how such status would affect its due diligence character, but the argument could be made that at the very least the ius cogens character of the preventive obligation or even only of the primary prohibition to which it attaches more forcefully obliges states to publicly explain how they took this obligation into account as part of their broader foreign policy decision-making vis-à-vis a certain situation of risk.

As to scope, the generically framed provisions containing the undertaking to prevent genocide and crimes against humanity are not expressly territorially limited. One of the noteworthy features of the 2007 *Bosnia Genocide* case concerned the ICJ's confirmation of Article I's independent and extraterritorial reach.[27] It held that, 'the substantive obligations arising from Articles I and III are not on their face limited by territory. They apply to a state wherever it may be acting or may be able to act in ways appropriate to meeting the obligations in question.'[28] Judge Leonid Skotnikov opposed the extraterritorial reading, which he found 'extraordinarily expansive'. Both Judges Leonid Skotnikov and Peter Tomka argued that, if an extraterritorial obligation was accepted this had to be linked to the exercise of jurisdiction or control.[29] The ICJ, instead, introduced a more flexible approach, and embraced a global duty to prevent.[30]

24 Ibid.

25 ICJ, *Bosnia Genocide* (n. 5), para. 210; Andrea Gattini, 'Breach of the Obligation to Prevent and Reparation Thereof in the ICJ's Genocide Judgement', *European Journal of International Law* 18 (2007), 695–713, at 697.

26 Ben-Naftali, 'The Obligation to Prevent and to Punish Genocide' 2009 (n. 9), 36.

27 As earlier found by the ICJ, *Application of the Convention on the Prevention and Punishment of the Crime of Genocide (Bosnia and Herzegovina v Serbia and Montenegro)*, Judgment on Preliminary Objections of 11 July 1996, ICJ Reports 1996, 595, para. 31.

28 ICJ, *Bosnia Genocide* (n. 5), para. 183.

29 Ibid., Separate Opinion of Judge Tomka, 310, para. 67; Ibid., Declaration of Judge Leonid Skotnikov, 366, 377–378 (Judge Leonid Skotnikov's obligation of result is closely linked to an obligation to prevent as envisaged in draft art. 4 of the articles on Crimes against Humanity (United Nations, International Law Commission (ILC), Crimes against humanity, A/CN.4/L.892, 26 May 2007, 4)); Judge Kreća opposed the interpretation of art. I in even more absolute terms in his Separate Opinion (ICJ, *Bosnia Genocide* (n. 5), Separate Opinion of Judge ad hoc Kreća, 457, paras 113–120).

30 ICJ, *Bosnia Genocide* (n. 5), para. 430; scholars have argued that this was stretching the interpretation of art. I, Gattini, 'Breach of the Obligation to Prevent and Reparation Thereof' 2007 (n. 25), 699.

Mitigating the universal reach of the obligation, the ICJ subsequently introduced the notion of due diligence and emphasised that responsibility for breaching the obligation would only be incurred if 'the State manifestly failed to take all measures to prevent genocide which were within its power'.[31] It thus used the notion of due diligence to limit the scope of the extraterritorial obligation and to introduce the idea of differentiated responsibility. The suggested parameter to differentiate was 'capacity to influence'. Factors that informed this capacity, as mentioned by the court, were: (i) geographical distance of the state from the scene of the events; and (ii) strength of political and other links between the state and the main actors in the events. Christian Tams has added to this that economic ties can also create relationships of dependence which may generate influence. He also pointed to the practical relevance of regularity of contact as a factor that will inform a state's effective ability to reach out in time.[32] In addition, Christian Tams referred to legal powers such as occupational regimes, that may be factors informing the notion of 'capacity to influence'. Taking this one step further, membership of a regional organisation could also be seen as a relationship that results in influence. Other special relations that may inform state's capacity to influence may flow from former colonial ties, which would generally be captured by the ICJ's reference to political ties. In addition to parameters that link a state's capacity to prevent harm to its relation with the perpetrators, one may also broaden the spectrum and focus on relations between states and victims of genocide or crimes against humanity.[33] For instance, diaspora bonds may also effectively enable a third state to take measures to protect that diaspora from genocide based on pre-existing relations and channels of communication with both the diaspora and the host state of the diaspora. Beyond the diaspora relation, the question can be raised as to whether refugee and asylum obligations vis-à-vis victims of genocide and crimes against humanity can come within the realm of an overarching obligation to prevent.[34] Hence, there is merit in understanding the capacity to influence as being broader than only concerning state-perpetrator relationships.

The concept of 'capacity to influence' also allows for more future-oriented approaches to the obligation to prevent genocide that would consider new types of duty bearers beyond the state, in particular social media companies like Facebook. Recent studies have shown that the role of new media in inciting violence goes

See also for analysis of the global duty, Christian Tams, 'Commentary on Article I', in Christian Tams/Lars Berster/Björn Schiffbauer (eds), *Convention on the Prevention and Punishment of the Crime of Genocide: A Commentary* (Munich: C. H. Beck/Hart/Nomos 2014), 46–48.

[31] ICJ, *Bosnia Genocide* (n. 5), para. 430.

[32] Tams, 'Commentary on Article I' 2014 (n. 30), 52.

[33] See, similarly, Brian Barbour/Brian Gorlick, 'Embracing the "Responsibility to Protect": A Repertoire of Measures Including Asylum for Potential Victims', *International Journal of Refugee Law* 20 (2008), 534–566, at 561–565.

[34] Sareta Ashraph/Makrina Finlay/Melinda Taylor, 'Asylum and the Duty to Protect the Yazidis from Genocide', 15 August 2018, available at: http://opiniojuris.org/2018/08/15/asylum-and-the-duty-to-protect-the-yazidis-from-genocide/ (accessed 16 April 2020).

much beyond offering a platform to extremists.[35] They map how incentive structures and social cues of algorithm-driven social media sites breed extremism organically, as posts figuring negative tribal emotions tend to score well and draw heavy engagement, thus radicalizing youth that is merely seeking to increase its numbers of followers or plaudits and likes. Platforms' actual capacity to influence and regulate online discussion is under scrutiny, and more generally debates on their role and responsibilities are in full flux, which may in turn also necessitate rethinking the concept of due diligence specifically as applied to non-state actors in relation to their potential independent obligation to prevent genocide and crimes against humanity.

4. The Contents of an Extraterritorial Obligation to Prevent and Its Relationship to Decision-making Processes

The due diligence character of the obligation to prevent genocide was also emphasised in another respect, namely as regards the contents of the obligation. The ICJ invoked the notion of due diligence to underline the need for assessment in concreto.[36] Serena Forlati also referred to the 'structural impossibility to identify once and for all what behaviours would be required to fulfil the obligation of prevention'.[37] The obligation to prevent is not static and it is inherently context-specific. The outer frontier that is fairly clear is that states may only act within the limits permitted by international law,[38] and hence the obligations to prevent genocide and crimes against humanity cannot be construed as independent bases for humanitarian intervention or other self-standing exceptions to the use of force.[39] At the other end of the spectrum, the obligation ultimately shrinks the room for complete passivity and full inaction.[40] Within these frontiers, the obligation to prevent does not contain a clear-cut positive obligation to resort to a specific type of action. Instead, it is highly discretionary, and it primarily obliges states to 'interrogate their actions and choose a course of conduct (and make public the reasons for it)'.[41] Hence at the core of the obligation to prevent lies the obligation to make informed decisions about the most appropriate course of conduct, coupled with an obligation to explain those decisions and subsequent conduct. Specific measures

[35] Max Fisher/Amanda Taub, 'How Everyday Social Media Users Become Real-World Extremists', *New York Times* (25 April 2018).

[36] ICJ, *Bosnia Genocide* (n. 5), para. 430.

[37] Serena Forlati, 'The Legal Obligation to Prevent Genocide', *Polish Yearbook of International Law* 31 (2001), 189–205, at 201.

[38] ICJ, *Bosnia Genocide* (n. 5), para. 430.

[39] Tams, 'Commentary on Article I' 2014 (n. 30), 51; But see Ben-Naftali, 'The Obligation to Prevent and to Punish Genocide' 2009 (n. 9), 43–44.

[40] Tams, 'Commentary on Article I' 2014 (n. 30), 54.

[41] Ibid., 53.

that states can choose to take may be of a diplomatic, social, or economic nature, or other, and they may include the imposition of targeted sanctions, or instead the lifting of an arms embargo to enable another state to prevent genocide.[42] The obligation to prevent genocide or crimes against humanity can also have implications for decision-making on the sending or continuation of peacekeeping missions.[43]

Measures with more direct economic impacts or of semi-military nature are not necessarily always the most important or effective though. Uncritical attitudes or silent support conveying a message that certain atrocities will de facto be tolerated or ignored are also often very conducive to creating the conditions in which mass atrocity takes place. In this context, the friendly reception of Rwandan Ministers at the Champs Elysées in the run up to the genocide in February 1994, as well as Rwanda's continued seating at the Security Council during the genocide, have been heavily criticised as conveying the wrong message. Less well-known, but also relevant in this respect, is the support of important segments of the international community for the Rwandan Patriotic Front before, during, and after the genocide, despite the fact that this actor's character may be less benign than often assumed.[44] In other situations, more decisive preventive action can even sort counterproductive effects. In relation to Syria, former Dutch diplomat Nikolaos van Dam has observed that the imposition of sanctions by western states, coupled with demands for accountability, has in fact resulted in diminished leverage over Assad and has thus eroded the West's capability to influence. This has resulted in less opportunities to effectively contribute to the prevention of further violence and atrocities.[45] Paradoxically therefore, it seems that in certain situations if a state takes measures to comply with the obligation to prevent this might reduce its capacity to influence and thereby lessen the intensity of the obligation as it applies to that state.

These examples illustrate the intensely discretionary nature of the obligation to prevent genocide and crimes against humanity, which is tied to the different views that exist in concrete situations of how best to handle a certain crisis. The examples thus underscore that, at its core, the obligations to prevent genocide and crimes against humanity concern an obligation to make well-informed decisions and to publicly explain action in atrocity situations in light of an overarching obligation to prevent rather than it being a precisely delineated substantive obligation. Such an understanding of the obligation corresponds with the view of due diligence as

[42] Ibid., 53; ICJ, *Case Concerning Application of the Convention on the Prevention and Punishment of the Crime of Genocide (Bosnia and Herzegovina v Serbia and Montenegro)*, Order for Provisional Measures of 13 September 1993, Separate Opinion of Judge ad hoc Lauterpacht, ICJ Reports 1993, 407.

[43] See for an analysis of how the obligation and ability to prevent was treated in Dutch courts in relation to Srebrenica, André Nollkaemper, 'Dual Attribution: Liability of the Netherlands for Conduct of Dutchbat in Srebrenica', *Journal of International Criminal Justice* 9 (2011), 1143–1157.

[44] See, generally, André Guichaoua, *From War to Genocide: Criminal Politics in Rwanda, 1990–1994*, (Madison: University of Wisconsin Press 2015).

[45] See, generally, Nikolaos van Dam, *Destroying a Nation: The Civil War in Syria* (London: I.B. Tauris 2017).

being a technique that transposes complex and controversial inquiries on content to less controversial questions on informed decision-making and process.[46] This then, evokes the question regarding a proper institutional framework to ensure and test how decision-making in third states with capacity to influence takes places, and whether the aim of preventing genocide and crimes against humanity has a proper place in broader foreign policy discussion as regarding a concrete situation. In democratic states, members of parliament may play an important role in putting situations on the agenda and verifying whether state responses and actions are adequate.[47] Ultimately, and *ex post facto*, the ICJ may check whether indeed a state has done all that could reasonably be expected to prevent atrocities in a given situation.

The question is whether there is a need for institutional machinery in between those extremes in which the obligation to prevent could be gradually clarified, or at least a platform that would encourage states to publicly justify their actions. In his preparations for a convention on crimes against humanity, the Special Rapporteur considered it best to have states select an appropriate monitoring mechanism, which might then also be connected to the Genocide Convention,[48] and the question of finding an appropriate institutional framework or platform in which due diligence can effectively be exercised remains open. Suggestions for a monitoring committee on the obligation to prevent genocide have been put forward,[49] but obviously these are highly contentious and seen as too intrusive in questions of foreign policy. Rather than a monitoring body therefore, and in conformity with the view of the core of the obligation to prevent being a procedural obligation to make informed decisions and to explain, the appropriate mechanism could also be a platform on which states with capacity to influence are invited to explain their specific conduct vis-à-vis a given situation. Without going into institutional details, the existence of such a platform linked to the Genocide and (future) Crimes against Humanity Convention would gradually clarify the notion of 'capacity to influence' while also recording how and what decisions states make in response to a certain situation taking account of their overarching obligations to prevent genocide and crimes against humanity.

[46] Martti Koskenniemi, as referred to in Tim Stephens and Duncan French, ILA, Study Group on Due Diligence in International Law, 'Second Report', 12 July 2016, 3.

[47] See, e.g., House of Commons Foreign Affairs Committee: Violence in Rakhine State and the UK's response, 6 December 2017. See more generally on the role of parliaments in foreign policy, Stelios Stavridis/Davor Jančić, *Parliamentary Diplomacy in Europe and Global Governance* (Leiden: Brill 2017).

[48] ILC, Provisional summary record of the 3348th meeting, A/CN.4/SR.3348, 2 June 2017, 6.

[49] See, e.g., Etienne Ruvebana, *Prevention of Genocide under International Law: An Analysis of the Obligations of States and the UN to Prevent Genocide at the Primary, Secondary and Tertiary Levels* (Cambridge: Intersentia 2014), 255.

5. When to Prevent Genocide: Risk, Due Diligence, and New Technology

The obligation to prevent genocide and crimes against humanity is temporally limited, and will be triggered by the existence of certain circumstances. According to the ICJ, the obligation is activated at the moment when a state is 'aware, or should normally have been aware, of the serious danger that acts of genocide would be committed'.[50] The threshold is therefore one of actual or constructive awareness of the risk of genocide, not certainty that genocide would in fact take place.[51]

Establishing that a state was in fact aware of the risk of genocide or crimes against humanity is a question of evidence. In the *Bosnia Genocide* case, the ICJ referred to documents detailing meetings between Slobodan Milosevic and third state officials[52] to determine that 'the dangers were known' to the Belgrade authorities, leading the court to hold that 'it must have been clear that there was a serious risk of genocide'.[53] Establishing that a state 'should normally have been aware' is a more complex matter, as it requires a determination of the knowledge that can be imputed to a state in the absence of evidence of actual knowledge. The ICJ provided no guidance on how this constructive knowledge is to be determined, and in the absence of such guidance two approaches can be suggested.

Under the first approach, the constructive knowledge element serves to cover those situations where actual knowledge cannot be proven, but where the accessibility and widespread availability of information is such that a reasonable person can be expected to have been aware. The second approach is more far reaching, and involves interpreting 'should normally have been aware' as imposing a positive obligation on states to take steps to inform themselves of situations of risk. Under this approach, the obligation to prevent genocide and crimes against humanity includes procedural obligations, such as the carrying out of risk assessments. The substantive obligations to prevent would therefore be activated not only when a state actually knew of the risk of genocide or crimes against humanity occurring, but also in situations where a diligently carried out risk assessment would have brought the risk to the state's attention.

5.1 Digital Technologies and Ascertaining Facts

For both approaches, the crucial question is what information was available to states concerning the risk of genocide or crimes against humanity. This can relate

[50] ICJ, *Bosnia Genocide* (n. 5), para. 431.
[51] Tams, 'Commentary on Article I' 2014 (n. 30), 49.
[52] ICJ, *Bosnia Genocide* (n. 5), paras 436–437.
[53] Ibid., para. 438.

to the information which was passively available to a state, under the first approach, and/or the information that would have come to the state's attention when actively carrying out a risk assessment, under the second approach. Traditional sources of information include diplomatic communications, public information, media coverage, and reports of governmental and non-governmental organisations;[54] however, these sources are increasingly supplemented by new sources of information arising as a result of technological developments. Digital technologies now allow for information to be gathered from areas that are otherwise hard to reach—due to security, infrastructure, etc.—and they allow for a larger volume of information to be gathered than was previously possible. This can contribute to a more accurate and granular understanding of events on the ground and potential risks. Ascertaining the range of information available to states therefore requires an understanding of what these technologies have to offer. A sample of three digital technologies will be outlined below: Satellite imagery, social media and radio monitoring, and mobile phone technology. Following a discussion on the types of information produced by these technologies, some key questions will be raised concerning how they may affect the triggering of prevention obligations.

Satellite imagery itself is not a new technology, and has been used by state intelligence agencies for many years. However, following a loosening up of regulations in the 1990s, satellite images have been increasingly used to document atrocities in geographical areas that are otherwise challenging or impossible to access.[55] Examples of such efforts include the documentation of prison camps in North Korea, and the documentation of conflict and violence in Sri Lanka, Nigeria,[56] Sudan,[57] and Myanmar.[58] In addition to documentation, there is now a move to use satellite imagery as a tool for preventing atrocities. When taken over a period of time, satellite images can show troop movements, troop build-up, and the strengthening of military infrastructure.[59] Such events are listed by the Office on Genocide Prevention and the Responsibility to Protect (OGPRP) as factors that can indicate

[54] Tams, 'Commentary on Article I' 2014 (n. 30), 49.

[55] Nathaniel A. Raymond/Brittany L. Card/Isaac L. Baker, 'A New Forensics: Developing Standard Remote Sensing Methodologies to Detect and Document Mass Atrocities', *Genocide Studies and Prevention* 8 (2014), 33–48, at 33.

[56] In relation to North Korea, Sri Lanka, and Nigeria, see Christoph Koettl, 'Sensors Everywhere: Using Satellite and Mobile Phones to Reduce Information Uncertainty in Human Rights Crisis Research', *Genocide Studies and Prevention* 11 (2018), 36–54, at 41–45.

[57] The report 'Sudan: Anatomy of a Conflict' was the first retrospective analysis of archival satellite imagery on a large scale to document a conflict over a multi-year time frame (Harvard Humanitarian Initiative, 'Sudan: Anatomy of a Conflict', June 2013, available at: https://hhi.harvard.edu/publications/sudan-anatomy-conflict (accessed 6 February 2019)).

[58] Human Rights Watch, 'Burma: Satellite Imagery Shows Mass Destruction', 19 September 2017, available at: https://www.hrw.org/news/2017/09/19/burma-satellite-imagery-shows-mass-destruction (accessed 6 February 2019); *The Guardian*, '"Everything is gone": satellite images in Myanmar show dozens of Rohingya villages bulldozed', 24 February 2018.

[59] Nathaniel Raymond/Benjamin Davies/Brittany Card/Zaid Al Achkar/Isaac Baker, 'While We Watched: Assessing the Impact of the Satellite Sentinel Project', *Georgetown Journal of International Affairs* 14 (2013), 185–191, at 187.

a risk of genocide or crimes against humanity.[60] Furthermore, satellite images can indicate bombardment patterns, damage to buildings, and fresh grave sites, all of which can help to identify when violence is escalating to the point where a risk of genocide or crimes against humanity is present.[61] In 2011, the Satellite Sentinel Project was established to use satellite imagery to monitor potential threats to civilians along the border between Sudan and the soon-to-be-independent South Sudan.[62] The Satellite Sentinel Project communicated regular reports to the international community concerning risks of genocide and crimes against humanity in South Sudan, thereby bringing this to the attention of states.

Another factor that the OGPRP lists as indicating a risk of genocide and crimes against humanity is an increase in inflammatory rhetoric, propaganda campaigns, or hate speech targeting protected groups or individuals.[63] Of the ten stages of genocide identified by the NGO GenocideWatch, dehumanisation through hate speech is listed as number four,[64] and hate speech is a phenomenon that can be historically detected in the run-up to many genocide and crimes against humanity events.[65] Identifying increases in hate speech is therefore important in understanding when a risk of such events arises. Digital technologies have allowed for more widespread monitoring of the media forms that are often used for circulating hate speech, including radio and social media.

Radio played an important part in disseminating hate speech prior to, and during, the genocide in Rwanda,[66] and radio is still a primary communication tool in many parts of the world. However, given the large number of stations and the many hours of broadcasts, monitoring the radio for hate speech can be prohibitively resource intensive. The UN programme Global Pulse sought to overcome this challenge by developing a digital tool for analysing radio content.[67] The tool converts verbal broadcasts into text, and then searches for keywords and phrases

[60] United Nations, Office on Genocide Prevention and the Responsibility to Protect (OGPRP), Framework of Analysis for Atrocity Crimes: A Tool for Prevention, 30 October 2014, 16–17.

[61] Raymond/Card/Baker, 'A New Forensics' 2014 (n. 55), 35.

[62] See generally, Raymond/Davies/Card/Al Achkar/Baker, 'While We Watched' 2013 (n. 59) and Ben Yunmo Wang/Nathaniel Raymond/Gabrielle Gould/Isaac Baker, 'Problems from Hell, Solution in the Heavens?: Identifying Obstacles and Opportunities for Employing Geospatial Technologies to Document and Mitigate Mass Atrocities', *Stability: International Journal of Security & Development* 2 (2013), 1–18.

[63] OGPRP, Framework of Analysis, 30 October 2014 (n. 60), 16–17.

[64] Gregory Stanton, 'The Ten Stages of Genocide', available at www.genocidewatch.org (accessed 24 January 2019). The stages correspond with Lemkin's writings on the different phases of genocide, Raphael Lemkin, *Axis Rule in Occupied Europe* (Washington D.C.: Carnegie Endowment for International Peace 1944).

[65] Gregory Gordon argues that a connection between hate speech and atrocities can be traced from ancient Egypt and ancient Rome, through World Wars I and II, through the genocide in Rwanda and the war in the Balkans, to the modern-day atrocities in Sudan, Myanmar, and Ivory Coast (Gregory Gordon, *Atrocity Speech Law* (Oxford: OUP 2017), 29–58).

[66] See, generally, Allan Thompson (ed.), *The Media and the Rwanda Genocide* (London: Pluto Press 2007); Catherine A. MacKinnon, 'Prosecutor v. Nahimana, Barayagwiza, & Ngeze. Case No. ICTR 99-52-T', *American Journal of International Law* 98 (2004), 325–330.

[67] UN Global Pulse, 'Using machine learning to analyse radio talk in Uganda', September 2017.

to identify sections of broadcast that merit closer analysis. The tool was piloted in Uganda for the purpose of gathering information relating to the Sustainable Development Goals, but by adapting the keywords and phrases, the technology could also be used to identify hate speech.

In addition to radio, any attempt to monitor hate speech must include the monitoring of social media. In Myanmar, for example, there was a spike in hate speech on Facebook prior to the 2017 escalation of violence against Rohingya Muslims.[68] Given social media's accessibility and its ever growing reach, hate speech posted on these platforms can reach a very large audience in a short time and play a significant role in fuelling tensions. As with radio, monitoring social media is challenging due to the amount of content; to take the video sharing platform YouTube as an example, 400 hours of video are uploaded every minute.[69]

More recent developments are moving from monitoring social media to also predicting the occurrence of hate speech. Software being developed by the NOHATE project will identify hate speech on social media and may eventually predict when an online discussion will escalate into hate speech.[70] This enables preventive measures to counter instances of hate speech. With the tools already in existence, and the tools under development, we will progress to the point when real-time information on rising levels of hate speech and the risks associated therewith can be made available to states more quickly.

Satellite imagery and radio and social media monitoring collect information indirectly, in the sense that those moving on the ground and those posting to social media do not intend to signal a risk of genocide or crimes against humanity. Information collected directly is also of great value, including speaking to individuals on the ground about events taking place in their surroundings and the possible risks they are facing. This can provide insights that other types of information do not, such as a pattern of attacks on a particular target group, patterns of discrimination, and significant differences in the socio-economic positions of different groups. These issues are also included in the OGPRP list of factors that can indicate a risk of genocide or crimes against humanity.[71] While gathering such information may traditionally have meant conducting face-to-face interviews and travelling to the region, mobile phone technology allows for such information to be gathered remotely, on a larger scale, and in a more cost effective manner.[72]

[68] Michael Safi, 'Revealed: Facebook hate speech exploded in Myanmar during Rohingya crisis', *The Guardian* (3 April 2018).

[69] Malachy Browne, 'YouTube Removes Videos Showing Atrocities in Syria', *The New York Times* (22 August 2007).

[70] Freie Universität Berlin, 'A Machine to fight the Hate: Researchers develop software to detect hate speech online', 7 March 2018, available at: https://www.fu-berlin.de/en/international/news-events/newsletter/2018/201801/hatespeech.html.

[71] OGPRP, Framework of Analysis, 30 October 2014 (n. 60), 11, 18.

[72] Nielsen/World Food Programme, 'Revolutionizing Data Collection: World Food Programme and Nielsen Use Scalable Mobile Surveys in Today's Changing Technological Landscape', 6 June 2015,

Initiatives of this type are being carried out by organisations such as the UN World Food Programme, which use messaging apps such as WhatsApp to collect information about food security, including photographs. The UN World Food Programme compiles the information it collects into reports and a vulnerability map, allowing for the information about food security in a region to be disseminated to states and other relevant actors. Such programmes could be (and possibly already have been) adapted to collect information relevant to atrocity prevention. Instead of inquiring about the price of a kilo of flour, individuals could be asked about violent events in their area, about who is the target of these attacks, how often attacks occur, etc. Such information can then be compiled and distributed to states to bring situations of risk to their attention.

5.2 Digital Technologies and Changing Procedural Obligations?

Digital technologies can increase the amount of information available to states, making it harder for states to argue that they did not, and should not, have known of the risk of genocide or crimes against humanity. While in the past states may have reasonably argued that they lacked actual or constructive knowledge of events taking place in remote and non-permissive regions, technology renders such arguments less credible, and increasingly so in the future.

If one accepts the second approach to the 'should have known' criterion, namely that states have the procedural obligation to actively conduct risk assessments concerning the risk of genocide or crimes against humanity, the impact of these digital technologies is possibly greater still. In an advisory opinion, the ITLOS Seabed Disputes Chamber noted that what is required by due diligence may change over time, and that 'measures considered sufficiently diligent at a certain moment may become not diligent enough in light, for instance, of new scientific or technological knowledge'.[73] With this in mind, questions can be raised regarding the scope and content of states' procedural obligations, and in particular, whether and to what extent states are required to utilise digital technologies when carrying out risk assessments. If a state fails to include satellite imagery in its risk assessment for an area, can that state be considered to have acted sufficiently diligently? Is a state obliged to monitor social media to determine whether there is an increase in hate speech? The same questions can be asked for other digital technologies also. Taking the inquiry one step further, one can consider whether an obligation to include digital technologies in risk assessments also involves an obligation to develop digital

available at: https://www.wfp.org/content/revolutionizing-data-collection-world-food-programme-nielsen-scalable-mobile-surveys-jun-2015 (accessed 6 February 2019).

73 ITLOS, *Responsibilities and Obligations in the Area Opinion* (n. 11), para. 117.

technologies that are fit for purpose. As discussed above, digital technologies developed for other purposes—such as monitoring the sustainable development goals or understanding food insecurity—could potentially be adapted to the atrocity prevention context. Are states under an obligation to take such a step? There will be a point when a state will be deemed to have sufficiently discharged its procedural obligations, but the increasing availability of digital technologies will play a role in determining when that point is reached.

6. The Obligation to Prevent Genocide and Crimes Against Humanity as a Due Diligence Obligation

The prohibitions of genocide and crimes against humanity are without any doubt ius cogens norms. Whether the obligation to prevent also has ius cogens status remains undecided, but the more interesting question for this chapter is whether the ius cogens status of the primary norm impacts on the due diligence nature of the obligation to prevent and renders this of a unique nature and completely different from other due diligence obligations in international law. This does not seem to be the case per se.

In the specific context of the obligation to prevent genocide and crimes against humanity, the function of the notion of due diligence was to insert some realism and place limits on the obligation's universal reach, as well as to introduce the concept of differentiated obligations corresponding with capacity. The concept of 'capacity to influence' also allows for the future consideration of other duty holders in addition to states, such as social media corporations.

Effectively, through the notion of due diligence the state's discretion to decide upon its own foreign policy is respected, while a dimension of accountability is introduced as a state is expected to make informed decisions that also take account of its obligation to prevent. Furthermore, the state needs to be able to explain its actions and how they contributed to prevention in situations where there is a real risk that genocide or crimes against humanity will be committed. The core of the obligation to prevent as a due diligence obligation is then the obligation to make informed decisions and to publicly explain how this is done.

In their article on risks in international law, Wouter Werner and Fleur Johns analysed the relationship between uncertainty, knowledge, and risk. They highlighted the belief that an increase in scientific knowledge would also enlarge the scope of social and legal responsibilities, especially the responsibility to prevent possible future harm.[74] In the particular context of preventing mass atrocity, the emergence of new technologies may certainly intensify due diligence obligations of

[74] Fleur Johns/Wouter Werner, 'The Risks of International Law', *Leiden Journal of International Law* 21 (2008), 783–786, at 784.

states, especially those with strong cyber- and other capacities. Yet, new technologies have led to overproduction of information and scientific knowledge, and this overproduction may in turn pose limits to the possibility of transforming uncertainty into manageable risks. Coupled with the highly discretionary nature of the obligation to prevent genocide and crimes against humanity, the question what is due in terms of preventive responses is not easily answered in the abstract. The emphasis lies perhaps foremost with the issue of diligence in the form of procedures and institutions. This then underscores the suggested need for a platform or other institutional mechanism connected to the Genocide and (future) Crimes against Humanity Convention. Such a forum would function as the site where the obligation to prevent can gradually be clarified and substantiated on the basis of concrete cases and situations. This line of thinking stresses the procedural nature of the obligation to prevent genocide and mass atrocity as a due diligence obligation and it is in that sense, it can ultimately be concluded, that the obligation or its due diligence nature is not fundamentally different or even unique. Its specialty rather flows from the gravity of the underlying norm, which makes it even more important to take the obligation seriously despite its inevitable elusiveness.

13

Due Diligence, the UN, and Peacekeeping

Nigel D. White

1. Introduction

The UN itself does not directly perform peacekeeping but relies on forms of 'outsourcing' to states and occasionally to private contractors. As there is a gap between the UN's commissioning and overall command of peacekeeping operations and its day-to-day control of peacekeepers, it is argued in this chapter that the UN should have due diligence obligations in regard to the conduct it has set in train. Peacekeepers may act for the UN but they remain very much soldiers of their sending states, meaning that the UN should be diligent to ensure that peacekeepers operate within an institutional and procedural framework that includes respect for, and protection of, the human rights of the civilian population of the host state. This chapter focuses on the application, acceptance, and implementation of human rights due diligence obligations in UN peacekeeping operations. It points to growing, but uneven, evidence of the development of standards and measures by the UN that would fit the meaning and purpose of due diligence, although there are very few instances of due diligence being used as a term within the UN. The argument in the chapter is that due diligence obligations are applicable to the UN as primary rules of international law rather than secondary rules of responsibility,[1] either through customary human rights law or the internal law of the UN or both, due to the fact that the principles of peacekeeping are themselves based on general principles of international law.

2. Should Due Diligence Apply to the UN?

In principle at least, most of what is written on due diligence obligations of states should be applicable to intergovernmental organisations (IGOs) possessing separate international legal personality and recognised as subjects of international law capable of exercising rights and duties on the international plane. Indeed, the International Law Association's Study Group on Due Diligence includes

[1] Timo Koivurova, 'Due Diligence', in: Rüdiger Wolfrum (ed.), *Max Planck Encyclopaedia of Public International Law* (Oxford: OUP 2010).

Nigel D. White, *Due Diligence, the UN, and Peacekeeping* In: *Due Diligence in the International Legal Order.* Edited by: Heike Krieger, Anne Peters, and Leonhard Kreuzer, Oxford University Press (2020). © The Several Contributors. DOI: 10.1093/oso/9780198869900.003.0013.

IGOs within its broad statement that 'due diligence is concerned with supplying a standard of care against which fault can be assessed', whereby 'a standard of reasonableness, of reasonable care', is applied to both states and IGOs 'that either commissioned the relevant act or which omitted to prevent its occurrence'.[2] Given that the UN 'commissions' various acts through its peacekeeping operations, the logic of due diligence should apply to it. Borrowing from Joanna Kulesza, who writes about a 'level of care',[3] the expectation is that the UN should take care to ensure that those actors it has mandated do not cause damage, injury, or loss, especially when that is as a result of their wrongful conduct.

A requirement that the UN act diligently to prevent harm should not impose over-onerous obligations. For responsibility to be incurred, an organisation must have 'manifestly failed to take all measures' that were 'within its power' to take'.[4] Nonetheless, recognising that due diligence obligations extend to the UN would certainly make it much more open to claims against it. A manifest failure to take preventive measures to protect civilians when the UN has a force on the ground, as in Srebrenica in 1995, would make the UN even more vulnerable to claims if due diligence obligations were attached to it. It might be argued that peacekeepers are not in a position to prevent genocide, due to their limited military capability, but it should be noted that the mandate of the United Nations Protection Force in 1995 included protecting safe areas.[5] The International Law Association's report highlights this conundrum, without solving it, by stating the 'due diligence requirements increase in situations in which the risks of harm are known to be particularly significant'.[6]

Under international human rights law a 'State's obligations in relation to the actions of third parties are often expressed in terms of due diligence', so that it may be 'held liable for human rights violations caused by a third party where the State has failed to exercise due diligence to prevent the violation or to respond as required'.[7] This aspect of due diligence is based on the state as the sovereign actor in its territory making it responsible for failing to take reasonable measures to prevent violations by private actors. This aspect is difficult to extend to the UN because it does not generally exercise sovereignty over a territory.[8] Obligations to prevent human rights abuses by private actors unconnected to the UN would go a step further than

[2] International Law Association (ILA), Study Group on Due Diligence in International Law, Second Report, 12 July 2016, 2.

[3] Joanna Kulesza, *Due Diligence in International Law* (Leiden: Nijhoff, 2016), 1.

[4] ILA, Study Group on Due Diligence, Second Report 2016 (n. 2), 8. Citing, inter alia, ICJ, *Application of the Convention on the Prevention and Punishment of the Crime of Genocide (Bosnia and Herzegovina v. Serbia and Montenegro)*, Judgment of 26 February 2007, ICJ Reports 2007, 43, para. 430.

[5] United Nations, Security Council, Resolution 836, S/RES/836, 4 June 1993.

[6] ILA, Study Group on Due Diligence, Second Report 2016 (n. 2), 12.

[7] Ibid., 32, citing Inter-American Court of Human Rights, *Velasquez Rodriguez Case*, Judgment of 29 July 1988, IACtHR (Ser. C) No. 4 (1988), para. 172.

[8] But see the judgment ECtHR, *Behrami v. France*, Grand Chamber Decision as to Admissibility of 2 May 2007, Application no. 71412/01, paras 70, 129–130, 133–134, 140.

the UN having due diligence obligations vis-à-vis peacekeepers drawn from states or even private security contractors it has engaged as part of its peace operations. However, where the UN exercises sufficient control, wider due diligence obligations should be engaged, for example if a peacekeeping force failed to take reasonable measures to prevent or stop violence by private individuals against civilians sheltered in its compounds or camps. The Human Rights Committee felt that human rights obligations under the Covenant extended to Troop Contributing Nations (TCNs) in a peacekeeping mission to ensure the human rights of persons within their power or effective control,[9] and therefore the customary equivalents should apply to the UN. In this light, and given the flexible nature of due diligence obligations, one might argue that the extent of due diligence obligations should be commensurate with the level of control exerted by an IGO. In other words, the UN has, in principle, obligations to take reasonable measures to prevent human rights abuse by peacekeepers or contractors operating under its mandate or control, and it may have such obligations to prevent human rights abuse by private actors if it is within its power to do so.

Since the UN itself does not directly perform peacekeeping but relies on forms of 'outsourcing' either to states and, occasionally, to private contractors, it can be argued that it should have due diligence obligations. In order to understand why, it is necessary to look at the consequences of the UN not having due diligence obligations in terms of its legal responsibility. Although the UN may be in effective control of the conduct that constituted a wrongful act by peacekeepers, and thereby can be directly responsible for that act,[10] normally the UN does not effectively control the impugned conduct, leaving a responsibility and accountability gap. Several factors indicate the normal lack of effective control by the UN: the practice of zonal deployment of peacekeeping forces, with each TCN having a significant level of control in their zone; the role of TCN commanders who commonly defer to their national governments rather than the commands of the UN Force Commander; conflicting national and UN rules of engagement leading to a preference for TCN rules of engagement due to the fact that military discipline lies with TCNs and not with the UN.

It could be argued that the absence of UN responsibility for the wrongful acts of peacekeepers does not prevent victims from seeking redress from TCNs and in that sense there is no gap in accountability. However, in the absence of due diligence, this would mean that the UN would not bear any legal responsibility for operations that it is responsible for creating and over which it does have a significant degree of control through the Security Council, Secretary-General, and Force

[9] United Nations, Human Rights Committee, General Comment 31, Nature of the General Legal Obligation on States Parties to the Covenant, CCPR/C/21/Rev.1/Add.13, 26 May 2004, para. 10.

[10] United Nations, International Law Commission (ILC), Report of the Work of the Sixty-Third Session, A/66/10, 23 April–3 June and 4 July–12 August 2011, 90.

Commander. The recognition of due diligence obligations would not only fill a gap in UN responsibility, but as primary obligations would also mean that the UN would have to take reasonable care to ensure that its operations were sufficiently resourced and controlled to fulfil their functions, including respecting and protecting human rights. Unfortunately, there is plenty of evidence that the UN has, in the past, deployed under-resourced and ill-prepared forces.[11] The recognition of the UN's due diligence obligations would provide legal standards against which to judge the preparedness of its deployments: did the UN exercise reasonable care and take adequate measures in the creation, mandating, and deployment of a force so as to prevent human rights abuses against civilians where it had the power to do so? Due diligence can fill a gap in an 'era of "privatized" international relations',[12] because although the UN does not effectively control many of the activities carried out under its authority, it still owes a duty of due diligence to those affected by such activities.

In any case, the benefit of due diligence is that it is not dependent upon effective control of the conduct that constitutes human rights abuse, given that it operates to require reasonable measures of prevention by the mandating organisation irrespective of whether a peacekeeper is truly regarded as a representative of the UN or of his or her sending state. To put it differently, the UN should not be able to deny that it has due diligence obligations for its peacekeeping forces even though it is not in effective control of all aspects of that force's conduct.[13] The conduct attributed to the state or the UN is the failure to take measures to prevent the abuses, not the abuses themselves.[14] It follows that the UN's due diligence obligations are not only to take measures to ensure that TCNs comply with their obligations under human rights law, but also directly to ensure that peacekeepers do not violate human rights and act to protect the human rights of others where they have the power to do so.

3. Do Due Diligence Obligations Bind the UN?

While the above section established that the conditions are present whereby due diligence obligations can and should apply to the UN, it remains to be established that the UN has duties under international law, including positive obligations under human rights law. In general terms it can be argued that the obligations on individual peacekeepers to protect human rights can be traced back not only to

[11] United Nations, Report of the High-Level Independent Panel on Peace Operations on Uniting our Strengths for Peace: Politics, Partnership and People (HIPPO Report), A/70/95-S/2015/446, 17 June 2015, para. 126.

[12] Kulesza, *Due Diligence* 2016 (n. 3), 1.

[13] Robert Barnidge, 'The Due Diligence Principle under International Law', *International Community Law Review* 8 (2006), 81–121, at 82.

[14] IACtHR, *Velasquez Rodriguez* (n. 7), para. 172.

their sending states and their duties under international law, but also in a separate act of constitutional validation to the UN Charter, and to the organisation itself. As an international legal person, a status implied from the provisions of the UN Charter indicating the organisation's autonomy from member states, the UN possesses separate rights and duties on the international plane.[15]

More substantially, the International Court of Justice has declared that the UN is a subject of international law and as 'as such' is 'bound by any obligations incumbent upon' it: under 'general rules of international law', under its constitution, or under international agreements to which it is a party.[16] Guglielmo Verdirame concludes that 'the most plausible interpretation' of the term 'general rules of international law' used by the court is that it is shorthand 'for customary international law of universal or quasi-universal applicability and for general principles of law'.[17] Furthermore, he suggests that subjecting the UN to 'this body of law, notwithstanding the absence of any evidence of [the UN] specifically consenting to each rule of it, is consistent with the approach adopted in the 1950s and 1960s towards newly independent states, when the view was taken that these new subjects of international law were bound by general custom'.[18] However, this does not make complete sense given that UN has been an international legal person since its inception in 1945, a status clarified by the International Court of Justice in 1949. This signifies that the organisation preceded the emergence of customary human rights law, a process the UN General Assembly itself initiated by the Universal Declaration of Human Rights in 1948. This calls into question the automatic attachment of customary human rights law to the UN. It also raises the question of whether consent to be bound, either expressly given or in the form of acquiescence, is required of the UN.

It is easy to agree with Verdirame that it would 'be extremely disruptive for the international system to tolerate the presence of actors that are endowed with legal personality, and thus with the legal capacity to operate upon the international plane, but are exempt from a body of universally or almost universally accepted rules'.[19] However, a consensual view of international law at least casts doubt upon the automatic attachment of customary human rights duties to the UN without its subsequent express or tacit consent.[20] While international legal personality gives

[15] ICJ, *Reparations for Injuries Suffered in the Service of the United Nations*, Advisory Opinion of 11 April 1949, ICJ Reports 1949, 174, 179.

[16] ICJ, *Interpretation of the Agreement of March 1951 between the WHO and Egypt*, Advisory Opinion of 20 December 1980, ICJ Reports 1980, 73, 90.

[17] Guglielmo Verdirame, *The UN and Human Rights: Who Guards the Guardians?* (Cambridge: CUP 2011), 71.

[18] Ibid.

[19] Ibid.

[20] Raphael M. Walden, 'The Subjective Element in the Formation of Customary International Law', *Israel Law Review* 12 (1977), 344–364, at 359.

the UN the capacity to hold duties and rights, the actual possession of specific obligations, including ones of due diligence, requires greater consideration.

Subject to caveats regarding its consent, due diligence obligations can attach to the UN in regards to its peacekeeping operations, first either by dint of customary rules of international law applicable to it as an international legal person, or, secondly, via its own internal constitutional order and the rules deriving from it.[21]

3.1 External Obligations

If due diligence is a general principle of customary international law it will apply to the UN on the basis of its international legal personality. If due diligence is not seen as a general principle itself, but is to be found in particular norms within particular regimes such as human rights law or international humanitarian law, then it is necessary to establish that those specific due diligence obligations have become part of customary international law, which then bind the UN. John Cerone, for instance, states that it is unclear whether the positive obligations contained in Article 2(1) of the International Covenant on Civil and Political Rights have counterparts in customary international law.[22] Having said that he argues for the application of human rights due diligence obligations to the UN at least when it is exercising sovereign powers over a territory, as it did in Kosovo,[23] presumably on the basis that such obligations are inherent in such powers.

3.2 Internal Obligations

The constituent treaty as developed in practice is an alternative—internal as opposed to external—source of due diligence obligations, in particular the human rights provisions of the UN Charter,[24] and the 'rules of the organisation' developing those provisions.[25] More specifically, it might also be argued that due diligence obligations flow from the general principles governing peacekeeping operations, namely consent, limited use of force, and impartiality. These principles are specific manifestations of fundamental principles of international law; of sovereignty,

[21] Henry Schermers/Niels Blokker, *International Institutional Law* (Leiden: Martinus Nijhoff 5th ed. 2011), 755.

[22] John Cerone, 'Reasonable Measures in Unreasonable Circumstances: A Legal Responsibility Framework for Human Rights Violations in Post-Conflict Territories under UN Administration', in Nigel D. White/Dirk Klaasen (eds), *The UN, Human Rights and Post-Conflict Situations* (Manchester: Manchester University Press 2005), 42–80, at 59.

[23] Ibid., 77.

[24] For example, Charter of the United Nations, 24 October 1945, 1 UNTS XVI, arts 24(2), 55, and 56.

[25] ILC, Articles on the Responsibility of International Organisations, YBILC, 2011, vol. II, Part Two, art. 2(b).

non-aggression, and non-intervention. This blurs the boundary between 'internal' and 'external' rules of international law, as the UN has crafted the basic principles governing peacekeeping from basic principles of the international legal order.

4. Consent as a Basis of Due Diligence

Peacekeeping forces are deployed and emplaced on the basis of the consent of the host state, normally reflected in a Status of Forces Agreement (SOFA) between the UN and the host state. The UN Standard SOFA of 1990 contains due diligence-type language when stating that the 'Special Representative/Commander shall take all appropriate measures to ensure the observance of (…) obligations'.[26] In addition to obligations arising from local laws, this due diligence-type obligation to ensure observance is crafted with reference to the UN's own internal legal order, namely the duties arising from the 'impartial and international nature' of peacekeeping, and not by reference to any external rules of international law.

However, an examination of recent operational SOFAs shows a growing acceptance by the UN of the applicability of some international laws to UN peacekeeping and, moreover, that the UN has due diligence obligations to ensure that peacekeepers comply with them. For instance, the 2004 SOFA agreed between the UN and the government of Haiti concerning the status of United Nations Stabilization Mission in Haiti (MINUSTAH) contains the above stated clause, but follows it with a paragraph stating the UN 'shall ensure that MINUSTAH shall conduct its operation in Haiti with full respect for the principles and rules of the international conventions applicable to the conduct of military personnel', referencing the four Geneva Conventions of 1949 and their Additional Protocols of 1977. It then uses due-diligence-type language to state that 'MINUSTAH shall ensure that the members of its military personnel are fully acquainted with the principles and rules of the above-mentioned international instruments'.[27]

These paragraphs refer to the principles and rules of conventions applicable to the conduct of military personnel and give the key international humanitarian law treaties as examples. It does not expressly mention human rights conventions, even though they are arguably more relevant to peacekeepers who are generally not engaged as combatants in an armed conflict. A similar provision is contained in the SOFA between the UN and the government of the Republic of South Sudan of 2011 as regards United Nations Mission in the Republic of South Sudan.[28]

[26] United Nations, General Assembly, Model Status-of-Forces Agreement for Peacekeeping Operations, A/45/594, 9 October 1990, para. 6.

[27] Agreement Between the United Nations and the Government of Haiti Concerning the Status of the United Nations Operation in Haiti, 9 July 2004, 2271 UNTS 251, para. 6.

[28] The Status of Forces Agreement Between the United Nations and the Government of the Republic of South Sudan Concerning the United Nations Mission in South Sudan, 8 August 2011, para. 6.

5. Impartiality as a Basis of Due Diligence

Impartiality might also be viewed as a fruitful source of due diligence obligations. The UN's position as peacekeeper in a host state is one of a protected international actor,[29] with immunity from local jurisdiction, and depends upon it being above the dispute and disputants. To achieve this, the UN must take measures to ensure that the state organs and agents it uses, and any private contractors, respect that principle. Furthermore, the evolution of impartiality suggests that peacekeepers cannot be passive in the face of human rights violations committed by others. As peacekeeping has become part of more complex 'peace operations' it is difficult for the force to remain completely neutral, and so this norm has been modified so that the force must be impartial in the implementation of its mandate, enabling it to take coercive action against 'spoilers' and others trying to undermine the peace process. The 'need for even-handedness towards the parties should not become an excuse for inaction in the face of behaviour that clearly works against the peace process (…) or the international norms and principles that a United Nations peacekeeping operation upholds'.[30]

However, while modern peacekeeping principles seem to reflect a move from neutrality to impartiality, the change does not appear to have been fully matched by actions on the ground, or in the understandings of their obligations by TCNs, or even the UN Secretariat.[31] While the intention after the Brahimi Report of 2000 was that peacekeepers should not again stand by in the face of egregious human rights violations,[32] the practical problems of establishing a credible gap between neutrality and impartiality has led to instances of peacekeepers remaining passive in the face of violence against civilians.

6. The Limitations Upon Force as a Basis of Due Diligence

Over the lifetime of peacekeeping operations there has been confusion as to the nature and level of force that peacekeepers are permitted to use. Despite a post-Cold War trend towards allowing more offensive action to be taken by peacekeepers, there is reluctance, especially from TCNs, to move away from peacekeeper self-defence as this makes the force less acceptable to the host state and the parties

[29] Convention on the Safety of United Nations and Associated Personnel, 9 December 1994, 2051 UNTS 363.

[30] United Nations, Secretariat, Department of Peacekeeping Operations/Department of Field Support, United Nations Peacekeeping Operations, Principles and Guidelines ('The Capstone Doctrine'), 2008, 14.

[31] Dominick Donald, 'Neutrality, Impartiality and UN Peacekeeping at the Beginning of the 21st Century', *International Peacekeeping* 9 (2002), 21–38, at 31–33.

[32] United Nations, Report of the Panel on United Nations Peace Operations (Brahimi Report), A/55/305-S/2000/809, 21 August 2000, paras 48–51.

within it. However, despite this reticence in practice, at the doctrinal level the UN has expanded the concept of self-defence. The Brahimi Report of 2000 did this by extending the language of self-defence from individual self-defence to defence of the mission.[33] This forms part of the doctrinal development of when legitimate force can be used by peacekeepers through the 'gradual expansion of the meaning of self-defence in Peacekeeping Operations (PKOs), from individual self-defence inherent to military personnel, to freedom of movement and defence of positions, to the defence of the mandate and the protection of third parties'.[34]

Increasing pressure is on peacekeepers to use force to protect civilians under attack or under threat of attack, and for them to protect the peace agreement and process from 'spoilers' who seek to undermine it. Thinking about this development in terms of due diligence, there is evidence (reviewed in the following section) that the UN takes measures to ensure that force is not used by peacekeepers in a way that violates basic rules of international human rights law or, where applicable, international humanitarian law: for example, specifying rules on when force should be used and providing assistance with the training of peacekeepers. However, it falls short of an objective standard in these circumstances, by not having rules on the use of force that are fully human rights compliant by, for example, allowing the use of potentially lethal force in defence of UN mission-essential property; by not directly training peacekeepers but relying on TCNs to do so under guidance by the UN; and by not providing remedies for abuse by peacekeepers or ensuring that TCNs provide remedies.[35]

7. Evidence of Due Diligence Usage and Acceptance in Peacekeeping

UN practice is certainly not consistent given that there are some clear instances in peacekeeping practice where due diligence should apply to the UN, but the UN does not appear to accept it has obligations in this regard. The failure to take measures to prevent cholera in Haiti seems to be a breach of a duty of care by the UN. While discussion of Haiti has been largely about the legality and legitimacy of the UN's use of immunity to protect itself from national courts,[36] the failure to screen the contingent from Nepal and to ensure that proper sanitation was installed in the camp occupied by UN peacekeepers from MINUSTAH,[37] demonstrate that the

[33] Ibid.

[34] Nicholas Tsagourias, 'Consent, Neutrality/Impartiality and the Use of Force in Peacekeeping Operations: Their Constitutional Dimension', *Journal of Conflict and Security Law* 11 (2006), 465–482, at 473.

[35] Nigel D. White, 'The Use of Weapons in Peace Operations', in Stuart Casey-Maslen (ed.), *Weapons under International Human Rights Law* (Cambridge: CUP 2014), 197.

[36] *Georges v. United Nations*, US Court of Appeals 2nd Circuit, No. 15-455-cv, 18 August 2016.

[37] See Alejando Cravioto, 'Final Report of the Independent Panel of Experts on the Cholera Outbreak in Haiti', 4 May 2011.

UN did not achieve the requisite level of care in fulfilling its obligations to respect the life and health of the people of Haiti. However, the UN has accepted only a 'moral responsibility to the victims of the cholera epidemic in Haiti',[38] indicating that there is still a long way to go towards the UN fully accepting that it is bound by obligations of due diligence.

Nevertheless, despite inconsistencies in practice, UN peacekeeping doctrine (reviewed below) demonstrates a growing acceptance by the UN that it is under an obligation to take measures to respect and protect human rights. However, the resultant due diligence framework remains quite basic. In particular, the UN's duties towards individuals remain under-developed. As a duty bearer, the UN's due diligence not only extends to taking measures to ensure that TCNs comply with their human rights obligations to protect the rights of individuals, but also means that the UN owes duties of due diligence to the rights holders, namely individuals within its power.

7.1. Memoranda of Understanding

There is a certain sharing of duties of prevention in the memoranda of understanding between the UN and TCNs, which provide that the TCN 'shall ensure' through pre-deployment training that all members of its national contingent understand and comply with UN standards of conduct. For its part, the UN shall provide to TCNs 'mission specific training material on United Nations standards of conduct, mission-specific rules and regulations, and relevant local laws and regulations'. Further, the UN 'shall conduct adequate and effective induction training and training during mission assignment to complement pre-deployment training'.[39] Although the question arises as to whether these are adequate measures to prevent human rights abuse, there is a certain sharing out of duties in that regard, but no recognition of the UN's duties vis-à-vis civilians. Furthermore, most duties lie with the TCNs not only as regards training but also the investigation of acts of misconduct by peacekeepers when the TCN has primary responsibility,[40] and in matters of discipline and criminal jurisdiction when the TCN has exclusive competence.[41]

[38] United Nations, General Assembly, The New United Nations Approach to Cholera in Haiti, A/RES/71/161, 13 January 2017. See also United Nations, General Assembly, Secretary-General's Report, 'A New Approach to Cholera in Haiti', A/71/620, 25 November 2016.

[39] Memorandum of Understanding Between the United Nations and [participating State] Contributing Resources to [the United Nations Peacekeeping Operation], A/C.5/63/18, 2008, para. 7.

[40] Ibid., para 7.10.

[41] Ibid., paras 7.5, 7.22, 7.24.

7.2. UN Peacekeeping Reports

At the doctrinal level, reports relating to peacekeeping produced or acknowledged by the UN can be examined in order to glean any signs of acceptance of human rights obligations by the UN, and moreover, whether this involves any obligations of due diligence to take reasonable measures to ensure that peacekeepers act in accordance with human rights.

The Brahimi Report of 2000, adopted against the backdrop of a failure by UN peacekeeping operations to protect civilians in Rwanda and Bosnia, has been pivotal to peacekeeping forces having stronger mandates to protect civilians. The Report expressly recognises the 'essential importance of the United Nations system adhering to and promoting international human rights instruments and standards and international humanitarian law in all aspects of its peace and security activities'.[42] In terms of measures, the Report mentions: 'improving respect for human rights through the monitoring, education and investigation of past and existing abuses'; training local police forces according to international human rights standards; having sufficient numbers of human rights specialists; the closer involvement of the UNOHCHR in 'planning and executing the elements of peace operations that address human rights'; and the importance of training military, police, and civilian personnel on human rights and international humanitarian law.[43] The Report strongly supports the development of an interim legal code by the UN based on human rights instruments, which could be applied by UN personnel in the legal vacuum often present in post-conflict states.[44] Overall the panel recommended a 'doctrinal shift (. . .) in complex peace operations to reflect an increased focus on strengthening rule of law institutions and improving respect for human rights in post-conflict environments'.[45] The Report, in effect, presents a range of measures that might in part be deemed to fulfil the UN's due diligence obligation 'to secure human rights'.[46]

The Capstone Doctrine of 2008 strengthens the idea that the UN itself has both negative and positive human rights obligations when it states that UN 'peacekeeping operations should be conducted in full respect of human rights and should seek to advance human rights through the implementation of their mandates'.[47] Further, UN 'peacekeeping personnel—whether military, police or civilian—should act in accordance with international human rights law and understand how the implementation of their tasks intersects with human rights'. This takes the form of a negative obligation: 'peacekeeping personnel should strive to ensure

42 Panel on Peace Operations, Brahimi Report, 21 August 2000 (n. 32), para. 6(e).
43 Ibid., paras 13, 38, 39, 40, 41, 244.
44 Ibid., para. 81.
45 Ibid., para. 47(b).
46 Ibid., para. 288.
47 Department of Peacekeeping Operations, Capstone Document, 2008 (n. 30), 14.

that they do not become perpetrators of human rights abuses'; and a positive obligation: 'they must be able to recognize human rights violations or abuse, and be prepared to respond appropriately within the limits of their mandate and their competence'.[48] The question then becomes whether the UN has acted diligently 'to ensure that human rights are promoted and protected by and within [its] field operations'.[49]

It is difficult to accept that the UN can meet its due diligence obligations when, by and large, training and equipment are largely the responsibility of TCNs,[50] albeit with substantial UN input into 'mandatory training in human rights, conduct and discipline, sexual exploitation and abuse and gender equality'.[51] While training improves the capability of peacekeepers and their ability to protect human rights, is it adequate to ensure that threats to civilians are significantly reduced? There is recognition that more is needed in the High Level Independent Panel on Peace Operations (HIPPO) Report of 2015, which stated that 'assessments of threats to civilians must drive capability requirements and planning'.[52] The UN's dependence on TCNs undermines its ability to take reasonable and effective measures to protect civilians, beyond the production of training materials for the use of TCNs, and the creation of standards of expected behaviour of peacekeepers. In its 2018 resolution on 'United Nations Peacekeeping Operations' it is worth noting that Security Council affirmed its support for the 'development of a comprehensive and integrated performance policy framework that identifies clear standards of performance for evaluating all United Nations civilian and uniformed personnel', while urging all TCNs to 'meet UN performance standards for personnel, training, and equipping'.[53] There is a drive by the UN to improve peacekeeping performance but the question remains as to how that might translate to meaningful due diligence obligations.

The HIPPO Report of 2015 focuses on issues of capability and resources of peace operations.[54] When deployed with a protection of civilians mandate, peace operations 'must do everything in their power to protect civilians under threat', through 'physical presence, deterrence and protective action'.[55] More specifically the report identified that resources and capability should be sufficient to enable: human rights monitoring, investigating, and reporting; taking decisive action to contain spreading violence or looting; providing havens to civilians fleeing violence; in

[48] Ibid., 15.
[49] Ibid., 27.
[50] United Nations, General Assembly, Comprehensive Review of the Whole Question of Peacekeeping Operations in All their Aspects, A/RES/49/37, 9 February 1995.
[51] UN Core Pre-Deployment Training Materials for United Nations Peacekeeping Operations (CPTM 2017), 6.
[52] HIPPO Report, 2015 (n. 11), para. 92.
[53] United Nations, Security Council, Resolution 2436, S/RES/2436, 21 September 2018, paras 1 and 3.
[54] HIPPO Report, 2015 (n. 11).
[55] Ibid., para. 83.

exceptional cases to support operations against armed groups. In addition to these measures that aim to protect civilians from third parties, the Report includes measures to prevent abuse by peacekeepers including human rights screening, and the barring of troops from TCNs with records of sexual or child abuse.[56]

The HIPPO Report makes reference to the UN Policy on 'Human Rights in United Nations Peace Operations and Political Missions' of 2011, which focuses in part on measures to be taken by mission leaders to protect the rights of civilians. In general they should 'anticipate, plan and prepare mission-wide plans for possible crises, escalation of violence and upsurges of human rights violations, within the limits of their mandate and capability', with 'internal procedures developed to ensure rapid preventive and protection responses'. Ultimately, in 'situations warranting measures to prevent or halt serious human rights violations, responses by the military component may include joint planning to rapidly deploy to volatile areas, support to human rights mobile teams, advocacy with potential perpetrators, proactive deterrent joint patrolling and—as a last resort—the use of force to protect civilians in accordance with the rules of engagement'.[57]

These measures identified in the HIPPO Report 2015 and the UN Policy of 2011, which extend significantly beyond training in human rights standards, have the potential to form a core of a UN due diligence doctrine detailing obligations of conduct. Given the limitations of peacekeeping, it is not possible for the UN to protect all civilians. This is recognised in the HIPPO Report especially when peacekeepers are deployed to situations of sustained armed conflict when the capabilities of the force will be reduced. In these situations the Report recommends the deployment of coalitions of the willing.[58] It could be argued that, when considering the possible due diligence obligations of the Security Council, it has the duty to take measures commensurate with the threat, so that peacekeeping forces are not placed in situations that warrant peace enforcement.

7.3. Security Council Mandates

With the above caveat in mind, do Security Council peacekeeping mandates manifest any signs of due-diligence-type obligations or measures that would reflect such? An examination of the thematic 'Protection of Civilians Resolutions' is somewhat disappointing in this regard in that they are not clearly binding decisions, they are confined to protecting civilians in armed conflicts, and they are

[56] Ibid., paras 87, 88, 91, 95, 213, 232, 264, 265, 289.

[57] United Nations, Office of the United Nations High Commissioner for Human Rights, Department of Peacekeeping Operations, Department of Political Affairs and Department of Field Support, Human Rights in United Nations Peace Operations and Political Missions, Ref. 2011.20, 1 September 2011, para. 87.

[58] HIPPO Report, 2015 (n. 11), para. 118.

generally not expressed in due-diligence terms.[59] Resolution 1894 of 2009 contains some provisions that suggest an approach closer to due diligence, for example, in commitments to prioritising the protecting of civilians in decisions concerning resources, risk assessments of the threats against civilians, and strategies and operational concepts specifically to address threats to civilians.[60]

The mandate of the United Nations African Union Hybrid Operation in Darfur (UNAMID), a joint UN-AU force deployed to Darfur in 2007, typically for a post-Brahimi peacekeeping operations contained a paragraph in which the Council acted under Chapter VII to decide that UNAMID was 'authorised to take necessary action, in the areas of deployment and as it deems within its capabilities' to 'protect civilians, without prejudice to the responsibility of the Government of Sudan'.[61] Any obligations created by this provision are ones of conduct not result as they are specifically linked to the judgment and capabilities of the force, but they lack real content as to concrete measures to protect the human rights of civilians under threat. Stronger language is found in the specific area of preventing sexual abuse by peacekeepers in the form of a request to the Secretary-General 'to take the necessary measures to achieve actual compliance in UNAMID' with the UN's zero-tolerance policy on sexual abuse, 'including the development of strategies and appropriate mechanisms to prevent, identify and respond to all forms of misconduct, including sexual exploitation and abuse', to 'ensure full compliance with the United Nations code of conduct'.[62]

The initial mandate of United Nations Multidimensional Integrated Stabilization Mission in the Central African Republic, deployed to the Central African Republic in 2014, has similar provisions on sexual abuse,[63] but also contains enhancements in the protection of civilians. The Council decided that the force's priority tasks were: to protect civilians 'from the threat of physical violence, within its capabilities and areas of deployment, including through active patrolling'; to provide specific protection for women and children including through the deployment of protection advisers; to identify and record attacks against civilians; and to 'design, implement and deliver' a 'mission-wide protection strategy'.[64] While by no means fully developed due diligence obligations, there is some movement towards the recognition that specific measures have to be taken not only to ensure that peacekeepers do not abuse the rights of civilians, but to protect the rights of civilians from abuse by others.[65]

59 See United Nations, Security Council, Resolution 1265, S/RES/1265, 17 September 1999, and United Nations, Security Council, Resolution 1674, S/RES/1674, 28 April 2006.
60 United Nations, Security Council, Resolution 1895, S/RES/1895, 18 November 2009, paras 19–24.
61 United Nations, Security Council, Resolution 1769, S/RES/1769, 31 July 2007, para. 15.
62 Ibid., para. 16.
63 United Nations, Security Council, Resolution 2149, S/RES/2149, 10 April 2014, para. 38.
64 Ibid., para. 30(a).
65 See also SC, Resolution 2436, 21 September 2018 (n. 53).

7.4. UN Secretary-General's Bulletins

The 1999 Bulletin outlines rules of international humanitarian law applicable to UN peacekeepers when they engage as combatants. The Bulletin contains a limited due diligence requirement on the UN, 'to ensure that members of the military personnel of the force are fully acquainted with the principles and rules (. . .) applicable to the conduct of military personnel'.[66]

The 2003 Bulletin on sexual abuse shows greater due diligence potential in that it is directed at providing measures of protection from sexual exploitation and abuse by UN peacekeepers. The Bulletin states that the Head of Mission 'shall be responsible for creating and maintaining an environment that prevents sexual exploitation and sexual abuse, and shall take appropriate measures for this purpose'. In particular, the Head of Mission 'shall inform his or her staff of the contents of the present bulletin'.[67] Furthermore, the Bulletin provides a limited amount of due diligence as regards third parties when the UN has entered into arrangements with them, whereby relevant UN officials shall inform them of the standards of conduct and 'shall receive a written undertaking from those entities or individuals that they accept these standards'. Furthermore, it provides that the 'failure of those entities or individuals to take preventive measures against sexual exploitation or sexual abuse, to investigate allegations thereof, or to take corrective action when sexual exploitation or sexual abuse has occurred, shall constitute grounds for termination of any cooperative arrangement with the United Nations'.[68]

The 2003 Bulletin has limited due diligence content, restricting appropriate measures to informing peacekeepers of the content of the Bulletin. In terms of remedies, the possibility of referral to national prosecuting authorities[69] is insufficient given the normal weaknesses of the host state's criminal justice system. Of further concern are the limited preventive measures to be taken when engaging non-UN entities, which are restricted to duties of informing such entities of the standards, and termination of the arrangements if those entities fail to comply with those standards.

Overall, the Bulletins show little evidence of the UN accepting it has due diligence obligations owed directly to the rights holders, namely individuals within the control or power of peacekeepers or third parties engaged by the UN.

[66] United Nations, Secretariat, Observance by United Nations Forces of International Humanitarian Law, ST/SGB/1999/13, 6 August 1999, section 3.

[67] United Nations, Secretariat, Special Measures for Protection from Sexual Exploitation and Sexual Abuse', ST/SGB/2003/13, 9 October 2003, section 4 'Duties of Heads of Department, Offices and Missions', para. 4.1.

[68] Ibid., section 6.

[69] Ibid., section 5.

7.5. The UN's Due Diligence Policy of 2013

The advent of the UN's Due Diligence Policy of 2013,[70] whereby the UN takes some measures to ensure that non-UN forces it supports are not committing war crimes, is a step forward in the sense of recognising due diligence is applicable to the UN. However, a piecemeal approach, exemplified by the 2013 Policy, is unduly distractive from a deeper understanding of due diligence and its relationship to the general principles of law governing peacekeeping. Nevertheless, the Policy of 2013 accepts the applicability of human rights law, international humanitarian law, and refugee law to the UN and, moreover, that the organisation must take measures to prevent and respond to violations by third parties.[71]

The Policy accepts that the UN must take precautions to assess the risk of violation and respond to violations, including intercession with the entity in question and, if necessary the removal of support. Specifically, when the UN is contemplating involvement with non-UN security forces it 'must therefore pursue a policy of due diligence' consisting of: an assessment of 'the risk of the recipient entity committing grave violations of international humanitarian law, human rights law or refugee law'; 'transparency with receiving entities about the legal obligations binding the Organization and the core principles governing provision of support'; and an 'effective implementation framework' including procedures for monitoring compliance and interceding.[72]

Standing alone this represents a positive and explicit development towards accepting that the UN has human rights due diligence obligations to take a series of precautionary, preventive, and responsive measures to ensure that a state or non-state security actor working alongside UN peacekeepers does not commit grave violations of human rights and other norms. While this Policy established that the UN owes due diligence obligations in its relationships with non-UN security actors, there is as yet no express commitment by the UN to extend such obligations to ensure precautionary and responsive measures are taken to address the potential or actual abusive actions of any non-UN actor who operates in areas to which peacekeepers are deployed.

8. Conclusion

This chapter has focused on the application, acceptance, and implementation of human rights due diligence obligations in UN peacekeeping operations. It has

[70] United Nations, General Assembly/Security Council, Human Rights Due Diligence Policy on United Nations Support to non-United Nations Security Forces', A/67/775-S/2013/110, 5 March 2013.
[71] Ibid., paras 1 and 3.
[72] Ibid., para. 2.

pointed to growing evidence of the development of standards and measures by the UN that would fit the meaning and purpose of due diligence, although there are very few instances of due diligence expressly being used as a term within the UN. This is not to say that such obligations are not applicable to the UN. It has been established that due diligence obligations are applicable either through customary human rights law, or the internal law of the UN, or both, due to the fact that the UN's principles of peacekeeping are themselves based on general principles of international law. Moreover, given the outsourced nature of UN peacekeeping, due diligence obligations are necessary to ensure respect for human rights by peacekeepers through the adoption of measures such as clear rules, training, education, risk assessment and mitigation, but also in terms of adequate resources and capabilities of a peacekeeping force. Furthermore, the ambit of due diligence extends to require that the UN puts in place reasonable measures to ensure that peacekeepers actively protect the human rights of civilians in their areas of deployment from violation by non-UN actors. Such measures, scattered unevenly and not always convincingly in UN doctrine, include proactive patrolling, rapid redeployments, safe havens, intercessions, detention of spoilers and, where absolutely necessary to protect the lives of civilians, the use of potentially lethal force.

The development of a coherent and consistent concept of due diligence for UN peacekeeping would involve the identification and enhancement of the UN's institutional due diligence obligations, for example through consistent Security Council decision-making, and by the adoption of clear procedural due diligence obligations such as human rights risk assessment by the UN Secretariat. There is evidence of emerging standards in this regard. Moreover, the approach adopted in the chapter considers the substantive human rights obligations the UN owes to rights holders especially civilians, and identifies the measures that can reasonably be taken by the UN and its peacekeepers to ensure those rights are protected, given the inherent limitations in the way forces are structured. Only by starting with the rights of vulnerable people can a truly inductive approach to the due diligence obligations of the UN be realised. Put simply, when the UN promises to protect civilians in countries to which it deploys peacekeepers it needs to take care to ensure that this happens.

14

Due Diligence in International Anti-terrorism Law

Developments in the Resolutions of the UN Security Council

Inger Österdahl[*]

1. Introduction

This chapter investigates the content of the due diligence principle in the area of international anti-terrorism law. The aim is to map out and clarify, as far as possible, what could reasonably be labelled the due diligence duties of states in this area. Currently, the substance of possible due diligence duties in the area of anti-terrorism law has been largely unexplored. At this point in international anti-terrorism law, one and only one due diligence duty would seem relatively uncontested, namely the rule stated in the *Corfu Channel* case of 1949 whereby every state is under the duty 'not to allow knowingly its territory [to] be used for acts contrary to the rights of other states'.[1] This general rule was further developed with respect to international anti-terrorism law in the Friendly Relations Declaration adopted by the UN General Assembly in 1970.[2] The Friendly Relations Declaration lays down that:

> [e]very State has the duty to refrain from organizing, instigating, assisting or participating in acts of civil strife or terrorist acts in another State or [even more importantly in the context of international anti-terrorism due diligence duties] acquiescing in organized activities within its territory directed towards the commission of such acts, when the acts referred to in the present paragraph involve a threat or use of force.[3]

[*] I would like to thank the Torsten Söderberg Foundation for enabling this research through a generous grant, R5/17.

[1] ICJ, *Corfu Channel Case (United Kingdom v. Albania)*, Judgment of 9 April 1949, ICJ Reports 1949, 4, p. 22.

[2] UN, General Assembly, Declaration on Principles of International Law concerning Friendly Relations and Co-operation among States in accordance with the Charter of the United Nations, A/RES/25/2625, 24 October 1970.

[3] Ibid.

Inger Österdahl, *Due Diligence in International Anti-terrorism Law* In: *Due Diligence in the International Legal Order*. Edited by: Heike Krieger, Anne Peters, and Leonhard Kreuzer, Oxford University Press (2020). © The Several Contributors. DOI: 10.1093/oso/9780198869900.003.0014.

This Friendly Relations Declaration rule is often cited explicitly or implicitly in the resolutions of the UN Security Council that deal with anti-terrorism measures. Regarding the quality of this due diligence duty, it would appear to be relatively uncontested at this moment that the duty is one of effort, or conduct, and not one of result.[4]

The purpose of this chapter then is to explore whether additional due diligence duties of states have developed or might be developing in the field of international anti-terrorism law. This will be done primarily by focusing on one of the most recent comprehensive UN Security Council resolutions dealing with measures against international terrorism: resolution 2396 (2017), which contains traces of several precursor resolutions adopted in this area since the late 1990s, in particular resolution 1267 (1999) and resolution 1373 (2001).[5] The subheadings to section 2 of this chapter correspond for the most part to the subheadings in resolution 2396.

2. Threats to International Peace and Security Caused by Terrorist Acts: Resolution 2396 (2017)

2.1 Criminalisation

In line with previous resolutions on the subject matter, the Security Council requires states to establish serious criminal offenses regarding the travel, recruitment,

[4] See, for instance, Elizabeth Nielsen, 'State Responsibility for Terrorist Groups', *University of California Davis Journal of International Law and Policy* 17 (2010), 151–191, at 181–192; Robert Barnidge Jr., 'States' Due Diligence Obligations with Regard to International Non-State Terrorist Organisations Post-11 September 2001: The Heavy Burden that States Must Bear', *Irish Studies in International Affairs* 16 (2005), 103–125, at 103–104; Joanna Kulesza, *Due Diligence in International Law* (Leiden: Brill Nijhoff 2016), 111–112, 136–137, 281–288; Marja Lehto, *Indirect Responsibility for Terrorist Acts: Redefinition of the Concept of Terrorism Beyond Violent Acts* (Leiden: Martinus Nijhoff 2009), 226–230; Riccardo Pisillo Mazzeschi, 'The Due Diligence Rule and the Nature of the International Responsibility of States', *German Yearbook of International Law* 35 (1992), 9–51, at 35; Robert Barnidge Jr., 'The Due Diligence Principle Under International Law', *International Community Law Review* 8 (2006), 81–121, at 114; Olivier Corten, 'The "Unwilling or Unable" Test: Has it Been, and Could it Be, Accepted?', *Leiden Journal of International Law* 29 (2016), 777–799, at 793; Timo Koivurova, 'Due Diligence', in Rüdiger Wolfrum (ed.), *Max Planck Encyclopedia of Public International Law* (Oxford: OUP 2010), para. 8; Myriam Feinberg, 'Terrorism Inside Out: Legislating for Humanity to Cooperate Against Terrorism', *North Carolina Journal of International Law* 42 (2017), 506–543, at 541; ICJ, *United States Diplomatic and Consular Staff in Tehran (United States of America v. Iran)*, Judgment of 24 May 1980, ICJ Reports 1980, 3, para. 68.

[5] UN, Security Council, Resolution 2396, S/RES/2396, 21 December 2017; UN, Security Council, Resolution 1267, S/RES/1267, 15 October 1999; UN, Security Council, Resolution 1373, S/RES/1373, 28 September 2001; on resolution 1267 (1999) and 1373 (2001) respectively, see Lisa Ginsburg 'The United Nations Security Council's Counter-Terrorism Al-Qaida Sanctions Regime: Resolution 1267 and the 1267 Committee', in Ben Saul (ed.), *Research Handbook on International Law and Terrorism* (Cheltenham; Northampton, Mass: Edward Elgar 2014), 608–625; and Luis Miguel Hinojosa-Martínez, 'A Critical Assessment of United Nations Security Council Resolution 1373', in Ben Saul (ed.), *Research Handbook on International Law and Terrorism* (Cheltenham; Northampton, Mass: Edward Elgar 2014), 626–650.

and financing of foreign terrorist fighters.[6] States shall ensure further that their domestic criminal laws and regulations provide the ability to prosecute and penalise criminal activities in a manner duly reflecting the seriousness of the offense.[7] Member states shall afford one another the greatest measure of assistance in connection with criminal investigations or proceedings relating to the financing or support of terrorist acts, including assistance in making available evidence in their possession necessary for proceedings.[8] The Security Council underscores that this includes physical and digital evidence, and underlines the importance of fulfilling this obligation with respect to investigations or proceedings involving foreign terrorist fighters.[9]

The Security Council calls on member states to cooperate and support each other's efforts to counter violent extremism conducive to terrorism.[10] Calls for cooperation among member states in their various efforts to eliminate terrorism has become a common element of the Security Council's resolutions.[11] The obligation to cooperate as it emerges from resolution 2396 fits well with the resolution's heavy emphasis on assistance and capacity building.[12]

On the subject of criminalisation, the United Nations Counter-Terrorism Executive Directorate (UNCTED), in the 2016 global survey of the implementation of resolution 1373 (2001), which is fully consistent with the three 2015 reports on the implementation of resolution 2178 (2014), finds that although most states have taken significant steps to develop an appropriate legal framework, in certain regions progress has been more limited.[13] Most states from western Europe and North America, to eastern Europe, and Central Asia and the Caucasus subregions

[6] Security Council, Resolution 2396, 21 December 2017 (n. 5), para. 1; UN, Security Council, Resolution 2178, S/RES/2178, 24 September 2014; see also Security Council, Resolution 1373, 28 September 2001 (n. 5), paras 1 (a), (b), (d).

[7] Security Council, Resolution 2396, 21 December 2017 (n. 5), paras 1, 17; Security Council, Resolution 2178, 24 September 2014 (n. 6); see also Security Council, Resolution 1373, 28 September 2001 (n. 5), para. 2 (e).

[8] Security Council, Resolution 2396, 21 December 2017 (n. 5), para. 23; see also Security Council, Resolution 1373, 28 September 2001 (n. 5), para. 2 (f).

[9] Security Council, Resolution 2396, 21 December 2017 (n. 5), para. 23.

[10] Ibid., para. 1; see also Security Council, Resolution 1373, 28 September 2001 (n. 5), paras 2 (f), 3 (b), (c), (e).

[11] Myriam Feinberg argues that the obligation to cooperate should form an inherent part of the existing obligation to prevent and punish terrorism; see Myriam Feinberg, 'Terrorism Inside Out: Legislating for Humanity to Cooperate Against Terrorism' 2017 (n. 4), 540 (focusing particularly on Security Council, Resolution 2178, 24 September 2014 (n. 6)).

[12] See the strong emphasis on capacity-building below in sections 2.2. and 2.3.

[13] UN, Security Council, Counter-Terrorism Committee Executive Directorate (UNCTED), Global Survey of the Implementation of Security Council Resolution 1373 (2001) by Member States, Compiled by the Counter-Terrorism Committee Executive Directorate (UNCTED) in 2016, S/2016/49, 20 January 2016, paras 7, 395; UN, Security Council, Counter-Terrorism Committee Executive Directorate (UNCTED), Implementation of Security Council Resolution 2178 (2014) by States Affected by Foreign Terrorist Fighters, A Compilation of Three Reports (S/2015/338, 14 May 2015; S/2015/683, 2 September 2015; S/2015/975, 29 December 2015).

have introduced comprehensive counterterrorism legislation.[14] However, as the UNCTED puts it, in subregions where progress is still required the degree to which the offences have been fully codified varies significantly and continues to require attention.[15] On the subject of bringing suspected terrorists and their supporters to justice in line with resolution 1373, the UNCTED finds that these requirements pose major challenges for states' criminal-justice systems.[16] Most of the more than ninety states visited by the UNCTED—conducted on behalf of the United Nations Security Council Counter-Terrorism Committee (UNCTC)—continue to experience difficulties in their efforts to implement these requirements.[17] The foreign terrorist fighter phenomenon, dealt with in resolution 2178, presents specific criminal justice challenges, the UNCTED finds.[18] Among the main challenges identified by the UNCTED are the use of classified information as evidence (including admissibility as evidence), investigation methods, collection of evidence from states of destination, international cooperation, the use of sophisticated technology by terrorists, conducting effective financial investigations, and links between terrorism and other forms of criminality.[19]

2.2 Border Security and Information Sharing

Border security and information sharing are a further important part of international anti-terrorism law.[20] The Security Council calls upon states to prevent the movement of terrorists by effective national border controls and controls on the issuance of identity papers and travel documents through measures for preventing counterfeiting, forgery, or the fraudulent use of identity papers and travel documents.[21] Member states are called upon to notify other concerned states in a timely manner regarding the travel, arrival, or deportation of captured or detained individuals whom they have reasonable grounds to believe are terrorists, including suspected foreign terrorist fighters.[22] Member states are further called upon to cooperate and respond expeditiously and appropriately and to share relevant information with Interpol.

[14] Security Council, Counter-Terrorism Committee Executive Directorate (UNCTED), Global Survey of the Implementation of Security Council Resolution 1373 (2001) by Member States, 20 January 2016 (n. 13), para. 395.

[15] Ibid.; incidentally, the UNCTED writes that, with the exception of Armenia, all states of Central Asia and the Caucasus have been affected by the phenomenon of foreign terrorist fighters, both as states of origin and as transit routes (ibid., para. 218).

[16] Ibid., para. 400.

[17] Ibid., paras 8, 400.

[18] Ibid., para. 401.

[19] Ibid.

[20] Security Council, Resolution 2396, 21 December 2017 (n. 5), paras 2–16.

[21] Ibid., para. 2; see also Security Council, Resolution 1373, 28 September 2001 (n. 5), para. 2 (g).

[22] Security Council, Resolution 2396, 21 December 2017 (n. 5), para. 3.

In all the paragraphs setting out duties relating to the exchange of information, the Security Council carefully points out that member states must act in accordance with the law—domestic and/or international—as is appropriate and sometimes including international human rights and humanitarian law. The obligation to respect the law is pointed out in eleven paragraphs in the preamble, and then in twenty-four of the fifty-one operative paragraphs in resolution 2396.[23] Member states are also called upon to take appropriate action to ensure that other member states—and their domestic law enforcement, intelligence, counterterrorism, and military entities—have access to relevant information about suspected terrorists, including foreign terrorist fighters.[24]

In order to increase access to information on terrorists, the Security Council urges member states to consider downgrading intelligence data about threats and related travel information connected to foreign terrorist fighters and individual terrorists; to appropriately provide such information domestically to front-line screeners, such as immigration, customs, and border security agencies; to appropriately share such information with other concerned states and relevant international organisations; and to share good practice in this regard.[25]

In somewhat more authoritative language, the Security Council decides that member states shall require airlines operating in their territories to provide advance passenger information (API) to the appropriate national authorities, and further calls upon member states to report any departures from their territories by suspected individuals, or attempts at entry into or transit through their territories, by sharing this information with the relevant state (in terms of the residency or nationality of the suspected individual). The Security Council also calls upon member states to share this information with the countries of return, transit or relocation, and with relevant international organisations as appropriate, and to ensure API is analysed by all relevant authorities.[26]

In this context, the Security Council refers back to commitments already undertaken by member states under resolution 2178 (2014) of the Security Council and under International Civil Aviation Organisation standards, but augments the degree of binding force of the earlier commitments by saying that the Council 'decides' (under Chapter VII of the UN Charter) that member states shall perform these commitments.[27] Thus, the commitments become binding, whereas before

[23] In Security Council, Resolution 1373, 28 September 2001 (n. 5), the only two instances among the operative paras where the need to respect human rights is pointed out is in connection with the exchange of information (operative para. 3 (b)) and in connection with the handling of asylum seekers (operative paras 3 (f), (g)). That states' measures to prevent and suppress the financing and preparation of any acts of terrorism must be 'lawful' is also pointed out in Security Council, Resolution 1373, 28 September 2001, (n. 5), preamble para. 8.

[24] Security Council, Resolution 2396, 21 December 2017 (n. 5), para. 7.

[25] Ibid., para. 8.

[26] Ibid., para. 11.

[27] See also International Civil Aviation Organisation, International Standards and Recommended Practices, Annex 9 to the Convention on International Civil Aviation, 15th edition October 2017.

they were expressed in hortatory terms; in resolution 2178 the Security Council 'called upon' member states to implement certain commitments, for example to require that airlines operating in their territories provide advance passenger information to the appropriate national authorities. Subsequently, in resolution 2396, it 'decided' that member states shall implement such commitments. 'Deciding', on the part of the Security Council, that member states must share sensitive information with each other and with international organisations might be unacceptable from the point of view of states.[28]

The Security Council furthermore decides that member states shall develop the capability to collect, process, and analyse—in furtherance of the International Civil Aviation Organisation standards and recommended practices—passenger name record (PNR) data and to ensure PNR data is used by and shared with all their competent national authorities.[29] In the same paragraph, the Security Council goes on to call upon member states, the UN, and other international, regional, and intraregional entities to provide technical assistance, resources, and capacity building to member states in order to implement such capabilities. The Security Council then in softer language encourages member states to share PNR data with other relevant or concerned member states with the purpose of detecting foreign terrorist fighters returning to their countries of origin or nationality, or traveling or relocating to a third country.

In the following paragraph 13, the Security Council goes on to decide that member states shall develop watch lists or databases of known and suspected terrorists.[30] The development of watch lists, in itself, could also be considered an obligation of result. The ultimate real result strived for in the area of international anti-terrorism law, however, is presumably the prevention of terrorism, in the sense that no further terrorist acts will be successfully carried out. Therefore, even if states were to fulfil their obligation to produce watch lists and databases, and that (hypothetically) these measures fail to substantially contribute to the preclusion of all terrorist acts, then the result achieved through the fulfilment of these obligations by states, even if complete and exemplary of their obligation of result, would turn out to be rather futile.[31]

The Security Council also decides that member states shall develop and implement systems to collect biometric data, which could include fingerprints, photographs, and facial recognition, among other biometric data, in order to responsibly and properly identify terrorists, including foreign terrorist fighters.[32] Member

[28] However, there are no explicit signs in the 'procès verbaux' that the binding duty to share sensitive information would be particularly unappealing to the states. On the contrary, the importance of information-sharing is emphasised by most speakers in the debate following the adoption of resolution 2396 (UN, Security Council, S/PV.8148, 21 December 2017).

[29] Security Council, Resolution 2396, 21 December 2017 (n. 5), para. 12.

[30] Ibid., para. 13.

[31] On the relativity of the distinction between duties of effort and duties of result in the context of due diligence, see further Kulesza, *Due Diligence* 2016 (n. 4), 136–138.

[32] Security Council, Resolution 2396, 21 December 2017 (n. 5), para. 15.

states and international, regional, and intra-regional entities are thereafter called upon to provide technical assistance, resources, and capacity building to other member states in order to implement such systems. And, lastly, member states are encouraged to share this data responsibly among other relevant member states, as appropriate, and with Interpol and other relevant international bodies. This paragraph could be said to be a typical example of the international anti-terrorism law of recent times, as it concerns the collection of information and data, involves assistance and capacity building, and the international sharing of the collected information.

As to implementation, the UNCTED in the earlier mentioned 2016 global survey finds that even though member states have significantly strengthened border-security measures in recent years, they continue to face a number of challenges, including the exploitation by terrorists of open borders, weaknesses in domestic and international information-sharing, and other vulnerabilities in border-control arrangements.[33] One of the greatest challenges the UNCTED notes is the need to effectively screen travellers at ports of entry, which is conducted through a combination of several mechanisms and depends on whether it is an air, maritime, or land border.[34] The UNCTED observes that despite the requirement of resolution 1373 (2001), data gathered from the country visits by the UNCTED on behalf of the UNCTC shows that only thirty-seven states currently have the capacity to effectively screen travellers at all ports of entry.[35] This is not entirely surprising, since only fifty-three states currently have API systems in place and only thirteen have fully linked their domestic immigration-screening process at the front line to the Interpol Stolen and Lost Travel Document database and Red Notices for suspected criminals and wanted persons, and to the Al-Qaida sanctions lists;[36] a further twenty-four states have taken significant steps towards achieving this.[37] Hence, it would seem as if that which the Security Council has 'decided' member states 'shall' perform in the area of border security and information will take some time to be carried into global effect.

Another area identified in the global survey that the UNCTED thinks requires attention is the adoption of comprehensive laws against the smuggling of terrorists.[38] The UNCTED notes that several states have no form of legislative measure at all in this regard,[39] and in particular those states most affected by the phenomenon of foreign terrorism.[40]

33 Security Council, Counter-Terrorism Committee Executive Directorate (UNCTED), Global Survey of the Implementation of Security Council Resolution 1373 (2001) by Member States, 20 January 2016 (n. 13), para. 424.
34 Ibid., para. 426.
35 Ibid.
36 Ibid.
37 Ibid.; thus, at best, a total of thirty-seven of 193 states.
38 Ibid., para. 427.
39 Ibid.
40 Ibid.

2.3 Judicial Measures and International Cooperation

Judicial measures and international cooperation are further cornerstones of international anti-terrorism law.[41] The Security Council calls upon member states, as well as the United Nations Office of Drugs and Crime (UNODC) and other relevant UN entities that support capacity building, to share best practices and technical expertise regarding the prosecution of foreign terrorist fighters.[42] The Security Council encourages enhancing member state cooperation with the private sector, especially with information and communication technology companies, in gathering digital data and evidence in cases related to terrorism and foreign terrorist fighters.[43]

On the issue of cooperation, the Security Council calls upon member states to improve international, regional, and infra-regional cooperation to prevent the undetected travel of foreign terrorist fighters and their families from or through their territories, and to share and adopt best practices to better analyse the patterns of such travel. Member states shall also act cooperatively to prevent terrorists from exploiting technology, communications, and other resources to support terrorist acts.[44] The Security Council underscores the need for member states to strengthen international judicial cooperation, including, where appropriate, to use applicable international instruments to which they are parties as a basis for mutual legal assistance and, again where appropriate, for extradition in terrorism cases. The Security Council reiterates its call on member states to consider strengthening the implementation of, and where appropriate to review possibilities for enhancing the effectiveness of, their respective bilateral and multilateral treaties concerning extradition and mutual legal assistance in criminal matters related to counter-terrorism; the Security Council further encourages member states, in the absence of applicable conventions or provisions, to cooperate whenever possible on the basis of reciprocity or on a case-by-case basis.[45]

The Security Council further reiterates its call upon member states to consider the possibility of allowing the transfer of criminal proceedings, as and when appropriate, in terrorism-related cases and recognises the role of the UNODC in providing technical assistance and expertise in this regard.

The Security Council calls upon member states precisely to help build the capacity of other member states, in this case to address the threat posed by returning or relocating foreign terrorist fighter and their families, prioritising those member states most affected by the threat (whoever they may be); to prevent and/or monitor

41 Security Council, Resolution 2396, 21 December 2017 (n. 5), paras 17–28.

42 Ibid., para. 20.

43 Ibid., para. 21; on the use of communications technologies by terrorist groups, see Security Council, Resolution 1373, 28 September 2001 (n. 5), para. 3 (a).

44 Security Council, Resolution 2396, 21 December 2017 (n. 5), para. 22.

45 Ibid., para. 24.

foreign terrorist fighters travelling across land and maritime borders; and to help collect and preserve evidence admissible in judicial proceedings.[46]

Hereafter the Security Council calls upon member states to improve domestic information sharing within their respective criminal justice systems—in contrast to the international information sharing between states that had thus far been the focus of the resolution—in order to more effectively monitor returning and relocating foreign terrorist fighters and other radicalised individuals.[47] Domestic information sharing would typically seem to be easier than information sharing between states.

As to preventing or recovering from terrorist attacks against so-called soft targets—namely locations that are relatively vulnerable to terrorist attacks due to their open access, structural characteristics, and limited security—the Security Council calls upon member states to establish or strengthen (where appropriate) national, regional, and international partnerships with stakeholders, both public and private, and to share information and experience in order to prevent, protect, mitigate, investigate, respond to, and recover from damage caused by terrorist attacks against soft targets.[48] The Council also urges states capable of assisting in the delivery of effective and targeted capacity development, training, and other necessary resources and technical assistance to do so, in order to enable all states to develop appropriate capacity to implement contingency and response plans with regard to attacks on soft targets. The strong emphasis on technical assistance throughout resolution 2396 would seem to illustrate among other things that this is the way in which the UN Security Council believes that the international anti-terrorism law will most likely be efficiently implemented at this stage of development.[49]

Again, the implementation of the obligations contained in the current subsection of resolution 2396 would seem to lag quite far behind the supposed expectations of the Security Council. In the global survey on the implementation of resolution 1373 (2001) and resolution 2178 (2014), the UNCTED notes that the increase in transnational crime, including terrorism, and the growth in borderless information technology over the past decade have significantly increased the need for international judicial cooperation.[50] Unfortunately for counter-terrorism

[46] Ibid., para. 25.

[47] Ibid., para. 26.

[48] Security Council, Resolution 2396, 21 December 2017 (n. 5), para. 27; soft target is not defined in the resolution; for the definition of soft target used here, see www.nato.int/cps/en/natohq/news_154976.htm (accessed 18 July 2019).

[49] Nielsen, 'State Responsibility for Terrorist Groups' 2010 (n. 4), 180: points out that despite a potentially aggressive role (Security Council, Resolution 1373, 28 September 2001 (n. 5), para. 8, hinting that enforcement action may be taken by the Security Council to ensure the full implementation of the resolution), the UNCTC early on changed to a non-aggressive capacity-based approach; see also Tal Becker, *Terrorism and the State: Rethinking the Rules of State Responsibility* (Oxford: Hart Publishing 2006), 125.

[50] Security Council, Counter-Terrorism Committee Executive Directorate (UNCTED), Global Survey of the Implementation of Security Council Resolution 1373 (2001) by Member States, 20 January 2001 (n. 13), para. 431.

efforts, however, the UNCTED finds that the responses from governments to these trends have not kept pace with the needs.[51] In general, the use of mutual legal assistance in criminal matters by member states is considered to be very low, especially in foreign terrorist fighter cases.[52] Most member states are covered by regional agreements on mutual legal assistance.[53] However, the level of engagement varies significantly by region, and cross-regional cooperation remains a big challenge.[54] As if that were not enough, the UNCTED then observes that there are far fewer bilateral or multilateral treaties or agreements on extradition than there are on mutual legal assistance.[55] The challenges faced in extradition procedures are similar to those faced in mutual legal assistance procedures.[56]

2.4 Prosecution, Rehabilitation, Reintegration, and Prevention Strategies

The next subsection in resolution 2396 relates to prosecution, rehabilitation, and reintegration strategies.[57] In this section the Security Council never uses any authoritative terms when it imposes different obligations on member states. Instead, they use expressions such as 'calls upon', 'emphasises', 'underscores', 'stresses', 'encourages', 'reiterates', and 'recognises'. Judging from the different font used in the heading of this section of the resolution, it would seem as if in adopting this section, and the following section of the resolution on UN Efforts on Returning and Relocating Foreign Terrorist Fighters, the Security Council is no longer acting under Chapter VII of the UN Charter. The font used in the headings of these two sections is the same as the one used in the first heading preceding the first operative paragraph, which reads: 'Acting under Chapter VII of the Charter of the United Nations.' The font, thus, would seem to indicate that the last two sections of the resolution are indeed sections and not subsections to the section titled 'Acting under Chapter VII . . . ', like the two subsections previously explored in this chapter.

However, judging merely from the text of the operative paragraphs of the last two sections of resolution 2396, the departure from Chapter VII is not evident. True, the term 'decides' is never used in these two sections, which would indicate a softer norm-making than that which potentially takes place under Chapter VII (which in its turn would indicate that the last two sections were not adopted under Chapter VII), but then the term 'decides' only occurs in four out of twenty-eight

51 Ibid.
52 Ibid.
53 Ibid., para. 432.
54 Ibid.
55 Ibid., para. 434.
56 Ibid.
57 Security Council, Resolution 2396, 21 December 2017 (n. 5), paras 29–41.

of the operative paragraphs having explicitly been adopted under Chapter VII. Moreover, it might be argued that the obligations for states laid down in the section on prosecution, rehabilitation, and reintegration strategies are of a softer and less precise character than the obligations laid down in the previous subsections of the resolution. However, this is only partially true, and the difference between what has been agreed upon within Chapter VII and beyond it is arguably one of degree and not kind.

In general, if there were no headings indicating whether a particular operative paragraph had been adopted under Chapter VII or not, it would be difficult—except for the four operative paragraphs that the Security Council begins with 'decides' (out of a total number of fifty operative paragraphs, not counting the fifty-first paragraph in which the Security Council 'decides' to remain seized of the matter)—to immediately judge whether the paragraph had been adopted under Chapter VII or not. Thus, even though an obligation might be formally binding under Chapter VII, in substance it might be rather difficult to pinpoint. Therefore, it can be argued that the obligations for the states prescribed outside Chapter VII in the case of resolution 2396 are not essentially different from those prescribed under Chapter VII. And, in principle, the Security Council may also adopt binding decisions outside Chapter VII.[58] Irrespective of whether the Security Council in resolution 2396 has agreed on obligations for states under or outside Chapter VII, the duties prescribed in the resolution are surprisingly extensive and numerous while their level of bindingness varies significantly. Indeed, the normative content of resolution 2396 would seem almost infinitely malleable.

In the first operative paragraph dealing with prosecution, rehabilitation, and reintegration strategies, the Security Council calls upon member states to assess and investigate suspected individuals entering those member states' territories whom they have reasonable grounds to believe are terrorists—including suspected foreign terrorist fighters and their accompanying family members, which includes spouses and children; to develop and implement comprehensive risk assessments for those individuals; and to take appropriate action, which includes considering appropriate prosecution, rehabilitation, and reintegration measures.[59]

The Security Council calls upon member states, emphasising that they are obliged, in accordance with resolution 1373, to ensure that any person who participates in the financing, planning, preparation, or perpetration of terrorist acts or supports them is brought to justice; to develop and implement comprehensive and tailored prosecution, rehabilitation, and reintegration strategies and protocols, in accordance with their obligations under international law, and to do so

[58] ICJ, *Legal Consequences for States of the Continued Presence of South Africa in Namibia (South West Africa) notwithstanding Security Council Resolution 276 (1970)*, Advisory Opinion of 21 June 1971, ICJ Reports 1971, 16, paras 111–114.

[59] Security Council, Resolution 2396, 21 December 2017 (n. 5), para. 29.

in consultation, as appropriate, with local communities, mental health and education practitioners, and other relevant civil society organisations and actors.[60] As civil society organisations may have relevant knowledge of, access to, and engagement with local communities, and are therefore likely to be able to confront the challenges of recruitment and radicalisation to violence, the Security Council encourages member states to engage proactively with civil society organisations when developing rehabilitation and reintegration strategies.[61] This paragraph of the resolution shows how the mandate of the Security Council has both broadened and 'softened' in the context of the concerted international effort to prevent terrorism and the relapse into terrorist action. The paragraph also illustrates how far down into national societies the Security Council's impositions reach.

In general, whether the Security Council is acting under Chapter VII or not, it could be noted that the obligations laid down in resolution 2396 are detailed and prescribe rather closely what states should do and what kinds of national governmental and non-governmental actors should be involved. It should also be noted that the issues the Security Council concerns itself with in this resolution—like mental health and education, as well as the potential contribution that can be made by local communities, civil society organisations, and actors in the rehabilitation and reintegration of former terrorists—are rather far from those issues relating to international peace and security traditionally associated with the action of the Security Council. Like an octopus, the Security Council stretches its long, but soft and flexible, arms deep into what has formerly been considered purely domestic if not local territory; nothing nowadays seems to be beyond the Security Council's normative reach. How powerful the Security Council's jaws are remains to be seen.

The Security Council encourages member states to collaborate in the pursuit of developing and implementing effective counter-narrative strategies in accordance with resolution 2354 (2017).[62] Still aiming at the national and local level, and thus close to citizens, the Security Council then reiterates that states should consider engaging, where appropriate, with religious authorities, community leaders, and other civil society actors that have relevant expertise in crafting and delivering effective counter-narratives and in countering narratives used by terrorists, including foreign terrorist fighters and their supporters.[63]

The Security Council then makes an explicit and interesting link between the reintegration and rehabilitation assistance provided to children and the goal of sustainable peace and security.[64] In this way, the Security Council also makes an explicit link between these specific aspects of its resolutions and its mandate under

60 Ibid., para. 30.
61 Ibid., para. 32.
62 Security Council, Resolution 2396, 21 December 2017 (n. 5), para. 34; Security Council, Resolution 2354, S/RES/2354, 24 May 2017.
63 Security Council, Resolution 2396, 21 December 2017 (n. 5), para. 35.
64 Ibid., para. 36.

the UN Charter. The Security Council recognises the particular importance of providing, through a whole government approach, timely and appropriate reintegration and rehabilitation assistance to children associated with foreign terrorist fighters returning or relocating from conflict zones—including through access to healthcare, psychosocial support, and education programmes that contribute to the well-being of children—and the relevance this has to sustainable peace and security. Again, hereafter, the Security Council encourages member states to develop appropriate legal safeguards to ensure that prosecution, rehabilitation, and reintegration strategies are in full compliance with their international law obligations, including cases involving children.[65]

In making sure that states act at an early stage to prevent terrorism from developing, the Security Council next calls upon member states to develop and implement risk-assessment tools to identify individuals who demonstrate signs of radicalisation towards violence and to develop intervention programmes that incorporate a gender perspective.[66] Conscious of the fact that such identification may become intrusive, the Security Council points out that the risk-assessment tools must be developed and implemented in compliance with applicable international and domestic law, which is a common reminder in resolution 2396, but also that states must not resort to discriminatory profiling practices prohibited by international law.[67] Here we seem to have another risk of a violation of the law identified by the Security Council.[68]

The Security Council addresses the issue of prisons as potential breeding grounds for terrorism and hence encourages member states to take all appropriate actions to maintain a safe and humane environment in prisons, to develop tools that can help address radicalisation towards violence and terrorist recruitment, and to develop risk assessments for prison inmates' susceptibility to terrorist recruitment and radicalisation towards violence, while taking into consideration, as appropriate, the UN Standard Minimum Rules for the Treatment of Prisoners, or the 'Nelson Mandela Rules'.[69] Finally, under the heading of 'prosecution, rehabilitation, and reintegration strategies' in resolution 2396, the Security Council encourages member states to take all appropriate action to prevent inmates who have been

[65] Ibid., para. 37.

[66] Ibid., para. 38.

[67] Ibid.; the requirement not to resort to such discriminatory profiling is also emphasised at para. 4.

[68] As the UN Special Rapporteur Fionnuala Ní Aoláin on the promotion and protection of human rights and fundamental freedoms while countering terrorism writes in her latest Annual Report (on the subject of 'Balance, necessity and proportionality in limiting rights while countering terrorism'): 'The measures taken must be the least intrusive possible to achieve their objective' (UN, Human Rights Council, Report of the Special Rapporteur on the promotion and protection of human rights and fundamental freedoms while countering terrorism on the human rights challenge of states of emergency in the context of countering terrorism, A/HRC/37/52, 27 February 2018, para. 48).

[69] Security Council, Resolution 2396, 21 December 2017 (n. 5), para. 40; UN, General Assembly, A/RES/70/175, 17 December 2015, Annex.

convicted of terrorism-related offenses from radicalising other prisoners towards violence, in compliance of course with domestic and international law.[70]

Regarding implementation, the UNCTED noted in the global survey on the implementation of resolution 1373 (2001) that although the prevention of terrorism and prosecution of terrorists are two distinct concepts, effective prosecution and prevention strategies are interrelated.[71] One challenge was to determine when to intervene.[72] The earlier the plot is thwarted, the less evidence there is to be used in court proceedings.[73] The development of a national and comprehensive counter-terrorism strategy can help to inform strategic choices made at the national level.[74] Interestingly, the UNCTED notes in another section of its survey—on the subject of national comprehensive counter-terrorism strategies—that currently only twenty-seven states have sufficiently comprehensive and integrated counter-terrorism strategies in place.[75] Of greater concern, however, is the fact that 134 states have either a minimal strategy or no strategy at all in place.[76] Moreover, forty-two of these states are considered to be among the group of seventy-eight states identified in the second foreign terrorist fighter report as being most affected by the foreign terrorist fighter phenomenon.[77]

In the area of prosecution, rehabilitation, and reintegration, as well as in all the other areas covered in resolution 2396, a major concern with respect to implementation repeatedly pointed to in the 2016 global survey on the implementation of resolution 1373 (2001) is the lack of respect for human rights and the rule of law. This is all the more problematic since, according to the UNCTED, not only is it a matter of states having to carry out their legal obligations but that failing to comply with their international legal obligations—including under the UN Charter, and in particular human rights, refugee, and humanitarian law—is one among many factors contributing to increased radicalisation and fosters a sense of impunity for potential human rights violations by states.[78] One core issue that remains a major matter of concern is the unclear legal definition of terrorist acts.[79] The UNCTED

[70] Security Council, Resolution 2396, 21 December 2017 (n. 5), para. 41.

[71] Security Council, Counter-Terrorism Committee Executive Directorate (UNCTED), Global Survey of the Implementation of Security Council Resolution 1373 (2001) by Member States, 20 January 2016 (n. 13), para. 405.

[72] Ibid.

[73] Ibid.

[74] Ibid.

[75] Ibid., para. 420.

[76] Ibid.; on the other hand, the demands of the UNCTED and ultimately of the Security Council as to the quality of a true national strategy are very strict: 'national strategies should (. . .) integrate law enforcement measures and measures to address the socioeconomic, political, educational, developmental, human rights and rule of law dimensions' (ibid., para. 392).

[77] Ibid., para. 420; Security Council, Counter-Terrorism Committee Executive Directorate (UNCTED), Implementation of Security Council Resolution 2178 (2014) by States Affected by Foreign Terrorist Fighters, A Compilation of Three Reports (n. 13), 46, paras 4, 5.

[78] Security Council, Counter-Terrorism Committee Executive Directorate (UNCTED), Global Survey of the Implementation of Security Council Resolution 1373 (2001) by Member States, 20 January 2016 (n. 13), para. 435.

[79] Ibid., para. 437.

says that it is aware of situations in several states, located in various regions, in which terrorism charges or administrative designations have been framed in vague terms, allowing for their misuse against legitimate conduct, such as the expression of political dissent or human rights advocacy.[80] In this regard, even EU member states are criticised in the global survey.[81] Western Europe is the only region in the global survey where most states seem to honour a good part of their human rights obligations when implementing their counter-terrorism obligations, and for that matter where most states seem to implement a reasonable part of their counter-terrorism obligations most of the time.[82]

Furthermore, compliance with international standards of due process and fair treatment also remains a matter of concern, notably wherever counter-terrorism measures are applied in a preventive manner.[83] Counter-terrorism measures may also have a negative impact on humanitarian action.[84] In terms of refugee law, the global survey finds that fifty states have adopted legislation to ensure compliance with the principle of non-refoulement, and that 'a number' of states have implemented measures to safeguard other forms of protection.[85] States must also ensure that they have in place a functioning refugee-status determination procedure that prevents the granting of asylum to individuals who have planned, facilitated, or participated in terrorist acts.[86] There are currently fifty-eight states that have implemented, or taken significant steps towards implementing, such procedures, and 145 states are parties to the Refugee Convention.[87] Here it must also be noted that international legal obligations, as well as national laws to the extent that such have been adopted, need to be implemented as a next step in order to be effective.

2.5 UN Efforts on Returning and Relocating Foreign Terrorist Fighters

In the final part of resolution 2396 on the subject of UN efforts to return and relocate foreign terrorist fighters, the Security Council turns to the numerous UN

[80] Ibid.; this is the case despite the existence for 'more than five years' of the model definition of terrorism put forward by the UN Special Rapporteur (UN, Human Rights Council, Report of the Special Rapporteur on the Promotion and Protection of Human Rights and Fundamental Freedoms while Countering Terrorism, Martin Scheinin: Ten areas of best practices in countering terrorism, A/HRC/16/51, 22 December 2010, para. 28).

[81] Security Council, Counter-Terrorism Committee Executive Directorate (UNCTED), Global Survey of the Implementation of Security Council Resolution 1373 (2001) by Member States, 20 January 2016 (n. 13), para. 358.

[82] Ibid., paras 353–373.

[83] Ibid., para. 438.

[84] Ibid., para. 440.

[85] Ibid., para. 429.

[86] Ibid., para. 428.

[87] Ibid.

Committees and other entities involved in the work against terrorism, as well as to member states.[88] First, the Security Council reaffirms that foreign terrorist fighters, and those who finance or otherwise facilitate their travel and subsequent activities, may be eligible for inclusion on the ISIL (Da'esh) & Al-Qaida Sanctions List maintained by the Committee pursuant to resolutions 1267 (1999), 1989 (2011), and 2253 (2015) and calls upon states to propose foreign terrorist fighters and those who facilitate or finance their travel and subsequent activities for possible designation.[89]

Turning to the Counter-Terrorism Committee, which also consists of representatives from every member of the Security Council and originally established under resolution 1373 (2001), the Security Council requests the UNCTC, with the support of the UNCTED, to review the 2015 Madrid Guiding Principles in light of the evolving threat of foreign terrorist fighters—particularly returnees, relocators, and their families—and other principal gaps that may hinder the abilities of states to appropriately detect, interdict, and where possible prosecute, rehabilitate, and reintegrate foreign terrorist fighter returnees and relocators and their families, as well as to continue to identify emerging good practices and to facilitate technical assistance upon request.[90] The Security Council has requested that it be updated by the 1267/1989/2253 Committee and the UNCTC on their respective efforts pursuant to resolution 2396.[91]

The Security Council encourages relevant UN entities, including UNODC and the United Nations Office of Counter-Terrorism (UNOCT) and in close consultation with the Counter-Terrorism Committee and UNCTED, to further enhance the provision and delivery of technical assistance for states, upon request, to better support the efforts of member states to implement resolution 2396.[92] The Security Council pragmatically acknowledges that the implementation of aspects of resolution 2396, especially PNR and biometric data collection, can be resource-intensive and may take an extended period of time to develop, which makes technical assistance crucial.[93]

Towards the very end of resolution 2396 there is a comprehensive paragraph that among other things contains a summary of what the Security Council considers to be the 'priorities of this resolution':[94] the establishment of effective API systems, the development of PNR capabilities, the development of effective biometric data

88 Security Council, Resolution 2396, 21 December 2017 (n. 5), paras 42–51.

89 Ibid., para. 42; Security Council, Resolution 1267, 15 October 1999 (n. 5); UN, Security Council, Resolution 1989, S/RES/1989, 17 June 2011; UN, Security Council, Resolution 2253, S/RES/2253, 17 December 2015.

90 Security Council, Resolution 2396, 21 December 2017 (n. 5), para. 44; see also UN, Security Council, Counter-Terrorism Committee, Madrid Guiding Principles: A Practical Tool for Member States to Stem the Flow of Foreign Terrorist Fighters, S/2015/939, 23 December 2015.

91 Security Council, Resolution 2396, 21 December 2017 (n. 5), para. 46.

92 Ibid., para. 47.

93 Ibid., para. 48.

94 Ibid., para. 50.

systems, the improvement of judicial procedures, and the development of comprehensive and tailored prosecution, rehabilitation, and reintegration strategies.[95] Some of these priorities have been expressed in stronger normative terms and some have been expressed more softly in the preceding parts of the resolution. Thus, the 'priorities' do not entirely coincide with (the few) obligations expressed in hard legal language which would otherwise be a natural conclusion to draw, at least from the point of view of an international lawyer. The prioritisation of 'these projects', as the Security Council puts it, shall be communicated by the UNOCT to all member states and relevant international, regional, and intra-regional bodies and the UNOCT is further requested to develop ways to measure the effectiveness of these projects. The Security Council, finally, calls upon member states, as and when appropriate, to provide the resources needed to implement these projects. The not very authoritative language used by the Security Council in this paragraph can be noted.

3. Conclusion

A host of obligations for states emanate from Security Council resolution 2396 (2017). The duties, as we have seen, range from the criminalisation of terrorist offenses and the prosecution of criminals to the processing of advance passenger information (API) and passenger name record (PNR) data from airlines, international (and domestic) information sharing, and cooperation and assistance, as well as engagement with local communities, mental health and educational institutions, religious leaders, and prisons. Some obligations are more specific, some are more general; some are more concrete, and some are more abstract; some are detailed, while some are less so. Some concern international measures, some concern domestic measures. Some tend to be more effort oriented whereas some tend to be more result oriented. Some of the obligations contained in resolution 2396 have been adopted under Chapter VII of the UN Charter and some have not. Still, having been adopted by the UN Security Council, all the obligations should be potentially binding.

Some obligations emanating from resolution 2396 are expressed in more commanding language, and some in softer terms. In a few instances—but (very) far from all—where obligations have been adopted under Chapter VII, the Security Council has 'decided' that member states 'shall' carry out their duties. In the case of obligations prescribed by the Security Council outside of Chapter VII, none are expressed in such terms. In comparison with the total number of obligations contained in resolution 2396, the ones expressed in 'binding' language make up a

[95] Ibid.

handful. Whether the different obligations contained in resolution 2396 should be classified as hard or soft is not evident.

Are there duties of due diligence in resolution 2396? All the norms contained in resolution 2396 aim at preventing and possibly punishing terrorism. Does that turn them into due diligence duties? Or, are all the obligations prescribed by resolution 2396 simply ordinary primary legal duties with no secondary due diligence characteristic necessarily belonging to them at all? I tend to lean toward the latter view. The analysis of resolution 2396 in this chapter shows that it is more a question of definition than a question of the quality of the obligations involved that determines whether the norms should best be qualified as duties of due diligence or duties *tout court*. The same goes for whether the obligations contained in resolution 2396—should they be qualified as duties of due diligence—would constitute duties of effort or duties of result; that too, I would argue, is a matter of definition; they could be either. Above in section 2.4 I ventured to label the quality of the normative content of resolution 2396 as infinitely malleable.

Regardless then of whether the obligations contained in resolution 2396 are classified as duties of due diligence, of effort or result, or just duties, hard or soft, in my view there is a general obligation that flows from resolution 2396: the obligation to prevent and punish terrorism. At least, considering all the resolutions adopted by the UN Security Council since 2001 in the area of counter-terrorism which directly or indirectly reflected in resolution 2396, it would be difficult to claim today that a general obligation to prevent and punish terrorism would not exist. This obligation reinforces the over-arching obligation of states under the Friendly Relations Declaration not to acquiesce in domestic terrorist activities directed towards other states and the obligation pronounced in the *Corfu Channel* case not to knowingly allow their territories to be used for acts contrary to the rights of other states. Apart from that, states still have the duty to accept and carry out the decisions of the UN Security Council. And, most important of all, states have the duty to fulfil all their international legal obligations. *Pacta* still *sunt servanda*.

Judging from the detailed global survey compiled in 2016 on the implementation by states of most of the obligations subsequently contained in resolution 2396, with the partial exception of western Europe, implementation is lacking across the board irrespective of in what form and in which language the obligations have been expressed in the preceding Security Council resolutions, most immediately resolution 1373 (2001) and 2178 (2014). Whatever the label, states have a myriad of international duties to fulfil in order to counter terrorist activities, and, judging from the Security Council's own investigations, they are largely not doing so. Besides—again with the partial exception of western Europe—neither are states in the main respecting their human rights, humanitarian, refugee, or rule of law obligations when implementing counter-terrorism measures. The conclusion to be drawn from this is that it is time for new questions to be asked.

15
Due Diligence in Cyber Activities

*Eric Talbot Jensen**

1. Introduction

When questioned recently concerning alleged hacking incidents by Russian citizens targeting servers and networks in other countries, Russian President Vladimir Putin responded:

> Hackers are free people, just like artists who wake up in the morning in a good mood and start painting. The hackers are the same. They would wake up, read about something going on in interstate relations and if they feel patriotic, they may try to contribute to the fight against those who speak badly about Russia.[1]

While openly acknowledging that such activities occur from within his territory, and implicitly divulging his knowledge of such activities, President Putin was unwilling to accept any responsibility on the part of Russia to prevent or even mitigate such cyber activities. The sentiments expressed by President Putin in the above quoted interview could have come from the leaders of any other cyber-capable state across the globe. Despite allegations that non-state actors, as well as coordinated transnational cyber actors such as Anonymous,[2] have engaged in major cyber operations from within states such as the US,[3] Russia,[4] China,[5] Israel,[6]

* Gratitude is acknowledged to Kyle Watkins for his superb research assistance and to the other authors and editors of this book who provided invaluable feedback.

[1] Ian Phillips/Vladimir Isachenkov, 'Putin: Russia doesn't hack but "patriotic" individuals might', *Washington Post* (1 June 2017).

[2] Katie Bo Williams, 'Anonymous declares war on ISIS', *Hill* (16 November 2015).

[3] Reuters, 'Iran hit by global cyber attack that left U.S. flag on screens', *Reuters* (7 April 2018), available at: www.reuters.com/article/us-iran-cyber-hackers/iran-hit-by-global-cyber-attack-that-left-u-s-flag-on-screens-idUSKBN1HE0MH (accessed 31 July 2019).

[4] See, for a discussion of the cyber-attacks on Estonia and Estonia's defensive response, Kertu Ruus, 'Cyber War I: Estonia Attacked from Russia', *European Affairs* 9 (2008), available at: www.europeaninstitute.org/index.php/42-european-affairs/winterspring-2008/67-cyber-war-i-estonia-attacked-from-russia (accessed 31 July 2019).

[5] Arjan Kharpul, 'Is China still hacking US? This cyber firm says yes', *CNBC* (19 October 2015), available at: www.cnbc.com/2015/10/19/china-hacking-us-companies-for-secrets-despite-cyber-pact-.html (accessed 31 July 2019).

[6] Alex Hern/Peter Beaumont, 'Israel hack uncovered Russian spies' use of Kaspersky in 2015, report says', *Guardian* (11 October 2017), available at: www.theguardian.com/technology/2017/oct/11/israel-hack-uncovered-russian-spies-use-kaspersky-lab-2015-report-us-software-federal-government (accessed 31 July 2019).

Eric Talbot Jensen, *Due Diligence in Cyber Activities* In: *Due Diligence in the International Legal Order*. Edited by: Heike Krieger, Anne Peters, and Leonhard Kreuzer, Oxford University Press (2020). © The Several Contributors.
DOI: 10.1093/oso/9780198869900.003.0015.

Syria,[7] and North Korea,[8] no government has accepted that it has a responsibility to exercise due diligence in order to prevent transboundary cyber harm originating from within its territory.

In fact, the most substantial self-limiting statement on the issue is possibly that of the 2015 United Nations Group of Governmental Experts on Developments in the Field of Information and Telecommunications in the Context of International Security (UN GGE).[9] The twenty states involved in the Group were only able, in a consensus report, to offer 'recommendations for consideration by states for voluntary, non-binding norms, rules or principles of responsible behaviour of states aimed at promoting an open, secure, stable, accessible and peaceful information and communications technology (ICT) environment'.[10] Among those 'voluntary, non-binding' recommendations was the statement that 'States should not knowingly allow their territory to be used for internationally wrongful acts using ICTs'.[11] Alluding to the international law principle of due diligence, a recommendation that states should exercise due diligence carries no legal obligation and little persuasion.

In other words, though there is undoubtedly a generally accepted principle of due diligence that applies to states, the sector-specific application of that principle to cyber operations fails to create meaningful constraints on states with respect to remedying, monitoring, or preventing transboundary cyber harm. The lack of acceptance of the due diligence principle with respect to cyber activities is currently creating an extremely dangerous and uncontrolled cyber environment that leaves the international community at risk of significant cyber consequences. In contrast, the acceptance of a robust application of cyber due diligence would dramatically decrease the instability of the cyber environment and strengthen international peace and security.

This chapter will proceed in five sections. Section 1 will briefly outline those aspects of the principle of due diligence that are relevant for the cyber context, relying on the 2014[12] and 2016[13] Reports of the International Law Association (ILA) Study Group on Due Diligence in International Law. This first section will include a discussion of the general principle of due diligence and its sector-specific application. Section 2 will analyse the current application of due diligence to cyber

[7] Discussing the attack that temporarily shut down the *New York Times* website, see Heather Kelly, 'Syrian group cited as New York Times outage continues', *CNN* (29 August 2013), available at: https://edition.cnn.com/2013/08/27/tech/web/new-york-times-website-attack/index.html (accessed 31 July 2019).

[8] Gordon Corera, 'NHS cyber-attack was "launched from North Korea"', *BBC* (16 June 2017), available at: www.bbc.com/news/technology-40297493 (accessed 31 July 2019).

[9] United Nations, Report of the Group of Governmental Experts on Developments in the Field of Information and Telecommunications in the Context of International Security, A/70/174, 22 July 2015.

[10] Ibid., para. 13.

[11] Ibid., para. 13(c).

[12] ILA, Study Group on Due Diligence in International Law, 'First Report', 7 March 2014.

[13] ILA, Study Group on Due Diligence in International Law, 'Second Report', 12 July 2016.

activities, including an examination of state practice and the major source of legal analysis in the area, the Tallinn Manual 2.0 on the International Law Applicable to Cyber Operations.[14] Section 3 will note the risks inherent to the current approach of a weak application of due diligence to cyber operations. Section 4 will suggest a way forward through strengthening the due diligence principle, although also including some cautionary notes. The chapter will conclude in section 5.

2. Due Diligence

The international law principle of due diligence has been fully developed in the contributions of the 2014 first report of the ILA's Study Group on Due Diligence in International Law,[15] and the subsequent second report from 2016,[16] as well as elsewhere in this book. Nevertheless, several key aspects deserve reemphasising here as they are particularly significant in analysing the application of the general principle of due diligence to cyber operations. One such point is that despite a general acceptance of a due diligence principle, '[p]recisely how the due diligence standard is applied is still subject to considerable discussion and debate'.[17] Indeed, both the first and the second report of the ILA describe due diligence as an 'open-ended standard or principle',[18] and as a 'flexible concept, the content of which varied depending on the circumstances of the case'.[19]

The accepted standard of care, when applying due diligence, is one of reasonableness,[20] though there is disagreement on whether this standard in any particular case is objective or subjective.[21] Regardless, the recognition that due diligence in a given situation may depend on state capabilities is important for the later discussion on cyber operations.

There are two other important aspects of the due diligence standard under international law with respect to cyber operations. First, international law allows for some *de minimis* imposition on the rights of other states.[22] In other words,

[14] Michael Schmitt, *Tallinn Manual 2.0 on the International Law Applicable to Cyber Operations* (Cambridge: CUP 2017).
[15] ILA, Study Group on Due Diligence, 'First Report' 2014 (n. 12).
[16] ILA, Study Group on Due Diligence, 'Second Report' 2016 (n. 13), 7.
[17] Ibid., 7.
[18] Ibid., 3.
[19] ILA, Study Group on Due Diligence, 'First Report' 2014 (n. 12), 2.
[20] ILA, Study Group on Due Diligence, 'Second Report' 2016 (n. 13), 8; Annegret Bendiek, 'Due Diligence in Cyberspace: Guidelines for International and European Cyber Policy and Cybersecurity Policy', *SWP Research Paper*, 7 May 2016, available at: www.swp-berlin.org/fileadmin/contents/products/research_papers/2016RP07_bdk.pdf (accessed 31 July 2019), 8; Luke Chircop, 'A Due Diligence Standard of Attribution in Cyberspace', *International and Comparative Law Quarterly* 67 (2018), 643–668, at 648.
[21] ILA, Study Group on Due Diligence, 'Second Report' 2016 (n. 13), 7–8.
[22] See Jutta Brunnée, 'Sic utere tuo ut alienum non laedas', in Rüdiger Wolfrum (ed.), *Max Planck Encyclopedia of Public International Law* (Oxford: OUP 2010), para. 7: 'The mere causation of transboundary harm does not transgress the *sic utere tuo* maxim.'

despite the seemingly comprehensive nature of this rule, international law allows that some harmful acts must be tolerated in the spirit of good neighbourliness.[23] Second, the principle of due diligence applies to the actions of non-state actors,[24] and 'there [is] a due diligence requirement to prevent and punish the unlawful acts of armed groups'.[25]

One of the most important contributions of the ILA's reports to a clearer understanding of due diligence is the recognition that the principle has a sector-specific nature to its application,[26] and that states will understand their due diligence duty differently depending on the sector in question. In each distinct sector of international law, such as cyber law for example, states will analyse the current state of the law and apply their due diligence obligation in accordance with that analysis.

3. Current Application to Cyber Operations

Both the 2014 and 2016 ILA Reports looked at the application of due diligence to various sectors of international law, but neither considered cyber operations (though both reports acknowledged that such an analysis was needed).[27] However, as briefly detailed in section 1 above, malicious cyber activities are on the rise and are now considered among the top national security risks identified by developed nations.[28]

One of the most concerning aspects of cyber technology is its pervasiveness and general accessibility. Unlike other potentially destabilising technologies such as nuclear weapons, autonomous weapon systems, artificial intelligence, and nanotechnology, cyber capabilities do not require state-like resources to be developed and employed.[29] Cyber technologies not only allow transnational criminal organisations, terrorist organisations, and other similar groups access to state-like levels of violence, but enable small like-minded collectives and even individuals to

[23] ILA, Study Group on Due Diligence, 'Second Report' 2016 (n. 13), 23.

[24] ICJ, *Case Concerning Armed Activities on the Territory of the Congo (DRC v. Uganda)*, Judgment of 19 December 2005, ICJ Reports 2005, 168, paras 299–301.

[25] ILA, Study Group on Due Diligence, 'First Report' 2014 (n. 12), 14, citing *British claims in the Spanish zone of Morocco*, 1925, vol. II, UNRIAA, 615–742; ILA, Study Group on Due Diligence, 'Second Report' 2016 (n. 13), 23, referring to Inter-American Court of Human Rights, *Velasquez Rodriguez Case*, Judgment of 29 July 1988, IACtHR (Ser. C), No. 4 (1988), para. 172.

[26] ILA, Study Group on Due Diligence, 'Second Report' 2016 (n. 13), 6, 48.

[27] ILA, Study Group on Due Diligence, 'First Report' 2014 (n. 12), 1; ILA, Study Group on Due Diligence, 'Second Report' 2016 (n. 13), 2.

[28] Alfred Ng, 'Cybersecurity is "greatest concern" at Senate threats hearing', *CNET* (13 February 2018), available at: www.cnet.com/news/cybersecurity-is-senate-threats-hearings-greatest-concern/ (accessed 31 July 2019); Richard Norton-Taylor, 'Top-tier threats to Britain's security', *Guardian* (18 October 2010), available at: www.theguardian.com/politics/2010/oct/18/top-tier-threats-to-britain (accessed 31 July 2019).

[29] Eric Talbot Jensen, 'The Future of the Law of Armed Conflict: Ostriches, Butterflies, and Nanobots', *Michigan Journal of International Law* 35 (2014), 253–317.

unleash dramatic global cyber consequences. This development is made even more complex by the potentially anonymous nature of the internet and the subsequent difficulties with timely attribution.

These facts result in a situation where a multitude of actors may be engaged in nefarious and harmful cyber actions from within any given state, pursuing a variety of objectives located in other states, and transiting those malicious acts through unknowing intermediary states. Hence, the legal history of cyber activities thus far has been one of very limited effective legal regulation, with the vast majority of legal activity being reactive criminal responses that has done very little to prevent or deter active cyber operations.

3.1 State Practice

Recent state practice has begun to demonstrate a recognition of this problem, but has been largely ineffective in the face of rampant cyber activities. In confronting state practice in the area of cyber operations, it is necessary to acknowledge that states are extremely active in this space, conducting many of the most impactful and malicious cyber activities. Various destructive cyber events have been attributed to the US,[30] Russia,[31] China,[32] Israel,[33] and North Korea,[34] to name just a few. While not the focus of this chapter, it is worth mentioning that international law already has a well-developed set of norms on state responsibility for handling cyber activities that violate international law.

For example, the 2015 UN GGE Report confirmed the finding in the 2013 UN GGE Report[35] that international law generally—and the Charter of the United Nations particularly—applied to states and their ICTs.[36] The 2015 UN GGE explicitly noted:

> [i]n their use of ICTs, States must observe, among other principles of international law, State sovereignty, sovereign equality, the settlement of disputes

[30] BBC, 'Edward Snowden: Leaks that exposed US spy programme', 17 January 2014, available at: www.bbc.com/news/world-us-canada-23123964 (accessed 31 July 2019).

[31] Ellen Nakashima, 'U.S., British governments warn businesses worldwide of Russian campaign to hack routers', *Washington Post* (16 April 2018), available at: www.washingtonpost.com/world/national-security/us-british-governments-say-russia-has-hacked-routers-used-by-businesses-globally/2018/04/16/90e8d34c-4181-11e8-8569-26fda6b404c7_story.html?noredirect=on&utm_term=.4fd9fd50976a (accessed 31 July 2019).

[32] Michael Schmidt/David Sanger, '5 in China Army Face U.S. Charges of Cyberattacks', *New York Times* (19 May 2014).

[33] Ellen Nakashima/Joby Warrick, 'Stuxnet Was Work of U.S. and Israeli Experts, Officials Say', *Washington Post* (2 June 2012).

[34] Gordon Corera, 'NHS cyber-attack was "launched from North Korea"', *BBC* (16 June 2017), available at: www.bbc.com/news/technology-40297493 (accessed 31 July 2019).

[35] UN GGE, ICT Developments in International Security, 24 June 2015 (n. 9).

[36] Ibid., para. 24.

> by peaceful means and non-intervention in the internal affairs of other States. Existing obligations under international law are applicable to State use of ICTs. States must comply with their obligations under international law to respect and protect human rights.[37]

However, in addition to the actions of states, the activities of non-state actors within a state's territory is a potentially more difficult concern. Moreover, this concern forces the international community to determine the extent to which the principle of due diligence requires states to monitor, prevent, and punish those non-state cyber activities that cause transboundary harm.

The UN GGE has provided some help in this area, though more should certainly be done. As previously mentioned, the UN GGE also agreed that 'States should not knowingly allow their territory to be used for internationally wrongful acts using ICTs',[38] an assertion echoed by the EU.[39] Further, the 2015 UN GGE reached a consensus on the issue that 'States have jurisdiction over the ICT infrastructure located within their territory'.[40] International law normally tries to keep a balance between authority and obligation.[41] Therefore, the assertion of jurisdiction over ICTs by states reciprocally implies that states must also exercise control over those ICTs.[42]

Some scholars have used this reciprocal nature to assert a strong version of due diligence in the cyber environment, including a duty to monitor and prevent. For example, Matthew Sklerov has argued that:

> States have an affirmative duty to prevent cyberattacks from their territory against other states. This duty actually encompasses several smaller duties, to include passing stringent criminal laws, conducting vigorous investigations, prosecuting attackers, and, during the investigation and prosecution, cooperating with the victim-states of cyberattacks that originated from within their borders.[43]

[37] Ibid., para. 28(b).
[38] Ibid., para. 13(c).
[39] EU, General Secretariat of the Council, Draft Council Conclusions on a Framework for a Joint EU Diplomatic Response to Malicious Cyber Activities ('Cyber Diplomacy Toolbox'), 7923/2/17 REV 2, 7 June 2017, 18.
[40] UN GGE, ICT Developments in International Security, 24 June 2015 (n. 9), para. 28(a).
[41] See Michael Schmitt, 'In Defense of Due Diligence in Cyberspace', *The Yale Journal Forum* 125 (2015), 68–81, at 71–72; see, for a discussion of the reciprocal nature of authority and obligations in international law, Martti Koskenniemi, 'Doctrines of State Responsibility', in James Crawford/Alain Pellet/Simon Olleson (eds), *The Law of International Responsibility* (Oxford: OUP 2010), 45–52, at 47–48.
[42] ILA, Study Group on Due Diligence, 'Second Report' 2016 (n. 13), 12.
[43] Matthew Sklerov, 'Solving the Dilemma of State Responses to Cyberattacks: A Justification for the Use of Active Defenses against States Who Neglect Their Duty to Prevent', *Military Law Review* 201 (2009), 1.

Even under Sklerov's view of due diligence, however, states would not be liable for every cyber act emanating from their territory. In addition to non-liability for *de minimis* acts, the standard of due diligence is still one of reasonableness.[44] Such considerations have led Michael Schmitt to convincingly argue that a clear understanding of the legal application of the due diligence principle would remove many of the objections states have to it.[45]

However, states have not gone that far in their cyber practice. As the ILA's second report notes, states usually only exercise due diligence to prevent harm if the state has knowledge of the situation.[46] Though some states, such as Germany,[47] India,[48] the Netherlands,[49] China, and Russia[50] have reflected a general requirement to ensure a state's ICT is not used for transboundary harm, there is little evidence that states have embraced this duty as a matter of international law.[51] In fact, the most important multilateral cyber treaty currently is the European Cybercrime Convention,[52] which, rather than establishing proactive requirements to monitor and prevent, is almost a purely procedural convention that establishes methodologies of cooperation in the aftermath of a cyber event to facilitate transnational investigation and prosecution. In practice, even parties to the Convention are often unhelpful when called upon to provide assistance to victim states.[53] On the other hand, the Convention does require Parties to take a number of measures at the national level to ensure that certain cyber acts—including gaining illegal access to a computer system, interfering with data, and computer-related fraud—are illegal. Increased acceptance of the Convention and adherence to its provisions may eventually lead to a general acceptance of the creation of domestic laws prohibiting certain cyber acts, but it appears that such a consensus is yet to exist.

In addition to the general unwillingness of states to accept a due diligence obligation with respect to its ICTs, states appear to be similarly hesitant to accept a

44 See above section 2.

45 Schmitt, 'In Defense of Due Diligence in Cyberspace' 2015 (n. 41), 74–76.

46 ILA, Study Group on Due Diligence, 'Second Report' 2016 (n. 13), 12.

47 Bundesinnenminister Thomas de Maizière, 'Sichere Informationsinfrastrukturen in einem Cyber-Raum der Chancen und der Freiheit', 2014, available at: www.bmi.bund.de/SharedDocs/reden/DE/2014/12/east-west-cyber-summit.html (accessed 31 July 2019).

48 Sean Kanuck, 'Sovereign Discourse on Cyber Conflict under International Law', *Texas Law Review* 88 (2010), 1571–1597.

49 United Nations, General Assembly, Resolution A/70/172, 22 July 2015, Developments in the field of information and telecommunications in the context of international security, Report of the Secretary-General, Submission by Kingdom of the Netherlands, 2015, 7.

50 United Nations, General Assembly, Letter from the Permanent Representatives of China, the Russian Federation, Tajikistan and Uzbekistan to the United Nations addressed to the Secretary-General, A/66/359, 12 September 2011.

51 See, for an analysis of the policies of the US, Germany, and China with respect to cyber due diligence, Scott Shackelford/Scott Russell/Andreas Kuehn, 'Unpacking the International Law on Cybersecurity Due Diligence: Lessons from the Public and Private Sectors', *Chicago Journal of International Law* 17 (2016), 26–43.

52 Council of Europe Convention on Cybercrime, 23 November 2001, ETS 2001, No. 185.

53 See, for a discussion of the lack of assistance by Russia despite calls for help with investigating the perpetrators by Estonia, Ruus, 'Cyber War I' 2008 (n. 4).

due diligence responsibility with respect to the cyber actions of non-state actors. However, the UN GGE was able to achieve consensus on the statement that 'States must not use proxies to commit internationally wrongful acts using ICTs, and should seek to ensure that their territory is not used by non-State actors to commit such acts.'[54]

The EU has endorsed the 'voluntary non-binding norms, rules and principles of responsible behaviour that have been articulated by the UN Group of Governmental Experts'. With specific reference to due diligence, it further urged that '[o]n a bilateral level, cyber dialogues will be further developed and complemented by efforts to facilitate cooperation with third countries to reinforce principles of due diligence and state responsibility in cyberspace'.[55]

Overall, the situation appears to be one where states are willing to make some carefully worded statements concerning the potential application of a relaxed due diligence obligation but are much less likely to actually exercise that obligation in a given set of facts. A complicating factor is the classified nature of cyber activities by states, making it more difficult to even assess state practice. State-sponsored cyber operations are almost always cloaked in secrecy. This allows states to keep the full knowledge of their cyber capabilities from their adversaries. It also allows states the ability to plausibly deny their responsibility for the cyber activities that they are suspected of being involved in. The result of this secrecy is that the international community will often hear about cyber activities but will not be privy to any of the significant details, such as the identity of the perpetrators or the methods with which the malicious cyber activities occurred. With state practice providing little clarity, the work of academics in the area has proved helpful.

3.2 Tallinn Manual

In response to the lack of clarity from states, a group of international cyber law experts gathered to discuss the applicability of international law to cyber operations. These discussions were conceived and supported by NATO's Cooperative Cyber Defence Centre of Excellence in Tallinn, Estonia, and were at least in part a response to the cyber attacks suffered by the Estonian government in 2007 from Russian hacktivists. The result of the initial discussions was the first Tallinn Manual[56,57] which analysed cyber warfare.

[54] UN GGE, ICT Developments in International Security, 24 June 2015 (n. 9), para. 28(e).

[55] European Union, Joint Communication to the European Parliament and the Council, Resilience, Deterrence and Defence, 'Building Strong Cybersecurity for the EU', JOIN/2017/0450 final, 13 September 2017, 18.

[56] Note that the author was a member of the group of experts for both the Tallinn Manual and the Tallinn Manual 2.0. For further analysis of Tallinn 2.0, including the principle of due diligence, see Eric Talbot Jensen, 'The Tallinn Manual 2.0: Highlights and Insights', *Georgetown Journal of International Law* 48 (2017), 735–778.

[57] Schmitt, *Tallinn Manual 2.0* 2017 (n. 14).

A similar but more diverse group was convened to broaden the legal analysis of the first Manual and to deal more broadly with cyber operations, with a particular focus on those operations that did not rise to the level of a use of force under the UN Charter. The resulting Tallinn Manual 2.0 is currently the most comprehensive and thorough analysis of cyber operations. The contributing experts recognise that states make law and their attempt was merely to identify how they thought current international law applied to cyber operations.[58] Appropriately, the Manual's experts sought and received significant input from states, all of which was comprehensively considered by the experts. However, the Manual's final conclusions are solely those of the experts. Though it is the actions and statements of states that will ultimately help to refine the application of international law to this cyber-specific sector, the Manual is nevertheless a helpful resource in determining the current state of the law.

The Tallinn Manuals are organised with black letter rules to which all the experts agreed, followed by a subsequent commentary that explains each rule, noting disagreements on issues among the experts and also identifying other views that the experts considered but rejected. The Tallinn Manual 2.0 has two separate rules devoted to due diligence. The first is a restatement of the broader due diligence rule but applied to cyber issues:

> A State must exercise due diligence in not allowing its territory, or territory or cyber infrastructure under its governmental control, to be used for cyber operations that affect the rights of, and produce serious adverse consequences for, other States.[59]

As a rule, all the Tallinn experts agreed with this application of the principle to cyber operations. The experts acknowledged the view, somewhat reflected in the UN GGE, that the principle of due diligence, while one that has general application, had not yet achieved the status of *lex lata* with respect to the sector-specific area of cyber operations.[60] However, none of the Tallinn experts took that view.[61] Instead, the experts determined that the due diligence principle did apply to cyber operations,[62] although acknowledging that the specifics of that application were contested. In line with this view adopted by the Tallinn Manual's experts, the EU, in its 2013 cybersecurity strategy,[63] stressed the importance of responsible state behaviour, cooperation, prevention, and resilience in cyberspace, which has led

[58] Ibid., 2–3.
[59] Ibid., 18, para. 3.
[60] Ibid., 19, paras 3–4.
[61] Ibid., 18, para. 3.
[62] Ibid., 19, para. 4.
[63] European Union, Joint Communication to the European Parliament, the Council, the European Economic and Social Committee and the Committee of the Regions, 'Cybersecurity Strategy of the European Union: An Open, Safe and Secure Cyberspace', JOIN/2013/0001 final, 7 February 2013.

Annegret Bendiek to conclude that '[t]o establish the digital single market, national regulations in civil law (data protection), commercial law (internet governance) and competition law (domestic market) must be worded in such a way as to fulfil due diligence obligations'.[64]

In discussing the details of the principle's application, the Tallinn experts agreed that the obligation to exercise due diligence applies throughout a state's entire territory,[65] which encompasses not only those overseas territories controlled by the state[66] but includes any governmental cyber infrastructure as well.[67] In accordance with the 'sector-specific' approach taken by the ILA Study Group, the Tallinn experts argued that many of the cyber-specific obligations were not based on a 'distinct primary obligation with respect to harmful cyber operations as such' but rather on 'the general principle of due diligence in the cyber context'.[68]

The Tallinn experts noted several areas where cyber operations required the thoughtful analysis and application of the due diligence principle. Perhaps the most important area concerns the standard that applies to the application of due diligence to a specific incident. After examining state practice, the Tallinn experts concluded that the standard of actual or constructive knowledge was the generally accepted standard with respect to implicating the due diligence obligation.[69] In other words, if a state has actual or constructive knowledge of a transboundary cyber harm originating from its territory, that state must exercise its due diligence obligation to remediate the harm. However, the experts concluded that in the cyber environment states do not accept the obligation to take preventive measures with its cyber infrastructure,[70] or even to monitor cyber infrastructure in order to gain awareness of any potential transboundary harm.[71] Once the state is aware of the transboundary harm, it is required to take 'all measures that are feasible in the circumstances to put an end to the cyber operations'.[72] Feasibility, in this context, is understood to mean that the state must take measures that are 'reasonably available and practical'.[73]

A cyber-unique area where the knowledge standard demonstrates gaps in coverage is the area of transiting data. Because of the nature of the internet, data will transit states through a set of protocols that allow the passage of data in ways that maximise the overall flow across the globally interconnected internet. As a matter of course, states neither monitor nor control that flow of transiting data.

64 Bendiek, 'Due Diligence in Cyberspace' 2016 (n. 20), 6.
65 Schmitt, *Tallinn Manual 2.0* 2017 (n. 14), 19, para. 8.
66 Ibid., 19, para. 9.
67 Ibid., 19–20, para. 10.
68 Ibid., 19, para. 6.
69 Ibid., 41, para. 39; Chircop, 'Due Diligence Standard of Attribution' 2018 (n. 20), 649.
70 Schmitt, *Tallinn Manual 2.0* 2017 (n. 14), 44–45, para. 7.
71 Ibid.
72 Ibid., 43, rule 7.
73 Ibid., 43, para 2.

Nevertheless, a robust reading of the due diligence obligation would demand those states through which data carrying malicious code is transiting to monitor and prevent it. The experts, however, refused to apply due diligence in this manner. Rather, they concluded that the due diligence obligation only arises when the transit state has actual or constructive knowledge of the passage of malicious code, and 'can take feasible measures to effectively terminate it'.[74] Others have noted that, despite the difficulty of establishing actual or constructive knowledge, 'there is no legal reason to consider that transit States do not have a duty of diligence and thus could escape their own obligations in this respect' if knowledge was established.[75]

Finally, the experts agree with the ILA Study Groups that not all transboundary cyber harm falls within the due diligence standard. The Tallinn experts agreed that some harm had to be tolerated,[76] and that only the harm resulting in serious adverse consequences was implicated in the obligation. Having come to this conclusion, the experts were unable to fully describe what 'serious adverse consequences' means and concluded that international law is unclear on this point.[77] But the experts did agree that it did not require 'physical damage to objects or injuries to individuals'.[78]

3.3 Interim Conclusion

It is clear that cyber operations are becoming an increasingly important part of national security. While cyber capabilities present great advancements and benefits, they also open up potential vulnerabilities. Often the cyber operations seeking to take advantage of these vulnerabilities originate from actors in states other than the target states and hence cause transboundary harm. Thus far, states have been unwilling to accept a robust application of the due diligence principle for the cyber sector, instead requiring knowledge (actual or constructive) on the part of a state to trigger the principle. The Tallinn experts were unable to find either general international law or a sector-specific application that would require states to act with heightened diligence.

[74] Ibid., 20, paras 13–14.

[75] Karine Bannelier-Christakis, 'Cyber Diligence: A Low-Intensity Due Diligence Principle for Low-Intensity Cyber Operations?', *Baltic Yearbook of International Law Vol. 14* (2014), 23–39, at 29.

[76] Schmitt, *Tallinn Manual 2.0* 2017 (n. 14), 26, para. 22.

[77] Ibid., 36–37, para. 25.

[78] Ibid., para. 28.

4. Risks Inherent to the Current Approach

Several aspects of cyber operations make the current application of due diligence by states ineffective in limiting transboundary harm. First, the anonymous nature of actions on the internet allow both state and non-state actors to conduct cyber operations with a significantly decreased fear of attribution than, for example, transnational environmental harm. Often, cyber forensics will eventually allow attribution, but in almost every case the attribution comes long after the cyber harm has occurred. For example, in December 2017, the US, the UK, Canada, Japan, and others eventually blamed North Korea for the WannaCry malware that was released in May 2017. When questioned about the length of time it took to attribute blame for the WannaCry malware to North Korea, a US government spokesperson stated:

> did we do it too slowly? No. My answer is, no. I think the most important thing is to do it right and not to do it fast (…). We can't get it wrong. We can't try to rush it.[79]

The passage of time between occurrence and attribution may present dramatically decreased potential costs to actors who engage in malicious cyber acts—both in potential criminal and civil liability. If state or non-state actors believe that their victims will be unable to identify them as the cyber actors for months or even years after the event, many will be willing to accept the potential risks in the hope that eventual responses to delayed attribution will be blunted by the passage of time, with focus deviating towards more recent events. This has led some states towards the decision to announce attribution at a much earlier stage than may have previously been done.

Acknowledging the difficulty posed by delayed or ineffective attribution, Luke Chircop has argued that a failure of due diligence could lead to attribution and thereby overcome this difficulty.[80] Under Chircop's view, if a victim state could point to a lack of due diligence on the part of the state from which the cyber operations originated, attribution might be assumed and therefore making that state potentially liable for the harm caused by the cyber act. Chircop's argument is persuasive, especially in a case where a state may use proxies to accomplish its cyber operations as a way to disclaim responsibility. However, perhaps because it might make it more difficult for states to avoid responsibility, it does not appear that states are enthusiastic about adopting this view. Allowing some increased level of

[79] Tom Bossert, 'Press Briefing on the Attribution of the WannaCry Malware Attack to North Korea', 19 December 2017, available at: www.whitehouse.gov/briefings-statements/press-briefing-on-the-attribution-of-the-wannacry-malware-attack-to-north-korea-121917/ (accessed 31 July 2019).

[80] Chircop, 'Due Diligence Standard of Attribution' 2018 (n. 20), 648–649.

attribution when there is a limited exercise of due diligence would encourage states to take their due diligence obligation more seriously.

An example that clearly illustrates the difficulty arising from the current approach to due diligence and the potential benefit of Chircop's approach is illustrated by a situation of transboundary harm, where the origin state, and not the victim state, controls and has jurisdiction over the computers and computer networks from which the transboundary harm originated. This means that the victim state is almost completely reliant on the willingness of the origin state to cooperate in post-event forensics; this fact cannot be assumed, as was demonstrated by Russia in the aftermath of the 2007 cyber incident in Estonia. The origin state is often in the best position to take effective action to both prevent and remediate the transboundary harm. As argued elsewhere:

> [r]ecognizing a cyber-specific obligation of due diligence to address emanation of such cyber harms might mitigate the attribution dilemma. That is, a primary rule of conduct requiring diligent management of territorial cyber infrastructure could give rise to the responsibility on the part of non-diligent States as proxies for unidentified or unreachable malicious actors.[81]

Failing this more vigorous application of due diligence, applying Chircop's approach of assuming attribution in the absence of due diligence would have allowed Estonia to attribute the acts to Russia, based on their lack of due diligence both in monitoring the initial attacks and in not responding to requests for information.

The second aspect of cyber operations that make the current application of due diligence by states ineffective is the instantaneous nature of cyber-enabled attacks. Unlike many other transboundary harms, cyber actions can take place almost instantaneously. The transition from 'mapping' a network or defining its boundaries and connections to inserting and triggering malicious code that could disable or destroy the network is often as simple as hitting 'enter' on the keyboard. In other words, the conversion from the domestic crime of unauthorised intrusion into a network to a violation of international law through the commission of a cyber 'use of force' can be as simple as triggering the 'payload' of malicious code that was imbedded in the cyber reconnaissance tool. This means that the temporal nature of cyber operations adds a level of complexity in determining both the characterisation and the intent of the cyber activity that undermine the effectiveness of traditional notions of due diligence.

Because the cyber harm can be instantaneous and devastating, the most effective way to mitigate such harms is to prevent them. One effective preventative approach is to strengthen the state responsibility of due diligence. In monitoring

[81] Eric Talbot Jensen/Sean Watts, 'A Cyber Duty of Due Diligence: Gentle Civilizer or Crude Destabilizer?', *Texas Law Review* 95 (2017), 1555–1577, at 1558.

their networks to identify potential harmful cyber activities, states will foster a pro-active approach to limiting cyber harms rather than merely relying on a post-event remediation approach to transboundary harm. Since the payload can be instantaneously triggered once it has been implanted in the system, the most effective approach to harmful malware is to keep it from getting into the system in the first place. Emphasising the principle of due diligence would greatly enhance the ability of states to stop the transboundary transmission of cyber malware.

A third aspect of cyber operations that makes the current application of due diligence by states ineffective in limiting transboundary harm is the standard of knowledge, whether actual or constructive, to trigger the obligation. Requiring the origin state to have actual or constructive knowledge of the transboundary harm—and not coupled with any obligation to monitor cyber networks—severely diminishes the application of the principle of due diligence and makes it practically ineffective. If the origin state's obligation to exercise due diligence does not accrue until the victim state has experienced the effects of the cyber harm, the due diligence principle becomes grounded in remediation. States have little incentive to seek out potential transboundary harms if there is no obligation to do so. If a state can legally allow the transboundary harm to occur and only take action to stop the harm once notified by the victim state, what would incentivise a state to invest the necessary resources to try to protect other states from potential cyber harms the proper exercising of a more robust due diligence obligation may provide actual or constructive knowledge of a potential transboundary harm long before it materialises? For example, had Russia been exercising an enhanced due diligence obligation in 2007, it may have become aware of the rising attacks on Estonia in time to mitigate much of the ensuing harm.

5. Ways Ahead

There is little doubt that despite the diminished role currently given to due diligence in the cyber context, it accords with states' desires. However, this need not be the case. A more robust application of due diligence in the cyber sector, one patterned after the application of the principle in other sectors, would significantly increase the responsibility of states to prevent malicious cyber acts and consequently enhance the ability of international law to provide order and stability in the international system. The enhancement of the principle of due diligence in the cyber context could be accomplished by transferring the more rigorous reliance on prevention from other sector-specific approaches and implant it into the cyber sector. While some academics have taken a different view,[82] the Tallinn Manual came to

[82] Bannelier-Christakis, 'Cyber Diligence' 2014 (n. 75), 9–12.

the conclusion that states currently accept no obligation to take preventive measures with regards to their cyber infrastructure,[83] or even monitor this infrastructure in order to be aware of any potential transboundary harm.[84] Recognising that this is the current state of the law does not require it to remain so. If states were to accept the duty to monitor their cyber networks more actively, they would provide themselves not only with increased knowledge but also foreknowledge of potential harms. States would then be better placed to take preventative action. Once a state gains knowledge of a developing cyber threat that would cause transboundary harm, that state would have to exercise due diligence in preventing the harm.

Strengthening the application of due diligence in the cyber sector could be accomplished in several ways. First, states could forge an international agreement on cyber due diligence and invite all states to join as parties. As Karine Bannelier-Christakis has suggested, the international community 'should think about the adoption in the future of a universal instrument on cybersecurity' in order to invigorate the principle of due diligence through common adoption.[85] Second, the UN could, possibly through additional meetings of the UN GGE, begin the process for authoritative statements that might lead to the eventual crystallisation of a new customary norm. Given the widespread effects of cyber harms, and as states consider their current vulnerability, a consensus may grow around a more rigorous obligation of due diligence. Third, states—including major cyber actors—could unilaterally begin to apply to their due diligence responsibilities, responsibilities that they readily accept in other areas of the law. Unilateral action carries some risks and cooperative action is certainly less costly, but for some states unilateral action may be preferable to no action. As more and more states, particularly those with advanced cyber capabilities, adopt unilateral measures to apply a robust due diligence obligation, other states will see the benefits of enhanced due diligence and the proposition might gather momentum. Regardless of what method is embraced, achieving an enhanced cyber due diligence obligation for states appears to be an important step towards greater international peace and security.

While advocating for due diligence in the cyber sector, it is clear that such a course of action is not without risks. Two particular risks are perhaps most troublesome. The first is the potential for states to use the duty to monitor and prevent cyber harms as the basis for censoring opponents and suppressing human rights, such as the freedom of expression. As noted by Ekaterina A. Drozdova:

> There are inherent dangers in a system for advanced monitoring, searching, tracking, and analyzing of communications. Though it could be very helpful against cyber crime and terrorism, it would also provide participating

[83] Schmitt, *Tallinn Manual 2.0* 2017 (n. 14), 44–45, para. 7.
[84] Ibid.; see above section 3.2.
[85] Bannelier-Christakis, 'Cyber Diligence' 2014 (n. 75), 18.

governments, especially authoritarian governments or agencies with little accountability, tools to violate civil liberties domestically and abroad.[86]

The evolution of due diligence certainly has the potential to develop in such a way as to justify the repression of human rights, a risk which has also been noted by states.[87] As the international community strengthens the obligation of states to monitor their ICTs, it must also ensure that strict safeguards are in place to prevent states from using this duty to censor communications that are critical of the government or government policies. Further, the required monitoring should not be used—on the basis of political rather than internet safety issues—to justify the targeting of specific individuals or groups and their expression. Vigorous oversight by the Human Rights Committee and other NGOs will certainly help prevent such abuses, but other mechanisms, specifically tailored to the review of domestic cyber policies, may become necessary.

The second risk is the possibility of increased use of potentially destabilising countermeasures. As the duty of due diligence becomes broader and more accepted, failures to exercise the obligation could constitute an internationally wrongful act. Victim states would then have the option of resorting to countermeasures to compel compliance. Generally speaking, countermeasures are illegal acts under international law but which are excused under exceptional circumstances if they are taken in response to an internationally wrongful act. Their only purpose must be to bring the violating state back into compliance with international law.[88] The Tallinn Manual conducted a thorough review of both cyber countermeasures and countermeasures in response to cyber actions.[89]

Chircop has argued that countermeasures could play a key role in state responses to cyber incidents, but with important limitations. He argues that if properly applied, countermeasures would be of limited effect in a cyber scenario because a strict reading of international law would only allow the use of countermeasures to urge compliance with the underlying due diligence standard, as opposed to targeting the specific cyber activity.[90] Others, however, take a broader position on the effectiveness of countermeasures,[91] including the Tallinn Manual. Regardless of the opinion of states on this particular issue, countermeasures must comply

[86] Ekaterina Drozdova, 'Civil Liberties and Security in Cyberspace', in Abraham Sofaer/Seymour Goodman (eds), *The Transnational Dimension of Cyber Crime and Terrorism* (Stanford: Hoover Institution Press 2001) 183–220, at 197; see also, in this regard, Bannelier-Christakis, 'Cyber Diligence' 2014 (n. 75), 31.

[87] European Union, Joint Communication, 'Building Strong Cybersecurity for the EU' 2017 (n. 55), 18.

[88] United Nations, International Law Commission (ILC), Commentary to the Draft Articles on State Responsibility, YBILC 2001, vol. II (part II), 30–143, art. 49, para. 1; Schmitt, *Tallinn Manual 2.0* 2017 (n. 14), 116, rule 21.

[89] Schmitt, *Tallinn Manual 2.0* 2017 (n. 14), 111–130, rules 20–23.

[90] Chircop, 'Due Diligence Standard of Attribution' 2018 (n. 20), 9–12.

[91] Schmitt, 'In Defense of Due Diligence in Cyberspace' 2015 (n. 41), 79.

with other broadly accepted limitations before being imposed. For example, states can take neither collective[92] nor anticipatory[93] countermeasures. Further, as mentioned above, countermeasures may only be used against states and not non-state actors;[94] they must also be proportionate.[95] Several of these well recognised limitations on the use of countermeasures present an interesting contrast to their accepted availability as a self-defence response.[96]

Despite these limitations, or perhaps because of them, cyber capabilities present states with an interesting set of additional tools to conduct international relations. Because cyber tools vastly expand the targets states are capable of effectively reaching, the measured use of cyber countermeasures could appeal to many states as a softer but effective way to urge a violating state back into compliance. In other words, cyber countermeasures could act as a real incentive for states to exercise their enhanced duty of due diligence.

For example, in response to the aforementioned WannaCry malware that was attributed to North Korea, a combined response with countermeasures by victim states might have sent a much stronger message to North Korea to desist from planning any future cyber activities and encourage greater compliance with international law. Similarly, countermeasures to ensure due diligence may have also been effective against Russia's employment of the NotPetya malware. Because of the complete lack of public acknowledgement of the use by states of cyber countermeasures, one can only speculate as to whether states have contemplated using them and if they think they would be effective. But it seems that cyber countermeasures would be an extremely useful tool when responding to at least some circumstances of internationally wrongful acts by other states.

However, an increase in the general use of countermeasures may carry with it an equally disturbing set of risks that could have a destabilising effect on international peace and security. As argued elsewhere:

> by presenting more opportunities for more States to allege more breaches of international law, due diligence potentially increases the frequency of States' resort to countermeasures and their accompanying destabilizing effects. Before fully embracing a more refined notion of cyber due diligence and the consequent increased opportunities to allege breach, States are well advised to consider carefully both practical limitations of the international regime of self-help and associated costs to international stability.[97]

[92] Schmitt, *Tallinn Manual 2.0* 2017 (n. 14), 126, para. 14.
[93] Ibid., 118, para. 5.
[94] Ibid., 113–114, paras 7–10.
[95] ILC, Commentaries to Articles on State Responsibility, 2001 (n. 88), art. 51 and art. 49, para. 1; Schmitt, *Tallinn Manual 2.0* 2017 (n. 14), 127, rule 23.
[96] Jensen/Watts, 'A Cyber Duty of Due Diligence' 2017 (n. 81), 1564.
[97] Ibid., 1577.

The Tallinn Manual also expresses concerns with a potential proliferation of countermeasures.[98] The tight constraints on countermeasures are in place to limit the natural tendency towards escalation that they might engender. This is particularly true of cyber countermeasures because of their instantaneous and often undetectable nature.[99] Strict adherence to the limitations on the use of countermeasures may mitigate this risk to some degree, but it still remains a potential risk.

6. Conclusion

It seems clear that due diligence is a fundamental principle of international law that requires states to not knowingly allow their 'territory to be used for acts contrary to the rights of other States'.[100] It is equally clear that this general principle functions differently based on sector-specific applications.

In the cyber environment, states currently have taken a less robust view of due diligence, resisting a preventive obligation and requiring actual or constructive knowledge before accepting the responsibility to intervene. Given the current factual situation of active cyber operations by both states and non-state actors, this creates an extremely dangerous and uncontrolled cyber environment that leaves the international community at risk of significant cyber consequences. If states were to accept a more robust application of cyber due diligence, including a duty to monitor and prevent, they would dramatically decrease the instability of the cyber environment and strengthen international peace and security. Though such a decision would also carry inherent risks, the stability and increased security to global cyber systems would far outweigh the consequences of these managed risks.

[98] Schmitt, *Tallinn Manual 2.0* 2017 (n. 14), 116, para. 16.

[99] Ibid., 117, para. 2.

[100] ICJ, *Corfu Channel Case (United Kingdom v. Albania)*, Judgment of 9 April 1949, ICJ Reports 1949, 4, p. 22.

PART IV

DUE DILIGENCE IN INTERNATIONAL ECONOMIC LAW

16

Due Diligence in International Investment Law

From the Law of Aliens to Responsible Investment

*Aniruddha Rajput**

1. Introduction

This chapter discusses the continued relevance and rising role of due diligence in international investment law. The nature of due diligence as a relative standard and its normative content as an obligation of 'conduct' and not 'result'[1] has informed the decisions of investment tribunals. At the same time, in turn, the jurisprudence of investment tribunals has contributed to the development of due diligence. In international investment law, due diligence has transformed from its original conceptualisation as an obligation on states regarding treatment of aliens to an obligation on foreign investors for responsible investments. To that extent, it functions as a balancing factor between responsibility of the host state and the duty of foreign investors. This chapter traces these developments and the potential future development of the principle of due diligence through five sections. The first section discusses due diligence as an obligation on host states. The second section discusses due diligence as an obligation on foreign investors. The third section presents the role due diligence has and the way it could develop in the future with regard to human rights and business, with focus upon the United Nations Guiding Principles on Businesses and Human Rights. The fourth section synthesises the preceding discussion to identify some general comments and conclusions that can be drawn therefrom. The chapter ends with some concluding observations in the final section.

* I thank Professor Attila Tanzi and Ms Camilla Gambarini for their helpful comments and Ms Somabha Bondopadhay for research assistance. The responsibility of the views expressed and errors is entirely mine.

[1] See for the discussion on the meaning and historical development of due diligence Giulio Bartolini, 'The Historical Roots of the Due Diligence Standard', chapter 2 of this book.

Aniruddha Rajput, *Due Diligence in International Investment Law* In: *Due Diligence in the International Legal Order*. Edited by: Heike Krieger, Anne Peters, and Leonhard Kreuzer, Oxford University Press (2020). © The Several Contributors. DOI: 10.1093/oso/9780198869900.003.0016.

2. Due Diligence Obligation of Host States

Host states incur an obligation of due diligence, as an obligation of conduct, towards foreign investors as an element emanating from certain rules of customary international law and treatment standards in bilateral investment treaties. In customary international law, due diligence has developed as an element of international minimum standard and denial of justice, which fall within the framework of the law of treatment of aliens. The treatment standard of full protection of security is based upon the requirement of due diligence behaviour of the host state and fair and equitable treatment encompasses some aspects of due diligence. The international minimum standard is violated if the authorities in the host state do not act with sufficient diligence. When the lack of diligence is attributed to the judiciary it constitutes denial of justice. Full protection and security contemplates that the host state undertakes necessary measures with diligence to provide physical protection and security to the foreign investor and the investment from persons or entities whose actions cannot be attributed to the state. Fair and equitable treatment encompasses due diligence. In this regard, due diligence includes the requirement of due process in actions of government and actions of judiciary, transparency, and legitimate expectations.

2.1 Due Diligence and International Minimum Standard

International minimum standard arose from the need for a host state to act with diligence in matters relating to investigation of offences committed against aliens in the host state. International minimum standard was defined in the famous *Neer* case, by the Mexico-US General Claims Commission as follows:

> [the] treatment of an alien, in order to constitute an international delinquency, should amount to an outrage, to bad faith, to wilful neglect of duty, or to an insufficiency of governmental action so far short of international standards that every reasonable and impartial man would readily recognize its insufficiency. Whether the insufficiency proceeds from deficient execution of an intelligent law or from the fact that the laws of the country do not empower the authorities to measure up to international standards is immaterial.[2]

In order to satisfy the international minimum standard, the host state has to show sufficiency of governmental action. It is fundamentally a question of the manner in which the government acted and whether it was sufficient in the circumstances.

[2] Mexico-US General Claims Commission, *L. F. H. Neer and Pauline Neer (USA v. United Mexican States)*, 15 October 1926, vol. IV, UNRIAA, 60, para. 4.

The Claims Commission further observed upon the due diligence requirement in investigation, as follows:

> In the light of the entire record in this case the Commission is not prepared to hold that the Mexican authorities have shown such lack of diligence or such lack of intelligent investigation in apprehending and punishing the culprits as would render Mexico liable before this Commission.[3]

International minimum standard would apply in a wide range of factual scenarios, as long as the conduct of a state is not committed with due diligence. International minimum standard is a standard of conduct. The host state is to ensure that it acts diligently, whether for the purpose of granting physical protection to the foreign investor or in relation to any other treatment of the foreign investor. There is no obligation of any definite outcome on the host state.[4] There are no precise contents of the international minimum standard. But it has been elaborated by investment tribunals while interpreting fair and equitable treatment.[5] A host state would be violating the international minimum standard if it does not act with due diligence; likewise, if the host state has acted with due diligence then it would not be responsible although the foreign investor has suffered any losses.

International minimum standard is a rule of customary international law.[6] But due diligence by itself is not a rule: it is a concept that is embedded in the international minimum standard.

2.2 Due Diligence and Denial of Justice

In addition to the international minimum standard, the international law on treatment of aliens includes denial of justice, which is also a customary international law rule.[7] Denial of justice is a rule of customary international law that imposes an obligation of conduct on the judiciary of a state.[8] Denial of justice is an obligation of conduct that does not impose absolute obligations. Due diligence as a

[3] Ibid., para. 5.

[4] See, for example, International Centre for Settlement of Investment Disputes (ICSID), *ECO Guatemala Holdings, LLC v. Republic of Guatemala*, ICSID Case No. ARB/10/23, Award, 19 December 2013, para. 454-5.

[5] ICSID, *El Paso v. Argentina*, ICSID Case No. ARB/03/15, Award of 31 October 2011, para. 335.

[6] ICSID, *Waste Management, Inc. v. United Mexican States*, ICSID Case No. ARB(AF)/00/3, Award of 30 April 2004, para. 92; ICSID, *Mondev Int'l, Ltd. v. United States*, ICSID Case No. ARB(AF)/99/2, Award of 11 October 2002.

[7] Muthucumaraswamy Sornarajah, *The International Law on Foreign Investment* (Cambridge: CUP 2nd ed. 2004), 138–142.

[8] For a detailed analysis of the principle see Alwyn Freeman, *The International Responsibility of States for Denial of Justice* (Cambridge: CUP 1st ed. 1938); Jan Paulsson, *Denial of Justice in International Law* (Cambridge: CUP 1st ed. 2005).

part of denial of justice expects a state to keep a workable judicial system available, so that claims can be properly examined and deeded in accordance with domestic or international law. There is no promise of a certain outcome.[9] Denial of justice would exist when 'relevant courts refuse to entertain a suit, if they subject it to undue delay, or if they administer justice in a seriously inadequate way'.[10] The threshold for establishing denial of justice is high.[11] In *Parkerings v. Lithuania*, the Tribunal did not find the host state in breach of due diligence due to its failure to interfere in the dispute between authorities of one of the cities and the foreign investor. The host state was responsible only to keep a judicial system available.[12] There is no obligation to ensure that the foreign investor would win every case.[13]

International minimum standard and denial of justice are customary international law rules that contain due diligence and are binding on a host state while treating a foreign investor. The elements of international minimum standard and denial of justice have been used to test the appropriateness of the conduct of the host state as a part of due diligence. Full protection and security and fair and equitable treatment are found in almost all the investment treaties. Both these treatment standards comprise of some aspects of due diligence.

2.3 Due Diligence and Full Protection and Security

Full protection and security is developed and informed by the international minimum standard. It relates to the obligation of a host state to grant physical protection and security to foreign investors from actions of third parties. In some cases, investment tribunals have included the legal protection and security in full protection and security—although not all tribunals share this position.[14] In either case, the responsibility of a host state does not go beyond due diligence. In *Lauder v. Czech Republic*, the Tribunal drew the relationship between full protection and security in the following words:

> The Arbitral Tribunal is of the opinion that the Treaty obliges the Parties to exercise such due diligence in the protection of foreign investment as reasonable

[9] United Nations Commission on International Trade Law (UNCITRAL), *Ronald S. Lauder v. Czech Republic*, Final Award of 3 September 2001, para. 314.

[10] Ibid., para. 102.

[11] UNCITRAL, *Chevron Corporation and Texaco Petroleum Corporation v. The Republic of Ecuador*, PCA Case No. 34877, Partial Award on Merits of 30 March 2010, para. 244.

[12] ICSID, *Parkerings-Compagniet AS v. Republic of Lithuania*, ICSID Case No. ARB/05/8, Award of 11 September 2007, paras 359–360.

[13] Ibid., paras 359–361.

[14] UNCITRAL, *Frontier Petrochemical v. Czech Republic*, Final Award of 12 November 2010, para. 263; ICSID, *Rumeli Telekom AS and Telsim Mobil Telekomunikasyon Hizmetleri AS v. Kazakhstan*, ICSID Case No. ARB/05/16, Award of 29 July 2008; ICJ, *Elettronica Sicula S.p.A. (ELSI) (United States of America v. Italy)*, Judgment of 20 July 1989, ICJ Reports 1989, para. 15.

> under the circumstances. However, the Treaty does not oblige the Parties to protect foreign investment against any possible loss of value caused by persons whose acts could not be attributed to the State. Such protection would indeed amount to strict liability, which cannot be imposed to a State absent any specific provision in the Treaty.[15]

Due diligence as part of full protection and security is an outcome of *jurisprudence constante*.[16] A state would be fulfilling its obligation under full protection and security if it acts with due diligence.[17] Full protection and security requires the host state 'to exercise such due diligence in the protection of foreign investment as reasonable under the circumstances'.[18] A state is expected to take all reasonable measures to protect assets and properties of the foreign investor.[19] It is not an obligation to 'prevent each and every injury'.[20] Under due diligence there is no strict liability for the harm caused.[21] Use of words such as 'constant' or 'full' do not change the standard of due diligence to 'strict liability'.[22] There is no strict liability of a state for harm because the presence of due diligence reduces the standard of responsibility from strict liability. Investment treaties do not expect host states to protect foreign investors from all losses caused by persons whose actions are not attributable to state. If due diligence is not applied, it would result in strict liability, which is not the desired standard.[23] If a state can establish that it has taken the best possible efforts in accordance with its police and military strengths to prevent the injury, the standard of full protection and security is satisfied.

[15] UNCITRAL, *Ronald S. Lauder* (n. 9), para. 310.

[16] ICSID, *Mamidoil Jetoil Greek Petroleum Products Societe S.A. v. Republic of Albania*, ICSID Case No. ARB/11/24, Award of 30 March 2015, para. 821. Cases where due diligence has been used as a part of Full Protection and Security: UNCITRAL, *Ronald S. Lauder* (n. 9), para. 308; ICSID, *Noble Ventures, Inc. v. Romania*, ICSID Case No. ARB/01/11, Award of 12 October 2005, para. 164; UNCITRAL *Saluka Investments B.V. v. the Czech Republic*, Partial Award of 17 March 2006, para. 483; ICSID, *Biwater Gauff (Tanzania) Ltd. v. United Republic of Tanzania*, ICSID Case No. ARB/05/22, Award of 24 July 2008, para. 725; ICSID, *Rumeli Telekom v. Republic of Kazakhstan* (n. 14), para. 668; ICSID, *Waguih Elie George Siag & Clorinda Vecchi v. the Arab Republic of Egypt*, ICSID Case No. ARB/05/15, Award of 1 June 2009, para. 447; ICSID, *Suez, Sociedad General de Aguas de Barcelona S.A. and Vivendi Universal S.A. v The Argentine Republic*, ICSID Case No. ARB/03/19, Decision on Liability of 30 July 2010 and ICSID, *AWG Group Ltd v. The Argentine Republic*, ICSID Case No. ARB/03/19, Decision on Liability of 30 July 2012, para. 161.

[17] ICSID, *Asian Agricultural Products Ltd. v. Sri Lanka*, ICSID Case No. ARB/87/3, Final Award of 27 June 1990, para. 67; ICSID, *Biwater Gauff v. Tanzania* (n. 16), paras 724–728; ICSID, *Plama Consortium Limited v. Republic of Bulgaria*, ICSID Case No. ARB/03/24, Award of 27 August 2008, para. 179.

[18] UNCITRAL, *Ronald S. Lauder* (n. 9), para. 308.

[19] UNCITRAL, *Saluka Investments B.V. v. the Czech Republic* (n. 16), para. 484.

[20] ICSID, *Mamidoil Jetoil Greek Petroleum v. Republic of Albania* (n. 16), para. 821.

[21] Ibid., para. 77; ICSID, *Técnicas Medioambientales Tecmed S.A. v. The United Mexican States*, ICSID Case No. ARB (AF)/00/2, Award of 29 May 2003, para. 177.

[22] ICSID, *Asian Agricultural v. Republic of Sri Lanka* (n. 17), para. 50.

[23] UNCITRAL, *Ronald S. Lauder* (n. 9), para. 308.

2.4 Due Diligence and Fair and Equitable Treatment

Fair and equitable treatment is a free-standing and flexible treatment standard. Host states are often found responsible for its breach, as compared to other treatment standards.[24] The standard by itself is devoid of contents. Investment tribunals have taken it as an invitation to interpret the standard liberally and identified its elements. Some of those elements are based on due diligence. One of the underlying descriptions of fair and equitable treatment by a tribunal represent it as an obligation of conduct: 'acts showing a willful neglect of duty, an insufficiency of action falling far below international standards, or even subjective bad faith'.[25]

Procedural propriety and due process are part of fair and equitable treatment. The requirement of due process may be violated by legislative or executive action. The due process requirement desires compliance with fair procedures. Responsibility would be invoked provided there is lack of procedure and serious procedural shortcomings and not for every violation of procedural shortcomings.[26] The standards of procedural fairness expected from executive and legislative action are lesser compared to denial of justice.[27] The standard of due process represents the standard of due diligence. Transparency in the application of laws, regulations, and policy is also an element of fair and equitable treatment, and the standard is satisfied if the host state applies them consistently and diligently.[28]

Legitimate expectations has emerged as the defining element of fair and equitable treatment. The investor has an expectation that the legal environment of the host state existing at the time of investment or its impressions based upon the representations by the host state would not be changed. If the change to that framework has been done by the host state with due diligence, it may not result into frustration of legitimate expectations of the foreign investor and thus not breach the fair and equitable treatment standard. In *Blusum v. Italy*, there was a change in a regulation which required a separate and additional registration of foreign investor in that sector. The investor claimed that the losses suffered by the foreign investor were due to the change in laws regarding registration and there was a legitimate expectation that these laws would not be changed. The Tribunal found that the government had acted with due diligence in completing the difficult task of compiling a full list in rapidly changing circumstances. Hence the host state was

[24] Rudolph Dolzer/Christoph Schreuer, *Principles of International Investment Law* (Oxford: OUP 2nd ed. 2012), 130.

[25] ICSID, *Genin v. Estonia*, ICSID Case No. ARB/99/2, Award of 25 June 2001, para. 367; also see ICSID, *Waste Management v. Mexico* (n. 6), paras 98, 40.

[26] Dolzer/Schreuer, *Investment Law* 2012 (n. 24), 140–145.

[27] UNCITRAL, *International Thunderbird Gaming Corporation v. United Mexico States*, Award of 26 January 2006, paras 197–201.

[28] ICSID, *MTD Equity Sdn Bhd and MTD Chile SA v. Republic of Chile*, ICSID Case No. ARB/01/7, Award of 25 May 2004, paras 163–166.

not responsible for violating the legitimate expectations of the foreign investor.[29] Likewise, in *Plama v. Bulgaria*, the tribunal observed that the investor failed to establish lack of due diligence in the treatment of the investor when the environmental laws were amended.[30]

Fair and equitable treatment also embodies international minimum standard[31] and denial of justice.[32] As discussed above, both include due diligence as an element for their breach.

A couple of tribunals have made an observation in passing that the host state has to conduct due diligence of impact of its actions on foreign investors.[33] It is difficult to sustain a positive obligation on the part of host state to conduct due diligence before undertaking regulations. However, if not just the conduct of due diligence but acting with due diligence would be a sufficient defence for a host state to defend its measure, although it is not under a legal obligation to conduct due diligence before adopting regulations.

3. Due Diligence Obligations of Foreign Investors

Due diligence not only works as an obligation of host states, but also on foreign investors. In *Plama v. Bulgaria*, the tribunal looked at the due diligence obligation of the host state as well as the foreign investor. It found that the host state was not in violation of its due diligence obligations while amending environmental laws.[34] However, it did find the investor not to have conducted due diligence regarding the tax legislation before taking the decision to invest.[35]

A foreign investor has to conduct due diligence prior to investment and act with due diligence during the life of the investment. This is an outcome of doctrine of illegality, whereby a foreign investor has to enter and conduct its operations as per the domestic laws of the host state.[36] The foreign investor assumes the risk for the actions it undertakes and has to make itself aware of the risks. If the change of laws

[29] ICSID, *Blusun S.A., Jean-Pierre Lecorcier and Michael Stein v. Italian Republic*, ICSID Case No. ARB/14/3, Final Award of 27 December 2016, para. 350.

[30] ICSID, *Plama Consortium v. Bulgaria* (n. 17), para. 222.

[31] UNCITRAL, *Ronald S. Lauder* (n. 9), para. 292.

[32] ICSID, *Mondev v. USA* (n. 6), paras 139–156; ICSID, *Wena Hotels v. Egypt*, ICSID Case No. ARB/98/4, Award of 8 December 2000, para. 84; ICSID, *Techmed v. Mexico*, ICSID Case No. ARB (AF)/00/2, Award of 29 May 2003, para. 177; ICSID, *Lowen v. US*, ICSID Case No. ARB(AF)/98/3, Award of 20 June 2003, paras 53, 121, 132; UNCITRAL, *White Industries Australia Limited v. The Republic of India*, Final Award of 30 November 2011, 41.

[33] ICSID, *Waguih v. The Arab Republic of Egypt* (n. 16), para. 447; ICSID, *Reinhard Unglaube v. Republic of Costa Rica*, ICSID Case No. ARB/09/20, Award of 16 May 2012, para. 247.

[34] ICSID, *Plama Consortium v. Bulgaria* (n. 17), para. 222.

[35] Ibid., para. 268.

[36] Aniruddha Rajput, *Protection of Foreign Investment in India and Investment Treaty Arbitration* (Alphen aan den Rijn: Wolters Kluwer 2018), 35–58.

in the home state could not be prospected through due diligence, then the investor could not be said to have assumed the risk.[37]

A foreign investor shall be aware of the risks involved in investing in the industry in a state and the overall political and economic situation in that state.[38] It is a prudent practice to conduct due diligence before investing and this is neither onerous nor unreasonable.[39] These assessments relate to the factual situation in the host state. A factual diligence exposes the benefits and drawbacks of the investment and appraises the investor of potential risks. If the investor is knowingly investing in a war-torn state, the investor cannot then claim that it was unaware of the risks involved. An investor has to make itself aware of political risks or corruption in a sector. The observations of the Tribunal in *Mamidoil Jetoil v. Albania* are self-explanatory:

> The Tribunal is conscious of the fact, which Respondent does not contest, that smuggling, fuel adulteration and tax evasion were serious problems in Albania as well as in the region at the time when Claimant made its investment. Claimant acknowledges that it was aware of this situation. It was part of the general business environment and investment conditions. Claimant decided to make its investment under these conditions of insecurity. Smuggling, fuel adulteration and tax evasion existed prior to the investment, and therefore were not specific to Claimant's investment. It is therefore not correct to allege that the problem distorted the conditions of the investment after it has been made.[40]

Investor would be responsible if due diligence of the impact of the investment activity on the environment is not conducted prior to the investment.[41]

While entering a jurisdiction, the foreign investor would have to do due diligence of the legal framework, which may be also called a 'legal due diligence'. Legal due diligence would be an assessment of the legal framework that existed at the time of investment and the possible changes in the framework that may take place during the life of the investment. The investor shall do due diligence of tax legislations in the host state,[42] as well as of all the relevant laws and procedures in the host state,[43] including all the permits and other permissions required to invest and conduct a business in a state.[44] In a case where the foreign investor invested despite

[37] UNCITRAL, *Saluka Investments B.V. v. the Czech Republic* (n. 16), para. 332.

[38] ICSID, *Churchill Mining PLC and Planet Mining Pty Ltd v. Republic of Indonesia*, ICSID Case No. ARB/12/14 and 12/40, Award of 6 December 2016, para. 517.

[39] ICSID, *Alasdair Ross Anderson et al. v. Republic of Costa Rica*, ICSID Case No. ARB(AF)/07/3, Award of 19 May 2010, para. 58.

[40] ICSID, *Mamidoil Jetoil Greek Petroleum v. Republic of Albania* (n. 16), para 823.

[41] ICSID, *Burlington Resources Inc. v. Republic of Ecuador*, ICSID Case No. ARB/08/5, Decision of 2 June 2010, para. 243.

[42] ICSID, *Plama Consortium v. Bulgaria* (n. 17), para. 268.

[43] ICSID, *Reinhard Unglaube v. Costa Rica* (n. 33), para. 258.

[44] ICSID, *Blusun v. Italian Republic* (n. 29), para. 392; ICSID, *Mamidoil Jetoil Greek Petroleum v. Republic of Albania* (n. 16), para. 690.

a constitutional challenge relating to the sector was pending in courts, the risk of the outcome of the decision was assumed by the investor and the state was not responsible since it had taken all steps in due diligence to conduct the judicial proceedings.[45] An element of due diligence is that the investor shall obtain legal advice about the domestic legal framework in the host state. Several areas are covered by domestic legal framework, such as: entry, structuring the investments, gaining permits and licenses, tax structures, environment legislations, and other regulatory set-ups. It is not a defence that the investor did not consider that they would need a lawyer's advice.[46]

This obligation of due diligence is as understood in private law as in corporate or commercial laws.[47] Failure to conduct due diligence would deprive the investor of protection under a bilateral investment treaty. The sufficiency of due diligence has to be seen in light of the due diligence of the consortium and its partners, wherever they are present.[48]

As a part of the doctrine of illegality, due diligence is a rule of international law, whereby an investor has a continuous duty to act in accordance with domestic law and international law. In the *Churchill Mining* case, the investor submitted thirty-four forged documents, which was treated as manifest failure of due diligence.[49] The Tribunal found that if the investor failed to carry out the investments in due diligence then the protection under the investment treaty would not be available.[50] The extent of due diligence required depends on the nature of the investment and the acts of the foreign investor. In cases of fraud and breach of good faith the entire claim would be rejected. Lack of due diligence compounds the seriousness of fraud.[51] The claims arising out of absence of due diligence would be inadmissible.[52] Investments made through bribery or in illegal transactions would not be protected.[53] Shareholders would have to take due care before investing in such a company, otherwise they would not get protection under an investment treaty.[54]

Due diligence obligation of foreign investors arises from various sources. The preambles of investment treaties show that the objective of investment treaties is investment protection as well as development of the host state. Investment treaties cannot be interpreted as exclusively imposing obligations on host states but also a corresponding responsibility on the foreign investor to contribute towards economic development of the host state. If the foreign investor indulges in actions

45 ICSID, *Blusun v. Italian Republic* (n. 29), para. 329 (e).
46 ICSID, *Mamidoil Jetoil Greek Petroleum v. Republic of Albania* (n. 16), para. 671.
47 ICSID, *Parkerings-Compagniet v. Lithuania* (n. 12), para. 333.
48 UNCITRAL, *National Grid v. Argentina*, Award of 3 November 2008, para. 103.
49 ICSID, *Churchill Mining v. Republic of Indonesia* (n. 38), para. 527.
50 Ibid., para. 589.
51 Ibid., paras 516–527.
52 Ibid., para. 528.
53 ICSID, *World Duty Free Company Limited v. Republic of Kenya*, ICSID Case No. ARB/00/7, Award of 4 October 2006, para. 173.
54 ICSID, *Alasdair Ross v. Republic of Costa Rica* (n. 39), paras 17–19, 53–58.

that are detrimental to the environment, health, labour standards, or overall developmental objectives of the host state, the protection under the investment treaty would not be available and at the same time there would be responsibility to compensate for the actions of the foreign investor.[55] A host state may enforce those breaches of due diligence of investors through counterclaims. Article 46 of the International Centre for Settlement of Investment Disputes (ICSID) Convention allows counterclaims: 'arising directly out of the subject-matter of the dispute provided that they are within the scope of the consent of the parties and are otherwise within the jurisdiction of the Centre'.[56] Even for arbitrations outside the ICSID, there is no restriction in investment treaties whereby host states do not have a right under an investment treaty.[57] With the overall need to protect and preserve public interest, especially when foreign investors are functioning in utility sectors, due diligence inevitably has a crucial role to play.[58]

Legitimate expectation, as a part of fair and equitable treatment, functions as an obligation on host state as well as on foreign investor. The scope of legitimate expectations of an investor is limited if the investor takes the risk of entering a particular jurisdiction knowing fully the circumstances in the economy and the nature of the legal framework.[59] Due diligence is meant to involve an assessment of economic, social, political, and security risks in the host state. An investment made despite this knowledge would not be made in due diligence and factually the investor would not be able to prove breach of the standards such as fair and equitable treatment and full protection and security.[60]

4. Businesses and Human Rights

The United Nations Guiding Principles on Businesses and Human Rights (the Ruggie Principles) contemplate the need of human rights due diligence to be conducted by business enterprises. All '[b]usiness enterprises should respect human rights'—which 'means that they should avoid infringing on the human rights of others and should address adverse human rights impacts with which they are

[55] ICSID, *Fraport AG Frankfurt Airport Services Worldwide v. The Republic of Philippines*, ICSID Case No. ARB/03/25, Award of 16 August 2007, para. 402.

[56] International Centre for Settlement of Investment Disputes Convention, 18 March 1965, 575 UNTS 159, art. 46.

[57] ICSID, *Urbaser S.A. and Consorcio de Aguas Bilbao Bizkaia, Bilbao Biskaia Ur Partzuergoa v. The Argentine Republic*, ICSID Case No. ARB/07/26, Award of 8 December, para. 1183.

[58] Attila Tanzi, 'On Balancing Foreign Investment Interests with Public Interests in Recent Arbitration Case Law in the Public Utilities Sector', *The Law and Practice of International Courts and Tribunals* 11 (2012), 47–76.

[59] ICSID, *Biwater Gauff v. Tanzania* (n. 16), para. 601; followed in ICSID, *Mamidoil Jetoil Greek Petroleum v. Republic of Albania* (n. 16), para. 631.

[60] This does not foreclose the possibility of violation of other treatment standards such as indirect expropriation.

involved'.[61] 'In order to identify, prevent, mitigate and account for (...) human rights impacts, business enterprises should carry out human rights due diligence.'[62] An investor would have to assess actual and potential human rights impacts, integrate and act upon those findings, track responses, and communicate how those impacts on human rights are addressed.[63] The extent of due diligence required would depend upon the size of the business enterprise, the risk of impact, and the nature and context of its operations.[64] The human rights due diligence is to be an ongoing endeavour since human rights risks change over time.[65] The Ruggie principles elaborate on the detailed procedures and process that need to be adopted by businesses to ensure compliance with human rights due diligence requirements.[66] They even contain the need and manner of communication of the due diligence and the impact of their activities on human rights.[67] This responsibility is prominent when an investor is functioning in a public utility sector, especially in light of the impact on public interest generally and human rights in particular.[68]

Investment tribunals have found it necessary for investors to conduct due diligence[69] before and during the investment. The general duty of due diligence would inevitably encompass human rights due diligence wherever appropriate and necessary. The Ruggie Principles, despite being non-binding, play a prominent role in substantiating the obligation of foreign investors to conduct due diligence before investing and during the life of the investment. Absence of due diligence could make investors claims inadmissible or expose to counterclaims. It is only natural that an investor shall conduct a human rights due diligence where the activities of the investor could potentially affect human rights. In case of failure to adhere to them, the investor will have to compensate and redress the infringements of human rights caused by its activities. In the past, investment tribunals have granted counterclaims on damage to environment and infrastructure.[70] Human rights violations can be a basis for counterclaims.[71] Thus, accordingly, failure of due diligence under the Ruggie Principles can be a basis for counterclaims by a state against a foreign investor. Additionally, states can make legislations that impose the Ruggie Principles or additional human rights obligations on foreign investors. Investors

[61] United Nations, Human Rights Council, United Nations Guiding Principles on Business and Human Rights, A/HRC/17/4, 16 June 2011, art. 11.

[62] Ibid., art. 17.

[63] Ibid., art. 17.

[64] Ibid., art. 17(b).

[65] Ibid., art. 17(c).

[66] Ibid., arts 18–20.

[67] Ibid., art. 21.

[68] Tanzi, 'Balancing Foreign Investment Interests with Public Interests' 2012 (n. 58), at 65–73.

[69] See above section 2.1.

[70] ICSID, *Burlington v. Republic of Ecuador* (n. 41), para. 175.

[71] ICSID, *Urbaser S.A. and Consorcio de Aguas Bilbao Bizkaia, Bilbao Biskaia Ur Partzuergoa v. The Argentine Republic*, ICSID Case No. ARB/07/26, Award of 8 December, paras 1182–1221 (the tribunal found that it had jurisdiction to entertain the counterclaim based on violation of human right, but ultimately declined jurisdiction).

would have to comply with them, unless those regulations are proved to be an arbitrary exercise of power aimed at defeating the rights of foreign investors. An investment tribunal will take into consideration all binding human rights obligations in the process of treaty interpretation.[72]

The discussion on business and human rights and the central role of due diligence in them is relevant because when foreign investors are involved there are bound to be some issues of human rights involved. More than that, it is the role that due diligence plays. The responsibility of due diligence of a host state and that of a foreign investor shows two kinds of due diligence that are involved in investment arbitration. First, an 'obligation of conduct' and second, 'obligation to conduct'. Due diligence as 'obligation of conduct' is as it developed in the international law on the treatment of aliens and its further developments in international investment law. Here the obligation is discharged if the behaviour meets certain standards. In international investment law this obligation of conduct is on the host state as well as the foreign investor. An 'obligation to conduct' due diligence is in the form of the conducting a due diligence before investment and during the life of an investment—the act of conducting a due diligence, as understood in private or corporate law. In other words, it is a 'standard' of international law in the case of 'obligation of conduct' and 'business process' in the case of 'obligation to conduct'. This obligation is essentially on foreign investors and not on the host states. Some commentators have criticised the Ruggie Principles for not making this distinction sufficiently clear and alleged that this may result in confusion for the investors.[73] In response to this criticism, on the limited point of human rights due diligence, John Gerard Ruggie and John Sherman argued that the focus of the United Nations Guiding Principles on Business and Human Rights is limited to the 'obligation to conduct'.[74] They do not specify whether they include 'obligation of conduct' or not. Although, for the author of the United Nations Guiding Principles on Business and Human Rights, this may be the case. The jurisprudence in investment arbitration has developed in a manner that it has introduced obligation of both kinds on foreign investors. This development in the field of international investment law, which can serve as a guide in other fields, as long as there are legal grounds to connect both aspects of due diligence. As was explained in the last two sections, there are sufficient grounds to do so in international investment law.

[72] ICSID, *Tulip Real Estate and Development Netherlands B.V. v. Republic of Turkey*, ICSID Case No. ARB/11/28, Decision on Annulment of 30 December 2015, para. 92.

[73] Jonathan Bonnitcha/Robert McCorquodale, 'The Concept of "Due Diligence" in the United Nations Guiding Principles on Business and Human Rights', *European Journal of International Law* 28 (2017), 899–919, at 908–911.

[74] John Gerard Ruggie/John Sherman, 'The Concept of "Due Diligence" in the United Nations Guiding Principles on Business and Human Rights: A Reply to Jonathan Bonnitcha and Robert McCorquodale', *European Journal of International Law* 28 (2017), 921–928, at 923–925.

5. Synthesis of the Jurisprudence on Due Diligence

The understanding of due diligence under private law or corporate law and public international law is different. In private law or corporate law, it is an assessment of the factual and legal situations and risks in the host state. In public international law, due diligence is a standard of behaviour expected from a party, failure to comply with which would result into international responsibility or absence of protection under international law. In private law, due diligence is meant to protect oneself. When investment tribunals refer to due diligence obligations of investors they are referring to the responsibility of investors to protect themselves—something in the nature of *caveat emptor* (buyer beware).[75] If the investor fails to conduct due diligence then the investor is at fault. In public international law and investment arbitration in particular, due diligence aims to protect others, i.e., the state is to act with due diligence to protect public interest. Likewise, in its operation in investment law, the private investor has to act diligently and not to act in a manner that causes harm to public interest. The duty of due diligence in private law is owed to oneself, but in public law towards public interest. Thus, even if the investor has to do due diligence prior to investment, it is protecting its own rights and interest, but once it comes into the domain of public international law, through the application of an investment treaty to that relationship due diligence obligations take up a public law character, where the duty is owed to the public at large.

An imbalance emerges to an extent that the host state is required only to comply with the public international law standard of due diligence, whereas the investor shall comply with the public as well as private international law standard. A tribunal gave reason for this imbalance. A foreign investor has several resources at its disposal. Moreover, when an investor participates in a bidding process for a contract of a technical nature, it is expected that the foreign investor would have the necessary expertise and would conduct due diligence in relation to the activities and consequences of participating in that field.[76]

Due diligence is understood as a subjective norm in investment law. In investment law, the due diligence of host states under customary international law and fair and equitable treatment and full protection and security, the standard is subjective. Imperfections in the administrative and other systems of a host state have been taken into account but have not been declared to be a violation of a stable and a transparent framework when it comes to the issuance of licenses and permits.[77] The tribunal in *Mamidoil Jetoil v. Albania* declared that a state has to 'exercise an objective minimum standard of due diligence that is linked to the circumstances

[75] UNCITRAL, *Guaracachi America, Inc. and Rurelec PLC v. The Plurinational State of Bolivia*, PCA Case No. 2011-17, Award of 31 January 2014, para. 465.

[76] ICSID, *Urbaser v. The Argentine Republic* (n. 71), para. 263.

[77] ICSID, *Mamidoil Jetoil Greek Petroleum v. Republic of Albania* (n. 16), para. 674.

within the State in question'.[78] The tribunal refers to the minimum standard of due diligence to be objective but then puts it into the overall context of the situation in the state and introduces a subject element. It appears that they eventually leant in favour of the subjective standard as the tribunal approved of the argument that tribunals would consider the state's level of development and stability as a relevant circumstance in determining whether there has been due diligence; and an investor cannot expect physical security in an area with endemic civil strike and poor governance.[79] The following observations are pertinent:

> General insecurity was also a consequence of weak government structures and institutions at the time of the investment. Albania was confronted with the general duty to confirm itself as a State and build efficient institutions to combat criminality in general and smuggling, fuel adulteration and tax evasion in particular. This is all the more so since the incriminated activities particularly prejudiced Respondent itself. In fact, the Tribunal has some difficulty in understanding in what way tax evasion by third parties injured Claimant's investment at all. While Claimant might have been entitled to expect that the general conditions of insecurity would improve over time, it was not entitled to expect that Respondent would protect its investment against the general insecurity that was inherent to the investment climate as opposed to specific instances of harassment.[80]

A similar position has been taken by another tribunal, where it was reiterated that the objective minimum standard was to be applied in light of the circumstances and resources of the host state.[81]

In investment law due diligence functions as a primary norm in all capacities. The addressees of due diligence would violate international law for their failure to comply with the due diligence obligation.

6. Conclusion

Due diligence in investment law has developed through jurisprudence that has coalesced around the notion of due diligence under customary law and its application as a prudent business practice in private law. The frequent use of due diligence with a direct or indirect link to investment protection treaties has contributed to the notion and importance of due diligence. In investment law, due diligence does not erode substantive standards but rather informs the existing standards

[78] Ibid., para. 364.
[79] Ibid., para. 364.
[80] Ibid., para 824.
[81] ICSID, *Pantechniki SA Contractors & Engineers (Greece) v. The Republic of Albania*, ICSID Case No. ARB/07/21, Award of 30 July 2009, paras 76–81.

as contained in customary law (international minimum standard and denial of justice) and treaty law (full protection and security and fair and equitable treatment). It may be too early to claim that it has achieved the status of some kind of an all-pervasive constitutional norm or become representative of 'multilateral interests', but it certainly is a new contribution to the field thus in a sense of an addition to the rule-based system in international relations. Due diligence in its current state is evidently influenced by the factual peculiarities and legal nuances of international investment law. Yet, its extrapolation in other areas of investment law is possible since these developments have contributed towards clarification of the notion and contents. They enrich the threshold for the understanding of the notion. The notion may then undergo changes as it adapts itself to the field of operation or its potential use in treaties.

The role of due diligence will rise henceforth. It creates parity in the rights and obligations of states and foreign investors. Its role would further increase in the jurisprudence and treaty practice since states are renegotiating treaties to increase the sphere of regulatory autonomy.

Due diligence, as it stands in international investment law today, has become a tool to protect rights of foreign investors as aliens and at the same time represents the responsibility of foreign investors to make responsible investments. The first aspect of due diligence as a tool for protection of rights was inherited from general international law, but the second aspect of responsibility of investors to make responsible investments is a contribution of international investment law. Due diligence operates in investment law in a variety of forms and as an obligation on states as well as foreign investors. Due diligence addresses one of the asymmetries in the system whereby the impression is that only the states owes responsibilities towards foreign investors under investment treaties. Due diligence is a tool that addresses this asymmetry to the extent that it adds responsibility on foreign investors as well. To that extent due diligence does perform a balancing function.

17

Due Diligence Debates in International Anti-corruption and Money Laundering Law

From Content to the Construction of Risk

Radha Ivory[*]

1. Introduction

In debates about due diligence in international law, questions about content can conceal questions about construction and consequence. Notions of due diligence connote standards of care—an absence of negligence.[1] Beyond that basic conceptualisation, the sources, subjects, and strictness of international due diligence norms are contested. Must states be diligent under the primary or secondary rules of public international law? Why are states subject to international duties to be careful and who else is covered by those obligations? How to calibrate the standard(s) of care in either case? These questions are important for clarifying the scope of obligations to avoid harm in the international lex lata. However, they can also distract from a fourth set of issues about attempts to coordinate state and non-state sectors to prevent potential dangers. Social scientists and theorists have problematised conceptions of risk and techniques of risk management in western industrialised societies. Drawing on that work, scholars of criminal law have identified regulatory practices that target 'risky' populations. As this literature shows, new techniques for risk management appear pragmatic and proportionate. However, they may also employ preventative and actuarial techniques of governance that depart, in some respects, from liberal notions about the role of the state and justifications for punishment. The matters at stake therefore also include: do international due diligence obligations fit a 'new' model of risk governance and, if so, to what effect?

[*] My thanks to the editors and other contributors for their insightful comments on an earlier draft of this chapter. The research was conducted in April 2018 and finalised in November 2018.

[1] See further Anne Peters/Heike Krieger/Leonhard Kreuzer, 'Due Diligence in the International Legal Order: Dissecting the Leitmotif of Current Accountability Debates', chapter 1 of this book, section 1.

Radha Ivory, *Due Diligence Debates in International Anti-corruption and Money Laundering Law* In: *Due Diligence in the International Legal Order.* Edited by: Heike Krieger, Anne Peters, and Leonhard Kreuzer, Oxford University Press (2020).
 DOI: 10.1093/oso/9780198869900.003.0017.

This chapter argues that international anti-corruption and money laundering laws are an important source of information about each of these diligence debates in public international law. First, the anti-corruption treaties and related money laundering standards oblige countries to reduce the likelihood that economic crimes will be perpetrated or facilitated by actors within their control. In this way, the anti-corruption treaties lend strength to the view that there is a general duty to prevent transboundary harms in public international law, which is reflected in particular primary due diligence obligations. Second, international anti-corruption and money laundering standards require due diligence of both state and non-state actors, the latter being charged with the supervision of other private parties. Therefore, the anti-corruption treaties and related anti-money laundering instruments create a cascading system of supervisory duties, running from state parties to legal entities and from legal entities to associated natural and legal persons. Third, both horizontal (state-to-state) and vertical (state-to-business) obligations are often discretionary and gauged by reference to notions of reasonableness and risk in particular situations.[2] Fourth, adopting a risk lens, a cascading system of due diligence rules and associated discretions may be viewed positively as a 'new' approach to governance and more sceptically as a 'new penal' or 'preventive' approach to justice. Raising these possibilities, the chapter contributes to a discussion about the content of international notions of due diligence. However, it also places that debate in a wider frame about concerns with the rightfulness and rationality of international efforts to regulate transnational business and financial flows.

2. Due Diligence Debates in Public International Law

Notions of due diligence are contested in international law and three familiar controversies are content-related. A first concerns the sources of rules that determine liability based on a state's failure to be careful. Must states be diligent under secondary rules of public international law, which specify when a country will be responsible for the conduct of non-state actors? Or do states have duties to be diligent under the primary rules of international law, which create obligations to undertake or refrain from particular behaviours? The debate is not quite over,[3] despite the International Law Commission's decision to omit a fault requirement from its Draft Articles on the Responsibility of States for Wrongful Acts (2001).[4]

[2] On transversal obligations as a feature of transnational criminal law, see generally Neil Boister, *An Introduction to Transnational Criminal Law* (Oxford: OUP 2nd ed. 2018), 18.

[3] See, e.g., Maja Seršić, 'Due Diligence—Fault-Based Responsibility or Autonomous Standard?', in Rüdiger Wolfrum/Maja Seršić/Trpimir Šošić (eds), *Contemporary Developments in International Law: Essays in Honour of Budislav Vukas* (Leiden: Brill 2016), 151–170.

[4] United Nations, International Law Commission (ILC), Report of the International Law Commission on the work of its fifty-third session, A/56/10, 23 April–1 June and 2 July–10 August 2001, YBILC 2001, vol. II (part II), 26–143 (text of Draft Articles on State Responsibility with Commentaries thereto), arts 2, 12, 34–36 (art. 2, paras 3, 10); see also ILC, Draft Articles on Prevention

The second due diligence debate is connected with a larger discussion about the subjects of public international law and the responsibility of states for the acts and omissions of non-state actors.[5] To what extent do due diligence norms circumvent the narrowness of rules that attribute states—as legal persons—with the behaviour of non-state actors? States are still only responsible for the conduct of their organs and agents, but may also be internationally liable if they did not take sufficient steps to control the behaviour of non-state actors.[6] Third, if states have duties to be diligent, what must they do to discharge that obligation? Due diligence norms have been described as obligations to take reasonable measures ('due or merited care').[7] They are not duties to attain or prevent an outcome 'in each and every case'.[8]

By contrast, the fourth emerging controversy is about the regulation of risk in public international law. Townley has latterly argued that due diligence obligations either create a cause of action for failures to manage risks or oblige states to take certain risk management measures.[9] But what are risks, other than 'potential dangers'?[10] And how desirable are methods of risk management, such as have been incorporated into international law? Outside doctrinal legal studies, scholars divide over whether (or to what extent) risks can be objectively ascertained.[11] In techno-scientific conceptions, risks are capable of identification through a calculation of probabilities using models or information about past events.[12] By contrast, social scientists and theorists problematise the construction of risk, particularly in advanced industrial societies.[13] Douglas matched concepts of risk with concepts of

of Transboundary Harm from Hazardous Activities, with Commentaries 2001, ILC, Report on the work of its fifty-third session, A/56/10, 23 April–1 June and 2 July–10 August 2001, YBILC 2001, vol. II (part II), 144–170.

[5] Jonathan Bonnitcha/Robert McCorquodale, 'The Concept of "Due Diligence" in the UN Guiding Principles on Business and Human Rights', *European Journal of International Law* 28 (2017), 899–919, 903; see generally Arno Hessbrügge, 'The Historical Evolution of the Doctrines of Attribution and Due Diligence in International Law', *NYU Journal of International Law and Politics* 36 (2004), 265–306; see also ITLOS Seabed Disputes Chamber, *Responsibilities and Obligations of States Sponsoring Persons and Entities with Respect to Activities in the Area*, Advisory Opinion of 1 February 2011, ITLOS Reports 2011, 10, para. 112.

[6] ILC, Commentaries on the Draft Articles on State Responsibility 2001 (n. 4), 29 (chapter II, para. 4); Brigitte Stern, 'The Elements of an Internationally Wrongful Act', in James Crawford/Alain Pellet/Simon Olleson (eds), *The Law of International Responsibility* (Oxford: OUP 2010), 193–218, at 208–209.

[7] International Law Association (ILA), Study Group on Due Diligence in International Law, Second Report, July 2016, 7–8 quoting Robert Barnidge, 'The Due Diligence Principle under International Law', *International Community Law Review* 8 (2006), 81–121, 118 and, in turn, Carsten Corino, 'Environmental Due Diligence', *European Environmental Law Review* 9 (2000) 120–124, at 120.

[8] ITLOS, *Responsibilities and Obligations in the Area Opinion* (n. 5), para. 110.

[9] Stephen Townley, 'The Rise of Risk in International Law', *Chicago Journal of International Law* 18 (2018), 594–646, at 618–626.

[10] Jakob Arnoldi, *Risk* (Cambridge: Polity 2009), 1.

[11] Deborah Lupton, 'Introduction: Risk and Sociocultural Theory', in Deborah Lupton (ed.), *Risk and Sociocultural Theory: New Directions and Perspectives* (Cambridge: CUP 1999), 1.

[12] Gabe Mythen, 'Sociology and the Art of Risk', *Sociology Compass* 2 (2008), 299–316, at 302; Rolf Lidskog/Goeran Sundqvist, 'Sociology of Risk', in Sabine Roeser et al. (eds), *Handbook of Risk Theory* (Dordrecht: Springer 2012), 1002–1024, at 1005.

[13] Lidskog/Sundqvist, 'Sociology of Risk' 2012 (n. 12), 1008–1009.

impurity and disorder, as interpreted through the normative systems of particular cultures.[14] Beck saw risks as arising from the peculiar capacities of modern technology to generate incalculable, cross-borders harms, as well as in the diminished ability of people to trust that 'the institutions of late modernity (government, industry, and science)'[15] will not themselves be the source of future dangers.[16] Still others, informed by Foucault,[17] characterise risk as 'a way (. . .) of ordering reality' and a component of governmental power.[18] From the eighteenth century, western states have construed their tasks as achieving the welfare and management of populations without immediate recourse to coercion.[19] Hence, they have sought to motivate individuals to exercise self-control, including by (scientifically or statistically) identifying categories of person who are 'at risk' of departing from societal norms and subjecting them to greater measures of restraint or supervision.[20] Such grand theories have the potential to extend debates about risk and due diligence in international law, as demonstrated with a review of norms on anti-money laundering and corruption.[21]

3. Due Diligence Debates in International Anti-corruption and Money Laundering Law

Each of these four due diligence debates can be enriched by reference to international 'hard' and 'soft' rules on corruption and money laundering.[22] Focusing on the anti-corruption treaties of the UN and the Organisation for Economic

[14] See, e.g., Mary Douglas, *Risk and Blame: Essays in Culture* (London: Routledge 1992), 26; see further Arnoldi, *Risk* 2009 (n. 10), 38–40; Lupton, 'Introduction' 1999 (n. 11), 3.

[15] Lupton, 'Introduction' 1999 (n. 11), 4.

[16] Arnoldi, *Risk* 2009 (n. 10), 46–53, 62–63; see, e.g., Ulrich Beck, *Risk Society: Towards a New Modernity* (London: Sage 1992), 21; Ulrich Beck, *World Risk Society* (Cambridge: Polity 1999), 3–6; see also Anthony Giddens, *Modernity and Self-Identity: Self and Society in the Late Modern Age* (Cambridge: Polity 1991), 20–21, 30–31.

[17] Michel Foucault, 'Governmentality', in Graham Burchell/Colin Gordon/Peter Miller (eds), *The Foucault Effect: Studies in Governmentality* (Chicago: University of Chicago Press 1991), 87–104, at 99–104.

[18] Mitchell Dean, *Governmentality: Power and Rule in Modern Society* (London: Sage Publications 1st ed. 1999), 177–178.

[19] Arnoldi, *Risk* 2009 (n. 10), 53–55; Lidskog/Sundqvist, 'Sociology of Risk' 2012 (n. 12), 1023; Lupton, 'Introduction' 1999 (n. 11), 4–5.

[20] Nikolas Rose, *Powers of Freedom: Reframing Political Thought* (Cambridge: CUP 1999), 237, 259–261; cf. Nikolas Rose/Joelle Abi-Rached, *Neuro: The New Brain Sciences and the Management of the Mind* (Princeton: Princeton University Press 2013), 14, 197.

[21] See also Fleur Johns/Wouter Werner, 'The Risks of International Law', *Leiden Journal of International Law* 21 (2008), 783–786.

[22] See, generally, Julio Bacio Terracino, *The International Legal Framework against Corruption: States' Obligations to Prevent and Repress Corruption* (Cambridge: Intersentia 2012), 47–79; Radha Ivory, *Corruption, Asset Recovery, and the Prevention of Property in Public International Law: The Human Rights of Bad Guys* (Cambridge: CUP 2014), 15–22; Cecily Rose, *International Anti-Corruption Norms: Their Creation and Influence on Domestic Legal Systems* (Oxford: OUP 2015), 13–58.

Co-operation and Development (OECD),[23] this part explains how international anti-corruption controls contribute to controversies about due diligence in public international law. In so doing, it also considers the anti-money laundering and counter-terrorist financial standards of the Financial Action Task Force (FATF).[24]

3.1 State-to-State Duties to Suppress Transboundary Economic Harms

First, the anti-corruption treaties lend strength to the ICJ's view that there is a general duty to prevent transboundary harms which is reflected in particular primary due diligence obligations. Most anti-corruption treaties do apply to conduct that is local in scope.[25] However, the preambles to the UN and OECD treaties also highlight the cross-border ramifications of corruption and its dangers to the international collective.[26] For example, the Convention on the Bribery of Foreign Public Officials in International Business Transactions (OECD Convention) 'considers that all countries share a responsibility to combat bribery in international business transactions'.[27] Developed in part to correct disadvantages to US businesses under the Foreign Corrupt Practices Act 1977,[28] the convention also depicts bribery as a 'distort[ion of] international competitive conditions'.[29] The United Nations Convention against Transnational Organised Crime similarly attempts to commit its parties to equivalent measures against racketeers who operate, in part, through corruption. Its parties are '[d]etermined to deny safe havens to those who engage in transnational organized crime by prosecuting their crimes wherever they occur and by cooperating at the international level'.[30] The United Nations

[23] See, e.g., Convention on Combating Bribery of Foreign Public Officials in International Business Transactions, 17 December 1997, DAFFE/IME/BR(97)20, 2802 UNTS 225 (OECD Convention); United Nations Convention against Transnational Organized Crime, 15 November 2000, 2225 UNTS 209; United Nations Conventions against Corruption, 31 October 2003, 2349 UNTS 41 (UNCAC).

[24] FATF, International Standards on Combating Money Laundering and the Financing of Terrorism & Proliferation: The FATF Recommendations, adopted 16 February 2012, updated October 2018, available at: http://www.fatf-gafi.org (accessed 4 February 2019); see further Ivory, *Human Rights of Bad Guys* 2014 (n. 22), 16 (table 2.1).

[25] See generally Boister, *Introduction to TCL* (n. 2), 146–147.

[26] Ivory, *Human Rights of Bad Guys* 2014 (n. 22), 4, 15–17.

[27] OECD Convention 1997, (n. 23), preamble.

[28] 15 US Code §§ 78dd-1; see, e.g., Kenneth Abbott/Duncan Snidal, 'Values and Interests: International Legalization in the Fight against Corruption', *The Journal of Legal Studies* 31 (2002), 141–178, at 154.

[29] OECD Convention, 1997 (n. 23), preamble.

[30] United Nations, Resolution adopted by the General Assembly, United Nations Convention against Transnational Organized Crime, A/RES/55/25, 8 January 2001, preamble; on the UNCAC, see also the Swiss Confederation and Stolen Asset Recovery Initiative, 'No Safe Havens: A Global Forum on Stolen Asset Recovery and Development: A Call to Collective Action', 8-9 June 2010, available at: https://documents.worldbank.org/en/publication/documents-reports/documentdetail/545101468251699476/no-safe-havens-a-global-forum-on-stolen-asset-recovery-and-development-a-call-for-collective-action (accessed 4 February 2019).

Convention against Corruption (UNCAC) still more clearly asserts that 'corruption is no longer a local matter but a transnational phenomenon that affects all societies and economies, making international cooperation to prevent and control it essential'.[31] Even references to apparently internal threats (e.g., 'to the stability and security of societies', 'good governance and economic development')[32] have international valence when read in light of development literatures. By creating inefficiencies and weakening institutional capacity, corruption is said to slow economic growth,[33] contribute to state fragility,[34] and enable violent extremism,[35] amongst other things.

Further, several of the treaties foresee non-criminal measures as a means to reduce opportunities and appetites for corruption in the public, private, and 'third' sectors. Entitled 'prevention', Chapter II UNCAC begins with requirements that states develop, implement, and periodically evaluate anti-corruption policies and practices.[36] They are to consider establishing 'preventive anti-corruption bodies' to carry out those policies, and increase anti-corruption awareness.[37] Within the public service, then, states are to take steps to 'strengthen systems' of human resource management as well as to consider or attempt to improve criteria for elected office, election funding, and conflict of interest management.[38] There are general duties to 'promote the integrity, honesty, and responsibility [of] (...) public officials', including with codes of conduct, asset declarations, and whistle-blower laws;[39] specific obligations pertain to the judiciary, legislature, and executive branch.[40] Within the private sector, states are to 'enhance accounting and auditing standards', including by mandating the disclosure of corporate beneficial ownership information and ensuring that enterprises have 'sufficient internal audit controls'.[41] Financial institutions are to be required 'to deter and detect all forms of money-laundering' *inter alia* by checking the depositor identities.[42] 'Civil society'

[31] UNCAC 2003 (n. 23), preamble.

[32] Ibid.; OECD Convention, 1997 (n. 23), preamble.

[33] For surveys and analysis, see Tina Søreide, *Corruption and Criminal Justice: Bridging Economic and Legal Perspectives* (Cheltenham: Edward Elgar 2016), 35–50; Benjamin Olken/Rohini Pande, 'Corruption in Developing Countries', *Annual Review of Economics* 4 (2012), 479–509, at 491–492.

[34] See, e.g., LSE-Oxford Commission on State Fragility, Growth and Development, 'Escaping the Fragility Trap', April 2018, available at: https://www.theigc.org/wp-content/uploads/2018/04/Escaping-the-fragility-trap.pdf (accessed 4 February 2019).

[35] See, e.g., Louise Shelley, *Dirty Entanglements: Corruption, Crime, and Terrorism* (Cambridge: CUP, 2014), 6–7; cf. Department for International Development, 'Why Corruption Matters: Understanding Causes, Effects and How to Address Them: Evidence Paper on Corruption', January 2015, available at: www.gov.uk/government/uploads/system/uploads/attachment_data/file/406346/corruption-evidence-paper-why-corruption-matters.pdf, 51–52 (accessed 4 February 2019); cf. Peter Andreas, 'Dirty Entanglements: Corruption, Crime, and Terrorism (Book review)', *Political Science Quarterly* 130 (2015), 350–352.

[36] UNCAC, 2003 (n. 23), art. 5.

[37] Ibid., art. 6.

[38] Ibid., art. 7.

[39] Ibid., art. 8.

[40] See Ibid., arts 8, 9, 11.

[41] Ibid., art. 12.

[42] Ibid., art. 52(1); see also UNCAC, 2003 (n. 23), art. 14.

is to be placed in a position to identify and protest against (governmental) corruption through access to (public) information.[43] Notably, the UNCAC seeks to 'respect[], promot[e] and protect[]' corruption-related freedoms of communication in language reminiscent of Article 19(3) International Covenant on Civil and Political Rights.[44]

Finally, in criminal matters, the treaties seek to establish each state party as a credible repressor of corruption, despite international mobility of goods, money, and people. Hence, the anti-corruption treaties do not create individual or corporate economic offences in public international law. They also do not hold states strictly liable for corrupt conduct committed by non-state actors within their jurisdictions. Rather, they both encourage and require the criminalisation of select misuses of power or office for private gain, as well as behaviours that allow offenders to enjoy ill-gotten gains or avoid prosecution.[45] States must prescribe these offences within their territories,[46] and, under some of the conventions, when they refuse to extradite a national (*aut dedere aut judicare*).[47] Extraterritorial jurisdiction is permitted but generally optional.[48] Some of the treaties regulate the circumstance in which states can refuse prosecution.[49] Several oblige states to ensure punishment according to international standards,[50] and most foresee confiscation or forfeiture.[51] There are corresponding duties to cooperate when suspects, offenders, assets, and information are located abroad.[52] To this end and others, the UNCAC contemplates a flow of education and training, information, and 'material support' within and between state parties.[53] Like the OECD Convention, it envisages treaty monitoring through state-to-state processes of peer review.[54]

Thus, anti-corruption and money laundering instruments construct a partially transboundary harm and create correlative duties of diligent crime control. States must ensure their institutions are able to enforce prohibitions on this conduct with certain preventive, suppressive, and remedial actions. Some of these measures are discretionary and/or qualified by reference to local factors. However, recalling the precautionary principle, they are prior to social scientific proof as to a particular state's 'level' of corruption or, indeed, the effectiveness of the treaties' measures.[55]

43 UNCAC, 2003 (n. 23), arts 10, 13.

44 Ibid., art. 13; see also Bacio Terracino, *International Legal Framework* (n. 22), 134–135.

45 Ivory, *Human Rights of Bad Guys* 2014 (n. 22), 8, 12-22, 63–90.

46 Ibid., 59-60; see, e.g., OECD Convention, 1997 (n. 23), art. 4(1); UNCAC, 2003 (n. 23), art. 42(1)(a).

47 See, e.g., UNCAC, 2003 (n. 23), art. 42(3).

48 Ivory, *Human Rights of Bad Guys* 2014 (n. 22), 60; see OECD Convention, 1997 (n. 23), art. 4(2).

49 Ivory, *Human Rights of Bad Guys* 2014 (n. 22), 96–99.

50 Ibid., 92; see, e.g., OECD Convention, 1997 (n. 23), art. 3(1).

51 Ivory, *Human Rights of Bad Guys* 2014 (n. 22), ch. 4; see, e.g., UNCAC, 2003 (n. 23), art. 14.

52 See e.g. UNCAC, 2003 (n. 23), ch. IV.

53 Ibid., ch. VI.

54 Ibid., art. 63; see also OECD Convention, 1997 (n. 23), art. 12.

55 On the precautionary principle, see Malgosia Fitzmaurice, 'Due Diligence in the Use of International Watercourses', chapter 8 of this book, section 4. On the problems with international anti-corruption and money laundering measures, see below section 3.4.

In addition, states must adhere to international procedures that are judged likely to enhance the effectiveness of all their domestic controls.

3.2 State-to-Business Duties to Regulate Non-State Actors

Second, advancing knowledge about the subjects of due diligence norms, the treaties indirectly require due diligence activities by non-state actors. In other words, states have obligations to ensure that certain legal entities within their jurisdictions manage themselves so as to detect and deter corruption and related financial flows. The OECD standards on corporate liability exemplify one such set of due diligence norms.[56] The OECD Convention requires countries to take steps to ensure that 'legal persons' may be held liable for foreign bribery and appropriately sanctioned.[57] The Convention does not say that corporate liability must be criminal,[58] nor does it specify the rules of attribution by which corporations are to incur offences under domestic law.[59] However, the OECD's Working Group on Bribery in International Transactions (OECD Working Group) recommends that corporations be held liable for the conduct of persons with 'flexible' levels of authority and despite variety in decision-making systems of legal persons.[60] If states choose only to identify corporations with culpable high-level managers, they should still ensure that companies will be responsible when those managers failed to prevent bribery at the 'lower level[s]'.[61] Since states must criminalise foreign bribery through intermediaries, these supervisory duties should extend to certain corporate 'third parties', like agents and (possibly) subsidiaries.[62]

Presuming that 'grand' corruption will nevertheless occur, several of the anti-corruption treaties seek to prohibit and prevent the concealment and reuse of illicit wealth.[63] The OECD Convention contains a qualified duty to criminalise

[56] See also UNCAC, 2003 (n. 23), art. 26.

[57] OECD Convention, 1997 (n. 23), arts 2, 3(2).

[58] Ibid., art. 3(2) and Commentaries on the Convention on Combating Bribery of Foreign Public Officials in International Business Transactions, 21 November 1997, DAFFE/IME/BR(97)20, 12–18, para. 20.

[59] Mark Pieth, 'Article 2: The Responsibility of Legal Persons for Bribery of Foreign Public Officials', in Mark Pieth/Lucinda Low/Nicola Bonucci (eds), *The OECD Convention on Bribery: A Commentary* (Cambridge: CUP 2nd ed. 2014), 212–251, at 226.

[60] See also OECD, Recommendation of the Council for Further Combating Bribery of Foreign Public Officials in International Business Transactions, 26 November 2009, annex I, para. B(a); see also G20, Leaders' Declaration: Shaping an Interconnected World, Annex: G20 High-Level Principles on the Liability of Legal Persons for Corruption, 8 July 2017, available at: https://www.g20germany.de/Webs/G20/EN/G20/Summit_documents/summit_documents_node.html, principle 4 (accessed 4 February 2019).

[61] OECD Recommendation, 2009 (n. 60), annex I, para. B(b).

[62] Ingeborg Zerbes, 'Article 1: The Offence of Bribery of Foreign Public Officials', in Mark Pieth/Lucinda Low/Nicola Bonucci (eds), *The OECD Convention on Bribery: A Commentary* (Cambridge: CUP 2nd ed. 2014), 59–211, at 153–156, 159–162; see also OECD Recommendation 2009 (n. 60), annex I, para. C.

[63] Ivory, *Human Rights of Bad Guys* 2014 (n. 22), 87–90.

corruption-related money laundering and to prohibit various forms of 'crooked' accounting.[64] The obligations of the UNCAC are yet more extensive. In addition to the private sector prevention provisions mentioned above, Chapter V (asset recovery) mandates the taking of domestic measures, 'to require financial institutions (…) to verify the identity of customers'.[65] Those verification duties increase for high-value accounts and increase again for the accounts of current and former politically exposed persons, 'their family members and close associates'.[66] Governments must assist their banks by issuing advisories or notifications about people, deposits, and transactions that deserve 'enhanced scrutiny'.[67] These measure must be 'in accordance with (…) domestic law and inspired by relevant initiatives (…) against money laundering'. The FATF, for one, discusses the above verification measures under the title of '[enhanced] customer due diligence'.[68] Its obligations are enforced by the members and members of affiliated bodies through 'soft' sanctions and peer review.[69] Both the FATF Recommendations and the UNCAC foresee the establishment of 'financial intelligence units' to 'collec[t], analy[se] and disseminat[e] (…)' suspicious transaction information, including to other states.[70]

Therefore, the anti-corruption treaties create a cascading system of supervisory duties. States are the primary subject of international 'corporate' due diligence obligations. However, there are at least two tiers of non-state actors who are the indirect objects of those standards: (1) the legal entities that may become liable for corruption or money laundering; and (2) the persons that those entities wrongfully fail to control. Reinforcing the prohibitions on corruption, anti-money laundering instruments require the collection and limited disclosure of information by financial institutions and their state supervisors. Hence, the instruments—soft and hard—entrench the notion that regulation of private actors is part of states' general duties to prevent harm.

[64] OECD Convention, 1997 (n. 24), arts 7–8.

[65] UNCAC, 2003 (n. 23), art. 52(1).

[66] Ibid.

[67] Ibid., art. 52(2).

[68] FATF, 2012 (n. 24), Recommendations 10 and 12 and Interpretive Notes thereto; see also Basel Committee on Banking Supervision (BCBS), Core Principles for Effective Banking Supervision, September 2012, available at: www.bis.org, para. 41, principle 29 (accessed 4 February 2019); The Wolfsberg Group, 'Anti-Money Laundering Principles for Private Banking', 2012, available at: https://www.wolfsberg-principles.com/sites/default/files/wb/pdfs/wolfsberg-standards/10.%20Wolfsberg-Private-Banking-Prinicples-May-2012.pdf, para. 1.3, appendix I (accessed 4 February 2019); on customer due diligence obligations in crime suppression conventions more generally, see also ILA, Study Group on Due Diligence in International Law, First Report, 7 March 2014, 22–23.

[69] See generally Rose, *International Anti-Corruption Norms* (n. 22), 199–214.

[70] FATF, 2012 (n. 24), Recommendation 25; UNCAC, 2003 (n. 23), art. 58.

3.3 The Calibration of State and Business Duties

Third, international anti-corruption and money laundering laws contextualise the standards of care for crime prevention and premise them on a calculation of risk. At the macro-level of state-to-state obligations, the treaty provisions are drafted in broad and often discretionary terms.[71] Monitoring bodies have also taken a staged approach to ascertaining state compliance.[72] Next, at the mezzo-level of state-to-business obligations, the OECD Working Group recommends that companies maintain systems to prohibit, prevent, detect, investigate, and discipline deviance. Yet, it acknowledges that the precise programmes, controls, or measures will vary depending on an entity's risk profile, as self-assessed.[73] Likewise, countries must have in place rules that shift levels of supervision of bank customers, accounts, and transactions to comply with international anti-money laundering norms. The UNCAC says that 'enhanced scrutiny shall be reasonably designed to detect suspicious transactions for the purpose of reporting to competent authorities and should not be so construed as to discourage or prohibit financial institutions from doing business with any legitimate customer'.[74] The FATF encourages banks to adopt a 'risk-based approach',[75] just as it calls on countries to deploy that general strategy in designing national anti-money laundering regimes.[76] Further, at the micro-level of business-to-business verification and assurance measures, US lawyers report a variety of practices, from contractual warranties to the engagement of private security firms to conduct background checks.[77] Likewise, money

[71] On the UNCAC and its 'escape hatches', see Lucinda Low, 'The United Nations Convention against Corruption: The Globalization of Anti-Corruption Standards' (conference paper), 4-5 May 2006, available at: www.steptoe.com/assets/attachments/2599.pdf (accessed 4 February 2019).

[72] For example, the OECD Working Group uses a notion of 'functional equivalence' to determine whether states have adequately implemented their anti-bribery standards. The OECD Working Group has conducted four rounds of review, each more probing than the next: Mark Pieth, 'Introduction', in Mark Pieth/Lucinda Low/Nicola Bonnuci (eds), *The OECD Convention against Bribery: A Commentary* (Cambridge: CUP 2nd ed. 2014), 3–56, at 22, 37; see also United Nations, Conference of the States Parties to the United Nations Convention against Corruption, Resolution 3/1 Review Mechanism, 9-13 November 2009, available at: https://www.unodc.org/unodc/en/treaties/CAC/CAC-COSP-session3-resolutions.html, paras 3 and 4 (accessed 4 February 2019).

[73] OECD Recommendations, 2009 (n. 60), annex II, introduction and para. A; see also G20, 'G20 High-Level Principles on Private Sector Transparency and Integrity', 2015, available at: http://www.g20.utoronto.ca/2015/G20-High-Level-Principles-on-Private-Sector-Transparency-and-Integrity.pdf (accessed 4 February 2019).

[74] UNCAC, 2003 (n. 23), art. 52(1).

[75] See also BCBS, 'Sound Management of Risks Related to Money Laundering and Financing of Terrorism', June 2017, available at: www.bis.org, para. 14 (accessed 4 February 2019); The Wolfsberg Group, 'Wolfsberg Statement: Guidance on a Risk Based Approach for Managing Money Laundering Risks', available at: https://www.wolfsberg-principles.com/publications/wolfsberg-standards (accessed 4 February 2019).

[76] FATF, 2012 (n. 24), Recommendations 1 and 10.

[77] Scott Killingsworth, 'The Privatization of Compliance, RAND Symposium: Transforming Compliance', in Michael Greenberg (ed.), *Transforming Compliance: Emerging Paradigms for Boards, Management, Compliance Officers, and Government* (RAND Corporation 2014), available at: https://www.rand.org/content/dam/rand/pubs/conf_proceedings/CF300/CF322/RAND_CF322.pdf, 33–45 (accessed 4 February 2019); Lucinda Low, 'Preventing and Defending against Vicarious and Successor

laundering reporting organisations may choose to execute their monitoring functions with the aid of information technologies and external research firms, as well as through in-house training, supervision, and reporting functions.[78]

In short, the treaties require countries and, indirectly, companies to be diligent to an extent appropriate to their assessed levels of risk. Again, recalling the precautionary principle, the corporate duty to prevent applies independently of proof about the occurrence of the offence within a particular institution. The implementing domestic laws are strictly beyond the scope of this chapter. Still, it is interesting to note that both US and UK anti-bribery guidelines use the language of risk assessment and 'due diligence'[79] and that 'third party due diligence' firms assist with company compliance in practice.

3.4 Due Diligence and Risk Governance

Fourth, the international anti-corruption and money laundering instruments demonstrate the importance of risk theories to debates about due diligence in international law. Here, the point is not so much that the instruments use the language of 'risk' in their requirements on non-state actors and corruption prevention in the public sector, as mentioned.[80] Rather, this language is one cause to consider the relevance of risk sociologies to discussions of international anti-corruption due diligence rules. For example, discourses of 'clean' and 'dirty' money are an instinctive match with Douglas' notion of risk as impurity, whereas the presentation of corruption as a crime of the global economy (and economic technology) resonates with Beck's accounts of the 'world risk society'.[81] There is also a panoptic quality of due diligence requirements that recalls Foucaultian accounts of private sector surveillance as a tool of governmentality by which individuals are encouraged to internalise a sense of being observed, as well to monitor others.[82]

Liability under National and International Bribery Regimes', in Mark Pieth/Lucinda Low/Nicola Bonucci (eds), *The OECD Convention on Bribery: A Commentary* (Cambridge: CUP 2nd ed. 2014), 611–683, at 628–629.

[78] Dennis Cox, *Handbook of Anti Money Laundering* (Chichester: Wiley 2014), 9–10, 277; Carolin Liss/Jason Sharman, 'Global Corporate Crime-Fighters: Private Transnational Responses to Piracy and Money Laundering', *Review of International Political Economy* 22 (2014), 693–718.

[79] UK Ministry of Justice, '*The Bribery Act 2010* (UK): Guidance', March 2011, available at: https://www.justice.gov/criminal-fraud/fcpa-resource-guide , principles 1.2, 4 (accessed 4 February 2019); US Department of Justice and US Securities and Exchange Commission, 'FCPA: A Resource Guide to the US Foreign Corrupt Practices Act', November 2012, available at: www.justice.gov/criminal/fraud/fcpa, 23, 58 (accessed 4 February 2019); see also, Rose, *International Anti-Corruption Norms* 2015 (n. 22), 78, 81; see also US Sentencing Commission, 'Federal Sentencing Guidelines', 2018, available at: https://www.ussc.gov/guidelines, §8B2.1 (accessed 4 February 2019).

[80] UNCAC, 2003 (n. 23), arts 7(1)(d), 9(2)(d).

[81] See also Anthony Giddens, 'Risk and Responsibility', *Modern Law Review* 62 (1999), 1–10, at 2–3 (discussing fraud and financial collapse in the context of Barings Bank).

[82] Larry Catá Backer, 'Global Panopticism: States, Corporations, and the Governance Effects of Monitoring Regimes', *Indiana Journal of Global Legal Studies* 15 (2008), 101–148, at 118–120; Hans Krause Hansen, 'Managing Corruption Risks', *Review of International Political Economy* 18 (2008),

The risk lens thereby points to a further set of debates about the desirability of particular approaches to regulation in the anti-corruption context and beyond.[83] The networked management of problems has a positive valence in the literature on 'new governance'.[84] According to this narrative, recent forms of interdependence and complexity have prompted shifts in dominant forms of government intervention.[85] One such 'new' strategy, cited by the likes of Ruggie, is the 'alignment' of the supervisory capacities in public law, civil society, and corporate governance systems of control.[86] Through soft or broadly drafted compliance requirements, states orchestrate rights-respecting conduct by persons within their jurisdictions; these actors in turn require compliance of other persons within their spheres of influence. These kinds of approaches seem pragmatic and might also encourage the achieving of economic efficiencies in parallel with democratic values,[87] like participation. In an echo of this debate, Pieth describes the anti-corruption and money laundering compliance regime as a 'text book example' of 'co-regulation'.[88] Elsewhere, he describes the advantages of the risk-based approach over rule-based regimes that may punish companies based on their failures to take prescribed measures, rather than their actual negligence.[89] As he piquantly notes, 'If banking and indeed, the wider financial community has to put up with an increasing density of regulation, it has—as a kind of counterweight—managed to convince supervisors of the benefits of a risk-based approach for both sides.'[90]

On the other hand, the 'new' and 'risk-based' features of international anti-corruption and money laundering norms are points for scepticism or even critique. There are threshold issues of ineffectiveness, with three prominent social scientists, for example, finding a lack of evidence that three rounds of FATF country supervision had any 'demonstrable impact on money laundering or the financing of terrorism'.[91] Others writing of UK and US financial and anti-discrimination controls

251–275; see also Christine Parker, *The Open Corporation: Effective Self-Regulation and Democracy* (Cambridge: CUP 2002), 14.

[83] See, generally, Radha Ivory, 'Beyond Transnational Criminal Law: Anti-Corruption as Global New Governance', *London Review of International Law* 6 (2018), 413–422.

[84] See, generally, Francis Fukuyama, 'Governance What Do We Know, and How Do We Know It?', *Annual Review of Political Science* 19 (2016), 89–115, at 96.

[85] See, e.g., Gráinne De Búrca, 'New Governance and Experimentalism: An Introduction', *Wisconsin Law Review* (2010), 227–238, at 232; Orly Lobel, 'The Renew Deal: The Fall of Regulation and the Rise of Governance in Contemporary Legal Thought', *Minnesota Law Review* 89 (2004), 342–470.

[86] John Gerard Ruggie, 'Global Governance and New Governance Theory: Lessons from Business and Human Rights', *Global Governance* 20 (2014), 5–17, at 9.

[87] See also Lobel, 'The Renew Deal' 2004 (n. 85), 344.

[88] Mark Pieth, *Wirtschaftsstrafrecht* (Basel: Helbing Lichtenhahn 2016), 169–170.

[89] Mark Pieth, 'International Standards against Money Laundering', in Mark Pieth/Gemma Aiolfi (eds), *A Comparative Guide to Anti-Money Laundering: A Critical Analysis of Systems in Singapore, Switzerland, the US and the UK* (Cheltenham: Edward Elgar 2004), 3–42, at 28.

[90] Ibid.

[91] Terrence Halliday/Michael Levi/Peter Reuter, 'Global Surveillance of Dirty Money: Assessing Assessments of Regimes to Control Money Laundering and Combat the Financing of Terrorism', 30 January 2014, available at: http://www.americanbarfoundation.org/publications/752, para. 26 (accessed 4 February 2019).

foreground a tension between deference to corporate expertise and meaningful restraints of corporate misbehaviour.[92] In common law states, some criminal lawyers and criminologist have been cautious of preventive and private policing strategies.[93] These developments are superficially justified by reference to goals of harm prevention and community safety.[94] However, they may test the principles of liberal criminal law (e.g., *nulla poena sine lege*)[95] and the role of modern governments in criminal justice.[96] The 'new penal state', which emerged in the 1970s and 1980s, is said not to be principally concerned with the adjudication of guilt or the rehabilitation of offenders. Rather, it seeks to manage perpetual crime risks by containing and surveilling 'risky' groups.[97] In the anti-corruption and money laundering sphere, more specifically, risk-based approaches are acknowledged to have resulted in financial exclusion, with global financial institutions withdrawing or restricting services to smaller institution from higher-risk jurisdictions.[98] Finally, it is significant that international economic and anti-money laundering laws are implemented via so-called regulatory technologies.[99] Not only does the collection of data entail potential for unauthorised use and disclosure, there may also be a process of co-construction at work as responsibility for 'fact finding' is transferred to technology (and its developers) and those technologies become ever more preferred (legitimised) as diviners of truth and integrity over humans and their appointed representatives.

4. Conclusion

The international instruments on corruption and money laundering illustrate the richness of debates about due diligence in public international law. Three familiar

[92] See, e.g., Julia Black, 'Paradoxes and Failures: New Governance Techniques and the Financial Crisis', *Modern Law Review* 75 (2012), 1037–1063; Lauren Edelman, *Working Law: Courts, Corporations, and Symbolic Civil Rights* (Chicago: Chicago University Press 2016) discussed further in Ivory, 'Beyond Transnational Criminal Law' (n. 83).

[93] See, generally, Andrew Ashworth/Lucia Zedner, 'Defending the Criminal Law: Reflections on the Changing Character of Crime, Procedure, and Sanctions', *Criminal Law and Philosophy* 2 (2008) 21–51, at 23, 44; Andrew Ashworth/Lucia Zedner, *Preventive Justice* (Oxford: OUP 2014), chs 1 and 11; Lorraine Mazzerolle/Janet Ransley, *Third Party Policing* (Cambridge: CUP 2016), at 179–180.

[94] Ashworth/Zedner, *Preventive Justice* 2014 (n. 93), 7–10, ch. 2.

[95] See generally Ashworth/Zedner, *Preventive Justice* 2014 (n. 93), ch. 11.

[96] David Garland, *The Culture of Control: Crime and Social Order in Contemporary Society* (Chicago: University of Chicago Press 2001), ch. 2.

[97] See, e.g., Malcolm Feeley/Jonathan Simon, 'The New Penology: Notes on the Emerging Strategy of Corrections and its Implications', *Criminology* 30 (1992), 449–470.

[98] World Bank, 'De-risking in the Financial Sector', 6 October 2016, available at: http://www.worldbank.org/en/topic/financialsector/brief/de-risking-in-the-financial-sector (accessed 4 February 2019).

[99] See generally Douglas Arner/Jànos Barberis/Ross Buckley, 'FinTech, RegTech, and the Reconceptualization of Financial Regulation', *Northwestern Journal of International Law & Business* 37 (2017), 371–414.

controversies—about sources, subjects, and standards of due diligence duties—are complemented by an emerging interest in the role of risk in international regulation. This review suggests that each of these four issues may be enriched by a study of efforts against corruption and money laundering. The cascade of due diligence obligations has pragmatic and progressive features, but is also associated with regulatory failures and departures from the principles of modern policing and liberal criminal justice. The chapter thus problematised the diffusion of supervisory approaches to economic crime through public international law. It embeds a call for further interdisciplinary inquiries into the rightfulness and rationality of international due diligence rules.

18

Due Diligence in International Tax Law

Reuven S. Avi-Yonah and Gianluca Mazzoni[*]

1. Introduction: Is There a Due Diligence Obligation in International Tax Law?

In international tax law prior to the financial crisis of 2008–2009, there was no due diligence concept that imposed on states, and derivatively on their financial institutions, an obligation not to harm other states by aiding and abetting tax evasion by residents of these other states. This was in part the result of a legal rule, the 'revenue rule', which stemmed from the eighteenth-century declaration of Lord Mansfield pronouncing that 'no country ever takes notice of the revenue laws of another [country]'.[1] In other words, states cannot be expected to aid other sovereign states in the collection of their taxes. In addition, as we will discuss in section 2, from the enactment of the portfolio interest exemption by the US in 1984 and the subsequent abolition of withholding taxes by EU member states, it was the clear policy of both the US and the EU to actively aid and abet tax evasion by each other's residents by allowing the payment of interest to foreign individuals and legal entities without either a withholding tax or the collection of any information about the identity of the beneficial owner of the interest that could be shared with the residence jurisdiction under tax treaties. This mutual race to the bottom culminated when the US adopted the 'qualified intermediary' regime in 2000, which affirmatively shielded the required information from the Internal Revenue Service (IRS), and the EU adopted the Saving Directive in 2003, which exempted payments to non-EU residents. The total lack of any due diligence obligation can be seen from the statement by UBS Group AG during the US Senate hearing on the 'UBS scandal' in 2009: that it was perfectly acceptable for the Swiss bank to rely on W8-BEN forms that indicated that the owner of an account was a tax-haven corporation when UBS had itself set up that corporation for a US resident and knew the identity of that resident.[2]

[*] We would like to thank Anne Peters and Leonhard Kreuzer for organising this project and for their meticulous editorial assistance.

[1] Court of King's Bench, *Holman v. Johnson*, 1775, English Reports 98 (1378–1865), 1120–1122, at 1121.

[2] US Senate, Permanent Subcommittee on Investigations, Staff Report, Tax Haven Banks and US Tax Compliance, 17 July 2008, available at: www.hsgac.senate.gov/imo/media/doc/REPORTTaxHavenBanksJuly1708FINALwPatEliseChgs92608.pdf (accessed 14 July 2019). On this and related

Reuven S. Avi-Yonah and Gianluca Mazzoni, *Due Diligence in International Tax Law* In: *Due Diligence in the International Legal Order*. Edited by: Heike Krieger, Anne Peters, and Leonhard Kreuzer, Oxford University Press (2020). © The Several Contributors. DOI: 10.1093/oso/9780198869900.003.0018.

This all changed in the wake of the UBS scandal and the 2008–2009 financial crisis. Both the US and the EU became aware that aiding and abetting tax evasion by each other's residents could lead to Americans pretending to be Europeans and Europeans pretending to be Americans in order to evade their tax obligations: in both the US and the EU, there was no withholding tax imposed on payments to non-residents, so if a resident of either the US or the EU could pretend to be a resident of the other, she could evade the withholding tax. In addition, the revenue pressure from the financial crisis and the subsequent public outrage at the banks that caused it first led to the enactment in the US of the Foreign Accounts Tax Compliance Act (FATCA) of 2010, then to the negotiation of Intergovernmental Agreements (IGAs) between the US and over a hundred other countries, and finally to the development by the Organisation for Economic Co-operation and Development (OECD) of the Common Reporting Standards (CRS) for the Automatic Exchange of Information (AEoI) under the Multilateral Agreement on Administrative Assistance in Tax Matters. The CRS have as of June 2018 been adopted by 123 jurisdictions (though not by the US).

2. Origins: Before 2010

In 1987 the US terminated its tax treaty with the Netherlands Antilles. The reason was that the treaty (technically an extension of the US-Netherlands treaty) had become a 'treaty with the world' (that is, allowing any non-resident to achieve treaty benefits without residing in a treaty jurisdiction): every US multinational could set up a finance subsidiary in the Antilles and use it to borrow funds from investors regardless of their country of residence, secure in the knowledge that there would be no withholding tax levied on the interest payments under Article 11 of the treaty.[3] The US became concerned that no country would be interested in negotiating tax treaties with it if their residents could use the Antilles treaty.[4]

investigations, see Elise Bean, *Financial Exposure: Carl Levin's Senate Investigations into Finance and Tax Abuse* (London: Palgrave Macmillan 2018).

3 104th US Congress, 2nd Session, Senate, Executive Report 104-135, Protocol Amending Article VIII of the 1948 Tax Convention With Respect to the Netherlands Antilles, 25 September 1996, at 4: 'Some U.S. companies established subsidiaries in the Netherlands Antilles in order to issue debt in the international capital markets. Under this structure, the Netherlands Antilles subsidiary issued so-called Eurobonds in the international market. The Netherlands Antilles subsidiary then loaned the proceeds of these Eurobonds to its U.S. parent or to another U.S. affiliate. The U.S. parent or affiliate thus issued to the Netherlands Antilles subsidiary a debt obligation that corresponded to the Eurobonds issued by the subsidiary. The Netherlands Antilles subsidiary receives interest from the U.S. parent or affiliate on the debt obligation of such parent or affiliate and pays interest on the Eurobonds it issued. The Netherlands Antilles subsidiary relies on Article VIII of the 1948 Convention as extended to the Netherlands Antilles in order to avoid the U.S. 30-percent withholding tax on the interest received from the U.S. parent or affiliate. The interest paid by the Netherlands Antilles subsidiary on the Eurobonds is not subject to any tax by the Netherlands Antilles.'

4 Omri Marian, 'Unilateral Responses to Tax Treaty Abuse: A Functional Approach', *Brooklyn Journal of International Law* 41 (2016), 1157–1183, at 1174: 'Two months after the termination of the

However, the termination of the treaty also caused concerns: how would the US itself (which was running a large budget deficit) and US corporations continue to borrow from overseas investors if the interests were subject to a 30% withholding tax? When a US corporation borrowed money from a foreign individual, any interest payments by the corporation to that individual would be subject to the 30% withholding tax. One answer was that those investors from treaty countries already benefitted from a lower rate of withholding tax (typically 10%, or even 0%). However, if the lower rate depended on a treaty, the investors would potentially be subject to the exchange of information provision (Article 26), which could mean that they would have to declare the US-source interest income to their country of residence.

The solution was to adopt the portfolio interest exemption, Internal Revenue Code §871(h), under which interest paid by US persons (the US treasury and US corporations, as well as US banks and other financial institutions) to lenders that do not own at least 10% of the stock of the borrowing corporation is unilaterally exempt from the withholding tax.[5] This enabled US persons to borrow without paying the withholding tax (which is typically shifted to the borrower, as interest rates are set in the global market) and also without jeopardising tax evasion by the lender, since the exemption does not depend on a treaty and therefore no information needs to be collected by the payors and no information was available for exchanging with residence countries.

The result was astonishing: over $300 billion were invested in the US from Latin America alone—a sum exceeding all official aid received by Latin American countries during the entire 1980s.[6] As the Deputy Assistant Secretary for Tax Analysis Charles McLure admitted, this was not foreseen by the Treasury and caused

treaty, O. Donaldson Chapoton, the Acting Assistant Treasury Secretary for Tax Policy (. . .) noted that the principal objection to treaty shopping was that it undermined the leverage the United States would otherwise bring to negotiations for new or revised treaties with the countries of residence of the treaty shoppers. It therefore posed a serious obstacle to the United States' efforts to bargain with trading partners for concessions, like low withholding tax rates on income derived by U.S. persons from those jurisdictions, which are so important to the international competitive standing of U.S. multinationals.'

[5] Reuven S. Avi-Yonah, *International Tax as International Law: An Analysis of the International Tax Regime* (Cambridge: CUP 2007), 70: 'This exemption specifies that all payments of U.S.-source interest to foreigners are exempt from the withholding tax as long as they are 'portfolio interest.' This exemption covers interest on deposits in banks (which is actually an even older exception), interest on bonds issued by the government, and interest on all bonds issued by private corporations; basically all interest is exempt from tax as long as it is so-called portfolio interest. Portfolio interest is interest that is paid to non-shareholders. The test is whether the shareholder owns 10% of the stock—that is, interest paid to foreign parents or to large foreign shareholders does not qualify for the portfolio interest exemption.'

[6] Ibid., at 71: 'The portfolio interest exception has had a dramatic effect. It is estimated that the first few years after 1984, more than $300 billion moved from Latin America to bank accounts in Miami. This money transfer was illegal from the Latin American countries' perspective because of local capital restrictions, but was attracted by the availability of interest free from withholding in bank accounts. In addition, deposits in American banks are guaranteed by the U.S. government and insured by the Federal Deposit Insurance Corporation, so it is a low-risk location. This quantity of money is large even by American standards, but by Latin American standards it is tremendously large: it was much more than all the World Bank and even private investment in Latin America at the time. The money went into Latin America and went back out to the U.S. bank accounts without benefiting Latin America. The attractiveness of American banks in the 1980s was one factor in why the 1980s were the 'lost decade' for

massive damage to Latin American countries.[7] In addition, tax competition has ensured that since 1984 no developed country has been able to collect a withholding tax on interest paid by its banks or corporations to non-residents, because if it tried to do so the funds would be shifted to the US.[8] For example, when Germany tried to impose a withholding tax on interest paid to non-residents because the Federal Constitutional Court held that it was a violation of equality requirements to withhold tax on wages but not on interest, the result was a massive flight of capital to Luxembourg that forced the German government to change course. The US and other OECD member countries have since benefitted from massive inflows of portfolio investment that is exempt from taxation 'at source' and that is generally not declared 'at residence', resulting in trillions of dollars of untaxed income.

However, from the beginning the US was concerned that the portfolio interest exemption could be used by US citizens and residents to move funds out of the US and then reinvest in US bonds via a secrecy jurisdiction. Because of this, the US took several steps to combat potential tax evasion by Americans: it severely restricted 'bearer bonds' that are not in a registered form; and it required that bonds issued by US corporations in Europe bear a legend that states they are not intended for sale to US citizens.[9] In addition, the portfolio interest exemption itself contains

Latin America in terms of development, because money given to them was transferred back into the United States.'

[7] Charles McLure, Jr., 'International Considerations in United States Tax Reform', in Munich Symposium on International Taxation (ed.), *Influence of Tax Differentials on International Competitiveness: Proceedings of the VIIIth Munich Symposium on International Taxation* (Boston: Kluwer Law and Taxation 1990), 1–24, at 22: 'I must admit that, as Deputy Assistant Secretary of the Treasury at the time this action [the adoption of the portfolio interest exemption] was taken, I did not fight early enough, long enough, or hard enough against its enactment,' mostly because of the effect on Latin American countries. See also Charles McLure, Jr., 'U.S. Tax Laws and Capital Flight from Latin America', *University of Miami Inter-American Law Review* 20 (1989), 321–357, at 349–350.

[8] Reuven S. Avi-Yonah, 'Globalization, Tax Competition, and the Fiscal Crisis of the Welfare State', *Harvard Law Review* 113 (2000), 1573–1676, at 1581: 'The United States' enactment of the portfolio interest exemption has resulted in a classic "race to the bottom". One after another, all the major economies have abolished their withholding taxes on interest for fear of losing mobile capital flows to the United States.' See also Charles Kingson/Cynthia Blum, *International Taxation* (New York: Aspen Law & Business 1998), 229.

[9] New York State Bar Association Tax Section, Report on Issues Relating to Restrictions Imposed on Offers and Sales of Bearer Bonds by the Tax Equity and Fiscal Responsibility Act of 1982, 1 October 2007, at 3–4: 'In 1982, Congress adopted restrictions on the issuance of debt instruments in bearer form, principally to enhance tax compliance by U.S. taxpayers and to restrict access to easily negotiable financial instruments that could be used to facilitate the 'laundering' of funds derived from illegal activities. Under these restrictions, issuers of debt instruments in bearer form generally are denied deductions for interest paid in respect of such instruments and are subject to an excise tax. Holders of bearer-form debt instruments also generally are subject to sanctions—a denial of capital gains treatment in respect of gains realized, and a denial of deductions for losses realized, on disposition of such instruments—unless the instruments are held in a manner that allows the instruments to satisfy information reporting requirements. In adopting these restrictions, however, Congress also recognized the importance of not unduly restricting liquidity in the financial markets and allowing U.S. issuers to issue securities in the international capital markets in an efficient manner. Thus, Congress reconciled these differing objectives by restricting the issuance of bearer-form debt instruments generally, but permitting their issuance outside the United States—i.e., under circumstances in which the instruments were unlikely to be sold to United States persons. The basic compromise adopted pursuant to Tax Equity and Fiscal Responsibility Act of 1982 and the Deficit Reduction Act of 1984 created a system pursuant to

a provision allowing the Treasury to suspend its application to countries that do not participate in information exchange.[10]

These steps, however, proved insufficient. Bearer bonds survived on the Eurobond market, and the legend was insufficient as it did not apply to the secondary sales of the bonds. Nor was the exchange-of-information limitation to the portfolio interest exemption ever applied.

To improve its policing of the withholding tax, the US in the early 2000s adopted the 'qualified intermediary' (QI) programme. Under the QI programme, banks could qualify to be QIs by signing an agreement to validate the identity of their customers. They would then pass on the information to the US withholding agents, but only in aggregate form without revealing the actual identities of the beneficial owners to anyone in the US. The reason for this latter provision, of course, was to ensure that the information was not available to the IRS to exchange in accordance with its obligation under the US tax treaties and therefore could not be used by other countries to combat tax evasion by their residents.[11]

The UBS scandal, which broke in 2009, showed that the QI programme was also insufficient to prevent 'round tripping' by US citizens. UBS sent representatives to visit locations in the US where the rich congregate and persuade them to set up corporations in tax havens like the Caymans. The tax-haven corporations then deposited funds into UBS (based in Zurich), which in turn invested them in the US. UBS claimed that the QI agreement it signed did not require it to disclose any of this information to the IRS as long as the accounts were in the name of the tax-haven corporations, even though it knew the corporations were beneficially owned by US citizens.[12]

which U.S. issuers were given a fundamental choice: (1) obtain the ability to issue securities globally by issuing them in registered form, subject to holder documentation requirements necessary to establish the identity of U.S. holders and the eligibility of non-U.S. holders for the portfolio interest exemption from U.S. withholding tax; or (2) minimize the need for holders to provide documentation by issuing the securities in bearer form, at the cost of not being able to issue those securities to U.S. investors.'

[10] US, Internal Revenue Code, Tax on Nonresident Alien Individuals, 26 USC §871(h)(6): 'If the Secretary determines that the exchange of information between the United States and a foreign country is inadequate to prevent evasion of the United States income tax by United States persons, the Secretary may provide in writing (and publish a statement) that the provisions of this subsection shall not apply to payments of interest to any person within such foreign country (or payments addressed to, or for the account of, persons within such foreign country).'

[11] Peter Connors/David Balaban, 'IRS Releases Final Qualified Intermediary Agreement', *Derivatives & Financial Instruments* 6 (2000), 335–341, at 335: 'The QI regime, which will be implemented on 1 January 2001, represents a new withholding tax system by which foreign financial institutions, or foreign branches of a US financial institution, can receive favorable withholding tax treatment (. . .) The QI rules were designed to reduce the burden on withholding agents by permitting them to rely on documentation furnished by a financial intermediary on behalf of its account holders without having to obtain specific information from each of these account holders. Under the QI rules, a financial intermediary who becomes a QI agrees to obtain reliable documentation from each of its account holders and to present that information in aggregate form to withholding agents (. . .) The QI rules are of particular importance to private banks and other financial institutions because a QI will generally be able to shield the identities of its non-US customers from US withholding agents and the IRS.'

[12] US Senate, Tax Haven Banks and US Tax Compliance, 2008 (n. 2), at 87–88: 'UBS (. . .) took steps to assist its U.S. clients to structure their Swiss accounts in ways that avoided U.S. reporting rules under

3. The Rise of Tax Due Diligence: From 2010 Onwards

The result of the UBS scandal was the enactment in 2010 of FATCA, under which any 'foreign financial institutions' (FFI) must take affirmative steps to discover who among its depositors is a US citizen or resident and disclose that information to the IRS. The penalty for not doing so is a hefty 30% withholding tax on any US-source income earned by the FFI in question. Since most FFIs are exposed to the US market in some way, this penalty has real teeth. To lighten the compliance burden, the US negotiated IGAs with several foreign governments under its tax treaties, according to which the foreign government collects the requisite information from its FFIs and shares it with the US either indirectly through local tax authorities (Model 1 Agreements) or directly to the IRS (Model 2 Agreements).[13]

As the first author has argued elsewhere, FATCA is the most spectacular and impressive recent example of the power of US leadership—or of constructive unilateralism—in international taxation. Indeed, the negotiation of IGAs by the US Treasury with foreign countries led to the development of standard information

the QI Program. UBS informed the Subcommittee that, after it joined the QI program in 2001, and informed its U.S. clients about its QI disclosure obligations, many of its U.S. clients elected to sell U.S. securities or open new accounts to avoid the QI reporting obligations attached (…) UBS also told the Subcommittee that, in 2001, about 250 of its U.S. clients with Swiss accounts took action to establish corporations, trusts, foundations, or other entities in non-U.S. countries, open new UBS accounts in the names of those foreign entities, and then, in a number of instances, transfer U.S. securities from the clients' personal accounts to those new accounts. The offshore entities included corporations, trusts, and foundations set up in the British Virgin Islands, Hong Kong, Liechtenstein, Panama, and Switzerland. UBS then accepted W-8BEN Forms from these offshore entities in which they claimed ownership of the assets had been transferred from the U.S. clients' personal accounts. UBS treated the new accounts as held by non-U.S. persons whose identities did not have to be disclosed to the IRS, even though UBS knew that the true beneficial owners were U.S. persons.'

[13] For a comparison of FATCA Model 1A and Model IGAs, see Maryte Somare/Viktoria Wöhrer, 'Two Different FATCA Model Intergovernmental Agreements: Which Is Preferable?: A Comparison of FATCA Model 1A and Model 2 Intergovernmental Agreements', *Bulletin for International Taxation* 68 (2014), 395–403. See, on the legal nature and the characteristics of IGAs, Allison Christians, 'The Dubious Legal Pedigree of IGAs (And Why It Matters)', *Tax Notes International* 69 (2013), 565–568, at 567, which argues that IGAs must be the 'sole' executive agreements—agreements undertaken by the president without congressional authorisation of any kind; Carol Tello, 'FATCA: Catalyst for Global Cooperation on Exchange of Tax Information', *Bulletin for International Taxation* 68 (2014), 88–102, at 93: 'For US purposes, the Treasury Department has adopted the position that an IGA, like a TIEA, is considered an executive agreement and not a treaty. A treaty requires the advice and consent of the Senate under art. 2(2), clause of the US Constitution'; Leopold Parada, 'Intergovernmental Agreements and the Implementation of FATCA in Europe', *World Tax Journal* 7 (2015), 201–240, at 209: 'Nonetheless, since the IGAs are not regarded as international agreements (at least not for both parties in the agreement), it is logical to have doubts regarding the rules that must be applied to interpret their provisions. A simple answer would be to affirm that the IGAs are instruments that depend on the existence of other instruments (i.e., DTCs or TIEAs); therefore, the interpretation rules must be in accordance to these instruments. In other words, when the exchange of information under the IGA is made in accordance to articles 26 or 27 of the OECD Model, the interpretation of the IGAs should be in accordance to this tax treaty. However, the reference to the DTCs and the IGAs is made only in terms of how the exchange of information must be made, but what about the interpretation of other provisions in the IGAs? Must they be interpreted independently in each contracting state? Can the rules of the Vienna Convention be applicable?'

exchange rules that culminated in the Multilateral Agreement on Administrative Assistance in Tax Matters, which has now been signed by over eighty countries and which provides for AEoI with no bank secrecy or dual criminality exceptions.[14]

On 15 July 2014, the OECD Council approved CRS, which calls on jurisdictions to obtain information from financial institutions and automatically exchange that information with other jurisdictions on an annual basis. CRS sets out the financial account information to be exchanged, namely all types of investment income (including interest, dividends, income from certain insurance contracts, and other similar types of income) but also account balances and sales proceeds from financial assets; the financial institutions required to provide a report, namely banks and custodians but also other financial institutions such as brokers, certain collective investment vehicles, and certain insurance companies; the different types of accounts and taxpayers covered, namely individuals and entities (including trusts and foundations) with the requirement to look through passive entities and report on the individuals that ultimately control these entities; as well as common due diligence procedures to be followed by financial institutions.

Reportable accounts are identified through a due diligence exercise, which consists mainly of an electronic record search (or a paper record search where the only indicia found is a 'hold mail' or 'in-care-of' address) of all electronically searchable data—performed in relation to account holders whose residence information is missing—for evidence (for example mailing address, fixed or mobile phone numbers, power of attorney granted) of the residence of such account holders in one of the jurisdictions where reporting and tax information exchanges apply. Borrowing the words of the Court of Justice of the European Union in *Digital Rights Ireland*, AEoI applies even to persons for whom there is no evidence capable of suggesting that their conduct might have a link, even an indirect or remote one, with tax evasion.[15] Therefore, in its current version, AEoI might be challenged because it does not respect the principle of sufficient cause, namely the verification of indicia for the non-compliant behaviour of taxpayers. In other words, AEoI could be considered disproportionate since it fails to narrow down reporting obligations to individuals suspected of tax evasion. In this regard, the European Data Protection Supervisor in its opinion of 8 July 2015 proposed a 'true' due diligence risk evaluation approach:

[14] Reuven S. Avi-Yonah, 'Constructive Unilateralism: US Leadership and International Taxation', 25 June 2015, *University of Michigan Public Law Research Paper* No. 463, available at: https://ssrn.com/abstract=2622868 (accessed 14 July 2019); for an examination of the primary features of the Convention on Mutual Administrative Assistance in Tax Matters, as amended by the 2010 Protocol, see Achim Pross/Raffaele Russo, 'The Amended Convention on Mutual Administrative Assistance in Tax Matters: A Powerful Tool To Counter Tax Avoidance and Evasion', *Bulletin for International Taxation* 66 (2012), 361–365.

[15] CJEU, *Digital Rights Ireland*, Grand Chamber Judgment of 8 April 2014, Joined Cases C-293/12 and C-594/12, para. 58.

> the [EU–Switzerland agreement on the automatic exchange of tax information] should have included provisions and criteria that explicitly link the reporting of personal data concerning financial accounts to possible tax evasion and that exempt low-risk accounts from reporting. In this respect, such criteria should be applicable *ex ante* to determine which accounts (and which information) would need to be reported. Only at that stage—once the relevance (or irrelevance) of the reporting for the purpose of countering tax evasion has been established—the electronic search might help determining the residence of the account holder.[16]

At the European level, Directive 2011/16 of 15 February 2011 recognises AEoI—defined as the systematic communication of predefined information to another member state, without prior request and at pre-established regular intervals[17]—as the most effective means of enhancing the correct assessment of taxes in cross-border situations and of fighting fraud. The directive provides for the mandatory exchange of five categories of income and assets, mainly of a non-financial nature: employment income, pension income, director fees, income and ownership of immovable property, and life insurance products. The scope has later been extended to financial account information, namely dividends, interest, gross proceeds from the sale or redemption of financial assets, and cash-value insurance contracts and account balances, cross-border tax rulings and advance pricing arrangements,[18] country-by-country reporting,[19] and tax planning schemes.

But FATCA and CRS also have significant built-in loopholes. On the one hand, FATCA can be avoided by using a bank with no US assets and therefore no US source income exposure. In addition, FATCA's disclosure requirements have been limited and weakened by its implementing regulations that provide a set of high dollar reporting thresholds and require the aggregation of account balances in different accounts only when the accounts are at the same financial institution. Thus, a US taxpayer can easily open multiple accounts at multiple banks and maintain account balances below the FATCA reporting thresholds.[20] On the other hand, on 19 February 2018, the OECD released a consultation document that assesses how

[16] European Data Protection Supervisor, Opinion 2/2015 on the EU-Switzerland agreement on the automatic exchange of tax information, 8 July 2015, para. 14, available at: https://edps.europa.eu/sites/edp/files/publication/15-07-08_eu_switzerland_en.pdf (accessed 14 July 2019). For the compatibility of reporting obligations under FATCA and CRS with the EU framework on privacy and data protection, see Reuven S. Avi-Yonah/Gianluca Mazzoni, 'Taxation and Human Rights: A Delicate Balance', 5 September 2016, *University of Michigan Public Law Research Paper No. 520*, available at SSRN: https://ssrn.com/abstract=2834883 (last accessed 14 July 2019).

[17] EU Council Directive 2011/16/EU of 15 February 2011 on Administrative Cooperation in the Field of Taxation and Repealing Directive 77/799/EEC, art. 3(9).

[18] EU Council Directive 2015/2376 of 8 December 2015 Amending Directive 2011/16/EU as Regards Mandatory Automatic Exchange of Information in the Field of Taxation.

[19] EU Council Directive 2016/881 of 25 May 2016 Amending Directive 2011/16/EU as Regards Mandatory Automatic Exchange of Information in the Field of Taxation.

[20] US Senate, Permanent Subcommittee on Investigations, Offshore Tax Evasion: The Effort to Collect Unpaid Taxes on Billions in Hidden Offshore Accounts, 26 February 2014, at 171–173.

'residence by investment' (RBI) or 'citizenship by investment' (CBI) schemes can potentially be exploited to avoid CRS reporting requirements.[21] Example 1 in the consultation document demonstrates how current CRS due diligence procedures are insufficient to effectively counter a case where an account holder falsely self-certifies their tax residency and omits to include all tax residence jurisdictions.[22] Practitioners suggested the following amendment to the current due diligence procedures so as to introduce a risk-based approach to the process of verifying tax residence status:

> Where an account holder seeks to rely on recently issued Documentary Evidence then a Financial Institution ought to treat the account as high risk and require supporting evidence of previous tax residence status, perhaps over the last 5 years. Recently Issued Documentary Evidence may be such documents relied on as may have been issued on or after 29 October 2014, to align with the proposed effective date of the MDR.[23]

The recent release of the Paradise Papers in late 2017, as well as the Panama Papers released the preceding year, demonstrates that the current regime is vulnerable to continuing evasion since it requires the cooperation of too many countries in order to be effective. Every tax haven has to sign on, otherwise money can be transferred to the non-cooperating tax havens. For instance, Panama had not yet confirmed its commitment to implement AEoI under the new standard. This aspect was also highlighted by OECD Secretary-General Angel Gurría when he stated, soon

[21] RBI or CBI are schemes that allow foreign individuals to obtain citizenship or temporary or permanent residence rights in exchange for local investments or against a flat fee. See Allison Christians, 'Buying In: Residence and Citizenship by Investment', *St. Louis University Law Journal* 62 (2017), 51–72.

[22] OECD, Consultation Document: Preventing Abuse of Residence by Investment Schemes to Circumvent the CRS, 19 February 2018, available at: www.oecd.org/tax/exchange-of-tax-information/consultation-document-preventing-abuse-of-residence-by-investment-schemes.pdf, at 3: 'X is an individual resident in jurisdiction F. In order to circumvent reporting under the CRS, X applies for 'residency status' in jurisdiction M under its RBI program. This status requires X to purchase a property in jurisdiction M worth at least 500,000 Euro or to rent a property for a minimum of 40,000 Euro per year. It allows X to obtain tax residency in jurisdiction M without being taxed on any income that is not sourced in or remitted to jurisdiction M. X opens a New Account with a Bank B in jurisdiction B and self-certifies to be resident for tax purposes in country M (including by presenting his tax residency certificate to Bank B in the on-boarding process). Although the CRS requires X to include all jurisdictions of residence for tax purposes in his self-certification, he omits to self-certify his tax residence in jurisdiction F. In addition, the AML/KYC documentation provided by X does not show any connection to jurisdiction F. Bank B will identify X as a resident of country M and report the income and other information about the account to the tax authorities of jurisdiction B that will exchange the CRS information with country M, in compliance with the CRS. However, X is not taxed on the income in jurisdiction M. X continues to be a resident of jurisdiction F but jurisdiction B does not exchange X's information with jurisdiction F, as a consequence of the outcome of the due diligence procedures applies by Bank B.' (accessed 14 July 2019).

[23] OECD, Public Input Received on Misuse of Residence by Investment Schemes to Circumvent the Common Reporting Standard, 17 April 2018, available at: www.oecd.org/tax/exchange-of-tax-information/public-input-received-misuse-of-residence-by-investment-schemes-to-circumvent-the-common-reporting-standard.pdf, at 60–65 (accessed 14 July 2019).

after the giant leak of more than 11.5 million financial and legal records, that 'our standards on tax transparency are robust; they need to be effectively implemented worldwide, by everyone, with no exceptions, so there's nowhere left to hide'.

4. Conclusion: From Rules to Standards

As we have seen, due diligence in international tax law is currently embodied in a specific set of rules imposed on FFIs by FATCA, CRS, and the EU Directives. The problem is that in the absence of an overarching standard of due diligence, these rules can be avoided, as exemplified by the RBI or CBI schemes outlined in section 3. For example, FATCA can be avoided by either using a bank with no US exposure, using several banks and dividing up the funds to avoid hitting the reporting limits, or by being born outside the US and self-certifying a non-US status. In the absence of a due diligence standard, FFIs can claim they have met their obligation in these cases even if they have reasons for suspicion. Similarly, CRS can be avoided by CBI and RBI schemes, if not too many questions are asked by the FFI. In addition, as explained above in the discussion of CRS, reliance on specific rules can lead to violations of privacy because the mechanical application of the rules ignores the specific circumstances of the taxpayer and whether the taxpayer poses an actual risk of tax evasion.

The solution is to create a due diligence standard over and above the specific rules and to hold those FFIs and states that regulate them to that standard. The OECD is the most likely institution to adopt this standard, perhaps as a preamble to CRS. Such a standard, like any due diligence standard, is based on the degree of risk in any particular situation. If an FFI is found to have neglected to ask the right questions despite a reason to be suspicious, the state that regulates the FFI should have an affirmative obligation to intervene, or else be held liable for violating its due diligence obligations. Only by openly adhering to such a due diligence standard can we avoid a repetition of the UBS scandal and achieve the goal of CRS: that every resident of every country that is liable to pay income tax be forced to do so. Otherwise, we risk undermining confidence in the income tax system, which for most countries is the main line of defence against rising inequality.

19

Due Diligence in International Trade Law

Markus Krajewski

1. Introduction

Due diligence is not a term of art in international trade law.[1] It is not mentioned in global or regional trade agreements and is not used in the relevant jurisprudence of the dispute settlement organs of the world trading system. In addition, the notion is largely absent from academic writings on international trade law. Equally, international trade law has so far not been used as a field of study or of reference in the general academic discourse on due diligence in public international law: the Report of the International Law Association's (ILA) Study Group on Due Diligence on International Law explicitly excludes trade law,[2] and it is not discussed in recent scholarly works on due diligence in international law.[3]

This finding is not only astonishing because a large subfield of public international law is absent from a significant and growing discourse in public international law; it is also especially noteworthy since international trade law seems to contain significant elements of due diligence. One could even argue that due diligence—broadly understood as the principle to ensure that a state's territory is not used to negatively impact the rights and interests of other states—is a cornerstone of international trade law. International trade has inevitable effects on other countries due to its very nature as a transboundary activity. It should hence be of no surprise that the international trade law regime established obligations requiring states to take the interests of other states into account when designing and implementing instruments aimed at the regulation of international trade.

The present chapter pursues two objectives: first, it aims at assessing and analysing elements of due diligence in existing international trade agreements. These elements include obligations to cooperate, to negotiate in good faith, to notify

[1] For the purposes of this chapter, international trade law comprises of the law of the World Trade Organisation (WTO), in particular the multilateral trade agreements administered by the WTO as well as the law of regional and bilateral free trade agreements (FTAs). International trade law can be distinguished from the law applicable to transnational commercial transactions (international commercial law) which is not part of public international law.

[2] International Law Association (ILA), Study Group on Due Diligence in International Law, First Report, 7 March 2014, 1.

[3] In her comprehensive study Joanna Kulesza, *Due Diligence in International Law* (Leiden: Brill 2016) does not discuss WTO law or other trade regimes.

Markus Krajewski, *Due Diligence in International Trade Law* In: *Due Diligence in the International Legal Order.* Edited by: Heike Krieger, Anne Peters, and Leonhard Kreuzer, Oxford University Press (2020).
DOI: 10.1093/oso/9780198869900.003.0019.

measures which could be harmful to other countries, to take the effects of measures on other countries' economies into account, and to address the activities of private parties which may have such negative effects on other countries. This part of the chapter also uses categorisations of the different due diligence elements in international trade law which would allow comparisons with due diligence in other fields of international law. The second objective of the chapter is to discuss due diligence elements applicable to the negotiation and implementation of trade agreements, especially the requirements of human rights and sustainable development impact assessments. The chapter will first establish the terminological and conceptual basis for addressing due diligence in international trade law even though the concept has not played a major role in the field.

2. General Reflections on Trade (Law) and Due Diligence

2.1 Terminology and Conceptualisation of Due Diligence in International Trade Law

The term 'due diligence' is not explicitly mentioned in any of the multilateral trade agreements administered by the World Trade Organization (WTO). It is safe to assume that 'due diligence' is equally not a term of art in bilateral and regional free trade agreements (FTAs). Due diligence does also not feature prominently in WTO jurisprudence. The Appellate Body only used it once to describe the contents of WTO obligations, i.e., Article 6.2 of the Agreement on Textiles and Clothing (ATC)[4] without going into a detailed analysis or linking the concept to international law in general.[5] Textual references to the notion of 'due diligence' in WTO jurisprudence and other WTO documents usually occur in the context of describing domestic legislation, often in the area of financial regulations[6] or with reference to the process of risk assessment of businesses in the context of private commercial transactions of investment decisions.[7]

In light of this finding, the chapter needs to adopt a working definition of 'due diligence' to assess if, and to which extent, international trade law contains elements of due diligence. The traditional understanding of due diligence in international law is that states must take other states' interests diligently into account and must use best efforts to prevent or minimise harm to the interests of other

[4] See below section 3.1.2.

[5] WTO, *US-Transitional Safeguard Measure on Combed Cotton Yarn from Pakistan*, Report of the Appellate Body of 8 October 2001, WT/DS192/AB/R, paras 76–79.

[6] See, e.g., WTO, *Argentina—Measures Relating to Trade in Goods and Services*, Report of the Appellate Body of 14 April 2016, WT/DS453/AB/R, para. 5.21.

[7] See, e.g., WTO, *EC and Certain Member States—Measures Affecting Trade in Large Civil Aircraft—Recourse to article 21.5 of the DSU*, Report of the Panel of 22 September 2016, WT/DS316/RW, paras 6.640, 6.643, 6.647, 6.649, 6.651.

states arising from activities conducted on the former state's territory.[8] This includes interests of other states with respect to the protection of their citizens and corporations. Hence, the chapter will discuss which aspects and elements of international trade law establish such obligations. As these due diligence requirements can be found inside the trade agreements themselves, they are referred to as the 'regime-internal due diligence dimension of international trade law'.

This regime-internal due diligence dimension of international trade law can be distinguished from a second discourse which also uses the notion of due diligence in the context of trade law. This discourse relates to the conclusion and implementation of trade agreements. It is argued that states are subject to due diligence obligations based on human rights or sustainable development principles requiring them to assess the impact of trade agreements on human rights or sustainable development. These due diligence obligations would therefore be based on normative principles established outside the international trade regime and contain requirements to take the effects of trade agreements on other international regimes into account when negotiating, concluding, and implementing an international agreement. Because these obligations are not established within, but outside of the trade regime, they are called 'regime-external' due diligence dimension of international trade law.

2.2 Exploring the (Missing) Link Between International Trade and Due Diligence

The relative absence of international trade from the recent debate(s) on due diligence in international law can be explained if one realises that two key elements which closely link international trade to the general concept of due diligence are not regulated by international trade law. First, transnational commercial activities inevitably affect other countries. Goods (and in the case of trade in services also people) cross the border and enter the territory of another state. They enter the domestic market and may have an immediate effect on the sale of domestic goods. However, they may also have negative effects on human health or consumer safety. Furthermore, trade may have effects on employment opportunities if domestic industries lose against their foreign competitors. In short: while trade can create tremendous benefits, it may also have direct negative effects on the importing country. This raises the question whether the exporting state has or should have a due diligence obligation to consider these negative effects and possibly react to them by prohibiting or reducing the export of those goods or services which cause

[8] Anne Peters/Heike Krieger/Leonhard Kreuzer, 'Due Diligence in the International Legal Order: Dissecting the Leitmotif of Current Accountability Debates', chapter 1 of this book, section 2; see also ILA, Study Group on Due Diligence in International Law, First Report 2014 (n. 2), 5–6.

such negative effects. This dimension of due diligence is especially prominent in international environmental law, the law of transboundary watercourses, and the law of the sea.[9] These areas of international law contain general obligations which require states to consider the negative effects of activities on their territories on territories of other states.

However, international trade law does not take such an approach. Unlike the Basel Convention on the Control of Transboundary Movements of Hazardous Wastes and their Disposal of 1989 which requires states under certain circumstances to prohibit the exportation of dangerous goods, international trade law puts the obligation to protect citizens against dangerous goods or other negative effects of trade on the importing state. The importing state may impose import bans or other restrictions based, e.g., on Article XX GATT which allows a deviation from the general GATT obligations inter alia if measures are necessary to protect human life or health. Hence, the general due obligation of taking another country's interests into account does not feature prominently in the main principles of trade law. Instead trade law permits the affected country, i.e., the importing country to address potential negative effects of trade through unilateral measures, but it does not require the exporting country to do so.

The second element of trade as an activity which seems to be linked to due diligence is the fact that trade is predominantly an activity which is carried out by private commercial actors. Due diligence requires states to address the effects of private behaviour or individuals on other states. For example, this element of due diligence can be found as an obligation of secondary rules in international human rights law.[10] Again, even though the key activity in international trade is an activity of private actors, international trade law generally does not address their behaviour.[11] International trade law typically applies to specific measures of states,[12] but it does not regulate private activities or address the effects of the behaviour of private entities.

Consequently, many of the controversies which have been discussed in the broader due diligence context[13] do not seem to be relevant with regard to trade law. As mentioned above, in light of the clear scope of application of international

[9] See Jorge E. Viñuales, 'Due Diligence in International Environmental Law', chapter 7 of this book, section 3.2.1; Malgosia Fitzmaurice, 'Due Diligence in the Use of International Watercourses', chapter 8 of this book, sections 2.1, 2.2, and 3; Irini Papanicolopulu 'Due Diligence in the Law of the Sea', chapter 9 of this book, sections 2.2 and 2.3.

[10] See Björnstjern Baade, 'Due Diligence and the Duty to Protect Human Rights', chapter 6 of this book, section 2.

[11] For an exception see below section 4.3.

[12] See most prominently General Agreement on Trade in Services, 15 April 1994, Marrakesh Agreement Establishing the World Trade Organization, Annex 1B, 1869 UNTS 183, 33 I.L.M. 1167, art. I (1): 'This Agreement applies to *measures by Members* affecting trade in services' (emphasis added). The same holds true for other agreements.

[13] See Radha Ivory, 'From Content to the Construction of Risk: Due Diligence Debates in International Anti-corruption and Money Laundering Law', chapter 17 of this book, section 2.

trade agreements, the responsibility of states for private actors' behaviour is usually not an issue in international trade law. Along the same lines, the question of attribution of the behaviour of private actors to states is also not relevant in trade law. More generally, international trade does not display a general principle of care. And finally, international commercial transactions do not produce any general risks which need to be addressed by the exporting state.

To summarise, international trade law does not display due diligence requirements as general principles which would then need to be translated into concrete norms. Instead, international trade law is an area of public international law which contains so many concrete rules that it is normally not necessary to rely on general principles. However, the specific obligations of international trade law can be seen as the concretisation of various general principles and the principle of due diligence could be one of them.

2.3 Distinguishing Obligations of Conduct and Obligations of Results: Measure-based versus Effects-based Rules in International Trade Law

As pointed out elsewhere in this book, Roberto Ago, the first Special Rapporteur on state responsibility of the International Law Commission introduced a distinction between obligations of conduct and obligations of results.[14] Even though this distinction was not included in the final Draft Articles on State Responsibility, it can still be considered a useful concept when discussing due diligence. It might therefore be appropriate to assess if the distinction between measure-based vs. effects-based rules exists in international trade law or if this distinction is at least a helpful categorisation in analysing the contents of international trade law from the perspective of due diligence.

The starting point of this analysis would be the question if the determination of a violation of WTO law is based on a particular measure itself or (also) on the measure's effects on trade. Even though international trade relations have significant effects on the economies of countries, WTO rules generally do not address these effects, but focus on concrete measures of states usually regardless of their effects on actual trade flows.[15] This is the case even though dispute settlement proceedings in the WTO require that the challenged measure must generally nullify or impair benefits accruing from the agreements as per Article XXIII GATT.[16]

[14] Helmut Aust/Prisca Feihle, 'Due Diligence in the History of the Codification of the Law of State Responsibility', chapter 3 of this book, section 2.2.

[15] Jelena Bäumler, 'Implementing the No Harm Principle in International Economic Law: A Comparison Between Measure-Based Rules and Effect-Based Rules', *Journal of International Economic Law* 20 (2017), 807–828, at 811.

[16] Ibid., 814.

However, since Article 3.8 of the WTO's Dispute Settlement Understanding (DSU) states that the infringement of any WTO obligation leads to prima facie consideration of nullification and impairment, the focus in WTO dispute settlement proceedings is usually on the legality of a particular measure and not on its effect.

Yet, the effects of a measure on trade become relevant if Members raise a so-called non-violation complaint which does not require that there is an actual breach of a WTO obligation. Similarly, the effects are relevant in the case of actionable subsidies according to Article 5 of the Agreement on Subsidies and Countervailing Measures (SCM).[17] In these cases, the respective state measures are not considered a violation of WTO law. Nevertheless, their negative effects on the economy of another WTO Member allows this Member to take certain actions in response. However, these effects-based rules do not amount to due diligence obligations, because the effects are relevant for the determination of the legality of particular measures, but not as a stand-alone obligation under WTO law.

3. Regime-internal Dimension: Categorising Due Diligence Obligations in WTO Law

Based on the above conceptual understanding, this section will focus on analysing the scope and contents of due diligence obligations in international trade law. Towards this end, different types of categorisation of WTO rules can be analysed allowing an assessment whether and to which extent due diligence obligations exist in international trade law.

3.1 Procedural Requirements

A first group of WTO requirements which could be analysed as possible exemplifications are procedural requirements. These include consultation and notification requirements, obligations to investigate, explain, and justify, or obligations to negotiate.

3.1.1 Consultation and Notification Requirements

Consultation and notification requirements could be seen as an element of due diligence because they provide an opportunity for Members to take the interests of other Members into account. Many WTO agreements require Members to consult with each other—often upon request by other Members. The most important requirement to consult is of course contained in the dispute settlement system as

[17] Ibid., 816–819.

per Article 4 of the Dispute Settlement Understanding. However, the function of this consultation requirement is not primarily aimed at considering the interests of another Member, but at finding solutions to a dispute before formally engaging a WTO dispute settlement organ.

Consultation requirements can also often be found in connection with provisions of an agreement allowing special trade restrictions or temporary measures, especially in the area of trade remedies. For example, Article 12.3. of the Agreement on Safeguards holds: 'A Member proposing to apply or extend a safeguard measure shall provide adequate opportunity for prior consultations with those Members having a substantial interest as exporters of the product concerned, (…)'. In *Korea—Dairy* the Panel stated that a WTO Member must conduct the consultations in 'good faith' and 'for the purpose of informing interested Members of its investigation, its conclusion and its proposed actions'.[18]

In a similar manner, Article 12 (1) b) of the Agreement on Agriculture (AoA) concerning the institution of new export prohibitions or restrictions on foodstuffs requires that a WTO Member 'shall consult, upon request, with any other Member having a substantial interest as an importer with respect to any matter related to the measure in question. The Member instituting such export prohibition or restriction shall provide, upon request, such a Member with necessary information'.

These consultation requirements serve the purpose of allowing a Member which could be negatively affected by a trade measure to either present arguments or evidence which could lead to a change of the imposing Members' policy or to be prepared and informed if and when such measures are imposed. However, the consultations do not require the Member imposing trade measures to take the substantial interests of the affected Member into account and possibly refrain from such measures because of these effects. WTO law only contains consultation requirements without any further obligations of the Member imposing trade restrictions. Therefore, such consultation requirements cannot be seen as an articulation of a due diligence principle, because the imposing Member state is not required to take the interests of the other Member actually into account when implementing the trade restrictions.

The same can be said concerning notification requirements to the competent WTO committees before imposing any special restrictions such as Article 12.1 of the Agreement on Safeguards which requires Members to notify the Committee on Safeguards of the steps taken towards the imposition of safeguard measures. Such notification requirements are usually not directed at other, affected WTO Members, but at the competent WTO body. While the notification to a WTO Committee gives other WTO Members the opportunity to be informed about such measures, it does not amount to due diligence vis-à-vis other Members.

[18] WTO, *Korea–Definitive Safeguard Measure on Imports of Certain Dairy Products*, Report of the Panel of 21 June 1999, WT/DS98/R, paras 7.152, 7.153.

3.1.2 Obligations of Investigation and Examination

The application of trade remedies such as anti-dumping and countervailing duties in WTO law generally requires an objective assessment by the competent domestic authority of the potential threat or injury that dumping or subsidies may have on the domestic industry of the state imposing trade remedies. This usually requires an impartial analysis of all the facts available and the opportunity for all affected stakeholders to present their views (see, e.g., Articles 3 and 5 of the Agreement on Implementation of Article VI of the General Agreement on Tariffs and Trade 1994—i.e., the Antidumping Agreement).

In *US—Hot-Rolled Steel*, the Appellate Body determined that an objective examination:

> requires that the domestic industry, and the effects of dumped imports, be investigated in an unbiased manner, without favouring the interests of any interested party, or group of interested parties, in the investigation. The duty of the investigating authorities to conduct an 'objective examination' recognises that the determination will be influenced by the objectivity, or any lack thereof, of the investigative process.[19]

More generally, an objective assessment 'includes an obligation to act in "good faith", respecting fundamental fairness'.[20]

In *US—Cotton Yarn*, the Appellate Body labelled a comparable obligation which required the assessment of a serious threat or injury to the domestic textiles industry under the now terminated Agreement on Textiles and Clothing explicitly as a 'due diligence' requirement.[21] Indeed, obligations to objectively investigate and examine are obligations of conduct as they do not require a particular result, but fair procedures. The required conduct involves elements of due diligence to the extent that interests of other parties need to be considered in an objective and impartial manner.

However, it should be noted that the due diligence in the context of trade remedies is not aimed at the interests of another WTO Member, but to the affected exporting and importing industries. For example, Article 3.4 of the Antidumping Agreement requires that '[t] he examination of the impact of the dumped imports on the domestic industry concerned shall include an evaluation of all relevant economic factors and indices having a bearing on the state of the industry (…)'. Indirectly though, the obligation to take the interests of the affected industries into

[19] WTO, *US —Anti-Dumping Measures on Certain Hot-Rolled Steel Products from Japan*, Report of the Appellate Body of 24 July 2001, WT/DS184/AB/R, para. 193.

[20] WTO, *EC—Measures Concerning Meat and Meat Products (Hormones)*, Report of the Appellate Body of 16 January 1998, WT/DS26/AB/R, WT/DS48/AB/R, para. 133.

[21] WTO, *US—Transitional Safeguard Measure on Combed Cotton Yarn from Pakistan*, Report of the Appellate Body of 8 October 2001, WT/DS192/AB/R, paras 76, 78.

account also benefits the exporting state which is the target of the trade remedies in question. Obligations to conduct anti-dumping and other trade remedies enquiry procedures in an objective and impartial manner can therefore be seen as a concretisation of the general due diligence standard in international law. As such it would belong to the category of conduct-based requirements, in particular procedural obligations to conduct investigations in an objective manner. This group of obligations is also closely connected to the obligations to directly consider the effects of a measure on another country.[22]

3.1.3 Obligations to Negotiate in Good Faith

The international trade system is shaped to a large extent by negotiations to further develop trade agreements aimed at trade liberalisation (see Article XXVIII bis GATT and XIX GATS) or to find solutions in the context of dispute settlement (Art. 4 DSU). These negotiations are largely of a voluntary nature and Members can chose to engage in such negotiations or stay away from them.

However, in *US—Shrimp*, the Appellate Body held that Article XX GATT may lead to an obligation to conduct negotiations in good faith. Article XX GATT provides for general exceptions or justifications of measures which would otherwise be inconsistent with the GATT. Amongst others, the introductory clause of Article XX GATT (the so-called 'chapeau') requires WTO Members to not apply the respective trade restrictions 'in a manner which would constitute a means of arbitrary or unjustifiable discrimination between countries where the same conditions prevail, or a disguised restriction on international trade', in order to benefit from the justification of Article XX GATT. The Appellate Body understood this part of Article XX GATT as an expression of the principle of good faith.[23] As the US negotiated exceptions from its trade restrictions with some, but not all affected countries, the Appellate Body saw this as a violation of the principle of good faith and considered the effect of this behaviour to be plainly discriminatory and unjustifiable.[24] The Appellate Body expected the US to make good faith efforts to reach international agreements that are comparable from one forum of negotiations to the other.[25]

The obligation to negotiate in a non-discriminatory manner to ensure a fair application of trade measures can be seen as an expression of the general principle to give due consideration to the interests of the other states and provide them with the opportunity to articulate their concerns and perspectives in such negotiations.

[22] See below section 3.2.

[23] WTO, *US—Import Prohibition of Certain Shrimp and Shrimp Products*, Report of the Appellate Body of 12 October 1998, WT/DS58/AB/R, para. 158.

[24] Ibid., para. 172.

[25] WTO, *US—Import Prohibition of Certain Shrimp and Shrimp Products—Recourse to Article 21.5 of the DSU by Malaysia*, Report of the Appellate Body of 22 October 2001, WT/DS58/AB/RW, para. 122.

As such the obligation to conduct negotiations in good faith can also be seen as an element of due diligence.

However, in a later part of the dispute the Appellate Body made it clear that Article XX GATT did not oblige WTO Members to actually conclude an agreement based on the negotiations. The Appellate Body held that

> requiring that a multilateral agreement be concluded by the United States in order to avoid 'arbitrary or unjustifiable discrimination' in applying its measure would (…) not be reasonable. For a variety of reasons, it may be possible to conclude an agreement with one group of countries but not another. The conclusion of a multilateral agreement requires the cooperation and commitment of many countries. In our view, the United States cannot be held to have engaged in 'arbitrary or unjustifiable discrimination' under Article XX solely because one international negotiation resulted in an agreement while another did not.[26]

The obligation to engage in non-discriminatory negotiations in good faith amounts to an obligation of conduct, as no concrete result is required. Hence, the obligation to negotiate in good faith on the basis of Article XX GATT contains elements of due diligence. Article XX GATT applies to restrictive measures which typically have negative effects on other states. These effects are exacerbated if the trade measures are applied in a discriminatory manner. Conducting negotiations in good faith are an appropriate measure to mitigate these effects by giving the affected countries an opportunity to articulate their interests. In fact, considering the effects of trade measures on other countries and their economies is not only the result of conduct-based obligations to negotiate in good faith but can also be found in other WTO provisions as will be shown in the next section.

3.2 Consideration of Effects on Other Countries

International trade law contains a number of obligations which directly require states to take the effects of their measures on the economies or other interests of other countries into account. Typically, these obligations can be found in the context of trade remedies and special protective measures.

For example, Article XII:2(a) GATT on trade restrictions aimed at safeguarding the balance of payments requires for the institution of import restrictions inter alia:

> Due regard shall be paid in either case to any special factors which may be affecting the reserves of such contracting party or its need for reserves, including,

[26] Ibid., para. 123.

where special external credits or other resources are available to it, the need to provide for the appropriate use of such credits or resources.

Similarly, Article 8 of the Agreement on Safeguard Measures (ASM) which addresses the level of concessions of safeguard measures holds that a member proposing a safeguard measure 'shall endeavour to maintain a substantially equivalent level of concessions and other obligations to that existing under GATT 1994 between it and the exporting Members which would be affected by such a measure'. These provisions oblige a WTO member seeking to apply trade restrictions as temporary measures either to address balance-of-payments difficulties or to react to a sudden increase of imports which lead to a serious injury or a threat thereof to consider the effects of such measures on other WTO members. These obligations may then be complemented with obligations to consult or to engage in negotiations.[27] In the case of the ASM, Article 8 is directly linked to the requirement of Article 12 ASM which requires good faith consultations. Again, these provisions contain obligations of conduct and not of result.

Another example would be Article 12 (1) (a) Agreement on Agriculture which holds that 'the Member instituting the export prohibition or restriction shall give due consideration to the effects of such prohibition or restriction on importing Members' food security'. This provision specifies which interests of the respective Member should be taken into account. It can be understood as a concretisation of the general principle of special and differential treatment of developing countries.

3.3 Requirements to Consider Private Party Behaviour

While the above obligations all concerned government measures, international trade law also contains requirements to take the behaviour or activities of private parties into account. However, the exact scope and extent of such obligations is not entirely clear. For example, in *Argentina-Hides and Leather*, the EU challenged certain Argentinian measures which amounted to de facto export restrictions administered by a body which included industry representatives. The question at hand was whether despite participation of the representatives of the industry the measure remained a government measure. The Panel held that it does not follow from Article XI:1 GATT that 'Members are under an obligation to exclude any possibility that governmental measures may enable private parties, directly or indirectly, to restrict trade, where those measures themselves are not trade restrictive.'[28] In this context, the Panel also noted that 'Article XI:1 does not incorporate an

[27] See, e.g., Agreement on Safeguard Measures, 15 April 1994, 1869 UNTS 154, art. 12.3.

[28] WTO, *Argentina—Measures Affecting the Export of Bovine Hides and the Import of Finished Leather*—Report of the Panel of 19 December 2000, WT/DS155/R, para. 11.19.

obligation to exercise "due diligence" in the introduction and maintenance of governmental measures beyond the need to ensure the conformity with Article XI:1 of those measures taken alone.'[29] This comment—although made in a footnote—is noteworthy for two reasons: first, it is one of the rare instances in which a WTO dispute settlement organ literally referred to the term 'due diligence'. Second, the statement clearly indicates that the WTO legal system can contain due diligence obligations.

A different example concerns private sanitary and phytosanitary standards. Many food safety standards are set by private industry associations or other non-governmental organisations. Even though these standards are formally not subject to the scrutiny of the Agreement on Sanitary and Phytosanitary Measures (SPS) they may have negative effects on trade.[30] Hence, Article 13 SPS requires that 'Members shall take such reasonable measures as may be available to them to ensure that non-governmental entities within their territories, as well as regional bodies in which relevant entities within their territories are members, comply with the relevant provisions of this Agreement.'

This provision is one of the clearest recognitions in international trade law that a state may bear some responsibility with regards to the behaviour of private parties. Article 13 SPS does not establish full state responsibility to private behaviour, but it indicates that the effects of such behaviour are not outside the scope of international trade law. The provision refers to reasonable measures to ensure that non-governmental organisations comply with the provisions of the SPS. Like the other provisions of international trade law discussed in this section, Article 13 SPS contains an obligation of conduct and does not require a particular result. However, a state which completely ignores the relevant behaviour of private entities would violate the obligation of Article 13 SPS. It can therefore also be seen as an exemplification of due diligence standard to prevent breaches of other states' legal rights by private parties operating in their territory in international trade law.[31]

WTO Members can meet those due diligence obligations through a number of measures including monitoring and evaluating the consistency of private standards with the principles of the SPS Agreement as well as evaluating any adverse effects of private standards on other countries. Furthermore, WTO Members could engage in dialogues with private entities aiming at persuading them to comply with the principles of SPS Agreement.[32] Again, a certain result cannot be guaranteed. Article 13 SPS therefore contains a due diligence standard of a procedural type.

[29] Ibid., para. 11.19, footnote 339.

[30] Moshe Hirsch, 'Private Food Safety Standards, Obligations of Governments, and Unresolved Questions in Contemporary WTO Law', *Hebrew University of Jerusalem Legal Studies Research Paper Series No. 17-18*, 22 March 2017, available at: https://ssrn.com/abstract=2938501 (accessed 24 February 2019).

[31] Ibid., 7.

[32] Ibid., 10.

4. Regime-external Dimension: Sustainability and Human Rights Impact Assessments of Trade Agreements as an Instrument of Due Diligence

While the analyses in the previous section addressed WTO obligations which require states to exercise due diligence vis-à-vis its domestic policies on the basis of trade law principles, this section addresses due diligence elements which apply to the drafting and implementation of trade agreements. As this concerns the 'lawmaking' of international trade law and not the contents of trade law obligations, this dimension of due diligence is considered 'regime-external'.

The most important and well-known principles in this sense are assessments of the impact of trade agreements on other international law principles and provisions, in particular in the fields of human rights or sustainable development. Sustainability and human rights impact assessments of trade agreements analyse the potential impact of an agreement on the human rights situation in the contracting parties. Questions such as whether a trade agreement should be concluded between two or more countries or whether particular contents should or should not be part of the agreement are at the centre of the impact assessments of trade agreements.

4.1 Concept and Normative Basis

The basis of sustainability and human rights impact assessments of trade agreements are principles and provisions in other international law regimes such as human rights or sustainable development. For example, human rights treaty bodies and special procedures of the Human Rights Council have consistently called upon states to conduct human rights impact assessments of trade and investment agreements.[33] In its 2016 Concluding observations on Canada the Committee on Economic, Social and Cultural Rights noted the importance of human rights impact assessments. It expressed its concern 'about the lack of impact assessments explicitly taking into account human rights prior to the negotiation of international trade and investments agreements'.[34] Similarly, the Working Group on the issue of human rights and transnational corporations and other business enterprises recommended in its 2017 report that '[s]tates should conduct an inclusive and transparent human rights impact assessment before concluding trade-investment agreements and insert explicit substantive human rights provisions in those

[33] James Harrison/Alessa Goller, 'Trade and Human Rights: What Does 'Impact Assessment' Have to Offer?', *Human Rights Law Review* 8 (2008), 587–615, at 589.

[34] United Nations, Committee on Economic, Social and Cultural Rights, Concluding observations on the sixth periodic report of Canada, E/C.12/CAN/CO/6, 6 March 2016, para. 15.

agreements to preserve adequate policy space to discharge their human rights obligations.'[35] Already in 2011, the Special Rapporteur on the Right to Food, Olivier De Schutter, proposed a set of guiding principles on human rights impact assessments of trade and investment agreements.[36]

The importance of assessing the impact of trade agreements on human rights before concluding a trade agreement is also recognised in EU law and practice. In July 2015, the European Commission adopted its own guidelines for human rights impact assessments of trade negotiations and trade agreements.[37] In 2015, the EU's General Court rendered a judgment which can be understood as establishing the obligation to conduct human rights impact assessments based on binding EU law. The court held that the Council of Ministers was required to examine 'carefully and impartially, all the relevant facts in order to ensure that the production of goods for export is not conducted to the detriment of the population of the territory concerned, or entails infringements of fundamental rights'[38] before concluding an additional protocol in the context of the EU-Morocco Free Trade Agreement on liberalisation of certain agricultural and fisheries products which also applied to Western Sahara.[39]

4.2 Sustainability and Human Rights Impact Assessments and the Life Cycle of a Trade Agreement

Sustainability and human rights impact assessments can be conducted at different moments in time: first, the impact of a trade agreement on human rights can be assessed before the negotiations start. A human rights impact assessment at such an early stage would address general questions and could assess whether negotiations about a trade agreement with the partner country in question should be pursued at all or whether certain elements of trade agreements (services, investment, intellectual property rights) should be kept out of the negotiations from the very beginning. While a human rights impact assessment before the formal beginning of

[35] United Nations, General Assembly, Report of the Working Group on the issue of human rights and transnational corporations and other business enterprises, A/72/162, 18 July 2017, para. 77.

[36] United Nations, Human Rights Council, Report of the Special Rapporteur on the Right to Food, Olivier de Schutter, Addendum—Guiding Principles on Human Rights Impact Assessments of Trade and Investment Agreements, A/HRC/19/59/Add.5, 19 December 2011.

[37] European Commission, Guidelines on the analysis of human rights impacts in impact assessments for trade-related policy initiatives, available at: http://trade.ec.europa.eu/doclib/docs/2015/july/tradoc_153591.pdf (accessed 24 February 2019); the Guidelines were adopted on 2 July 2015, see European Commission, New Guidelines on the analysis of human rights impacts in impact assessments, available at http://trade.ec.europa.eu/doclib/press/index.cfm?id=1344 (accessed 24 February 2019).

[38] General Court, Case T-512/12, *Front Polisario v. Council*, Judgment of 10 December 2015, ECLI:EU:T:2015:953, para. 228.

[39] The decision was overturned by the Court of Justice on 21 December 2016 on procedural grounds without addressing the substantive human rights issues relied upon by the General Court, see ECJ, Case C-104/16 P, *Council v Front Polisario*, Judgment of 21 December 2016, ECLI:EU:C:2016:973.

negotiations could influence the agenda at an early stage, it might be difficult to provide a detailed assessment as the concrete impact of the trade agreement on human rights can only be analysed if the details are known.

This is why a sustainability and human rights impact assessment could also be conducted after the end of the negotiations and before the agreement is signed and ratified. This would allow a much more comprehensive analysis. However, it might be difficult for the human rights impact assessment to have a real impact on the actual contents of the agreement. At such a late stage in the process, there is usually high pressure on all organs and institutions involved not to suggest that the agreement cannot be signed.

The impact of the trade agreement on human rights could also be assessed during the negotiations of certain elements and aspects of the agreement have already been agreed upon, but a final outcome has not yet been reached. The outcome of the human rights impact assessment could therefore still influence the negotiations. However, often the most controversial parts of an agreement are negotiated at the end and even if there seems to be consensus on certain parts of a trade agreement, this consensus may only be provisional. Lastly, it is important to conduct regular human rights impact assessments also after the conclusion of the agreement and during its operation (ex post human rights impact assessment).[40] In this context, the trade agreements need elements and clauses which would allow a revision of termination of the agreement should it have negative effects on human rights.

While there is no single method for human rights impact assessment,[41] the procedure should be guided by a human rights-based approach. According to the 2011 Guidelines of the Special Rapporteur on the Right to Food, the credibility and effectiveness of human rights impact assessments depends on the fulfilment of the following minimum conditions: independence, transparency, inclusive participation, expertise, funding, and status.[42] It should also be kept in mind that human rights impact assessments cannot be based on simple quantitative analyses. Instead a whole range of factors and potential developments need to be taken into account some of which could be quantified through the use of numerical benchmarks. However, other effects of a trade agreement on human rights can only be described and analysed in a qualitative way. In any case, oversimplifications should be

[40] UN Guiding Principles on Human Rights Impact Assessments of Trade and Investment Agreements, 2011 (n. 36), Section 3.3. See also Jadranka Petrovic, 'Intersecting Trade, Politics and Human Rights: The Negotiation Phase of the Australia-China Free Trade Agreement', *Journal of World Trade* 51 (2017), 67–104, and Malayna Raftopoulos, 'REDD+ and Human Rights— Addressing the Urgent Need for a Full Community-based Human Rights Impact Assessment', *International Journal of Human Rights* 4 (2016), 509–530.

[41] Harrison/Goller, 'Trade and Human Rights' 2008 (n. 33), 593.

[42] UN Guiding Principles on Human Rights Impact Assessments of Trade and Investment Agreements, 2011 (n. 36), Section 4.

avoided.[43] In the end, a human rights impact assessment might not yield in a clear recommendation whether to conclude or not to conclude an agreement but can suggest areas of conflict between the agreement and the protection of human rights or sustainable development which could be mitigated through careful drafting of the agreement.

4.3 Sustainability and Human Rights Impact Assessments as an Element of Due Diligence in Making and Implementing International Agreements

The ultimate aim of sustainability and human rights impact assessments of trade agreements is to avoid or minimise actual or potential conflicts between international trade law and other international law regimes. These impact assessments therefore aim at avoiding inter-regime conflicts and can be seen as an element of prevention and precaution. Sustainability and human rights impact assessments do not require certain results or outcomes. Instead they require states to take their obligations under other international legal regimes into account when negotiating and implementing trade agreements. Hence, sustainability and human rights impact assessments are an expression of a general due diligence standard requiring states to take certain interests and legal principles into account and giving them due consideration without determining the ultimate outcome of such an exercise. Sustainability and human rights impact assessments can therefore also be understood as an exemplification of a due diligence principle in international trade law.

5. Conclusion

Based on the analysis in this chapter it seems possible to offer a few preliminary observations on due diligence and international trade law. First, it is clear that due diligence is not a general principle or overarching rule of international trade law which would be applicable to all obligations. This may be partly due to the fact that general principles do not play such an important role in applying trade law as in other areas of international law, because international trade law transposes its underlying general principles usually into concrete rules. Reference to the principle and its roots in general international law do not seem to be necessary to understand

[43] For example, the graphical description of the impact of the negotiations on a plurilateral Agreement on Trade in Services on human rights used in the Sustainability Impact Assessment commissioned by the European Union is not convincing as it based on the perception of NGOs and stakeholders. See European Commission, Trade Sustainability Impact Assessment in support of negotiations on a plurilateral Trade in Services Agreement, 2017, available at: www.trade-sia.com/tisa/wp-content/uploads/sites/7/2014/02/TiSA-Final-Report.pdf, 108 (accessed 24 February 2019).

and interpret the relevant rules in international trade law. Also, with respect to those international trade rules which address private behaviour, due diligence is not a necessary concept of understanding and applying those rules. In short, the usefulness of the concept of due diligence to interpret and analyse international trade law is limited due to the relatively concrete nature of trade law obligations.

Nevertheless, secondly, international trade law obligations can be understood as concretisations of general due diligence principles. Therefore, studying the contents and application of certain international trade law rules might be helpful to better understand the idea of due diligence in general international law.

Third, due diligence with respect to international trade law reaches beyond the interpretation and application of international trade law and is linked to the processes of law-making. Due diligence can be seen as one of the key concepts behind human rights and sustainable development impact assessments. Assessing the impact of future and existing trade agreements on other areas of international law such as human rights law, labour standards, or multilateral environmental agreements is based on the idea of exercising due diligence when drafting and implementing specific international treaty obligations. In this regard, due diligence can be seen as a tool to avoid inter-regime conflicts. This understanding of due diligence is not limited to international trade law. As a matter of fact, assessing the impact of an international agreement on other areas of international law could be seen as one element of a general law of international due diligence.

20

Due Diligence in World Bank Project Financing

Diane A. Desierto[*]

1. Introduction

Due diligence practices and methods used in the context of World Bank project financing constitute a significant application of due diligence as an evolving international law norm. As an intergovernmental organisation mandated to advance economic growth, poverty reduction, and social development through projects undertaken in its member countries,[1] the World Bank Group and its International Finance Corporation (IFC) are described as significant 'law-making and law-governed institutions'[2] in the international economic system. These institutions' particular usages of due diligence bear scrutiny not only to map the contours of due diligence as an international law norm, but to evaluate how the World Bank has reached its authoritative decisions as to what it deems to be relevant risks affecting the Bank's sovereign and private development projects that purposely require due diligence. I submit that the due diligence practices and methods for the assessment of environmental and social risks attendant to World Bank and IFC projects reflect the continuing legal position of these international financial institutions that they create their own distinct *lex specialis*, quite problematically distancing themselves from expressly admitting the binding nature of international human rights law[3] and especially due diligence requirements under business and human rights.[4] As

* With thanks for research support from the Klau Center for Civil and Human Rights and the Kellogg Institute of International Studies at the Keough School of Global Affairs, University of Notre Dame.

[1] See Antje Vetterlein, 'Economic Growth, Poverty Reduction, and the Role of Social Policies: The Evolution of the World Bank's Social Development Approach', *Global Governance* 13 (2007), 513–533, at 516–518.

[2] Daniel Bradlow/Andria Naudé-Fourie, 'The Operational Policies of the World Bank and the International Finance Corporation', *International Organizations Law Review* 10 (2013), 3–80, at 3.

[3] United Nations Office of the High Commissioner for Human Rights, '"The World Bank is a Human Rights-free Zone" – UN Expert on Extreme Poverty Expresses Deep Concern', Press Release, 29 September 2015, available at: https://www.ohchr.org/EN/NewsEvents/Pages/DisplayNews.aspx?NewsID=16517&LangID=E (accessed 30 May 2019).

[4] Jonathan Bonnitcha/Robert McCorquodale, 'The Concept of "Due Diligence" in the UN Guiding Principles on Business and Human Rights', *European Journal of International Law* 28 (2017), 899–919, at 901–906.

Diane A. Desierto, *Due Diligence in World Bank Project Financing* In: *Due Diligence in the International Legal Order.*
Edited by: Heike Krieger, Anne Peters, and Leonhard Kreuzer, Oxford University Press (2020).
DOI: 10.1093/oso/9780198869900.003.0020.

I show in this chapter, while there is demonstrably a significant hardening of environmental and social risk identification and corresponding due diligence practices and methods of the World Bank and the IFC in their respective operational policies, these institutions nevertheless still reject the full applicability of international environmental, social, and human rights law standards to Bank projects. The Bank's own track record in its projects, as seen from the corpus of Inspection Panel reports, demonstrate that while the most vulnerable stakeholders of these projects—local communities, indigenous peoples, minorities, among others—might possess some degree of public participation,[5] they ultimately depend on the robustness of the World Bank's environmental and social risk due diligence practices to oversee Bank projects and managing community impacts. As the current body of Inspection Panel decisions itself shows, however, the human rights outcomes remain variably challenging for these most affected stakeholders in a climate of continuing denial of the full applicability of international human rights law to World Bank and IFC due diligence practices.[6] I further show in this chapter that in some instances it appears that the Bank could (or has) taken into consideration a borrowing country's international environmental, social, or human rights law commitments in designing an environmental and social risk assessment for a Bank project, but without explicitly holding the Bank bound by the same treaty or legal norms. Finally, I observe how the World Bank's own nascent Environment and Social Framework (ESF) could serve as a functional and interpretive gateway for operationally intermediating international human rights law in the due diligence practices of the World Bank, by expanding the scope of the sources of a borrowing country's environmental, labour, and social regulatory framework.

2. Project Financing and Its Risks

Preliminarily, it should be recalled that project finance refers to the 'financing of the construction or development of a project where the lenders rely primarily on the expected cash flow generated by the operation of the project for repayment of their loans as well as for the value of the project's assets'.[7] Project finance is distinguished from other modes of financing, 'in which the general assets of a sponsoring company, often owning several projects, are wholly or in part the subject

[5] Laurence Boisson de Chazournes, 'Public Participation in Decision-Making: The World Bank Inspection Panel', *Studies in Transnational Legal Policy* 31 (1999), 84–94, at 89.

[6] See NYU Law School Clinic on International Organizations, 'The World Bank Inspection Panel and International Human Rights Law', 2017, available at: https://www.iilj.org/wp-content/uploads/2017/08/The-World-Bank-Inspection-Panel-FINAL-REPORT.pdf (accessed 30 May 2019).

[7] Harold Moore/Evelyn Giaccio, 'International Project Finance', *North Carolina Journal of International Law and Commercial Regulation* 11 (1987), 597–612, at 597–598.

of claims by the lender in the event of a failure to repay the loan'.[8] The distinction matters, because project finance loans are made on a

> non-recourse or limited recourse basis. Whereas lenders normally assess a loan proposition based on the creditworthiness of the borrower reflected by his asset portfolio and aggregate earning capacity, the lender in a project finance is willing to look primarily to the expected income stream of the project for his repayment. If the project fails or the expected income stream fails to materialize, the liability for the repayment of the loan does not pass to the project sponsors or operators—except to the extent expressly assumed by them.[9]

International project finance could involve a mixed universe of private sector companies as project operators, international development financing institutions (including multilateral development banks (MDBs)), state-owned enterprises, or sovereign lenders among others.[10] Project finance transactions are thus very complex. As one author stated: 'It may take a much longer period of time to structure, negotiate, and document project financing than traditional financing, and the legal fees and related costs associated with project financing can be very high.'[11]

Among the critical transactions in international project finance is the conduct of due diligence by the project lenders. Due diligence, in this context, refers to 'the process of reviewing and analysing the various project participants and contracts for the purpose of determining risks present in a project'.[12] The main purpose of due diligence in international project financing is risk identification. To this aim, it is required to conduct an 'interdisciplinary process of legal, technical, environmental, and financial specialties, designed to detect events that might result in total or partial project failure'.[13] Precisely because the nature of lending in project financing makes repayment dependent on the project's future expected income stream, project lenders must undertake as comprehensive an assessment of foreseeable risks as possible, balancing such risks against the stream of expected returns from project revenues and all other income derived from the multi-year operation of the project:

[8] Sheldon Leader, 'Project Finance and Human Rights', in Juan Bohoslavsky/Jernej Cernic (eds), *Making Sovereign Financing and Human Rights Work* (London: Hart Publishing 2016), 199–212, at 200.

[9] Alexander Loke, 'Risk Management and Credit Support in Project Finance', *Singapore Journal of International and Comparative Law* 2 (1998), 37–75, at 37.

[10] See Edward Yescombe, *Principles of Project Finance* (Oxford: Elsevier Academic Press 2nd ed. 2014), 61–78.

[11] Katharine Baragona, 'Project Finance', *Transnational Lawyer* 18 (2004), 139–158, at 139.

[12] Scott Hoffman, *The Law and Business of International Project Finance* (Cambridge: CUP 2007), 327.

[13] Ibid., 59.

> the lender's responsibility for full investigation and surveillance extends to the whole process of the financing of the project, including the reasonably foreseeable consequences. A lender is therefore under the duty to consider factors such as the likely environmental effects of the project, the consequence of the project for indigenous peoples in affected areas, possible damage to archaeological or culture heritage sites and so forth.[14]

Among the many risks that frequently affect international projects are completion risks (also known as 'development, delay, cost-overrun, or construction risk');[15] operating risks (e.g., facility under-performance or excessive operating and/or maintaining costs);[16] supply risks (the sufficiency of inputs for the project, depending on 'the nature of the project itself');[17] currency risks;[18] as well as political risks (such as war and civil disturbance).[19] Most crucially, environmental and social risks also comprise part of the general risks affecting international projects. Environmental and social risks include:

> a) liability for the discharge of contaminants into the environment; b) liability for non-compliance with environmental, health, and safety laws, and permits; c) uncertainty in environmental permitting; d) changes in laws and enforcement priorities that tend to make environmental requirements more stringent over time; and e) potential exposure to challenges brought against the project by affected populations or the interested non-governmental organizations (NGOs) on their behalf.[20]

For the purposes of this chapter, I focus on due diligence with respect to the assessment of environmental threats and social risks,[21] considering both the risk of transboundary harm and the evolving nature of social and technical regulation,[22] as distinctly evidenced by the practices of the World Bank Group in financing international projects for development,[23] in order to draw a practice-based illustrative

[14] Xiuli Han, 'Crisis Prevention for China as a Sovereign Creditor and the UNCTAD Principles', in Carlos Esposito/Yuefen Li/Juan Pablo Bohoslavsky (eds), *Sovereign Financing and International Law: The UNCTAD Principles on Responsible Sovereign Lending and Borrowing* (Oxford: OUP 2013), 261–286, at 275.

[15] John Dewar/Oliver Irwin, 'Project Risks', in John Dewar (ed.), *International Project Finance: Law and Practice* (Oxford: OUP 2011), 81–112, at 83.

[16] Ibid., 88.

[17] Ibid., 89.

[18] Ibid., 91.

[19] Ibid., 94.

[20] Ibid., 99.

[21] See Pierre-Marie Dupuy/Jorge E. Viñuales, *International Environmental Law* (Cambridge: CUP 2nd ed. 2018), 314–315.

[22] Patricia Birnie/Alan Boyle/Catherine Redgwell, *International Law and the Environment* (Oxford: OUP 2009 3rd ed.), 147–148.

[23] See Diane Desierto, *Public Policy in International Economic Law: The ICESCR in Trade, Finance, and Investment* (Oxford: OUP 2015), 253–280.

nexus with the broader concept of due diligence in international law. To this aim, I examine due diligence in World Bank project financing from two polar ends of the spectrum of its practices. First, I examine conceptual and practice-based trends that have emerged from the World Bank Inspection Panel's scrutiny of failed or defective due diligence processes for environmental threats and social risks in World Bank-financed projects, which, as of writing this, involve 131 cases since 1994.[24] As seen in the next section, the Inspection Panel's investigation reports demonstrate an accretion of evolving internal practice-based understanding of due diligence—one that often readily melds interdisciplinary lenses and approaches to 'due diligence' in the Panel's findings. Second, I then turn to the Bank's codified due diligence policies and the particular turn towards the assessment of environmental and social risks. This, in my view, necessarily crystallised in tandem with the Bank's own record at the Inspection Panel, where the bulk of due diligence problems have arisen from the defects or failures of Bank-financed projects to anticipate, plan for, adjust, or appropriately respond to environmental hazards, the welfare and rights of indigenous peoples, and related social risks of long-term displacement of inhabitants impacted by these projects. I then briefly contrast these approaches with other MDBs that have some environmental and social policies in place,[25] but which neither have the particular institutional template of the Bank's Inspection Panel procedures, nor the same experiences as the Bank as it evolved its cohesive ESF for Bank financing of investment projects. In conclusion, I submit that the World Bank's particular operations-based conception of due diligence in project financing signifies an entrenched institutional understanding of transboundary harm that is demonstrably broad (encompassing environmental, social, labour, economic, cultural, and related human rights risks), all the more so since the Bank determines impacts on multiple stakeholders (and most especially local communities) affected by World Bank-financed projects well beyond the traditional actors in an international project finance transaction.

3. Inspection Panel Review of Due Diligence in World Bank Projects

Established in 1993 by the World Bank, the Inspection Panel provides an accountability dimension to the Bank's project financing practices, since it 'functions as

[24] World Bank Inspection Panel Cases, data accessed, available at: https://inspectionpanel.org/panel-cases (accessed 1 February 2019).

[25] On this aspect see Gunther Handl, 'The Legal Mandate of Multilateral Development Banks as Agents for Change for Sustainable Development', *American Journal of International Law* 92 (October 1998), 642–665; Eisuke Suzuki/Suresh Nanwani, 'Responsibility of International Organizations: The Accountability Mechanisms of Multilateral Development Banks', *Michigan Journal of International Law* 27 (2005), 177–226.

an organ reviewing acts and omissions of the Management of the World Bank as a response to requests from private parties [hereinafter requesters] affected by World Bank projects'.[26] The Inspection Panel is a non-judicial body that is designed to be an independent mechanism, comprised of diverse interdisciplinary professionals on five-year terms, who are never allowed to be employed by the Bank after their terms finish.[27] The precise mandate of the Inspection Panel is to:

> [ensure] that the voices of people who may be adversely affected by Bank-financed projects are heard, and to promote accountability at the Bank (...) The Panel does not investigate unless it receives a formal, written Request for Inspection. The Panel has the power to review Bank-funded projects, and determine whether Bank Management is following the World Bank's operational policies and procedures (...) which were put in place in order to provide social and economic benefits, and to avoid harm to people or to the environment.[28]

Once the Panel has made its findings to the Bank's Board of Executive Directors, Bank Management must prepare a response with recommendations and actions to address the Panel's findings of non-compliance and harm.[29]

The 131 cases brought before the Inspection Panel show evolving interdisciplinary methodologies to determine flaws in the due diligence processes underlying World Bank-financed projects. Not all these requests for inspection proceeded to a full-blown investigation. Several were either not registered or dismissed,[30] or

[26] Kristian Fauchald, 'Hardening the Legal Softness of the World Bank through an Inspection Panel?', *Scandinavian Studies in Law* 58 (2013), 101–128, at 102.

[27] See Daniel Bradlow, 'International Organizations and Private Complaints: The Case of the World Bank Inspection Panel', *Virginia Journal of International Law* 34 (1994), 553–614, at 553–555.

[28] World Bank Inspection Panel, *Filing a Request for Inspection*, available at: https://inspectionpanel.org/how-to-file-complaint (accessed 1 February 2019).

[29] IBRD Resolution No. 93-10 and IDA Resolution No. 93-6, dated 22 September 1993, creating the World Bank Inspection Panel, available at: https://inspectionpanel.org/sites/ip-ms8.extcc.com/files/documents/Resolution1993.pdf, paras 22–27 (accessed 30 May 2019).

[30] See, among others, Inspection Panel, *Ethiopia: Compensation for Expropriation and Extension of IDA Credits to Ethiopia (Not Registered)*, 4 April 1995, available at: https://inspectionpanel.org/panel-cases/compensation-expropriation-and-extension-ida-credits-ethiopia-not-registered (accessed 30 May 2019); *Tanzania: Power VI Project*, Report and Recommendation, 15 August 1995, available at: https://inspectionpanel.org/panel-cases/power-vi-project (accessed 30 May 2019); *Chile: Financing of Hydroelectric Dams in the Bio-Bio River (Not Registered)*, 17 November 1995, available at: https://inspectionpanel.org/panel-cases/financing-hydroelectric-dams-bio-bio-river-not-registered (accessed 30 May 2019); *Bangladesh Jute Sector Adjustment Credit*, 14 March 1997, available at: https://inspectionpanel.org/sites/inspectionpanel.org/files/ip/PanelCases/6-Eligibility%20Report%20%28English%29.pdf (accessed 30 May 2019); *Lesotho/South Africa: Phase 1B of Lesotho Highlands Water Project*, Panel Report and Recommendation, 18 August 1998, available at: https://inspectionpanel.org/sites/inspectionpanel.org/files/ip/PanelCases/12-Eligibility%20Report%20%28English%29.pdf (accessed 30 May 2019); *Argentina: Special Structural Adjustment Loan*, Inspection Panel Report and Recommendation, 16 December 1999, available at: https://inspectionpanel.org/sites/inspectionpanel.org/files/ip/PanelCases/17-Eligibility%20Report%20%28English%29.pdf (accessed 30 May 2019); *Brazil: Land Reform and Poverty Alleviation Pilot Project*, Report and Recommendation on Second Request for Inspection, 17 December 1999, available at: https://inspectionpanel.org/sites/

the Bank Management deemed the request ineligible for further consideration because loan proceeds had already been disbursed.[31] For the most part, however, the Inspection Panel consistently emphasises the importance of expanding its risk assessment to include short- and long-term environmental risks, community displacements and resettlement feasibilities, the unique legal rights of indigenous peoples to natural resources, and the need to *timely* embed these main considerations at the outset of project planning for all Bank-financed projects.

In the first Inspection Panel Report, on a proposed hydroelectric and access road project in Nepal,[32] the Panel investigated issues regarding the Bank's economic analysis of investment operations, environmental assessment, information disclosures, involuntary resettlements, and indigenous peoples. The Panel explicitly found that it was necessary to create a panel of social and environmental experts for the project on: (i) environmental impacts and flooding risks; (ii) the displacement of families because of the project and the need for resettlement plans; and (iii) that indigenous peoples affected by the project should have 'informed participation through public consultations, security over land tenure, and an action program with socially and culturally appropriate components'.[33] Another Inspection Panel Report on natural resources management in one part of the Amazon Basin (Rondônia, Brazil) found increased deforestation, invasions of indigenous and extractive areas, and many legal and operational policy challenges to the long-term sustainability of protected areas for indigenous peoples, and required the Bank to address these challenges.[34] Another report, relating to a bridge project in Jamuna, Bangladesh, found that the project design did not take into account char dwellers (thousands who live on mid-channel islands in the Jamuna river) in the process of planning, designing, and implementing resettlement plans as well as preventive and mitigative environmental measures, and required revisions to the Bank's Erosion and Flood Policy for the project 'to meet [Bank operational] policy requirements' and held that a 'full and informed participation of affected people

inspectionpanel.org/files/ip/PanelCases/18-Eligibility%20Report%20%28English%29.pdf (accessed 30 May 2019).

[31] See among others Inspection Panel, *Management Response to Request for Inspection Panel Review of Itaparica Resettlement and Irrigation Project*, 28 April 1997, available at: https://inspectionpanel.org/sites/inspectionpanel.org/files/ip/PanelCases/9-Management%20Response%20%28English%29.pdf (accessed 30 May 2019).

[32] Inspection Panel, *Report on Request for Inspection, Nepal: Proposed Arun III Hydroelectric Project and Restructuring of the Arun III Access Road Project*, Request No. RQ94/01, 16 December 1994, available at: https://inspectionpanel.org/sites/inspectionpanel.org/files/ip/PanelCases/1-Eligibility%20Report.pdf (accessed 30 May 2019).

[33] Inspection Panel, *Proposed Arun III Hydroelectric Project, Investigation Report*, 21 June 1995, available at: https://inspectionpanel.org/sites/inspectionpanel.org/files/ip/PanelCases/1-Investigation%20Report%20%28English%29.pdf, 32–34 (part 7—Findings) (accessed 30 May 2019).

[34] Inspection Panel, *Report on Progress Review of Implementation of Brazil: Rondônia Natural Resources Management Project*, 25 March 1997, available at: https://inspectionpanel.org/sites/inspectionpanel.org/files/ip/PanelCases/4-Progress%20Report.pdf, 13–14 (accessed 30 May 2019).

would be needed to ensure its success'.[35] In another case, this time involving the Yacyretá Hydroelectric Project in Argentina and Paraguay, the Inspection Panel found that site selection alone 'locked the project into a series of inevitable and irreversible impacts, including flooding over 100,000 hectares and affecting over 50,000 people in two major urban areas'.[36] The Panel also learned that the basic 'imbalance' between the 99.8% completion of the civil and electro-mechanical works for the Project, vis-à-vis less than one third completion of complementary works such as environmental plans and resettlement plans, resulted in the project 'incur[ring] important environmental and social liabilities that are causing frictions which could have been foreseen and avoided'.[37] This problem was further exacerbated because of 'the usual Bank practice'[38] of wholly focusing on financing civil and electro-mechanical works, leaving environmental and resettlement plans to counterpart funding by other project financiers. The same disproportionate emphasis by Bank Management (neglecting funding for environmental and social impacts) was again detected by the Inspection Panel over a power generation project in India, where senior regional management was found to have focused mainly on accelerating loan approvals, while 'not granting the same relevance to Resettlement and Rehabilitation and Environmental Action matters as to other project components'.[39]

The Inspection Panel has also emphasised the importance of timely and meaningful consultations with affected indigenous peoples, *well before* project formulation and implementation. In its report and recommendation over the World Bank financing for the India Ecodevelopment Park (Rajiv Gandhi Nagarahole National Park), the Panel found (and the Bank Management acknowledged) that consultations were not made with indigenous peoples at the appraisal stage for the project, and neither was there an indigenous peoples' development plan prepared at the same time to properly evaluate 'the tension between biodiversity protection objectives and the condition and aspirations of the indigenous people at Rajiv Gandhi National Park'.[40] In another project involving environmental management in Lake Victoria, Kenya, the Inspection Panel emphasised that:

[35] Inspection Panel, *Report and Recommendation to the Executive Directors of the International Development Association on Request for Inspection, Bangladesh: Jamuna Bridge Project,* 26 November 1996, available at: https://inspectionpanel.org/panel-cases/jamuna-new-multipurpose-bridge-project, 18, para. 56 (accessed 30 May 2019).

[36] Inspection Panel, *Review of Problems and Assessment of Action Plans, Argentina and Paraguay: Yacyretá Hydroelectric Project,* available at: https://inspectionpanel.org/sites/inspectionpanel.org/files/ip/PanelCases/7-Review%20and%20Assessment%20%28English%29.pdf, 57, para. 252 (accessed 30 May 2019).

[37] Ibid., 57, para. 253.

[38] Ibid., 57, para. 255.

[39] Inspection Panel, *India: NTPC Power Generation Project,* Report on Investigation, 22 December 1997, available at: https://inspectionpanel.org/sites/inspectionpanel.org/files/ip/PanelCases/10-Investigation%20Report%20%28English%29.pdf, 8, para. 16 (accessed 30 May 2019).

[40] Inspection Panel, *India Ecodevelopment Park (Rajiv Gandhi Nagaharole National Park,* Report and Recommendation on Request for Inspection, 21 October 1998, available at: https://inspectionpanel.

> consultations should have been undertaken not only with the experts but the potentially affected people (…) involving them in the design [of the project] could have avoided a lot of unnecessary misunderstanding (…). Thus, Management is left with a situation in which there was no prior review of the environmental consequences of the method and the environmental and other data needed for a subsequent assessment of the method have not been obtained. This appears to contradict Operational Directive 4.01 concerning the 'purpose and nature of [environmental assessment]', including to improve decision making and to ensure that the project options under consideration are environmentally sound and sustainable.[41]

Notably, the Panel underscored the obligatory nature of the Bank's social and environmental policies as the benchmark for determining Bank Management's compliance. In the *China: Western Poverty Reduction Project* case (a massive project involving voluntary resettlement of 57,775 poor farmers practicing high-altitude rain-fed agriculture, to a new irrigation project in the drylands of the Haixi Tibetan and Mongolian Autonomous Prefecture in Dulan County), the Panel noted that some members of Bank Management staff argued that 'the Bank's Operational Directives and other policies were simply idealized policy statements, and should largely be seen as a set of goals to be striven after (…) policies allow for flexibility of interpretation'.[42] The Panel rejected this position, stressing that the Bank's Operational Directives 'are the primary source of Bank policy for purposes of assessing compliance'.[43] Ultimately, the Panel identified several violations of Bank Operational Directives pertaining to environmental assessment, indigenous peoples, and involuntary resettlement, among others.[44]

It is also worth noting the few instances when the Panel has found the due diligence assessments in projects to be somewhat in compliance with the Bank Operational Directives and policies on environmental assessment and/or community impacts. With respect to a mining development project in Ecuador, the Panel found that while it appeared that the Bank Management was 'substantially in compliance' with Bank Operational Directives and policies on environmental assessment, the very limited scope of the initial environmental assessment (which

org/sites/inspectionpanel.org/files/ip/PanelCases/11-Eligibility%20Report%20%28English%29.pdf, paras v. and vi. of the Executive Summary (accessed 30 May 2019).

41 Inspection Panel, *Kenya: Lake Victoria Environmental Management Project*, Investigation Report, 15 December 2000, available at: https://inspectionpanel.org/sites/inspectionpanel.org/files/ip/PanelCases/19-Investigation%20Report%20%28English%29.pdf, 18, paras 46 and 47 (accessed 30 May 2019).

42 Inspection Panel, *The Qinghai Project: China: Western Poverty Reduction Project*, Investigation Report, 28 April 2000, available at: https://inspectionpanel.org/sites/inspectionpanel.org/files/ip/PanelCases/16-Investigation%20Report%20%28English%29.pdf, xiv, para. 10 (accessed 30 May 2019).

43 Ibid., xv, para. 15.

44 Ibid., i of Investigation Report.

did not provide adequate baseline environmental data necessary for ongoing assessments) made such compliance easy to begin with:

> the [environmental assessment] was written almost entirely from an abiotic environment point of view, focusing on the effects of pollution caused by artisanal mining activities. It does not address issues of the living environment; it does not cover the biological environment; and it is virtually silent on the extraordinarily rich biodiversity of Ecuador (…) the [environmental assessment] does not elaborate on possible future negative impacts of the Project on the natural environment, caused in this case by potential future mining activities.[45]

With respect to the Chad-Cameroon Oil Pipeline Project (dubbed by the Panel as 'the largest energy infrastructure development on the African continent'),[46] the Panel expanded the scope of its assessment of the project's due diligence to include subject matter such as oil spills, groundwater contamination, air pollution, natural habitats, forestry, pest management, consultations with local communities, involuntary resettlement, indigenous peoples, cultural property, governance and human rights, economic evaluations, and poverty reduction.[47] The Panel found that the pipeline project largely complied with environmental assessment requirements and made necessary preparatory planning and mitigation measures for feared environmental externalities. It did find, however, that certain consultations with affected groups and local communities that were 'conducted in the presence of security forces (…)[were] incompatible with the Bank's policy requirements (…) [Full] and informed consultation is impossible if those consulted perceive that they could be penalized for expressing their opposition to, or honest opinions about, a Bank financed project.'[48] Moreover, while the Panel stressed that:

> [it] is not within the Panel's mandate to assess the status of governance and human rights in Chad in general or in isolation (…). However, the Panel felt obliged to examine whether issues of proper governance or human rights violations in Chad were such as to impede the implementation of the Project in a manner compatible with the Bank's policies … the situation is far from ideal. It raises questions about

[45] Inspection Panel, *Ecuador: Mining Development and Environmental Control Technical Assistance Project*, Investigation Report, 23 February 2001, available at: https://inspectionpanel.org/sites/inspectionpanel.org/files/ip/PanelCases/20-Investigation%20Report%20%28English%29.pdf, para. 34 (accessed 30 May 2019).

[46] Inspection Panel, *Chad-Cameroon Petroleum and Pipeline Project*, Investigation Report, 17 July 2002, available at: https://inspectionpanel.org/sites/inspectionpanel.org/files/ip/PanelCases/22-Investigation%20Report%20%28English%29.pdf, para. 1 of the Executive Summary (accessed 30 May 2019).

[47] Ibid., paras 16–54.

[48] Ibid., para. 26.

> compliance with Bank policies, in particular with those that relate to informed and open consultation, and it warrants renewed monitoring by the Bank.[49]

As seen from various investigation reports of the Inspection Panel, the due diligence processes expected for the appropriate environmental, social, and economic risk assessment of World Bank projects require conducting timely, informed, and free consultations with affected communities well *before* the start of project implementation as well as during project implementation, with regular monitoring from the Bank as the project lender. The scope of the risk assessment is necessarily extensive as to subject-matter, multidimensional as to tools and methods used for risk analysis, interrelated in the approach to identifying individual and collective environmental and social risks, and continuing as part of the Bank Management's project oversight. At the very least, these internal practices suggest a high threshold in the Inspection Panel's expectations for designing the substance and procedure involved in due diligence compliance mechanisms aimed at holistically assessing risks in World Bank-financed projects.

4. Due Diligence Processes at the World Bank and Other Multilateral Development Banks

MDBs provide capital specifically targeted towards countries' economic development and related social goals:

> multilateral development banks are bodies or agencies created by international agreement among multiple nations whose purpose is to promote development among all or certain member states. These development goals focus primarily on the economic and social benefits to be achieved through the investment, as well as corollary matters such as protection of the environment and sustainability. Unlike [export credit agencies], [MDBs] are generally funded or financed by contributions from member states party to the multilateral agreement or other arrangement creating such [MDB].[50]

Due to the wide scope of their development mandates, due diligence processes for MDB-financed projects necessarily involve broader dimensions beyond standard project risks, covering, in particular, the assessment of environmental, labour, and social risks in the states hosting MDB-financed projects within their territories.

Given its own record of operational practices on risk assessments in financing development projects as discussed in the previous section, the World Bank Group

[49] Ibid., paras 35 and 37.

[50] John Dewar, *International Project Finance: Law and Practice* (Oxford: OUP 2011), at 218.

has chosen to prescribe its own detailed due diligence processes in its ESF, setting environmental and social standards for investment project financing,[51] composed of four main pillars: (i) the Bank's Vision for Sustainable Development (indicating the World Bank's policy understanding and vision for environmental and social sustainability of its projects); (ii) the World Bank Environmental and Social Policy for Investment Project Financing (which sets out the mandatory requirements that apply to the World Bank Group); (iii) the specific Environmental and Social Standards (with annexes, that are mandatory requirements imposed on the borrower and the projects financed by the World Bank); and (iv) the Bank Directive on Addressing Risks and Impacts on Disadvantaged or Vulnerable Groups. The World Bank ESF cohesively articulates, restates, and further develops the World Bank Group's previous and current due diligence practices for assessing environmental and social risks.[52]

4.1 Vision for Sustainable Development

The World Bank Group's Vision for Sustainable Development recognises that 'the corporate goals of ending extreme poverty and promoting shared prosperity in all its partner countries'[53] ultimately requires being 'globally committed to environmental sustainability, including stronger collective action to support climate change mitigation and adaptation',[54] as well as ensuring inclusion ('empowering all people to participate in, and benefit from, the development process')[55] and supporting 'the realization of human rights expressed in the Universal Declaration of Human Rights'.[56] To this end, the World Bank Group stresses that it 'uses its convening ability, financial instruments, and intellectual resources to embed this commitment to environmental and social sustainability across all its activities, which range from the Bank's global engagement in issues such as climate change, disaster risk management, and gender equality, to ensuring that environmental and social considerations are reflected in all sector strategies, operational policies, and country dialogues.'[57] The vision for sustainable development—explicitly premised on international human rights law and fully embedding sustainable development

[51] As of 1 October 2018, the World Bank Group's Environmental and Social Framework (ESF) is now being implemented to all new World Bank investment project financing. See full text of the 2017 ESF, available at: http://documents.worldbank.org/curated/en/383011492423734099/pdf/114278-WP-REVISED-PUBLIC-Environmental-and-Social-Framework.pdf (accessed 30 May 2019).

[52] See International Finance Corporation, Understanding IFC's Environmental and Social Due Diligence Process, available at: https://www.ifc.org/wps/wcm/connect/aa10e586-be7e-46b8-91c3-cc5e98af6f3d/IFC+Process.pdf?MOD=AJPERES&CVID=jUzk.Hj (accessed 1 September 2018).

[53] World Bank ESF 2017 (n. 2), 1, para. 1.

[54] Ibid., 1, para. 2.

[55] Ibid., 1, para. 3.

[56] Ibid., 1, para. 3.

[57] Ibid., 4, para. 4.

in all its civil, political, economic, social, cultural, environmental dimensions—is arguably the most comprehensive among other MDBs.[58] The World Bank ESF has in turn inspired other recent environmental and social policy or operational frameworks in new MDBs, such as those from the New Development Bank (established by the 'BRICS' countries Brazil, Russia, India, China, and South Africa),[59] and the recently established Asian Infrastructure Investment Bank (led by China and joined by over twenty states, for the purpose of collectively funding infrastructure investments in the Asian region).[60]

4.2 Environmental and Social Policy for Investment Project Financing

The second pillar of the World Bank's ESF is its Environmental and Social Policy for Investment Project Financing, which sets out the 'mandatory requirements that apply to the Bank'.[61] The Bank deliberately 'undertake[s] its own due diligence of proposed projects, proportionate to the nature and potential significance of

[58] See among others, the Environmental and Social Policy of the European Bank for Reconstruction and Development (EBRD), May 2014, available at: https://www.ebrd.com/news/publications/policies/environmental-and-social-policy-esp.html, 2, para. 8 ('The EBRD recognizes the ratification of international environmental and social agreements, treaties and conventions by its countries of operations. Within its mandate, the EBRD will seek to structure the projects it finances so that they are guided by the relevant principles and substantive requirements of international law (…)') (accessed 30 May 2019); Safeguard Policy Statement of the Asian Development Bank, June 2009, available at: https://www.adb.org/sites/default/files/institutional-document/32056/safeguard-policy-statement-june2009.pdf, 4 ('Safeguard policies are generally understood to be operational policies that seek to avoid, minimize, or mitigate adverse environmental and social impacts, including protecting the rights of those likely to be affected or marginalized by the development process. ADB's safeguard policy framework consists of three operational policies on the environment, Indigenous Peoples, and involuntary resettlement.') (accessed 30 May 2019); Inter-American Development Bank, Environment and Safeguards Compliance Policy, 19 January 2006, available at: http://idbdocs.iadb.org/wsdocs/getdocument.aspx?docnum=665902, 2, para. 2.3 ('This Policy is grounded in the principles of sustainable development as set out in the Declaration of Rio 92, Agenda 21 (…). Sustainability goals, in this context, depend on the alignment of social and economic development goals with long-term environmental sustainability (…) this policy encompasses social, cultural and economic aspects … this policy identifies environment as a dimension of development to be mainstreamed and internalized across all sectors.') (accessed 30 May 2019); African Development Bank Group, Policy on the Environment, February 2004, available at: https://www.afdb.org/fileadmin/uploads/afdb/Documents/Policy-Documents/10000027-EN-BANK-GROUP-POLICY-ON-THE-ENVIRONMENT.PDF, 2–3 ('The new policy on the environment, therefore, focuses more on integrating social, economic and environmental objectives rather than protecting and conserving the physical environment for its own sake (…). The Bank also has to ensure that provisions contained in various [multilateral environmental agreements] are implemented taking into account specific constraints in the [regional member countries](…)') (accessed 30 May 2019).

[59] See New Development Bank, Operations Division Environment and Social Framework, Version 2016, available at: https://www.ndb.int/wp-content/uploads/2017/02/ndb-environment-social-framework-20160330.pdf (accessed 30 May 2019).

[60] Asian Infrastructure Investment Bank, Environmental and Social Framework, February 2016, available at: https://www.aiib.org/en/policies-strategies/_download/environment-framework/20160226043633542.pdf (accessed 30 May 2019).

[61] World Bank ESF 2017 (n. 2), ix.

the environmental and social risks and impacts related to the project', including 'carry[ing] out early and continuing engagement and meaningful consultation with stakeholders, in particular affected communities, and (...) providing project-based grievance mechanisms'.[62] The World Bank assists borrowing states to identify 'appropriate methods and tools to assess and manage the potential environmental and social risks and impacts of the project',[63] as well as to set out specific conditions for the Bank's support for the project in the borrowing state, through an Environmental and Social Commitment Plan (ESCP). The Bank will refer to the ESCP, apart from all other aspects of the ESF, in monitoring the environmental and social performance of the project in the borrowing state. The ESCP is part of the borrower's legal agreement with the Bank, and sets out the 'material measures and actions required for the project to meet the [Bank's Environmental and Social Standards] over a specified timeframe'.[64]

The World Bank's due diligence process for investment project financing enumerates the following environmental and social risks as part of its assessment:

> (a) Environmental risks and impacts, including: (i) those identified in the World Bank Group Environmental, Health, and Safety Guidelines (EHSGs); (ii) those related to community safety (including dam safety and safe use of pesticides); (iii) those related to climate change and other transboundary or global risks and impacts; (iv) any material threat to the protection, conservation, maintenance, and restoration of natural habitats and biodiversity; and (v) those related to ecosystem services and the use of living natural resources, such as fisheries and forests; and
>
> (b) Social risks and impacts, including: (i) threats to human security through the escalation of personal, communal, or interstate conflict, crime, or violence; (ii) risks that project impacts fall disproportionately on individuals or groups who, because of their particular circumstances, may be disadvantaged or vulnerable; (iii) any prejudice or discrimination towards individuals or groups in providing access to development resources and project benefits, particularly in the case of those who may be disadvantaged or vulnerable; (iv) negative economic and social impacts relating to the involuntary taking of land or restrictions on land use; (v) risks or impacts associated with land and natural resource tenure and use, including (as relevant) potential project impacts on local land use patterns and tenurial arrangements, land access and availability, food security and land values, and any corresponding risks related to conflict or contestation over land and natural resources; (vi)

[62] Ibid., 3, paras 3(a) and 3(b).
[63] Ibid., 4, paras 3(c) to 3(e).
[64] Ibid., 9, para. 46.

> impacts on the health, safety and well-being of workers and project-affected communities; and (vii) risks to cultural heritage.[65]

The Bank's due diligence process yields its determination on the classification of a project as either 'high risk, substantial risk, moderate risk, or low risk'.[66] The ultimate purpose of the Bank's environmental and social due diligence is to 'assist the Bank in deciding whether to provide support for the proposed project and, if so, the way in which environmental and social risks and impacts will be addressed in the assessment, development, and implementation of the project'.[67] Broadly described, the due diligence process of the Bank includes functions such as:

> (a) reviewing the information provided by the Borrower relating to the environmental and social risks and impacts of the project and requesting additional and relevant information where there are gaps that prevent the Bank from completing its due diligence; and (b) providing guidance to assist the Borrower in developing appropriate measures consistent with the mitigation hierarchy to address environmental and social risks and impacts in accordance with the [Environmental and Social Standards of the Bank].[68]

Apart from these, the Bank also takes into account the:

> (a) risks and impacts inherent to the type of project and the specific context in which the proposed project will be developed and implemented; and (b) the capacity and commitment of the Borrower to develop and implement the project in accordance with the [Environmental and Social Standards of the Bank].[69]

The Bank's due diligence process includes extensive stakeholder consultations, particularly with affected communities, indigenous peoples, and other local community organisations.[70] In the course of its due diligence, the Bank can also use independent verification of information, such as from independent experts, local communities, or non-governmental organisations.[71]

Separately from the Bank's due diligence risk assessment above, the World Bank also requires its borrower states to conduct their own environmental and social assessments for the prospective projects on which they seek Bank financing.[72] In implementing Bank-funded projects, borrower states are subject to the Bank's ten

65 Ibid., 4, paras 4(a) and 4(b).
66 Ibid., 6, para. 20.
67 Ibid., 7, para. 30.
68 Ibid., 7, para. 32.
69 Ibid., 8, para. 33.
70 Ibid., 10, paras 53–55.
71 Ibid., 11, para. 58.
72 Ibid., 6, para. 15.

Environmental and Social Standards, inter alia including assessment and management of environmental and social risks and impacts; labour and working conditions; resource efficiency and pollution prevention and management; as well as community health and safety.[73] The borrower state's environmental and social assessment should be based on current information, including an accurate description and delineation of the project, as well as on appropriately detailed environmental and social baseline data (. . .).'[74]

The Bank applies the following mitigation hierarchy when adverse environmental and social impacts are found:

> (a) Anticipate and avoid risks and impacts;
> (b) Where avoidance is not possible, minimize or reduce risks and impacts to acceptable levels;
> (c) Once risks and impacts have been minimized or reduced, mitigate (which may include measures to assist affected parties to improve or at least restore their livelihoods as relevant in the particular project setting); and
> (d) Where significant residual impacts remain, compensate for or offset them, where technically and financially feasible.[75]

Most critically, the Bank requires the borrower state's environmental and social assessments to be premised on the widest set of environmental legal and policy frameworks, including:

> a) the country's applicable policy framework, national laws and regulations, and institutional capabilities (including implementation) relating to environment and social issues; variations in country conditions and project context; country environmental or social studies; national environmental or social action plans; and *obligations of the country directly applicable to the project under relevant international treaties and agreements*; b) applicable requirements under the [Bank's Environmental and Social Standards]; and c) the [Bank's Environmental, Health, and Safety Guidelines] and other relevant Good International Industry Practice.[76]

The Bank recommends tools and methods to the borrower state to carry out environmental and social assessment and to document the results from their assessment.[77] Finally, the operational timeframe and modalities for implementation of

[73] Ibid., 4, para. 5.
[74] Ibid., 18, para. 24.
[75] Ibid., 19, para. 27.
[76] Ibid., 19, para. 26 (emphasis added).
[77] These include, among others, an environmental and social impact assessment and an environmental and social audit, ibid., 23–24, paras 5(a) to 5(j).

any investment project in the borrower state are set by the Bank, in a manner that purposely takes into account:

> the nature and significance of the potential environmental and social risks and impacts, the timing for development and implementation of the project, the capacity of the Borrower and other entities involved in developing and implementing the project, and the specific measures and actions to be put in place or taken by the Borrower to address such risks and impacts.[78]

The Bank's Environmental, Health, and Safety Guidelines set performance levels and measures that are ordinarily applicable to Bank-financed projects, and is the baseline of implementation expected by the Bank—the borrower state, if it chooses, can impose a higher or more stringent set of environmental, health, and safety guidelines.[79] Finally, the borrower state is always required by the Bank to provide a grievance mechanism for all project-affected parties, especially on environmental and social performance.[80] Separate from the borrower state-initiated grievance mechanism, the World Bank also has its own corporate grievance redress service to receive complaints on all project-related concerns, as well as the Bank's independent Inspection Panel that can conduct inspections to determine whether harm has occurred as a result of project noncompliance with Bank policies and procedures, including especially the ESCP, the Environmental, Health, and Safety Guidelines, and the rest of the Bank's ESF.[81]

4.3. Bank Directive on Addressing Risks and Impacts on Disadvantaged or Vulnerable Groups

The 2016 Bank Directive Addressing Risks and Impacts on Disadvantaged or Vulnerable Individuals or Groups established directions for the World Bank 'regarding due diligence obligations relating to the identification of, and mitigation of risks and impacts on, individuals or groups because of their particular circumstances, [who] may be disadvantaged or vulnerable'.[82] The Bank's task team determines in its due diligence process whether the borrowing state's assessment properly identified the disadvantaged or vulnerable individuals or groups, and whether there are appropriate differentiated mitigation measures incorporated into the Bank's project 'so that adverse impacts do not fall disproportionately on the disadvantaged or vulnerable, and they are not disadvantaged in sharing any

[78] Ibid., 6, para. 16.
[79] Ibid., 6, para. 19.
[80] Ibid., 11, para. 60.
[81] For an analysis of the Inspection Panel's practice see above section 3.
[82] World Bank ESF 2017 (n. 2), para. 1.

development benefits resulting from the project'.[83] The 2018 Environmental and Social Directive for Investment Project Financing[84] recently succeeded and expanded the 2016 Bank Directive.[85] It also committed the Bank to assess environmental and social risks as part of its own due diligence process and to, inter alia, assesses the adequacy of the capacity of institutions responsible for the management of environmental and social risks and impacts.[86]

4.4 Convergence of Due Diligence Standards Regarding Environmental and Social Risks

Since the World Bank's adoption of the 2018 revised comprehensive Environmental and Social Framework, the Bank has steadily made its due diligence documents publicly available, including in particular recent Environmental and Social Review Summaries for various projects.[87] A 2015 expert study commissioned by the World Bank concluded that there are many similarities between the World Bank's environmental and social safeguard frameworks (including due diligence processes therein) and that of other MDBs.[88] This suggests, at the very least, that there is some growing normative convergence between the World Bank and other MDBs on the

[83] Ibid., para. 6.

[84] World Bank Group, Environmental and Social Directive for Investment Project Financing, 3 October 2018, available at: https://policies.worldbank.org/sites/ppf3/PPFDocuments/18479bc9036d43f980875b7ba94cd934.pdf (accessed 30 May 2019).

[85] World Bank Group, Bank Directive on Addressing Risks and Impacts on Disadvantaged or Vulnerable Individuals or Groups, 4 August 2016.

[86] Ibid., at footnote 56, para. 5.

[87] See among others World Bank Group, Environmental Social and Review Summary: Network Reinforcement and Access Project P16670, Zambia, Africa, 24 October 2018, available at: http://documents.worldbank.org/curated/en/252311540385185729/Environmental-and-Social-Review-Summary-ESRS-Network-Reinforcement-and-Access-Project-P166170 (accessed 30 May 2019); Morocco-Noor Solar Power Projects environmental assessment: Environmental and Social Review Summary, 8 March 2018, available at: http://documents.worldbank.org/curated/en/565341517589494999/Environmental-and-social-review-summary (accessed 30 May 2019); Zambia—West Lunga Scaling Solar Energy Project: Environmental and Social Review Summary, 1 January 2017, available at: http://documents.worldbank.org/curated/en/186661485338957768/Environmental-and-social-review-summary (accessed 30 May 2019); Grenada Digital Governance for Resilience—Environmental and Social Review Summary, 24 October 2018, available at: http://documents.worldbank.org/curated/en/310541540411444931/Environmental-and-Social-Review-Summary-ESRS-Grenada-Digital-Governance-for-Resilience-P167588 (accessed 30 May 2019); Tunisia-Italy Power Interconnection Project Preparation Technical Assistance—Environmental and Social Review Summary, 5 July 2018, available at: http://documents.worldbank.org/curated/en/541431531167022689/Environmental-and-social-review-summary (accessed 30 May 2019); Africa Environmental Health and Pollution Management Program—Environmental and Social Review Summary, 2018 October 27, available at: http://documents.worldbank.org/curated/en/850361540664230193/Environmental-and-Social-Review-Summary-ESRS-Africa-Environmental-Health-and-Pollution-Management-Program-P167788 (accessed 30 May 2019).

[88] Harvey Himberg, *Comparative Review of Multilateral Development Bank Safeguard Systems*, May 2015, available at: https://consultations.worldbank.org/sites/default/files/consultation-template/review-and-update-world-bank-safeguard-policies/fr/related/mdb_safeguard_comparison_main_report_and_annexes_may_2015.pdf (accessed 30 May 2019).

conduct of due diligence for environmental and social risks. The due diligence processes give some consideration for the recipient state's environmental and human rights treaty commitments, but it has not yet been made explicit that either the World Bank or other MDBs deliberately internalise these treaty commitments as their normative baseline. Rather, the World Bank and other MDBs have still driven due diligence processes from the authoritativeness of their internal institutional mandates under their respective articles of agreement, acknowledging some similarities with concepts in environmental and human rights treaties without purposely treating the latter to be obligatory on these institutions.[89]

5. Conclusion

International project finance due diligence processes focus on risk assessment, but not all institutional lenders or sovereign lenders evaluate risk or conduct due diligence review in a uniform way. The World Bank's due diligence process in its investment project financing operations is significant practice for public international lawyers to consider, in that it purposely internalises states' existing environmental and social treaty obligations and commitments under international human rights law, and deliberately operationalises these obligations and commitments through the World Bank's Environmental and Social Framework implemented in every Bank-funded project. The fact that the Bank recognises a broader understanding of project risks to include environmental and social risks, as well as direct and indirect impacts to affected, displaced, or vulnerable communities, indigenous peoples, and other groups, itself exemplifies that the World Bank Group frames its development duties with consciousness towards international human rights and the international rule of law. While not all MDBs completely replicate the World Bank's ESF, the growing consideration for some of the environmental and social treaty obligations of borrowing states into MDB-funded development projects suggests that in the area of international project finance due diligence may be headed towards possible convergence with international human rights obligations, particularly in environmental and social treaty commitments of states. For the present, however, the World Bank and other international financial institutions declare that they are themselves not bound by the hard law of states' human rights, environmental, and climate change treaty obligations.

[89] See World Bank, The International Bill of Rights and IFC Sustainability Framework, 2016, available at: http://documents.worldbank.org/curated/en/470681480669101836/pdf/110689-IBHR-and-IFC-Policies-PS-DRAFT.pdf (accessed 1 February 2019).

CONCLUSION

21
Due Diligence and Structural Change in the International Legal Order

Heike Krieger and Anne Peters

1. Introduction

Due diligence, the expectation or requirement to exercise care (*diligentia*) or circumspection, is on the rise in all fields of international law, ranging from international environmental law over peace and security law to international economic law, as the contributions to this book have shown.[1] The rise of this regulatory technique[2] seems to reflect both the doctrinal and the political challenges the international legal order has to meet in order to reach its objectives and purposes. Due diligence is therefore an indicator for identifying transformations of the international legal order as a whole. This seems true although the concept of due diligence has been described as both a characteristic of the law of coordination[3] and of the law of cooperation.[4] With its reference to what is 'due', the concept may just refer to the normative ambitions of any given legal order without itself determining the characteristics of that order. Nevertheless, we deem the spread of the concept of 'due diligence' across international law (in fields as diverse as climate change law and or anti-terrorism law) to manifest a new preference for handling accountability.[5] Since securing accountability is a major defining purpose of any legal

[1] See for the meaning of due diligence (and its opposite: negligence) Anne Peters/Heike Krieger/Leonhard Kreuzer, 'Due Diligence in the International Legal Order: Dissecting the Leitmotif of Current Accountability Debates', chapter 1 of this book, section 1. Citing the *Encyclopædia Britannica*, we defined due diligence as 'a standard of vigilance, attentiveness, and care often exercised in various professional and societal settings'. We emphasised that due diligence is a *modality* attached to a duty of care for someone or something else (including the duty to prevent and mitigate harm).

[2] By 'regulatory technique', we understand the legal art (*techné*, as opposed to mechanics or managerialism) of framing legal rules and regimes and thereby contributing to the ordering and development of the global society with legal means.

[3] See Giulio Bartolini, 'The Historical Roots of the Due Diligence Standard', chapter 2 of this book, section 2.

[4] Pierre d'Argent/Alexia de Vaucleroy, 'Le contenu de l'omission illicite: la non utilisation de moyens raisonnables', in Société Française pour le Droit International (SFDI)/Sarah Cassella (eds), *Le standard de due diligence et la responsabilité internationale* (Paris: Pedone 2018), 255–278, at 255.

[5] In the introduction to this book, we defined 'accountability', relying on Mark Bovens, as the relationship between an actor and a forum in which the actor has to explain and justify its conduct against acknowledged benchmarks, and where the actor faces (reputational, political, or even legal) sanctions if

Heike Krieger and Anne Peters, *Due Diligence and Structural Change in the International Legal Order* In: *Due Diligence in the International Legal Order*. Edited by: Heike Krieger, Anne Peters, and Leonhard Kreuzer, Oxford University Press (2020).
 DOI: 10.1093/oso/9780198869900.003.0021.

order, it stands to reason to assume that the dissemination of due diligence is one sign of possibly ongoing structural transformations within this order.

Based on the contributions to this book, the present chapter looks into different emanations of due diligence across international law in order to answer the question which legal functions due diligence performs and whether and how its rise can be interpreted as a response to, a manifestation of, and a catalyst for structural change in international law. We first recapitulate the most visible international legal principle that incorporates and manifests the idea of due diligence which is the so-called no harm rule. In this context, due diligence has changed sides: While it historically served to contain accountability, due diligence now helps to create accountability (as we explain in section 2). Whereas the no harm rule and its variations address man-made risks, the next section looks at humans as risks. In this context, due diligence, imposed on states, closes the accountability gap which arises from the fact that 'risky' humans are for the most part not held personally liable under international law (section 3). Having identified due diligence's two functions of risk-management and securing accountability, section 4 looks at further tasks of due diligence in various branches of international law (such as defining audits and impact assessments, or operationalising obligations of progressive realisation). Section 5 discusses whether a common understanding of due diligence throughout the different areas of international law and possibly across different types of legal persons (states, international organisations, other) can be traced and, if so, whether this warrants qualifying due diligence as an overarching principle of international law. It judges that this is not the case. Section 6 shows which 'structural' work due diligence indeed performs and also sheds some light on its dark sides. Section 7 concludes that while due diligence is shaping the international law of a global risk society and helps to secure accountability, it also menaces to mellow firm obligations.

2. The No Harm Rule: From Restricting to Creating Accountability through Due Diligence

The traditional field of application of due diligence has been the international no harm rule. In this context, the function of due diligence has moved from restricting liability to creating accountability. A major factor in this process is the rise of a global risk society.

the explanation does not satisfy the recipients of accountability, see Peters/Krieger/Kreuzer, 'Dissecting the Leitmotif' (n. 1), section 1. In international law, the *legal* accountability is mainly secured by the rules on the international legal responsibility of states and other international persons, and through so-called liability for lawful acts, see (n. 13) of this chapter.

2.1. Due Diligence and the Global Risk Society

Modernisation has generated new technical risks—small scale and large scale.[6] Specific and limited risks in the industrial society are displaced by global unpredictable risks which transgress temporal, spatial, or social boundaries, such as nuclear power, environmental pollution, and climate change. All these risks have a both scientific/technical and a social/cultural dimension. The risk concept underlying the no harm rule refers predominantly to a positivist scientific framework based on the laws of nature and causality. Here risks are related to the physical world, are systematically accessible, subject to scientific proof, and measurable in scientific terms.[7] In a social cultural framework, risks or rather perceptions thereof are above all conceived of as social phenomena. This has fostered a perception of the unpredictable behaviour of certain groups of human beings as a legally relevant risk.[8] And because risks are socially constructed in specific cultural contexts, they differ across different cultures.[9] Diverging legal approaches to terrorism illustrate the social and cultural contingency of risk.

Risks are aggravated by globalisation due to interconnection in economic, security, or social matters. Even where activities are not meant to cross borders they may spill over state frontiers not least in relation to global commons. The multitude and diversity of actors (states with highly diverging factual capacities, international organisations, and non-state actors) increase the uncertainty and the risks.[10]

The rise of risk, uncertainty, and complexity has affected and altered decision-making processes.[11] This does not only concern political processes but also legal structures. In order to address globalised risks, we need alternative argumentative strategies for allocating accountability. Also, the spatial and temporal points of reference of legal rules need to shift. Instead of only settling disputes (which are often territorially defined), international law must manage future risks which are decoupled from space. In these circumstances, retrospective responsibility based on clear concepts of damage, causality, attribution, and knowledge may not fit. The

[6] Ulrich Beck, *Risk Society: Towards a New Modernity* (London/Thousand Oaks/New Delhi: Sage Publications 1992).

[7] Cf. Oliver Lepsius, 'The Problem of De-individualisation in the Risk Society', in Gordon R. Woodman/Diethelm Klippel (eds), *Risk and the Law* (London/New York: Routledge-Cavendish 2008), 36–52, at 37.

[8] Manfred Max Wambach (ed.), *Der Mensch als Risiko* (Frankfurt am Main: Suhrkamp 1983).

[9] Niklas Möller, 'The Concepts of Risk and Safety', in Sabine Roeser/Rafaela Hillerbrand/Per Sadin/Martin Peterson (eds), *Handbook of Risk Theory* (Dordrecht/Heidelberg/London/New York: Springer 2012), 55–85, at 70; Oliver Kessler, 'Is Risk Changing the Politics of International Legal Argumentation?', *Leiden Journal of International Law* 21 (2008), 863–884, at 866–868.

[10] On the impact of interdependence and responsibility see also André Nollkaemper/Dov Jacobs, 'Shared Responsibility in International Law: A Conceptual Framework', *Michigan Journal of International Law* 34 (2013), 359–438, at 370; for the role of diversity ibid., 374.

[11] Kessler, 'International Legal Argumentation?' 2008 (n. 9), 864, 865, 868.

legal regulation of accountability needs new techniques, in particular risk mitigation strategies which also focus on risk management and not only on retrospective responsibility. In this context, the due diligence standard appears to have turned into an apt if not the dominant legal tool, as the chapters in this book show.

2.2. Techniques of Allocating Accountability in the Face of Risks

Generally speaking, international law offers two regimes for legal accountability:[12] the rules on state responsibility for wrongful acts, as secondary rules; and the rules on liability for lawful acts, as primary rules.[13] In the face of risks, states can choose between different regulatory approaches. First of all, they can simply decide to prohibit a specific risky behaviour so that a transgression of the prohibition will give rise to state responsibility. States tend to impose prohibitions where there is a high probability that a risk will materialise, where this will entail serious harm and where causality is obvious. Bans on specific types of weapons reflect this approach.

In contrast, where risks seem tolerable, states may refrain from prohibiting the relevant behaviour but will only deal with the consequences. International law basically offers three ways to do so and to handle accountability for such tolerated risks. States may decide not to impose any liability (option 1), to create strict liability (option 2), or to create liability for negligent behaviour based on the no harm rule and the due diligence standard (option 3).[14] An example for the first approach (international rules which, in principle, allow states to do harm, i.e., do *not* ask states to do no harm) are the export and import rules of the World Trade Organization (WTO) regime.[15] This regime does not require the exporting state to take measures against the risk arising from dangerous goods or against negative effects of trade. Rather, it is for the importing states to avert risks or harm. The WTO treaties allow the importing states to take measures such as import bans within the confines of Article XX GATT, in order to protect specific public interests such as human life or health.[16] This risk distribution reflects all states' basic interest in international trade relations. Unlike in cases of transboundary (environmental) harm, cross-border effects are the very essence of international trade relations, and

[12] See for the concept of accountability (n. 5) of this chapter.

[13] See for this distinction and terminology United Nations, International Law Commission, Draft Articles on Prevention of Transboundary Harm from Hazardous Activities, with commentaries, UN GAOR 56th Sess., Supp. No. 10, A/56/10, 23 April–1 June, 2 July–10 August 2001, art. 1, commentary, para. 6, YBILC 2001, vol. II (part II), 150. The term liability is not coherently used in international law. In some cases, the term denotes international (state) responsibility for wrongful acts (as in art. 91 Additional Protocol I to the Geneva Conventions, 8 June 1977, 1125 UNTS 3; art. 139 United Nations Convention on the Law of the Sea (UNCLOS), 10 December 1982, 1833 UNTS 3; art. 4(4) Annex III to UNCLOS).

[14] Discussed below in section 2.3.

[15] Markus Krajewski, 'Due Diligence in International Trade Law', chapter 19 of this book, section 2.2.

[16] Ibid.

international law protects exactly this. It is therefore consistent to leave the protection of countervailing public interests against risks to the importing states.

Once states decide that liability for risks should be created, they have the abovementioned options 2 and 3. Thus, they may impose 'strict' liability (option 2). By strict liability, we understand liability for harm, once a risk materialised, *independently of negligent or diligent* behaviour of the actor which produced the risk.[17] Strict liability is rare in international law.[18] Some examples in international environmental law concern activities seen as particularly dangerous or new,[19] where scientific knowledge on their effects and the risks is limited. Here only the state engaging in the activities bears the burden should the risk materialise. Strict liability is warranted where other states cannot be expected or may simply not be able to take protective measures to avert harm coming from elsewhere. The Outer Space regime reflects these considerations. Article VII of the Convention on Principles Governing the Activities of States in the Exploration and Use of Outer Space, including the Moon and other Celestial Bodies,[20] and Article II of the Convention on International Liability for Damage Caused by Space Objects[21] establish strict liability.[22] Further examples are Article 8(2) and (3) of the Convention on the Regulation of Antarctic Mineral Resource Activities.[23]

An older International Law Commission (ILC) project had dealt with 'International liability for injurious consequences arising out of acts not prohibited by international law'.[24] Liability for 'acts not prohibited' is, in other words, liability for *lawful* acts.[25] However, this project faced numerous conceptual problems at

[17] A similar term is 'absolute liability' which may be even more rigid because no exceptions are allowed. See for the terminology Kirsten Schmalenbach, 'Verantwortlichkeit und Haftung', in Alexander Proelß (ed.), *Internationales Umweltrecht* (Berlin/Boston: De Gruyter 2017), 211–242, at 215.

[18] In contrast, in domestic laws, strict liability seems to enjoy a renaissance, see Hans-Bern Schaefer/Frank Mueller-Langer, 'Strict Liability Versus Negligence', in Gerrit De Geest (ed.), *Encyclopedia of Law and Economics* (Cheltenham: Edward Elgar 2nd ed. 2012), 5, 6.

[19] Alexandre Kiss/Dinah Shelton, 'Strict Liability in International Environmental Law', in Tafsir Malick Ndiaye/Rüdiger Wolfrum (eds), *Law of the Sea, Environmental Law and Settlement of Disputes: Liber Amicorum Judge Thomas A Mensah* (Leiden/Boston: Martinus Nijhoff 2007), 1131–1151, at 1135–1138.

[20] Treaty on Principles Governing the Activities of States in the Exploration and Use of Outer Space, Including the Moon and Other Celestial Bodies, 27 January 1967, 610 UNTS 205.

[21] 'A launching state shall be absolutely liable to pay compensation for damage caused by its space object on the surface on the earth or to aircraft in flight.' Convention on the International Liability for Damage Caused by Space Objects, 29 March 1972, 961 UNTS 187, 24 UST 2389, TIAS 7762, UN Reg No I-13810.

[22] See also United Nations, General Assembly, Principles Relevant to the Use of Nuclear Power Sources in Outer Space, A/Res/47/68, 23 February 1993, Principle 9.

[23] Convention on the Regulation of Antarctic Mineral Resource Activities, 2 June 1988 (did not enter into effect), SATCM IV-12-10.

[24] United Nations, International Law Commission, Eighth report on international liability for injurious consequences arising out of acts not prohibited by international law, by Mr Julio Barboza, Special Rapporteur, A/CN.4/443; YBILC 1992, vol. II (part I).

[25] This type of liability is also sometimes called 'strict liability'. As mentioned above, in a slightly different terminology, 'strict liability' (or 'absolute liability') is the liability independent of negligence or diligence, see (n. 17).

its interface with the traditional law on state responsibility including the question as to whether 'fault' is required to establish state responsibility for environmental harm.[26] In response, the ILC split the liability project and first focused on harm prevention rules which resulted in the Draft Articles on Prevention of Transboundary Harm from Hazardous Activities, adopted in 2001.[27] Only five years later, in 2006, the ILC adopted the Draft Principles on the Allocation of Loss in Case of Transboundary Harm Arising out of Hazardous Activities.[28] The first set of principles (2001) laid out primary obligations for averting risks. Although the separation of the normative framework into two different sets of provisions suggests a neat distinguishability between prevention of harm and legal consequences once harm did occur, the concepts of 'harm prevention' and 'liability' (responsibility) continue to overlap.[29] In other words, ex post liability is blurred with risk management.

2.3. The Traditional No Harm Rule

Instead of exceptional strict liability, responsibility for lack of due diligence has become normal across international law. Here, due diligence works as a legal tool to *restrict* or to *create* accountability.[30]

We will first look at the accountability-restricting function of due diligence as one element of the so-called no harm rule. The historical starting point of the modern no harm rule, as reflected in the *Trail Smelter* decision of 1941, was the duty to act *diligently* not to cause harm.[31] We consider that the environmental no

[26] Jutta Brunnée, 'Procedure and Substance in International Environmental Law', *Recueil des Cours de l'Académie de Droit International de la Haye* 405 (2020) 77–240, at 156.

[27] ILC, Draft Articles on Prevention, 2001 (n. 13); Brunnée, 'Procedure and Substance' 2020 (n. 26), 156.

[28] United Nations, International Law Commission, Draft principles on the allocation of loss in the case of transboundary harm arising out of hazardous activities, with commentaries, UN GAOR 61st Sess., A/61/10, 1 May–9 June and 3 July–11 August 2006, 106–182; YBILC 2006, vol. II (part II), 59–90.

[29] Compare, e.g., ILC, Draft Articles on Prevention, 2001 (n. 13), art. 3, and ILC Draft Principles on Allocation of Loss, 2006, art. 5(a) (n. 28). The obligation to notify in art. 5(a) has a preventive dimension, too. In scholarship, Attila Tanzi defines 'liability' as 'situations according to which States have a duty to take *reparatory* and, at the same time, *preventive* measures vis-à-vis other States for damage caused, or likely to be caused, by activities—carried out, either directly by them, or by private operators—which are harmful though not prohibited under international law'. Attila Tanzi, 'Liability for Lawful Acts', in Rüdiger Wolfrum (ed.), *Max Planck Encyclopedia of Public International Law* (Oxford: OUP 2010), para. 1.

[30] See for the terms liability, responsibility, accountability above (n. 5) and (n. 13), with accompanying text.

[31] The arbitral tribunal did not use the word 'diligence' though. The tribunal found that 'no State has the right to use or permit the use of its territory in such a manner as to cause injury by fumes in or to the territory of another or the properties or persons therein, when the case is of serious consequence and the injury is established by clear and convincing evidence', *Trail Smelter Arbitration*, Decision of 11 March 1941, UNRIAA, vol. III, 1938–1982, 1965. See for a due diligence-oriented interpretation of the arbitral award, e.g., Jutta Brunnée, 'Community Obligations in International Environmental Law: Procedural Aspects', in Eyal Benvenisti/Georg Nolte (eds), *Community Interests*

harm rule has evolved out of the broader 'obligation to protect within the territory the rights of other States' as the arbiter Max Huber had put it already in the *Palmas* award of 1925 (i.e., as an obligation to avoid 'neighbourhood nuisances').[32] This obligation, and thus also the traditional no harm rule ('*neminem laedere*'), was arguably based on the due diligence standard, although neither of the two leading awards on no harm (*Palmas* and *Trail Smelter*) explicitly cited due diligence. Due diligence was however mentioned in another arbitral award of the time, *British Property in Spanish Morocco* (issued in 1925),[33] and was supported by contemporary literature.[34] It is therefore plausible that due diligence formed the undercurrent of the two leading decisions on *neminem laedere*, too. Clyde Eagleton, writing in 1928, asserted:

> While it might appear to follow from the exclusive control which the state has over its own territories that it should be responsible for all injurious acts occurring therein, the community of nations, with a proper understanding of the imperfections of human endeavour, has *alleviated* the force of the principle in practice by the rules of due diligence and local redress.[35]

Here—and this is crucial—the due diligence standard limits state responsibility to negligent behaviour by exonerating a state that acted diligently enough, with 'due' diligence.

The standard's traditional and restrictive function is in line with a proper understanding of the doctrinal distinction between obligations of conduct and obligations of result. In fact, the obligation to behave diligently is often characterised as an obligation of conduct. The distinction between these two types of obligations was introduced by Roberto Ago in his 1977 ILC Report on State responsibility,[36] and further developed by Pierre-Marie Dupuy:

Across International Law (Oxford: OUP 2018), 151–175, at 159. In the literature, this understanding of the no harm rule is sometimes disputed. Some commentators consider that the arbitral decision pronounced a strict prohibition, see, e.g., Alexander Proelß, 'Prinzipien des internationalen Umweltrechts', in Proelß 2017 (n. 17), 71–102, at 76. Other authors think the award established a form of strict liability (independently of diligence or negligence), e.g., Paulina Starski, 'Right to Self-Defense, Attribution and the Non-State Actor—Birth of the "Unable or Unwilling" Standard?', *Heidelberg Journal of International Law* 75 (2015), 455–501, at 482.

[32] *Palmas* award (n. 154); see in this sense Brunnée, 'Procedure and Substance' 2020 (n. 26), 121, 126.

[33] Max Huber, *Affaire des biens britanniques au Maroc espagnol (Spain v. UK)*, 1 May 1925, UNRIAA, vol. II, 645.

[34] See, e.g., Edwin M. Borchard, *The Diplomatic Protection of Citizens Abroad or the Law of International Claims* (New York: The Banks Law Publishing 1915), 217: 'The failure of a government to use due diligence to prevent a private injury is a well-recognized ground of international responsibility.'

[35] Clyde Eagleton, *The Responsibility of States in International Law* (New York: New York University Press 1928), 94 (emphasis added); see further Bartolini, 'Historical Roots' (n. 3).

[36] See Helmut Philipp Aust/Prisca Feihle, 'Due Diligence in the History of the Codification of the Law of State Responsibility' chapter 3 of this book, section 2.2; Roberto Ago, Sixth Report on State Responsibility, A/CN.4/302 and Add.1, 2, 3, 15 April, 7 June, 5 and 14 July 1977, YBILC 1977, vol. II (part I), at 8, para. 12. Ago's understanding was not included in the final version of the Articles on

> [A]n obligation of conduct is (…) an obligation to endeavour or to try to reach a certain result. Typical in this respect is the obligation of a doctor in relation to a patient. He or she must do everything that a reasonable person and competent physician can do in order to look after a patient. In contrast, in the case of an obligation of result, (…) there is a burden on the person who owes such an obligation to attain a precise result. When I buy a car, the seller has the obligation, after I have paid for it, to provide me with the car.[37]

Dupuy's conceptualisation of obligations of conduct has come to dominate the international legal discourse on due diligence. For instance, the Max Planck Encyclopedia refers to 'due diligence obligations' as

> primary obligations that require States (…) to endeavour to reach the result set out in the obligation. A breach of these obligations consists not of failing to achieve the desired result but failing to take the necessary, diligent steps towards that end.[38]

On this basis, many international lawyers tend to equate 'the principle of due diligence' with an obligation of conduct and in turn with the no harm rule as laid down in the *Trail Smelter* arbitration and the *Corfu Channel* case.[39] However, only negligent conduct (that is conduct lacking due diligence) causing (significant) transboundary harm is legally relevant.[40]

The due diligence standard applies to rules which have developed out of the no harm rule across international law, decoupled from 'neighbourly relations'. According to the International Court of Justice (ICJ), 'the general obligation of States to ensure that activities within their jurisdiction and control respect the environment *of other States or of areas beyond national control* is now part of the corpus of international law relating to the environment'.[41] Both under this 'general'

State Responsibility but continues to unfold relevance in legal analysis, see e.g., International Law Association (ILA), Study Group on Due Diligence in International Law, Second Report, July 2016, 17.

[37] Pierre-Marie Dupuy, 'Reviewing the Difficulties of Codification: On Ago's Classification of Obligations of Means and Obligations of Result in Relation to State Responsibility', *European Journal of International Law* 10 (1999), 371–385, at 375.

[38] Timo Koivurova, 'Due Diligence', in Rüdiger Wolfrum (ed.), *Max Planck Encyclopedia of Public International Law* (Oxford: OUP 2010), para. 3.

[39] ILA, 'Second Report' 2016 (n. 36), 5–6; Koivurova, 'Due Diligence' 2010 (n. 38), para. 3; see also Krajewski, 'International Trade Law' (n. 15), section 3.1.

[40] In the words of the commentary on the ILC, Draft Articles on Prevention, 2001 (n. 13), UN GAOR A/56/10, 23 April–1 June, 2 July–10 August 2001, commentary to art. 3, p. 154, para. 7: 'The duty of due diligence involved (…) is not intended to guarantee that significant harm be totally prevented, if it is not possible to do so. In that eventuality, the State of origin is required, as noted above, to exert its *best possible efforts* to minimize the risk. In this sense, it does not guarantee that the harm would not occur' (emphasis added). See also Brunnée, 'Procedure and Substance' 2020 (n. 26), at 123, 129.

[41] ICJ, *Legality of the Threat or Use of Nuclear Weapons*, Advisory Opinion of 8 July 1996, ICJ Reports 1996, 226, para. 241; ICJ, *Gabcikovo-Nagymaros Project* (*Hungary v. Slovakia*), Judgment of 25 September 1997, ICJ Reports 1997, 7, para. 53; ICJ, *Pulp Mills on the River Uruguay Case (Argentina v. Uruguay)*, Judgment of 20 April 2010, ICJ Reports 2010, 14, para. 193.

rule, and under most international environmental law treaties, due diligence is the relevant standard for the aversion (and prevention)[42] of ecologic harm.[43] Also the United Nations Convention on the Law of the Sea (UNCLOS) contains, as Irini Papanicolopulu demonstrates, manifold obligations of states to ensure the protection both of the marine environment and human life at sea on the basis of the due diligence standard.[44] Moreover, state obligations to prevent harm arising from state activities are acknowledged with regard to the outer space,[45] the ozone layer,[46] the climate,[47] cyberspace,[48] and arguably in relation to global health.[49] All these protective (and preventive) duties require that the states exercise due diligence.

The no harm rule is breached only when negligent conduct *and* an unwanted result are present: The breach consists in failing to avoid the bad result (or failing to maintain or achieve the desired result) and in failing to take the necessary, diligent steps towards that end.[50] Put differently, the traditional no harm rule combines an obligation of conduct and an obligation of result.[51] It cannot be simply equated with the concept of due diligence. Due diligence here is only a modality and a yardstick for assessing whether and when a state has violated its obligation not to cause harm.[52] Finally, the function of due diligence to restrict or limit accountability in

[42] On the harm prevention rule see below section 2.4.

[43] See Peters/Krieger/Kreuzer, 'Dissecting the Leitmotif', (n. 1), section 5. The wording of the treaties mostly does not explicitly mention 'due diligence' but terms such as 'appropriate measures' and the like.

[44] See Irini Papanicolopulu, 'Due Diligence in the Law of the Sea', chapter 9 of this book, section 2.1, with reference to, e.g., art. 194 UNCLOS, 1982 (n. 13). According to Papanicolopulu, the following conventions contain due diligence obligations although the term due diligence is never mentioned: International Convention for the Prevention of Marine Pollution from Ships of 2 November 1973, IUCN ID: TRE-000113; Convention on the Prevention of Marine Pollution by Dumping of Wastes and Other Matter, 29 December 1972, 1046 UNTS 138; International Convention for the Control and Management of Ships' Ballast Water and Sediments, 13 February 2004 (entered into force on 8 September 2017), IMO Doc. BMW/CONF/36.

[45] 'States Parties (...) shall (...) conduct exploration of them so as to avoid their harmful contamination and also adverse changes in the environment of the Earth resulting from the introduction of extraterrestrial matter and, where necessary, shall adopt appropriate measures for this purpose', Outer Space Treaty, 1967 (n. 20), art. ix.

[46] Preamble of the Montreal Protocol on Substances that Deplete the Ozone Layer, 16 September 1987, 1522 UNTS 1989.

[47] See Lavanya Rajamani, 'Due Diligence in International Climate Change Law', chapter 10 of this book.

[48] Eric Talbot Jensen, 'Due Diligence in Cyber Activities', chapter 15 of this book.

[49] Antonio Coco/Talita de Souza Dias, 'Due Diligence and COVID-19: States' Duties to Prevent and Halt the Coronavirus Outbreak' Parts I–III, *EJIL: Talk!*, 24 and 25 March 2020, available at: https://www.ejiltalk.org/part-i-due-diligence-and-covid-19-states-duties-to-prevent-and-halt-the-coronavirus-outbreak/ (accessed 14 April 2020). The International Health Regulations of the WHO of 2005 do not contain the words 'due diligence' but in substance embody due diligence obligations, for example, the obligation to build up a public health response capacity, International Health Regulations 2005, 2509 UNTS 70, art. 13.

[50] '[T]he means to be employed are means to that end and are not themselves the primary objective.' Rüdiger Wolfrum, 'Obligations of Result vs Obligations of Conduct', in Mahnoush H. Arsanjani/Jacob Cogan/Robert Sloane/Siegfried Wiessner (eds), *Looking to the Future: Essays on International Law in Honor of W. Michael Reisman* (Leiden/Boston: Martinus Nijhoff 2011), 363–383, at 381.

[51] See ibid., 368, 380, 381.

[52] See Papanicolopulu, 'Law of the Sea' (n. 44), with reference to Riccardo Pisillo Mazzeschi, 'Le chemin étrange de la due diligence d'un concept mysterieux à un concept surevalué', in SFDI/Cassella 2018 (n. 4), 323–337, at 334.

the context of the traditional no harm rule shows in the harm mitigation duties. Due diligence requires states to take appropriate measures for either removing or mitigating any harm.[53] The mere fact that harm occurred does not constitute an internationally wrongful act as long as the state exercised due diligence. In that situation, states are not obliged to cease behaviour, to re-establish the prior situation, or to compensate, as they would be in the regime of state responsibility.[54] Instead, the occurrence of harm triggers new primary obligations which are again circumscribed and limited by the due diligence standard. Then, the rules on state responsibility only come into play when harm is not diligently mitigated.[55]

2.4. The New Harm Prevention Rule

Due diligence also has a role in the harm prevention rule. The specific content of this more recent rule and its relationship to the traditional no harm rule is not yet fully clear.[56] In *Pulp Mills* and in *Costa Rica v. Nicaragua/Nicaragua v. Costa Rica*, the ICJ recalled a state's obligation to exercise due diligence in preventing significant transboundary harm.[57] The Court seemed to keep apart two rules: a harm prevention duty which it equated with result-independent procedural obligations,[58] and a duty to diligently not cause harm.[59] The latter duty is breached only when the state did not behave diligently *and* when this negligence indeed caused significant transboundary harm. Based on this distinction, the Court held Costa Rica and Nicaragua responsible for violating their procedural obligations, but not for violating the substantive duty not to cause harm because in the end no significant transboundary harm had occurred. A lack of diligence was not sufficient for finding a violation of the traditional no harm rule.[60]

[53] Tanzi, 'Liability' 2010 (n. 29), paras 3 and 11.

[54] Ibid., paras 11 and 14.

[55] Ibid., para. 14; cf. Brunnée, 'Procedure and Substance' 2020 (n. 26), 157.

[56] See for different understandings Proelß, 'Prinzipien' 2017 (n. 31), 78; Brunnée, 'Procedure and Substance' 2020 (n. 26), 115, 146; Ulrich Beyerlin/Thilo Marauhn, *International Environmental Law* (Portland/Oxford/London: Hart Publishing et al. 2012), 40–41; Leslie-Anne Duvic-Paoli argues that the harm prevention rule is broader and more comprehensive than the traditional no harm rule, see Leslie-Anne Duvic-Paoli, *The Prevention Principle in International Environmental Law* (Cambridge: CUP 2018), 21–24.

[57] ICJ, *Pulp Mills Case* (n. 41), para. 101: 'A State is thus obliged to use all the means at its disposal in order to avoid activities which take place in its territory, or in any area under its jurisdiction, causing significant damage to the environment of another State'; ICJ, *Certain Activities Carried Out by Nicaragua in the Border Area (Costa Rica v. Nicaragua)* and *Construction of a Road in Costa Rica along the San Juan River (Nicaragua v. Costa Rica)*, Judgment of 16 December 2015, ICJ Reports 2015, 665, para. 153.

[58] ICJ, *Certain Activities* (n. 57), paras 153 and 161–162 on the procedural obligation to carry out an environmental impact assessment.

[59] Ibid., para. 217.

[60] Ibid., paras 117–118 and 217. The ICJ's approach may be explained by a misreading of art. 14(3) United Nations, International Law Commission, Draft Articles on Responsibility of States for Internationally Wrongful Acts (ARSIWA), UN GAOR A/56/10, 23 April–1 June, 2 July–10 August 2001, 59, which runs: 'The breach of an international obligation requiring a State to prevent a given event occurs *when the event occurs* and extends over the entire period during which the event continues

But what does the harm prevention rule actually demand? Jutta Brunnée suggests that it requires states to act diligently in the face of a risk of significant harm.[61] From this perspective, 'causation of actual harm (. . .) is not an element of the primary rule'.[62] Brunnée sees the preventive duties not through the lens of liability but as means to avert risks. This approach explicitly turns the harm prevention rule (and maybe even its root, the no harm rule) into an instrument of risk management.

We submit that the detachment of a due diligence obligation from the result, in other words: the complete 'proceduralisation' of the obligation, is adequate only in specific constellations. Adequacy hinges, we claim, on the possibility to identify and pinpoint the result, and whether this result is good or bad. If the result is easy to identify, then the procedural and preventive obligations should not be completely detached from that result (cf. Article 14(3) ILC Articles on the Responsibility of States for Internationally Wrongful Acts (ARSIWA)). For example, with regard to the obligation to prevent genocide, the ICJ had held that 'a State can be held responsible for breaching the obligation to prevent genocide only if genocide was actually committed'.[63] Conditioning the breach of the obligation to prevent on the occurrence of the (bad) event is adequate here, given that it is fairly easy to determine (factually) whether the event did take place or not.

If however the due diligence obligation consists in reaching or maintaining a complex situation which is difficult to quantify (e.g., a certain level of education or a low level of corruption) and which moreover extends over time (and is not a spot-on event), then the 'success' is difficult to measure. Here, the preventive and other procedural obligations (e.g., under anti-corruption law or under human rights law) should indeed be detached from the result. This then means, firstly, a state violates its obligations if it fails to act diligently, even if the level of corruption is low or the level of literacy high—despite the laxity of the state.[64] Conversely (and as a flipside), a state is released from international responsibility if it takes reasonable (diligent) measures, even if the desired outcome is not reached, in our example: when a state is not entirely 'clean' from corruption, or when full literacy is not reached in the population. Secondly, the state cannot avoid responsibility simply by showing that—in our example: corruption or children missing school—would persist despite all of its efforts to prevent it.[65] Thus, although diligent preventive action would

and remains not in conformity with that obligation' (emphasis added). See for the detailed argument Brunnée, 'Procedure and Substance' 2020 (n. 26), 141, 142.

[61] Brunnée, 'Procedure and Substance' 2020 (n. 26), 147.

[62] Ibid.

[63] ICJ, *Application of the Convention on the Prevention and Punishment of the Crime of Genocide (Bosnia and Herzegovina v. Serbia and Montenegro)*, Judgment of 26 February 2007, ICJ Reports 2007, 43, para. 431.

[64] A follow-up question then is what the content of state responsibility is in the event of a breach of purely procedural duties. Reparation hardly fits, but cessation and satisfaction would be an option.

[65] In the *Bosnian Genocide* case, the ICJ found that an obligation to prevent genocide exists even if the state cannot be certain whether the preventive measures will be successful or not. In that case, success would have been the prevention of genocide. See ICJ, *Bosnian Genocide* (n. 63), para. 461.

presumably not have eliminated the problems, the lack of diligence still counts. If a breach of international law were denied here, the state would be able to avoid responsibility too easily.[66] It is at this point that the gist of the obligation are the means and processes that the state must employ. The due diligence standard here creates accountability.

2.5. The Precautionary Approach

In conjunction with the precautionary approach, due diligence seems to have turned into result-independent obligations,[67] although it is not clear what the actual source of these obligations is: a putative (customary) rule of precaution[68] or a due diligence norm itself.[69] The precautionary approach requires states to avoid environmentally sensitive activities and to take precautionary measures, even where there are only plausible indications of potential hazards and when scientific evidence as to the negative impact of the activity is inconclusive. The International Tribunal for the Law of the Sea (ITLOS) put it as follows: 'A sponsoring State would not meet its obligation of due diligence if it disregarded those risks. Such disregard would amount to a failure to comply with the precautionary approach.'[70]

Unlike the traditional no harm rule, the precautionary approach neither asks for a damage nor for a strong scientific evidence of causality.[71] And in contrast to the harm prevention rule which still presupposes knowledge about a cause-effect relation, the precautionary approach applies even where the likelihood of the materialisation of a risk is uncertain.[72] The irrelevance of scientific certainty, of damage, and of causality means that the legal obligation boils down to a duty to act diligently.[73] Importantly, a lack of diligence triggers state responsibility *even if no harm occurs*. Therefore, due diligence no longer limits accountability, but can generate it.

[66] In the *Bosnian Genocide* case, the ICJ examined this question solely for the *scope* of responsibility—that is, in order to determine whether Serbia owed reparations. *Only* at this point the ICJ examined whether genocide would have occurred even despite efforts to prevent it, see ibid., para. 462. Because this could not be shown, the ICJ did not believe financial compensation by Serbia to be appropriate.

[67] Jorge E. Viñuales, 'Due Diligence in International Environmental Law', chapter 7 of this book, section 3.2.5.

[68] See for the reluctance of the ICJ to espouse this qualification below (n. 174).

[69] Viñuales, 'International Environmental Law' (n. 67).

[70] ITLOS Seabed Disputes Chamber, *Responsibilities and Obligations of States Sponsoring Persons and Entities with Respect to Activities in the Area*, Advisory Opinion of 1 February 2011, ITLOS Reports 2011, para. 131.

[71] Meinhard Schröder, 'Precautionary Approach/Principle', in Rüdiger Wolfrum (ed.), *Max Planck Encyclopedia of Public International Law* (Oxford: OUP 2010), para. 4.

[72] See, in particular, Principle 15 of the Rio Declaration, United Nations, General Assembly, Rio Declaration on Environment and Development, A/CONF.151/26, 13 June 1992, Rev. 1: 'Where there are threats of serious or irreversible damage, lack of full scientific certainty shall not be used as a reason for postponing cost-effective measures to prevent environmental degradation'.

[73] See Viñuales, 'International Environmental Law' (n. 67).

The precautionary approach has been developed in environmental law where risks can be scientifically measured. It guides decision-making processes in situations of scientific uncertainty about potentially high risks which may entail irreversible damage. The approach has been transferred to socially constructed risks where scientific evidence plays no role.[74] Radha Ivory has pointed out that inter-state obligations under the United Nations Convention against Corruption (UNCAC), the OECD Convention on the Bribery of Foreign Public Officials in International Business Transactions, and the United Nations Convention against Transnational Organised Crime (UNTOC) also reflect a precautionary approach in that they establish free-standing duties of diligent crime control. They are not based on 'social scientific proof as to a particular state's "level" of corruption or, indeed, the effectiveness of the treaties' measures'. Moreover, 'the corporate duty [i.e., the duty incumbent on non-state actors] to prevent applies independently of proof about the occurrence of the offence within a particular institution'.[75]

Overall, the precautionary approach mainly seeks to preventively channel risks. It is less concerned with retrospectively allocating responsibility, based solely on inadequate conduct. Due diligence here functions as a new legal tool for augmenting accountability and demonstrates that regulating risks requires alternative accountability approaches.

2.6. Procedural Obligations and Due Diligence

In various subfields of international law, procedural duties (duties to notify, warn, inform, or consult) are tied to the due diligence standard.[76] However, not all procedural obligations (e.g., of notification or consultation) have to do with due diligence. For example, in international trade law, such obligations are expressions of the bona fide principle but neither require to take the interest of the other state parties into account, nor can they be seen as obligations to prevent or mitigate harm.[77]

Procedural obligations may be seen as a concretisation of the substantive due diligence standard or as result-independent obligations creating accountability. Such procedural obligations are either developed by courts, in particular when interpreting customary international law, or explicitly laid down by state parties in

[74] On the risks involved in such an approach see below section 6.

[75] See Radha Ivory, 'Due Diligence Debates in International Anti-corruption and Money Laundering Law', chapter 17 of this book, section 3.3.

[76] Brunnée, 'Community Obligations' 2018 (n. 31), 154, 157; see Malgosia Fitzmaurice, 'Due Diligence in the Use of International Watercourses', chapter 8 of this book, section 3; Schröder, 'Precautionary Approach/Principle' 2010 (n. 71), para. 12. See in global health law, International Health Regulations 2005, 2509 UNTS 70, arts 5, 6, 7, and 44. See David P. Fidler, 'From International Sanitary Conventions to Global Health Security: The New International Health Regulations', *Chinese Journal of International Law* 4 (2005), 325–392.

[77] See Krajewski, 'International Trade Law' (n. 15), section 3.1.3.

international treaties. Thus, under some treaties, procedural duties (such as planning obligations) seem to have turned into result-independent obligations creating accountability.[78] In multilateral environmental agreements, substantive due diligence obligations coupled with specifically enumerated procedural obligations allow long-term regimes to continuously evolve.[79]

Still, the law is blurred by inconclusive ICJ decisions and a lack of practice.[80] The *Pulp Mills* judgment seems inconsistent: On the one hand, the Court suggested that an environmental impact assessment is needed to comply with due diligence, but simultaneously categorised the obligation to conduct an environmental impact assessment as 'a requirement under general international law', i.e., as a free-standing duty.[81] In the same judgment, the ICJ held that both types of duties: the substantive duties (to manage soil and woodland so as not to impair water quality, and the like) and procedural duties (to notify plans, to warn, and so on) are independent from each other and can be independently breached or complied with.[82]

If one conceives the harm prevention rule as a duty to act diligently in the face of the risk of transboundary harm, the procedural duties (such as the duty to conduct an environmental impact assessment), spell out and shape what is required to act diligently. In such an understanding, breaching the procedural duties cannot be considered as a diligent behaviour. *Procedural* flaws would then violate the harm prevention rule even if no transboundary harm is actually caused. The procedural obligations are thus *distinct* from specific preventive obligations which will (at least in the understanding of Article 14(3) ARWISA)[83] be breached only when harm has occurred. Along this line, Jutta Brunnée has stressed that under customary international law, due diligence links procedure and substance. Procedural obligations 'are also part of the harm prevention rule, via its due diligence standard'.[84]

To conclude, due diligence has acquired a key function in the context of the no harm rule and its progeny, and has become mainly a tool for securing accountability.

78 See Björnstjern Baade, 'Due Diligence and the Duty to Protect Human Rights', chapter 6 of this book, section 6; Papanicolopulu, 'Law of the Sea' (n. 44), section 3.2; Rajamani, 'International Climate Change Law'(n. 47), section 1.

79 This applies, in particular, to the so-called framework-protocol model including the Convention on Long-Range Transboundary Air Pollution, 13 November 1979, 1302 UNTS 217; Vienna Convention for the Protection of the Ozone Layer, 22 March 1985, 1513 UNTS 293; United Nations Framework Convention on Climate Change, 9 May 1992, 1771 UNTS 107; Brunnée, 'Procedure and Substance' 2020 (n. 26), 191.

80 Brunnée, 'Community Obligations' 2018 (n. 31), 174.

81 ICJ, *Pulp Mills Case* (n. 41), para. 204. The qualification (as a free-standing obligation) was espoused by the ITLOS Seabed Dispute Chamber, ITLOS, *Activities in the Area* (n. 70), para. 147. See Brunnée, 'Procedure and Substance' 2020 (n. 26), 133.

82 Although the ICJ analysed the relation between substantive and procedural duties in the context of a treaty regime, it made them sound relevant for customary international law as well; ICJ, *Pulp Mills Case* (n. 41), paras 77–79; Brunnée, 'Community Obligations' 2018 (n. 31), 157.

83 See on art. 14(3) ARSIWA and for a possible understanding of result-independent preventive obligations above (n. 60) with accompanying text.

84 Brunnée, 'Procedure and Substance' 2020 (n. 26), 149.

3. Humans as Risk: Due Diligence for Closing the Accountability Gap

The no harm rule and its variations and emanations as analysed in the preceding section apply to harm caused both by states and by non-state actors. This section looks specifically at harm stemming from non-state actors including armed groups, mercenaries, private military companies, terrorists, and also banks and multinational enterprises, and highlights the key role of due diligence where risks emanate from private actors. The pertinent rules may or may not be directly related to the no harm rule but they are in structural terms similar. In some cases, the damage caused by private actors is strictly speaking not transboundary, although it affects rights and interests of other states. Moreover, most treaties do not contain any duties to mitigate harm. Instead, violations of the treaty provisions usually immediately set in motion the regime of state responsibility. The application of the due diligence standard in the relevant primary obligations works as a catalyst for closing accountability gaps in relation to activities of non-state actors. By holding states accountable for activities of non-state actors only in case of state negligence, the due diligence standard assuages the obligations of prevention and makes them acceptable for states.

An early manifestation of the due diligence standard is the obligation on states to protect foreigners and their properties who suffered harm from activities of private individuals inside the territorial state.[85] This basic rule about the treatment of (intra-territorial) aliens has been transferred to international investment law. Here the due diligence standard mitigates the obligations of host states 'to provide full protection and security' and 'fair and equitable treatment'.[86] Another area is diplomatic and consular law.[87] Article 22(2) of the 1961 Vienna Convention on Diplomatic Relations obliges the receiving state 'to take all appropriate steps to protect the premises of the mission'. In the *United States Diplomatic and Consular Staff in Tehran* case of 1980, the ICJ held the Iranian Government responsible for a violation of this provision and in this context applied the due diligence standard.[88]

As a historically important marker, the *Alabama* arbitration award confirmed the relevance of the due diligence standard in the realm of the law of neutrality.[89]

[85] See Bartolini, 'Historical Roots' (n. 3), section 2.1.

[86] Aniruddha Rajput, 'Due Diligence in International Investment Law', chapter 16 of this book, section 2. Whether the due diligence standard also applies to the international minimum standard of treatment is disputed: ibid., section 2.1; ILA Study Group on Due Diligence in International Law, First Report, 7 March 2014, 9.

[87] See Bartolini, 'Historical Roots' (n. 3), section 2.2; Tanzi, 'Liability' 2010 (n. 29), para. 1.

[88] ICJ, *United States Diplomatic and Consular Staff in Tehran (United States of America v. Iran)*, Judgment of 24 May 1980, ICJ Reports 1980, 3, para. 63: 'On 4 November 1979 the Iranian Government failed altogether to take any "appropriate steps" to protect the premises, staff and archives of the United States' mission against attack by the militants, and to take any steps either to prevent this attack or to stop it before it reached its completion.' See also ibid., para. 67.

[89] *Alabama Claims of the United States of America against Great Britain*, Award of 14 September 1872, UNRIAA 29, 124–134

The arbitration stimulated the codification of duties of neutral governments to adopt appropriate efforts to prevent the use of its territory for activities by private parties or belligerents that would be potentially detrimental to other states.[90] Article 1(1) of the 1928 Havana Convention on Duties and Rights of States in the Event of Civil Strife formulated as a broad rule that state parties must 'use all means at their disposal to prevent the inhabitants of their territory, nationals or aliens from participating in (…) in civil strife'.[91] The basic norm 'that the state must not tolerate the use of its territory for hostile military operations against another state' has constantly been refined.[92] It has been confirmed in the *Corfu Channel* case[93] and is currently seen as a fundamental rule in anti-terrorism law.[94]

While initially the protective duties sought to address unusual or even criminal attacks on (physical) security,[95] state obligations to protect have been much extended and normalised, also relating to economic damage. Radha Ivory explained how international anti-corruption treaties and money laundering law have introduced a cascading system of obligations of supervision which requires state parties to diligently oversee legal entities which in turn have to oversee associated natural and legal persons. Thereby, the obligation to regulate activities of private actors becomes part of states' general duties to prevent harm.[96] A comparable system of cascading duties mitigated by the due diligence standard also exists in international tax law.[97]

Supervisory duties tempered by a due diligence standard also arise where a state delegates specific tasks to non-state actors whose acts are not attributable to the former under the international rules of state responsibility. An important example are the obligations of sponsoring states in relation to deep seabed mining activities in the Area under the United Nations Convention for the Law of the Sea (UNCLOS). In its 2011 advisory opinion, the Seabed Disputes Chamber of the

[90] See Bartolini, 'Historical Roots' (n. 3), section 2.2. See, e.g., art. 8 of the Convention concerning the Rights and Duties of Neutral Powers in Naval War (XIII), 18 October 1907, translated in James Scott (ed.), *The Proceedings of the Hague Peace Conference: The Conference of 1907*, vol. I (New York: OUP 1920), 672–677: 'A neutral Government is bound to employ the means at its disposal to prevent the fitting out or arming of any vessel within its jurisdiction which it has reason to believe is intended to cruise, or engage in hostile operations, against a Power with which that Government is at peace. It is also bound to display the same vigilance to prevent the departure from its jurisdiction of any vessel intended to cruise, or engage in hostile operations, which had been adapted entirely or partly within the said jurisdiction for use in war.'

[91] Convention on Duties and Rights of States in the Event of Civil Strife, 20 February 1928, 134 LNTS 47.

[92] Riccardo Pisillo Mazzeschi, 'The Due Diligence Rule and the Nature of the International Responsibility of States', *German Yearbook of International Law* 35 (1992), 9–51, at 35.

[93] ICJ, *Corfu Channel Case (United Kingdom of Great Britain and Northern Ireland v. Albania)*, Judgment of 9 April 1949, ICJ Reports 1949, 4, p. 22.

[94] See Österdahl, 'Due Diligence in International Anti-terrorism Law: Developments in the Resolutions of the UN Security Council', chapter 14 of this book, section 1.

[95] Cf. Mazzeschi, 'The Due Diligence Rule' 1992 (n. 92), 22.

[96] See Ivory, 'International Anti-corruption and Money Laundering Law' (n. 75), section 3.1.

[97] See Reuven S. Avi-Yonah/Gianluca Mazzoni, 'Due Diligence in International Tax Law', chapter 18 of this book, section 3.

International Tribunal for the Law of the Sea distinguished between the states' obligations to ensure compliance by sponsored contractors[98] and direct obligations of the states themselves.[99] Both types of obligations are mitigated by the due diligence standard.[100]

Various international instruments protect such specific community interests or values against harmful activities of private actors. These instruments then oblige the state parties, as the ICJ puts it, 'to take certain steps to prevent the acts it [the treaty] seeks to prohibit'.[101] The most important examples are Article I of the Genocide Convention, common Article 1 of the Geneva Conventions I-IV and Article 1 of the Additional Protocol I,[102] and arguably also Article 2 of the ILC Draft Articles on Crimes against Humanity.[103] The obligations under these umbrella clauses do not only embody state obligations concerning private persons under the state parties' control. Rather, these umbrella provisions possess an additional 'external dimension':[104] They have an extraterritorial scope of application,[105] and additionally lay down the state parties' obligation to ensure that other states and other actors respect the treaty too.[106] The International Committee of the Red Cross (ICRC) commentaries call this a 'a general duty of due diligence'.[107]

For the obligation to prevent genocide, the catalyst function of the due diligence standard to activate prevention duties for securing some accountability for harmful behaviour of non-state actors has become particularly evident. In the *Bosnian Genocide* case, the Court could not successfully establish Serbia-Montenegro's responsibility, neither on the basis of attribution under Articles 4 and 8 ARSIWA, nor on any other ground of attribution,[108] nor on the basis of complicity under Article III e) of the Genocide Convention itself or under Article 16 ARSIWA.[109] Therefore, as a kind of last resort, the Court developed and elaborated on the duty to prevent under Article I of the Genocide Convention as an autonomous obligation of the state parties.[110] The Court took a restrictive approach by limiting its considerations to the specific case.[111] It further mitigated the duty to prevent by explicitly referring

[98] The operators must comply with the terms of the contract and with obligations set out in UNCLOS and related instruments, UNCLOS, 1982 (n. 13), art. 139(1).

[99] ITLOS, *Activities in the Area* (n. 70), para. 121.

[100] Ibid., para. 109.

[101] ICJ, *Bosnian Genocide* (n. 63), para. 429.

[102] ICRC (ed.), *Updated Commentary on the First Geneva Convention* (Cambridge: CUP 2016), para. 166.

[103] See Larissa van den Herik/Emma Irving, 'Due Diligence and the Obligation to Prevent Genocide and Crimes Against Humanity', chapter 12 of this book, section 3.

[104] ICRC, *Commentary* 2016 (n. 102), para. 153.

[105] Ibid., para. 183.

[106] See van den Herik/Irving, 'Obligation to Prevent Genocide' (n. 103); Marco Longobardo, 'Due Diligence in International Humanitarian Law', chapter 11 of this book, section 2.2.

[107] ICRC, *Commentary* (n. 102), para. 150.

[108] ICJ, *Bosnian Genocide* (n. 63), paras 381–382 and 414–415.

[109] Ibid., paras 420 and 424.

[110] Ibid., para. 427.

[111] Ibid., para. 429.

to the due diligence standard.[112] The ICJ thereby sought to strike a balance between avoiding impunity on the one hand and overburdening third states in the face of atrocities committed outside their effective (territorial) control on the other hand. It is worth repeating that due diligence does not lead to the attribution of genocidal acts to the state (in that case Serbia-Montenegro) but circumscribes a separate and specific own obligation of prevention of the state.

The prevailing view, also espoused by the ICRC, is that common Article 1 of the Geneva Conventions I-IV works in a similar way[113] and is also limited by the due diligence standard.[114] The duty to ensure respect falls on all states even if they are not a party to an armed conflict. The ICRC commentary argues that the extraterritorial reach of the duty to ensure respect flows from its erga omnes partes nature as an obligation that protects a fundamental value of the international community and which therefore creates a legal interest of each and every contracting party in compliance.[115]

4. Other Functions of Due Diligence in International Law

Broadening the analysis of due diligence norms even more allows us to identify further diverse tasks of due diligence in various branches of international law.

4.1. Human Rights Law and the Duty to Protect

The states' duty to protect international human rights is often broadly understood as an obligation of due diligence or an obligation of conduct because it 'requires the state to act in protection of a right, including against private actors, without having to guarantee success'.[116] Here, 'the term "due diligence" is used to describe the standard of conduct necessary to comply with a duty to protect'.[117] However,

[112] Ibid., para. 430.

[113] ICRC, *Commentary* 2016 (n. 102), para. 120; Longobardo, 'International Humanitarian Law' (n. 106), section 2.2.

[114] ICRC, *Commentary* 2016 (n. 102), para. 153.

[115] Ibid., para. 119.

[116] Baade, 'Duty to Protect Human Rights' (n. 78), section 2.1, with reference to William A. Schabas, *The European Convention on Human Rights: A Commentary* (Oxford: OUP 2015), 125. See *mutatis mutandis* Koivurova, 'Due Diligence' 2010 (n. 38), para. 33: 'Hence, a violation of a human right by a non-State entity may also trigger a State's legal responsibility where it has failed to act with due diligence in preventing and punishing the non-State actor.'

[117] See Baade, 'Duty to protect human rights' (n. 78), section 1, with reference to ILA, Study Group on Due Diligence, 'First Report' 2014 (n. 86), 14; Koivurova, 'Due Diligence' 2010 (n. 38), para. 5; United Nations, Commission on Human Rights, The Due Diligence Standard as a Tool for the Elimination of Violence against Women, Report of the Special Rapporteur on violence against women, its causes and consequences (Yakin Ertürk), E/CN.4/2006/61, 20 January 2006, para. 14: 'yardstick'.

a closer analysis reveals that in human rights law, 'due diligence' diverges somewhat from the due diligence standard in duties of prevention in other areas of international law.

Negative and positive human rights obligations differ in content. The 'negative' duty to respect obliges the state to refrain from a specific activity that infringes human rights. In contrast, in order to comply with the positive duty to protect, the state must take one of several adequate measures. The European Court of Human Rights (ECtHR) has conceptualised this difference in terms of obligations of result versus obligations of conduct.[118] While other human rights monitoring institutions[119] explicitly refer to due diligence, the ECtHR has apparently not used the term 'due diligence' at all for describing the scope and content of the duty to protect human rights. Arguably, the functions of the due diligence standard, its strictness, and the elements of the balancing process are not identical in other areas of international law and under the European Convention on Human Rights (ECHR) on which our analysis focuses.[120]

Due diligence as discussed in the preceding sections operates on an inter-state level and restricts or creates accountability basically towards other states. In contrast, the primary purpose of the ECHR is to hold the member states accountable to individuals. This form of accountability is secured with help of a specific mechanism and in a specific legal vocabulary. The ECtHR controls whether an act or omission of the state fails to strike a fair balance between the individual rights and the public interest, using a proportionality test. With regard to positive state obligations honouring the duty to protect, the balancing exercise considers numerous factors. One of them is the foreseeable risk to the human right at stake and the state's capacity to act. These factors need to be balanced against countervailing public interests or against human rights of other individuals. As Björnstjern Baade emphasises, 'these factors are not separate requirements *before* a reasonableness or proportionality test is conducted; they are part of the same

[118] ECtHR, *Plattform 'Ärzte für das Leben' v. Austria*, Judgment of 21 June 1988, Application No. 10126/82, para. 34: 'In this area the obligation they enter into under Article 11 of the Convention is an obligation as to measures to be taken and not as to results to be achieved.'

[119] See, e.g., IACtHR, *Opinión Consultativa Solicitada por la República de Colombia: Medio Ambiente y Derechos*, Advisory Opinion of 15 November 2017, OC-23/17, paras 149–152; United Nations, Human Rights Committee, General Comment No. 36 on article 6 of the International Covenant on Civil and Political Rights, on the right to life, 30 October 2018, CCPR/C/GC/36, para. 21: 'State parties are thus under a due diligence obligation to undertake reasonable positive measures, which do not impose on them disproportionate burdens.' United Nations, Committee on Economic, Social and Cultural Rights, General Comment No. 24 (2017) on state obligations under the International Covenant on Economic, Social and Cultural Rights in the context of business activities, E/C.12/GC/24, 10 August 2017, e.g., paras 15–17, 31–33.

[120] But see, leaning towards an overarching duty to protect and a corresponding due diligence standard: Anja Seibert-Fohr, 'From Complicity to Due Diligence: When Do States incur Responsibility for their Involvement in Serious International Wrongdoing?', *German Yearbook of International Law* 60 (2017), 667–707, 706.

assessment'.[121] In doctrinal terms, considerations of risk and capacity limit the states' headway.[122]

In this balancing exercise, the standard is usually much stricter than elsewhere in international law which means that the states' leeway is smaller. First, as Björnstjern Baade shows, 'the number of measures available to effectively protect a human right is finite. Among these, states may generally choose; however, at times only one available measure may be sufficiently effective'. The balancing exercise often 'crystallised into the duty to take (…) one specific measure'[123] because the risks and the context involved are very specific and allow determining what is exactly required to protect a human right. Then, states are not only obliged to take whatever adequate measure but must even fulfil some minimum obligations. It can therefore not be said that positive obligations under the ECHR only require best efforts. Rather, the positive obligations encompass a duty to prevent human rights violations from taking place. Second, the very importance of the rights at stake considerably limits states' latitude.[124] Under certain circumstances, the human rights-based duties might even amount to obligations of result.

Here a similarity shines up with the domain of general international law where ius cogens obligations should also have the effect of raising the requirements of due diligence. However, there is so far no practice in this direction. For example, under Article I of the Genocide Convention, the requirements for concrete measure for fulfilling the duty to prevent genocide still seem to be comparatively lenient.[125]

Further, the elements of the balancing process differ from those under due diligence in general international law. In human rights law, balancing may involve conflicting public interests and the human rights of other individuals. Protection against harmful activities of non-state actors in itself impacts on human rights of those others. The balancing exercise, for example between one person's right to privacy and another person's right to free speech is highly value-laden. The experience that national courts and international monitoring bodies have often reached different conclusions in such tripolar constellations shows that the perception of risks is culturally contingent. Positive obligations may strongly interfere with the national legal system and with political choices which result from democratic processes on the domestic level. It is no coincidence that some ECtHR decisions on positive obligations are among the most contested ones. The member states' margin of appreciation in relation to their positive obligations is therefore an important tool for respecting democratic self-government.[126] In human rights law, due diligence

[121] See Baade 'Duty to Protect Human Rights' (n. 78), section 3.

[122] Heike Krieger, 'Funktionen von Grund- und Menschenrechten', in Oliver Dörr/Rainer Grote/Thilo Marauhn (eds), *Konkordanzkommentar zum europäischen und deutschen Grundrechtsschutz* (Tübingen: Mohr Siebeck 2nd ed. 2013), 287–365, at 327–328.

[123] See Baade, 'Duty to Protect Human Rights' (n. 78), section 4.2.

[124] Ibid.; see also Krieger, 'Funktionen' 2013 (n. 122), 328.

[125] See van den Herik/Irving, 'Obligation to Prevent Genocide' (n. 103), section 6.

[126] Krieger, 'Funktionen' 2013 (n. 122), 329.

is more closely linked to 'proportionality' which arguably is a general principle of international law and even of international constitutional law.[127] Against this background, 'due diligence' in the human rights context might mean something else than in other fields of international law—although the family resemblance of course remains. So the use of the identical term 'due diligence' somewhat obscures that we are dealing with diverging meanings and functions of a legal concept.

4.2. Goal-oriented Obligations

Within human rights law, the due diligence standard seems to play an obvious role for the operationalisation of goal-oriented obligations (obligations of progressive realisation) which are dominant in the ICESCR (cf. Article 2(1)). These oblige states to 'set into motion an evolutionary process leading into a particular direction. (...) The process may mean to lead to a concrete result albeit in some (distant) future.'[128] Goal-oriented obligations can also be found in the climate law regime,[129] in other multilateral (environmental) agreements,[130] and in further areas of international law.[131] Goal-oriented obligations do not prescribe a specific conduct through which a goal shall be reached but only define the goal itself. They leave states a broad discretion in how to reach it. This legal technique is adequate where possible measures are too diverse to be agreed upon in a specific treaty rule. The broad range of possible measures may stem from uncertainties about future developments and about the effects of particular measures. In addition, states may be in legitimate disagreement about the adequacy of measures because of diverging cultural, social, economic, and political contexts.[132] As with the precautionary approach, it is not easy to determine when progressive obligations are breached and when the usual consequences of state responsibility are triggered. The standard legal structure of 'action-causality-damage-reparation' does not seem to fit. Instead, the progressive obligations are so programmatic and open that they hardly allow for retrospective accountability.[133] Because of this particular legal structure, the obligations

[127] Anne Peters, 'Proportionality as a Global Constitutional Principle', in Anthony F. Lang Jr./ Antje Wiener (eds), *Handbook on Global Constitutionalism* (Cheltenham and Northampton, Massachusetts: Edward Elgar 2017), 248–264.

[128] Wolfrum, 'Obligations' 2011 (n. 50), 367.

[129] Rajamani, 'International Climate Change Law' (n. 47), section 3.1.

[130] E.g., Convention on the Protection of the Alps (Alpine Convention), 7 November 1991, OJ EC 1996 L 61, 32–36, art. 2.

[131] For example, in the law of the United Nations, see Charter of the United Nations, 24 October 1945, 1 UNTS XVI, art. 55(a).

[132] Jochen Rauber, 'Zukunftsorientierung und Prozeduralisierung im öffentlichen Recht—Parallelen in der Entwicklung von innerstaatlicher und völkerrechtlicher Ordnung', *Archiv des öffentlichen Rechts* 143 (2018), 67–121, at 85–86.

[133] See, however, for a proposal to operationalise progressive obligations and to apply tests of causality in this context: Anne Peters, 'Corruption as a Violation of International Human Rights', *European Journal of International Law* 29 (2018), 1251–1287.

of progressive realisation, notably in the field of social human rights, have for a long time been characterised as mere political promises and hortatory norms, especially by authors of the western world.[134] Now the due diligence standard, which requires states to take all appropriate means, makes these programmatic norms legally operational by setting a benchmark against which efforts can be assessed in legal terms. It may thereby create legal accountability.

4.3. Due Diligence Audits

'Due diligence' in international economic law may relate to the conduct of legal audits. In this context, the term attaches to a different practice than in the other areas of international law discussed so far.

The meaning of 'due diligence' is here borrowed from private corporate law in relation to business transaction and corporate finance.[135] In that sphere, we might speak of 'doing due diligence' as opposed to 'acting with due diligence'.[136] Doing due diligence is an exercise of risk mitigation by conducting a legal, environmental, and/or social audit before envisaged projects and other (legal) undertakings in order to avoid a bad outcome. The bad outcomes to be fended off include not only potential breaches of the law but encompass all kinds of negative results. Therefore, 'doing due diligence' is partly outside the realm of the law. Still, from the perspective of a corporation, the diligence exercise seeks to avoid its legal liability or other legal problems. For example, an investor is expected to assess the present and possible future legal framework of the state where the investment shall take place. An investor who did not conduct due diligence will lose its protection under a bilateral investment treaty.[137] Thus, in investment law, due diligence actually secures the investors' claims for damages. Here, due diligence is primarily exercised to protect the actor itself, and not, as in the constellations described above, other actors' interests.

'Due diligence' is also used when examining a potential target for project financing, as a legal, environmental, or social audit in international project finance. Project leaders must identify and assess foreseeable risk against expected returns from project revenues. In particular, the World Bank's due diligence process in its investment project financing operations scrutinises the human rights, environmental, and social treaty commitments and compliance of the states involved.

[134] Egbert W. Vierdag, 'The Legal Nature of the Rights Granted by the International Covenant on Economic, Social and Cultural Rights', *Netherlands Yearbook of International Law* 9 (1978), 69–105, at 105, concluding that 'the rights granted by the International Covenant on Economic, Social and Cultural Rights are of such a nature as to be legally negligible'.

[135] Cf. Rajput, 'International Investment Law' (n. 86), section 6.

[136] Neil McDonald, 'The Role of Due Diligence in International Law', *International and Comparative Law Quarterly* 68 (2019), 1041–1054, at 1042.

[137] Rajput, 'International Investment Law' (n. 86), section 3.

The World Bank 'recognises a broader understanding of project risks to include environmental and social risks, as well as direct and indirect impacts to affected, displaced, or vulnerable communities, indigenous peoples, and other groups', as Diane Desierto pointed out.[138] Here, the conduct of due diligence mitigates the accountability gap which arises because the World Bank and other international financial institutions do not consider themselves to be bound by states' human rights, environmental, and social international obligations.[139] Due diligence—at least partly—complements the international legal obligations of the states hosting the projects.[140]

A similar function of 'due diligence' may be traced in international trade law. Markus Krajewski claimed that already the drafting and conclusion of trade agreements requires due diligence with regard to international human rights and other obligations.[141] Here, due diligence denotes the 'assessments of the impact of trade agreements on other international law principles and provisions, in particular in the fields of human rights or sustainable development' in order to 'analyse the potential impact of an agreement on the human rights situation in the contracting parties. Questions such as whether a trade agreement should be concluded between two or more countries or whether particular contents should or should not be part of the agreement are at the centre of the impact assessments of trade agreements.'[142] This impact assessment in international trade law embodies a kind of 'external due diligence dimension'.

Due diligence as a form of legal audit has also appeared within the UN in relation to peacekeeping. Under the UN Human Rights Due Diligence Policy,[143] the UN must conduct a risk assessment before cooperating with non-UN security forces. The due diligence exercise must assess whether these forces are likely to commit grave violations of international humanitarian law, human rights law, or refugee law. This policy also includes 'transparency with receiving entities about the legal obligations binding the Organization and the core principles governing provision of support'; and an 'effective implementation framework' including procedures for monitoring compliance and interceding.[144]

[138] Diane Desierto, 'Due Diligence in World Bank Project Financing', chapter 20 of this book, section 5.

[139] See for the official position former General Counsel to the IMF François Gianviti, 'Economic, Social and Cultural Human Rights and the International Monetary Fund', in Philip Alston (ed.), *Non-State Actors and Human Rights* (Oxford: OUP 2005), 113–140, at 135. But see, e.g., Willem van Genugten, *The World Bank Group, the IMF and Human Rights* (Cambridge: Intersentia, 2015).

[140] Desierto, 'World Bank Project Financing' (n. 138), section 4.

[141] See in this sense also United Nations, Special Rapporteur on the right to food (Olivier de Schutter), Guiding Principles on Human Rights Impact Assessments of Trade and Investment Agreements, A/HRC/19/59/Add. 5, 19 December 2011.

[142] Krajewski, 'International Trade Law' (n. 15), section 4.

[143] United Nations Secretary General Ban Ki-moon, 'Human Rights Due Diligence Policy on United Nations Support to Non-United Nations Security Forces', A/67/775–S/2013/110, 5 March 2013.

[144] Ibid., para. 2; Nigel D. White, 'Due Diligence, the UN and Peacekeeping', chapter 13 of this book, section 7.5.

The mentioned forms of legal audit encompass an element of risk governance or risk management in that they delineate certain spheres of accountability in order to mitigate (legal) and other risks. However, in general, no legal consequences, in particular no sanctions, are attached to failures in preventing risks from materialising. Negligence on the side of the World Bank in project-related due diligence does so far not create legal accountability even if harm occurs. The same is true for the UN Human Rights Due Diligence Policy. In sum, the work that the audits called 'due diligence' performs starkly differ from the functions of 'due diligence' as a standard of behaviour in the context of the no harm rule and its emanations.

5. Due Diligence as a General Principle?

Our investigation of the various manifestations of due diligence in different areas of international law raises the question whether a common understanding of due diligence can be traced which might warrant the conclusion that it qualifies as a general principle, either as a formal source of international law in terms of Article 38(1) lit. c) ICJ Statute or in a looser sense as a 'general principle of law'. We have seen that the term 'due diligence' has a wide array of different meanings and fulfils diverging functions in hugely diverse legal regimes. It is most coherently employed in the context of the no harm rule and for the allocation of accountability for man-made risks (including humans themselves as risk) in relation to (transboundary) harm. Here, the standard disseminated from some unspecified obligations under international customary law to specific treaty regimes. This spread reflects that (new) risks and insecurities have triggered new strategies for allocating accountability. Due to its openness and its inherent feature of balancing to identify what is 'due', due diligence appears as a particularly suitable legal tool for assigning accountability in international relations. Traditional forms of retrospective responsibility need to be complemented by preventive methods of risk allocation and by prospective risk management. This consideration might speak in favour of envisaging due diligence as a general principle in this particular context. Due diligence might establish a baseline of accountability of states and other actors. This regulatory approach might be transferred to other constellations and might serve as a normative basis for procedural obligations under customary international law. Conceiving of due diligence as a general principle could contribute to the overall coherence of the international legal order.[145]

However, a number of considerations speak against qualifying due diligence as a general principle of international law. A preliminary point is that due diligence

[145] Such coherence is desirable because it strengthens the normative power of the international legal order, its quality as 'law'. See Anne Peters, 'The Refinement of International Law: From Fragmentation to Regime Interaction and Politicization', *International Journal of Constitutional Law* 15 (2017), 671–704.

is no free-standing obligation, but is a modality and a standard of behaviour. It can therefore be only a 'component part' of other rules: '[S]pecific primary rules ... require a particular act or omission by ... states which *might* require ... to act with due diligence in order to act consistently with the rule.'[146] This ancillary character of due diligence would not per se prevent it from becoming a general principle, as the recognition of 'good faith' as a general principle of international law shows.[147] A problem rather is that what is required (what is 'due'), can only be defined by reference to other substantive rules and to the object and purpose of the specific regulatory regime.

In this vein, elemental considerations on standards of attribution under the law of state responsibility apply *mutatis mutandis*. In his Commentaries on the Articles on State Responsibility, Special Rapporteur James Crawford explained that the Articles avoid terms such as 'subjective' and 'objective' elements:

> Whether responsibility is 'objective' or 'subjective' in this sense depends on the circumstances, including the content of the primary obligation in question. The articles lay down no general rule in that regard. The same is true of other standards, whether they involve some degree of fault, culpability, negligence or want of due diligence. Such standards vary from one context to another for reasons which essentially relate to the object and purpose of the treaty provision or other rule giving rise to the primary obligation.[148]

In the same manner, in the *Bosnian Genocide* case, the ICJ cautioned against a generalisation of due diligence-based prevention duties:

> The content of the duty to prevent varies from one instrument to another, according to the wording of the relevant provisions, and depending on the nature of the acts to be prevented. The decision of the Court does not, in this case, purport to establish a general jurisprudence applicable to all cases where a treaty instrument, or other binding legal norm, includes an obligation for States to prevent certain acts.[149]

Anyone who wants to identify and circumscribe the due diligence obligations (both procedural and substantive) must always look at the substantive standards of the specific regime. In consequence, due diligence as a general principle would not add much but simply state an unspecified duty of good behaviour.

146 McDonald, 'The Role of Due Diligence' 2019 (n. 136), 1047.

147 Guillaume Futhazar/Anne Peters, 'Good Faith', in Jorge Viñuales (ed.), *The Friendly Relations Declaration* (Cambridge: CUP 2020), 189–228.

148 United Nations, International Law Commission, Commentary to the Draft Articles on State Responsibility, YBILC 2001, vol. II (part II), 30–143, art. 2, para. 34.

149 ICJ, *Bosnian Genocide* (n. 63), para. 429.

More importantly, the acknowledgment of due diligence as a general principle of international law would create an additional legal argumentative burden for states when they intend to apply a different liability standard. Turning the due diligence standard into a general principle, into an overarching obligation to behave diligently in international relations, would imply that due diligence is normatively more desirable than other standards (such as absolute harm prevention on the one side or mere avoidance of gross recklessness on the other side). The imposition of a uniform standard of behaviour (which the conceptualisation of due diligence as a general principle of international law suggests) might be inadequate, and it would also restrict the states' freedom to work out the most appropriate allocation of accountability. The ongoing negotiations on autonomous weapons are a case in point. States and academics are recommending various mechanisms for creating accountability here. Proposals range from a complete ban to a broad permission and include strict liability, a presumption of liability, and prevention or harm mitigation duties based on the due diligence standard.[150] Eventually, the future standard of conduct chosen for the primary obligations of states will depend on risk assessments and political viability. But none of these standards is per se normatively more desirable than any other. In view of the widely diverging functions of due diligence and its dependence on the primary rules which it accompanies, due diligence should not be conceived as a general principle of international law.[151] Rather, due diligence is as an emanation or sibling of other structural principles, such as good neighbourliness and good faith.

6. The Rise of Due Diligence and Structural Change in the International Order

Although due diligence does not qualify as an overarching general principle of international law, it still seems to mirror some structural change in the international legal order, as speculated in our introductory chapter.[152] The structure of the international legal order is mainly determined by who counts as a legal person, what counts as a legal source, and by patterns in the content of the norms. Structural questions implied in the rise of due diligence are the firmness of the international rule of law, international legal personhood, deformalisation, proceduralisation,

[150] Robin Geiss, 'Autonomous Weapons Systems: Risk Management and State Responsibility', Third CCW meeting of experts on lethal autonomous weapons systems (LAWS) Geneva, 11–15 April 2016, available at https://www.unog.ch/80256EDD006B8954/(httpAssets)/00C95F16D6FC38E4C1257F9D0039B84D/$file/Geiss-CCW-Website.pdf (accessed 14 April 2020).

[151] It is therefore immaterial whether due diligence is indeed sufficiently widespread in representative legal orders to qualify as a general principle in the sense of Article 38(1) lit. c) ICJ Statute, cf. Alain Pellet/Daniel Müller, 'Article 38', in Andreas Zimmermann/Christian J. Tams et al. (eds), *The Statute of the International Court of Justice: A Commentary* (Oxford: OUP 3rd ed. 2019), 922–931, at 925.

[152] Peters/Krieger/Kreuzer, 'Dissecting the Leitmotif' (n. 1), section 8.

and related themes. Due diligence seems to be at once a response to, a manifestation of, and a catalyst for structural change in international law. This section seeks to corroborate our initial hypothesis on the basis of the book chapters' findings.

6.1. A Compensation for Curtailing Sovereign Freedoms

Since 1945, international law has developed into a dense legal order which has considerably curbed states' freedom of action in view of ever-increasing interdependencies. There is not much space left for the Lotus principle that '[r]estrictions on the independence of States cannot (...) be presumed'.[153] Still, states need a certain leeway for pursuing legitimate interests. Due diligence has become one of the legal tools granting such leeway. Thereby, states' freedom of action has been transformed from a pre-legal concept into a legally circumscribed and curtailed form of discretion.

Second, due diligence allocates accountability for risks on the grounds of predictability of those risks and the state's capacity to control or mitigate them. Due diligence thus makes clear that other states, depending on the circumstances, must tolerate harm to a certain extent. Not all transboundary harmful effects of sovereign acts count, but only those which result from negligent behaviour. Moreover, this 'milder' accountability standard takes the lawfulness or legitimacy of a state's harmful activity into account. The due diligence standard makes room for a balancing process between the states' freedom to act based on their sovereignty and other interests. While acknowledging that acts of states may legitimately unfold effects beyond a state's territory, due diligence underlines that such sovereign 'uses' of state territory are limited by the states' corollary duty to respect the rights of other states or certain legally protected common goods and values.[154]

The opaque notion of sovereignty is here only a placeholder for legitimate or legally recognised interests states may pursue. Such interests are, *inter alia*, exemplified in Article 3 No. 4 of the Southern African Development Community 2000 Revised Protocol on Shared Watercourses[155] which states that 'State Parties shall maintain a proper balance between resource development for a higher standard of living for their people and conservation and enhancement of the environment to promote sustainable development.' The same logic feeds the differentiated due diligence standard in international climate law. Article 4(1) of the Paris Agreement

[153] PCIJ, *The Case of the S.S. Lotus (France v. Turkey)*, Judgment of 7 September 1927, Series A, No. 10, at 18.

[154] Arbitrator Max Huber, *Case of the Island of Palmas (Netherlands v. USA)*, Award of 4 April 1928, vol. II, UNRIIA, 829–871, at 829, 838; Jelena Bäumler, *Schädigungsverbot* (Berlin/Heidelberg: Springer 2017), 53–55.

[155] Southern African Development Community, Revised Protocol on Shared Watercourses, 7 August 2000, available at: https://www.sadc.int/files/3413/6698/6218/Revised_Protocol_on_Shared_Watercourses_-_2000_-_English.pdf (accessed 14 April 2020).

laying down the objectives and goals of the regime refers, *inter alia*, to 'efforts to eradicate poverty' while Article 2(2) permits to consider 'different national circumstances.'[156] This gives developing states more leeway for setting national policy priorities by weighing interests in poverty eradication and development against concerns of climate protection. The balancing process informs the parameters which will then define the due diligence standard in the concrete case.

To conclude, due diligence exemplifies the paradigmatic shift from the 'state of nature' among states to a legally regulated sphere. At the same time, due diligence re-introduces a wriggle room which superficially operates as a compensation for losses of 'natural' sovereign freedom. This might be the price to pay for legalisation and risks to undermine its benefits.

6.2. A Tool to Manage Risk and Uncertainty in the Face of Connectivity and Diversity of International Actors

The reluctance to introduce rules on strict liability or to apply the rules of state responsibility to far-reaching environmental harm has to do with the complexity of assessing the costs of such environmental damage (where even the scientific parameters for calculating harm are uncertain), in particular in relation to the measure taken by states concerned. The negotiations over the Chernobyl accident and the ensuing treaty-making efforts demonstrate the states' preference for preventive measures and liability regulations based on the due diligence standard.[157] Restitution in kind based on causality seems to overburden all actors involved. Here, the due diligence standard renders factual complexities manageable for legal regulation and evaluation.

As shown above, the due diligence standard also allows allocating accountability for risks where several actors are in a position to avert the harm. Due diligence facilitates dealing with high connectivity, in the constellation that activities of states and non-state actors are either meant to cross borders or have spillover effects. Where multiple actors may cause, contribute to, or prevent harm (or the risk of harm), a responsibility regime based on a direct causal link between action or omission and harm, combined with insular rules on the attribution of conduct to a state will not suffice to legally capture the multifarious factual interrelations.[158] On the other hand, rigid standards in form of strict liability would not allow to

[156] Rajamani, 'International Climate Change Law' (n. 47), section 3.3.

[157] Kiss/Shelton, 'Strict Liability' 2007 (n. 19), 1135; Brunnée, 'Procedure and Substance' 2020 (n. 26), 152. Lavanya Rajamani shows how difficult the assessment of the contributions of the state parties to climate harm is. As the contributions are a relevant parameter for identifying what is 'due', the due diligence standard becomes difficult to apply, see Rajamani, 'International Climate Change Law' (n. 47), section 3.3.

[158] Cf. Seibert-Fohr, 'From Complicity to Due Diligence' (n. 120), 667.

properly take account of the nuanced quantity and quality of the various contributions of states and non-state actors involved. Instead, we need criteria to link the materialisation of a risk to one or several of the relevant actors. What matters is not direct causality between action and damage but the proximity of an actor to a risk.[159] Two typical elements of the due diligence standard—fact-based predictability of a risk and capacity to control or mitigate the risk—offer manageable criteria to establish such legally relevant proximity. And by relating the risk management capacity (the second element) primarily to jurisdiction (or effective control over territory), the due diligence standard uses a traditional, yet fairly obvious and thus foreseeable criterion, while also allowing for differentiated and graded obligations and responsibility.

In the *Bosnian Genocide* case, the ICJ also concentrated on the 'capacity to influence' as the relevant criterion that triggers the (due diligence-)obligation to prevent genocide.[160] Beyond jurisdiction and control, relevant factors include 'geographical distance of the state from the scene of the events, and the strength of political and other links between the state and the main actors in the events'.[161] The ICRC commentary also relies on the capacity to influence for defining the due diligence standard under common Article 1 of the Geneva Conventions.[162]

In international environmental law, one relevant factor for defining the risk management capacity of a state is its 'economic level'.[163] And in international climate law, risk proximity is contingent both on states' resources for action and on their past contributions to climate harm. Resort to these criteria reflects the overall approach of common yet differentiated responsibilities within the climate protection regime which acknowledges that respect for sovereign formal equality allows to take account of the vast factual discrepancies between developed and developing states (Article 2(2) Paris Agreement).[164] The standard of common but differentiated responsibilities, firstly, 'does clarify that, in the context of the climate regime, the degree of care expected of an industrialized state with sophisticated environmental management systems is different from that expected of less developed states'.[165] Second, attention to past climate damaging behaviour introduces an element of responsibility into risk allocation.

Further, anti-corruption treaties and related anti-money laundering instruments likewise address the variety of states and non-state actors with cascades of due diligence obligations attached to the diverse capacities and responsibilities of all actors involved.[166] The diversified obligations of sponsoring states in relation

[159] Federica Violi, 'The Function of the Triad 'Territory', 'Jurisdiction', and 'Control' in Due Diligence Obligations', chapter 5 of this book, section 2.
[160] ICJ, *Bosnian Genocide* (n. 63), para. 430.
[161] van den Herik/Irving, 'Obligation to Prevent Genocide' (n. 103), section 3.
[162] ICRC, Commentary 2016 (n. 102), paras 164–165.
[163] ILC, Draft Articles on Prevention (n. 13), art. 3, commentary, para. 13.
[164] Rajamani, 'International Climate Change Law' (n. 47), section 3.3.
[165] Brunnée, 'Procedure and Substance' 2020 (n. 26), 201.
[166] Ivory, 'International Anti-corruption and Money Laundering Law' (n. 75), section 4.

to deep seabed mining activities in the Area under UNCLOS are another case in point.[167]

To conclude, the due diligence standard is flexible enough to allow ongoing adaptation. Due diligence also takes into account the diversity of state actors. It permits to grade legal responsibility based on distinct degrees of risk proximity.[168] Overall, due diligence works against a too summarial and formalist allocation of accountability among international actors which are increasingly connected. Seen from the perspective of the international rule of law, this adds an element of material justice which can be seen as a core component of the rule of law.

6.3. A Tool for Progressive Interpretation in Times of Contestation

Being an open legal concept, due diligence is an entry point for progressive interpretations of international law. The term 'due' is a dynamic reference, because the question what is 'due' requires a factual and a normative answer which may change over time.

On the level of facts, 'due-ness' takes technical developments of risk ascertainment into account which may raise the requirements over time. What is due depends on the state of the art in any given moment.[169] High complexity, lack of knowledge, and uncertainties about the appropriate measures to be taken make it difficult if not impossible to reach consensus on an abstract standard and on the exact content of duties of prevention on the international level. With the advancement of scientific knowledge, specific regulatory approaches and rules may quickly become outdated. Although specific obligations would increase legal certainty and foreseeability, they would soon require cumbersome treaty revisions. The broad due diligence standard leaves room for development without treaty amendments, leaving the particularisation of the benchmark to the stage of treaty application. On that level, the circumstances of the case at hand allow decision-makers to identify more clearly what is concretely 'due'.[170]

In the normative dimension, the term 'due' links the specification of the standard to the object and purpose of a given treaty and to rules and principles within and outside a given treaty regime. Due diligence thereby permits to align diverging obligations of the state owing a diligent behaviour and may thus develop the law. The climate protection regime is an example. Lavanya Rajamani has pointed out that a

[167] ITLOS, *Activities in the Area* (n. 70), para. 109.

[168] Violi, 'The Function of the Triad' (n. 159), section 6.

[169] 'It may change over time as measures considered sufficiently diligent at a certain moment may become not diligent enough in light, for instance, of new scientific or technological knowledge' see ITLOS, *Activities in the Area* (n. 70), para. 117.

[170] Rauber, 'Zukunftsorientierung und Prozeduralisierung' 2018 (n. 132), 85–87.

systematic and teleological interpretation of the Paris Agreement helps to specify the due diligence standard under the Agreement. Cross-cutting normative expectations as laid down in context-setting provisions of the preamble and in Articles 3 and 4 ('progression', 'highest possible ambition', and 'leadership') limit the states' broad discretion under the due diligence standard in relation to their self-selected nationally determined contributions.[171]

The normative openness of the due diligence standard facilitates treaty negotiations because at least some of the conflicting interests do not need to be enshrined in explicit legal rules. In this regard, due diligence works as a tool for managing contestations. In the design of a treaty, contravening interests may be made explicit, for example in the preamble or in programmatic articles, but their accommodation is transferred to a later point in the process of implementing and applying a treaty.[172] The problem with this deferral technique are the resulting discrepancies flowing from the fact that the law is mainly applied by decentralised national authorities.

The value judgment what is 'due' is influenced by the legitimate expectations of the actors involved. Here, social, political, and ethical considerations enter.[173] The normative openness of the due diligence standard has repeatedly turned it into a conduit for drawing policy considerations *de lege ferenda* into the realm of *lex lata*. Due diligence then performs a bridge function. This shows in the precautionary approach whose legal status as international customary law is disputed.[174] In connection with the due diligence standard which the ITLOS Seabed Dispute Chamber qualified as a 'general obligation',[175] the Chamber could in its *Advisory Opinion on Deep Seabed Mining* operationalise the idea of precaution which in turn solidified the precautionary approach in international environmental law.[176] Thus, a policy approach was transformed into a legal obligation through the due diligence concept. This is a contribution to the international rule of law.

[171] Rajamani, 'International Climate Change Law' (n. 47), section 3.2.

[172] See, for international climate law, Sandrine Maljean-Dubois, 'Climate Change Litigation', in Hélène Ruiz Fabri (ed.), *Max Planck Encyclopedia of International Procedural Law* (Oxford: OUP 2018), para. 20: 'This broad interpretation of due diligence, the customary nature of which is established, has significant consequences for States. Due to its "umbrella" character, due diligence could make up for the potential shortcomings of treaties.'

[173] Peters/Krieger/Kreuzer, 'Dissecting the Leitmotif' (n. 1), section 1.

[174] The ICJ in *Pulp Mills* still refrained from a clear pronouncement on the customary law status of the precautionary approach although both parties raised the issue. See ICJ, *Pulp Mills Case* (n. 41), para. 164 and, e.g., verbatim record 2009/21 of public sitting held on Tuesday 29 September 2009, Mr. Sands, p. 27.

[175] ITLOS, *Activities in the Area* (n. 70), para. 131; see also ICJ, *Pulp Mills Case* (n. 41), para. 110.

[176] Fitzmaurice, 'International Watercourses' (n. 76), section 4; Viñuales, 'International Environmental Law' (n. 67), section 3.3.3.

6.4. Stabilising the International Order through Proceduralisation

The creation of free-standing procedural and institutional obligations stemming from the due diligence standard has considerably contributed to a proceduralisation of international law.[177] By proceduralisation, we mean the extension and refinement of rules on procedures (i.e., about steps and ways to proceed) as opposed to substantive rights, obligations, commands, prohibitions, or guarantees. Generally speaking, legal procedures encompass, *inter alia*, meetings, voting, reporting, documentation, and the like. In international law, we observe a proliferation of (mostly binding) procedural rules which constitute and shape the processes of law-making and law enforcement. The idea of a proceduralisation of (international) law suggests, descriptively, that legal actors are contending themselves with structuring the procedures and processes of law-making and law enforcement through binding procedural rules (e.g., on hearings, participation, obligations to explain and give reasons, voting-modes, monitoring, verification, and the like), and—normatively—that this is on balance not bad.

Denser proceduralisation may have a strong stabilising effect for the international order. First of all, procedures generally protect the weaker participants in any given relationship, because they prevent powerful players to change the rules of the game at their whim. Importantly, procedures thus outbalance the power disparities, for example by giving equally long speech slots to all sides or asking for written justification by all sides. The antidote to sheer powerplay is especially important in international relations where the disparities of strength and influence are huge. Next, the observance of prescribed procedures may generate legitimacy (acceptability and acceptance), because the procedures help to reach better outcomes. Procedures also tend to increase accountability, because they create, compile, and publicise knowledge and thus allow outsiders to hold actors to account. This accountability not only relates to past deeds but also to shaping the future. For example, information exchange and scientific assessment procedures enable states to take informed decisions. Because the due diligence standard demands that the circumstances of each case of application is examined and specified and that scientific progress is taken into account, the standard offers more guidance than its textual openness makes believe.[178] At the same time, the leeway offered by due

[177] See for the idea of proceduralisation Rauber, 'Zukunftsorientierung und Prozeduralisierung' 2018 (n. 132), 102–119. See further Oddný Mjöll Arnardóttir, 'The "Procedural Turn" under the European Convention on Human Rights and Presumptions of Convention Compliance', *International Journal of Constitutional Law* 15 (2017), 9–35; Isabelle van Damme, 'Procedural Review in WTO Law', in Janneke Gerards/Eva Brems (eds), *Procedural Review in European Fundamental Human Rights Cases* (Cambridge: CUP 2017), 209–241; Thomas Kleinlein, 'The Procedural Approach of the European Court of Human Rights: Between Subsidiarity and Dynamic Evolution', *International and Comparative Law Quarterly* 68 (2019), 91–110.

[178] Rauber, 'Zukunftsorientierung und Prozeduralisierung' 2018 (n. 132), 102.

diligence is narrowed where customary or treaty rules specify concrete measures for complying with the due diligence standard, such as conducting an environmental impact assessment or enacting national legislation.[179] More importantly, the extensive procedural obligations in many treaty regimes, in particular on information exchange and scientific assessment processes, re-enforce the future orientation of those regimes.

> The adoption of the underlying treaty thus marks not the endpoint of the international legal process but its beginning ... [The provisions] entail a duty for parties to engage in ongoing negotiations aimed at developing the regime as needed to meet its objective [and] provide iterated, institutionalised opportunities for negotiation and law-making.[180]

Over time, these processes and procedures within long-term treaty regimes build consensus about how to assess and deal with the risk addressed in the treaties. The processes allow for timely action and quicker regime development and make regimes more resilient.[181] Thus, broadly framed due diligence obligations and related procedural obligations may work as a starting point for creating more specific substantive obligations under a particular treaty regime over time.[182]

Simultaneously, reporting duties and other duties to publicly justify policy decisions create accountability through transparency and combine types and forms of legal and political accountability. Together with consultation duties, these obligations re-enforce states' general obligations to co-operate under the UN Charter, such as foreseen in Article 55 UN Charter. Even where states are for various reasons not able to agree on common substantive standards, the web of procedural duties guarantees that they continuously interact, thereby preserving space for future agreement. Due diligence thus is a framework for an 'interactional' international law.[183]

However, mere references to 'due diligence' in treaty texts and soft law do not always encompass due diligence procedures. Such procedures are fleshed out or being developed in practice only in some issue areas as we have seen. Where the due diligence standard is not itself 'proceduralised', powerful states might simply define what is 'due'. There is the danger that states and other international persons simply proclaim due diligence and then do what they want. So the growing reliance

[179] Brunnée, 'Community Interests' 2018 (n. 31), 167: 'One important advantage of treaty-based procedural requirements is that their "triggers", scope and content can be specified and nuanced for more than is possible under the general due diligence framework.'

[180] Ibid., 166, 168.

[181] Ibid., 169.

[182] Brunnée, 'Procedure and Substance' 2020 (n. 26), 189, 193.

[183] Jutta Brunnée/Stephen Toope, *Legitimacy and Legality in International Law* (Cambridge: CUP 2010).

on due diligence comes with risks for the international rule of law and global governance to which we now turn.

6.5. Undermining the Governance Capacity of the Law

Broad (indeterminate) normative standards, such as due diligence, may undermine the capacity of the law to govern behaviour, because the vague and blurry terms of those norms give plenty of leeway to those interpreting and applying them. This undermines the international rule of law. Tom Franck has emphasised that the compliance-pull of legal rules depends on their determinacy.[184] In national law, determinacy is often produced by a thick practice of agencies and courts which apply the broad and vague legal terms to the facts.[185] In international law, the problem of indeterminacy persists because there are much fewer—if any—court decisions which render more concrete a broad standard such as due diligence. For example, in customary international environmental law, there is little court practice so that the standards remain vague and undefined. And in areas where a bulk of case law exists—such as in human rights law—highly detailed findings strongly depend on the facts of the specific case. This is particularly relevant for the member states' positive obligation to protect which must be delivered diligently. After all, the ECtHR once claimed that it 'does not have to develop a general theory of the positive obligations which may flow from the Convention'.[186] This absence of a 'general theory' makes it difficult to generalise court findings and thus to foresee how the next decision involving due diligence will come out. More than the welcome nuanced allocation of responsibility after the fact,[187] the unpredictability on the level of primary obligations risks to destabilise the legal order.

Moreover, the due diligence standard is a double-edged sword. On the one hand, it may help to strengthen and develop stricter obligations within treaty regimes. On the other hand, when due diligence obligations are introduced (through secondary law or interpretation) into treaty regimes which had previously provided for substantive standards, due diligence may dilute the strictness of those regimes by re-opening states' discretion. This may give room for more 'subjective, self-selected and self-justifying' processes and 'self-serving' narratives and thereby contribute to a detachment of states from international legal commitments.[188] If states are unwilling to accept that stricter standards may be gradually developed through subsequent practice within the institutional framework of procedural duties, the due

[184] Thomas Franck, *The Power of Legitimacy Among Nations* (Oxford: OUP 1990), 50, 52.
[185] Rauber, 'Zukunftsorientierung und Prozeduralisierung' 2018 (n. 132), 103.
[186] ECtHR, *Plattform 'Ärzte für das Leben'* (n. 118), para. 31.
[187] See above section 2.2.
[188] For the complex processes under the climate protection regime in this regard, see Rajamani, 'International Climate Change Law' (n. 47), section 4.

diligence standard may remain malleable.[189] In this respect, the Paris Agreement will be a testing ground. The Agreement turned away from the Kyoto Protocol's approach to lay down binding substantive obligations and, instead, uses broadly framed substantive standards and due diligence in climate change mitigation.[190] As Lavanya Rajamani explained, there is a certain danger that processes of dilution might unfold under the Paris Agreement.[191] Overall, due diligence may work towards an erosion of global governance.

6.6. Disparaging Human Beings as Risks

A final drawback of due diligence lies in its contribution to perceiving humans as risk, commonsensical since the 11th of September 2001. Given that human behaviour is always uncertain and unpredictable,[192] the social construction of the behaviour of *certain groups* of human beings is not without problem. Natural science-based risk assessment asks how the law can deal with scientific uncertainty. In contrast, the assessment of social risks involves the allocation of responsibility and the distribution of costs and benefits.

Already the *Alabama* arbitral decision of 1872, dealing with the law of neutrality, asked neutral states to exercise due diligence with regard to risks arising from belligerents. The award thus espoused a 'precautionary approach' *avant la lettre*.[193] In the nineteenth century, conceiving human beings as risk raised no specific concerns. Unpredictable cross-border activities of human beings did not enjoy any specific protection, since human rights law was not yet in place. This has, of course, fundamentally changed. The recognition of fundamental liberties (both in national law and in international law) counsels against applying a regulatory technique developed for natural, technical risks to human beings.[194]

Moreover, the context-dependency also suggests caution in applying the due diligence standard to humans seen as risks. For example, the refugee crisis has fuelled political discourses in which refugees are not seen as individuals who need protection out of humanitarian considerations but just as a group posing security, economic, and social risks.[195] Such changes in perception have already affected

189 For such an attitude in the Katowice process, see ibid.; see also Fitzmaurice, 'International Watercourses' (n. 76), section 6; Österdahl, 'International Anti-terrorism Law' (n. 94), section 3.

190 Brunnée, 'Procedure and Substance' 2020 (n. 26), 197–202.

191 Rajamani, 'International Climate Change Law' (n. 47), section 4.

192 Lepsius, 'De-individualisation' 2008 (n. 7), 36.

193 Tribunal of arbitration, *Alabama* (n. 89), 125–134; cf. Viñuales, 'International Environmental Law' (n. 67), section 2.1.

194 Lepsius, 'De-individualisation' 2008 (n. 7), 37.

195 For a process of securitisation of refugee law at the cost of its humanitarian roots: Philip Rudge, 'European Initiatives on Asylum', in Danièle Joly/Robin Cohen (eds), *Reluctant Hosts: Europe and its Refugees* (Aldershot: Avebury 1989), at 212; Jef Huysman, 'The EU and The Securitization of Migration', *Journal of Common Market Studies* 39 (2000), 751–777; Thanos Zartaloudis, 'Asylum, Refugee and Immigration Law Studies: A Critical Supplement', in Rafiqul Islam/Jahin Hossain Bhuiyan (eds), *An*

legal regimes. For example, norm contestations and even changes of the rules on rescue at sea[196] to which the due diligence standard applies, have arguably been triggered by the perception of refugees as a risk group.

Another question is which actors have framed a certain human behaviour in terms of risk and for what purposes. An example is the application of due diligence to cyberspace. Russia and China have focused on the risk of cyber terrorism in order to forge an international consensus to restrict freedom of expression on the internet.[197] The International Code of Conduct for Information Security of September 2011 may be seen as such an attempt to legitimise restrictions of free speech that actually disregard international human rights obligations.[198] A duty to monitor and prevent cyber harms may also serve as a justification for further disproportionate surveillance measures.[199] In response, the EU has explicitly acknowledged that cyber-surveillance technologies exported from EU states might be abused by the importers for violating human rights.[200] In sum, treating human out-groups ranging from refugees to cyber-pirates with due diligence itself risks to eviscerate acknowledged human rights standards.

Introduction to International Refugee Law (2013), 319–356, at 332; Monika Wohlfeld, 'Is Migration a Security Issue?', in Omar Grech/Monika Wohlfeld (eds), *Migration in the Mediterranean: Human Rights, Security and Development Perspectives* (2014), 61–77, at 68–69; Ayelet Shachar, 'Bordering Migration/Migrating Borders', *Berkeley Journal of International Law* 37 (2019), 93–147, at 134–135.

[196] Thomas Gammeltoft-Hansen/Tanja Aalberts, 'Search and Rescue as Geopolitics of International Law', in Tanja Aalberts/Thomas Gammeltoft-Hansen (eds), *The Changing Practices of International Law* (2018), 188–207, at 194–195; Daniel Ghezelbash/Violeta Moreno-Lax/Natalie Klein/Brian Opeskin, 'Securitization of Search and Rescue at Sea', *International and Comparative Law Quarterly* 67 (2018), 315–351, at 319, 349–350.

[197] Heike Krieger, 'Conceptualizing Cyberwar: Changing the Law by Imagining Extreme Conditions', in Thomas Eger/Stefan Oeter/Stefan Voigt (eds), *International Law and the Rule of Law under Extreme Conditions: An Economic Perspective* (Tübingen: Mohr Siebeck 2017), 195–212, at 209.

[198] United Nations, General Assembly, International Code of Conduct for Information Security, Annex to the Letter dated 12 September 2011 from the Permanent Representatives of China, the Russian Federation, Tajikistan and Uzbekistan to the United Nations addressed to the Secretary-General, Developments in the field of information and telecommunications in the context of international security, A/66/359, 14 September 2011. Lit.c) of the Code of Conduct pledges: '(c) To cooperate in combating (…) terrorist activities that use information and communications technologies, including networks, and in curbing the dissemination of information that incites terrorism, secessionism or extremism or that undermines other countries' political, economic and social stability, as well as their spiritual and cultural environment'. There are further elements in the Code which aim to grant states sufficient discretion to restrict the freedom of expression in the interest of national security and culture in relation to the use of the cyberspace, e.g., lit.e) and f): '(e) To reaffirm all the rights and responsibilities of States to protect, in accordance with relevant laws and regulations, their information space and critical information infrastructure from threats, disturbance, attack and sabotage; (f) To fully respect rights and freedom in information space, including rights and freedom to search for, acquire and disseminate information on the premise of complying with relevant national laws and regulations.'

[199] Jensen, 'Cyber Activities' (n. 48), section 5.

[200] European Union, European Commission/High Representative of the Union for Foreign Affairs and Security Policy, Joint Communication to the European Parliament and the Council, 'Resilience, Deterrence and Defence: Building Strong Cybersecurity for the EU', 13 September 2017, at 19.

7. Conclusion

This book has demonstrated that the spread of due diligence 'slang'[201] across in international law points to fairly similar phenomena. Depending on the regime and the context, due diligence has comparable but different legal functions. The rise of due diligence has allowed international law to adapt to the challenges of a global risk society. This development is often positively connoted. It permits international law to deal with non-state actors as if they were international legal persons or at least to integrate them into legal regimes. It helps to close accountability gaps and aims to prevent large-scale risks from materialising. However, altering legal structures and diluting legal categories comes at a price.

A minor point is that diligence, just like negligence, is first of all a mental state—something that only natural as opposed to juridical (moral) persons have. Due diligence language thus (if only subtly) might reinforce the ever-present anthropomorphism which bedevils the representations of the state, the most powerful person in international law.[202] Arguably, this imagery risks to make us forget that—after all—states are only instrumental for securing the wellbeing of humans.[203] States formally represent their populations' interests on the international plane, seem to be vessels for the forging of identity, and they are pragmatically the currently 'best available structure to advance individual welfare'[204]—but they are not ends in themselves. Ultimately, the legal understanding of both diligence and negligence has probably been sufficiently de-personalised for minimising the danger of anthropomorphic, Leviathan-type imaginations in the working of international law.

A more serious drawback of the proliferation of due diligence is the rule of law. The international rule of law is affected because due diligence tends to undermine previsibility and legal certainty. It is difficult to gauge in advance and ascertain after the fact whether a due diligence standard has been breached or not. While the flexibility and openness of the due diligence concept may enable states to reach a compromise in treaty negotiations, it simultaneously increases the risk that states by furthering due diligence obligations try to replace, escape, or circumvent 'hard' legal commitments on substance. After all, when applying broad and undetermined legal concepts, such as due diligence, states gain more leeway to interpret these obligations in line with their perceived national interest. Thus, a compromise reached in treaty negotiations may still be undermined in the course of the

[201] To speak with Bartolini, 'Historical Roots' (n. 3), section 2.3.

[202] Cf. Jean d'Aspremont, 'The Doctrine of Fundamental Rights of States and Anthropomorphic Thinking in International Law', *Cambridge Journal of International Law* 4 (2015), 501–520.

[203] Anne Peters, 'Humanity as the A and Ω of Sovereignty', *European Journal of International Law* 20 (2009), 513–544.

[204] Steven Ratner, *The Thin Justice of International Law* (Oxford: OUP 2015), 86.

application of the agreement. The resulting legal insecurity per se cuts against the (international) rule of law.

Next, due diligence is both a response to, and a stimulus for, a (further) opening up of the circle of international legal persons. The traditional and probably still major field of application of due diligence relates to the activities of private actors which have thereby, as mentioned, been at least indirectly brought under the purview of international law. Thus, due diligence also contributes to the rise of 'informal' international law, notably professional and industrial standards which are often issued by transnational non-state actors such as professional associations, business interest groups, frequently in collaboration with NGOs, or with government agencies.[205] Such standards are often crucial for determining which conduct is actually 'due' in a given issue area, and they heavily influence the interpretation of the relevant hard law. However, informal law-making processes are often associated with negatively connoted concepts, such as managerialism and technocracy. These processes must answer calls for new forms of legitimising global governance since these are not covered by state consent.

This search for alternative forms of legitimacy may rely on due diligence as one manifestation of the on-going proceduralisation of law.[206] Proceduralisation gives an answer to three overlapping problems that beset contemporary law: the problem of information, the problem of governance, and the problem of legitimacy. As Jochen Rauber has shown, these three basic problems not only affect international law but all law including on the domestic level.[207] The positive assessment of proceduralisation builds on the recognition that the law (notably international law) can no longer (if it ever could) fully determine legal outcomes in substance. The primary task of the law should therefore be the circumscription of the ways how to reach these outcomes. An important driver of this approach is the disagreement among the members of a pluralist and even deeply divided international society about proper outcomes. The impossibility to reach consensus about substantive outcomes is exacerbated by the complexity of problems and lack of knowledge about their nature and scope, let alone about ways to solve them. In this constellation, negotiators may find it easier to agree on procedures, because these are less burdened with ideology and are to some extent open-ended. The underlying idea is that fair procedures will also lead to normatively acceptable and in fact accepted outcomes.[208] Thus, the elements of deliberation inherent in the procedural approach complement more traditional forms of justifying international law. Seen as a new key procedure, due diligence might bolster the legitimacy of

[205] Anne Peters/Lucy Köchlin/Till Förster/Gretta Fenner Zinkernagel (eds), *Non-state Actors as Standard Setters* (Cambridge: CUP 2009).

[206] See for the concept above (n. 177).

[207] Rauber, 'Zukunftsorientierung und Prozeduralisierung' 2018 (n. 132), 102.

[208] Niklas Luhmann, *Legitimation durch Verfahren* (Frankfurt: Suhrkamp 10th ed. 1983).

international law. However, this presupposes that due diligence is indeed fleshed out as a procedure and is not used only as a buzzword.

Finally, due diligence responds to the deficiencies of the extant rules on international responsibility especially in the face of the combined effects of the conduct of multiple actors in an interconnected world.[209] For example, in the international law of cyberspace, due diligence circumvents the key problem of attribution and the problem of the qualification of the behaviour at issue as an unlawful act.[210] More generally, Anja Seibert-Fohr has argued that 'due diligence' creates a new, third type of *ex ante* state responsibility below the thresholds of responsibility as a 'perpetrator' and as an 'accomplice'. Complicity (Article 16 ARSIWA) requires connection (namely 'aid or assistance') between the wrongdoer and the complicit state, and also the latter's 'knowledge of the circumstances of the internationally wrongful act'. When such knowledge is absent and/or the connection between the principal wrongdoer and another state is too remote or altogether lacking, a form of 'indirect participation' should suffice, and this is the place for due diligence standards.[211] As the guarantee of accountability, notably in the formal form of international legal responsibility, is a core component of the rule of law, due diligence here strengthens the international rule of law.

Seen from the perspective of global constitutionalism, the rise of due diligence, as a tort law- and criminal law-based institution, at first sight might suggest an undue 'privatisation' or 'de-constitutionalisation' of the international legal order. However, in the era of global capitalism, constitutionalisation can and should not be confined to states. The framework of 'societal constitutionalism', i.e., the acknowledgment that actors of civil society (both non-profit and business) are endowed with a natural authority to produce non-state law including constitutional law, has more explanatory power.[212] The most tangible markers of this type of constitutionalisation are the new instruments to hold business actors to account for human rights abuses, the rule-of-law oriented reforms of transnational investor-state arbitration (strengthening institutional independence of arbitrators, improved review, increased options for the state side to institute proceedings, tightened obligations of the investor), and finally the international actors' battle

[209] See on the shortcomings of the established secondary rules of international law André Nollkaemper/Ilias Plakokefalos (eds), *The Principles of Shared Responsibility in International Law* (Cambridge: CUP 2014); André Nollkaemper/Dov Jacobs (eds), *Distribution of Responsibilities in International Law* (Cambridge: CUP 2015); André Nollkaemper/Ilias Plakokefalos (eds), *The Practice of Shared Responsibility in International Law* (Cambridge: CUP 2017).

[210] Karine Bannelier, 'Obligations de diligence dans le cyberspace: Qui a peur de la cyber-diligence', *Revue belge de droit international* 50 (2017), 612–665. See also Jensen, 'Cyber Activities' (n. 48), section 4.

[211] Seibert-Fohr, 'From Complicity to Due Diligence' (n. 120), 707.

[212] Gunther Teubner, 'Societal Constitutionalism: Alternatives to State-Centred Constitutional Theory?' in Christian Joerges/Inger-Johanne Sand/Gunther Teubner (eds), *Transnational Governance and Constitutionalism* (Oxford: Hart Publishing 2004), 3–28.

against corruption (the antagonist of the rule of law).[213] These moves to some extent defy and erode the public/private split by extending constitutional concepts (and bonds) to the private (economic) sphere. All this shows that constitutionalism and constitutionalisation should no longer be confined to the traditional 'public' sphere, but that it may and must be extended to the business sphere, not blindly, but in a mitigated way, adapted to the specific logics of that sphere of society.[214] Against this background, the rise of due diligence both in inter-state constellations and in 'diagonal' state/non-state constellations such as human rights, investment protection, international criminal law, and anti-terrorism law can be interpreted as one feature of a global societal constitutionalism.

Overall, due diligence is responding to the current technological and ecological insecurity, to the global political and economic power shift, and to probably growing ideational and ideological strife. But in doing so, it not only meets these developments but might even push them further, by offering cheap talk and empty rituals. Due diligence is as janus-faced as current international law as a whole: oscillating between a hollow hope and guarantor of peace and justice.

[213] Foreword by former United Nations Secretary-General Kofi Annan to the United Nations Convention against Corruption 2003: 'Corruption (. . .) undermines democracy and the rule of law (. . .) is a major obstacle to poverty alleviation and development.' Published in United Nations, Office on Drugs and Crime, United Nations Convention against Corruption available at: https://www.unodc.org/documents/brussels/UN_Convention_Against_Corruption.pdf (accessed 14 April 2020). See in this sense also the preamble of United Nations, General Assembly, United Nations Convention against Corruption, A/RES/58/4, 31 October 2003, and the preamble of United Nations Convention against Corruption itself, 2349 UNTS 145.

[214] Anne Peters, 'Constitutionalization', in Sahib Singh/Jean d'Aspremont (eds), *Concepts for International Law: Contributions to Disciplinary Thought* (Cheltenham: Edward Elgar 2019), 141–153, at 149–151; Horatia Muir Watt, 'Private International Law Beyond the Schism', *Transnational Legal Theory* 2 (2011), 347–427, at 417–418, 426.

Index

For the benefit of digital users, indexed terms that span two pages (e.g., 52–53) may, on occasion, appear on only one of those pages.

abuse
 by foreign forces 86–87
 of human rights 100, 218–19, 220, 226, 227–28
 of immunities of international organisations 71–74; *see also* immunity
 of rights 51–52
 by peacekeepers 218–19, 225, 228–29, 230, 231
 by private actors 190, 218–19
 sexual 228–29, 230, 231
 by state organs 100
accountability 3–4, 8, 13, 14, 16, 17, 18, 19
 allocating 353–56, 374, 378–79
 in the climate change regime 172
 demand for 208
 gap 63, 71, 72, 219, 352, 365–68, 372–73, 387
 to individuals 74, 369–70
 of international organisations 3–4, 16, 61, 63, 71, 72, 74; *see also* international organisation
 through due diligence 215, 352–64; *see also* due diligence, as a tool creating accountability
 through procedural obligations 363–64
 through transparency 383
 of the World Bank 333–34
Ago, Roberto 6–7, 14, 42–44, 46–47, 48, 49, 50, 51, 58, 149, 316, 357
aid or assistance
 by a state in the commission of an internationally wrongful act by an international organisation 66, 68, 70; *see also* complicity
 to other states in the commission of an internationally wrongful act 3–4, 8, 43–44, 54–57, 58, 367–68, 389; *see also* complicity
aiding or abetting tax evasion by residents 302, 303
al-Assad, Baschar Hafiz 208
Al-Qaida 240, 248–49
Amazon Basin (Rondônia, Brazil) 335–36
American-Mexican General Claims Commission 26–27, 29, 274
Angel Gurria, Jose 310–11
anti-terrorism law
 border security in 237–40
 capacity building in 236, 239–40, 241; *see also* capacity, building of
 duty to prevent and punish terrorism 251; *see also* duty to prevent
 extradition in 241, 242–43
 information sharing in 237–40, 242, 250
 mutual legal assistance in 241, 242–43
 risk assessment in 246
arbitration 23–24, 27, 42, 89–91, 112, 113, 115, 116–17, 121–22, 123–24, 284, 285, 358, 365–66, 389–90
Argentina 135, 138, 141–42, 322–23, 335–36
Asian Infrastructure Investment Bank 340–41
attribution
 absence of 184–85
 of the conduct of an armed group 184–85
 of the conduct of private actors 315–16
 of cyber operations 255–56, 263–64
 of wrongful acts 23, 25, 43–44, 47, 48, 50, 53, 55, 367–68, 375, 378–79
audit control 293–94, 374
 sanctions following 374
Australia 78–79
aut dedere aut judicare 294
automatic exchange of information 303, 307–8, 309, 310–11
autonomous weapons 376
autonomy
 of international organisations 59–60, 72–73, 220–21
 of states 164, 168, 169–70

Bangladesh 335–36
Bannelier-Christakis, Karine 266
bearer bonds 305–6
Beck, Ulrich 290–91, 298

belligerent parties 28
Bendiek, Annegret 260–61
Berkes, Antal 81–82
best efforts 4–6, 53–54, 72–73, 134–35, 165, 168–69, 170–71, 313–14, 370
bonus pater familias 35–36
Bosnia 200–1, 202–4, 205, 210, 218, 227
Brahimi Report 224–25, 227
Brazil 335–36, 340–41
bribery 281, 292–93, 295, 298, 363
British-Chilean Mixed Commission 39
British-Mexican Claims Commission 39
Brunnée, Jutta 138–40, 177–78, 361, 364
burden of proof 133, 141–42, 198

Canada 29, 114–15, 263, 324–25
capacity 2, 4–6, 12, 14, 37, 62, 70, 77–78, 87, 99, 111, 124–26, 153–54, 155–56, 166–67, 172–77, 179, 221–22, 240, 241–42, 331, 343, 345, 377, 378–79, 384
  to act 97, 101, 369–70
  building of 32, 97, 99, 105, 236, 239–40, 241
  of businesses 94–95
  to implement contingency plans 242
  to influence 14, 87, 186, 200–1, 206–7, 208–9, 215, 379
  institutional 12, 31, 32, 105–6, 201–3, 211–12, 292–93, 341–42, 345–46
  to pay compensation 71
  of private actors 153–54
  to protect 81–82
  reduced 77–78
  technological 39
Capstone Doctrine 227–28
Caribbean 81
cascading system of duties 289, 296
causality, *see* harm, causation of
Caymans 306
Central African Republic 230
Cerone, John 222
Chad 338–39
China 84–85, 252–53, 256, 258, 337, 340–41, 386
Chircop, Luke 263–64, 267–68
circumstances precluding wrongfulness 156–57
circumvention 66
citizenship by investment (CBI) 309–10, 311
civilians, protection of 15–16, 189–90, 228–30
civil society 94–95, 108, 119, 244–45, 293–94, 299, 389–90
civil war 36, 39, 113, 125–26
climate change 77–78, 163, 340–41, 347, 351–52, 353, 384–85
  common but differentiated responsibilities 15, 165–66, 169–70, 172–73, 174–75, 176–77, 379
  global warming, *see* global warming
  greenhouse gas, *see* greenhouse gas
  impacts of 16–17, 88–89, 342
code of conduct 230, 293–94, 386
Colombia 81
Committee on Safeguards 318
community interests 97, 367
compensation 62, 70, 71, 129–30, 133–34, 147–48, 378
compliance 57, 66, 68, 79–80, 89–91, 95, 108, 134–35, 150, 152–53, 158–60, 161, 167–68, 172, 174, 183–84, 186–87, 190, 192–93, 194, 197, 198, 199, 230, 232, 245–47, 248, 267–68, 278, 282–83, 297–98, 299, 303, 307, 332, 334, 337–39, 366–67, 368, 372–73, 384
complicity 8, 53, 56
  aid or assistance to other states in the commission of an internationally wrongful act 3–4, 8, 43–44, 54–57, 58, 367–68, 389
  aid or assistance by a state in the commission of an internationally wrongful act by an international organisation 66, 68, 70
compulsory labour 32
conduct of hostilities 15–16, 30, 183, 187–89, 195–96, 198
conduct of military personnel 223, 231
consular law 365
control 27, 28, 36, 65–66, 67–68, 75, 101, 116, 122, 136–37, 142, 149, 150–52, 153–54, 156–57, 158, 160–61, 162, 195, 204–5, 217, 231, 240, 257, 260, 261–62, 289–91, 292–93, 294–95, 296, 299, 358–59, 363, 367, 377, 378–79
  administrative 137–38, 152–53
  de facto 84–85
  degree of 13–14, 186, 219–20
  direction and 65–66
  effective 63, 77–79, 80, 81–83, 85–87, 89–91, 99, 113, 218–20, 367–68, 378–79
  lack of 78–79
  level of 4–6, 39–40, 77–78, 218–19
  overall 184–85
  over information and communication technology (ICT) 257, 264
  over territory 23–24, 77–78, 79–81, 89–91, 357
  physical 82–83, 87
cooperation 8, 55–56, 57, 64, 69–70, 71, 129–30, 132, 134, 136–37, 144, 145, 236–37, 241–43, 250, 258, 259, 260–61, 292–93, 310–11, 321, 358
corporate duty to prevent 298
corporate liability 295

corporate social responsibility 1;
 see also Ruggie Principles
corruption, anti-corruption 4–6, 16, 17, 280, 288, 361–62, 363, 366, 379–80, 389–90
Crawford, James 14, 43–44, 48, 50–51, 52, 58, 375
crime, economic 289, 300–1
crimes against humanity
 duty of vigilance 201–2
 obligation to prevent
  duty bearer 201–2, 204–7
  scope 201–2, 203, 205, 215–16
  status 205, 215
customer due diligence 295–96
cyber activities 16, 252
 applicability of international law 258
 attribution of 255–56, 263–64
 control over 253, 257, 260, 261–62, 264, 269
 cyber war and 259
 investigation of 257, 258
 knowledge of 258, 259, 260, 261–62, 265–66, 268
 liability for 258, 263–64
 monitor 253, 257, 258, 261–62, 264–67, 269; *see also* duty to monitor
 prevention of 252–53, 254–55, 256, 257, 258, 260–62, 264–66, 267, 269
 risk of 253, 263, 266, 267, 268, 269
 state responsibility for 252–53, 256, 258–59, 263–66, 269
 territorial aspects of 252–53, 257, 258–59, 260, 261, 264, 269
cyber harm, *see* harm, cyber
 countermeasures against 267–69
 limitation of 267–68, 269
 mitigation of 252–53, 264–65, 269
 remediation of 264–65
 self-defense against 267–68
cyber infrastructure 260, 261, 264, 265–66
cyberspace 16, 259, 260–61, 358–59, 386, 389
Czechoslovakia 143

damage 2, 25, 82–83, 112–13, 114–15, 116, 122–24, 127–28, 132–33, 137–38, 150, 151–52, 154–55, 189, 193, 211–12, 218, 242, 262, 283–84, 304–5, 332, 353–54, 355, 362, 363, 365, 366, 371–72, 378–79; *see also* harm
data collection 105, 249, 299–300
denial of justice, *see* international investment law
Desierto, Diane 372–73
developed country 153–54, 163–64, 165–66, 167–68, 169–70, 172–73, 174–75, 304–5, 379–80
diligentia quam in suis 4–6, 34–35
discretion 12, 27, 59, 89–91, 120–21, 159–60, 164, 165, 169–70, 172–73, 179–80, 195–96, 215, 289, 294–95, 297–98, 357, 358, 371–72, 377, 380–81, 384–85; *see also* margin of appreciation
dispute settlement 23–24, 61–62, 256–57, 312, 316–18, 320, 322–23
Douglas, Mary 290–91, 298
downstream states 15, 132–33
Draft Articles on Crimes Against Humanity 2019 202–4, 367
Draft Articles on the Prevention of Transboundary Harm from Hazardous Activities 2001 7–8, 82–83, 114–15, 122, 125, 134, 137, 355–56
Draft Articles on the Responsibility of International Organizations (ARIO) 2011 14, 60, 61–62, 63, 65–68, 70, 71, 72–73
Draft Articles on the Responsibility of States for Internationally Wrongful Acts (ARSIWA) 2001 3–4, 7–8, 14, 43–57, 58, 154–55, 194, 289–90, 316, 361, 367–68, 389
Drozdova, Ekatarina A. 266
due diligence
 as a baseline for accountability 374
 in corporate law 279, 281; *see also* Ruggie Principles
 'doing' 4–6, 372
 as an element of an international minimum standard 4–6, 35, 133, 197, 274–76, 285–87
 evolution of 43–44, 47, 51, 128, 267
 as a general principle 8–9, 27, 53, 195, 217, 221, 222–23, 232–33, 252–53, 259, 266, 325–26, 374–76
 as a legal parameter 27, 81–82
 as an objective standard 195, 253–54, 282
 in private law 279, 281–82, 284
 reasonability standard and 25–27, 34–36, 40, 53–54, 97, 98–99, 100, 105, 129–35, 136–37, 144–46, 152, 161, 183–84, 199, 208–9, 210, 217–20, 227, 228, 232–33, 254, 258, 289–90
 as a result-independent obligation 363–64
 role in the law of state responsibility 51–52
 as a subjective standard 57, 175–76, 285–86
 as a tool creating accountability 215, 352–64
 as a tool for managing contestation 381
 as a tool restricting accountability 356–57, 359–60
due process 248, 274, 278

Dupuy, Pierre-Marie 357, 358
duty of vigilance 2, 26–27, 46, 122, 137–38, 152–53, 191–92, 201–2
duty to communicate 166, 168–69, 172, 241, 249–50, 282–83
duty to control 89–91, 113, 116, 122, 136–37, 149, 150–55, 156–57, 158, 160–61, 162, 257, 289–90, 294–95, 296
duty to cooperate 71, 132, 134–35, 136, 166, 236–37, 241, 242–43, 257, 258, 259, 260–61, 264, 292–93, 294, 312–13, 321, 351–52
duty to criminalise 25–26, 32, 150, 187, 236–37, 250, 257, 294, 295–96
duty to explain 12, 197, 205, 207–9, 215, 317, 382
duty to inform 8, 106, 152–53, 210, 231, 363; *see also* information exchange
duty to investigate 25–26, 96, 102, 106, 152–53, 156–57, 187, 226, 231, 242, 244, 258, 274–75, 297–98, 317, 319
duty to mitigate risk 14, 16, 77–78, 92–97, 103, 104, 133–34, 144, 166, 242, 252–53, 264–65, 374, 377, 378–79
duty to monitor 12, 77–78, 105, 136–37, 152–53, 186, 209, 210–15, 232, 241–42, 253, 257, 258, 261–62, 264–67, 269, 323, 373, 382, 386
duty to notify 12, 138–40, 237, 312–13, 318, 363, 364
duty to prevent 2, 137–40, 191–92, 203–4, 205, 375
  corporate 298
  cyberattacks 257
  due diligence with regard to the 2, 116–17, 118–19, 137–38, 177–78, 292–93, 298, 367–68
  environmental harm 116–17, 118–19, 177–78
  genocide 16, 68–69, 72–73, 75, 186, 200, 218, 361, 367–68, 370, 379
    content of 202–4, 207–9
    due diligence character 215–16
    duty bearer 206–7
    nature and scope of 204–7
  human rights violations 370
  mass atrocity 202–3
  slavery 150–51
  terrorism 251
  transboundary harm 7–8, 114–15, 138–40, 150–51, 257, 258, 261, 264, 265–66, 289, 292–93, 360, 364
  as a tool for risk management 361
duty to prosecute 2, 32, 187, 235–36, 244–47, 250, 257, 258
duty to protect
  aliens 37
  environment 127–28, 151–52
  foreigners 25–26, 32, 35, 365
  global health 358–59
  human rights 92–93, 94, 96, 97, 98, 100, 101, 102, 103, 107, 368–71
  individuals 184–85, 189–90, 193, 195, 315
  other states 29, 356–57
  outer space 358–59
  ozone layer 358–59
  victims of armed conflict 183
duty to regulate private actors 296, 366
duty to supervise 14, 59, 65–66, 68, 74, 289, 295, 296, 299–79, 366
Duvic-Paoli, Leslie Anne 145–46

Eagleton, Clyde 23–24, 29, 33–34, 356–57
Ecuador 337–38
electronic record search 308
environmental impact assessment 10–11, 106, 120, 130, 138–40, 152–53, 335–36, 364, 382–83
environmental protection 84, 111–12, 116, 117, 119, 122–23, 124, 127–28, 129–30, 132, 135, 136–46, 149–50, 151–52
equality 136, 304–5
  of belligerents 197
  gender 106–7, 228, 340–41
  sovereign 80–81, 379
equity 132, 141, 174–75, 176–77
Eritrea-Ethiopia Claims Commission 190
Estonia 259, 264, 265
European Commission 325
European Council of Ministers 325
European Court of Human Rights (ECtHR) 64, 80–81, 93, 94, 95–96, 98–99, 102, 103–5, 369–71, 384
European Court of Justice (ECJ) 308
European Space Agency (ESA) 64
European Union (EU) 88–89, 247–48, 257, 260–61, 302, 303, 309, 311, 322–23, 325, 386
evidence 38, 102, 103–4, 210, 217, 219–20, 221, 225, 231, 232–33, 308, 310, 362, 363
  in cases related to terrorism 235–37, 241–42, 247
  of knowledge 210
  lack of 96, 299–300
  of significant transboundary harm 114, 138–40, 143
exclusive economic zone 155–56
extradition 241, 242–43, 294

fault 6–8, 23, 43–44, 46, 50, 52, 97, 123–24, 194, 217–18, 285, 289–90, 355–56, 375

Financial Action Task Force 17, 291–92, 295–96, 297–98, 299–300
financial crisis 302, 303
financial institutions 293–94, 295–96, 297–98, 299–300, 302, 304, 307, 308, 329–30, 347, 372–73
fishing vessels 149–50
flag state 84–85, 149–51, 159–60, 161
flexibility 3, 13, 23–24, 28, 30–31, 32, 40, 41, 80–81, 133, 134–35, 144–46, 152–53, 164, 166–68, 174, 176, 179–80, 196–97, 198–99, 337, 387–88
force majeure 66–67, 156–57
Forlati, Serena 207–8
Foucault, Michel 290–91, 298
Friendly Relations Declaration 234, 235, 251

García-Amador, Francisco V. 14, 42–47, 48, 51–52, 54, 58
gender-based violence 93–94, 100, 104–7
genocide
  prevention of 16, 68–69, 72–73, 75, 186, 200, 218, 361, 367–68, 370, 379
  risk of 209–14
  see duty to prevent, genocide
Genocide Watch 212
German Federal Constitutional Court 304–5
Germany 64, 258, 304–5
global administrative law 18–19
global commons 353
global constitutionalism 18–19, 389–90
  social 389–90
global governance 18–19, 384–85, 388
  erosion of 384–85
global warming 178; *see also* climate change
good faith 2–3, 15, 34–35, 56, 57, 69–72, 136–37, 138–40, 165, 171, 179–80, 281, 312–13, 318, 319, 320–21, 322, 374–75, 376
good governance 1, 292–93
good neighbourliness 1, 8–9, 136–37, 254–55, 376
good willingness 34–35
greenhouse gas
  emission 167, 168, 171–72, 175, 178
  mitigation 163–64, 165, 166, 167–69, 172, 174–75
  see climate change
Guantanamo Bay 78–79

hacking 252
Haiti 61–62, 73, 223, 225–26
harm
  causation of 59–60, 61, 62, 63, 67–68, 71–72, 129–30, 132–34, 135, 137–38, 140, 141–42, 144, 257, 262, 263–64, 265–66, 277, 283–84, 285, 353–54, 356–57, 358, 359–60, 361, 362, 364, 365, 378–79
  to civilians 187–88
  climate 165, 173, 174–76, 177–78, 179–80
  cost of 378, 385
  cyber 252–53, 254–55, 256, 257, 258, 261, 262, 263–66; *see also* cyber harm
  ecologic 358–59
  economic 292–95, 385–86
  environmental 81–83, 84–85, 116–17, 118–19, 121–22, 123, 125–26, 129–30, 141–42
  financial 61
  foreseeable 103
  by international organisations 59–60, 61, 63, 68, 71–72, 74
  liability for 277, 355, 367–68
  mitigation of 264–65, 269, 359–60, 376
  pollution-related 133
  precaution against 188, 363
  relationship to due diligence 133–34, 137–38, 145
  remediation of 261, 264–65
  risk of 81, 116–17, 122–23, 138–40, 177–78, 332–33, 378–79
  significant 114–15, 116–17, 119–20, 129–30, 132–34, 135, 137–38, 143, 144–46, 177–78, 361
  threshold of 122–23, 177–78
  tolerance of 134, 254–55, 262, 377
  without violating international law 61, 68, 71–72
Higgins, Rosalyn 72
highest possible ambition 169–70, 173, 178–79, 380–81
High Level Independent Panel on Peace Operations Report (HIPPO) 228–29
human rights, *see* international human rights law
human rights impact assessment 17, 233, 324–27
humans as risks 365–68, 385; *see also* risk, humans as
Hungary 143

ILC, *see* International Law Commission
ILC Special Rapporteur 6–7, 14, 42–45, 46–47, 48, 58, 149, 203–4, 209, 316, 324–25, 326–27, 375
illegal fishing 147–48
immunity
  of international organisations 59–60, 61–62, 63, 64, 70, 71–74, 224, 225–26; *see also* international organisation
  of the UN 224, 225–26

impact assessment 364, 373, 382–83; *see also* environmental impact assessment; human rights impact assessment; trade, international law of, elements of due diligence in
impartiality 222–23, 224
incitement 65–66, 68–69
India 175–76, 258, 335–36, 340–41
information exchange 305–6, 307–8, 382–83; *see also* duty to inform
  mandatory 309
  standard information exchange rules 307–8
injuries to aliens 25–26, 42, 43–46, 47
Institut de Droit International 26, 28
interactional international law 383
Inter-American Commission on Human Rights 104–5
Inter-American Court of Human Rights (IACtHR) 81–82, 94, 96, 97, 98
interdependence 299
intergenerational equity 141
intergovernmental organisations (IGOs) 217–18, 329–30
Intergovernmental Panel on Climate Change 178
International Centre for Settlement of Investment Disputes (ICSID) 281–82
International Civil Aviation Organisation (ICAO) 238–39
International Committee of the Red Cross 189, 193, 367, 368, 379
International Court of Justice (ICJ) 1, 4–6, 11, 16, 55–56, 69–70, 75, 82–83, 86–87, 127–28, 132, 137–40, 141, 143, 145–46, 148, 186, 200–1, 202–5, 206, 207–9, 210, 221, 292–93, 358–59, 360, 361, 364, 365, 367–68, 374, 375, 379
International Criminal Tribunal for the former Yugoslavia 86–87
International Finance Corporation (IFC) 329–30
international humanitarian law
  applicable for UN peacekeeping 225, 227, 229, 231, 232, 353
  compliance with 187, 194, 197–99
  duty to ensure respect for 186–87, 195
  duty to protect civilians from violations of 186, 189–91, 194
  prevention of violations of 192
international human rights law 2, 7–8, 10–11, 14, 16, 17, 31–33, 42–43, 44–45, 51, 59, 64, 78–81, 92–108, 121, 127–28, 152–53, 159, 191–92, 209, 217, 218–19, 220–21, 222, 225, 227–28, 232–33, 247–48, 251, 266, 267, 282–84, 314, 315, 324–28, 332, 338, 340–41, 346–47, 368–71, 384, 386, 389–90
international investment law
  denial of justice 274, 275–76, 278
  fair and equitable treatment 274, 275, 278–79, 282, 285–86, 365
  full protection and security 274, 276–77, 280, 282, 285–86, 365
  international minimum standard 274–75, 276, 279, 285–86
  obligations/responsibility of foreign investors 273, 274, 275–76, 277, 278–85, 287
    assessment of legal framework 280–81
    responsible investments 273, 287
    risk assessment 279–81, 282–83, 285
  obligations of host states 273, 274–79, 281–82, 284–86
    international delinquency 274
  treatment of aliens 273, 274, 275–76, 284, 287
International Law Association (ILA) 142, 218, 253–54, 255, 261, 262
  Study Group on Due Diligence in International Law 253–54, 261, 262, 312
International Law Commission (ILC) 6–8, 14, 42–47, 51, 53, 55–56, 58, 60, 62, 68, 70, 72, 73, 82–83, 114–15, 122, 125, 129–30, 133, 134, 137, 149, 173, 177–78, 201, 202–3, 205, 289–90, 316, 357, 361, 367
international law of the sea 15, 63, 75–76, 84–86, 125, 129–30, 147–62, 314–15
  control as *ratione materiae* 85
  flag state 84–85
  jurisdiction as *ratione loci* 85
  sovereign rights 84–85
  spatial dimension of control 85
  zonal approach 84–85
international legal order
  coherence of the 374
  structural change in the 17–19, 352, 376–86
  transformation of the 19, 127–28, 351–52
International Monetary Fund (IMF) 64
international organisation 3–4, 13–14, 17, 117–18, 121–22
  accountability of 59–61, 63, 70, 71, 72
  aid or assistance by a state in the commission of an internationally wrongful act by an 66
  autonomy of 59–60, 62, 72–73, 220–21
  immunity of 59–60, 70–73, 224, 225–26
  responsibility of 60–64, 219–20

international relations 2–3, 219–20, 286–87, 374, 376, 382–83
international rule of law 4, 247–48, 251, 347, 380, 381, 383–84, 387–88, 389–90
International seabed area 147–48, 150–51
International Tribunal for the Law of the Sea (ITLOS) 1, 11, 15, 125, 140–41, 142, 147–48, 149, 151–52, 171, 177–78, 201–2, 214–15, 362, 366–67, 381
international tax law
  tax evasion 131, 280, 286, 302, 303, 304, 306, 308, 309, 310–11
  withholding tax 302–5, 306, 307
internationally wrongful act 52–54, 56, 66, 217–18, 257, 258–59, 264, 267, 268, 359–60, 389
Interpol 237, 239–40
intervention, prohibition of 59, 69, 72–73, 222–23, 256–57
investment tribunal 273, 275–77, 278–80, 281, 283–84, 285–86
Islamic State of Iraq and Levant (ISIL) 248–49
Israel 191, 252–53, 256
Italian-Venezuelan Mixed Claims Commission 40
ius cogens 205, 215, 370; *see also* peremptory norms
Ivory, Radha 17, 363, 366

Japan 263
Johns, Fleur 215–16
jurisdiction 14, 23–24, 29, 63, 75–77, 79–89, 91, 94, 96, 113, 116, 121–22, 123, 127–28, 137–38, 150–52, 153–54, 158, 160–61, 202–3, 205, 257, 264, 302, 303, 305–6, 308, 309–10, 358–59, 378–79
justice 35, 88–89, 93–94, 119, 120–21, 236–37, 242, 244–45, 274, 275–76, 278, 279, 286–87, 289, 299–301, 380, 390; *see also* international investment law, denial of justice

Kenya 336
knowledge 38–39, 55–57, 76–77, 98, 126, 152, 210, 214–15, 353–54, 362, 380, 388–89
  actual 210, 214, 259, 260, 263, 266
  constructive 210, 214, 261–62, 265
  evidence of 210
Kosovo 222
Krajewski, Markus 373
Kulesza, Joanna 217–18

Latin America 40, 304–5
law enforcement 79–80, 89–91, 106, 111, 117–18, 123–24, 137–38, 152–53, 156–57, 191–92, 238, 332, 382
League of Nations 25, 26–27, 33–34, 35
  Committee of Jurists 26–27
  Conference on Codification 25, 26–27, 33–34, 35
legitimacy of international law 18–19, 382–83, 388–89
  through proceduralisation 382–83, 388–89; *see also* proceduralisation
liability 4–6, 72, 82–83, 84, 107, 112–13, 123–24, 125, 129–30, 133, 178–79, 199, 258, 263, 276–77, 289–90, 294, 295, 331, 332, 352, 354–56, 361, 372, 376, 378–79
litigation 113
Lord Mansfield 302

margin of appreciation 30, 101, 370–71; *see also* discretion
marine environment 150–51, 156, 358–59
McCaffrey, Stephen 133, 134, 135, 144–45
McLure, Charles 304–5
medical care 30, 32, 95–96, 189–90, 192, 193
Mexico 25–27, 29, 274, 275
Milošević, Slobodan 210
modernisation 353
Moldova 80–81
money-laundering 16, 17, 288, 366, 379–80
Mongolia 337
monitoring
  abuses of human rights 227, 228–29, 232
  climate change-related risks 77–78
  compliance 232
  cyber harm 253, 264, 266–67
  cyber infrastructure 264–65
  data 136–37
  of environmental and social performance 341–42
  mechanisms of 152–53, 186, 195, 209, 214–15
  of project implementation 338–39
  social media 210–11, 212–13
  terrorist fighter 241–42
  transiting data 261–62
  of treaties 294, 297–98
morality 2–3
multilateral development banks 331, 332–33, 339–47
multinational enterprises 89–91, 154, 282–83, 293–94, 324–25, 331, 365
Murphy, Sean 202–3
Myanmar 211–12, 213

nationally determined contributions (NDC) 168–71, 173, 175–76, 178–80, 380–81
NATO's Cooperative Cyber Defence Centre of Excellence 259

natural hazards 93, 97
negligence 2, 3–7, 46, 52, 95–96, 113, 124, 194, 288, 299, 360, 365, 374, 375, 387
Nepal 225–26, 335–36
Netherlands 258, 303
Netherlands Antilles 303
neutrality 4–6, 27, 36, 37, 112–13, 183, 224, 365–66
  appropriate efforts to prevent 365–66
Nigeria 211–12
no harm principle, no harm rule 1, 119–20, 129–30, 132, 133–34, 135, 138–40, 145–46, 359–60, 361, 362, 365, 374; *see also* principle of prevention
non-governmental organisation (NGO) 94–95, 210–11, 267, 323, 332, 343, 388
non-navigational uses of international watercourses 129
non-state actors 89–91, 206–7, 252–53, 254–55, 257, 258–59, 263, 267–68, 294, 296, 298, 353, 363, 365, 366–67, 370–71, 378–80, 387
  capacity of 160–61
  collaboration with 156
  conduct of 54, 149, 252–53, 289–90, 294
  countermeasures against 267–68
  harm emanating from 2, 93, 252–53
  international law, participation of 89–91
normative expectation 2, 164, 169–70, 171, 173, 178–79, 380–81
norm contestation 385–86
North Korea 211–12, 252–53, 256, 263, 268
nulla poena sine lege 299–300

objectivity, objective standard 34, 38, 43–44, 46, 47, 48, 51, 52–53, 150, 151–52, 161, 162, 176–77, 194, 225, 254, 285–86, 319
obligations
  of conduct 13, 15–16, 23–24, 28, 50–51, 53–54, 76, 97, 135, 138, 149, 155–56, 157, 163–66, 168–71, 172–78, 179–80, 183–84, 190, 194, 195, 200–1, 204–5, 229, 230, 264, 274, 275–76, 278, 284, 316, 319, 321, 322, 323, 357–60, 368–69
  erga omnes 128, 186, 368
  extraterritorial 87–88, 113, 200–8, 367
  negative 27, 28, 65–66, 184–85, 191, 197–98
  positive 3, 27, 29, 30–32, 80–81, 97, 107, 207–8, 210, 220–21, 222, 227–28, 279, 370–71, 384
  procedural 3, 12, 32, 93, 102, 106–7, 120–21, 130, 132, 134, 135, 136, 137–40, 143, 144, 145–46, 157–58, 163, 194, 198, 200–2, 214–15, 233, 317, 319–20; *see also* procedural obligations
  of result 23–24, 29, 49, 50–51, 53–54, 107, 132, 135, 138, 150, 155–57, 163–71, 173, 179, 184–85, 187, 190, 196–97, 199, 200–1, 204–5, 239, 251, 316, 357, 359–60, 369
  substantive 138–40, 163–73, 205, 208–9, 210, 383, 384–85
occupation, law of 30, 75–76, 86–87, 191–92, 195, 197–98
  administration of occupied territory 191–92
  duty to restore and ensure public order and civil life 191–92, 195, 197–98
  occupying power 86–87, 183–84, 191–92, 197–98
OECD 291–93, 294, 295–96, 297–98, 303, 304–5, 308, 309–11, 363
OECD Common Reporting Standards 17, 303, 308, 309–10, 311
Office on Genocide Prevention and the Responsibility to Protect 211–12, 213
official misconduct 93, 96
omission 16, 23–24, 48, 65–66, 67–68, 70, 142, 154–55, 289–90, 333–34
opinio iuris 11
organised crime 292–93, 363
outer space 355, 358–59

Panama 36, 310–11
Panama Papers 310–11
Papanicolopulu, Irini 15, 358–59
Paradise Papers 310–11
Paraguay 335–36
peace-keeping
  acts of misconduct 226, 230
  capability 228–30
  nature and level of force 224–25
  prevention of sexual abuse 230, 231
  protection of civilians 218, 225, 227–30, 232–33
  training for 225, 227, 228
  Troop Contributing Nations (TCNs) 219–20, 224–25, 226, 228–29
peremptory norms, breach of 8, 56–57, 67, 68–69, 128, 205; *see also* ius cogens
Pieth, Mark 299
Pisillo Mazzeschi, Riccardo 149
polluter-pays-principle 122–23, 141
pollution 158, 338, 353
  avoidance of 133
  prevention of 150–52, 156, 343–44
portfolio investment 304–5
  interest exemption 302, 304, 305–6

positive obligations 3, 29, 30–32, 67–68, 80, 97, 107, 149, 159, 184, 207–8, 210, 220–21, 222, 279, 370–71, 384
precautionary principle/approach 15, 116–17, 125–26, 140–43, 152–53, 177–78, 294–95, 298, 362–63, 371–72, 381, 385
prevention obligation, *see* duty to prevent
preventive policing 299–300
principle of distinction 187
principle of equitable utilisation 129–30, 132, 133–34, 136, 143, 144, 145
principle of prevention 116–17, 119, 129–30, 137–38, 144; *see also* duty to prevent
privacy 100, 311, 370–71
private military companies 217, 218–20, 224, 365
procedural obligations 3, 12, 32, 93, 102, 106–7, 120–21, 130, 132, 134, 135, 136, 137–40, 143, 144, 145–46, 157–58, 163, 194, 198, 200–2, 214–15, 233, 317, 319–20; *see also* obligations, procedural
  increasing accountability 374; *see also* accountability
  increasing transparency 383
  as part of the harm prevention rule 359–60
  proliferation of 382
  as result-independent obligations 360, 361
  stabilising effect of 382–84
proceduralisation 3, 17–18, 158, 194, 198, 361, 376–77, 382–84, 388–89
  legitimacy through 382–83, 388–89
progression
  normative expectation of 169–70, 173, 178–79
progressive realisation 31–32, 352, 371–72
proof
  burden of 133, 141–42, 198
  standard of 205
property 89–91, 191–92, 225, 309
  cultural 188–89, 338
  defence of 225
  intellectual 325–26
  protection of 25, 98–99, 191
  respect for 39
proportionality 97, 187–88, 369–71
prosecution 12, 31, 187, 241, 243–48, 249–50, 257, 258, 294; *see also* duty to prosecute
protection, *see* duty to protect
public interest 2, 281–83, 285, 354–55, 369–71
Putin, Vladimir 252–53

racketeer 292–93
Rajamani, Lavanya 15, 380–81, 384–85
Rauber, Jochen 388–89
reasonability 25–27, 34–36, 40, 53–54, 97, 98–99, 100, 105, 129–35, 136–37, 144–46, 152, 161, 183–84, 199, 208–9, 210, 217–20, 227, 228, 232–33, 254, 258, 289–90; *see also* due diligence, reasonability standard and
rebels 36, 39, 40
redress 61–62, 222–23, 283–84, 345, 357
refugee law 232, 248, 373
remedy 71–72, 93, 94–95, 104, 129–30, 144, 225, 231, 253, 261, 264–65, 294–95, 318, 319–20, 321
reparations 62, 67, 68, 71, 371–72
  for injuries to aliens 43–45
residence by investment (RBI) 309–10, 311
resilience 172, 260–61
responsibility of international organisations, *see* international organisation, responsibility of
responsibility of states, *see* state responsibility of international organisations
revenue rule 302
review
  of domestic cyber policies 267
  of mitigation measures 167–68
  project risks 331, 339, 347
right-holders 111, 118–21, 127
right to an environment of a certain quality 121
right to free speech 370–71
right to life 81, 93–94, 96, 102, 106
right to notification and consultation 120, 136, 137–40, 143
right to personal integrity 81
right to safe working environment 160
right to work 159–60
riots 39
riparian states 129–30, 134, 136, 144
risk
  -based approach 297–98, 299–300, 309–10
  construction of 290–91, 353, 363
  of crimes against humanity 210–15
  as damage 112–13, 114–15, 122–24, 127–28
  definition of 116–17
  degree of 177–78, 311
  evaluation 4–6, 308
  foreseeable 97, 98, 196, 331, 369–70, 372–73
  genocide, of 200–1, 210–15
  governance 17, 288, 298–300, 374
  humans as 352, 365–68, 385
  level of 38–39, 112–13
  magnitude of 116–17, 122–23
  management 2, 17, 288, 290–91, 340–41, 352, 353–54, 355–56, 361, 374, 378–79
  notion of 76, 298

risk (*cont.*)
obligation of states to take steps to inform themselves of situations of 210
predictability and knowledge of the 4–6, 13–14, 76–77, 98, 210, 377, 378–79, 384
proximity 76–77, 79–80, 81–83, 91, 378–79, 380
risky groups 288, 299–300, 352
of significant harm 116–17, 138–40, 177–78, 361
socially constructed 353, 363
society 2, 18–19, 298, 352, 387
technical 353, 385
tolerated 354–55
risk assessment 122–23, 200–1, 210–11, 214–15, 232–33, 246, 298, 313, 329–30, 331, 332–33, 334–36, 337–38, 339, 342, 343–46, 347, 385
Rohingya 213
Ruggie, John Gerard 281
Ruggie Principles 11, 94–95, 273, 282–84, 299
rule of law, *see* international rule of law
Russia 80–81, 252–53, 256, 264, 265, 340–41, 386
Rwanda 212–13, 227

safe haven 232–33, 292–93
safety of navigation 151, 158, 160
safety of vessels and structures 152
sanctions/penalties 105, 152–53, 156–57, 207–8, 235–36, 240, 248–49, 295–96, 307, 338, 374
Satellite Sentinel Project 211–12
Schmitt, Michael 258
De Schutter, Oliver 324–25
scientific proof 294–95, 353, 363
scientific uncertainty 177–78, 363, 385
Seabed Dispute Chamber 140–41, 147–48, 152–55, 157–58, 201–2, 214–15, 366–67, 381
secondary rules 3, 6–7, 8, 14, 42–44, 47, 49, 50–51, 58, 65, 149, 186, 217, 288, 289–90, 315, 354
Seibert-Fohr, Anja 389
self-determination 179–80
Sherman, John 284
Sklerov, Matthew 257
Skotnikov, Leonid 205
slavery 31–33, 105, 150–51
social media 206–7, 210–11, 212, 213, 214–15
soft law 11, 14–15, 18–19, 106, 111, 129–30, 291–92, 295–96, 383–84
South Africa 340–41
South Sudan 211–12, 223
sovereignty 1, 4–6, 8–9, 14, 23–24, 28–29, 40, 49, 69, 77–78, 84–85, 107, 127–28, 160–61, 191, 218–19, 222–23, 256–57, 377–78
principle of sovereign equality 256–57
territorial 23–24, 28–29, 77–78, 84–85
Spain 40
Srebrenica 218
Sri Lanka 211–12
state responsibility
avoidance of 195–97, 198, 199, 263–64
case-specific standard 48
in cyberspace 252–53, 256, 259, 264–65, 267–68
for failure to prevent genocide 204–5
for failure to prevent or punish certain acts 48, 53
for failure to supervise international organisations 65–71, 74
general principles 49, 51–52, 55
history of 43–44, 51, 53, 56, 58
in-between substantive questions and general principles 51–52, 55
objective nature 35, 43–44, 46, 47, 48, 52–53, 194
subjectivity 43–44, 46–47, 48, 50–53, 54, 55–56, 57, 58
Status of Forces Agreement (SOFA) 223
subjects of international law 54, 117–18, 121–22, 217–18, 221–22, 388
Sudan 211–12, 230
Supreme Court of Israel 191
surveillance 35, 36, 100, 298, 332, 386
sustainable development 17, 131, 132, 143, 176–77, 312–13, 314, 324–25, 326–27, 328, 339–41, 373, 377–78
Sustainable Development Goals 212–13, 214–15
Switzerland 113–14, 309
Syria 208, 252–53

Tallinn Manual 16, 253–54, 259–62, 265–66, 267–68, 269
Tams, Christian 206
Tanzi, Attila 136
territory 2, 4–6, 14, 15–16, 23–24, 26–27, 28–29, 31–32, 37, 59, 69, 75–83, 84–85, 86–91, 96, 99, 113, 114, 119–20, 121–22, 125–26, 127–28, 200–3, 204–5, 206, 218–19, 222, 234, 238–39, 241, 244, 245, 251, 252–53, 257, 258–59, 260, 261, 264, 269, 294, 312, 313–15, 323, 325, 339, 353–54, 356–57, 365–66, 367–68, 377, 378–79; *see also* control, over territory
third states 28, 208–9, 266, 367–68

three rules of Washington 28
Tibet 337
Tomka, Peter 205
torture 96, 99–100
totalitarianism 107
Toufayan, Mark 202–3, 204–5
Townley, Stephen 290–91
trade, international law of
effects-based rules 316, 317
elements of due diligence in 312–14
consultation and notification requirements 317–18, 320, 363
impact assessments 312–13, 324–27, 328, 373
obligation of investigation and examination 319–20
obligation to consider negative effects 312–13, 314–15, 317, 318, 321, 323, 326
obligation to negotiate in good faith 312–13, 318, 319, 320–21, 322
obligation to take the effects of measures on other countries' economies into account 312, 313–14, 315, 317–18, 319–22, 327
measure-based rules 316
'regime-external' due diligence dimension of 314, 324–27
'regime-internal' due diligence dimension of 313–14, 317
remedies in 318, 319–20, 321
restrictions in 318, 320, 321, 322–23
violation of 316–17, 320, 323
transboundary pollution 150–51
Transdniestrian 80
transparency 163–64, 170–71, 172, 176, 198, 232, 274, 278, 310–11, 326–27, 373, 383
tax 310–11

UBS 302, 303, 306, 307, 311
Uganda 212–13
Unable or unwilling 158–59
UN African Union Hybrid Operation in Darfur (UNAMID) 230
UN Committee on Economic, Social and Cultural Rights 64, 94, 324–25
UN Counter-Terrorism Executive Directorate (UNCTED) 236–37, 240, 242–43, 247–48, 249
UN Efforts on Returning and Relocating Foreign Terrorist Fighters 243, 248–50
UN General Assembly 70, 71–72, 221, 234
UN Group of Governmental Experts on Developments in the Field of Information and Telecommunications in the Context of International Security (UN GGE) 253, 256, 257, 258–59, 260–61, 266
UN Guiding Principles on Business and Human Rights, *see* Ruggie Principles
UN Human Rights Committee 218–19, 267
UN Human Rights Council 324–25
UN Human Rights Due Diligence Policy 232, 373, 374
United Kingdom 34–35, 38, 71–72, 112–13, 114–15, 263, 298, 299–300
United Nations 217, 291–93
Charter 116, 220–21, 222–23, 238–39, 243, 245–46, 247–48, 250, 256, 260, 383
General Assembly 70, 71–72, 221, 234
Secretary-General 71–72, 73, 219–20, 230
Security Council 17, 207–8, 219–20, 228, 229–30, 233, 234
United States 34–35, 38, 61–62, 112–14, 124, 168, 175–76, 252–53, 256, 263, 292–93, 297–98, 299–300, 302, 303, 304–6, 307–8, 309–10, 311, 320, 321
UN Mission in the Republic of South Sudan 223
UN Multidimensional Integrated Stabilization Mission in the Central African Republic 230
UN Office of Counter-Terrorism (UNOCT) 249, 250
UN Office of Drugs and Crime (UNODC) 241, 249
UN Policy on 'Human Rights in United Nations Peace Operations and Political Missions' 229
UN Programme Global Pulse 212–13
UN Secretary-General's Bulletins 231
UN Security Council Counter-Terrorism Committee (UNCTC) 236–37, 240, 249
UN Special Rapporteur 324–25, 326–27
UN Stabilization Mission in Haiti (MINUSTAH) 223, 225–26
UN Standard Minimum Rules for the Treatment of Prisoners 246–47
UN World Food Programme 214
Uruguay 135, 138, 141–42
US Civil War 36, 113
US Internal Revenue Service 302, 306, 307
US-Spanish Claims Commission 40
US Supreme Court 29

van Dam, Nikolaos 208
Venezuela 40
Verdirame, Guglielmo 221–22
Vinuales, Jorge E. 14–15, 177–78

war crimes 187, 232
watercourses, international
  procedural obligations 135–40, 143–46
  shared freshwater ecosystems 136
  shared resources 132, 144–45
  upstream and downstream states 15, 132–33
Werner, Wouter 215–16
Western Sahara 325
Working Group on the issue of human rights and transnational corporations and other business enterprises 324–25
World Bank 64, 329
  Inspection Panel 329–30, 332–36, 337, 342, 343
  Project financing
    applicability of international environmental, social, and human rights law standards 329–30
    definition 330–31
    due diligence by the project lenders 331, 339
    due diligence obligations in
      classification of risks 339
      mitigation 340–41, 342–43
      risk assessment 329–30, 331, 332, 333–34, 337–39, 341–43, 372–73
    standards for 338
    transactions 331
World Health Organization (WHO) 69–70
World Trade Organization (WTO) 313–24
  dispute settlement 316–18, 320
  obligations of 313, 316–17, 322
World War II 31, 42